The Official CompTIA® A+® Core 1 Student Guide (Exam 220-1001)

The Official CompTIA® A+® Core 1 Student Guide (Exam 220-1001)

COURSE EDITION: 1.01

Acknowledgements

James Pengelly, Author
Pamela J. Taylor, Author
Brian Sullivan, Media Designer
Peter Bauer, Content Editor

Thomas Reilly, Vice President Learning
Katie Hoenicke, Director of Product Management
James Chesterfield, Manager, Learning Content and Design
Becky Mann, Senior Manager, Product Development

Notices

DISCLAIMER

While CompTIA, Inc. takes care to ensure the accuracy and quality of these materials, we cannot guarantee their accuracy, and all materials are provided without any warranty whatsoever, including, but not limited to, the implied warranties of merchantability or fitness for a particular purpose. The use of screenshots, photographs of another entity's products, or another entity's product name or service in this book is for editorial purposes only. No such use should be construed to imply sponsorship or endorsement of the book by nor any affiliation of such entity with CompTIA. This courseware may contain links to sites on the Internet that are owned and operated by third parties (the "External Sites"). CompTIA is not responsible for the availability of, or the content located on or through, any External Site. Please contact CompTIA if you have any concerns regarding such links or External Sites.

TRADEMARK NOTICES

CompTIA®, A+®, and the CompTIA logo are registered trademarks of CompTIA, Inc., in the U.S. and other countries. All other product and service names used may be common law or registered trademarks of their respective proprietors.

COPYRIGHT NOTICE

Copyright © 2019 CompTIA, Inc. All rights reserved. Screenshots used for illustrative purposes are the property of the software proprietor. Except as permitted under the Copyright Act of 1976, no part of this publication may be reproduced or distributed in any form or by any means, or stored in a database or retrieval system, without the prior written permission of CompTIA, 3500 Lacey Road, Suite 100, Downers Grove, IL 60515-5439.

This book conveys no rights in the software or other products about which it was written; all use or licensing of such software or other products is the responsibility of the user according to terms and conditions of the owner. If you believe that this book, related materials, or any other CompTIA materials are being reproduced or transmitted without permission, please call 1-866-835-8020 or visit **www.help.comptia.org**.

Table of Contents

Lesson 1: Installing and Configuring PC Components... 1
    Topic A: Use Appropriate Safety Procedures... 2
    Topic B: PC Components.. 13
    Topic C: Common Connection Interfaces.. 34
    Topic D: Install Peripheral Devices.. 52
    Topic E: Troubleshooting Methodology... 63

Lesson 2: Installing, Configuring, and Troubleshooting Display and Multimedia Devices.. 75
    Topic A: Install and Configure Display Devices... 76
    Topic B: Troubleshoot Display Devices... 96
    Topic C: Install and Configure Multimedia Devices... 104

Lesson 3: Installing, Configuring, and Troubleshooting Storage Devices............ 113
    Topic A: Install System Memory... 114
    Topic B: Install and Configure Mass Storage Devices... 127
    Topic C: Install and Configure Removable Storage... 140
    Topic D: Configure RAID... 149
    Topic E: Troubleshoot Storage Devices... 156

Lesson 4: Installing, Configuring, and Troubleshooting Internal System Components... 169
    Topic A: Install and Upgrade CPUs... 170
    Topic B: Configure and Update BIOS/UEFI.. 185
    Topic C: Install Power Supplies... 197
    Topic D: Troubleshoot Internal System Components.. 208
    Topic E: Configure a Custom PC.. 223

Lesson 5: Network Infrastructure Concepts.. 235
    Topic A: Wired Networks.. 236

Topic B: Network Hardware Devices.. 254
Topic C: Wireless Networks.. 264
Topic D: Internet Connection Types.. 270
Topic E: Network Configuration Concepts... 278
Topic F: Network Services... 293

Lesson 6: Configuring and Troubleshooting Networks................................311
Topic A: Configure Network Connection Settings...312
Topic B: Install and Configure SOHO Networks... 327
Topic C: Configure SOHO Network Security...347
Topic D: Configure Remote Access... 366
Topic E: Troubleshoot Network Connections.. 374
Topic F: Install and Configure IoT Devices...387

Lesson 7: Implementing Client Virtualization and Cloud Computing........ 397
Topic A: Configure Client-Side Virtualization...398
Topic B: Cloud Computing Concepts.. 407

Lesson 8: Supporting and Troubleshooting Laptops....................................417
Topic A: Use Laptop Features.. 418
Topic B: Install and Configure Laptop Hardware.. 426
Topic C: Troubleshoot Common Laptop Issues.. 439

Lesson 9: Supporting and Troubleshooting Mobile Devices....................... 453
Topic A: Mobile Device Types..454
Topic B: Connect and Configure Mobile Device Accessories........................463
Topic C: Configure Mobile Device Network Connectivity..............................470
Topic D: Support Mobile Apps...483

Lesson 10: Installing, Configuring, and Troubleshooting Print Devices....495
Topic A: Maintain Laser Printers... 496
Topic B: Maintain Inkjet Printers... 506
Topic C: Maintain Impact, Thermal, and 3D Printers......................................512

Topic D: Install and Configure Printers.. 521

Topic E: Troubleshoot Print Device Issues.. 546

Topic F: Install and Configure Imaging Devices..559

Appendix A: Mapping Course Content to CompTIA® A+® Core 1 (Exam 220-1001)..569

Solutions...587

Glossary.. 623

Index... 671

About This Course

CompTIA A+ certified professionals are proven problem solvers. They support today's core technologies from security to cloud to data management and more. CompTIA A+ is the industry standard for launching IT careers into today's digital world. It is the only industry recognized credential with performance-based items to prove pros can think on their feet to perform critical IT support tasks in the moment. It is trusted by employers around the world to identify the go-to person in end point management and technical support roles. CompTIA A+ is regularly re-invented by IT experts to ensure that it validates core skills and abilities demanded in the workplace.

The Official CompTIA® A+® Core 1 (Exam 220-1001) course provides the background knowledge and skills you will require to be a successful A+ technician. It will help you prepare to take the CompTIA A+ Core Series certification examination (exam number 220-1001), in order to become a CompTIA A+ Certified Professional.

Course Description

Target Student
This course is designed for individuals who have basic computer user skills and who are interested in obtaining a job as an entry-level IT technician. This course is also designed for students who are seeking the CompTIA A+ certification and who want to prepare for the CompTIA A+ Core 1 220-1001 Certification Exam.

Prerequisites
To ensure your success in this course, you should have experience with basic computer user skills, be able to complete tasks in a Microsoft® Windows® environment, be able to search for, browse, and access information on the Internet, and have basic knowledge of computing concepts. You can obtain this level of skills and knowledge by taking the following official CompTIA courses:

- *The Official CompTIA® IT Fundamentals+ (Exam FC0-U61)*

Note: The prerequisites for this course might differ significantly from the prerequisites for the CompTIA certification exams. For the most up-to-date information about the exam prerequisites, complete the form on this page: **https://certification.comptia.org/training/exam-objectives**

Course Objectives
In this course, you will install, configure, optimize, troubleshoot, repair, upgrade, and perform preventive maintenance on personal computers and digital devices. You will:

- Install and configure PC system unit components and peripheral devices.
- Install, configure, and troubleshoot display and multimedia devices.
- Install, configure, and troubleshoot storage devices.
- Install, configure, and troubleshoot internal system components.
- Explain network infrastructure concepts.
- Configure and troubleshoot network connections.
- Implement client virtualization and cloud computing.
- Support and troubleshoot laptops.
- Support and troubleshoot mobile devices.
- Install, configure, and troubleshoot print devices.

The CompTIA CHOICE Home Screen

Logon and access information for your CHOICE environment will be provided with your class experience. The platform is your entry point to the learning experience, of which this course manual is only one part.

On the Home screen, you can access the Course screens for your specific courses. Visit the Course screen both during and after class to make use of the world of support and instructional resources that make up the learning experience.

Each Course screen will give you access to the following resources:

- **Classroom**: A link to your training provider's classroom environment.
- **eBook**: An interactive electronic version of the printed book for your course.
- **Files**: Any course files available to download.
- **Checklists**: Step-by-step procedures and general guidelines you can use as a reference during and after class.
- **Videos**: Brief videos, developed exclusively for CompTIA by ITPro.TV, provide demonstrations of key activities in the course. These are a good alternative to view if you do not have access to all equipment mentioned in the course.
- **Assessment**: A series of different assessments for each lesson as well as an overall course self-assessment.

Depending on the nature of your course and the components chosen by your learning provider, the CHOICE Course screen may also include access to elements such as:

- LogicalLABs, a virtual technical environment for your course.
- CertMaster Practice, an adaptive knowledge assessment and practice test platform.
- Various partner resources related to the courseware.
- Related certifications or credentials.
- A link to your training provider's website.
- Notices from the CHOICE administrator.
- Newsletters and other communications from your learning provider.
- Mentoring services.

Visit your CHOICE Home screen often to connect, communicate, and extend your learning experience!

How to Use This Book

As You Learn

This book is divided into lessons and topics, covering a subject or a set of related subjects. In most cases, lessons are arranged in order of increasing proficiency.

The results-oriented topics include relevant and supporting information you need to master the content. Each topic has various types of activities designed to enable you to solidify your understanding of the informational material presented in the course. Information is provided for reference and reflection to facilitate understanding and practice.

Data files for various activities as well as other supporting files for the course are available by download from the CHOICE Course screen. In addition to sample data for the course exercises, the course files may contain media components to enhance your learning and additional reference materials for use both during and after the course.

Checklists of procedures and guidelines can be used during class and as after-class references when you're back on the job and need to refresh your understanding.

At the back of the book, you will find a glossary of the definitions of the terms and concepts used throughout the course. You will also find an index to assist in locating information within the instructional components of the book. In many electronic versions of the book, you can click links on key words in the content to move to the associated glossary definition, and on page references in the index to move to that term in the content. To return to the previous location in the document after clicking a link, use the appropriate functionality in your PDF viewing software.

As You Review

Any method of instruction is only as effective as the time and effort you, the student, are willing to invest in it. In addition, some of the information that you learn in class may not be important to you immediately, but it may become important later. For this reason, we encourage you to spend some time reviewing the content of the course after your time in the classroom.

As a Reference

The organization and layout of this book make it an easy-to-use resource for future reference. Taking advantage of the glossary, index, and table of contents, you can use this book as a first source of definitions, background information, and summaries.

Course Icons

Watch throughout the material for the following visual cues.

Student Icon	Student Icon Descriptive Text
	A **Note** provides additional information, guidance, or hints about a topic or task.
	A **Caution** note makes you aware of places where you need to be particularly careful with your actions, settings, or decisions, so that you can be sure to get the desired results of an activity or task.
	Video notes show you where an associated video is particularly relevant to the content. These videos can be accessed through the Video tile in CHOICE.
	Checklists provide job aids you can use after class as a reference to perform skills back on the job. Access checklists from your CHOICE Course screen.
	Additional **Practice Questions** are available in the Assessment tile in your CHOICE Course screen.

Lesson 1
Installing and Configuring PC Components

LESSON INTRODUCTION

A very large percentage of the work that most IT technicians do entails working with hardware, including installing, upgrading, repairing, configuring, maintaining, optimizing, and troubleshooting computer components.

In this lesson, you will turn your attention to the computer's system components and peripheral devices. You will see how they are connected and configured to create a customizable PC platform.

LESSON OBJECTIVES

In this lesson, you will:

- Use appropriate safety procedures for avoiding hazards associated with PC support and minimize the risk of damage from ESD.
- Identify PC components.
- Identify common connection interfaces and the cables and connectors used with them.
- Install peripheral devices.
- Identify procedures and techniques to employ when troubleshooting.

Topic A
Use Appropriate Safety Procedures

To complete PC support tasks without damaging the equipment that you are servicing or causing physical injury to yourself or others, there are several tools to use and operational procedures to follow in order to get the job done quickly, safely, and correctly. In this topic, you will identify the best practices for PC technicians to follow to promote electrical and environmental safety.

LOCAL GOVERNMENT REGULATIONS

When performing PC maintenance work, you may need to take account of compliance with government regulations. Regulations that typically affect PC maintenance or the installation of new equipment are:

- Health and safety laws: Keeping the workplace free from hazards.
- Building codes: Ensuring that fire prevention and electrical systems are intact and safe.
- Environmental regulations: Disposing of waste correctly.

For example, in the United States, the most common safety regulations are those issued by the federal government, such as the Occupational Safety and Health Administration (OSHA), and state standards regarding employee safety. OSHA-compliant employers must provide:

- A workplace that is free from recognized hazards that could cause serious physical harm.
- Personal protective equipment designed to protect employees from certain hazards.
- Communication—in the form of labeling, Material Safety Data Sheets (MSDSs), and training about hazardous materials.

While specific regulations may vary from country to country and state to state, in general employers are responsible for providing a safe and healthy working environment for their employees. Employees have a responsibility to use equipment in the workplace in accordance with the guidelines given to them and to report any hazards. Employees should also not interfere with any safety systems, including signs or warnings or devices such as firefighting equipment. Employees should not introduce or install devices, equipment, or materials to the workplace without authorization or without making an assessment of the installation.

HEALTH AND SAFETY PROCEDURES

A company's health and safety procedures should be set out in a handbook, possibly as part of an employee's induction handbook. Health and safety procedures should:

- Identify what to do in the event of a fire or other emergency.
- Identify responsible persons (for example, for overall health and safety, nominated first aiders, fire marshals, and so on).
- Identify hazardous areas in the workspace and precautions to take when entering them.
- Describe best practice for use and care of the workspace and equipment within it.

- Establish an incident reporting procedure for detecting and eliminating workplace hazards and accidents.

GENERAL EMERGENCY PROCEDURES

Here is a general procedure for emergency situations:

1. Raise the alarm and contact the emergency services, giving them a description of the emergency and your location.
2. If possible, make the scene safe. For example, if you are faced with a fire, establish that you have an escape route, or if faced with electrical shock, disconnect the power (if it is safe for you to do so).
3. If you have training and it is safe to do so, do what you can to tackle the emergency (for example, give first aid or use firefighting equipment).

Of course, circumstances might dictate that you do something differently. It is vital that you keep calm and do not act rashly.

ELECTRICAL HAZARDS

The most prevalent physical hazards that computer technicians face are electrical hazards. Electricity is necessary to run a computer, but it can also damage sensitive computer equipment, and in some cases, pose a danger to humans. Following established best practices for promoting electrical safety will protect not only the computer equipment that you work on, but also your personal safety and the safety of others.

Electrical equipment can give an electric shock if it is broken, faulty, or installed incorrectly. An electric shock can cause muscle spasms, severe burns, or even kill (electrocution).

Electrical currents can pass through metal and most liquids, so neither should be allowed to come into contact with any electrical device installations. Damaged components or cables are also a risk and should be replaced or isolated immediately. It is important to test electrical devices regularly. The frequency will depend on the environment in which the device is used. In some countries, **portable appliance testing (PAT)** carried out by a qualified electrician or technician ensures that a device is safe to use.

The human body is an electrical conductor and a resistor, so a current will pass through it and make it heat up, manifesting as a burn if the current is strong enough. A current can interfere with the body's nervous system, which also uses electrical signals. This might manifest as spasm or paralysis or in a severe case cause a heart attack. Collateral injuries occur when involuntary muscle contractions caused by the shock cause the body to fall or come in contact with sharp edges or electrically live parts.

Electricity can hurt you even if you are careful and avoid becoming part of an electrical ground circuit. The heat generated by an electric arc or electrical equipment can burn your skin or set your clothes on fire.

Note: High voltages (over about 30V) are more dangerous because they have the power to push more current through you (skin's resistance drops at higher voltages), but it is the current that causes the actual damage. This is why static electricity is not dangerous to you, despite the high voltages. More current will flow if a larger area of your body is exposed.

FUSES

An electrical device must be fitted with a **fuse** appropriate to its power output. A fuse blows if there is a problem with the electrical supply, breaking the circuit to the power source. Fuses come in different ratings, such as 3A, 5A, and 13A. A device's instructions will indicate what rating of fuse to use, but most computer equipment is rated at 3A or 5A. If the fuse fitted is rated too low, it will blow too easily; if the rating is too high, it may not blow when it should (it will allow too much current to pass through the device).

If multiple devices need to be attached to a single power point, a power strip of sockets should be used. If too many devices are attached to a single point, there is a risk that they will overheat and cause a fire. "Daisy-chaining" one power strip to another is dangerous. The total amperage of devices connected to the strip must not exceed the strip's maximum load (typically 12 amps).

EQUIPMENT GROUNDING

Electrical equipment must also be **grounded** (or earthed). If there is a fault that causes metal parts in the equipment to become live, a ground provides a path of least resistance for the electrical current to flow away harmlessly. Most computer products (PCs, printers, and so on) are connected to the building ground via the power plug. However, the large metal equipment racks often used to house servers and network equipment must also be grounded. Do not disconnect the ground wire. If it has to be removed, make sure it is replaced by a competent electrician.

Grounding terminals and wires. (Image by phadventure © 123RF.com.)

HIGH VOLTAGE DEVICE SAFETY

Most of the internal circuitry in a computer is low voltage (12 V or less) and low current, so there is not much of a threat to your personal safety. However, there are exceptions to this, and these exceptions can be very dangerous. Power supplies, CRT monitors, the inverter card in an LCD display's fluorescent backlight, and laser printers can carry dangerously high levels of voltage. Charges held in capacitors can persist for hours after the power supply is turned off. You should not open these units unless you have been specifically trained to do so. Adhere to all printed warnings, and never remove or break open any safety devices that carry such a warning.

Caution: Never insert anything into the power supply fan to get it to rotate. This approach does not work, and it is dangerous.

ELECTRICAL FIRE SAFETY

Faulty electrical equipment can pose a fire risk. If the equipment allows more current to flow through a cable than the cable is rated for, the cable will heat up. This could ignite flammable material close to the cable. If an electrical wire does start a fire, it is important to use the correct type of extinguisher to put it out. Many extinguishers use water or foam, which can be dangerous if used near live electrical equipment. The best type to use is a Carbon Dioxide (CO_2) gas extinguisher. CO_2 extinguishers have a black label. Dry powder extinguishers can also be used, though these can damage electronic equipment.

Caution: Care must be taken in confined spaces as the CO_2 plus smoke from the fire will quickly replace the available oxygen, making it hard to breathe.

You should also ensure that the electricity supply is turned off. This should happen automatically (the fuses for the circuit should trip), but make sure you know the location of the power master switches for a building.

GUIDELINES FOR WORKING SAFELY WITH ELECTRICAL SYSTEMS

*Note: All of the Guidelines for this lesson are available as checklists from the **Checklist** tile on the CHOICE Course screen.*

Consider these guidelines as you prepare to work with electrical equipment.

ELECTRICAL SAFETY

Follow these guidelines to work safely with electrical systems:

- Do not work on electrical systems unless you have a good understanding of the risks and appropriate safety procedures.
- Do not attempt repair work when you are tired; you may make careless mistakes, and your primary diagnostic tool, deductive reasoning, will not be operating at full capacity.
- Do not assume anything without checking it out for yourself. A ground wire might have been disconnected or never properly installed, for example.
- Disconnect the power to a circuit if you must handle it.
- Hold down the power button on the device to ensure the circuits are drained of residual power.
- Test live parts with a multimeter to ensure that no voltage is present.
- Always use properly insulated tools and never grip a tool by its metal parts.

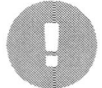
Note: It is especially important not to touch the live parts of multimeter probes, as these may be connected to an energized circuit. Handle the probes by the insulated sheaths only.

- Take care not to touch any part of a circuit with both hands to reduce the risk of a serious shock. This is called the "hand in pocket" rule. It reduces the chance that the current will pass through your chest and cause a heart attack.
- Make sure your hands and the surrounding area are dry. Sweat can make your hands more conductive.

- Do not leave any spill hazards in the vicinity and ensure you are not standing on a wet floor.
- Do not wear jewelry, a wrist watch, or other items such as name badges that may dangle from your neck or wrist, as they can cause a short circuit or become trapped by moving parts.

ENVIRONMENTAL SAFETY

In addition to electrical hazards, there are other environmental issues that computer technicians must deal with on a regular basis. The health and safety of you and those around you should always be your highest priority. Recognizing potential environmental hazards and properly dealing with them in a safe manner is a critical responsibility for a CompTIA® A+® technician.

Category	Description
Trip hazards	A **trip hazard** is caused by putting any object in pathways where people walk.
Lifting and carrying risks	Lifting a heavy object in the wrong way can damage your back or cause muscle strains and ligament damage. You may also drop the object and injure yourself or damage the object. Lifting and manual handling risks are not limited to particularly heavy objects. An object that is large or awkward to carry could cause you to trip over or walk into something else. An object that has sharp or rough edges or contains a hot or corrosive liquid could cause you to cut or hurt yourself.

TOXIC WASTE HANDLING

The conditions surrounding computer equipment can be an issue when there is a large number of airborne particles flowing in and around various devices. Contaminants can be either gaseous, such as ozone; particles, such as dust; or organic, which comes from industrial processing of fossil fuels or plastics. There is also a risk of poisonous or corrosive chemicals leaking from faulty equipment. Special care must be taken in respect of the following device types:

- **CRT monitors**: A cathode ray tube (CRT) is an older type of computer monitor. These are very heavy and bulky and can contain substantial amounts of hazardous materials, notably lead. They also contain a glass vacuum tube and high-voltage capacitors. While the tube is designed to be shatter resistant, it is still potentially very hazardous if dropped. The capacitors represent a high risk of electric shock.
- **Batteries**: Swollen or leaking batteries from laptop computers or within cell phones and tablets must be handled very carefully and stored within appropriate containers. Use gloves and safety goggles to minimize any risk of burns from corrosive material.
- **Electronic devices (PCs, cell phones, and tablets)**: Many components in electronic devices contain toxins and heavy metals, such as lead, mercury, and arsenic. These toxins may be present in batteries, in circuit boards, and in plastics used in the case. These toxins are harmful to human health if ingested and damaging to the environment. This means that you must not dispose of electronic devices as general waste in landfill or incinerators. If an electronic device cannot be donated for reuse, it must be disposed of through an approved waste management and recycling facility.
- **Toner kits and cartridges**: Photocopier and laser printer toner is an extremely fine powder. The products in toner powder are not classed as hazardous to health but

any dust in substantial concentration is a nuisance as it may cause respiratory tract irritation.

GUIDELINES FOR WORKING SAFELY AMONG ENVIRONMENTAL HAZARDS

Here are some guidelines to help you work safely when environmental hazards are present.

ENVIRONMENTAL SAFETY

Follow these guidelines to work safely among environmental hazards:

- When installing equipment, ensure that cabling is secured, using cable ties or cable management products if necessary. Check that cables running under a desk cannot be kicked out by a user's feet. Do not run cabling across walkways or, if there is no option but to do so, use a cord protector to cover the cabling.
- When servicing equipment, do not leave devices (PC cases for instance) in walkways or near the edge of a desk (where it could be knocked off). Be careful about putting down heavy or bulky equipment (ensure that it cannot topple).
- When you need to lift or carry items, be aware of what your weight limitations are, as well as any restrictions and guidance set forth in your job description or site safety handbook. Weight limitations will vary depending on context. For example, a 50 pound limitation for lifting and carrying an object while holding it close to your body is not the same as lifting an object from a shelf above your head.
- If necessary, you should obtain protective clothing (gloves and possibly goggles) for handling equipment and materials that can be hazardous.
- Lift heavy objects safely. To do so:
  1. Plant your feet around the object with one foot slightly toward the direction in which you are going to move.
  2. Bend your knees to reach the object while keeping your back as straight as is possible and comfortable and your chin up.
  3. Find a firm grip on the object then lift smoothly by straightening your legs—do not jerk the object up.
  4. Carry the object while keeping your back straight.
- Lower heavy objects safely, by reversing the lifting process; keep your chin up and bend at the knees. Take care not to trap your fingers or to lower the object onto your feet.
- If you cannot lift an object because it is too awkward or heavy, then get help from a coworker, or use a cart to relocate the equipment. If you use a cart, make sure the equipment is tightly secured during transport. Do not stack loose items on a cart. If you need to carry an object for some distance, make sure that the route is unobstructed and that the pathway (including stairs or doorways) is wide and tall enough.
- Follow these guidelines when working with toxic materials.
  - Never disassemble a CRT and never try to stack old units on top of one another.
  - Use gloves and safety goggles to minimize any risk of burns from corrosive materials from batteries, cell phones, and tablets.
  - Use an air filter mask that fits over your mouth and nose when servicing toner kits and cartridges to avoid breathing in the particles. People who suffer from asthma or bronchitis should avoid changing toner cartridges where possible. Loose toner must be collected carefully using an approved toner vacuum and sealed within a strong plastic waste container. Get the manufacturer's advice about disposing of loose toner safely. It must not be sent directly to a landfill.

ESD

Static electricity is a high voltage (potential difference) stored in an insulated body. **Electrostatic discharge (ESD)** occurs when a path is created that allows electrons to rush from a statically charged body to another with an unequal charge. The electricity is released with a spark. The charge follows the path of least resistance, so it can occur between an electrical ground, such as a doorknob or a computer chassis, and a charged body, such as a human hand.

Although the voltage is high, the amount of ESD current sustained is very low, so static electricity is not that harmful. It can, however, be slightly painful. You might have felt a small shock when reaching for a metal door handle for instance. You can feel a discharge of over about 2500V. A discharge of 20,000V or more could produce a visible spark. Walking over an untreated carpet in dry conditions could create a charge of around 35,000V.

The human body is mostly water and so does not generate or store static electricity very well. Unfortunately, our clothes are often made of synthetic materials, such as nylon and polyester, which act as good generators of static electricity and provide insulating layers that allow charges to accumulate. Humidity and climate also affect the likelihood of ESD. The risk increases during dry, cool conditions when humidity is low. In humid conditions, such as before or during a storm, the residual charge can bleed into the environment before it can increase sufficiently to be harmful to electrical components.

An electronic component, such as a memory or logic chip, is composed of fine, conductive metal oxides deposited on a small piece of silicon. Its dimensions are measured in fractions of a micron (one millionth of a meter). Any static electricity discharged into this structure will flash-over (spark) between the conductive tracks, damaging or even vaporizing them. A transistor designed to work with 1-3V can be damaged by a charge of under 100V, though most have ESD protection circuits that improve this tolerance.

A static discharge may make a chip completely unusable. If not, it is likely to fail at some later time. Damage occurring in this way can be hidden for many months and might only manifest itself in occasional failures.

COMPONENT HANDLING

By eliminating unnecessary activities that create static charges and by removing unnecessary materials that are known charge generators, you can protect against ESD-related damage and injuries. There are several other prevention techniques that you can use to protect yourself and equipment when you are working with computer components.

- **Self-grounding**, or manual dissipation of static buildup by touching a grounded object prior to touching any electronic equipment. You can accomplish this by touching an unpainted part of a metal computer chassis or other component.
- Using an anti-ESD wrist strap or leg strap can dissipate static charges more effectively than self-grounding. The band should fit snugly around your wrist or ankle to maximize contact with the skin. Do not wear it over clothing. The strap ground is made either using a grounding plug that plugs into a wall socket or a crocodile clip that attaches to a grounded point or an unpainted part of the computer's metal chassis.

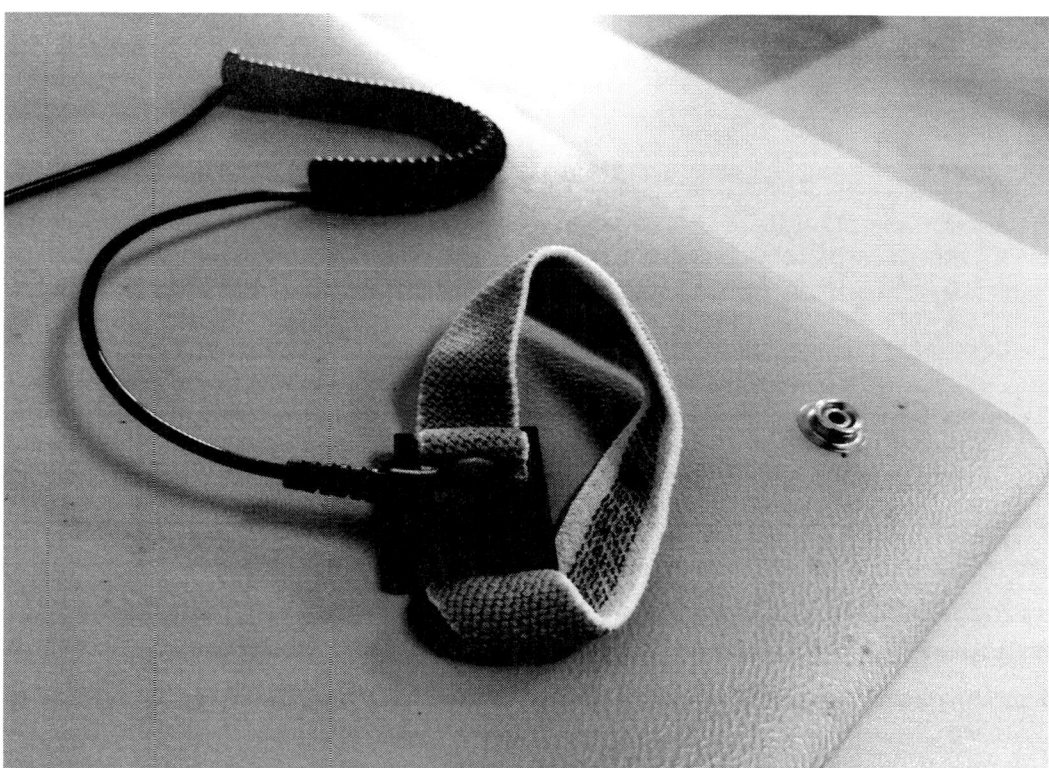

Electrostatic Discharge ESD wrist strap on ESD mat. (Image by Audrius Merfeldas © 123RF.com.)

- An anti-ESD service mat is also useful. Sensitive components can be placed on the mat safely. The mats contain a snap that you connect to the wrist or leg strap. If the technician's clothing has the potential to produce static charges, an ESD smock, which covers from the waist up, can be helpful.

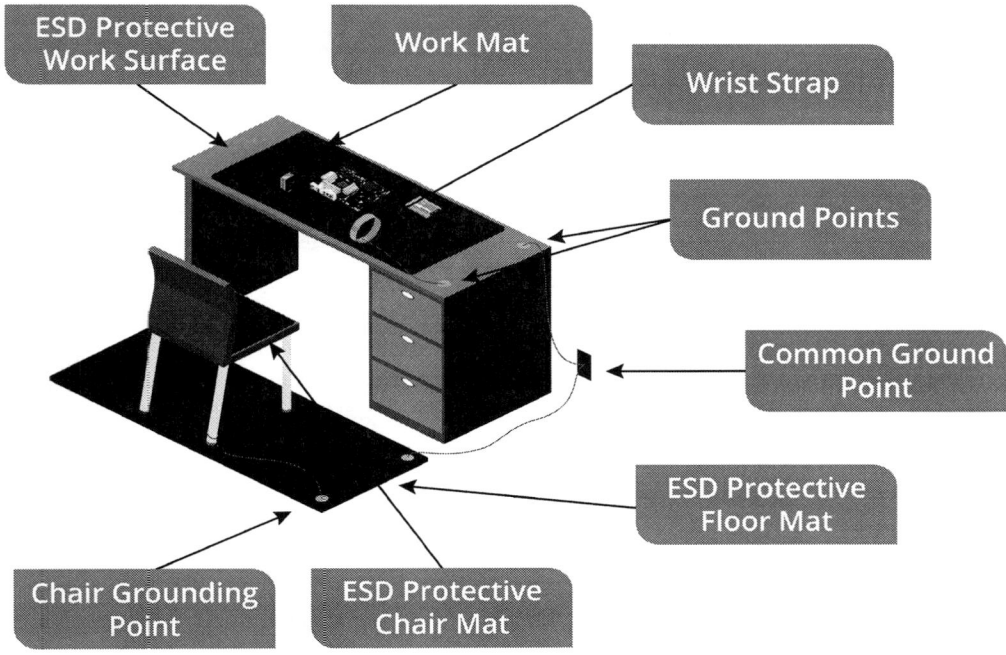

An example of a basic electrostatic discharge (ESD) workstation. (Image © 123RF.com.)

- Electronic components, assemblies, and spare parts, known as **field replaceable units (FRUs)** are often shipped in **antistatic bags** to protect them from ESD damage.

ANTISTATIC BAG TYPES

Antistatic packaging includes either anti-ESD shielding or dissipative material.

- Anti-ESD Shielding—this packaging reduces the risk of ESD because it is coated with a conductive material (such as a nickel compound). This material prevents static electricity from discharging through the inside of the bag. These bags are usually a shiny grey metallic color. To protect the contents of the bag fully, you should seal it, or at least fold the top over and seal that down.
- Dissipative Packaging—this light pink or blue packaging reduces the build-up of static in the general vicinity of the contents by being slightly more conductive than normal. A plastic bag or foam packaging may be sprayed with an anti-static coating or have anti-static materials added to the plastic compound. This is used to package non-static-sensitive components packed in proximity to static-sensitive components.

GUIDELINES FOR PROTECTING COMPONENTS FROM ESD DAMAGE

Here are some guidelines to help you protect your electronic components from ESD damage.

ESD PROTECTION

Follow these guidelines to protect electronic components from damage due to ESD:

- Use proper component handling and storage procedures whenever you are performing PC maintenance work.
- To protect components and equipment from ESD damage:
  - Make sure that your body and clothing are drained of static electricity before starting work.
  - If possible, work in an uncarpeted area.
  - The simplest (but least effective) means of self-grounding is to touch an unpainted metal part of the PC, such as the power supply unit, before you handle a sensitive component. This is only a temporary solution and a static charge could build up again.

Caution: Do not leave the PC plugged in if you open the case for servicing. Your safety is more important than the risk of damaging some PC components.

- Where possible, handle vulnerable components by holding the edges of the plastic mounting card, and avoid touching the surfaces of the chips themselves.
- Use ESD wrist or ankle straps and dissipative floor mats.

Note: Ensure that the strap has a working current-limiting resistor for safety (straps should be tested daily). Do not use a grounding plug if there is any suspicion of a fault in the socket or in the building's electrical wiring, or if the wiring is not regularly inspected and tested.

*Note: To learn more, check the **Video** tile on the CHOICE Course screen for any videos that supplement the content for this lesson.*

Activity 1-1
Implementing an Anti-ESD Service Kit

BEFORE YOU BEGIN
Your instructor will provide you with an anti-static kit.
You will be performing this activity at your WORKBENCH PC.

SCENARIO
You are assisting with introducing recently hired employees to the safety culture. You will need to demonstrate safe use of an anti-static kit and answer questions about safety procedures and hazards.

1. **Describe the equipment you should use to prevent static electricity on your body from damaging the equipment on which you are working.**

2. Your instructor will provide you with an anti-static service kit. Prepare it for use and allow your instructor to check that you have connected everything correctly.
   You can refer to the figure in the **Component Handling** section for assistance.

3. **True or False? If you are using an anti-static floor mat, you do not need any other anti-ESD service equipment.**

4. **In which atmospheric conditions is the risk of ESD highest?**

5. **Electrical injuries include electrocution, shock, and collateral injury. Would you be injured if you are not part of the electrical ground current?**

6. **Which computer component presents the most danger from electrical shock?**

   ○ System boards

   ○ Hard drives

   ○ Power supplies

   ○ System unit

7. **What component helps to protect users of electrical equipment against a short circuit?**

   ○ Resistor

   ○ Fuse

   ○ Power supply

   ○ ESD wrist strap

8. **What care should you take when lifting a heavy object?**

9. **What should you do before transporting a bulky object?**

Topic B
PC Components

EXAM OBJECTIVES COVERED
1001-3.5 Given a scenario, install and configure motherboards, CPUs, and add-on cards.

If you are not familiar with the various components that a computer is made up of, it can seem like a jigsaw puzzle. Like most puzzles, each part of a computer connects to other parts in a specific place, but generally, you will find that the pieces fit together almost exactly the same way from one system to another. To help you put the puzzle together, you need to understand what these pieces look like and what they do.

SYSTEM CASE TYPES

A **desktop computer** refers to a PC that is not designed to be used on the move. The components of a desktop computer system are divided between those that are designed to be handled by the user (peripheral devices) and those that would be damaged or dangerous if exposed.

The **system case** (or **chassis**) is a plastic and metal box that houses this second class of components, such as the motherboard, Central Processing Unit (CPU), memory, adapter cards, disk drives, and power supply unit. System units are also often referred to as boxes, main units, or base units.

There are two basic types of system unit: Tower and Small Form Factor (SFF). These types are available in different sizes. Be aware that while a small case may be desirable because it takes up less space, it has less room inside for installing extra devices and is less effective at cooling.

A **tower case** is designed to sit vertically on a surface, so that it is taller than it is wide. Tower cases come in four basic sizes: full, mid, mini, and slim line.

- Full tower cases are usually used for PC servers. These require the extra internal space for additional hard disks, adapter cards, and redundant power supply units.
- Mid tower cases are used for high-end user PCs. These PCs do require extra devices and adapter cards, but not as many as a server.
- Mini tower cases are usually used for office or home PCs where the requirement for additional internal devices and adapter cards is limited.
- Slimline cases require low-profile adapter cards but can be oriented horizontally or vertically.

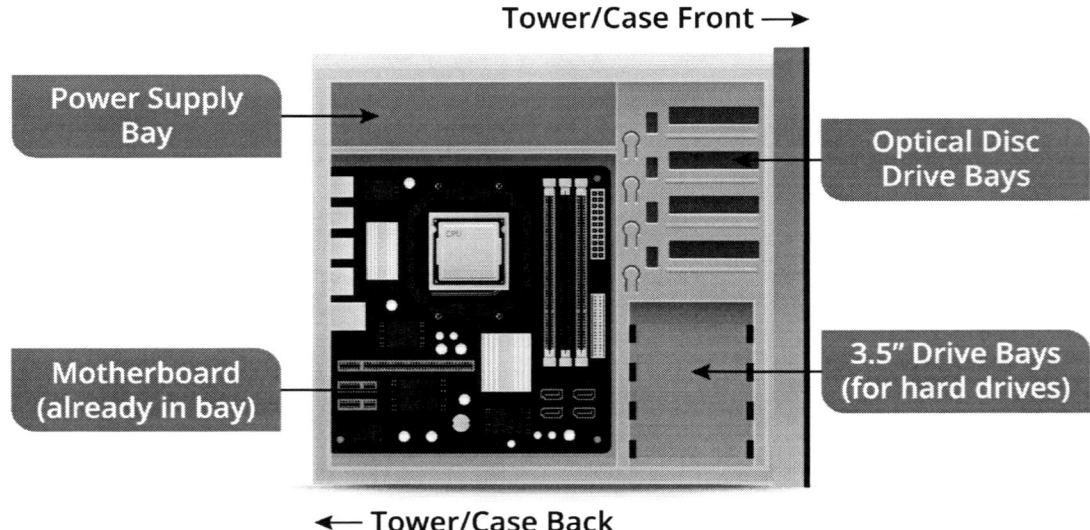

Computer tower with main panel removed showing an attached motherboard and areas for optical disc drives, 3.5" drive bays, and a power supply bay. (Image © 123RF.com.)

Small Form Factor (SFF) case designs are semi-portable, space-saving designs typically used for domestic entertainment or Media Center systems that will not look out of place in a living room. They are usually cube-like or super slimline. SFF cases can hold only a limited number of components.

Desktop computers can also be purchased as **all-in-one units**. All-in-one means that all the computer components, except the keyboard and mouse, are contained within the monitor case.

All-in-one PC. (Image © 123RF.com.)

PARTS OF THE SYSTEM CASE

To perform PC maintenance and component upgrades, you must understand how to open a desktop computer's case.

- Each case has a **cover**, which is removed by either undoing the screws at the back or pressing together clips that release it. Cases based on the slimline design have a hinged cover that releases to allow access to the motherboard.
- The **front panel** provides access to the removable media drives, a power on/off switch, a reset switch, and LEDs (Light Emitting Diodes) to indicate drive operation. The front cover can be removed but may require the side panel to be removed first in order to access the screws or clips that secure it.

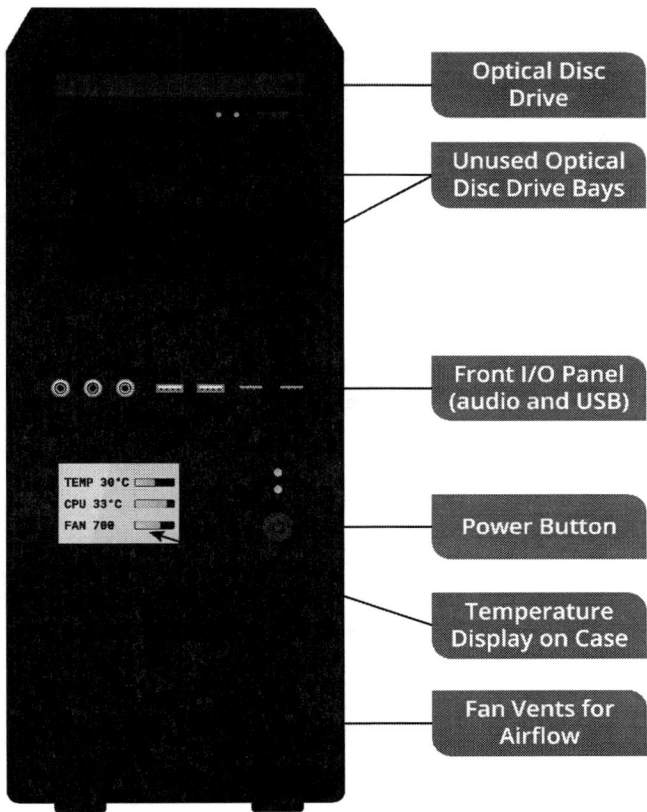

Front of case. (Image © 123RF.com.)

 Note: *Some cases feature tool-free access (that is, they are secured by clips). Some cases use proprietary screw fittings to prevent unauthorized access to the internal components.*

- The **rear panel** has cut-out slots aligned with the position of **adapter card** slots. These slots should either be covered by an adapter card or a metal strip known as a **blanking plate**. Uncovered slots can disrupt the proper flow of air around components in the PC and cause overheating and also increase the amount of dust in the system.

  There is also a cut-out aligned with the motherboard's Input/Output (I/O) ports. These allow for the connection of peripheral devices.

  The rear panel provides access to the Power Supply Unit (PSU) sockets. The PSU has an integral fan exhaust. Care should be taken that it is not obstructed, as this will adversely affect cooling. There may be an additional case fan.

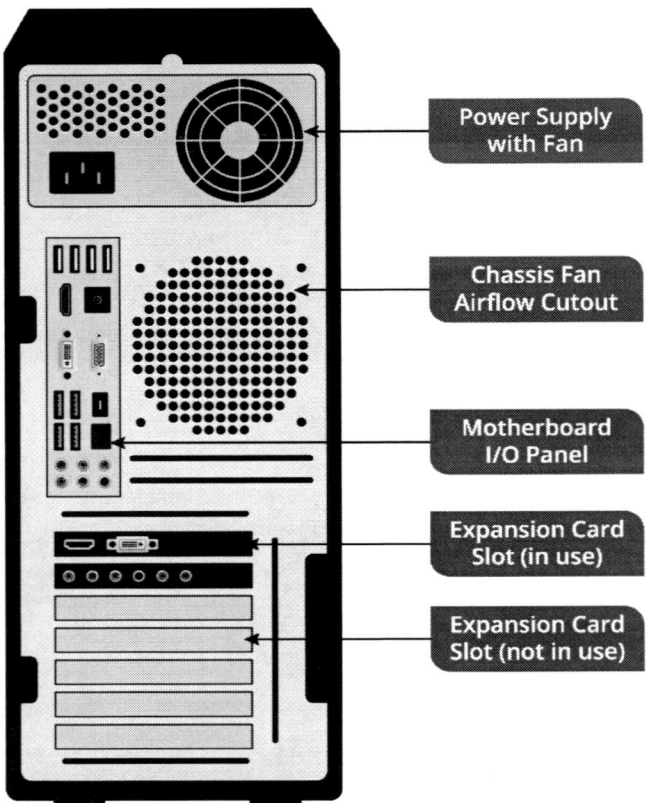

Rear panel of a PC. (Image © 123RF.com.)

REPAIR OR REPLACE?

PC components that are easily user-replaceable (or upgradeable) are referred to as **field replaceable units (FRUs)**. Due to economic factors, most components of a PC are not worth repairing; instead they are simply replaced with a new unit ("swapped out").

GUIDELINES FOR PC DISASSEMBLY

Here are some guidelines for disassembling PCs.

PC DISASSEMBLY

Before you start to disassemble a PC, consider the following guidelines:
- Back up all data stored on the internal drive(s) to protect important data.
- Create a clean work environment with plenty of working space where you can set the PC at a comfortable height.
- Gather all necessary tools and equipment. A notepad and pen may be useful for making diagrams and notes. A digital camera is also useful for recording the layout of components.
- Make sure that all devices are powered off and unplugged from the building power before disconnecting them.
- Take anti-static precautions to minimize the chance of damaging sensitive components. Place static-sensitive components, such as processors and memory, in anti-static bags.

*Note: To learn more, check the **Video** tile on the CHOICE Course screen for any videos that supplement the content for this lesson.*

Access the Checklist tile on your CHOICE Course screen for reference information and job aids on How to Disassemble a Personal Computer.

MOTHERBOARDS

A printed circuit board, variously called the **motherboard**, **mobo**, **system board**, or **main board**, houses the processor, chipset, memory, and expansion slots. The type of motherboard influences system speed and upgrade capabilities. There are many motherboard manufacturers, including AOpen (Acer), ASRock, ASUSTek, Biostar, EVGA Corporation, Gigabyte, Intel, MSI, Shuttle, Tyan, and Via.

The motherboard is attached to the case by using **standoffs**. These hold the motherboard firmly and ensure no other part of it touches the case. The standoffs are positioned in holes that line up in the same position in the case and the motherboard (as long as they use compatible form factors). Standoffs are either brass ones secured by screws or plastic ones that snap into place.

MOTHERBOARD FORM FACTORS

The form factor of the motherboard describes its shape, layout, and the type of case and power supply that can be used. Two motherboards may have exactly the same functionality but different form factors; the difference is the layout of the components on the motherboard.

The following table describes common motherboard form factors.

Form Factor	Description
ATX	• The Advanced Technology Extended (ATX) specification was developed by Intel in 1995 to provide a new design for PC motherboards, updating the previous AT form factor. • Full size ATX boards are 12 inches wide by 9.6 inches deep (or 305 x 244 mm). • ATX boards can contain up to seven expansion slots.
Micro-ATX	• The Micro-ATX (mATX) standard specifies a 9.6-inch (244 x 244 mm) square board. • mATX boards have fewer expansion slots than ATX boards (up to 4 compared to a maximum of 7 for full-sized ATX boards).

Note: Most mATX boards can be mounted in ATX cases.

Form Factor	Description
Mini-ITX	• Small Form Factor (SFF) PCs are becoming popular as home machines (and in image-conscious offices). SFF PCs often use Via's Mini-ITX form factor. • Mini-ITX is 6.7 inches (170 x 170 mm) square with one expansion slot. *Note: Most mini-ITX boards can be mounted in ATX cases.*
Other ITX-based form factors	There are also smaller nano-, pico-, and mobile-ITX form factors, but these are used for embedded systems and portables, rather than PCs. *Note: No commercial motherboards were ever produced from the original plain ITX specification.*

MOTHERBOARD CONNECTOR TYPES

All motherboards have connectors for the same sort of components: CPU, memory, disk drives, peripherals, and so on. However, the type and number of these connectors depends upon the motherboard model.

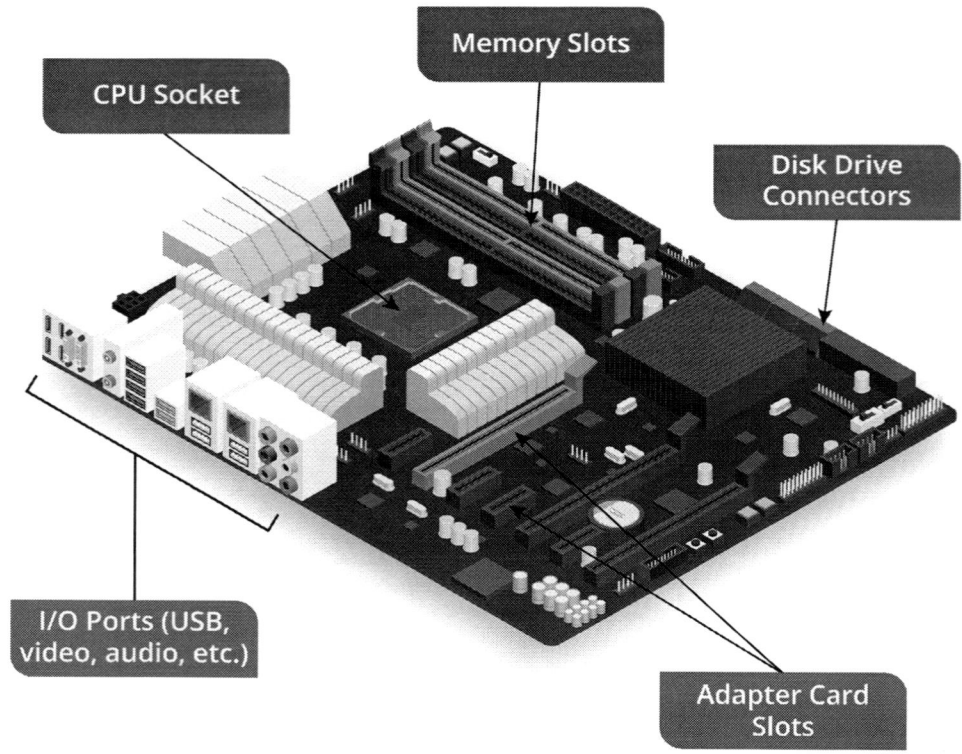

Motherboard connectors. (Image © 123RF.com.)

CPU SOCKETS

New motherboards are generally released to support new CPU designs. Most PC CPUs are manufactured by Intel and AMD, and these vendors use different socket designs.

Also, because technology changes rapidly, a given motherboard will only support a limited number of CPU models. CPU models are closely tied to the chipset and memory subsystem. This means that there is less scope for upgrading the CPU than used to be the case. You could not, for instance, take a motherboard designed for the Core 2 CPU and plug an AMD Phenom CPU into it. Both the physical interface (socket) and system architecture have diverged along proprietary lines since the old socket 7 interface.

The CPU is typically inserted into a squarish socket, located close to the memory sockets, and then covered by a heatsink and fan.

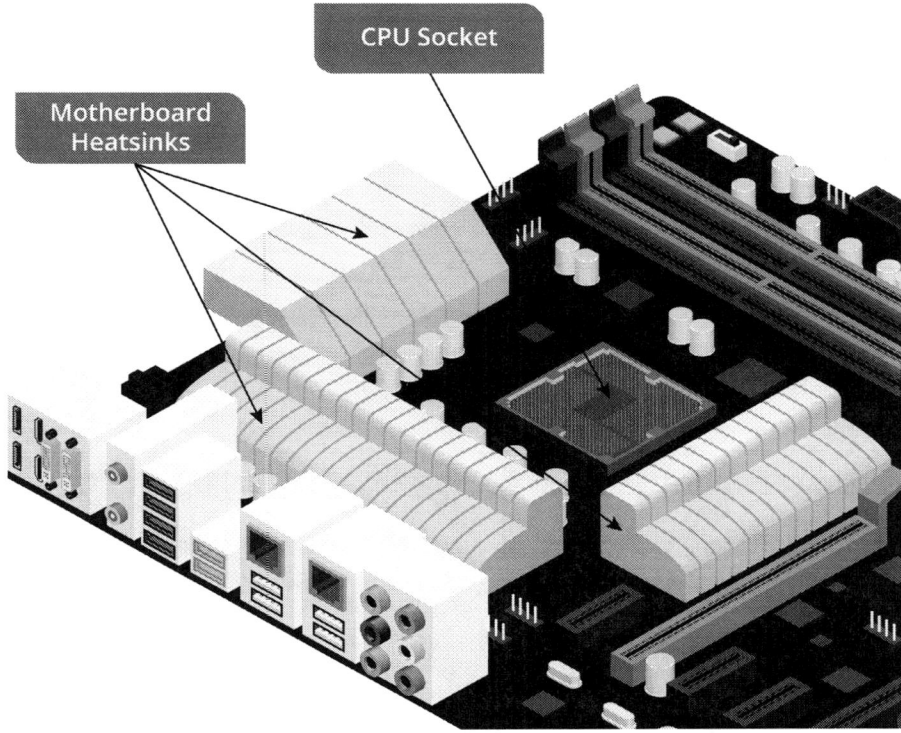

Motherboard CPU socket and heatsinks. (Image © 123RF.com.)

MEMORY SLOTS

All the software and data processed by a computer is ultimately stored as binary code; strings of ones and zeroes. This program code is stored in system memory.

System memory uses a type of memory technology called **Random Access Memory (RAM)**. Program code is loaded into RAM so that it can be accessed and executed by the processor. RAM also holds data, such as the contents of a spreadsheet or document, while it is being modified. System RAM is volatile; it loses its contents when power is removed.

System RAM is normally packaged as Dual Inline Memory Modules (DIMMs) fitted to motherboard slots. DIMM slots have catches at either end, are located close to the CPU socket, and are often color-coded. Note that there are various RAM technologies (DDR3 versus DDR4, for instance) and the DIMMs are specific to a particular DDR version. A label next to the slots should identify the type of DIMMs supported.

The capabilities of the memory controller and number of physical slots determine how much memory can be fitted.

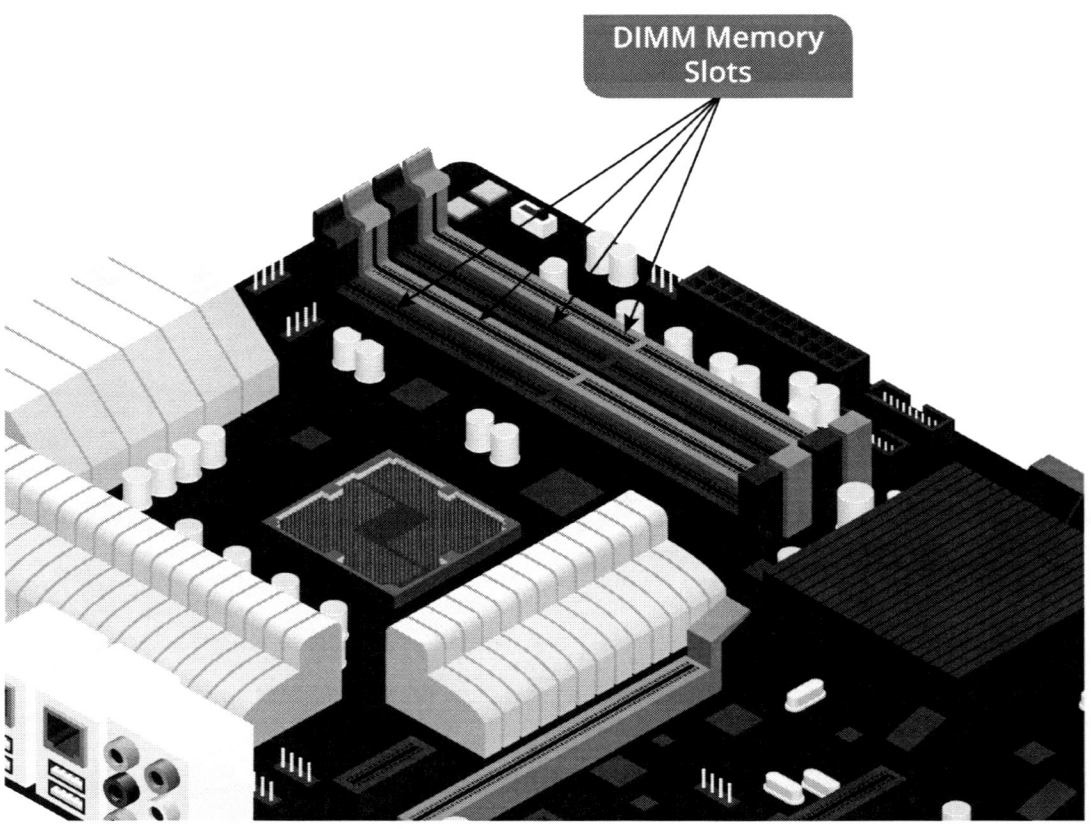

Motherboard DIMM system memory slots. (Image © 123RF.com.)

CHIPSET AND MEMORY ARCHITECTURE

The **chipset** consists of several controllers that handle the transfer of data between the CPU and various devices. Examples of controllers include the following:

- System memory controller.
- Input/Output (I/O) controller to handle disk drives and expansion buses.
- Controllers for any integrated video, sound, and network (cabled and wireless) interfaces.

 Note: Intel and AMD manufacture all the CPUs used in PCs, but there are various chipset vendors. Some of the major names include ATI (now owned by AMD), NVIDIA, SiS, ULi, and VIA.

The chipset is soldered onto the motherboard and cannot be upgraded. The type of chipset on the motherboard can affect the choice of processor and multiprocessing support, type and amount of system memory supported, and type(s) of system bus supported.

The link between the CPU and system memory is a key factor in determining system performance. Historically, PCs used a chipset split into two sections: the northbridge and the southbridge. The main function of the northbridge is as the system memory controller, connecting the processor to RAM. The southbridge is designed to control all of the I/O functions not handled by the northbridge. These are older, slower technologies, such as USB.

As memory, video, and fixed disk technologies improved, the northbridge/southbridge architecture became a bottleneck to performance. Newer CPUs and chipsets use different designs, with Intel and AMD both introducing different architectures. The general trend is for subsystems that require a lot of bandwidth—notably the system memory controller and graphics controller—to be incorporated on the same chip as the CPU itself (referred to as "on die").

CMOS AND RTC BATTERIES

On older computers, **CMOS** RAM stored the PC's basic configuration and any settings made via the CMOS/system firmware setup program. CMOS stands for Complementary Metal-Oxide Semiconductor, which describes the manufacturing process used to make the RAM chip.

CMOS devices require very little power to operate and use a small battery to maintain their settings. The **CMOS battery** is a coin cell lithium battery. These batteries typically last for 5-10 years.

On current motherboards, configuration data is stored in a Non-Volatile RAM (NVRAM) chip such as flash memory, rather than in CMOS RAM. Flash memory does not require battery-backup. A CMOS battery is still used to power the **Real Time Clock (RTC)**, however, and may be referred to as the **RTC battery** or **clock battery**. The RTC keeps track of the actual date and time.

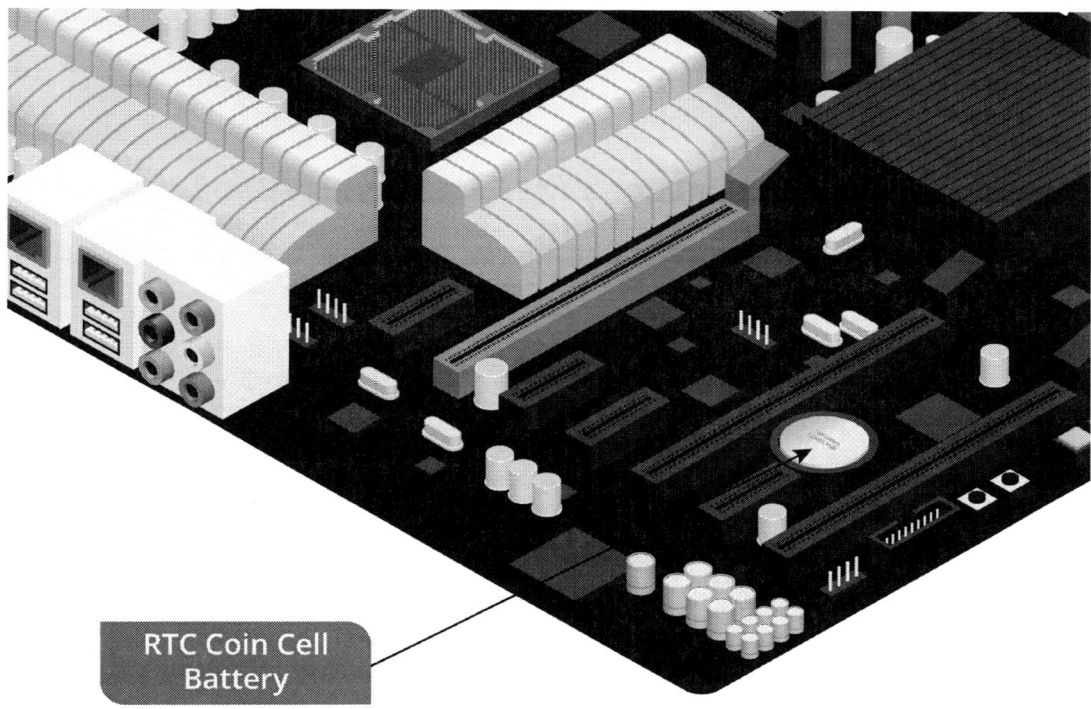

RTC coin cell battery on the motherboard. (Image © 123RF.com.)

BUS ARCHITECTURE

Computers transmit data using electrical signals and process and store it using components called transistors and capacitors. An electrical pathway on the motherboard or through cabling that carries the signals is referred to as a **bus**. Physically, a bus is implemented on the motherboard as tiny wires (called **traces**) running between components. The bus carries information being processed by the computer (data) and information about where the data is located in memory (address). The bus also carries power to a component and the timing signals that synchronize data transfers between components.

The term "bus architecture" usually means an expansion bus, used to connect peripheral devices. However, a variety of buses exist within a PC. Also, the way that bus designs are implemented has changed considerably as PC technology has developed and improved.

INTERNAL AND EXTERNAL BUSES

One way of categorizing types of buses is to divide them into internal and external. An internal bus, or **local** bus, connects core components, such as the CPU, memory, and the system controllers.

An external bus, or **expansion bus**, allows additional components to be connected to the computer. These components could be peripheral devices (located outside the case) or adapter cards (located inside the case).

External bus technologies do not necessarily extend outside the computer case. For example, PCI, the most popular expansion bus standard, provides connections to internal adapter cards only. A genuinely external bus (like SCSI, USB, or Firewire) extends the bus wires outside the computer case using cabling. The distinction between internal and external bus types has also become a lot less clear as one bus technology will be used to perform both types of role (for example, PCI Express).

EXPANSION SLOTS

Expansion slots enable you to install plug-in adapter cards in a computer to extend the range of functions it can perform. There are several expansion bus types and many different types of adapter card.

Computers can support more than one expansion bus. PCs use a multi-bus design, to support older technologies and allow for upgrades. For example, a PC might support PCI and PCI Express for adding internal adapter cards plus USB to allow the connection of peripherals.

RISER CARDS

Some PC case designs are slimline, meaning that there is not enough space for full height expansion cards. This problem is addressed by providing a **riser card** at right angles to the main board, enabling you to connect additional adapters to the system in an orientation that is parallel to the motherboard and thus save space within the system case.

 Note: Another option is to use low profile adapter cards. A low profile card is about half the height of a standard card and so fits within a slimline case.

Historically, the LPX and NLX form factors were designed as riser architectures. Most manufacturers just use the ATX riser card specification. This specifies a 2x11 connector plus a PCI connector for the riser card.

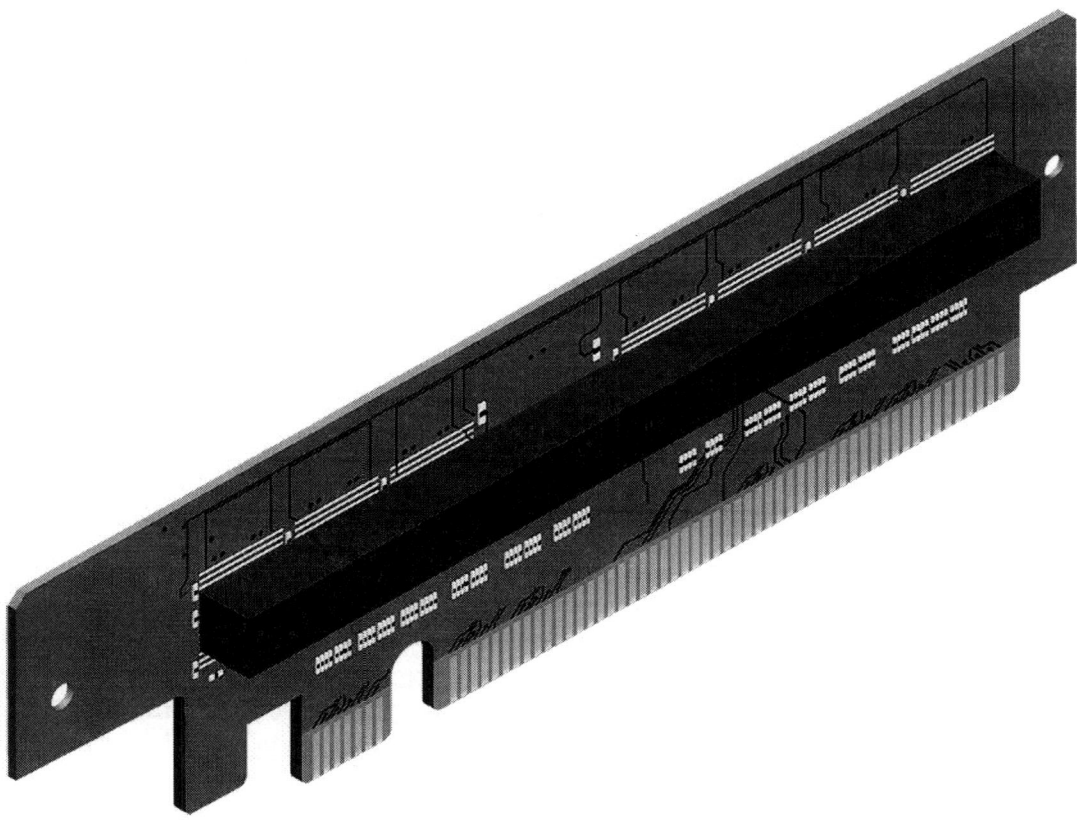

A riser card. (Image © 123RF.com.)

 ***Note:* Daughter board** *is a general computing and electronics term for any circuit board that plugs into another circuit board. In personal computing, a daughter board can be used as a more general term for adapter cards. Sometimes, in casual usage, the term is used interchangeably with the term riser card, but technically they are not the same.*

SYSTEM CLOCK AND BUS SPEED

The **system clock** synchronizes the operation of all parts of the PC and provides the basic timing signal for the CPU. Clock speeds are measured in Megahertz (MHz) or Gigahertz (GHz). The clock consists of a clock generator that sets up a timing signal and clock multipliers that take the timing signal produced by the generator and apply a multiplication factor to produce different timing signals for different types of buses. This means that one type of bus can work at a different speed (or frequency) to another type of bus.

PCI BUS

The **Peripheral Component Interconnect (PCI) bus** was introduced in 1994 with the Pentium processor. It is still an important technology in terms of adapter card provision, though it is being superseded by PCI Express. Several versions of PCI have been released subsequently to the first commercial version (2.0). Information about PCI standards is published at pcisig.org. The different capabilities are summarized here.

BUS WIDTH AND CLOCK SPEED

- PCI supports up to 5 devices (though each device can have up to 8 different functions) and allocates system resources by using Plug-and-Play. Bandwidth on the PCI bus is shared between all devices. PCI supports **bus mastering**, meaning that the device can control the bus to transfer data to and from memory, without requiring the CPU. The PCI architecture is a 32-bit-wide parallel bus working at 33.3 MHz, achieving a transfer rate of up to 133 MBps (that is, 32 bits divided by 8 to get 4 bytes, then multiplied by the clock rate of 33.3).
- Later versions allowed for 66 MHz operation (giving a 32-bit bus 266 MBps bandwidth) and a 64-bit wide bus (266 MBps at 33.3 MHz or 533 MBps at 66 MHz). 64-bit and 66 MHz cards and buses are not commonly found on desktop PCs, however.

ADAPTER CARD AND SLOT FORM FACTORS

Originally, PCI cards were designed for 5V signaling, but the PCI 2.1 specification also allows for 3.3V and dual voltage cards. In order to prevent the wrong type of PCI card from being inserted (for example, a 3.3V card in a 5V PCI slot), the keying for the three types of cards is different.

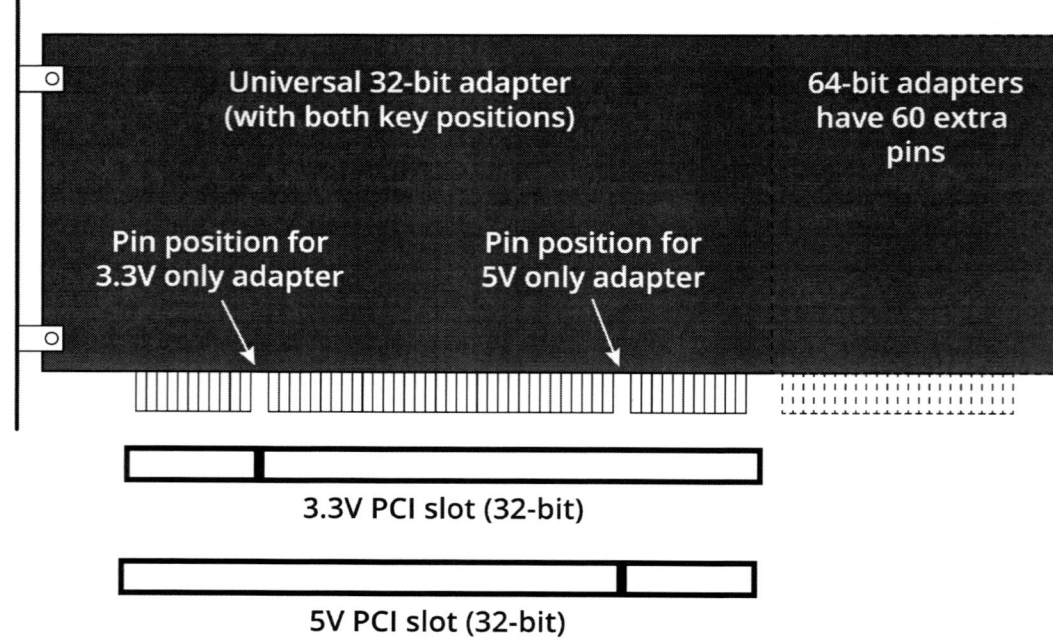

PCI card and slot form factors. The exact number of pins is not shown in this image. (Image © 123RF.com.)

On a 5V card and slot, the key is at pins 50-51; on a 3.3V adapter, the key is at pins 12-13.

64-bit compatible slots and adapters have an extra 60 pins, making the slots distinctively longer. A 32-bit card can be inserted into a 64-bit slot (as long as it is not a 5V card).

 Note: *PCI 2.3 deprecates the use of 5V cards and most cards are universal. The vast majority of cards and slots for desktop systems are 32-bit. 64-bit PCI is more a feature of server-level systems.*

Regardless of the voltage used for signaling, PCI slots can deliver up to 25W of power to an adapter.

A dual voltage (universal) adapter has both keys.

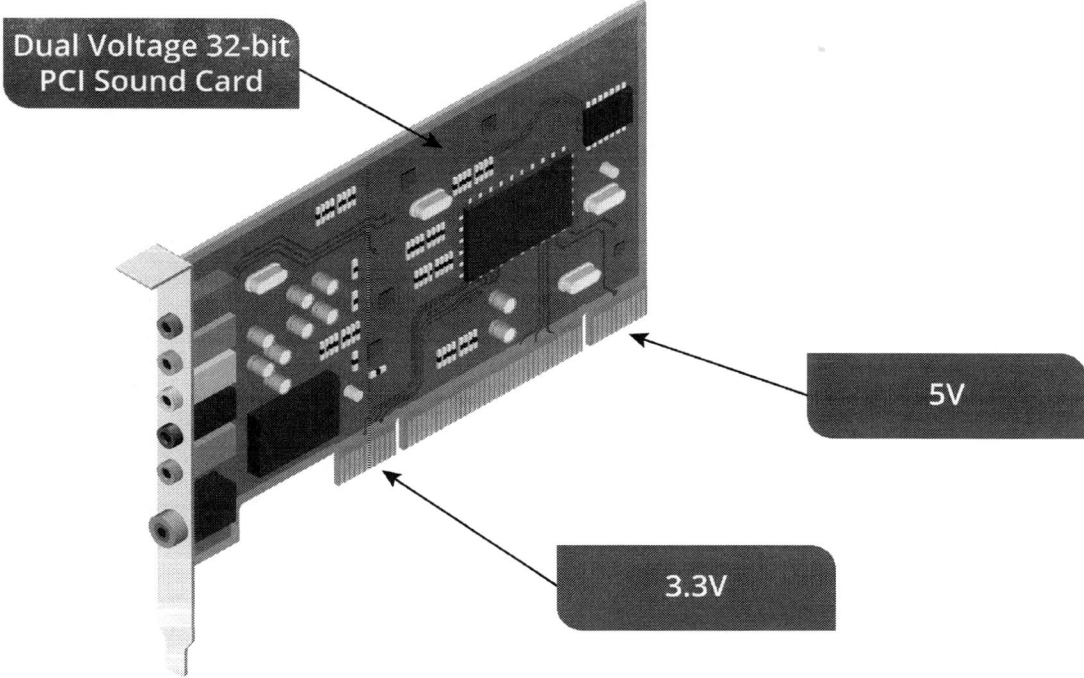

32-bit PCI sound card with dual voltage. (Image © 123RF.com.)

PCI EXPRESS BUS

As CPU and memory bus speeds increased over the years, PCI represented a substantial bottleneck to computer performance. PCI is a parallel interface. Parallel interface speeds are limited by the problem of timing each signal (data skew). They are also more complex and costly to implement. Another performance barrier is the fact that the bandwidth of the PCI bus is shared between all the components connected to it, and only one component can make use of the bus at any one time. This is a particular problem for video, disk access, and networking.

Various fixes were implemented to remove critical bottlenecks. These fixes added to the complexity of chip design, and over time the PCI bus simply became inadequate. **PCI Express (PCIe)** was released by Intel in 2004 as the replacement for the PCI architecture. PCIe uses point-to-point serial communications, meaning that each component can have a dedicated link to any other component. Connections are made via a switch, which routes data between components and can provide Quality of Service (QoS) to any component that needs it (for example, to prioritize real-time video over non-time critical data).

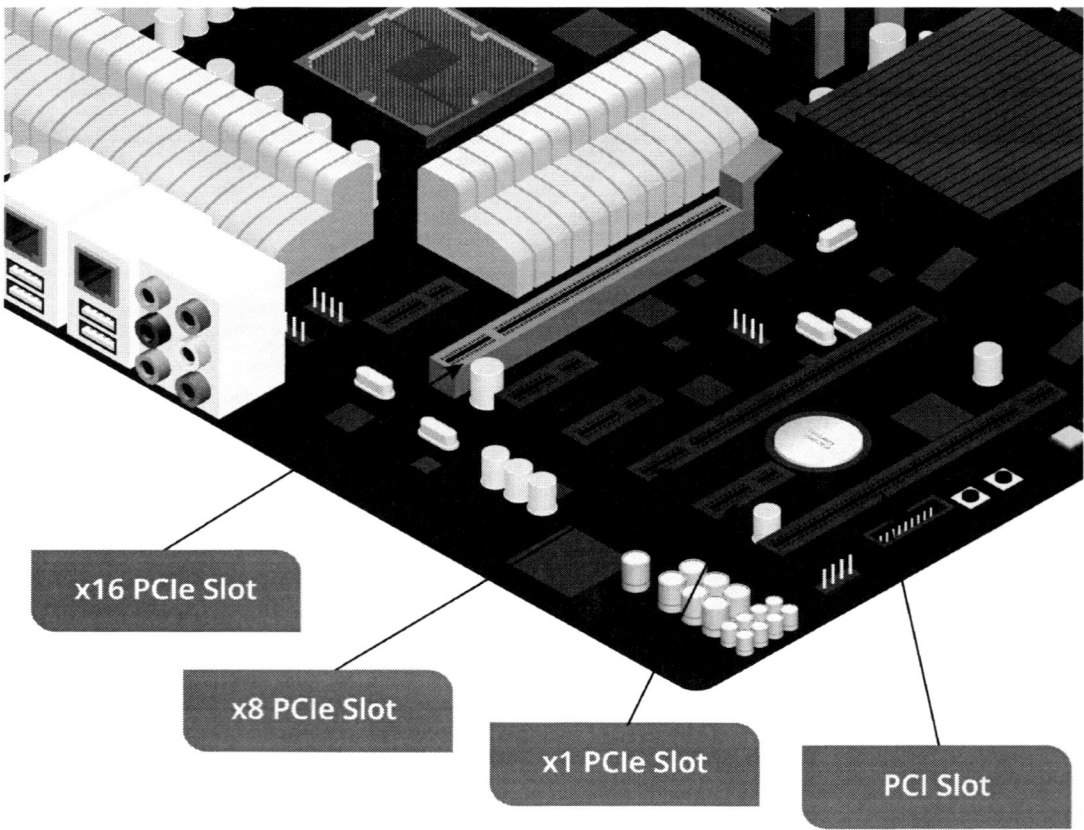

Motherboard PCI and PCI Express expansion slots. (Image © 123RF.com.)

Each point-to-point connection is referred to as a **link**. The link sends both data and control/timing instructions. A link can make use of one or more **lanes**. Each lane consists of two wire pairs (four wires in total) using low voltage differential signaling. One pair is used to transmit and the other to receive (bi-directional).

- A given component can support a specific number of lanes (usually x1, x4, x8, or x16), and the switch negotiates the maximum possible number of lanes to use (for example, x8 and x16 devices would use 8 lanes). Each lane supports a transfer rate of 250 MBps in each direction. Most graphics cards use x16 links (4 GBps in each direction).
- A card will fit in any port with an equal or greater number of lanes. For example, a x8 card will fit in a x8 or x16 socket (up-plugging) and work at x8, but it will not fit in a x1 or x4 slot (down-plugging). x4, x8, and x16 slots are physically the same length but parts of the slot will be blanked out for x4 and x8.

PCIe is software compatible with PCI, meaning that PCI ports can be included on a motherboard (to support legacy adapter cards) but PCI cards cannot be fitted into PCIe sockets.

PCIe can supply up to 75W to a device via the motherboard slot. An extra 75W power can be supplied via a PCIe power connector. PCIe also features power management functions and support for hot swappable and hot pluggable adapters.

PCIe VERSIONS

The original PCIe standard has been subject to several version updates. PCI Express 2 compatible motherboards and adapters support transfer rates of 500 MBps per lane. Version 2.0 motherboards and adapters are interchangeable with earlier version 1.1

devices, though the added performance benefits are realized only if both components support version 2.

PCIe 2.1 specifies a power draw from the slot of up to 150W and an 8-pin auxiliary power connector delivering another 150W. This change introduced potential compatibility problems with v1.0 devices but these can often be fixed via a firmware update.

PCIe 3 further increases transfer rates to around 1 GBps per lane while maintaining backward-compatibility. The PCIe 4 standard doubles transfer rates again, to roughly 2 GBps per lane, whereas PCIe 5, while still being finalized at the time of writing, will almost double it again (to nearly 4 GBps per lane).

> **Note:** You will also see the term GigaTransfers per second (GT/s) used to describe PCIe speeds. These values do not exclude the bits transmitted as signaling and encoding overhead.

STORAGE BUS (SATA AND IDE)

A **storage bus** is a special type of expansion bus dedicated to communicating with storage devices, such as hard disks, solid state drives, and optical drives (CD/DVD/Blu-ray). Host Bus Adapters (HBAs) provide a connection point for internal mass storage devices, such as hard drives, optical drives, and tape drives. There used to be two main bus standards for attaching internal storage devices to a PC: Parallel ATA (PATA), which is also known as Integrated Drive Electronics (IDE) or Enhanced IDE (EIDE), and Small Computer System Interface (SCSI).

Both IDE and SCSI used parallel transfers of data per clock signal to improve bandwidth. As circuitry and encoding methods have improved, these parallel transmission technologies have been superseded by faster serial bus types. Consequently, IDE and SCSI have now largely been replaced by SATA (Serial ATA).

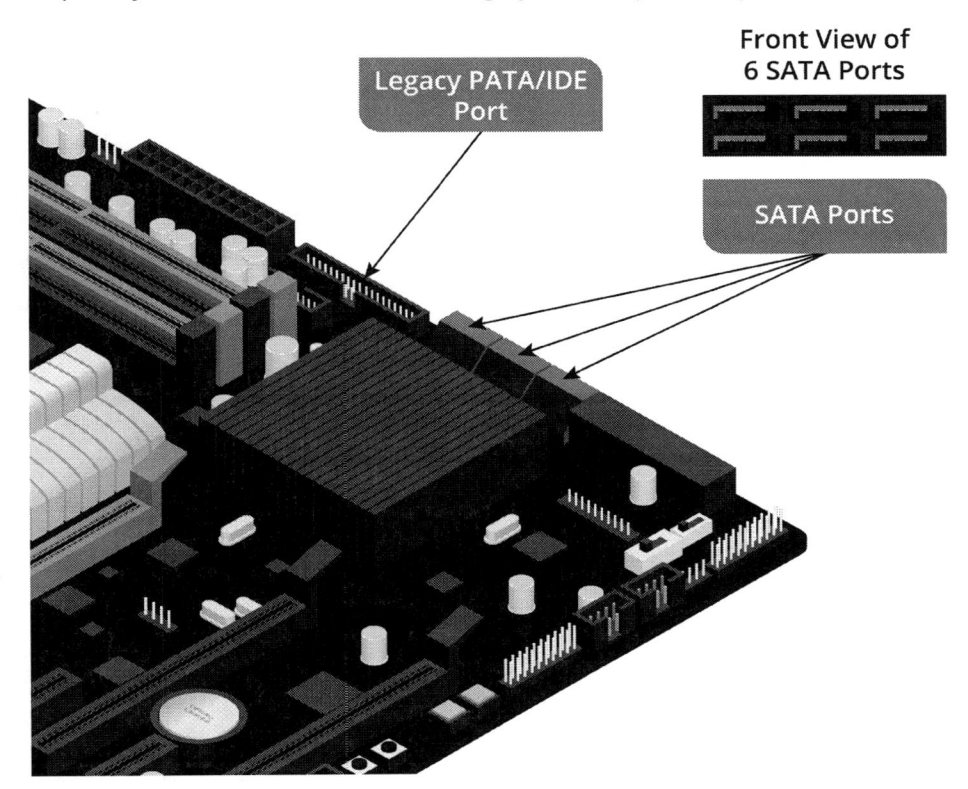

Motherboard SATA and legacy PATA/IDE ports. (Image © 123RF.com.)

A SATA port accepts a compact 7-pin connector and can be used to attach a single device. Most full size motherboards have 4 built-in SATA ports.

> **Note:** What is called IDE today is technically Enhanced IDE (EIDE). Original IDE specifications were published even further in the past.

OTHER MOTHERBOARD CONNECTORS

In addition to slots and sockets for the major components, motherboards also include connectors for things like case buttons and fans.

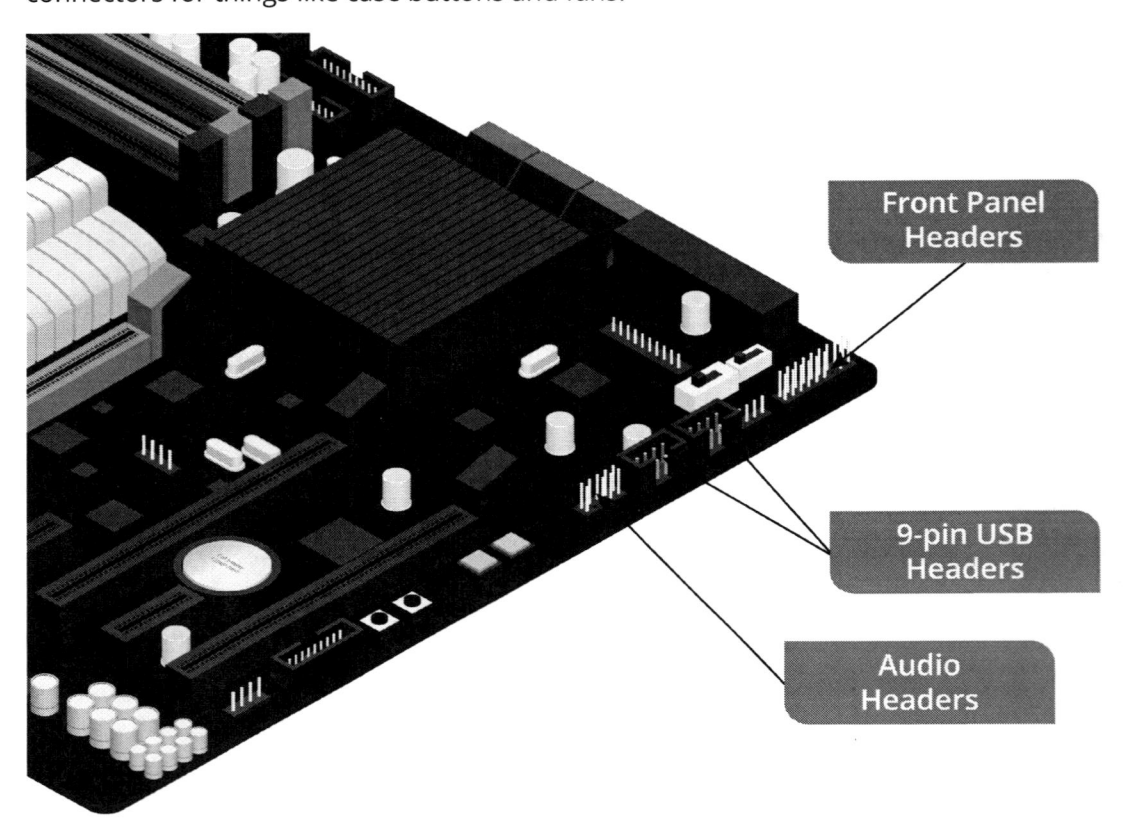

Motherboard front panel, USB, and audio headers. (Image © 123RF.com.)

These connector types are described in the following table.

Connector Type	Description
Internal USB connectors	A computer will normally feature one or two front USB ports to connect peripherals, as well as more on the back. Internal USB connections are made via 9-pin headers, which accept up to two 4-pin port connections (the 9th pin is to orient the cable correctly).

Connector Type	Description
Front panel connectors	Components on the front panel of the case connect to headers on the motherboard. Typically, front panel connectors can include:
	• Power button (soft power): On modern computers, the power button sends a signal to the PC that can be interpreted by the OS (as a command to shut down for instance) rather than actually switching the PC off. Holding down the power button for a few seconds will cut the power, however.
	• Drive (HDD) activity lights: These show when an internal hard disk is being accessed.
	• Audio ports: These allow headphones and a microphone to be connected to the computer.
	When disassembling the system, you should make a diagram of how these connectors are plugged in (position and orientation). If you do not have a diagram, you will have to refer to the motherboard documentation or go by any labels printed on the wires and headers. These are not always very easy to follow, however, which is why you should always make a diagram (or take a digital photo) to refer to.
Power and fan connectors	The motherboard also contains various connection points for the power supply and fans.
	• The power connector is usually a 24-pin white or black block.
	• Fan connectors are smaller. There will be one for the CPU and one or more for the case fans.
	There is no current standard that dictates the size and form factor of fan connectors. Common connectors include:
	• A 3-pin Molex KK connector, commonly used to connect a fan directly to the motherboard.
	• A 4-pin Molex KK connector that is similar in function to the 3-pin KK connector, except that it has an extra pin to provide the ability to control the speed of the fan.
	• A 4-pin Molex connector that connects directly to the system's power supply.

Note: In some systems, the system firmware monitors the fan speed. In order for this to happen, the power supply requires an external fan connector that is attached to the motherboard. The fan does not draw power from the connector; it only is used to provide information to the system firmware. Based on the information received, the system can increase the fan speed for improved cooling or decrease the fan speed when less cooling is needed so that the system operates more quietly.

JUMPER SETTINGS

When upgrading components such as the CPU, you may have to change the position of **jumpers** on the motherboard. A jumper is a small plastic clip containing a metal conductor that fits over two contacts on the motherboard. The position of the clip completes a circuit that configures the motherboard in one way or another.

Note: *There may be a motherboard reset jumper. Setting this may allow you to restore the system from a failed firmware update, forgotten system supervisor password, and so on.*

Activity 1-2
Discussing PC Components

SCENARIO
Answer the following questions to check your understanding of the topic.

1. Describe how you would open a PC case to access the motherboard.

2. At the rear of a system case are slots for adapter card ports. Why should these be covered with blanking plates if not in use?

3. You have been servicing a computer but when you have finished you find that it will not turn on. There was no power problem before and you have verified that the computer is connected to a working electrical outlet.

   What is the most likely explanation?

4. What is the main function of the chipset?

5. True or false? The Real Time Clock controls the timing of signals between the CPU and other components.

6. What type of socket is used to install system memory?

7. **You have a x8 PCIe storage adapter card—can you fit this in a x16 slot?**

8. **What is the bandwidth of a PCIe v2.0 x16 graphics adapter?**

9. You also need to help new hires identify the different types of motherboards used in computers deployed throughout the company.

   What type of motherboard is displayed here, and what characteristics did you use to help you identify the board type?

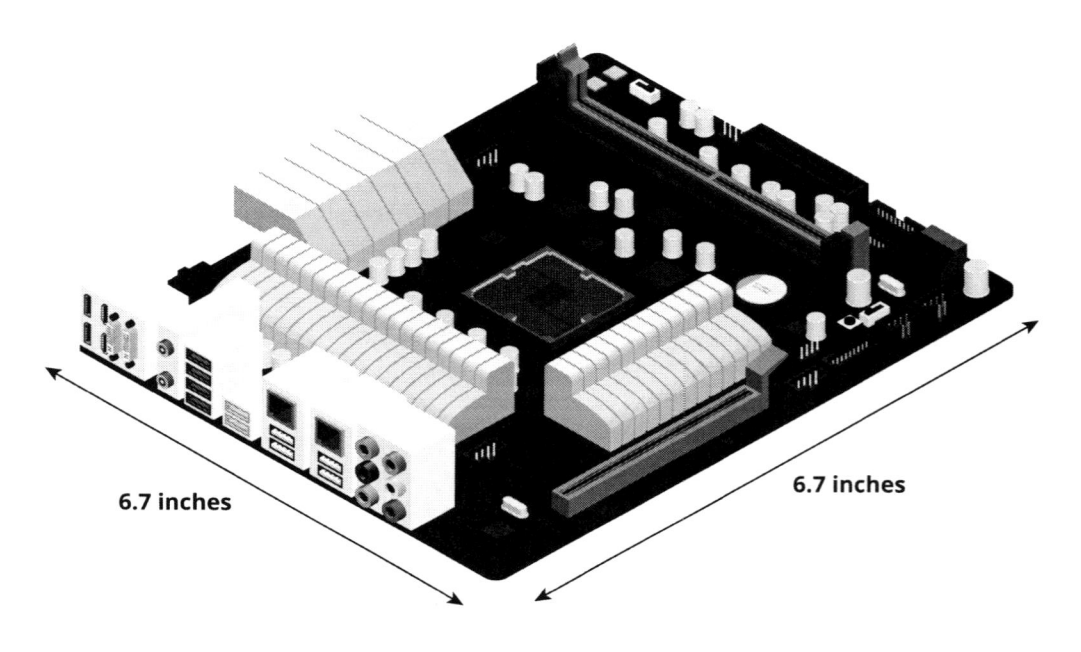

   6.7 inches

   6.7 inches

10. **What type of motherboard is displayed here, and what characteristics did you use to help you identify the board type?**

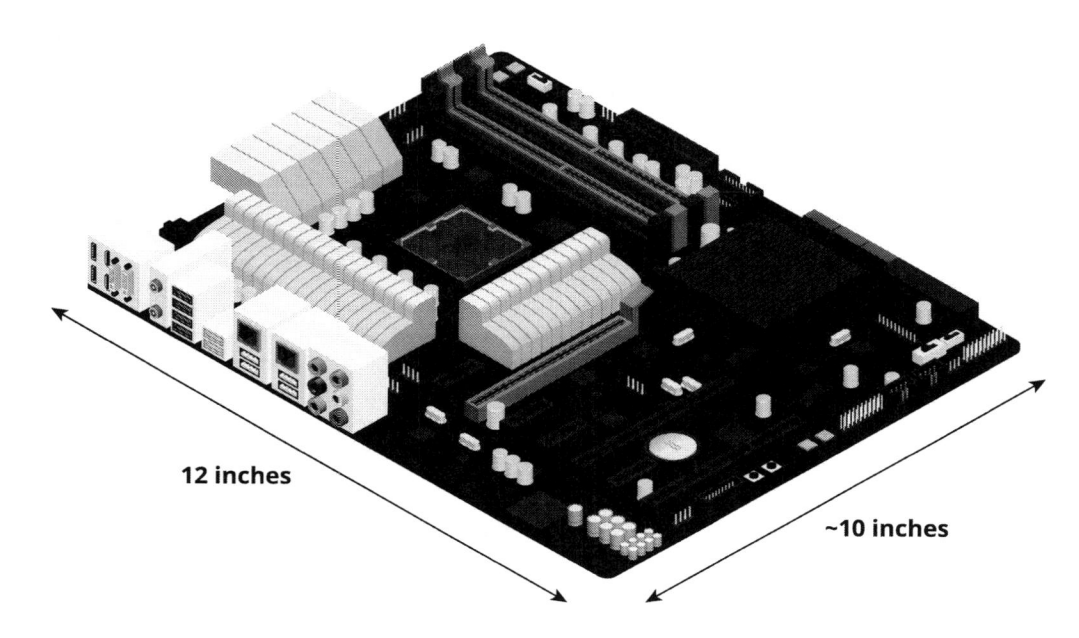

12 inches

~10 inches

Topic C
Common Connection Interfaces

EXAM OBJECTIVES COVERED
1001-3.1 Explain basic cable types, features, and their purposes.
1001-3.2 Identify common connector types.
1001-3.5 Given a scenario, install and configure motherboards, CPUs, and add-on cards.

You need to be able to identify how components are connected together to form a complete computer system. In this topic, you will compare PC and device connection interfaces and their characteristics.

A PC is made up of many different components. All of these components need to be able to communicate with each other so that the computer can function properly. As PC designs have evolved over the years, several connection technologies have been implemented to provide communication among computer components. As a computer technician, identifying the methods used to connect devices to a computer will enable you to install, upgrade, and replace PC components quickly and effectively.

INTERFACES, PORTS, AND CONNECTIONS

Some people might use the terms interface, port, and connection interchangeably, but there are some differences among the three.

INTERFACE
An **interface** is the point at which two devices connect and communicate with each other.

PORT
A **Port** is a hardware interface that you can use to connect devices to a computer. The port can also be referred to as an endpoint.
- The port transfers electronic signals between the device and the system unit.
- A port is either an electrically wired socket or plug, or it can be a wireless transmission device.
- Ports can vary by shape, by color, by the number and layout of the pins or connectors contained within the port, by the signals the port carries, and by the port's location.
- Ports exist for both internal and external devices. External ports often have a graphical representation of the type of device that should be connected to it, such as a small picture of a monitor adjacent to the video port.

CONNECTIONS
Computer **connections** are the physical access points that enable a computer to communicate with internal or external devices. They include the ports on both the computer and the connected devices, plus a transmission medium, which is either a cable with connectors at each end or a wireless technology. Personal computer connections can be categorized by the technology or standard that was used to develop the device.

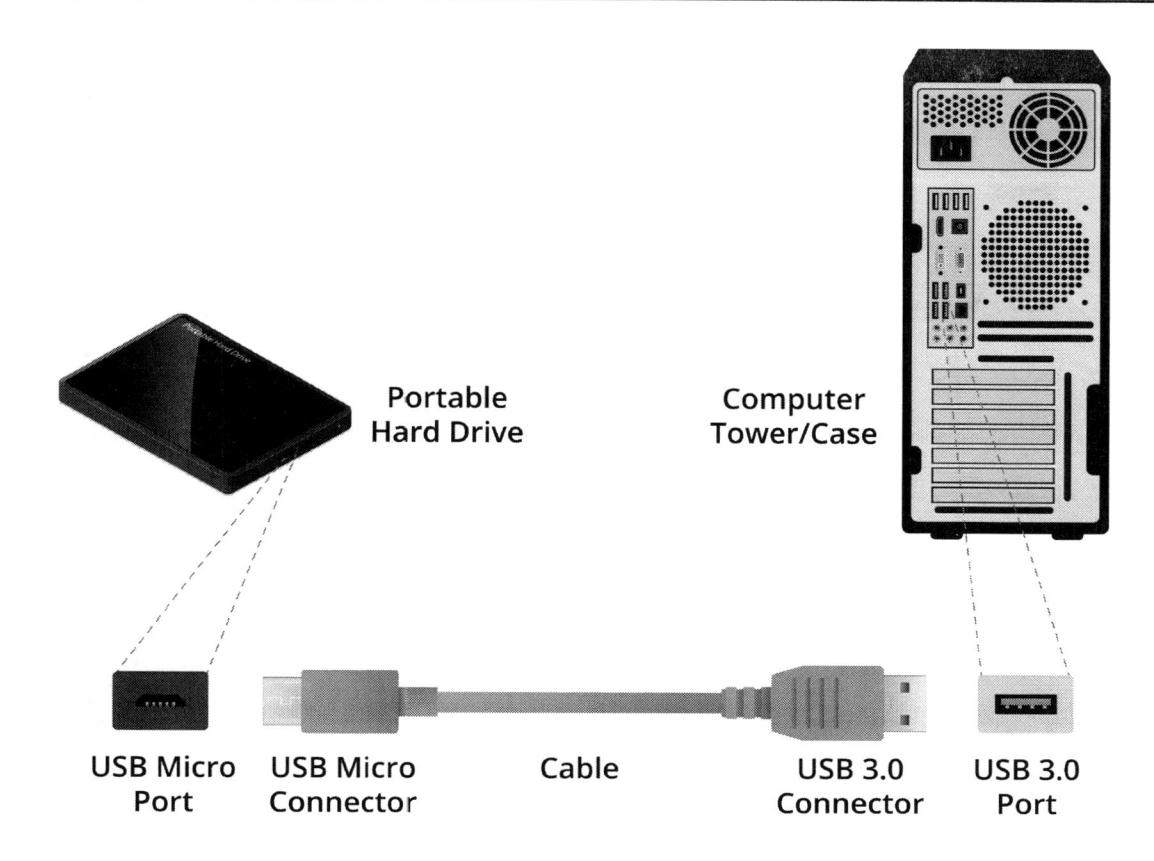

A computer connection between an external USB hard drive and a desktop computer. (Image © 123RF.com.)

Ports are often described as being **male**, meaning they have pin connectors, or **female**, meaning they have hole connectors. This gender orientation means that it is virtually impossible to connect them incorrectly. Many connectors and ports are also **keyed** to prevent them from being inserted the wrong way around.

I/O PORTS AND CABLES

Input and output **(I/O) ports** allow additional devices to be connected to the PC. Some ports are designed for a particular type of device (such as a graphics port). Other ports (such as USB) support different device types.

External ports are positioned at the rear or front of the PC through cut-outs in the case. They can be provided on the motherboard or with an expansion card.

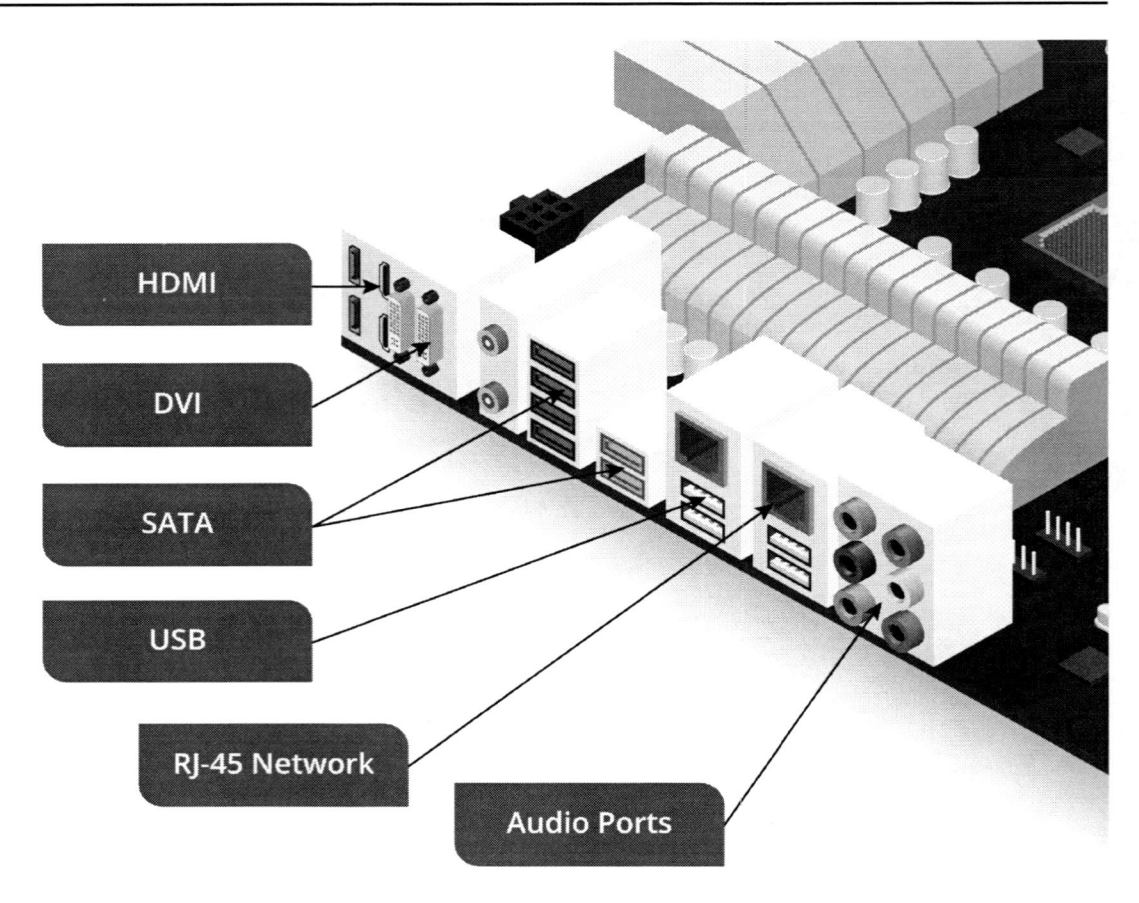

I/O ports on a motherboard. (Image © 123RF.com.)

USB CONNECTORS

The **Universal Serial Bus (USB)** has become the standard means of connecting peripheral devices to a computer. It is an example of a multipurpose cable that can be used to attach a wide range of peripherals and storage devices.

> *Note: USB has not historically been used as a display interface (to attach a monitor). That is changing as the USB-C connector (discussed later) is becoming more widely adopted.*

A USB bus consists of a **host controller** and up to 127 devices.

> *Note: To overcome the limitations of sharing bandwidth, most PC chipsets feature multiple USB controllers, each of which has only three or four ports.*

A device can be a **hub** (providing ports for additional devices) or function. Functions are divided into classes, such as human interface (keyboards and mice), mass storage (disk drives), printer, audio device, and so on.

USB STANDARDS

There have been several iterations of the USB standard. Each new version introduces better data rates. A version update may also define new connector form factors and other improvements. The **USB 2.0 (HighSpeed) standard** specifies a data rate of 480 Mbps. Note that this bandwidth is shared between all devices attached to the same host.

The USB 3.0 standard introduces a **SuperSpeed mode**. SuperSpeed improves the bus bandwidth tenfold (to 5 Gbps or 5000 Mbps) and makes the link full duplex, so a device can send and receive at up to 5 Gbps simultaneously. USB 3.1 defines a **SuperSpeed+ mode** with a data rate of 10 Gbps. USB 3.2 promises 20 Gbps, but only over USB-C ports and cabling (discussed later).

> *Note: USB 3 controllers actually feature two sub-controllers. One controller handles SuperSpeed-capable devices while the other supports legacy HighSpeed, FullSpeed, and LowSpeed USB v1.1 and v2.0 devices. Consequently legacy devices will not slow down SuperSpeed-capable devices. There are changes to the way the bus works to try to improve "real-world" bandwidth too.*

USB 3.x receptacles and connectors often have a blue connector tab or housing to distinguish them.

USB POWER

Power is supplied by the host at 5V and a single device may draw up to 500 mA (milli-amps) or 2.5 W (increased to 4.5 W with the USB 3.0 specification). Devices that require more power than this, such as printers, must be connected to an external power supply.

> *Note: Devices supporting fast charging can supply 7.5 W if the port is in charging mode (no data transfer is possible in charging mode). Devices conforming to the USB Power Delivery version 2.0 specification are able to deliver up to 100 W of power.*

USB ON THE GO (OTG)

USB On the Go (OTG) allows a port to function either as a host or as a device. For example, a port on a smartphone might operate as a device when connected to a PC but as a host when connected to a keyboard.

USB CONNECTORS AND PORTS

USB connectors are *always* inserted with the USB symbol facing up. There have been several versions of the USB standard and these versions have often introduced new connector form factors.

The main connectors for USB 2.0 are:

- Type A (4-pin)—for connection to the host. The connector and port are shaped like flat rectangles.
- Type B (4-pin)—for connection to a device. The connector and port are square, with a beveled top. There are also small form factor versions of the type B connector and port:
    - Type B Mini (5-pin)—a smaller connector for connection to a device. This type of connector was seen on early digital cameras but is no longer widely used. The additional pin supports USB OTG.

        > *Note: There were also a number of non-standard mini B connectors used on various digital camera models.*

    - Type B Micro (5-pin)—an updated connector for smaller devices, such as smartphones and tablets. The micro connector is distinctively flatter than the older mini type connector.

USB 2.0

Type A Type B Type B Mini Type B Micro

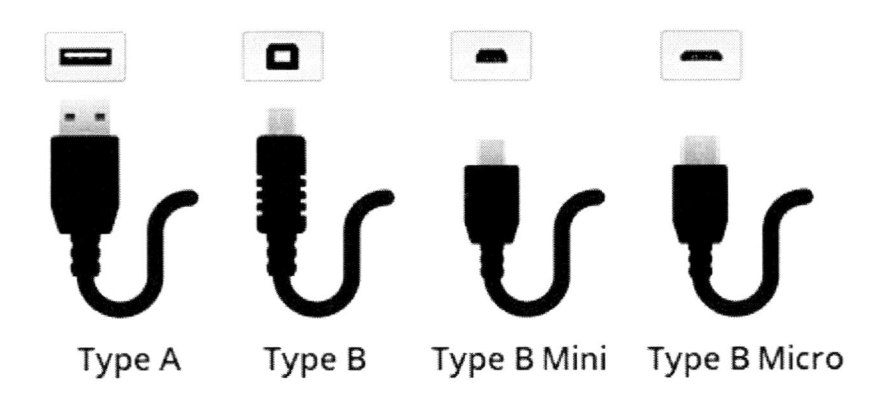

USB 2.0 ports and connectors. (Image © 123RF.com.)

A USB cable can feature Type A to Type A connectors but most convert from one type to another (Type A to Type B or Type A to Micro Type B for instance).

In USB 3.0, there are 9-pin versions of the Type A, Type B, and Type B Micro connectors. USB 3.0 Type A connections are physically compatible with USB 1.1 and 2.0 connections, but the Type B/Type B Micro connections are not. So, for example, you could plug a USB 2.0 Type A cable into a USB 3.0 port, but you could not plug a USB 3.0 Type B cable into a USB 2.0 Type B port.

USB 3.0 and 3.1

Type A Type B Type B Micro Type C

USB 3.0 and 3.1 connectors and ports (from left to right): Type A, Type B, Micro Type B, Type C. (Image © 123RF.com.)

As you can see, USB has historically featured a bewildering range of connector types. USB 3.1 defines a new USB-C 24-pin connector type. This should provide a single consistent hardware interface for the standard. The connector is reversible, meaning it can be inserted either way up. The connector design is also more secure and robust. USB-C can use the same type of connector at both ends or you can obtain USB-C to USB Type A or Type B converter cables.

CABLE LENGTH

The maximum cable length for LowSpeed devices is 3m while for FullSpeed and HighSpeed the limit is 5m. Vendors may provide longer cables however. SuperSpeed-capable cables do not have an official maximum length but up to about 3m is recommended.

OTHER PERIPHERAL CONNECTOR TYPES

USB is the dominant interface for PC peripherals, but you may also come across cabled devices requiring different connections.

THUNDERBOLT (TB)

The **Thunderbolt (TB)** interface was developed by Intel® and is primarily used on Apple® workstations and laptops. Thunderbolt® can be used as a display interface (like DisplayPort or HDMI) and as a general peripheral interface (like USB). In its first two versions, Thunderbolt uses the same physical interface as MiniDP and is compatible with DisplayPort, so that displays with a MiniDP port can be connected to a host via Thunderbolt. Thunderbolt ports are distinguished from MiniDP by a lightning bolt icon.

The USB-C form factor adopted for Thunderbolt 3. (Image © 123RF.com.)

Version 2 of the standard supports links of up to 20 Gbps. Up to six devices can be connected to a single port by daisy-chaining the devices. You can also use a dock or hub device to channel a variety of ports (TB, USB, HDMI, and Ethernet, for instance) via a single Thunderbolt port on the host PC or laptop.

Thunderbolt version 3 changes the physical interface to use the same port, connector, and cabling as USB-C. Converter cables are available to connect Thunderbolt 1 or 2 devices to Thunderbolt 3 ports. A USB device plugged into a Thunderbolt 3 port will function normally but Thunderbolt devices will not work if connected to a USB port that is not Thunderbolt-enabled. Thunderbolt 3 supports up to 40 Gbps over a short, high-quality cable (up to 0.5m/1.6ft).

LIGHTNING

Apple's iPhone® and iPad® mobile devices use a proprietary 8-pin **Lightning** port and connector. The Lightning connector is reversible (can be inserted either way up).

Apple Lightning connector and port. (Image © 123RF.com.)

The Lightning port is found only on Apple's mobile devices. To connect such a device to a PC, you need a suitable adapter cable, such as Lightning-to-USB A or Lightning-to-USB C.

SERIAL PORTS (RS-232 AND DB-9)

The **serial port** (or **RS-232**) is so-called because data is transmitted over one wire one bit at a time. Start, stop, and parity bits are used to format and verify data transmission. While modern interfaces like USB are also serial, an RS-232 interface uses much less sophisticated signaling methods. Consequently, an RS-232 serial port supports data rates up to about 115 Kbps only.

9-pin serial connector and port. (Image © 123RF.com.)

Serial ports are generally associated with connecting external modems, used to establish dial-up Internet connections, though even this function has largely been superseded by USB. You may also come across serial ports on network equipment, where a serial connection can be used to manage the device.

RS-232 (Recommended Standard #232) specifies a 25-pin hardware interface, but in practice, PC manufacturers used the cheaper 9-pin D-shell (**DB-9**) male port shown above.

In Windows®, the serial port is referred to as a **Communications (COM) port**.

> **Note:** You might also come across the term PS/2. This was a serial interface used to attach mice and keyboards. PS/2 ports use a 6-pin mini-DIN format.

STORAGE CONNECTOR TYPES

USB and Thunderbolt are examples of multipurpose cables used to attach different kinds of external peripheral device (though it is also possible to use USB cabling within the system case). Internal storage devices use different types of interface, though.

- **SATA and eSATA connectors.**

    Serial Advanced Technology Attachment (SATA) is the standard means of attaching internal storage drives to a desktop PC. Each SATA host adapter port supports a single device.

    Internal SATA cables can be up to 1 m (39"). The cables are terminated with compact 7-pin connectors.

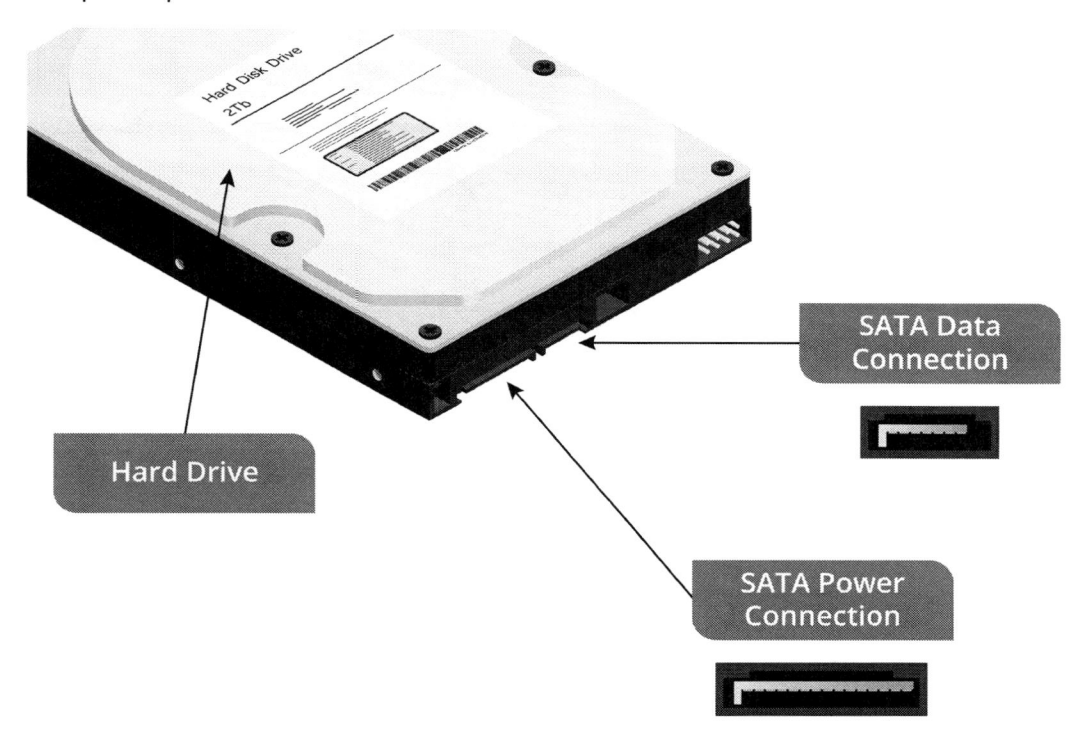

SATA data and power ports on a hard drive. (Image © 123RF.com.)

There is also an **eSATA standard** for the attachment of external drives, with a 2 m (78") cable. You must use an eSATA cable to connect to an external eSATA port; you cannot use an internal SATA cable. **eSATAp** is a non-standard powered port used by some vendors that is compatible with both USB and SATA (with an eSATAp cable). The USB interface dominates the external drive market, however.

> **Note:** The main drawback of eSATA compared to USB or Thunderbolt external drives is that power is not supplied over the cable. This is not so much of an issue for 3.5" drives, which require a separate power supply anyways, but it limits the usefulness of eSATA for 2.5" portable drives.

- **SCSI.**

    Modern connection interfaces use serial communications. These serial links can achieve Mbps and Gbps speeds because of improved signaling and encoding methods. Back when serial interfaces were much slower, PC vendors used parallel data transmission to support better transfer rates. While a serial interface essentially transfers 1 bit at a time, a parallel interface transfers 8 bits (1 byte) or more. This requires more wires in the cable and more pins in the connectors, meaning parallel interfaces are very bulky.

Internal PC storage devices often used Parallel ATA (PATA)/Enhanced Integrated Drive Electronics (EIDE) connections. This supported transfer rates up to about 133 MBps. Workstations and servers requiring more speed would use the **Small Computer Systems Interface (SCSI)** bus instead. SCSI could support up to 320 MBps data rates. While you will not come across any new systems shipping with SCSI connections, you might need to support legacy systems that use SCSI.

SCSI could be used for both internal devices and external peripherals (such as scanners and printers) but you are very, very unlikely to find it used anywhere except for the connection of internal disk drives. While early SCSI types used 50-pin connectors, you are only likely to come across High Density (HD) 68-pin connectors or Single Connector Attachment (SCA) 80-pin connectors. SCA incorporates both a power connector and configuration wires, allowing for hot swappable drives.

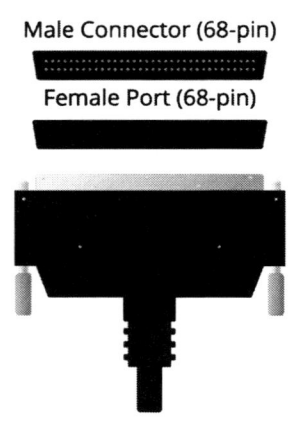

Male Connector (68-pin)

Female Port (68-pin)

Internal and external male HD connectors. (Image © 123RF.com.)

Also, you should note that while parallel SCSI as a physical interface has almost completely disappeared, the software interface and command set are used in many other storage technologies, including Serial Attached SCSI (SAS), Firewire, and Storage Area Networks (SAN).

- **Molex connectors.**

  As well as a data connection, an internal hard drive needs to be connected to the computer power supply. A computer power supply will come with a number of peripheral power connectors. For older devices, this power connection is made using **Molex connectors** and ports. A Molex connector is usually white and has 4 pins plus red, yellow, and black wires.

A Molex connector. (Image © 123RF.com.)

> **Note:** *SATA drives are more likely to use the SATA power connector. Some devices might have both types of power connectors.*

NETWORK CONNECTOR TYPES

Network connections also use dedicated cable types, rather than multipurpose cabling such as USB and Thunderbolt.

- **RJ-45.**

    Most computers have a network adapter already installed as part of the motherboard chipset. The network adapter will have an RJ-45 port to connect the computer to the network, via another RJ-45 port in the network equipment. This port will be marked "LAN" (Local Area Network).

    An **RJ-45 (Registered Jack) connector** is used with twisted pair cable for Ethernet local area networking products. Twisted pair is a type of copper cabling where pairs of insulated conductors are twisted around one another, to minimize electrical interference.

    RJ-45 port and connector. (Image © 123RF.com.)

    RJ-45 connectors are used with 4-pair (8-wire) cables. The connectors are also referred to as 8P8C, standing for 8-position/8-contact. This means that all eight "potential" wire positions are supplied with contacts, so that they can all carry signals if needed.

- **RJ-11.**

Smaller **RJ-11 connectors** are used with 2- or 3-pair UTP or with flat ribbon "silver satin" phone cables. Typically only one pair carries the dial tone and voice circuit (also called the Tip and Ring wires after the way older phono plugs were wired). The other pair is usually unused but can be deployed for a secondary circuit. RJ-11 connectors are used for telephone systems (for example, to connect a modem to a phone jack).

RJ-11 port and connector. (Image © 123RF.com.)

Note: *An RJ-11 connector only has two contacts (6P2C); to use more pairs, an RJ-14 (6P4C) connector is required. This is physically the same size as RJ-11 but has more wired contacts.*

EXPANSION CARDS

Expansion cards (or add-on cards) can be installed on the motherboard to add functions or ports not provided as part of the chipset. An expansion card can be fitted to an appropriate slot (PCI or PCIe) on the motherboard.

- **I/O Adapters and Storage Cards.**

    Most Input/Output (I/O) bus functions are provided on the motherboard, which will typically have USB ports for external peripherals and SATA ports for internal storage drives. An adapter card can be installed to provide additional ports or a bus type that is not supported on the motherboard. Typical examples include an eSATA host adapter to make external storage ports available, a flash memory card reader, a card with extra USB ports, or a card supporting wireless peripherals, such as Bluetooth®.

- **Network Interface Cards (NICs).**

    Most computers have a network adapter already installed as part of the motherboard chipset. However, there may be occasions when you need to install an add-on Network Interface Card (NIC) or need to upgrade an adapter to use a different type of network, bandwidth, or cabling.

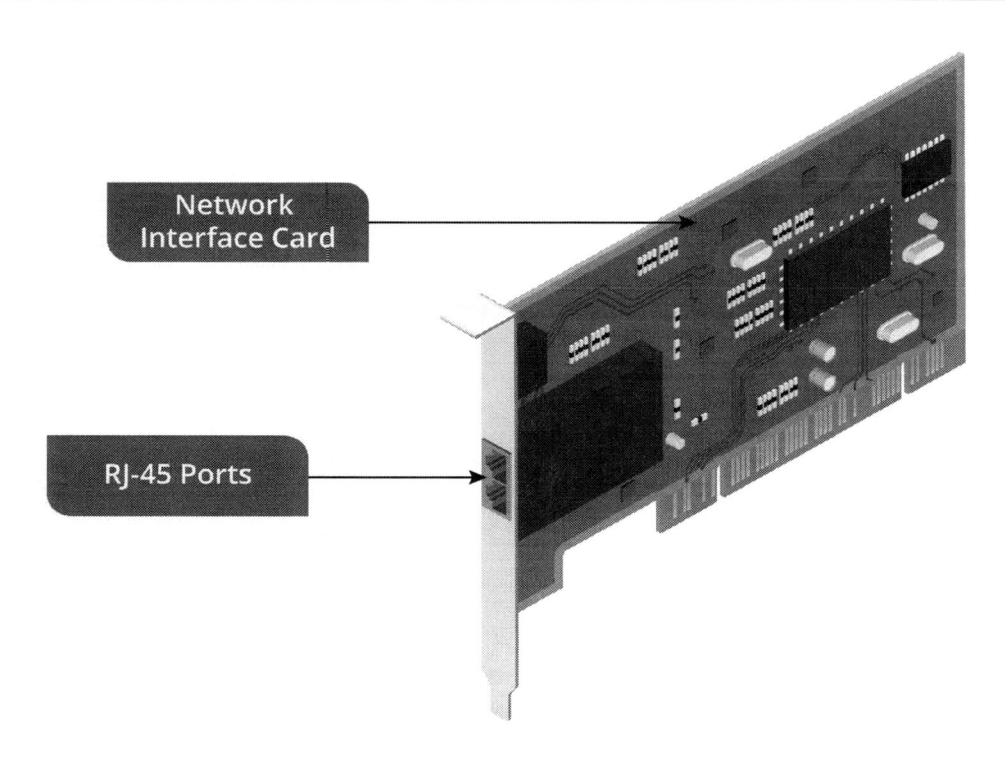

RJ-45 ports on a Network Interface Card (NIC). (Image © 123RF.com.)

A Wi-Fi adapter can be added to connect to a wireless network. Wi-Fi adapters are developed to different 802.11 standards (802.11a/b/g/n/ac).

*Note: To learn more, check the **Video** tile on the CHOICE Course screen for any videos that supplement the content for this lesson.*

Access the Checklist tile on your CHOICE Course screen for reference information and job aids on How to Install and Remove Expansion Cards.

Activity 1-3
Identifying Connection Interfaces

SCENARIO
Answer the following questions to check your understanding of the topic.

1. In this graphic, identify the (A) audio ports, (B) video ports, and (C) USB ports.

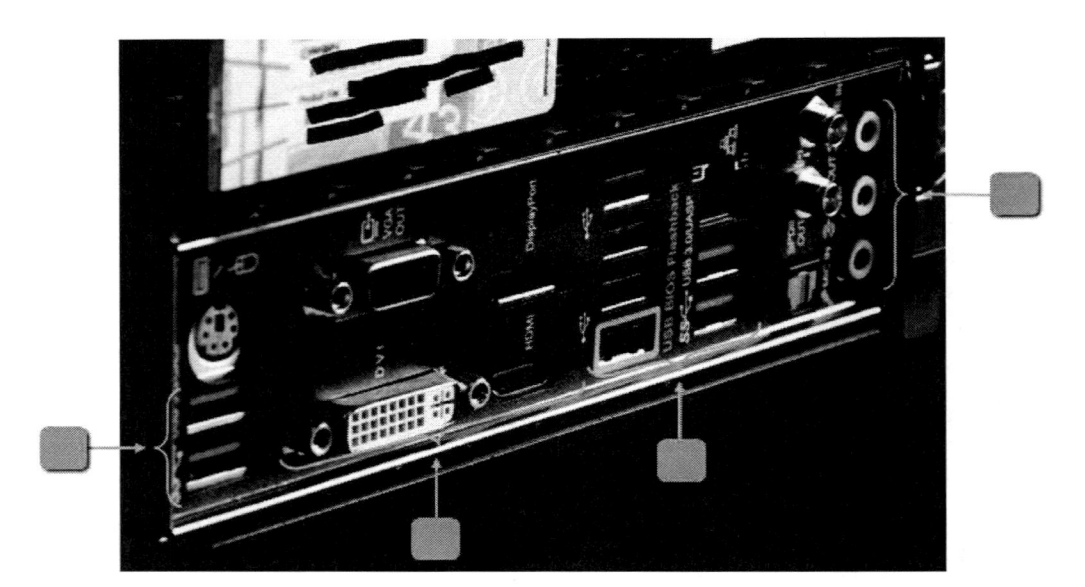

2. You are speaking with a junior technician. He is not sure what is meant by a "keyed" connector. Can you tell him?

3. What is the nominal data rate of a USB port supporting SuperSpeed+?

4. True or false? USB-C ports and cables are compatible with Apple Lightning ports and cables.

5. What type of device would you connect a Molex cable to?

6. Why would you install an I/O adapter card?

Activity 1-4

Demonstrating PC Disassembly and Reassembly

BEFORE YOU BEGIN

Your instructor will provide you with a WORKBENCH PC system to use to complete this activity. Make sure you find out the account credentials used to sign in. If a PC is not available for use in this activity, use the reference images provided instead.

You will perform this activity at your WORKBENCH PC.

SCENARIO

You are responsible for familiarizing new technical support staff on the hardware used by the company. You are going to show how to remove the PC case to compile information about the components installed to add to system inventory documentation.

> **Note:** *Activities may vary slightly if the software vendor has issued digital updates. Your instructor will notify you of any changes.*

---

1. Open a PC case and identify components on the motherboard.
    a) The PC should be powered off and cables to devices should all be disconnected. If not, shut down the PC then remove all the cables, starting with the power connector.
    b) Carefully lift the system unit onto your workbench and remove the system case cover.
    Use this image if you don't have a computer to open.

c) Without touching anything inside the system unit, identify the following components. You can move cables if they obstruct your view, but be careful not to dislodge them from their connectors. If you do not have access to a PC, identify the location of components in the image above instead. You will not be able to see as much as with a physical inspection, so do not worry if you cannot identify exact numbers and types.
- CPU
- Memory slots (number and type—DDR3 or DDR4 for instance)
- Expansion slots (number of each type)
- Drive ports (number of each type)
- Power connectors (P1 and fans)
- RTC battery
- Front panel connectors

2. Draw a diagram showing the layout of the components you identified above.

3. Write down any problems you might suspect with the way the system is built (for example, cables not connected to devices, scorch marks, excessive dust or dirt, and so on).

4. When you have finished, replace the system case cover.

5. Identify the external ports.

Your system likely has a different number of ports, different ports, and different locations for some items. Use this image if you don't have a physical PC to examine.

6. **What ports can you identify?**

7. Demonstrate how to identify external ports on your WORKBENCH PC.
   a) Inspect the PC and complete the table below to show the number of available ports (remember that there could be connectors on the back and the front of the PC).

Port Type	Number/Notes
USB 2	
USB 3	
Thunderbolt (MiniDP or USB type)	
Network (RJ-45)	
Other (display connectors, for instance)	

   b) Check the ports carefully to ensure that none are damaged (for example, pins that are broken, bent, or missing or mounting bolts that are loose or missing).

8. Check the case labeling for the following information (this would be used to obtain support):

Information	Details
Vendor (OEM)	
Model Number	
Serial Number/ Service Tag	

9. Finally, demonstrate how to set up the PC for use again.
   a) If the cabling is fine, connect the devices in the following order, taking care not to damage the connectors and to secure them properly (note that some devices might not be available to you—check with your instructor if you are unsure):
      - Mouse
      - Keyboard
      - Display screen
      - Microphone and speakers
      - Display power plug
      - PC power plug
   b) Check the routing of cables so that there are no trip hazards. Optionally, adjust the monitor so that it is the correct height for use (the top edge should be at eye level).
   c) When your instructor has checked the system, press the power button to turn it on.
   d) As the PC powers up, listen and look for the following signs that the computer is operating normally.
      - Power LED comes on.
      - Fans start spinning.

- Hard disk activity—LED flickers and there may be some soft noise but grinding or clicking indicates a problem.
- System firmware messages on the screen—if you do not see anything, check the display is connected and switched on.
- Windows logo on the screen.

e) Verify that the keyboard and mouse work. Sign in to the PC using the credentials provided.

10. Your instructor might provide you with examples of device connections and interfaces and ask you or other participants to identify them.

Topic D
Install Peripheral Devices

EXAM OBJECTIVES COVERED
1001-3.6 Explain the purposes and uses of various peripheral types.

Much of the work that you will perform as a PC technician will involve installing and configuring various hardware and software components. As an IT professional, you will often find yourself setting up end-user workstations or helping those end users with the hardware they need to make their daily lives easier. Installing and configuring peripheral components—like keyboards and mice, or even more specialized devices—are some of the more common tasks that you will perform.

INPUT DEVICES

Input devices—or **Human Interface Devices (HIDs)**—are peripherals that enable the user to enter data and select commands. Computers need user input such as directions or commands and user interaction with the programs that are included in order to produce something of use.

Keyboards and pointing devices are the standard input devices for personal computers these days, but there is an ever-growing number of input devices available for the user to interact with in a variety of ways. As well as command input, security systems often require different ways for users to input credentials to access an account or authorize a payment.

KEYBOARDS

The **keyboard** is the longest serving type of input device. Historically, keyboards were connected via the 6-pin mini-DIN PS/2 port. This is colored purple to differentiate it from the identical form factor mouse connector. All keyboards are now USB or wireless (typically Bluetooth), though.

Extended PC keyboards feature a number of special command keys (Alt and Ctrl plus keys such as Print Screen, NumLock, Scroll Lock, Start, Shortcut, and Function). A numeric keypad can be used to allow faster entry of numeric data or as an additional set of arrow keys (the function is toggled by NumLock). Multimedia keyboards may also feature programmable keys and buttons that can be used for web browsing, playing CDs/DVDs, and so on.

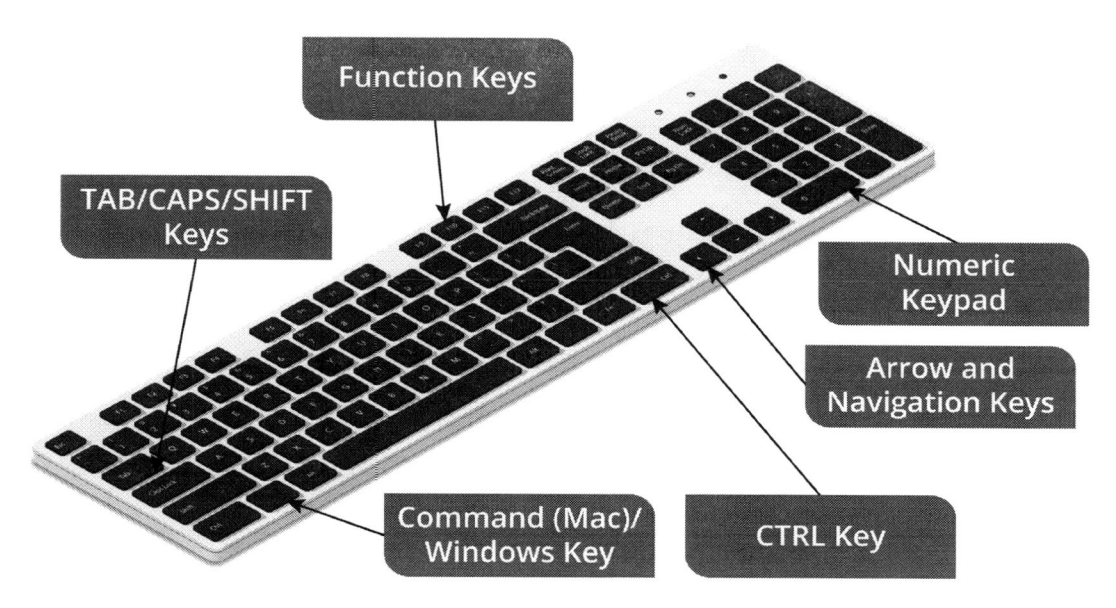

An extended keyboard. (Image © 123RF.com.)

When selecting a keyboard for a user, in addition to considering its ergonomics, you should also consider whether the keyboard offers additional features (such as customizable hot keys and scrolling) as well as wireless connectivity.

An ergonomic keyboard. (Image by Dmitriy Melnikov © 123RF.com.)

Most keyboards designed for use with Latin scripts use the QWERTY key layout. There are different layouts though, such as the small differences between US and UK layouts, the Dvorak alternative layout for Latin script, and keyboards for different scripts, such as Cyrillic. It is important that the keyboard type is set correctly in the OS.

In Windows, the type of keyboard layout is configured through the **Language** applet in Control Panel/Settings so that the computer knows which symbol to use when a particular key or key combination is pressed.

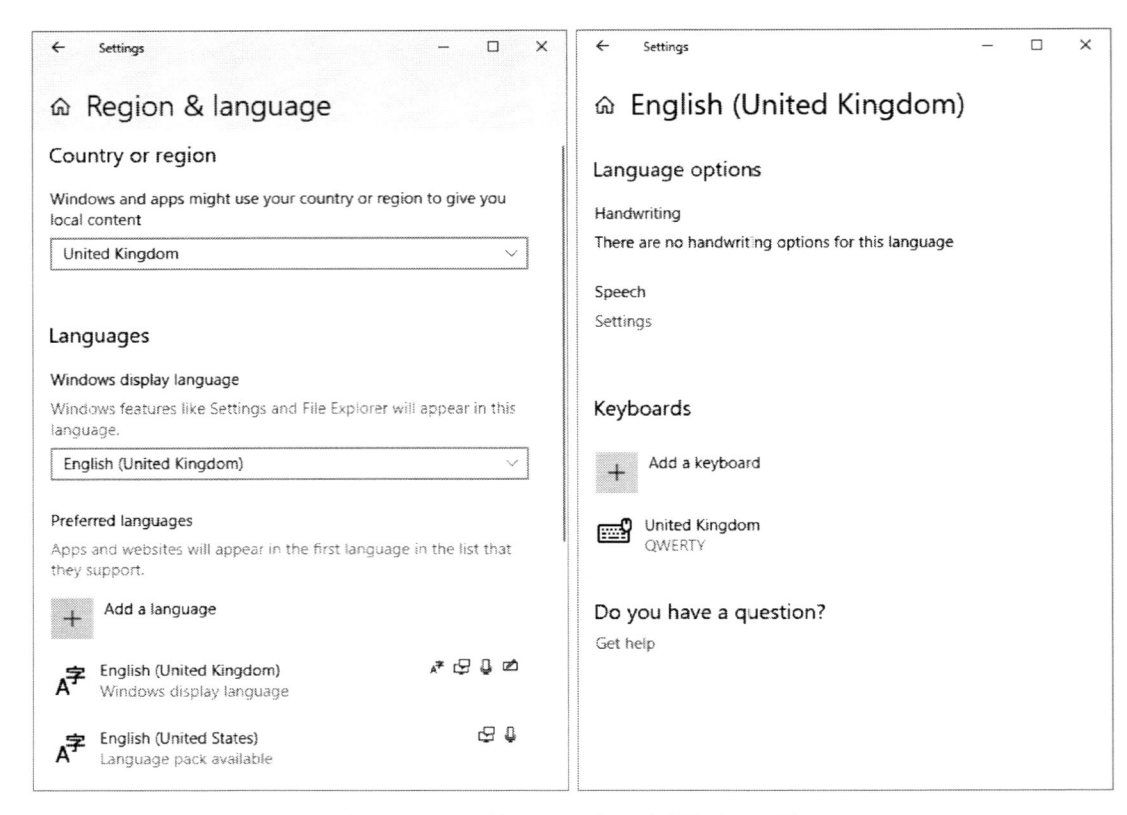

Language and input options in Windows 10.

POINTING DEVICES

While a keyboard can be used to navigate a window (using **Tab** and arrow keys, for instance), most operating systems are designed to be used with some sort of **pointing device**. A pointing device is usually used to move a cursor to select and manipulate objects on the screen.

MOUSE

The **mouse** is the main type of pointing device for graphical software. Mice use the same interfaces as keyboards (the PS/2 port for a mouse is color-coded green, though). There are three main types:

- Mechanical mouse—this contains rollers to detect the movement of a ball housed within the mouse case. As the user moves the mouse on a mat or other firm surface, the ball is moved and the rollers and circuitry translate that motion to move a cursor on the screen. Mechanical mice are no longer in production.
- Optical mouse—this uses LEDs to detect movement over a surface.
- Laser mouse—this uses an infrared laser, which gives greater precision than an optical mouse.

A basic mouse, with a scroll wheel and four buttons (two main buttons on top and two side buttons). (Image © 123RF.com.)

Another distinguishing feature of different mouse models is the number of buttons (between two and four), which can be customized to different functions, and the presence of a scroll wheel, used (obviously) for scrolling and as a clickable extra button. Mice are also distinguished by their size and shape. Smaller mice are useful with portable systems; some mice are marketed on the basis of their ergonomic shape.

TOUCHPAD

A **touchpad** is a small, touch-sensitive pad where you run your finger across the surface to send electronic signals to the computer to control the pointer on the screen. Touchpads can have buttons like a mouse or trackball, or the touch pad can be configured to detect finger taps on its surface and process those signals like button clicks.

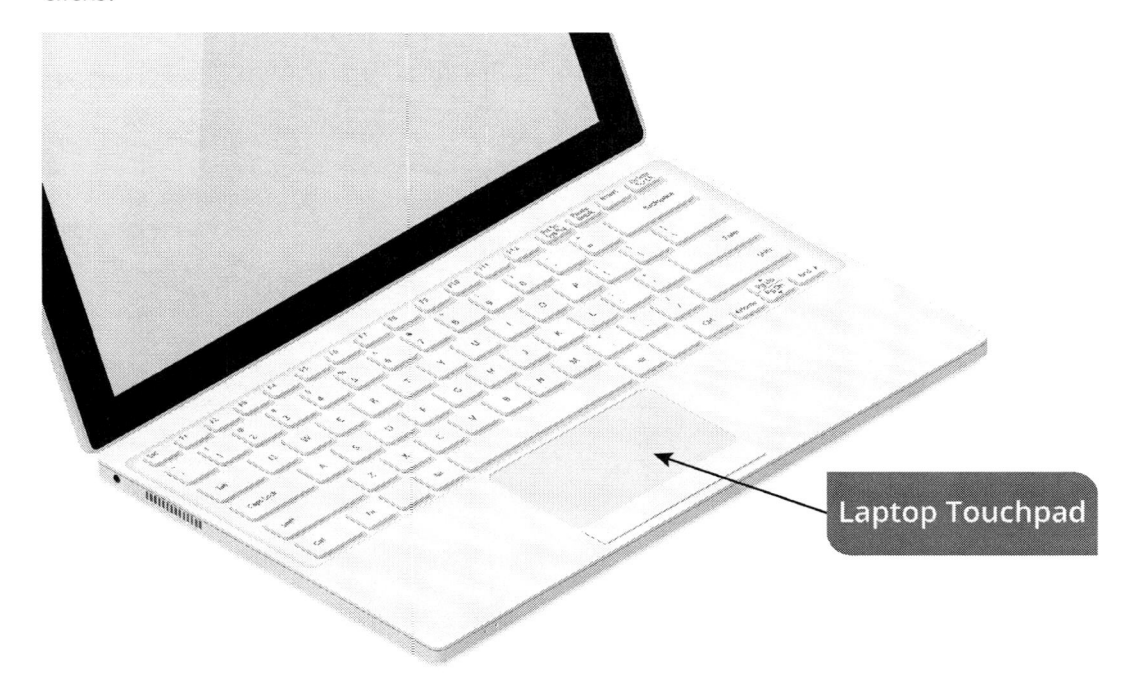

Touchpad on a laptop. (Image © 123RF.com.)

Touchpads are most closely associated with laptop computers but it is possible to use them as peripheral devices with PCs, too. An external touchpad is connected using USB or Bluetooth.

GAME CONTROLLERS

PC games are mostly designed for use with the mouse and keyboard but some games (flight simulators, for instance) benefit from the use of a game controller, such as a **joystick** or **game pad**. There are also controllers for specific game types, such as steering wheels for driving games and light guns for shooting games. As with most other peripherals, wired game controllers are connected using USB, whereas wireless models use Bluetooth. Joysticks can also be used as input devices by people who have difficulty using a mouse or keyboard.

A game controller. (Image © 123RF.com.)

KVM SWITCHES

A **Keyboard, Video, Mouse (KVM) switch** allows multiple computers (typically servers) to be controlled via a single keyboard, mouse, and monitor. Some switches designed for home use also support speaker and microphone ports. Each computer's ports are cabled to the switch, then a single cable runs from the switch to the input and output devices.

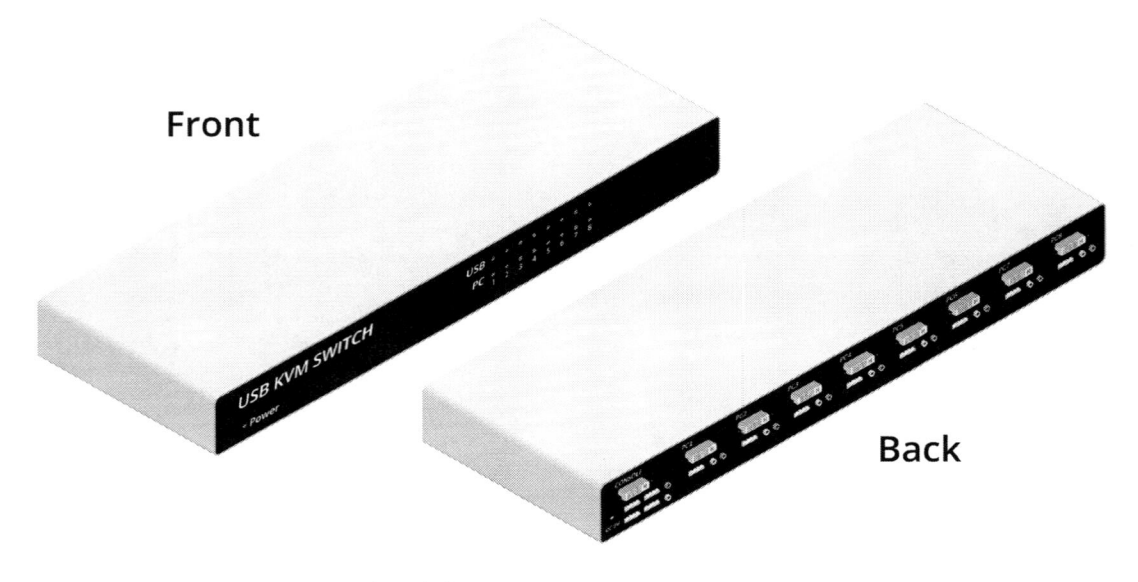

A KVM switch with front and back views. (Image © 123RF.com.)

Simple desktop KVM switches support two devices; control is usually switched using a key sequence such as **Scroll Lock** + **Scroll Lock** + an arrow key (such as **Right Arrow**).

Server-level KVM switches may support 10 or more ports and have more sophisticated controls.

SECURITY INPUT DEVICES

Security input devices provide protection against unauthorized access to computing devices and resources. Commonly implemented security input devices include biometric devices and card readers.

BIOMETRIC AUTHENTICATION DEVICES

Biometric devices are used to perform authentication. **Authentication** means identifying someone as a valid user of the computer or network.

Biometrics is an automated method of recognizing a person based on a physiological or behavioral characteristic unique to the individual, such as a retina pattern, fingerprint, or voice pattern. Biometric technologies are becoming the foundation of an extensive array of highly secure identification and personal verification solutions. Biometric input devices can add an additional layer of physical security or information security by verifying the identity of the person attempting to gain access to a location or device.

Biometric devices will need to be installed and configured, and then initialized for the specific end user who will be using the device. The initial biometric authentication "object" for the user (be it a fingerprint, retina scan, pass phrase, etc.) must first be captured and stored. Then the user will have to test the device to make sure that it accurately verifies his or her identity against the authentication object, permitting them access to the location or device.

Touching a fingerprint scanner. (Image © 123RF.com.)

Whether or not a biometric device is being deployed will likely be a decision made based on an organizational security policy or standard. If biometric devices will be deployed at individual workstations, you will need to determine the specific biometric device's connector requirements; as most use a USB connection, you will need to make sure that the user's computer has an available USB port to connect the device.

SMART CARD READERS

A **smart card reader** provides a slot or NFC (contactless) interface to interact with a **smart card**. The reader is typically a peripheral device attached via a USB port but may be built into some laptop models. The microprocessor embedded in the smart card is used to store a digital certificate to prove the identity of the holder. The use of the certificate token is combined with a PIN or password to protect against loss or theft.

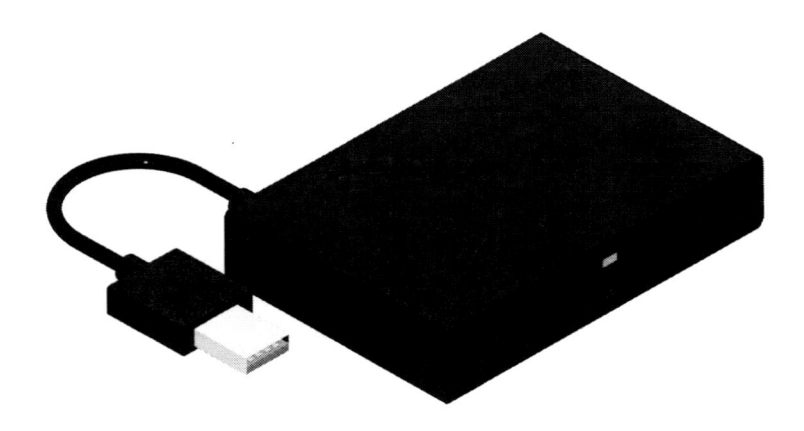

A smart card reader. (Image © 123RF.com.)

MAGNETIC STRIP/CHIP READERS

In the days before microprocessors could be made small enough to embed in a plastic wafer, the account number and other details of a credit or bank card were encoded in a magnetic strip. All bank-issued cards retain these magnetic strips for compatibility with legacy systems. When the card is swiped through a magnetic reader, the reader obtains the account details from the card. As with smart card readers, these would be attached as a USB peripheral.

A chip reader works in the same way as a smartcard reader but is designed to work specifically with bank cards to support Point of Sale (POS) systems.

NFC AND TAP PAY DEVICES

As mentioned above, a smart card can be contact-based or contactless. Many contactless readers use the **Near Field Communications (NFC) protocol**. NFC is a very short range radio link based on **Radio Frequency ID (RFID)**. NFC normally works at up to 2 inches (6cm) at data rates of 106, 212, and 424 Kbps.

As well as cards, NFC sensors are now often integrated with smartphones, allowing their use as a kind of "electronic wallet." As with a chip reader, an NFC/tap pay terminal would be attached to the computer via a USB cable as part of a POS system.

NFC mobile payment between a smartphone and a payment processor. (Image © 123RF.com.)

SIGNATURE PADS

Signature recognition uses a signature pad and a database of approved signatures. A user signs the signature pad, and the recognition system analyzes the individual behavior of the person signing, such as the strokes used and the pressure applied while signing, to verify the identity of the user.

If not hard-wired into a system (such as a security system), a signature capture pad used with a smaller device like a personal computer typically connects via a USB connection.

A signature pad and pen. (Image © 123RF.com.)

INSTALLATION AND CONFIGURATION CONSIDERATIONS

Peripheral devices for Windows computers are **Plug-and-Play**. This means that they can be added to the computer and the operating system will detect the device automatically and prompt you to configure it using a hardware or device setup wizard. Most devices also come with setup programs which will do the same job. They are required if the OS does not ship with the drivers required by the device.

SYSTEM RESOURCES

When you install a new device, such as a network card, sound card, or internal modem into a PC, it must be allocated a set of **system resources** that enable it to communicate with the CPU and memory without conflicting with other devices. This process is handled by Plug-and-Play.

Resource	Description
Memory Range/I/O Address	Every device in the PC has its own set of unique memory addresses in an area called the **I/O address** map. The I/O address is a means for the CPU to communicate with a device. The address map is a block of system memory 65,536 bytes (64 KB) in size. The I/O port is referred to using its hexadecimal (or port) address in the range of 0000-FFFF.
Interrupts (IRQ)	An I/O address tells the CPU where to look in memory to communicate with a device, but it must also know when to communicate with it! This is accomplished by the device raising an **Interrupt Request (IRQ)**. Under the early PC architecture, each device was allocated an IRQ "line" from 0 to 15. Allocating the same IRQ to two devices was the cause of many problems on these early computers. Modern PCs use more advanced interrupt controllers to facilitate interrupts from multiple devices on a bus such as PCI or PCIe. Some core system components are still allocated IRQs from the 0 to 15 range, though.

HOT SWAP

Most devices connected over USB are hot swappable. This means that the device can be added to or removed from the computer while it is switched on. Devices attached via legacy interfaces may need the PC to be restarted.

> *Note: You may also see the term hot pluggable used. Technically, a hot pluggable device can be installed while the system is running but cannot necessarily be removed safely without shutting down the computer. A fully hot swappable device can be added or removed without an OS restart.*

DRIVERS

Before connecting a device, you may need to install its **driver** using the vendor-supplied software. A driver is software that creates an interface between the device and the operating system. It may also include tools for configuring and optimizing the device. Many devices have drivers that are shipped along with Windows or made available over Windows Update, but even in that case the vendor may be able to supply a more up-to-date driver. Output devices such as monitors and speakers do not generally require drivers, but input devices such as mice, keyboards, and touchscreens do.

CONNECTIONS

Assuming the correct driver is available to the OS, adding and removing external peripherals is then just a case of plugging or unplugging the connector into the correct type of socket. USB has simple push/pull connectors that are keyed to prevent incorrect insertion. Connectors for legacy ports often have screws to hold them in place. RJ-11 and RJ-45 connectors have a plastic clip that must be pressed down to remove.

CONFIGURATION

The OS will detect and install the device automatically. You can then use Device Manager, Control Panel, Windows Settings, or the vendor-supplied software to configure user settings.

GUIDELINES FOR INSTALLING PERIPHERAL DEVICES

Follow these guidelines for working with peripheral devices.

INSTALLING PERIPHERAL DEVICES

Here are some guidelines for you to consider when you are adding or removing peripheral devices:

- Always read the manufacturer's instructions and check that the device is compatible with the PC and operating system.
- Hold the connector, not the cable, when removing a lead.
- Inspect the connector and port for damage (notably broken or bent pins) before attaching a lead.
- Take care to align the connector carefully and do not use excessive force, to avoid damaging the pins.
- Check whether the device requires an external power source.

*Note: To learn more, check the **Video** tile on the CHOICE Course screen for any videos that supplement the content for this lesson.*

Access the Checklist tile on your CHOICE Course screen for reference information and job aids on How to Install and Remove Peripheral Devices.

Activity 1-5
Discussing Peripheral Device Installation

SCENARIO
Answer the following questions to check your understanding of the topic.

1. A remote user has requested a Dvorak keyboard for use with her Windows 10 computer. The device has arrived and the user connected it to a USB port. She contacts support saying that the keyboard "isn't typing properly."

   What is the likely cause of this issue?

2. You are contacted by another remote user. The user has a laptop and desktop computer. The user wants to know if there is a device that would allow them to use the same peripheral devices with both systems without having to switch cables over all the time.

   What is your answer?

3. You are supporting a client setting up a Point of Sale system.

   Which peripheral device types or functions should she consider?

4. You have finished copying some files to a USB memory stick.

   What should you do before unplugging the stick?

Topic E
Troubleshooting Methodology

EXAM OBJECTIVES COVERED
1001-5.1 Given a scenario, use the best practice methodology to resolve problems.

Often, computer technicians spend a large percentage of their time troubleshooting the various software and hardware components used in computers, networks, and printers. Before you can even begin to troubleshoot a physical problem with a piece of hardware or diagnose an error thrown up by a software program, you need to understand the basics of troubleshooting and some best practices used.

The most elaborate toolkit and expensive diagnostic software can be useless if you do not have a consistent plan for solving problems. Even experienced technicians can sometimes overlook obvious problems or solutions. Troubleshooting can be extremely challenging, but if you follow common best practices and basic troubleshooting procedures, you will often be able to determine the specific cause of a problem, as well as possible solutions to the problem.

TROUBLESHOOTING BASICS

To some extent, being an effective troubleshooter simply involves having a detailed knowledge of how something is supposed to work and of the sort of things that typically go wrong. However, the more complex a system is, the less likely it is that this sort of information will be at hand, so it is important to develop general troubleshooting skills to approach new and unexpected situations confidently.

Troubleshooting is a process of problem solving. It is important to realize that problems have causes, symptoms, and consequences. For example:

- A computer system has a fault in the hard disk drive (cause).
- Because the disk drive is faulty, the computer is displaying a "blue screen" (symptom).
- Because of the fault, the user cannot do any work (consequence).

From a business point-of-view, resolving the consequences of the problem is more important than solving the original cause. For example, the most effective solution might be to provide the user with another workstation, then get the drive replaced.

It is also important to realize that the cause of a specific problem might be the symptom of a larger problem. This is particularly true if the same problem recurs. For example, you might ask why the disk drive is faulty—is it a one-off error or are there problems in the environment, supply chain, and so on?

PROBLEM MANAGEMENT

Any organization that has to deal with more than a few problems every week will have a system in place for **problem management**. The basis of problem management is the identification, prioritization, and ownership of **incidents**. The process of problem management is as follows:

1. A user contacts the help desk, perhaps by phone or email. An operator or technician is assigned to the incident and a job ticket is generated.

2. The user describes the problem to the operator, who may ask clarifying questions. The operator categorizes the problem, assesses how urgent it is, and how long it will take to fix.
3. The operator may take the user through initial troubleshooting steps. If these do not work, the job may be escalated to deskside support or a senior technician.
4. Troubleshooting continues until the problem is resolved. At that point, the user is contacted to confirm that the problem has been fixed. The job ticket is updated with details of the problem and how it was resolved. The ticket is then considered closed.

At each stage, the problem management system can track the ownership of the problem (who is dealing with it) and its status (what has been done). At each stage of problem management, you need to consider and be guided by corporate policies, procedures, and impacts before making changes. An enterprise network is, by definition, highly interconnected. Even small changes can have major, unintended impacts, so it is imperative that you follow established change management procedures and know when to seek authority to make a change.

THE COMPTIA A+ TROUBLESHOOTING MODEL

Here are the steps in CompTIA's A+ troubleshooting model:
1. Identify the problem.
   - Question user and identify user changes to computer.
   - Perform backups before making changes.
   - Inquire regarding environmental or infrastructure changes.
   - Review system and application logs.
2. Establish a theory of probable cause (question the obvious and if necessary conduct internal or external research based on symptoms).
3. Test the theory to determine cause:
   - Once theory is confirmed, determine next steps to resolve problem.
   - If theory is not confirmed, re-establish new theory or escalate.
4. Establish a plan of action to resolve the problem and implement the solution.
5. Verify full system functionality, and if applicable, implement preventative measures.
6. Document findings, actions, and outcomes.

These steps and the approach and attitude you should apply when troubleshooting are explained in a bit more detail in the next section.

> *Note: A methodical process is the ideal, but troubleshooting in help desk and IT support departments is often a time-critical process. In the real world, you often have to balance being methodical with being efficient.*

CUSTOMER SERVICE AND COMMUNICATIONS SKILLS

Employers value "soft skills," such as being able to communicate and use questioning, as highly as technical skills. Troubleshooting is one area where soft skills are vital:
- A user may be upset or angry—perhaps they have lost work or cannot get an expensive, new computer to work.
- A user may not be technically knowledgeable.

It is your job to calm the user and to help him or her give you the information you need to diagnose and solve the problem. You need to be able to ask questions that the user can answer simply, without having to know anything about the computer or its software, and guide him or her through basic troubleshooting steps. When speaking with a user, try to be calm and polite. Do not interrupt when the user is speaking. Do not use technical language (jargon) or abbreviations that are likely to confuse.

OPEN AND CLOSED QUESTIONING

The basis of getting troubleshooting information from users is asking good questions. Questions are commonly divided into two types:

- Open questions invite someone to explain in their own words. Examples are, "What is the problem?", "What happens when you try to switch the computer on?", "Were you able to complete this task before, and if so, when did you notice there was an issue?", and "What types of changes have you noticed since the last time you completed this task?"
- Closed questions invite a Yes/No answer or a fixed response. Examples include, "Can you see any text on the screen?" or "What does the error message say?"

Open questions are good to start with as they help to avoid making your own assumptions about what is wrong and encourage the user to give you all the information that he or she is able to. However, you should not trust the user's judgment completely. The user may be inexperienced or have formed a false impression of what is going wrong. Try to establish factual information rather than asking for the user's opinion.

Closed questions can be used to "drill down" into the nature of the problem and guide a user towards giving you information that is useful.

DEVELOPING A TROUBLESHOOTING MINDSET

Troubleshooting is not just the application of technical knowledge and expertise; the approach you choose to take is equally important.

- Be calm—if you are calm, it instills confidence in the customer and will also prevent you from making rash decisions.
- Take breaks—troubleshooting requires a great deal of concentration. After a long period of working on the same task, the mind can become fatigued and concentration is reduced. Consider taking breaks or leaving the problem for a while to refresh your mind.
- Challenge assumptions—a problem may be reported that is similar to one that you have experienced before, but you should not assume that the problem is identical. Although the symptoms may be similar, the problem and its solution could be completely different. Always treat each problem as a new challenge. Be prepared to try something different. If you have decided what the problem is, but cannot seem to solve it, it may be that you are incorrect. Be prepared to start again from the beginning with an open mind.
- Assess costs and impacts—remember, you must account for corporate policies and evaluate the impact of a problem. A particular problem might be a stimulating challenge, but if resolving it is not the highest priority in terms of business needs, you need to give up on finding "The Answer" and use a shortcut to get to a solution. When assessing whether to repair a part, consider the cost of the part and the cost of your time to perform the repair. In many circumstances, replacement is the most effective option.
- Know when to give up!—you will not always be able to fix the problem yourself. Be prepared to pass the problem on rather than wasting the customer's time!

PROBLEM IDENTIFICATION

When troubleshooting, unless the problem is very simple, it is best to work methodically to ensure that you diagnose the correct problem and choose the best way to resolve it.

The traditional method for problem solving is to find the cause of the problem and then to seek to remove or resolve that cause. If you switch your television on and the screen remains dark, you would seek out the cause and then remove it. Finding the actual cause may involve identifying several possible causes and then checking them out one by one to determine a probable cause. If your television stops working, you could ask yourself, "Is the problem in the television?", "Has the fuse blown?", "Is there a problem at the broadcasting station rather than with my television?". With all problems we run through a list of possibilities before making a decision. The trick is to do this methodically (so that possible causes are not overlooked) and efficiently (so that the problem can be solved quickly).

Troubleshooting is not just a problem-solving process, though. It requires effective decision-making. Sometimes there is no simple solution to a problem. There may be several solutions and which is best might not be obvious. An apparent solution might solve the symptoms of the problem but not the cause. A solution might be impractical or too costly. Finally, a solution might be the cause of further problems, which could be even worse than the original problem.

BE PREPARED

Before you visit a user or customer to fix a problem, ensure that you have all the necessary hardware and software tools, documentation, and any other information you may need to avoid repeated and unnecessary trips between your office and the customer's location.

If you are instructing a user over the phone or by email, make sure you offer clear, concise, and accurate instructions.

If troubleshooting requires that the system be taken offline, make sure that this is scheduled appropriately and sensitively. Remember that troubleshooting may involve more than fixing a particular problem; it is about maintaining the resources that users need to do their work.

PERFORM BACKUPS

Consider the importance of data stored on the local computer when performing troubleshooting or maintenance. Check when a backup was last made. If a backup has not been made, perform one before changing the system configuration, if at all possible. The simplest way of making a backup before troubleshooting is to use drive imaging software.

QUESTION THE USER

The first report of a problem will typically come from a user or another technician, and they will be one of the best sources of information, if you can ask the right questions. Before you begin examining settings in Windows or taking the PC apart, spend some time gathering as much information as you can about the problem. Ensure you ask the user to describe *all* of the circumstances. Some good questions to ask include:

- What are the exact error messages appearing on the screen or coming from the speaker? Remember that the error could reveal a symptom, not a cause.
- Has anyone else experienced the same problem?
- How long has the problem been occurring?
- What changes have been made recently to the system? Were these changes initiated by you, or via another support request?

  The latest change to a system is very often the cause of the problem. If something worked previously, then excepting mechanical failures, it is likely that the problem has arisen because of some user-initiated change or some environmental or infrastructure change. If something has never worked, a different approach is required.

- Has anything been tried to solve the problem?

SOURCES OF INFORMATION

Of course, you cannot always rely on the user to let you know everything that has happened. To diagnose a problem, you may also need to use the following techniques:

- Make a physical inspection—look and listen. You may be able to see or hear a fault (scorched motherboard, "sick"-sounding disk drive, no fan noise, and so on).
- If the symptoms of the problem are no longer apparent, a basic technique is to reproduce the problem—that is, repeat the exact circumstances that produced the failure or error. Some problems are intermittent, though, which means that they cannot be repeated reliably. Issues that are transitory or difficult to reproduce are often the hardest to troubleshoot.
- Check system and application logs or diagnostic software for information.
- Check the system documentation, such as installation or maintenance logs, for useful information.
- Consult any other technicians that might have worked on the system recently or might be working at the moment on some related issue. Consider that environmental or infrastructure changes might have been instigated by a different group within the company. Perhaps you are responsible for application support and the network infrastructure group has made some changes without issuing proper notice.

DETERMINATION OF PROBABLE CAUSES

If you obtain accurate answers to your initial questions, you will have determined the severity of the problem (how many are affected), a rough idea of where to look (hardware or OS for instance), and whether to look for a recent change or an oversight in configuration.

You diagnose a problem by identifying the symptoms. From knowing what causes such symptoms, you can consider possible cause to determine the most probable cause and then devise tests to show whether it is the cause or not. Sometimes symptoms derive from more than one cause; while this type of problem is rarer, it is much harder to troubleshoot. A computer system comprises a number of components. Fault finding needs to identify which component is faulty.

QUESTIONING THE OBVIOUS

There are two good ways to consider a computer problem systematically:

- Step through what should happen, either yourself or by observing the user, and identify the point at which there is a failure or error.
- Work up or down layers—for example, power, hardware components, drivers/firmware, software, network, user actions.

With either approach, do not overlook the obvious—sometimes seemingly intractable problems are caused by the simplest things.

Note: A basic technique when troubleshooting a cable, connector, or device is to have a "known good" duplicate on hand. This is another copy of the same cable or device that you know works that you can use to test by substitution. This approach very quickly identifies "non-causes."

Unless a problem is trivial, break the troubleshooting process into compartments or categories. If you can isolate your investigation to a particular subsystem by eliminating "non-causes," you can troubleshoot the problem more quickly. For example, when troubleshooting a PC, you might work as follows:

1. Decide whether the problem is hardware or software related (Hardware).
2. Decide which hardware subsystem is affected (Disk).

3. Decide whether the problem is in the disk unit or connectors and cabling (Connector).
4. Test your theory.

When you have drilled down like this, the problem should become obvious. Of course, you could have made the wrong choice at any point, so you must be prepared to go back and follow a different path.

> **Note:** *If you are really unlucky, two (or more) components may be faulty. Another difficulty lies in assessing whether a component itself is faulty or whether it is not working because of a related component.*

RESEARCHING THE PROBLEM

One of the most useful troubleshooting skills is being able to do research; to find information quickly. Learn to use web and database search tools so that you can locate information that is relevant and useful. Identify different knowledge sources available to you. Consider both internally available documentation and problem logs and external support resources, such as vendor support or forums.

RE-ESTABLISHING A NEW THEORY

If your theory is not proven by the tests you make or the research you undertake, you must establish a new theory. If one does not suggest itself from what you have discovered so far, there may be more lengthy procedures you can use to diagnose a cause—remember to assess business needs before embarking on very lengthy and possibly disruptive tests. Is there a simpler workaround that you are overlooking?

If a problem is particularly intractable, you can do the reverse of the above process and take the system down to its base configuration (the minimum needed to run). When (if) this is working, you can then add peripherals and devices or software subsystems one-by-one, testing after each, until eventually the problem is located. This is time-consuming, but may be necessary if nothing else is providing a solution.

PROBLEM ESCALATION

Be aware that you may not have all the answers all the time. Consider consulting your colleagues, Internet discussion groups, or manufacturers' help lines. This will not only help you to solve the problem more quickly or identify a better solution than you had considered yourself, but will also increase your knowledge and experience.

If you cannot solve a problem yourself, it is better to escalate it than to waste a lot of time trying to come up with an answer. Formal escalation routes depend on the type of support service you are operating and the terms of any warranties or service contracts that apply. Some obvious escalation routes include:

- Senior staff/Knowledge Experts/Subject Matter Experts/technical staff/developers/programmers/administrators within your company.
- Suppliers and manufacturers—warranty and support contracts and helplines or web contact portals.
- Other support contractors/consultants, websites, and social media.

Choosing whether to escalate a problem is complex as you have to balance the need to resolve a problem in a timely fashion with what might be additional costs and the burdens/priorities that senior staff are already coping with. You should be guided by policies and practices in the company you work for. When you escalate a problem, make sure that what you have found out or attempted so far is documented. Failing that, describe the problem clearly to whoever is taking over or providing you with assistance.

If you are completing troubleshooting steps under instruction from another technician —the vendor's support service, for instance—make sure you properly understand the steps you are being asked to take, especially if it requires disassembly of a component or reconfiguration of software that you are not familiar with.

SOLUTION IMPLEMENTATION AND TESTING

If you have established and tested a theory of cause, it should be apparent what steps are required to resolve the issue. There are typically three solutions to an IT problem:

- Repair—you need to determine whether the cost of repair makes this the best option.
- Replace—often more expensive and may be time-consuming if a part is not available. There may also be an opportunity to upgrade the part or software.
- Workaround—as any software developer will tell you, not all problems are critical. If neither repair nor replacement is cost-effective, it may be best either to find a workaround or just to document the issue and move on.

> **Note:** *If a part or system is under warranty, you can return the broken part for a replacement. To do this, you normally need to obtain a Returned Materials Authorization (RMA) ticket from the vendor.*

When you consider solutions, you have to assess the cost and time required. Another consideration is potential effects on the rest of the system that your plan of action may have and whether you have authorization to proceed. A typical example is applying a software patch, which might fix a given problem but cause other programs not to work. This is where an effective change and configuration management system comes into play, as it should help you to understand how different systems are interconnected and cause you to seek the proper authorization for your plan.

IMPLEMENT THE SOLUTION

If you do not have authorization to implement a solution, you will need to escalate the problem to more senior personnel. If applying the solution is disruptive to the wider network or business, you also need to consider the most appropriate time to schedule the reconfiguration work and plan how to notify other network users. When you make a change to the system as part of implementing a solution, test after each change. If the change does not fix the problem, reverse it and then try something else. If you make a series of changes without recording what you have done, you could find yourself in a tricky position.

VERIFICATION AND DOCUMENTATION

When you apply a solution, test that it fixes the reported problem and that the system as a whole continues to function normally. Tests could involve any of the following:

- Trying to use a component.
- Substituting the component for a "known good" one.
- Inspecting a component to see whether it is properly connected or damaged or whether any status or indicator lights show a problem.
- Disabling or uninstalling the component (if it might be the cause of a wider problem).
- Consulting documentation and software tools such as Device Manager to confirm a component is configured properly.
- Updating software or a device driver.

Before you can consider a problem closed, you should both be satisfied in your own mind that you have resolved it and get the customer's acceptance that it has been fixed. Restate what the problem was and how it was resolved then confirm with the customer that the incident log can be closed.

PREVENTIVE MEASURES

To fully solve a problem, you should try to eliminate any factors that could cause the problem to reoccur. For example, if the power cable on a PC blows a fuse, you should not only replace the fuse, but also check to see if there are any power problems in the building that may have caused the fuse to blow in the first place. If a computer is infected with a virus, ensure that the antivirus software is updating itself regularly and users are trained to avoid malware risks.

DOCUMENT FINDINGS, ACTIONS, AND OUTCOMES

Most troubleshooting takes place within the context of a ticket system. This shows who is responsible for any particular problem and what its status is. This gives you the opportunity to add a complete description of the problem and its solution (findings, actions, and outcomes).

This is very useful for future troubleshooting, as problems fitting into the same category can be reviewed to see if the same solution applies. Troubleshooting steps can be gathered into a "Knowledge Base" or Frequently Asked Questions (FAQ) of support articles. It also helps to analyze IT infrastructure by gathering statistics on what types of problems occur and how frequently.

The other value of a log is that it demonstrates what the support department is doing to help the business. This is particularly important for third-party support companies, who need to prove the value achieved in service contracts. When you complete a problem log, remember that people other than you may come to rely on it. Also, logs may be presented to customers as proof of troubleshooting activity. Write clearly and concisely, checking for spelling and grammar errors.

Activity 1-6
Discussing Troubleshooting Methodology

SCENARIO
Answer the following questions to check your understanding of the topic.

1. You are dealing with a support request and think that you have identified the probable cause of the reported problem.

   What should be your next troubleshooting step?

2. **If you have to open the system case to troubleshoot a computer, what should you check before proceeding?**

3. You receive a support call from a user.

   What should be your first troubleshooting step?

4. **Why does it help to categorize a problem when troubleshooting?**

5. **If another technician says to you, "We'll have to strip this back to base?", what do they mean, and at which specific step of troubleshooting are you likely to be?**

6. **What should you do if you cannot determine the cause of a problem?**

7. You think you have discovered the solution to a problem in a product Knowledge Base, and the solution involves installing a software patch.

   What should be your next troubleshooting step?

8. **After applying a troubleshooting repair, replacement, or upgrade, what should you do next?**

9. **What is the last step in the best practice methodology for troubleshooting and how might it be implemented?**

Summary

In this lesson, you identified core hardware components, various connection interfaces, and a troubleshooting methodology, and you installed peripheral components.

Will there be any specialty input devices that you will need to install or configure at your workplace? How might this affect your day-to-day activities as an IT professional?

Which part of the CompTIA A+ Troubleshooting Model do you expect to find most challenging, and why?

Practice Question: Additional practice questions are available on the CompTIA CHOICE platform within the **Assessments** tile.

Lesson 2
Installing, Configuring, and Troubleshooting Display and Multimedia Devices

LESSON INTRODUCTION

This lesson focuses on installing, configuring, and troubleshooting display and multimedia devices. The video and audio subsystems provide the main ways that information is output from the computer and presented to the user. Multimedia devices can also be used as inputs—to record sound from a microphone, import pictures from a scanner or camera, or capture video from a webcam.

LESSON OBJECTIVES

In this lesson, you will:

- Install and configure display devices.
- Troubleshoot display device issues.
- Install and configure multimedia devices.

Topic A
Install and Configure Display Devices

EXAM OBJECTIVES COVERED
1001-3.1 Explain basic cable types, features, and their purposes.
1001-3.5 Given a scenario, install and configure motherboards, CPUs, and add-on cards.
1001-3.6 Explain the purposes and uses of various peripheral types.

Output devices are those that transmit information from the computer system to the user, whether as video/graphics (display), audio (speakers), or hard copy (printer). The video subsystem is the main type of output provided with a PC. Graphics output is provided by some sort of display unit or monitor plus a video card, which generates the signals to drive the monitor.

DISPLAY DEVICE TYPES

Display devices include monitors, projectors, and VR headsets. You will work most often with monitors, as they are required by practically every desktop and portable computer.

Some notable manufacturers of display devices include ViewSonic®, Iiyama, Sony, Panasonic, Toshiba, LG, Acer®, Sanyo, and Mitsubishi.

MONITORS

Historically, computer monitors used the same sort of cathode ray tube (CRT) technology as consumer television sets. A CRT requires an analog signal from the display adapter to form the picture. CRTs are also very bulky. In the last decade or so, flat panel displays have replaced CRTs. Flat panels use digital signaling, are much thinner and lighter, and use less power than CRTs.

LCDs

Flat panel **Liquid Crystal Displays (LCDs)** are the standard display type for PC systems and laptops. Liquid crystals are chemicals whose properties change with the application of voltage. In modern types of LCD, voltages "twist" the molecules in the liquid crystal to block the passage of light to some degree to set the pixel to the required color.

Each picture element (pixel) in a color LCD comprises cells (or subpixels) with filters to generate the three primary colors (red, green, and blue). Each pixel is addressed by a transistor to vary the intensity of each cell, therefore creating the gamut (range of colors) that the display can generate. In the types of flat panel used for computer displays, the liquid crystal elements and transistors are placed on a **Thin Film Transistor (TFT)** and such LCD panels are often just referred to as "TFTs." TFTs designed for use with PCs are usually of two types:

- **Twisted Nematic (TN)**—produces acceptable results and good response times. Low response times make the display prone to motion blur and "trails."
- **In-Plane Switching (IPS)**—the different arrangement of the cells in IPS panels delivers better color reproduction at a wider range of viewing angles (especially vertical viewing angles) than TN-type displays. The trade-off is slightly worse response times.

TFTs are driven by a digital signal, but many older models come with analog-digital converters so they can accept an analog signal from an interface such as Video Graphics Array (VGA).

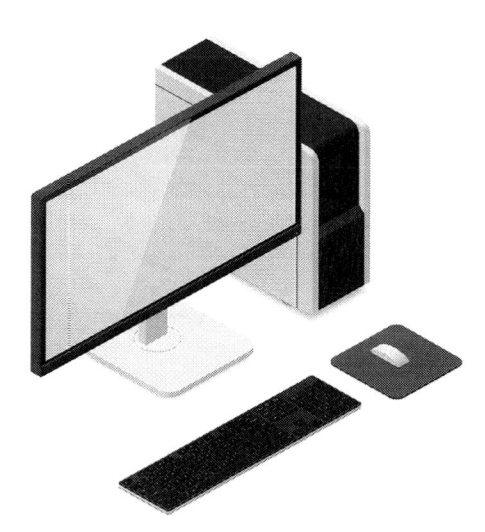

A desktop computer with a TFT display. (Image © 123RF.com.)

LCD BACKLIGHTS

A TFT panel must be illuminated to produce a clear image. In cheaper displays, the **backlight** is a **Cold Cathode Fluorescent (CCFL)** bulb. In most modern TFTs, the backlight is provided by an array of Light Emitting Diodes (LED) rather than a fluorescent bulb. There are a number of different types of LED lighting:

- Edge lit—the LEDs are arranged around the screen rather than behind it. A diffuser is used to try to make the light evenly bright across the whole of the screen.
- Backlit—the LEDs are positioned in an array behind the TFT. This should illuminate the panel more evenly. The disadvantage is that the panel will be slightly thicker. A full array LED backlight can also allow for local dimming, where the LEDs can be selectively dimmed in zones, improving contrast ratio (and power efficiency).
- Color temperature—the backlight can either generate a uniform white light (WLED) or be composed of some combination of RGB or GB LEDs, to allow for different color "temperatures."

OLED DISPLAYS

An **OLED (Organic LED)** display is a newer type of device, often used for small screens (in smartphones, for instance), though more full-scale OLED monitors are starting to appear. One advantage of OLED is that it does not require a separate backlight, making the representation of "True Black" much better and allowing the display to be thinner, lighter, and consume less power. Also, OLEDs can be made from plastic with no requirement for a layer of glass. This means that the display can be curved to different shapes. Manufacturers are even experimenting with flexible, roll-up displays.

DIGITAL PROJECTORS

A **video projector** is a large format display, suitable for use in a presentation or at a meeting. The image is projected onto a screen or wall using a lens system. Some types of projectors are portable; others are fixed in place.

A DLP projector. (Image © 123RF.com.)

Like display monitors, projectors can use different imaging technologies:
- Cathode Ray Tube (CRT)—you may come across legacy projectors using this analog format, but they are not widely marketed anymore.
- Liquid Crystal Display (LCD)—this is a similar technology to that used in display screens except that the lamp used to project the image is much more powerful than a backlight.
- **Digital Light Processing (DLP)**—developed by Texas Instruments. Each pixel in a DLP device is represented by a mirror, which can be tilted towards or away from the lamp, and color filters to create the required shade.
- Laser projector—a lampless projector still uses LCD or DLP imaging but replaces the bulb light source with laser light. Some systems use three lasers (red, green, and blue) while others use a single laser with splitters and phosphors to generate different shades.

Note: Take care when handling projectors. During use, the bulb becomes very hot and while it is hot will be very fragile. Allow a projector to cool completely before attempting to move it.

VR HEADSETS

A **Virtual Reality (VR) headset** is a device that fits over your eyes and ears. It aims to replace sights and sounds from the real world with images and noises generated by a computer application. The headset also comes with handheld controllers to allow you to move the avatar representing you in the virtual space and interact with the virtual environment.

VR is mostly used for games but has other obvious applications for meetings and social networking that is likely to see it more widely adopted in business networks in the next few years. There are two main types of headsets: **tethered VR headsets** are self-contained devices, whereas **mobile VR headsets** are designed to use a specific smartphone model (or range of models) to provide the display.

Tethered headsets, such as the HTC Vive® and Oculus Rift, require an HDMI port plus a number of USB ports on the host PC. While not current at the time of writing, it is likely that most systems will adopt a single USB-C cable in the near future. Tethered VR headsets have substantial system requirements for the CPU, graphics adapter, and system memory.

Note: Make sure the surrounding area is free from obstructions and trip hazards so that the wearer is less likely to hurt themselves or damage anything in the nearby environment.

DISPLAY DEVICE SETTINGS AND FEATURES

Display devices are evaluated on the following characteristics:

- **Resolution and analog versus digital output. Resolution** is the number of **pixels** (picture elements) used to create the image. Resolution is quoted as the number of horizontal and vertical pixels (for example, if the resolution is 640x480, the image is 640 pixels wide by 480 pixels high). Each pixel can be a different color. The total number of colors supported in the image is referred to as the **color depth** (or bit depth). Early (very early) computer monitors had limited color support, such as 8-bit (256 colors). Modern TFTs will support either 18-bit or 24-bit (or higher) color.

    A video card (the component that generates the screen image) can support a number of resolutions (limited by the card's bandwidth; higher resolutions require more data). If the resolution set is greater than the monitor's maximum resolution, then the display will be unstable or will not show anything.

    While **analog display** devices (such as legacy Cathode Ray Tube [CRT] monitors) can support a range of resolutions, **digital display** devices such as TFTs have a **native resolution**, based on the number of pixels in the display. An analog device such as CRT can support a number of output resolutions without losing quality (the "crispness" of an image). TFTs only support lower resolutions by interpolating the image, which makes it look "fuzzy."

- **Screen size and aspect ratio.** For flat panels, the quoted screen size is always the viewable area, measured diagonally. Most screens are around 20" but premium models are available up to 30." **Aspect ratio** is the width of the screen divided by the height. Flat panels are either 4:3 or widescreen (16:9 or 16:10), with widescreen models now dominating the market. One feature of some flat panels is the ability to pivot the display through 90 degrees (making it 3:4 or 9:16).

    > **Note:** Consumer widescreen (for DVD movies) is 16:9, but many PC widescreen display formats are 16:10 to leave room for on-screen controls above or below the movie.

- **Refresh rate.** In an analog device, **refresh rate** is the speed at which the CRT redraws the image, measured in hertz (Hz). If the refresh rate is not high enough (below about 70 Hz), there will be a noticeable flicker as the image is redrawn. This can cause eyestrain and headache. TFTs are not refreshed in the same way and do not suffer from flicker, but the refresh rate in a TFT still has an impact on the quality of the image (in particular, how smoothly objects in motion are displayed).

    Whereas refresh rate is the number of times the display device updates the display (regardless of whether the image is changed or not), the **frame rate** is the number of times the image in a video stream changes per second. This can be expressed in Hertz or Frames per Second (fps). The refresh rate needs to be synched to the frame rate. For example, a display device with a 120 Hz refresh rate displays a 30 fps video stream at a ratio of 4:1. Standard TFTs have a refresh rate of 60 Hz with more expensive models featuring 120 or 240 Hz.

- **Response rate** is the time taken for a pixel to change color, measured in milliseconds (ms). The best quality TFTs have a response rate of 8 ms or lower. High response rates (over 20 ms) can lead to "ghosting" or "trails" when the image changes quickly.

- **Brightness, contrast ratio, and illuminance. Luminance** is the perceived brightness of a display screen, measured in candelas per square meter (cd/m^2). Typically, TFTs are between 200 and 300 cd/m^2 though panels designed for home entertainment or gaming may be 500 cd/m^2 or better. **Contrast ratio** is a measure of luminance of white compared to black. Higher ratios (above 600:1) indicate that displays can display "true blacks" and better saturated (more intense) colors.

When evaluating projectors, the critical performance factor is **illuminance** or light projecting power rather than luminance/brightness. With a flat panel, you want to evaluate how bright it appears when you look at it. With a projector, you want to evaluate the brightness of the image it projects onto another surface. Projectors are normally rated in lumens (or more specifically ANSI lumens, which represents a particular set of test conditions). A projector rated at around 3000 lumens will be able to display clear images with a small amount of ambient light (a room with the curtains closed and overhead lighting dimmed, for instance). A projector rated at 6000 lumens would be able to display a clear image in a sunlit room. Do note that the larger the image, the greater the projecting power needs to be to maintain the same image clarity.

- **Viewing angle and privacy filters.** The image on a flat panel darkens and distorts to some degree if not viewed straight on. Although this is not an issue for desktop use, it can affect use of the screen for viewing movies or as a presentation device. Manufacturers may quote acceptable viewing angles in marketing literature, but these values are not usually comparable to one another. As mentioned above, IPS-type flat panels perform better at wide angles than TN-type panels.

  A **privacy filter** prevents anyone but the user from reading the screen. IPS-type TFTs are designed to be viewed from wide angles. This is fine for home entertainment use but raises the risk that someone would be able to observe confidential information shown on a user's monitor. A privacy filter restricts the viewing angle to the person directly in front of the screen.

- **Coatings.** A display can come with either a matte or a gloss coating. A **gloss coating** helps the display to appear "richer" but also reflects more light, which can cause problems with screen glare and reflections of background objects. A **matte coating** may be superficially less impressive but is generally better suited to office work. **Anti-glare covers** are available if the ambient lighting causes problems with the display.

VGA STANDARDS

IBM® created **Video Graphics Array (VGA)** as a standard for the resolution and color depth of computer displays. VGA specifies a resolution of 640x480 with 16 colors (4-bit color) at 60 Hz. VGA also specifies other lower resolution modes with more colors, but 640x480 is what is commonly referred to as "VGA."

Increasing any one of resolution, color depth, or refresh rate increases the amount of bandwidth required for the video signal and the amount of processing that the CPU or Graphics Processing Unit (GPU) must do and the amount of system or graphics memory required.

The VGA standard is long obsolete but was further developed by the Video Electronics Standards Association (VESA) as **Super VGA (SVGA)**. SVGA was originally 800x600 @ 4-bit or 8-bit color. This was very quickly extended as the capabilities of graphics cards and monitors increased with the de facto XGA standard providing 1024x768 resolution, better color depths, and higher refresh rates. Resolutions for modern display systems use some variant of the XGA "standard" (in fact, these are labels rather than standards) or a High Definition (HD) resolution, similar to that found on consumer electronics and media. Some of the more popular XGA and HD resolutions in use are as follows.

Standard	Resolution	Aspect Ratio
WXGA (Widescreen XGA)	1280x800	Widescreen (16:10)
SXGA (Super XGA)	1280x1024	5:4
HD	1366x768	Widescreen (16:9)
WSXGA	1440x900	Widescreen (16:10)
HD+	1600x900	Widescreen (16:9)

Standard	Resolution	Aspect Ratio
Full HD	1920x1080	Widescreen (16:9)
QHD (Quad HD)	2560x1440	Widescreen (16:9)
4K UHD (Ultra HD)	3840x2160	Widescreen (16:9)

DISPLAY DEVICE CONNECTIONS AND CABLES

There are many different types of video connectors and cabling. An individual model of any one video card, monitor, or projector will often support more than one cable type. When computers were primarily used with CRT monitors, the graphics adapter would generate an analog video signal to drive the monitor. Now that most screens use TFT technology, the video signal is usually digital. Many digital monitors can take an incoming analog video signal but need to convert it back to digital (so the signal is being converted from digital to analog and then from analog back to digital).

VGA PORTS AND CONNECTORS

The distinctive blue, 15-pin **Video Graphics Array (VGA) port** (HD15F/DE-15) was the standard analog video interface for PC devices for a very long time. Up until a few years ago, even new video cards and monitors usually included it, though it is starting to be phased out completely now.

The connector is a D-shell type (HD15M) with screws to secure it to the port. The screws very frequently become stuck or the housing bolt comes undone when you try to unscrew the connector.

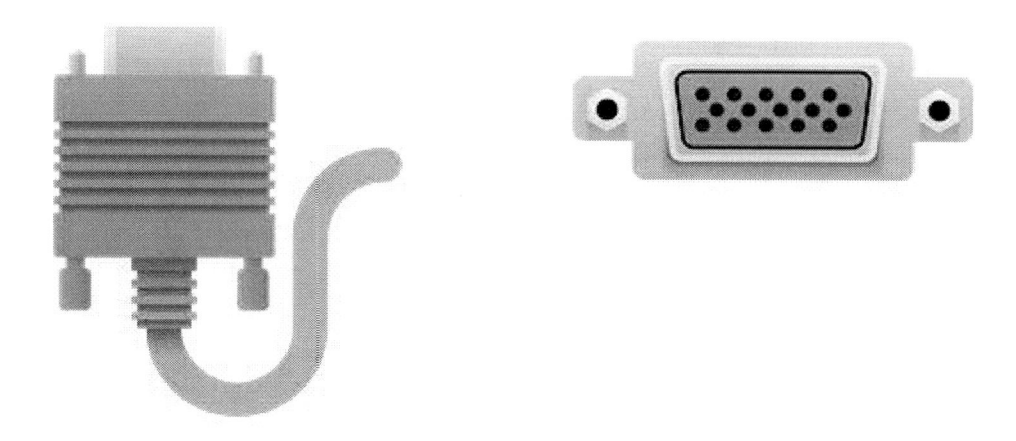

A VGA connector and port. (Image © 123RF.com.)

The interface is analog, meaning that it carries a continuous, variable signal for Red, Green, and Blue (RGB) component video.

Better quality cables (generally speaking, the thicker the better) use shielded coaxial wiring and support longer lengths at better resolutions. Low quality cable may only be able to support 800x600. The cable may be marketed with the highest resolution it can support—UXGA (1600x1200), for instance. Most VGA cable does not exceed 5 m but a good quality cable might be able to support sub-HD resolutions at lengths of up to 30 m.

DVI PORTS AND CONNECTORS

Digital Visual Interface (DVI) is a video cable type designed for flat panel display equipment. While popular for a short period after its introduction in 1999, DVI is now being phased out in favor of better-established technologies, such as HDMI®, DisplayPort™, and Thunderbolt™. You are unlikely to see DVI used on new display devices or computers.

There are five types of DVI, supporting different configurations for bandwidth and analog/digital signaling. The pin configuration of the connectors identifies what type of DVI is supported by a particular port.

- DVI-A
- DVI-D (single link)
- DVI-I (single link)
- DVI-D (dual link)
- DVI-I (dual link)

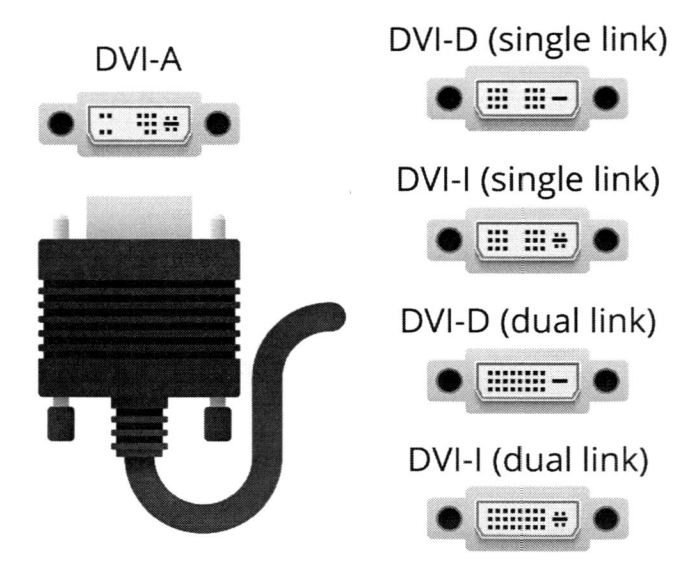

DVI port and connector types. (Image © 123RF.com.)

DVI-I supports both analog equipment (such as CRTs) and digital. DVI-A supports only analog equipment and DVI-D supports only digital.

DVI bandwidth in single-link mode is 3.7 Gbps, enough for full HD resolution (1920x1200) at a frame rate of 60 fps. More bandwidth can be obtained through connectors that support dual-link mode. Dual-link supports over 7.4 Gbps, enough for HDTV @ 85 fps. A single-link connector can be plugged into a dual-link port, but not vice versa.

There are economy and premium brands of DVI cable. Cables have to support an HD signal at a length of at least 5 m (16.5 ft). Better quality cable will support longer lengths. The quality cable uses thicker wiring and better shielding.

HDMI PORTS AND CONNECTORS

The **High Definition Multimedia Interface (HDMI)** is the most widely used graphic device interface. It is ubiquitous on consumer electronics, such as televisions and Blu-ray players, as well as computer equipment. HDMI supports both video and audio digital streams, plus remote control (CEC) and digital content protection (HDCP).

> **Note:** HMDI carries only a digital signal. It does not support analog monitors.

HDMI cabling is specified to different HDMI versions with different bandwidth capabilities. Notably, version 1.4 adds support for 4K (4096x2160@24Hz). 4K is the format used in digital cinemas and consequently represents something of a Holy Grail for home cinema enthusiasts. The Ultra HD (3840x2160) format is often also branded "4K."

Version 1.4 also allows the controller (typically a computer) and display device (an IP-capable TV, for instance) to establish a Fast Ethernet (100 Mbps) network link over an HDMI With Ethernet cable.

At the time of writing, HDMI is on version 2.1. This supports 48 Gbps bandwidth, or up to 10K at 120 Hz.

HDMI uses a proprietary 19-pin (Type A) connector. There is a Type B connector (29-pin) to support dual-link connections but it is not widely used.

HDMI Type A port and connector. (Image © 123RF.com.)

HDMI v1.3 introduced the Mini HDMI connector (Type C) for use on portable devices, such as camcorders. This is more compact but has the same number of pins. HDMI v1.4 also introduced the even smaller Micro HDMI connector (Type D), still with 19 pins.

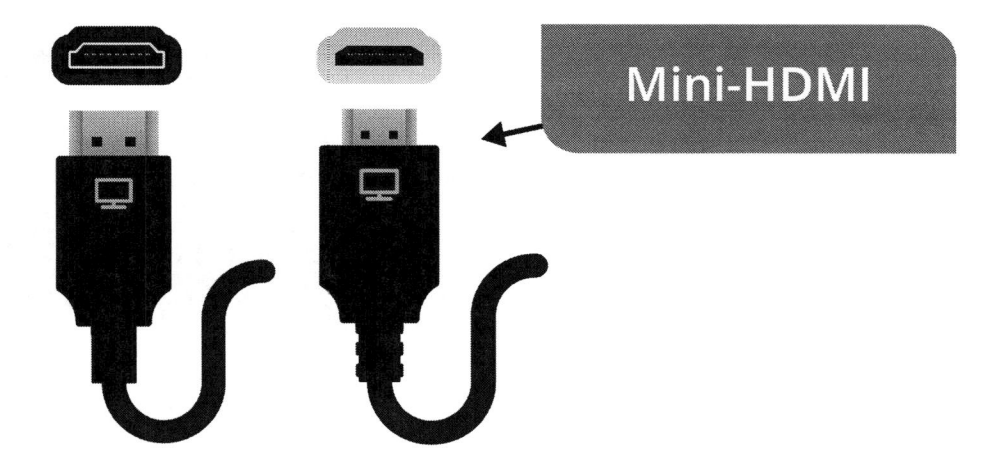

From left to right: HDMI connector and port, Mini-HDMI connector and port. (Image © 123RF.com.)

HDMI cable is rated as either Standard (Category 1) or High Speed (Category 2). High Speed cable supports greater lengths and is required for v1.4 features, such as 4K and

3D. HDMI version 2.0 and 2.1 specify Premium High Speed (up to 18 Gbps) and Ultra High Speed (up to 48 Gbps) cable ratings.

HDMI is backward-compatible with DVI-D using a suitable adapter cable. This means that (for example) a DVI-D graphics adapter could be connected to an HDMI port on the display device.

DISPLAYPORT PORTS AND CONNECTORS

HDMI was principally developed by consumer electronics companies (Hitachi, Panasonic, Sony, and so on) and requires a royalty to use. **DisplayPort** was developed by the Video Electronics Standards Association (VESA), the organization largely representing PC graphics adapter and display technology companies. It is a royalty-free standard intended to complement HDMI.

Unlike other video and audio standards, it transmits packetized data, in the same sort of way as PCI Express. Like PCI Express, bandwidth can be allocated in bonded lanes (up to 4). Each lane can be given a different data rate. In v1.2 of the standard, each lane can be allocated a 1.62, 2.7, or 5.4 Gbps data rate. The maximum data rate for a 4-lane link is 17.28 Gbps. Like HDMI v1.4, there is support for 48-bit color, 3D, 4K/UHD, and HDCP. There is also an auxiliary channel that allows (for example) a microphone-enabled display to feed the audio signal back to the PC without additional cabling.

DisplayPort supports both copper and fiber-optic cabling. DisplayPort-certified copper cable must be capable of supporting 2560x1600 (WQXGA resolution) over 2 m. It also supports multiple monitors "daisy-chained" on the same cable.

A DP++ DisplayPort port and connector. (Image © 123RF.com.)

DisplayPort uses a 20-pin connector. A DP++ port allows a connection with DVI-D and HDMI devices (using a suitable adapter cable). There is also a mini DisplayPort format (MiniDP or mDP), developed by Apple and licensed to other vendors.

THUNDERBOLT AND USB-C PORTS AND CONNECTORS

Historically, computer video used dedicated cable types such as HDMI or DisplayPort. Modern computer display equipment is quickly adopting the USB-C connector interface. USB-C can carry HDMI or DisplayPort signaling (with an adapter cable) but would usually be used with Thunderbolt 3 signaling for video support.

A USB-C connector with Thunderbolt 3 support. (Image © 123RF.com.)

Note: Not all USB-C ports support Thunderbolt 3. Look for the flash icon on the port or confirm using the system documentation.

VIDEO ADAPTERS AND CONVERTERS

Many video cards provide support for older display standards. It might be that the video card itself is quite old but it can be useful for newer video cards to support interfaces that might only be found on older monitors and projectors. If there is no port common to both the computer and the monitor, you may be able to use a converter or adapter cable to connect them.

It will often be the case where the graphics adapter comes with a physical interface that is not supported by the display device. In this scenario, you can use a converter cable or adapter plug to connect the devices:

DVI TO HDMI

DVI is not supported on many consumer devices so you may use this type of adapter to connect a laptop to a TV set. There is no signal conversion involved so this can be performed by a passive cable.

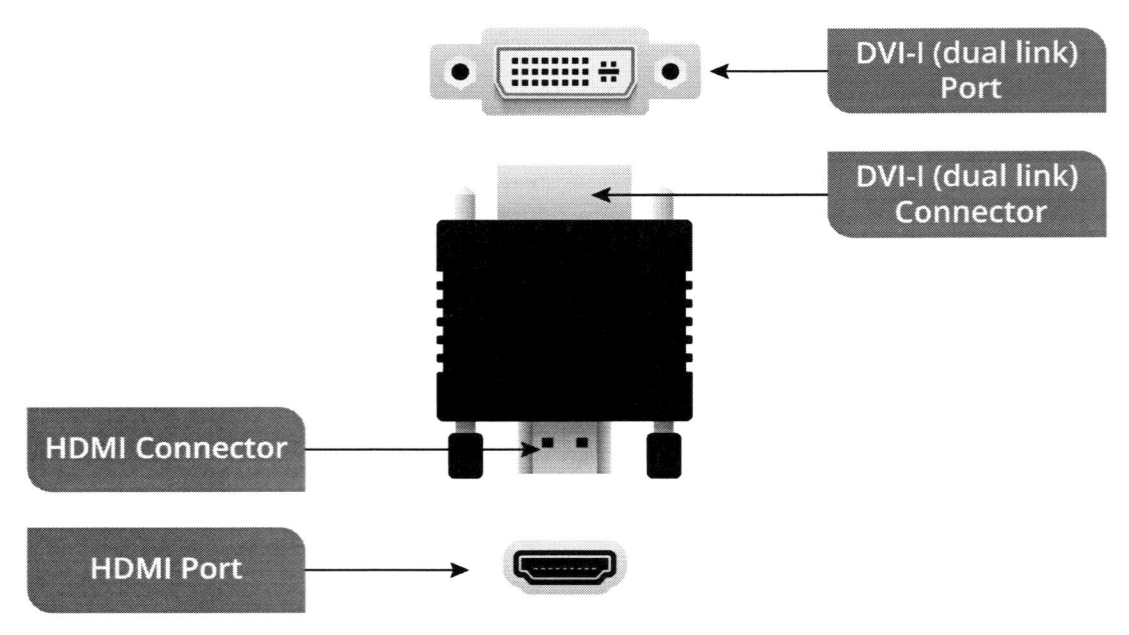

HDMI to DVI-I adapter. (Image © 123RF.com.)

DVI OR HDMI TO VGA

Older flat panels may only come with VGA ports so this type of converter can be used to connect them up to newer computing devices. Unless going from DVI-I (analog) to VGA, this type of converter requires an active Digital to Analog Converter (DAC) chip. Note that the converter will not be accepted by HDCP-protected content.

For instance, a VGA to DVI-I adapter would carry an analog signal only, while an HDMI to VGA converter cable converts between digital and analog inputs or outputs.

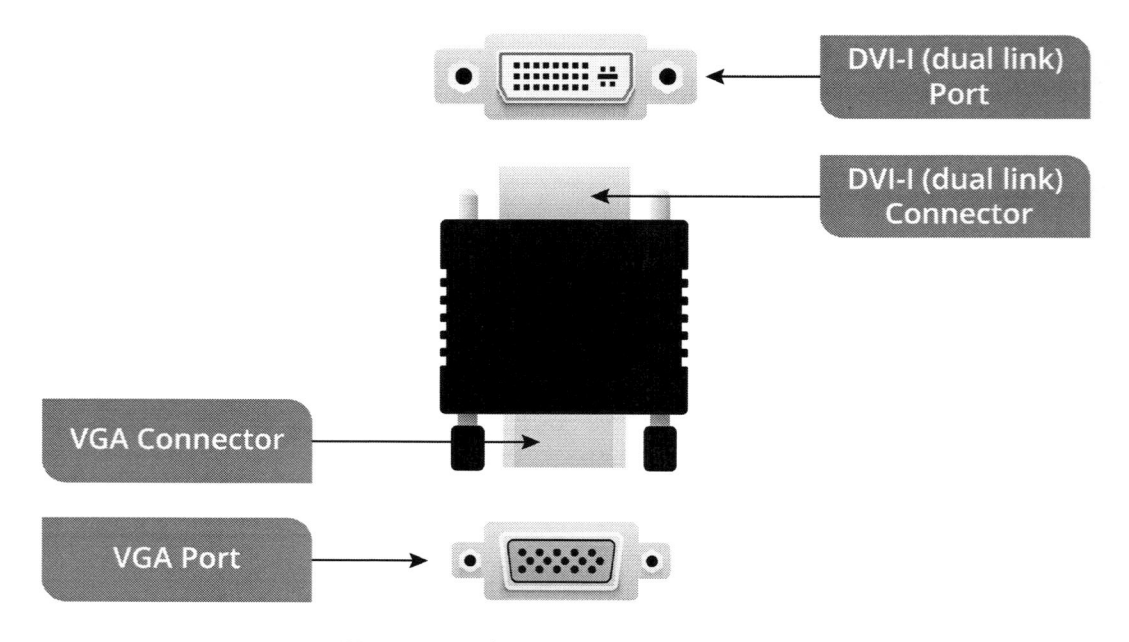

VGA to DVI-I adapter. (Image © 123RF.com.)

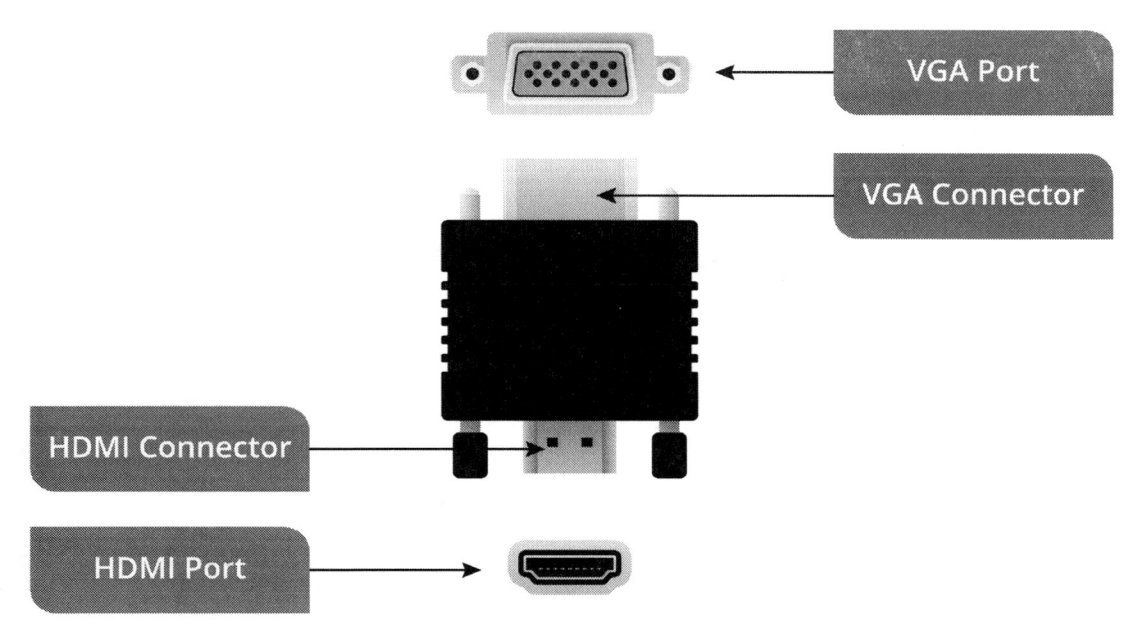

HDMI to VGA adapter. (Image © 123RF.com.)

DISPLAYPORT/THUNDERBOLT TO DVI

This type of adapter would allow you to connect a computing device of a "certain age" to newer display devices (or vice versa). No signal conversion is involved so only a simple passive cable with appropriate connectors on each end is required.

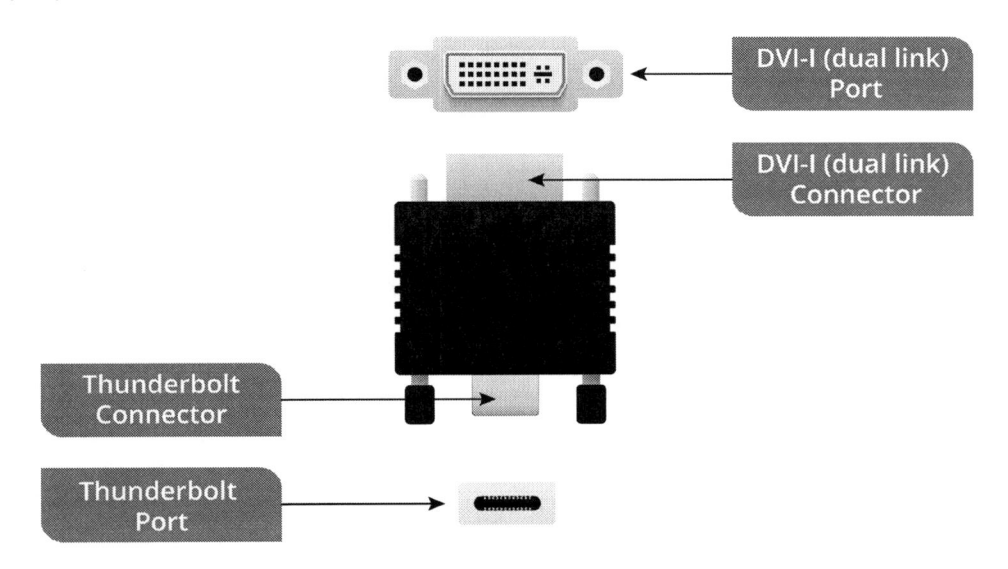

A Thunderbolt to DVI-I adapter. (Image © 123RF.com.)

VIDEO CARDS

The **video card** (or **graphics adapter**) generates the signal to send to the monitor or projector. The video card may make use of the system CPU and memory, but most add-in cards are highly sophisticated pieces of equipment, essentially computers in their own right.

> **Note:** Be aware that the terms video, graphics, and display are used interchangeably to refer to these adapters (or cards).

Low-end graphics adapters are likely to be included with the motherboard chipset or as part of the CPU itself. This is also referred to as an **onboard adapter**. If a computer is to be used for 3D gaming, Computer Aided Design (CAD), or digital artwork, a better quality adapter is required. This can be installed as an **add-on card** via a PCIe slot. Most graphics adapters are based on chipsets by ATI/AMD (Radeon chipset), NVIDIA (GeForce and nForce chipsets), SiS, VIA, and Intel.

ADAPTER COMPONENTS

The core of a video adapter is the **Graphics Processing Unit (GPU)**. This is a microprocessor like the CPU, but designed and optimized for processing instructions that render 2D and 3D images on-screen. High-end cards are differentiated based on the following features:

- **Clock speed**—as with the CPU, the clock speed is the basic measure of performance, but the internal architecture (pipeline) of the GPU is another important factor.
- **Shader units**—support the special effects built into games and other software. These units perform calculations that allow for 3D shading, realistic shadows and lighting, surface textures, translucency, and so on.
- **Frame rate**—the basic test for a GPU is the frame rate it can produce for a particular game or application. 25 fps is about the minimum to make a game playable.

3D cards need a substantial amount of memory for processing and texture effects. A dedicated card may be fitted with up to 12 GB GDDR RAM at the high-end; around 2 GB would be more typical of current mid-range performance cards. The width and speed of the memory bus between the graphics RAM and GPU are also important. Low end cards use shared memory (that is, the adapter uses the system RAM). Some cards may use a mix of dedicated and shared memory.

Note:
Graphics Double Data Rate (GDDR) memory technology is similar to the DDR modules used for system RAM.

Most modern cards use a PCIe x16 interface. Dual cards, using two (or more) slots, are also available. With NVIDIA cards, this is accomplished using Scalable Link Interface (SLI); AMD/ATI dual cards are branded CrossFire.

SUPPORT FOR DISPLAY INTERFACES

Modern cards will support at least one digital interface (DVI, HDMI, DisplayPort, or Thunderbolt). Some cards may support other interfaces, such as VGA, but such support for analog display interfaces is increasingly unlikely. Having multiple connectors on the card also allows for the attachment of multiple display devices, even if the connectors are different types.

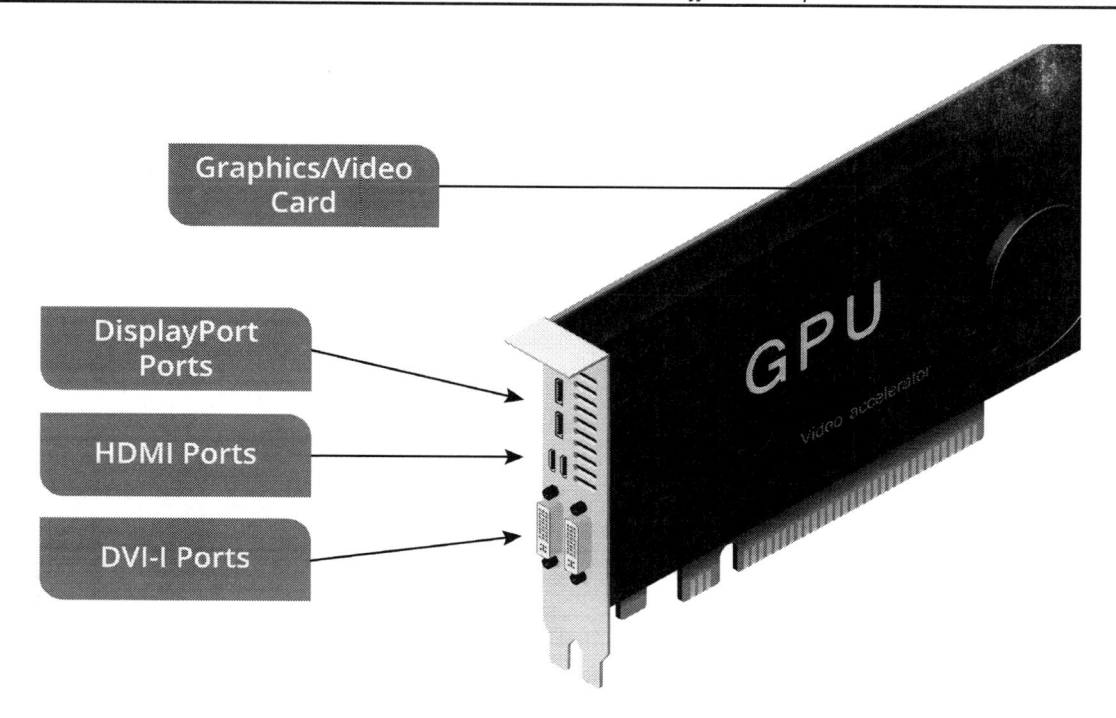

A video/graphics card with DisplayPort, HDMI, and DVI-I ports. (Image © 123RF.com.)

GRAPHICS APIs

To work with 3D games and design applications, graphics cards need to be compliant with the specified version of one of the major graphics application programming interfaces (APIs):

- DirectX®—Microsoft's specification. DirectX also specifies sound and multimedia APIs.
- OpenGL®—developed by Silicon Graphics.

CONFIGURATION TOOLS FOR DISPLAY DEVICES

Once the adapter card has been installed and the monitor connected via a suitable cable, Windows should detect the devices and make them available for use via Plug and Play.

If the computer has an onboard adapter, you may need to disable it via the system setup (BIOS) program after installing an add-on card. In some cases though, the utility supplied with the adapter will support selecting the default input and specifying use of a particular adapter for a particular task or process.

Basic display settings, such as the resolution, can be configured via a built-in operating system tool, such as Windows Settings or Windows Control Panel. Alternatively, an adapter card might ship with a dedicated management utility. You would normally access this via an icon in the notification area.

Intel utility for configuring graphics properties.

You may also need to use controls on the monitor itself to adjust the image or select the appropriate input channel. For example, if there is no image on the screen, check that the monitor is set to use the HDMI port that the computer is connected to, rather than an empty DVI port. These **On-Screen Display (OSD)** menus are operated using buttons on the monitor case. As well as input control, you can usually find settings for brightness, color/contrast, and power saving.

MULTIPLE DISPLAYS

A computer can be set up to use two (or more) display devices. In terms of hardware, the PC requires a graphics adapter with multiple display ports, multiple graphics adapters, or monitors with input and output DisplayPort or Thunderbolt connectors for daisy-chaining.

> *Note: The adapter and monitors must support Multi-Stream Transport (MST) to use daisy chaining. To set up the chain, connect the first cable from the graphics adapter port to the "IN" port on the first monitor. Connect a second cable from the "OUT" port on the first monitor to the "IN" port on the second monitor.*

Dual monitors can be used in one of three modes, configured via Windows display properties:

- Display the same image on both devices—select the **Duplicate these displays** option (this mode is useful for delivering presentations).

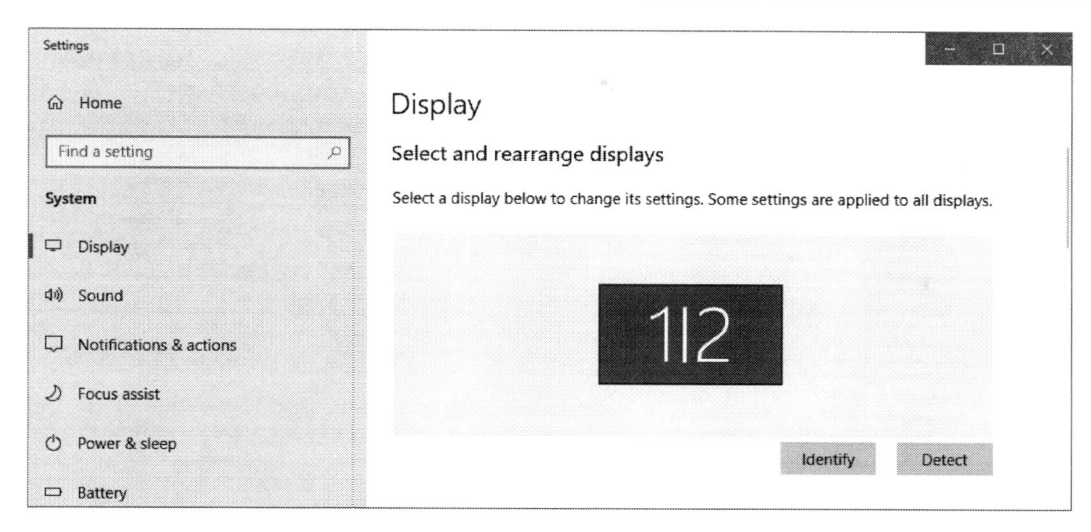

Configuring dual monitors in Windows 10 to duplicate the display. (Screenshot used with permission from Microsoft.)

- Display the desktop over both devices—select **Extend these displays** (this mode makes more screen "real estate" available and is useful for design, publishing, and programming work). Drag the displays in the box to position them correctly. You can put them to the left and right or above and below one another.

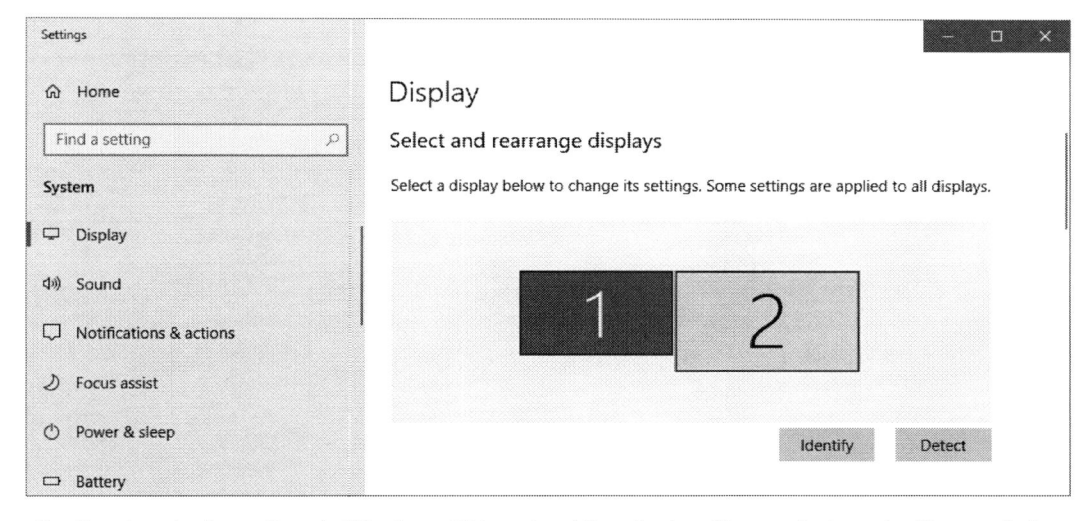

Configuring dual monitors in Windows 10 to extend the display. (Screenshot used with permission from Microsoft.)

- Display the desktop on one device only—select either **Show only on 1** or **Show only on 2**.

> **Note:** In Windows 10, you can select a multi-monitor mode quickly using **Windows + P**. This causes a prompt to appear on the right side of the primary display listing the options **PC screen only**, **Duplicate**, **Extend**, and **Second screen only**.

> **Note:** To learn more, check the **Video** tile on the CHOICE Course screen for any videos that supplement the content for this lesson.

> **Access the Checklist tile on your CHOICE Course screen for reference information and job aids on How to Install and Configure Display Devices.**

Activity 2-1
Discussing Display Device Installation and Configuration

SCENARIO
Answer the following questions to check your understanding of the topic.

1. Look at the following exhibit.

   What two types of display cabling can be connected to this laptop?

2. **Which ports are present on the graphics card shown below?**

3. **Which interfaces does the adapter cable shown below support?**

4. A customer is shopping for a computer game for her daughter and wants to know if you can explain the reference to "DirectX" on the packaging?

5. You are configuring two monitors in extended desktop mode.

   What should you configure in the Display dialog box?

Activity 2-2
Installing a Graphics Adapter

BEFORE YOU BEGIN

What you do in this activity will depend on the components available to you. Check with your instructor which of the following steps you should perform.

You will perform this activity on your WORKBENCH PC.

SCENARIO

A common upgrade on machines used for playing games or doing Computer Aided Design or graphics intensive work is to upgrade the graphics adapter. Another upgrade that can be performed is to add a second adapter to the system so that two monitors can be used. This requires that both adapters support dual displays.

1. Record information about the graphics adapter make and model currently installed, including the driver version.
   a) Start and log on to the PC then press the **Windows+X** keys and select **Device Manager**.
   b) In **Device Manager**, expand the **Display adapters** node, and record the installed adapter name.
      - Adapter make and model: _____

      If there are multiple display adapters, record information about all of them.
   c) Right-click the adapter and select **Properties**. Select the **Driver** tab, then record the **Driver Provider** and **Driver Version** information.
      - Driver provider: _____
      - Driver version: _____

      Again, if there are multiple display adapters, do this for each of them.

2. Access the PC's internal components safely.
   a) Shut down the PC and then disconnect the power cable and all peripheral cables. Take the usual ESD precautions.
   b) Remove the system case cover.

3. Complete this step or one of the next two steps, as suggested by your instructor.
   a) If your system has onboard graphics, identify a free expansion slot that will accommodate the type of adapter you are installing.
   b) Remove the blanking plate from the slot.
   c) Insert the card into the slot, checking carefully to make sure that it is properly seated and that any locking catches are in place.

4. Complete this step, the previous step, or the next step, as suggested by your instructor.
   a) Remove your existing adapter (remember that there may be a plastic clip to release as well as the mounting screw).
   b) Swap adapters with a classmate, and install the new one.

5. Complete either this step or one of the previous steps, as suggested by your instructor.
   a) Install a second graphics adapter alongside your existing one.

   A second graphics adapter can be installed so that two monitors can be used at the same time. This type of setup is favored by graphics professionals where having lots of screen "real estate" is extremely productive. It can also be used with presenting software.

   > **Note:** Another use for twin adapters is for high performance gaming systems where two cards are installed to double performance. Another dual-monitor option is to obtain a "multi-head" card with two or more outputs.

6. Verify the installation and configure display settings.
   a) Close the system case.
   b) Reconnect the peripheral devices. When connecting the display, make sure you connect the cable to a display port on the new adapter, if you installed a second adapter alongside an integrated one or existing card.
   c) Reconnect the power cable and start the PC.
   d) When the PC reboots, the new adapter should be detected automatically. If it is not, install the driver software that comes with the card.
   e) Right-click the **Desktop** and select **Display settings**. Select the **Advanced display settings** link, and record the following information:
      - Refresh rate: _____
      - Bit depth: _____
   f) Select the **Display adapter properties** link. Record the following information:
      - Chip type: _____
      - Total Available Graphics Memory: _____
      - Dedicated Video Memory: _____
   g) Select **List All Modes** to list the combinations of resolution and refresh rate supported by the monitor.
   h) Select **Cancel** to close each dialog box.
   i) In the **Settings** app, select the **Back** button.
   j) Experiment with different text DPI settings by using the **Change the size of text** list box.

   These are useful on very high resolution monitors where the on-screen menus can look very small as the default setting (96 dpi).
   k) If you installed a second display adapter, configure the display across the two monitors, experimenting with the options available. When you have finished, set the display back to one monitor. Disconnect the second monitor and connect it back onto the other PC.

7. At the end of the activity, if you installed a second adapter, open the computer and remove it then hand it back to your instructor. Revert any other changes as suggested by your instructor.

Topic B
Troubleshoot Display Devices

EXAM OBJECTIVES COVERED
1001-5.4 Given a scenario, troubleshoot video, projector, and display issues.

As well as installing and configuring display devices, you also need to know how to identify and resolve issues related to using them.

COMMON DISPLAY ISSUES

Common display issues include:
- No image is displayed on the monitor.
- Image is dim.
- Image flickers or is distorted.
- Images have low resolution or color depth.
- Images and icons are oversized.
- Incorrect color patterns.
- Dead pixels.
- Image is burned into the monitor.
- Unexpected objects or patterns appear on the monitor.
- Overheating.
- Protected content.

GUIDELINES FOR TROUBLESHOOTING DISPLAY DEVICES

*Note: All of the Guidelines for this lesson are available as checklists from the **Checklist** tile on the CHOICE Course screen.*

Here are some guidelines to follow to help troubleshoot display devices.

TROUBLESHOOT DISPLAY CONFIGURATION ISSUES
Follow these guidelines when you are troubleshooting display device configuration issues.
- **No image.** If no image is displayed on the monitor, try these actions:
  - Make sure that the monitor is plugged in and turned on. Check that the monitor is not in standby mode (press a key or cycle the power to the monitor to activate it).
  - Check the connection between the video card and monitor. Make sure the cable is connected securely at both ends and is not loose. Make sure that the cable has not become stretched or crimped. If there are dual display ports, check that the cable is connected to the right port.
  - If the monitor supports different display inputs (VGA and HDMI, for instance), check that it is switched to the correct one using the On-Screen Display (OSD) controls.
  - Try the monitor with a different PC and see if it works.

- **Dim image.** If the image is dim, check the brightness and contrast controls to make sure they are not turned all the way down. It is possible that a power saving mode is dimming the display. It is also possible that an adaptive brightness, auto-brightness, or eye-saving feature of the device or operating system has been enabled. These reduce brightness and contrast and can use lower blue light levels. This type of feature might activate automatically at a certain time of day or could use an ambient light sensor to trigger when the room is dark.
- **Image quality.** If there is a problem with image quality, such as a flickering or misshapen image or missing colors, try these actions:
  - Check the video cable and connector. If the connector is not securely inserted at both ends, this could cause flickering. If a pin is bent and not lining up with the video card connector, this can cause a missing color. If the cable is poor quality, higher resolutions may not be supported.
  - If video playback does not work, try lowering or disabling hardware acceleration (using the slider on the **Troubleshoot** tab). If this solves the problem, check for an updated display driver.

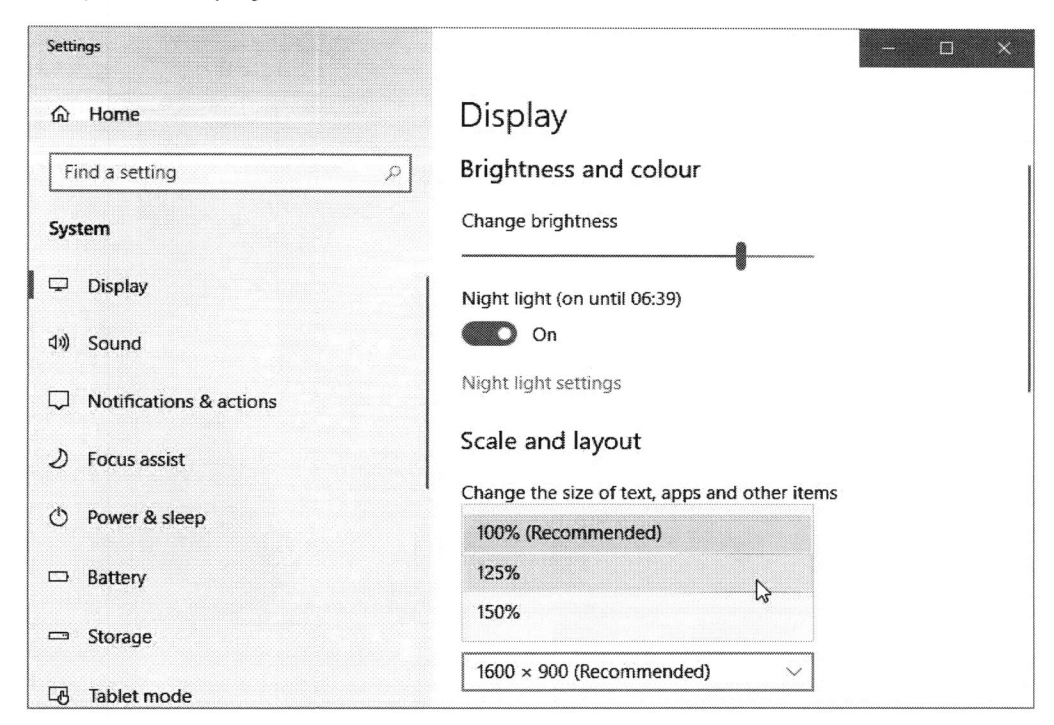

Configuring scaling on a Windows 10 PC. (Screenshot used with permission from Microsoft.)
  - Increasing DPI makes text larger at a particular resolution. This is useful for flat panels that support high native resolutions (using a lower interpolated resolution would make the display "fuzzy"). However, this can cause graphics rendering problems with older software. Also, Windows may set a high DPI automatically when using a high resolution display device.
  - If using a CRT monitor, check refresh rate and resolution settings for the video driver. If resolution is too high or refresh rate is too low this can cause the screen to flicker. On a TFT, check that there is no problem with the backlight.

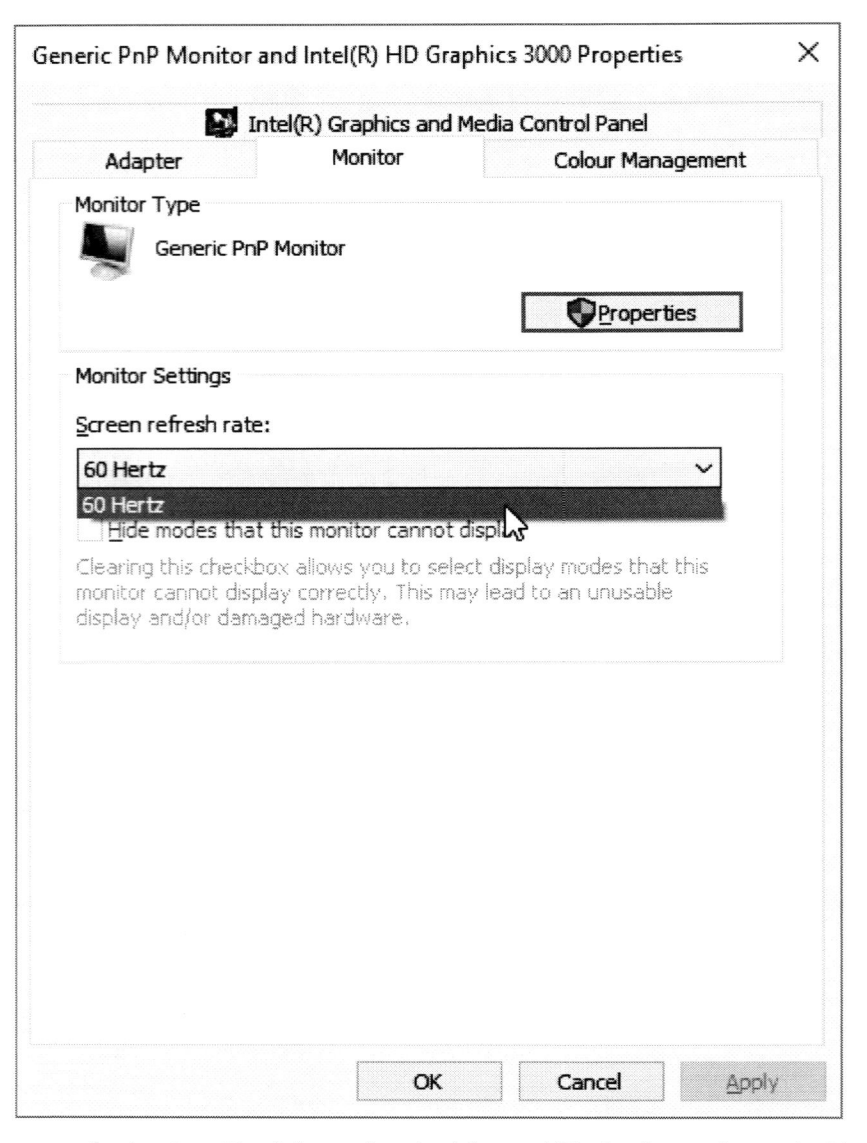

The screen refresh rate setting is located under Advanced Display Properties on the Monitor tab. (Screenshot used with permission from Microsoft.)

- If a CRT image geometry is distorted (a pincushion effect where the edges appear to bulge, for instance), try adjusting the monitor's image control knobs.
- If a TFT image is distorted, check that the panel has not been bent or physically damaged.
- If a projector image is distorted, try to ensure the projector lens is lined up with the display screen or whiteboard. The position of the lens within the projector may be adjustable using a knob or dial. If the lens is above or below the screen, there may be a keystone effect where the top of the image is wider or narrower than the bottom. If the projector or lens cannot be repositioned, there may be a keystone correction control, accessed via the OSD menu, that allows you to adjust the digital image to compensate for this.
- **VGA mode.** If there is a problem with low resolution or color depth:
  - Low resolution or color depth (VGA rather than SVGA) can make the image look blocky or grainy.
  - If a computer boots in VGA mode without this being specified in the boot configuration, check the display driver.

> **Note:** *Windows 10 does not actually support VGA resolution anymore. The minimum resolution is SVGA (800x600).*

- **Oversized images and icons.** If images and icons appear oversized:
  - One way for screen objects to look "too large" is to use a low resolution, such as VGA.
  - Another way is to use a high DPI scaling setting, as described previously.
  - You should also check whether a zoom tool is in use. Windows comes with accessibility features to allow the screen to be magnified. A user might unwittingly activate the screen magnifier (especially if it is configured with a hot key activation) and not know how to turn it off.

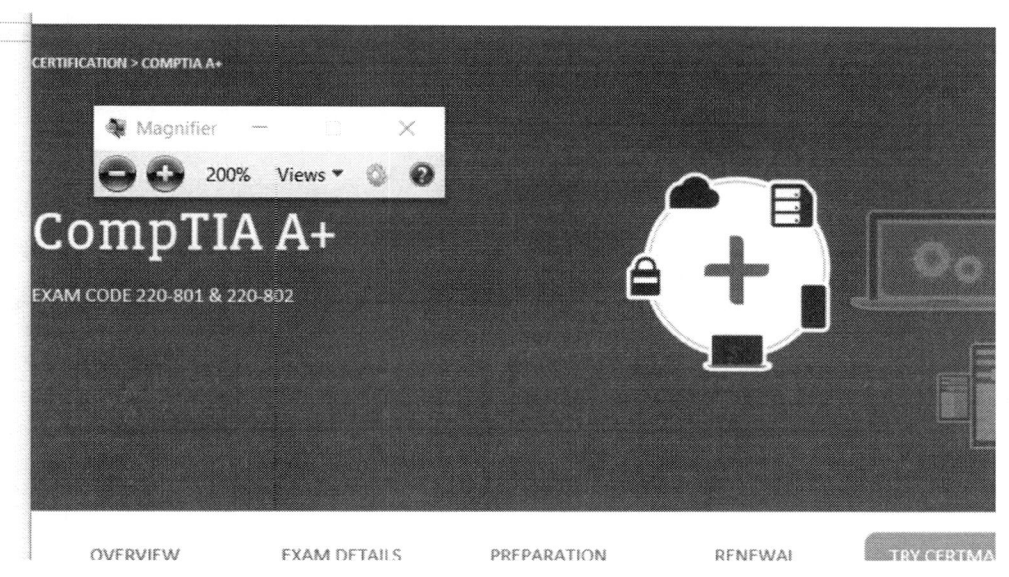

A user may not realize that the Magnifier tool is activated. (Screenshot used with permission from Microsoft.)

- **Color issues.** If there is a problem with color:
  - If a computer is used to produce digital art, it is very important that the display be calibrated to scanning devices and print output. **Color calibration** (or workflow) refers to a process of adjusting screen and scanner settings so that color input and output are balanced. Color settings should be configured with the assistance of a color profile. You can use the **Color Management** applet in Control Panel along with test card color patterns and spectrophotometers to define a color profile and verify that the display matches it.

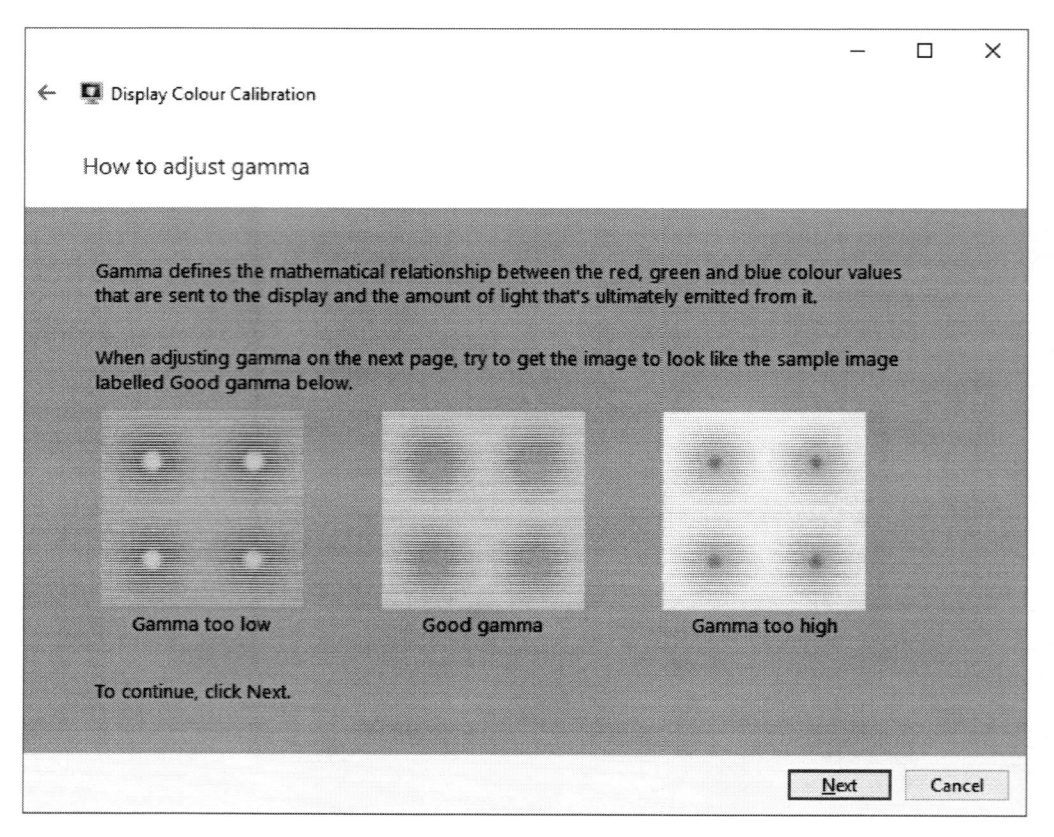

Display Color Calibration utility in Windows 10. (Screenshot used with permission from Microsoft.)

- You may also come across color glitches, such as purple or green horizontal lines or colors changing unexpectedly. These are usually caused by a faulty or loose connector or cabling that is either faulty or insufficient quality for the current image resolution. Try replacing the cable. If this does not fix the issue, there could be a hardware fault.

> **Note:** On a laptop, one simple test is to check whether the problem manifests on both the built-in display and on an external monitor. If the problem only appears on the external monitor, suspect the cable or connector/port.

TROUBLESHOOT ADAPTER AND MONITOR FAULTS

Many display problems are caused by errors in configuration, but you must also be alert to the possibility of hardware faults in the graphics adapter or monitor. In addition to the possible effects of a faulty cable or connector, be aware of these issues and possible solutions:

- **Dead pixels.** If you have dead pixels:
  - Defects in a flat panel monitor may cause individual pixels to be "stuck" or "dead." If a TFT panel has stuck (constantly bright) pixels, and the panel cannot be replaced under warranty, there are software utilities available to cycle the pixel through a series of relatively extreme color states to try to reactivate it.

    > **Note:** Many vendors stipulate that they will only replace a screen if the number of manufacturing defects exceeds a stated threshold.

  - Fixed pixels can also sometimes be reactivated by gently pressing or tapping the affected area of the screen with a stylus or pencil eraser, though there is the risk of causing further damage or scratching the screen. Dead pixels (solid black) cannot usually be fixed.

- **Burn-In.** If you have burn-in:
  - Burn-in is where a static image is displayed for so long that the monitor's picture elements are damaged and a ghost image is "burned" permanently onto the display. Older monitors were highly prone to burn-in, which is why most operating systems include the option for an automatic screen saver to activate after so many minutes inactivity.
  - Modern flat panel monitors are not so susceptible to burn-in, though it is still worth using a screen saver or power saving mode just in case. Some plasma screens are vulnerable to burn-in and additional care should be taken when using a consumer TV device as display screen.
- **Artifacts.** There are two main sources of unexpected objects or patterns appearing on the screen.
  - If the artifacts are "static" and completely out of context with their surroundings, the likelihood is that the cause is a faulty adapter.
  - Some TFTs can suffer from "image persistence," where the crystals become slightly less responsive because they have been left in the same state for an extended period. The problem can usually be solved by turning off the display for a few hours.
  - In terms of 3D graphics performance and possible motion trails or slowdown (especially with computer games), you need to ensure the card is one that is capable of playing the game and that the latest driver and version of DirectX are installed.
  - If there are still issues with frame rates (the speed at which images are displayed), try disabling video effects or using a lower resolution.
  - Make sure that you are using the correct (and latest) drivers for your video card. The FAQs will list any issues with particular applications that the driver addresses.
- **Unexpected shutdowns.** If you are experiencing unexpected shutdowns:
  - A faulty display adapter or display adapter driver is a common cause of STOP errors, or Blue Screens of Death (BSoD). If the problem occurs only in specific circumstances, the fault could lie in some sort of compatibility between the driver and a particular program (typically a 3D game).
  - If the problem occurs more randomly or at bootup, the issue is more likely to be a fault in the adapter itself. 3D graphics cards come bundled with high performance GPUs and memory and as such are prone to overheating, especially in laptops. Make sure the system is being adequately cooled as prolonged overheating will cause permanent damage to the card.
- **Protected content.** If you encounter an error that indicates unauthorized content or an HDCP error:
  - DVI, HDMI, DisplayPort, and Thunderbolt all provide support for the Digital Rights Management (DRM) mechanism High-bandwidth Digital Content Protection (HDCP). HDCP allows a content source (such as a Blu-ray disc) to disable itself if the display adapter and monitor and/or speaker system do not support HDCP and fail to authenticate themselves with the playback source. There have been various iterations of HDCP (at time of writing the current version is 2.2) and backward-compatibility can be problematic as authentication may fail between devices that support different versions of the standard.

Activity 2-3
Discussing Display Device Troubleshooting

SCENARIO
Answer the following questions to check your understanding of the topic.

1. Imagine that the display you installed is not showing the color blue.

   Which component(s) would you prioritize for fault-finding?

2. **What is the most likely cause of a flickering display?**

3. **What would you do if the image from a projector appeared narrower at the top than at the bottom?**

4. You need to set up a system to show content-protected video.

   Which display connector types would be suitable?

Activity 2-4
Troubleshooting Monitor Issues

BEFORE YOU BEGIN
Your instructor has altered the display settings for your monitor. The computer is running and the lock screen is displayed.

This activity will be performed on your WORKBENCH PC.

SCENARIO
An employee recently had to move the location of his workstation. The employee reports that, since the move, the display does not appear in the center of the monitor. The images are too dark, making them difficult to see, and he cannot see as much on the screen as he would like. The employee needs you to resolve these issues so that he can get back to work.

1. Log on to Windows, and examine the video output.

2. Adjust the monitor display.
   a) Referring to the monitor's documentation as necessary, locate the physical controls or On Screen Display (OSD) menu to adjust the brightness of the display image.
   b) Adjust the brightness so that the monitor is comfortable to view.
   c) Adjust the contrast so that you can view all the screen elements easily.

3. Change the resolution.
   a) To open the **Screen Resolution** window, if you are using a Windows 7 computer, right-click the desktop and select **Screen resolution**. If you are using a Windows 10 computer, right-click the desktop and select **Display settings**.
   b) In the **Resolution** section, select the current resolution to display the drop-down list.
   c) In the **Screen Resolution** window, select the appropriate resolution.
   d) If you are using Windows 7, select **OK**.
   e) In the **Display Settings** message box, select **Keep changes** to set the new resolution.

4. Adjust the horizontal and vertical positions of the image.
   a) Referring to the documentation as necessary, locate the controls to adjust the size and centering of the display image.
   b) Adjust the vertical display position so that the display is centered top-to-bottom on the screen.
   c) Adjust the horizontal display position so that the display is centered side-to-side on the screen.
   d) Adjust the height and width of the image so that there is either no border or the smallest border allowed.

Topic C
Install and Configure Multimedia Devices

EXAM OBJECTIVES COVERED
1001-3.6 Explain the purposes and uses of various peripheral types.

Multimedia refers to devices used to play and record audio and video from different inputs and outputs. You will need to be able to support a wide range of multimedia devices, including speakers, microphones, headsets, and cameras.

AUDIO SUBSYSTEMS

A computer's **audio subsystem** is made up of a **sound card** (to process audio signals and provide interfaces for connecting equipment) and one or more input (microphone) and output (speaker) devices.

SOUND CARDS

The basis of a sound (or audio) card is the **Digital Signal Processor (DSP) chip**, which contains one or more **Digital-to-Analog Converters (DACs)**. DACs convert the digital signals generated by the CPU to an analog electrical signal that can drive the speakers. The DSP also provides functions for playing digital sound (synthesis) and driving MIDI compatible devices. The quality of audio playback is determined by the card's **frequency response**, which is the volume that can be produced at different frequencies.

A basic sound chip may be provided as part of the motherboard chipset, but better quality audio functions can be provided as a PCI or PCIe expansion card, or as an external adapter connected by USB. Pro-level cards may also feature onboard memory, flash memory storing sound samples (wavetables), and multiple jacks for different input sources.

> **Note:** *Locating recording functions within the computer case creates lots of problems with noise. Consequently, most audio interfaces designed for professional use are now external units connected via USB or Thunderbolt.*

As with graphics cards, sound cards are designed to support sound APIs. Cards designed for use with Windows should support Microsoft's DirectSound3D (part of DirectX). Cards designed for use with games should also support Open AL and EAX, which provide extensions to DS3D for special sound effects.

Creative, Terratec, RealTek, and Turtle Beach are the most notable vendors of consumer sound cards, while M-Audio, RME, and Apogee are noted for their professional-level cards.

AUDIO CONNECTORS

Most audio connectors are 3.5 mm (⅛ inch) mono or stereo jacks (also referred to as phone plugs or mini TRS [Tip, Ring, Sleeve] connectors). A standard sound card will have several of these for different equipment.

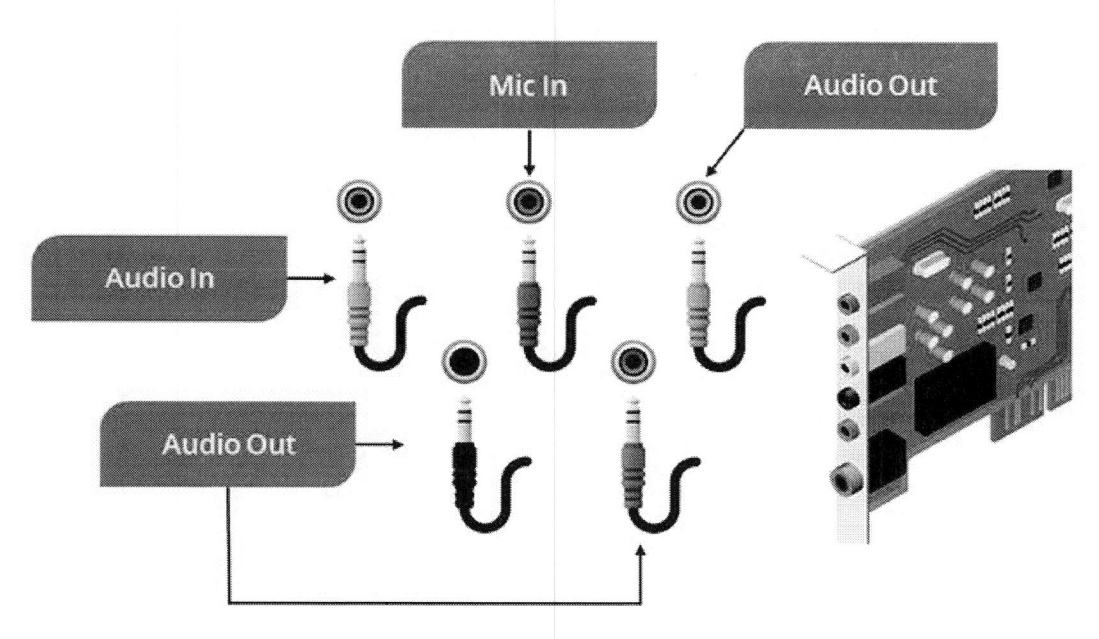

Audio jacks on a sound card. (Image © 123RF.com.)

Jack	Description
Audio in (light blue)	Audio in (or line in) is a low-level (1V) stereo signal as supplied by most tape decks, video players, tuners, CD players, and so on.
Microphone input (pink)	This is generally a mono-only analog input.
Audio out (lime)	Audio out (or line out) is a low-level (1V) analog stereo signal suitable for feeding into amplified speakers or headphones.
Audio out (black)	Carries the signal for rear speakers in a surround sound system.
Audio out (orange)	Carries the signal for the subwoofer in a surround sound system.

Higher end sound cards will include an **Sony/Phillips Digital Interface (S/PDIF) jack**. S/PDIF can either use coax cabling with RCA (or phono) connectors or fiber optic cabling and connectors, which can either be in a square form factor (TOSLINK) or use 3.5mm jacks. S/PDIF is most often used to carry digital data for surround-sound speaker systems.

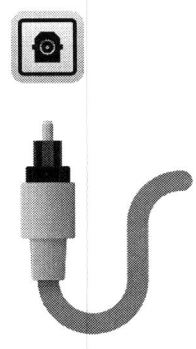

A TOSLINK connector and port. (Image © 123RF.com.)

Note: *RCA connectors are distinguished by a collar surrounding the connector, which makes the fit between plug and socket more secure.*

AUDIO OUTPUT DEVICES

Audio playback is achieved via speakers or headphones, which are connected to the sound card via an analog or digital audio jack. Both analog and digital speakers are available (or speakers may support both analog and digital inputs).

Sound cards supporting multiple output channels with an appropriate speaker system can provide various levels of playback, from mono (on legacy systems) or stereo to some type of **surround sound**. Surround sound uses multiple speakers positioned around the listener to provide a "cinematic" audio experience.

- A 5.1 digital system (Dolby Digital or Digital Theater System [DTS]) has three front center, left, and right speakers, two left and right rear speakers, and a subwoofer for bass sounds.
- A 7.1 system (Dolby Digital Plus or DTS-HD) has two extra side speakers. A speaker system will usually have controls for adjusting volume, bass, and treble plus optionally EQ or preset sound effects.

Note: *A sound card will also feature internal channels (or voices). These represent the number of sounds that the card can play and mix at once (polyphony). This is important for music recording and working with sound effects used by some games.*

Note: *Most graphics adapters support audio over HDMI (or Thunderbolt), allowing surround sound output without a separate connection to a sound card. An HDMI cable would be connected from the graphics adapter port to the TV and then the TV would be connected to the surround sound speaker system.*

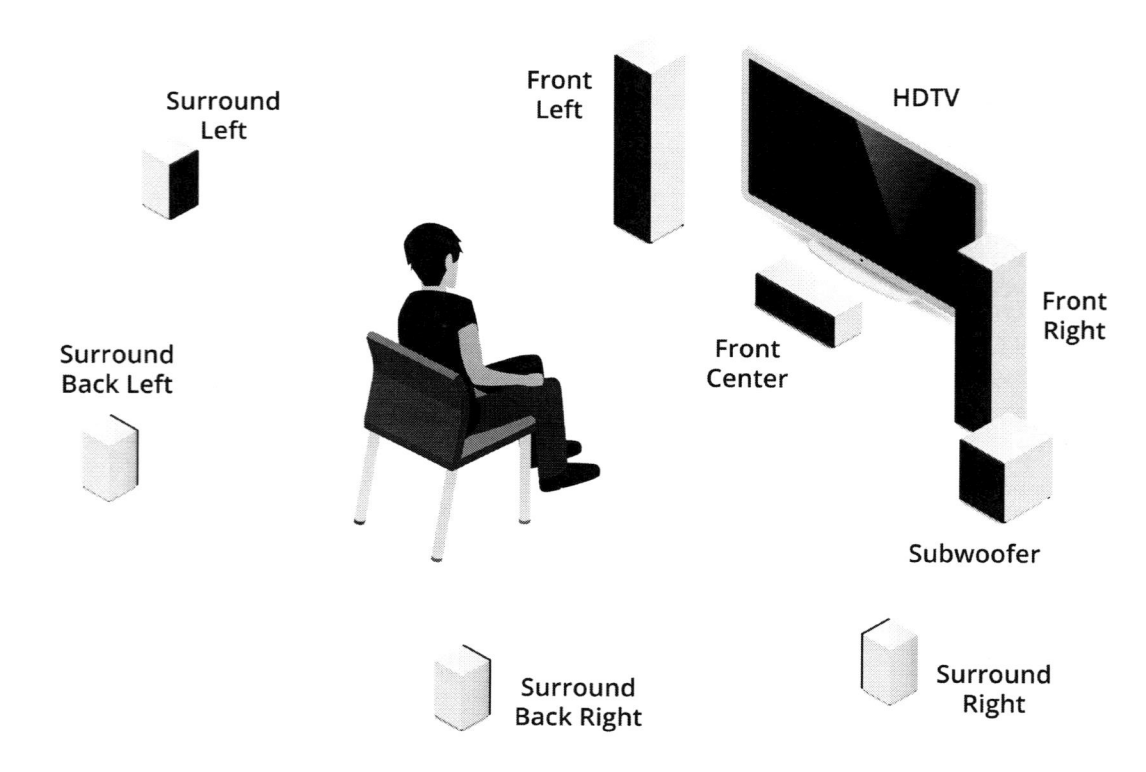

Surround sound configuration for a home theater. (Image © 123RF.com.)

MIDI EQUIPMENT

As well as playing sound via speakers, a card supporting **Musical Instrument Digital Interface (MIDI)** functions can be used to control MIDI equipment (such as a synthesizer or drum machine).

Instead of exchanging the sound wave, the devices exchange information about how to play a sound, in terms of sample (a sound pattern stored in a wavetable), volume, pitch, tempo, and so on. For example, you could use a keyboard to play with samples stored on the PC or use sequencing software to program a drum machine.

MIDI devices use 5-pin DIN connectors or USB connectors.

SOUND RECORDING EQUIPMENT

To record an analog sound wave, the sound card must **sample** the wave. The sampler divides the wave up into a number of slices per second (sampling rate) and records information about each slice (resolution). The higher the sampling rate (measured in Kilohertz [KHz]) and resolution (measured in bits), the better the representation of the source is. CD-quality audio is sampled at 16-bit/44.1 KHz, but professional cards may sample at 24-bit/192 KHz or better.

The card's circuitry and cabling introduce some degree of noise or distortion into the sampled audio. Noise levels are measured using **Total Harmonic Distortion (THD)** and **Signal-to-Noise Ratio (SNR)**. THD is measured as a percentage and SNR in decibels (dB). For both, smaller values represent better performance.

> **Note:** When using a PC to record music, the acoustic performance of components such as the hard drive and fans is very important, so as not to cause interference with analog inputs. Locate an internal sound card in the slot farthest from any other components.

A sound card can be fitted with several ports to connect different types of recording equipment.

HEADSETS

A **headset** combines headphones and a microphone in a single device. They are mostly used with Voice over IP (VoIP) calling, meeting, and conferencing applications. Most headsets are connected to the computer via a USB port or via a wireless interface, such as Bluetooth®.

AUDIO SETTINGS

To set up the audio subsystem, connect the microphone, headset, or speakers to the appropriate ports on the card or motherboard. Use the **Sound** applet in Control Panel or Windows Settings to test the hardware and configure settings.

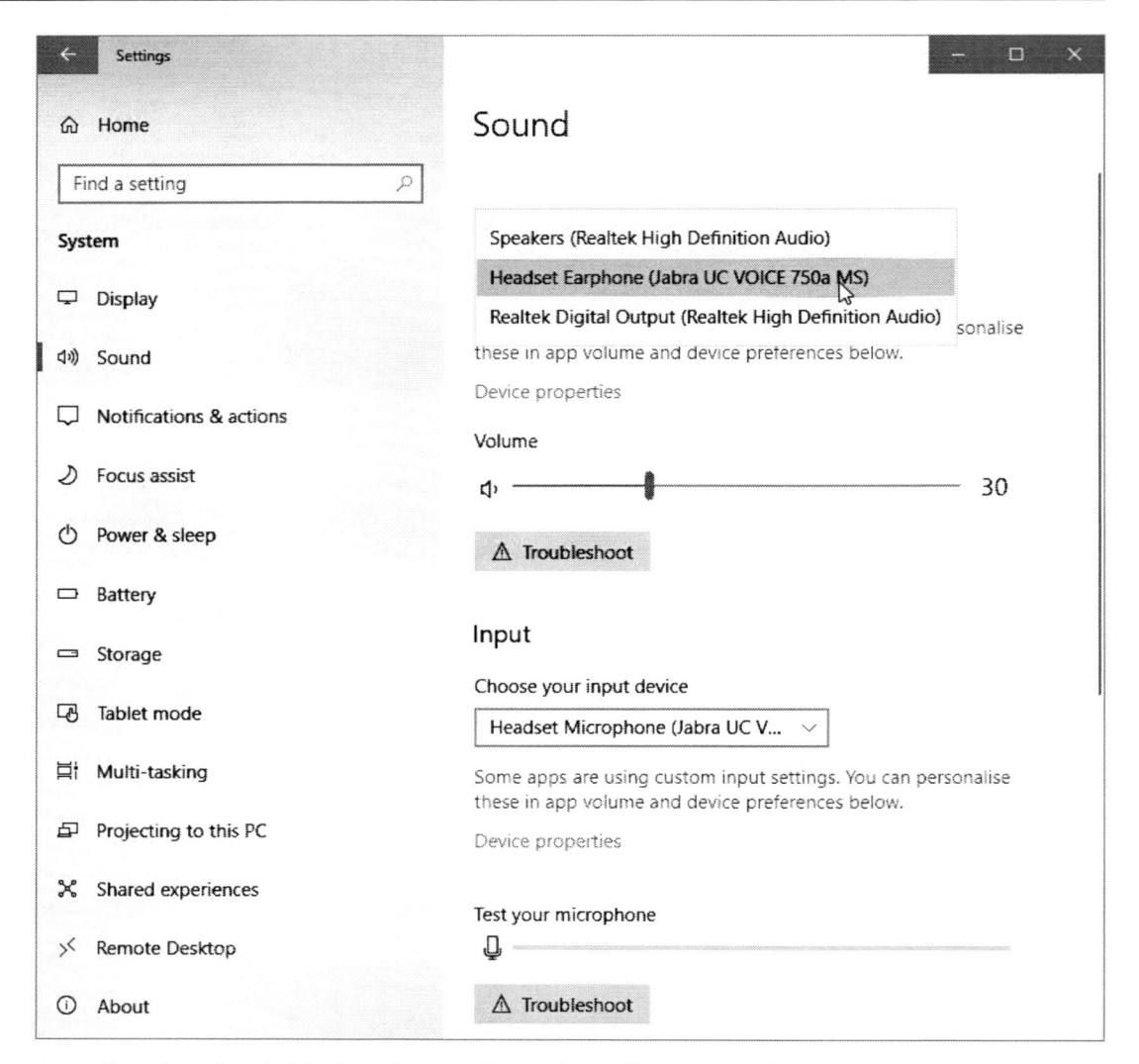

Using Sound settings in Windows 10 to configure the audio output and input devices. (Screenshot used with permission from Microsoft.)

If you have multiple devices connected at the same time, you can choose the defaults here and test levels for audio input and output.

If you have a multimedia keyboard, there are usually keys on that for adjusting the volume. Also, laptops have push-buttons and special function (Fn) keys to adjust the volume.

In Windows, use the **Speakers** icon in the Notification Area to control the volume and switch between playback devices.

Windows volume control. (Screenshot used with permission from Microsoft.)

WEBCAMS

Webcams record video images using a CMOS or CCD sensor and usually feature a microphone to record audio. Most webcams now support HD recording but may come with quite low quality lenses and records at up to about 30 frames per second (fps). Higher quality devices for professional recording and 4K resolution are available. Webcams are used for online video conferencing, as feeds for websites, and as surveillance devices.

Built-in and USB-attached webcam options. (Image © 123RF.com.)

Webcams can be built into a laptop computer chassis or connected as a peripheral device via an external USB port. Some webcams may come with Wi-Fi networking functionality.

> *Note: With webcams—and especially built-in webcams—it is important to enforce app permissions to prevent privacy abuses. While an application such as a browser might need to use the webcam for video conferencing from a particular service provider, that does not mean that other websites should be able to activate the camera.*

DIGITAL CAMERAS

Digital cameras are primarily still cameras, though many can record HD video too. They record an image using a light-sensitive CCD or CMOS array and store it on digital media (a flash memory card). Properties of 35 mm film, such as ISO sensitivity, can be set through software. Digital compact cameras dispense with traditional viewfinders and allow the user to compose each shot using a preview image on an LCD display screen. In other respects, digital cameras have the same features and functions as film cameras.

From left to right: A compact action camera, a DSLR digital camera. (Image © 123RF.com.)

The digicam market is divided into consumer models (replicating the features of compact 35 mm film cameras), professional **Digital Single Lens Reflex (DSLR)** models (preserving the traditional viewfinder method of picture composition and supporting replaceable lenses and manual adjustments), and **prosumer** models (ranging from high end compacts to entry-level DSLRs). Additionally, smartphones and tablets now come with a camera function.

> **Note:** *There are also mirrorless cameras, which support interchangeable lenses but do not use an optical viewfinder.*

Apart from its lens, shutter speed, and feature set, the basic quality measurement of a digital camera is its **resolution**, expressed in **megapixels** (MP). The following table lists the best output that can be expected from images of a particular resolution.

Resolution	Uses
Less than 1 MP	On-screen viewing only.
1 to 2 MP	On-screen viewing and small prints (up to about 7 inches).
3 MP	Larger prints (up to about 12 inches, or letter sized).
4 to 8 MP and higher	Poster prints (30 inches and larger).

> **Note:** *In point of fact, image resolution is now less important than the physical size of the sensor. Compact digicams support high resolution but have tiny sensors, while DSLRs have high resolution and larger sensors (the best quality have a "full frame" sensor; the same size as a frame of 35 mm film).*

Another important factor is the type of memory card used by the camera. Cameras can only use one type of card. Most cameras convert images to compressed (JPEG) file format to save space. JPEG is a lossy compression algorithm, meaning that even at the highest quality setting, some image information is discarded. Professional and prosumer models can typically record uncompressed (RAW) data, but this requires about 2-3 times as much space per picture.

Picture files can be transferred to a PC using the removable memory card or the camera can be connected directly using USB or (on some models) over Wi-Fi wireless networking. Many printers also support memory card slots or connectivity for direct printing from a camera without requiring a PC.

Activity 2-5
Discussing Multimedia Device Installation and Configuration

SCENARIO
Answer the following questions to check your understanding of the topic.

1. What size and color connector would you look for to plug a basic microphone into a PC?

2. You have installed a new sound card in a computer designed for home entertainment. What type of connector would you use to connect a digital surround sound speaker system to the new card?

3. What type of speaker unit is the ".1" in a 5.1 or 7.1 surround sound system and where do you suggest this speaker be placed?

4. What type of interface would allow a software program running on the PC to operate a synthesizer connected as a peripheral device?

5. What sampling rate from a sound card would you require if you want to be able to record CD-quality sound?

Summary

In this lesson, you supported display and multimedia devices by installing, configuring, and troubleshooting them. It is likely that you will be called upon to support display devices often as a computer technician.

What types of monitors do you have experience with? What types of connections have you used to connect those monitors to computers?

In your current job role, have you had to troubleshoot display device problems? If so, what did you do and how did you resolve the issues?

Practice Question: Additional practice questions are available on the CompTIA CHOICE platform within the **Assessments** tile.

Lesson 3
Installing, Configuring, and Troubleshooting Storage Devices

LESSON INTRODUCTION

As a computer technician, your responsibilities are likely to include installing and maintaining many different types of computer components, including storage devices. By identifying the various types of storage devices that can be found in most personal computers, you will be better prepared to select, install, and maintain storage devices in personal computers.

Data storage comes in a variety of types and sizes and for different purposes. Temporary data storage in RAM and permanent storage on hard disk drives, optical drives (CD/DVD/Blu-ray™), and flash memory drives and cards are the main types of storage you will encounter.

LESSON OBJECTIVES

In this lesson, you will:

- Install system memory.
- Install and configure mass storage devices.
- Install and configure removable storage devices.
- Configure RAID.
- Troubleshoot storage device issues.

Topic A
Install System Memory

EXAM OBJECTIVES COVERED
1001-3.3 Given a scenario, install RAM types.

Just as some people say you can never be too rich, you can never have too much memory. Adding memory is one of the simplest and most cost-effective ways to increase a computer's performance, whether it is on a brand-new system loaded with high-performance applications or an older system that performs a few basic tasks.

SYSTEM MEMORY

System memory is the main storage area for programs and data when the computer is running. System memory is a type of volatile memory called Random Access Memory (RAM). System memory is necessary because it is much faster than accessing data in a mass storage system, such as a hard disk. System memory provides a fast storage medium for the operating system and applications but it is **volatile**, meaning that data cannot be stored without a power supply.

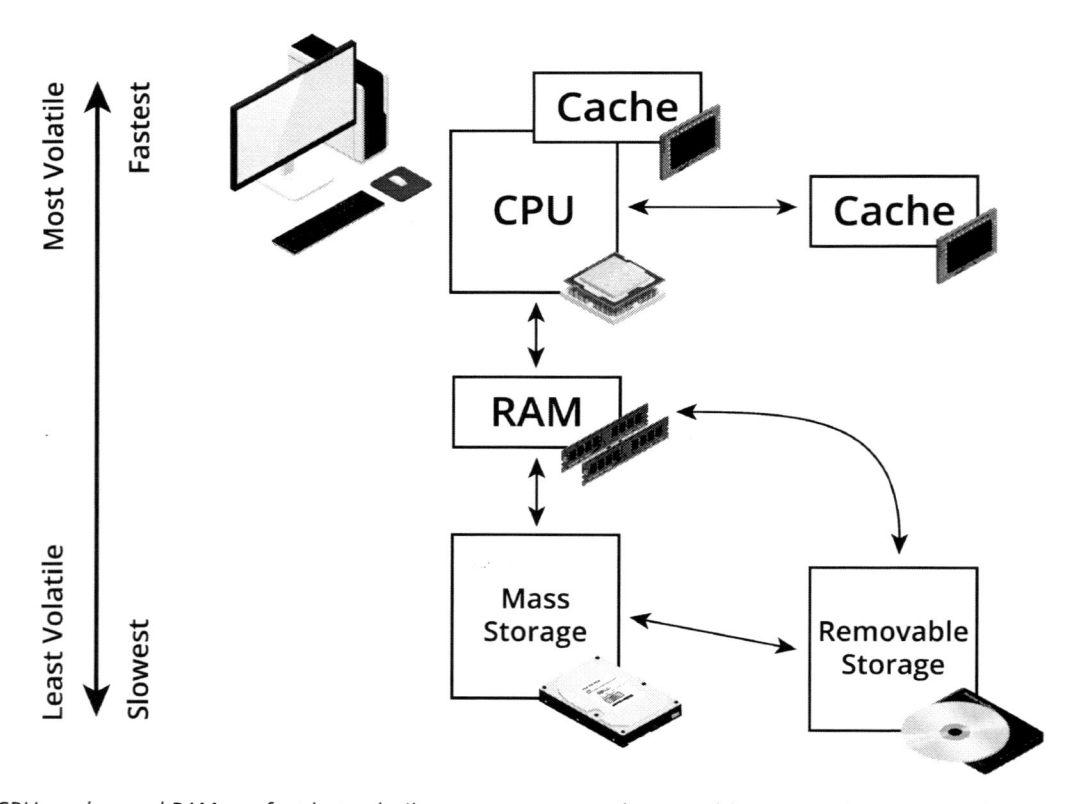

CPU, cache, and RAM are fast but volatile; mass storage and removable storage devices provide slower but permanent data retrieval. (Image © 123RF.com.)

> **Note:** Non-volatile memory does not require a constant power source to store data. Examples include read-only memory (ROM) and flash memory.

A large quantity of system memory is essential for running a PC. It determines its ability to work with multiple applications at the same time and larger files. Each new generation of software tends to take up more memory space. If there is not enough system RAM, the memory space can be extended by using disk space (virtual memory), but as noted previously, accessing the disk is very slow compared to accessing RAM.

RAM TYPES

Several different RAM technologies have been used for system memory in PCs over the years.

RAM Type	Description
Dynamic RAM (DRAM)	DRAM stores each data bit as an electrical charge within a single bit cell. A bit cell consists of a capacitor to hold a charge (the cell represents 1 if there is a charge and 0 if there is not) and a transistor to read the contents of the capacitor.
	The electrical charge gradually dissipates, causing the memory cell to lose its information. In order to preserve the information, dynamic memory has to be refreshed periodically by accessing each bit cell at regular intervals. The refresh cycles slow down the operation of DRAM but it supports high densities (more MB per memory module) and is relatively low cost.
	Many types of DRAM have been developed and become obsolete.
Synchronous DRAM (SDRAM)	In the mid-1990s, variants of SDRAM were used for system memory. SDRAM is so-called because it is synchronized to the system clock. It has a 64-bit data bus. Consequently, if the bus is running at 66 MHz, the bandwidth available to an SDRAM memory controller is 66.6*64 or 4266 megabits per second. Dividing by 8 gives the bandwidth in megabytes per second (533 MBps).

Some notable RAM vendors include Kingston®, Crucial™ (Micron), Corsair, PNY, and Integral™.

DDR SDRAM

Double Data Rate SDRAM (DDR SDRAM) is an updated type of SDRAM (released to market in 2001) where data is transferred twice in one cycle ("double-pumped"). There are four DDR standards, matching different system clock speeds.

RAM Type	Memory Clock (MHz)	Bus Clock (MHz)	Data Rate MT/s)	Transfer Rate (Gbps)
DDR-200/ PC-1600	100	100	200	1.6
DDR-266/ PC-2100	133	133	266	2.1
DDR-333/ PC-2700	167	167	333	2.7

RAM Type	Memory Clock (MHz)	Bus Clock (MHz)	Data Rate MT/s)	Transfer Rate (Gbps)
DDR-400/PC-3200	200	200	400	3.2

SDRAM is referred to by the bus clock speed (PC100, PC133, and so forth). DDR chips are labeled using the maximum theoretical bandwidth (PC1600, PC2100, and so on) largely for marketing reasons. For example, consider DDR-200 PC-1600 memory:

- The internal memory clock speed and I/O bus speed are both 100 MHz.
- The data rate is double this as there are two operations per clock "tick." This is expressed in units called MegaTransfers per Second (200 MT/s). This gives the DDR-200 designation.
- The peak transfer rate is 1600 MBps (200 MT/s x 8 bytes per transfer). This gives the "PC-1600" designation. 1600 MBps is equivalent to 1.6 GBps. Note that the peak transfer rate does not represent "real world" performance; it is a maximum theoretical rate.

DDR2/DDR3/DDR4 SDRAM

DDR has been superseded by DDR2 (from 2003), DDR3 (from 2007), and DDR4 (from 2014) SDRAM. These increase bandwidth by multiplying the bus speed, as opposed to the speed at which the actual memory chips work. This produces scalable speed improvements without making the chips too unreliable or too hot.

The drawback is increased latency, as data takes longer to access on each chip. Latency is offset by improving the memory circuitry.

RAM Type	Memory Clock (MHz)	Bus Clock (MHz)	Data Rate (MT/s)	Transfer Rate (Gbps)
DDR2	100 to 266	200 to 533	400 to 1066	3.2 to 8.533
DDR3	100 to 266	400 to 1066	800 to 2133	6.4 to 17.066
DDR4	200 to 400	800 to 1600	1600 to 3200	12.8 to 25.6

The following represent specific examples of DDR standards:

- DDR2-1066/PC28500—the memory works at 266 MHz and the bus at 533 MHz, which with the double data rate gives 1066 MT/s and nominal transfer rate of 8.533 GBps. This is the best available DDR2 standard.
- DDR3-1600/PC312800—the memory works at 200 MHz and the bus at 800 MHz, which with the double data rate gives 1600 MT/s and nominal transfer rate of 12.8 GBps.
- DDR4-1600/PC4-12800—the memory works at 200 MHz and the bus at 800 MHz, which with the double data rate gives 1600 MT/s and nominal transfer rate of 12.8 GBps. The only advantage over DDR3-1600 is the lower voltage, reducing power consumption.
- DDR4-2400/PC4-19200—the memory works at 300 MHz and the bus at 1200 MHz, which with the double data rate gives 2400 MT/s and nominal transfer rate of 19.2 GBps, exceeding anything available for DDR3.

Note: Clock speeds ending 33 or 66 are usually rounded down; technically they are 33⅓ and 66⅔. In the case of DDR2-667, the memory manufacturers just didn't like the look of "DDR2-666" so they rounded up.

> **Note:** When specifying high performance RAM you may want to compare the performance timings. These are quoted as a series of numbers in the form 5-5-5-15. Each number represents a different timing statistic. The lower the numbers, the better the performance. Each DDR standard has timing variants. For example, DDR3-1333G has 8-8-8-12 timing, whereas DDR3-1600G8 has 8-8-8-10 and DDR3-1600K has 11-11-11-13. More information on SDRAM standards can be obtained from *jedec.org*.

> **Note:** You may also come across GDDRx memory, which is a type of DDRx optimized for use on graphics cards.

MEMORY MODULES

A RAM module, or **memory module**, is a printed circuit board that holds a group of memory chips that act as a single unit. Memory modules reside in slots on the motherboard, and they are removable and replaceable. Memory modules are defined by their design and by the number and type of chips they contain.

DUAL INLINE MEMORY MODULES

DDR for desktop system memory is packaged in 184-pin **Dual Inline Memory Module (DIMMs)**. The notches (keys) on the module prevent it from being inserted into a slot the wrong way around.

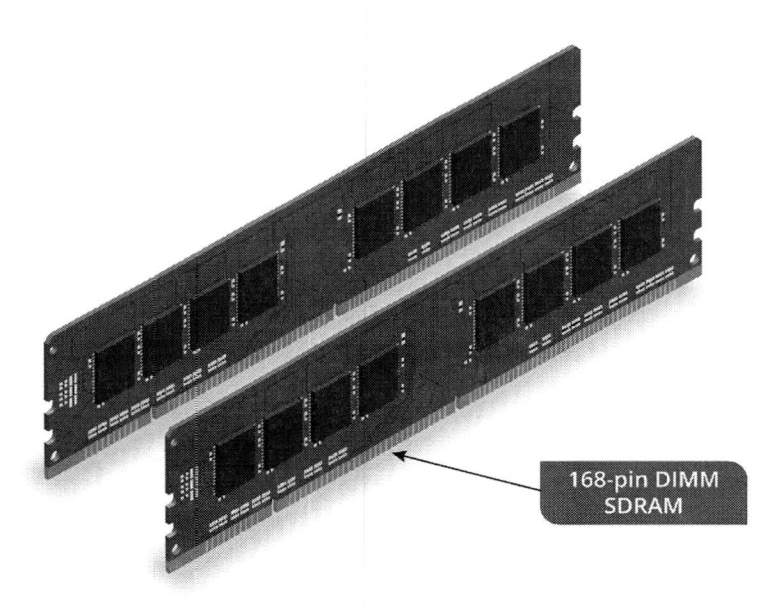

SDRAM packaged in 168-pin DIMMs. (Image © 123RF.com.)

> **Note:** Memory slots look similar to expansion slots but have catches on each end to secure the memory modules.

DDR2 and DDR3 are both packaged in 240-pin DIMMs but are not compatible. The modules and slots are keyed differently to prevent a module from being inserted into an incompatible slot. Faster modules typically feature heatsinks, because of the higher clock speeds.

DDR4 DIMMs have 288 pins. The modules are the same size as previous standards but the pins are more closely spaced. Again, the key position prevents a DDR4 module from being inserted into an incompatible DDR3 or DDR2 motherboard slot. DDR4 works at 1.2 V so is more power-efficient than previous standards.

RAM Type	Pins	Voltage
DDR	184	2.5 to 2.6V
DDR2	240	1.8 to 1.9V
DDR3	240	1.35 to 1.5V
DDR4	288	1.2V

LAPTOP MEMORY

Laptop RAM is packaged in a smaller module called **Small Outline DIMM (SODIMM)**. Both DDR and DDR2 use 200-pin packages, but the key position for DDR2 is slightly different to prevent insertion in a slot designed for DDR. DDR3 uses a 204-pin package while DDR4 is 260-pin.

The memory is typically fitted into slots that pop-up at a 45° angle to allow the chips to be inserted or removed.

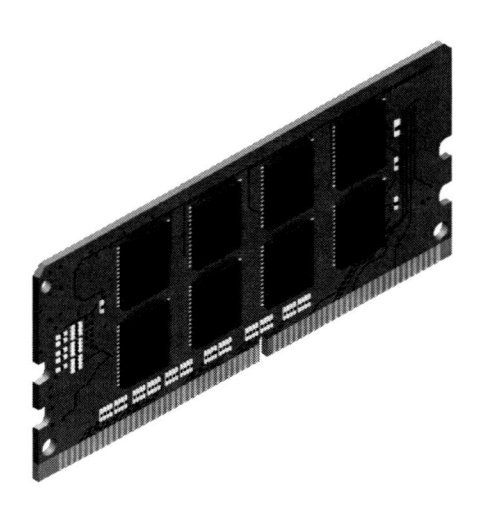

SODIMM. (Image © 123RF.com.)

DUAL-CHANNEL MEMORY

In the 2000s, the increasing speed and architectural improvements of CPU technologies led to memory becoming a bottleneck to system performance. To address this, Intel® and AMD developed a dual-channel memory architecture for DDRx RAM. Dual-channel was originally used primarily on server-level hardware but is commonly being employed on desktop systems and laptops too.

Single-channel memory means that there is one 64-bit bus between the CPU and RAM. With a **dual-channel memory** controller, there can effectively be two pathways through the bus to the CPU, meaning that 128 bits of data can be transferred per "transaction" rather than 64 bits. In fact, in most configurations they continue to operate as two independent 64-bit pathways, but this still increases the bandwidth available. Ordinary RAM modules are used (that is, there are no "dual-channel" DDR memory modules).

> *Note: DDRx memory is sold in "kits" for dual-channel applications but there is nothing special about the modules themselves, other than being identical.*

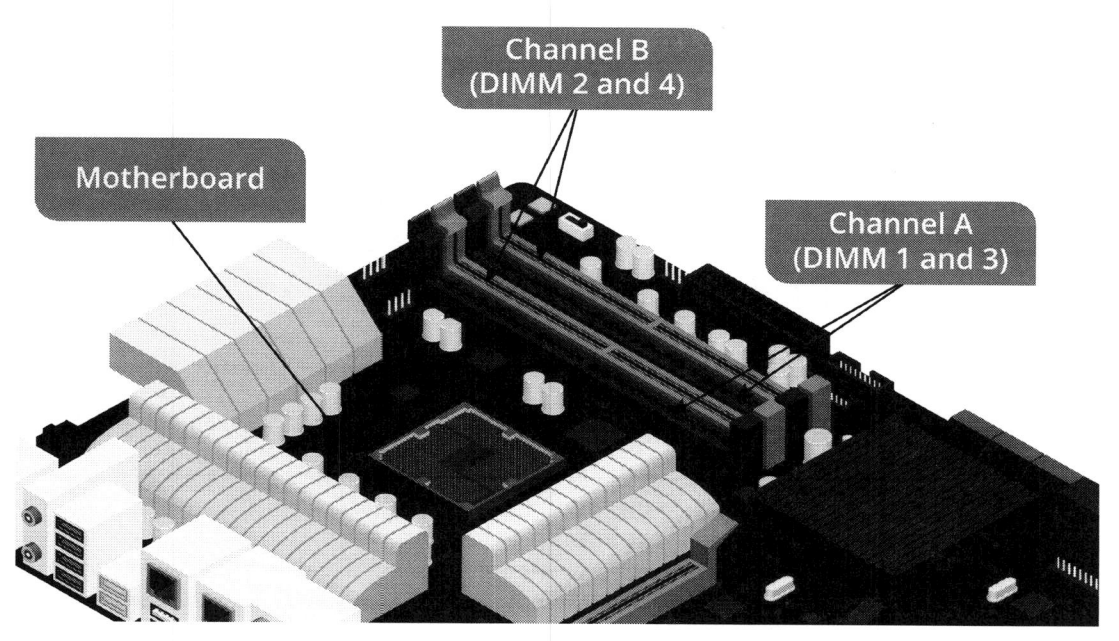

Motherboard DIMM slots (dual channel). Slots 1 and 3 (black slots) make up one channel, while slots 2 and 4 (grey slots) make up a separate channel. (Image © 123RF.com.)

For example, a dual-channel motherboard might have four DIMM slots arranged in color-coded pairs. Each pair represents one channel; each slot represents one of the two sockets in each channel. The memory modules installed should be identical in terms of speed and capacity. If only two slots are used, to enable dual-channel, the modules must be installed in socket 1 of each channel. You will need to consult the system documentation carefully to identify the appropriate slots to use. For motherboards supporting Intel CPUs and some AMD CPUs, the first sockets in both channels are slots 1 and 3. For most AMD CPU-based motherboards, it would mean filling slots 1 and 2. Unfortunately, there is no standardized color-coding. As well as using different colors, some motherboard manufacturers use the same color for the same channel; others use the same color for the same socket. Check the documentation carefully.

Adding an odd number of modules or adding mismatched DIMMs will cause the system to operate in single-channel mode. Dual-channel mode may also need to be enabled via the PC firmware's system setup program.

Some of Intel's CPUs and supporting chipsets have triple- or quadruple-channel memory controllers. AMD is starting to release quadruple-channel controllers too. In these architectures, if the full complement of modules is not installed, the system will revert to dual- or single-channel operation.

PARITY AND ECC RAM

Motherboards used to use a simple error detection method called **parity checking**. Each byte of data in memory is accompanied by a ninth bit. This bit is set to 1 or 0 to make the total number of bits set to 1 in the byte an odd or even number, depending on the type of parity checking being performed. When the byte is read, its parity is checked to ensure that the parity value is still odd (or even). If this is not the case, a bit must have become corrupted.

System memory for most desktops is **non-parity**; that is, it does not perform error checking (except for the startup memory count). For systems that require a high level of reliability (such as workstations and servers), **Error Checking and Correcting (ECC)**

memory is available. ECC memory is enhanced parity circuitry that can detect internal data errors and make corrections. ECC will detect and correct single-bit errors and allow the system to continue functioning normally. It will also detect errors of 2, 3 or 4 bits but will not correct them; instead, it will generate an error message and halt the system.

ECC memory has an extra chip and a 72-bit data bus rather than 64-bit. The motherboard must support the use of ECC memory modules (and the option to use them must typically be enabled in system setup). ECC memory cannot be mixed with non-ECC modules.

> *Note:* An ECC DIMM will have an odd number of memory chips, whereas non-parity DIMMs will have an even number of memory chips.

MEMORY INSTALLATION AND UPGRADE

Upgrading the memory is a common task for any PC technician. If the motherboard supports it but the system is not configured to use it, enabling a dual-channel configuration is the best way of extracting more performance from existing components. Increasing the bus speed would require purchasing a new motherboard and memory modules (and possibly CPU).

> *Note:* When you are purchasing a computer, it is a good idea to get the fastest memory bus you can afford, as this is the component that is most difficult to upgrade later.

MEMORY COMPATIBILITY ISSUES

In terms of compatibility, always consult the motherboard user guide, but consider the following general guidelines:

- The DIMM format must match the motherboard (you cannot install DDR modules in DDR2 slots, for instance).
- Different capacity modules can be installed (with the exception of most multi-channel configurations). Most vendors recommend installing the largest module in the lowest numbered slot.
- Modules from different vendors can be mixed, though this may cause problems with multi-channel configurations.
- For best performance, the modules should be the same speed as the motherboard. Different speeds can be mixed; that is, you can add modules that are faster or slower than the motherboard slots or mix modules of different speeds. The system will only operate at the best speed supported by all installed components (memory modules and controller), so this is not generally a good idea.
- For best performance and reliability, configure multi-channel systems with identical memory modules for each channel.
- ECC memory cannot be mixed with non-parity memory and must be supported by the motherboard. Similarly, registered memory cannot be mixed with unbuffered modules and must be supported by the motherboard.

Memory modules are quite easy to insert and remove (unless cabling within the case makes them inaccessible). The key point here is to ensure that the memory is suitable for the system and in the correct configuration.

Note: To learn more, check the **Video** tile on the CHOICE Course screen for any videos that supplement the content for this lesson.

Access the Checklist tile on your CHOICE Course screen for reference information and job aids on How to Install and Upgrade Memory.

Activity 3-1
Discussing System Memory Installation

SCENARIO
Answer the following questions to check your understanding of the content presented in this topic.

1. **What are the principal characteristics of DRAM technology?**

2. **Why is Synchronous DRAM so-called?**

3. **What is the clock speed of PC2100 DDR SDRAM?**

4. **How many pins are there on a DIMM stick of DDR2 SDRAM?**

5. **How can you distinguish memory slots on the motherboard?**

6. **How is laptop system memory typically packaged?**

7. You are configuring a system with dual-channel memory. You have two modules and there are four slots.

   How would you determine which slots to use?

8. **Your PC's system bus is 800 MHz. You have one 1 GB stick of PC3-12800 installed already. You have a 1 GB stick of PC3-8500 available. Should you add it to the system?**

9. Additional memory was installed in a user's system, and now it will not boot.

   What steps would you take to resolve this job ticket?

Activity 3-2
Upgrading Memory

BEFORE YOU BEGIN
Your instructor will give you a system memory module or kit to install. Remember that memory modules are particularly susceptible to ESD, so handle the modules carefully by the plastic edges and avoid touching the chips.

Perform this activity on your WORKBENCH PC.

SCENARIO
Adding extra system memory is one of the simplest (and cheapest) means of improving system performance. More memory means less slow pagefile access when multiple applications are running or when large files are being manipulated.

1. Use the Windows **System Properties** page and the CPUID CPU-Z utility to report system information and configuration.
   a) Open **System Properties** to confirm the amount of RAM currently installed.
   b) Run the **CPUID CPU-Z** utility by using its desktop shortcut and select **Yes** when prompted by User Account Control (UAC).
      The first tab shows information about the CPU.
   c) Select the **Memory** tab.

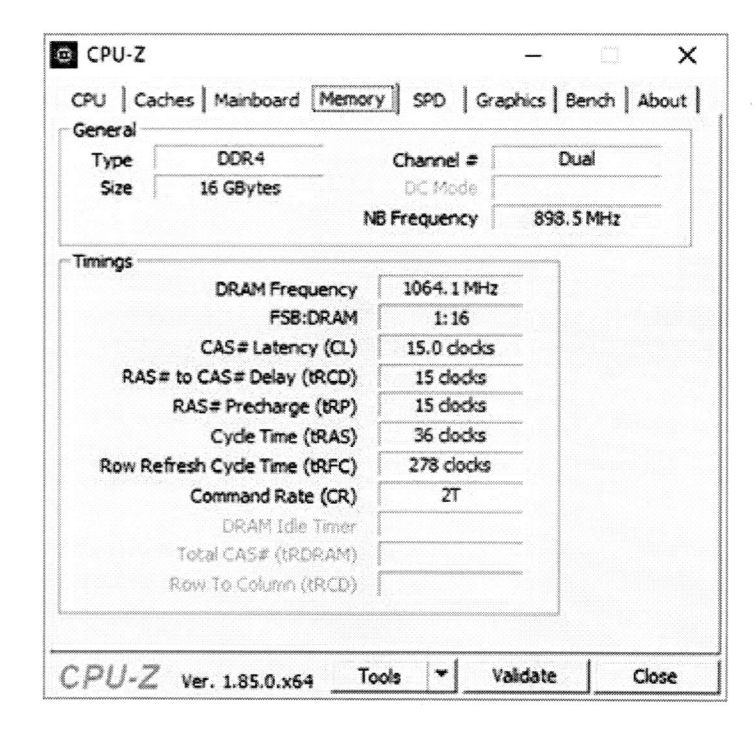

   This tab shows the total amount of system memory, its type and timings as well as whether it is configured in dual-channel mode.

d) Make a note of the DRAM frequency:
e) Select the **SPD** tab.

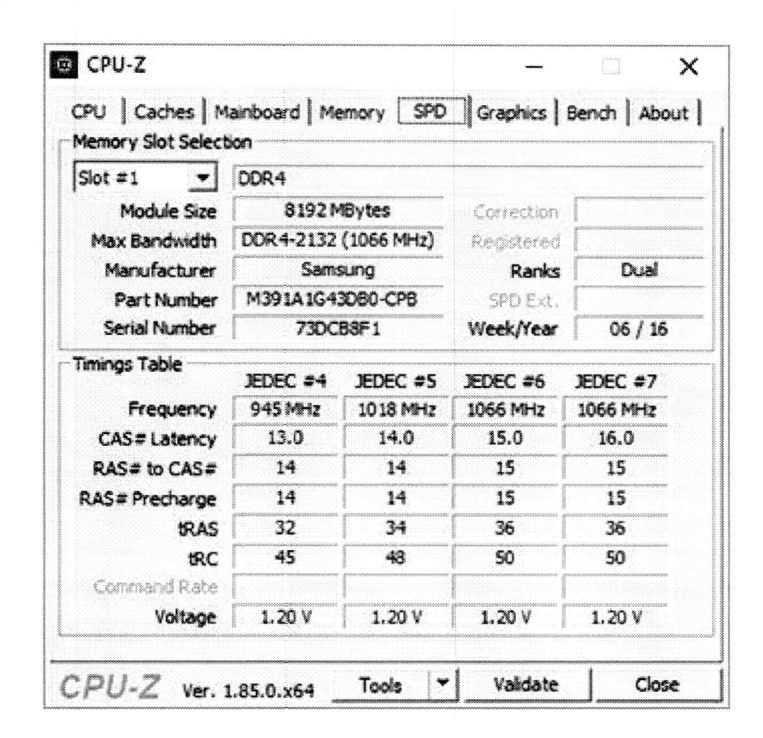

SPD stands for **Serial Presence Detect**. This chip reports the configuration of a memory module installed in a particular slot on the motherboard. You can use this to find out if there are spare slots available for upgrade; useful if your system documentation has not been kept up-to-date.

f) Note which slot(s) the memory module(s) are installed in, and if the system is in dual-channel mode which slots comprise sockets in different channels.
- Slots where memory installed: _____
- Slots comprising sockets in different channels: _____

g) Optionally, select the **Graphics** tab to view information about the video adapter and any graphics memory it might have installed.
h) Select **Close**.

2. Perform a memory module upgrade, and verify the procedure.
   a) Power down the PC, disconnect the power cable, and take the usual ESD precautions.
   b) Remove the case cover.
   c) Confirm that there is a free memory slot and that the memory you have been given is of the correct type.

   > **Note:** *If your instructor has additional memory available for you to install in the PC, they will give it to you now. If not, you can remove the existing memory module and reinstall it. Be sure to follow ESD best practices when you work with RAM modules.*

   d) Release the clips on the memory slot, and push the module into place, taking care to handle it by the plastic parts, rather than touching the chips.

   The clips should snap back into place when the module is properly inserted.

   e) Double-check that the module is seated correctly, and then close the system case.
   f) Reconnect the power cable and start the PC. As the PC boots, look to see if there is a memory check (most computers skip this sort of check these days). If there is an error, power off the PC again, and check that you have seated the module correctly.
   g) Log on to Windows and double-check in **System Properties** that the RAM has been recognized.

       h) Run the **CPUID CPU-Z** utility again and check the memory configuration. Is it still running at the same speed?
           Answers will vary depending on the DIMM used to upgrade the PC.
       i) Close the **System Information** and **CPU-Z** windows.

3. If necessary, uninstall the added memory and return it to your instructor.
   a) Power down the PC, disconnect the power cable, and take the usual ESD precautions.
   b) Uninstall the extra module and hand it back to your instructor.
   c) Close the system case, reconnect the power cable, and restart the PC.
   d) Log in to Windows.

Topic B

Install and Configure Mass Storage Devices

EXAM OBJECTIVES COVERED
1001-3.1 Explain basic cable types, features, and their purposes.
1001-3.4 Given a scenario, select, install and configure storage devices.

Mass storage devices such as hard disks are one of the most common system components you will install. In this topic, you will install and configure hard disk drives (HDDs) and solid state drives (SSDs). Users rely on local persistent storage devices to keep their applications and data current and available. As a CompTIA® A+® technician, your responsibilities are likely to include installing and configuring different types of storage devices to provide your users with the data-storage capabilities that they need to perform their jobs.

STORAGE DEVICES

System memory provides a fast storage medium for the operating system and applications but is volatile, meaning that data cannot be stored without a power supply. Non-volatile storage devices (or **mass storage devices**) hold data when the system is powered off. Removable mass storage devices and removable media allow data to be archived from the PC and transferred between PCs.

Mass storage devices use magnetic, optical, or solid state technology to store data. At least some storage devices are fitted as internal components. In the case of internal devices that use removable storage media, the drive is positioned at the front of the case so that the media can be inserted and removed. Hard drives do not need user access and so do not need to be positioned near a faceplate.

External storage devices are also popular for backup and data transfer or to provide a drive type not available as an internal unit. A device such as an external hard drive would typically be connected to the computer via a USB port.

HARD DISK DRIVES

Even with the advances in the speed and capacity of other types of storage technology, the **hard disk drive (HDD)** remains the primary method of persistent storage for PC data. On a workstation PC, the hard disk drive will store the operating system files, application program files, system software files (such as drivers), and user data. On a server PC, the hard disks will store individual user files and shared sources of information, such as databases. Advances in hard disk technology have enabled disks of up to 8 terabytes (8000 GB) to be produced, although smaller capacities are more common for performance and reliability reasons.

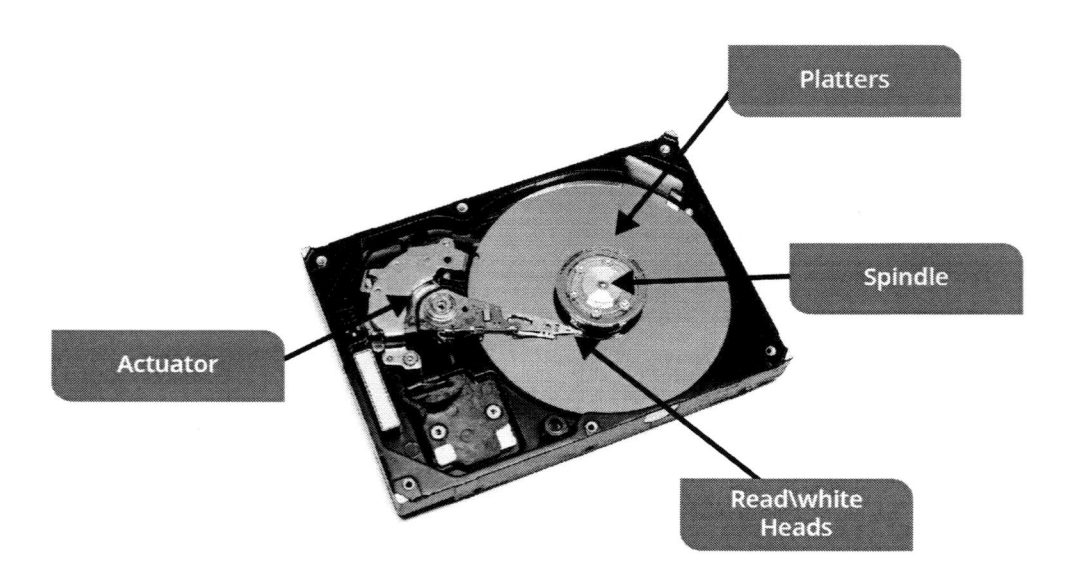

HDD with drive circuitry and casing removed showing 1) Platters; 2) Spindle; 3) Read/write heads; 4) Actuator. (Image by mkphotoshu © 123RF.com.)

In an HDD, data is stored on several metal or glass platters that are coated with a magnetic substance. The top and bottom of each platter is accessed by its own read/write head, moved by an actuator mechanism.

These heads do not actually touch the surface of the platters. The platters are mounted on a spindle and spun at high speed and the heads "float" above them at a distance of less than a millionth of an inch. The disk unit is kept sealed to maintain a constant air pressure (important for keeping the drive heads at the correct distance from the platters) and to prevent the entry of dust.

Each side of each platter is divided into circular **tracks** and each track contains several **sectors**, each with a capacity of 512 bytes. This low-level formatting is also referred to as the drive geometry.

There are two main formats for HDDs. 3.5" units are the mainstream type used in PCs. 2.5" form factors are used for laptops and as portable external drives. There is also a 1.8" form factor but it is not widely used. 2.5" HDDs can also vary in height, with 15 mm, 9.5 mm, 7 mm, and 5 mm form factors available.

DRIVE BAYS AND CADDIES

A drive can be fitted using a caddy. You screw the drive into the caddy and then screw the caddy into the case. A caddy can also allow you to fit a drive of a different size to the bay. For example, you can fit a 2.5" drive in a 3.5" bay by using an adapter caddy. Some caddies use rails so that you can pull the drive out without having to open the case.

HDD PERFORMANCE FACTORS

Several factors determine overall hard disk performance. One factor is the speed at which the disks can spin, measured in Revolutions Per Minute (RPM). The higher the RPM, the faster the drive is. High performance drives are rated at 15,000 or 10,000 rpm; average performance is 7,200 or 5,400 rpm.

RPM is one factor determining **access time** (measured in milliseconds), which is the delay that occurs as the read/write head locates a particular track position (**seek time**) and sector location (**rotational latency**) on the drive. A high performance drive will have an access time below 3 ms; a typical drive might have an access time of around 6 ms.

The **internal transfer rate** (or data or disk transfer rate) of a drive is a measure of how fast read/write operations are performed on the disk platters. A 15 K drive should support an internal transfer rate of up to about 180 MBps, while 7.2 K drives will be around 110 MBps. The **external transfer rate** (often simply described as the transfer rate) measures how fast data can be transferred to the CPU across the bus. Cache memory can help to sustain better transfer rates. A high performance disk may feature an 8 MB or better cache.

> **Note:** Generally, the burst transfer rate is quoted. This is the maximum possible transfer rate under ideal conditions and cannot be sustained over a long period.

The other crucial factor that impacts HDD performance is reliability. Reliability is rated by various statistics, including **Early-life Failure Rate**, **Mean Time Between Failure (MTBF)**, which is the number of hours that a device should operate (under optimum conditions) before a critical incident can be expected, and **life expectancy**, which is the duration for which the device can be expected to remain reliable. All drives now feature **Self-Monitoring Analysis and Reporting Technology (S.M.A.R.T.)** to pass status information and alerts back to monitoring software. This can provide advance warning that a drive is about to fail.

Some of the major hard drive vendors include Seagate, Western Digital, Maxtor, Hitachi, Fujitsu, Toshiba, and Samsung.

STORAGE ADAPTERS AND CABLES

Host Bus Adapters (HBAs) provide a connection point for internal mass storage devices, such as hard drives, optical drives, and tape drives. The interface between the drive, host adapter, and the rest of the system is a type of bus. There used to be two main bus standards for attaching internal storage devices to a PC—Parallel ATA (PATA) and Small Computer System Interface (SCSI)—but these have now largely been replaced by SATA.

> **Note:** HBAs are also commonly referred to as **drive controllers**. Technically, the controller is the circuitry in the disk unit that allows it to put data on the bus, which the HBA shuttles to the CPU or RAM.

SATA

Serial Advanced Technology Attachment (SATA) is the standard means of attaching internal storage drives to a desktop PC. It has superseded the legacy Parallel ATA (PATA) technology.

As the name suggests, SATA transfers data in serial format. This allows for thin, flexible cables of up to 1 m (39"). The cables are terminated with compact 7-pin connectors. Each SATA host adapter port supports a single device. SATA is a **hot swappable** interface. This means that a compatible drive can be connected or disconnected while the system is running.

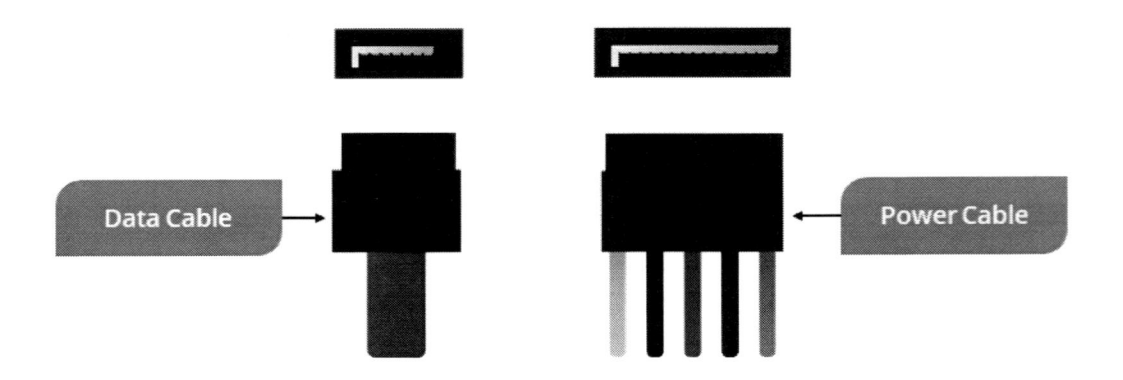

SATA connectors and ports (from left to right): SATA data, SATA power (with 3.3V orange wire). (Image © 123RF.com.)

The first commercially available SATA standard supported speeds of up to 1.5 Gbps. This standard was quickly augmented by SATA revision 2 (3 Gbps) and then SATA revision 3 (6 Gbps).

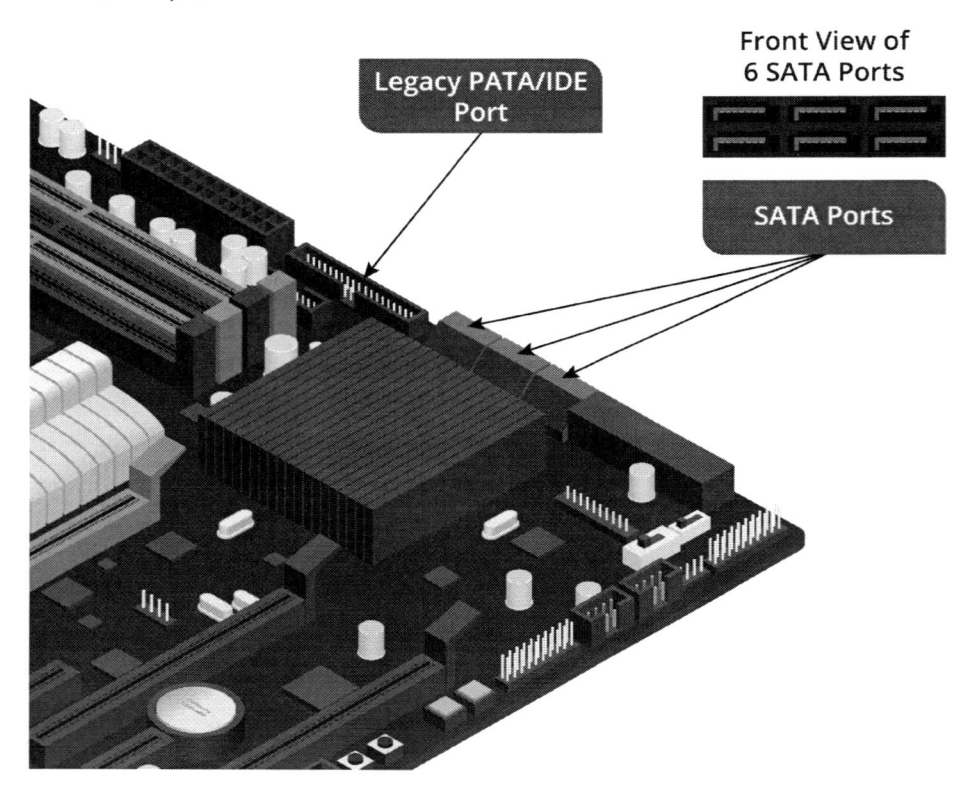

Motherboard SATA and legacy PATA/IDE ports. (Image © 123RF.com.)

More information on SATA standards can be obtained from **www.sata-io.org**.

> **Note:** *While SATA dominates the PC market,* **Serial Attached SCSI (SAS)** *is also very popular in the server market. It supports over 16,000 devices, offers point-to-point links (as opposed to shared bandwidth), has none of the termination issues that complicated legacy SCSI, and supports higher bandwidths (up to 12 Gbps).*

SOLID STATE DRIVES

Flash memory is being incorporated onto a new generation of **Solid State Drives (SSDs)** designed to replicate or supplement the function of the hard drive.

A 2.5" form factor solid state drive with SATA interface. (Image © 123RF.com.)

The advantages of flash memory-based SSDs are:

- The lack of moving parts makes them quieter, more power efficient, and less prone to catastrophic failure or damage due to shock (dropping or moving a device rapidly, for instance).
- Read times are better because seek time and consequently the effect of file fragmentation is eliminated.
- They are less susceptible to data loss in the event of power failure.
- Most drives still feature DRAM-based write cache to improve performance. In the event of a power failure, unwritten cache would be lost. However, the DRAM cache may be backed up by a battery to cover this eventuality.

The main disadvantage is the high cost; a 64 GB SSD costs a bit more than a 2 TB HDD (a 1 TB SSD can cost the same as a top-end server).

SSD INTERFACES AND FORM FACTORS

An SSD might be installed as the computer's only internal drive or as a system drive for use with an additional hard drive. The SSD would normally be used to install the OS and software applications, whereas the HDD would be used for user data files. In this configuration, both drives are available to the user.

An SSD might be installed to a SATA port as with a mechanical HDD. This is any easy way to upgrade the 2.5" drive in a laptop as the device form factor is exactly the same. The main drawback is that the 6 Gbps SATA interface can be a bottleneck to the best performing SSDs. Consequently, modern SSDs often use the PCI Express (PCIe) bus directly. Where SATA uses the **Advanced Host Controller Interface (AHCI)** logical interface to communicate with the bus, PCIe-based SSDs use the **Non-Volatile Memory Host Controller Interface Specification (NVMHCI)** or **NVM Express (NVMe)** for short.

A PCIe-based SSD can either be implemented as a regular PCIe adapter card or Add-in Card (AiC) or it can use the M.2 adapter interface. M.2 can use up to 4 PCIe **lanes**. Note that M.2 adapters are not hot-swappable or hot-pluggable. An M.2 adapter is considerably smaller than a PCIe adapter so the interface is often used on laptops as well as PC motherboards. M.2 supplies power over the bus so there is no need for a separate power cable. M.2 adapters can be different lengths (42 mm, 60 mm, 80 mm, or 110 mm), so you should check that any given adapter will fit on your motherboard. Labels indicate the adapter sizes supported.

> **Note:** Note that M.2 is a physical form factor and so you can obtain M.2 SSDs that use the SATA/AHCI bus. These will not perform as well as NVMe-based M.2 SSDs. On the motherboard, an M.2 socket may be able to support both types of drive or only one; check the documentation. The key position on the connector is different for SATA and NVMe models. Also note that M.2 can be used for wireless adapters too.

> **Note:** SATA 3.2 defines SATA Express (SATAe) as a means of interfacing with a 2-lane PCI Express bus. It uses a different connector, but the port is backwards-compatible with "ordinary" SATA cabling. You might also come across the U.2 (or SFF-8369) interface. U.2 uses the same physical interface as SATA Express and is hot-swappable, but supports up to 4 PCIe lanes, like M.2.

SSD PERFORMANCE FACTORS

SSDs normally outperform HDDs but there are situations where they can perform worse than HDDs; when serving large (GB) files, for example.

When making a detailed comparison between different types of storage technology, you need to compare performance against different types of data transfer. For example, read and write performance are not equivalent. There are also differences between sequential access (reading data from the same "block" as might happen when transferring a large file) and random access (reading data from different locations on the drive or transferring lots of small files for instance). Along with the data throughput and latency/access time, you may need to consider the number of Input/Output Operations per Second (IOPS) that can be achieved by a device for different kinds of data transfer operation.

Flash chips are also susceptible to their own type of degradation over the course of many write operations, so the drive firmware and operating system must use **wear leveling** routines to prevent any single storage location from being overused and optimize the life of the device.

HYBRID DRIVES

Solid state storage may also be incorporated on a **hybrid drive**. In a hybrid drive, the SSD portion functions as a large cache, containing data that is accessed frequently. The magnetic disc is only spun up when non-cached data is accessed. Version 3.2 of the SATA standard defines a set of commands to allow the host computer to specify how the cache should be used (also referred to as **host-hinted mode**). Alternatively, the drive firmware can run self-optimizing routines. The user does not have direct control over files stored on the cache.

DUAL-DRIVE CONFIGURATIONS

Another option is for separate SSD and HDD units to be installed in a dual-drive configuration. In this case, the system chipset and storage drivers, usually based on Intel Smart Response Technology (SRT), make the caching decisions. Again, the user does not have control over the use of the SSD.

> **Note:** SRT can only use caches up to 64 GB (at the time of writing). If the SSD is larger, SRT can reserve part of the drive for caching and the remainder of the capacity is then available to the user and can be manipulated via the OS disk and file management tools.

LEGACY STORAGE TECHNOLOGIES

While SATA is the dominant connection method for most drive types, you may come across systems using much older host bus adapters, such as IDE and SCSI. It is important that you know how to configure these older technologies.

IDE/PATA

The **Parallel Advanced Technology Attachment (PATA)** interface was the principal mass storage interface for desktop PCs for many years. The interface was (and still is) also referred to as IDE (Integrated Drive Electronics) or EIDE (Extended IDE). As the name suggests, an EIDE bus uses parallel data transfers, meaning 16 bits is transferred for each clock tick.

A motherboard supporting PATA may come with one or two host adapters or **channels**, called IDE1 and IDE2 or primary (PRI IDE) and secondary (SEC IDE). A single PATA channel is now more typical if the motherboard also supports SATA. Each PATA channel supports two devices, 0 and 1, though they are usually labeled master and slave.

A PATA drive features a 40-pin port but typically uses 80-wire shielded cables, which are required for UDMA4 or better transfer modes. PATA cable is supposed to be up to 46 cm (18") long. Each PATA cable typically has three connectors, one for the motherboard and one for each device. Most cables are "Cable Select," allowing the master and slave device to be identified by the position of the connector on the cable. Pin 1 on the cable must be oriented with pin 1 on the connector. On the cable, pin 1 is identified with a red stripe. The connectors are also keyed to prevent them from being inserted the wrong way around.

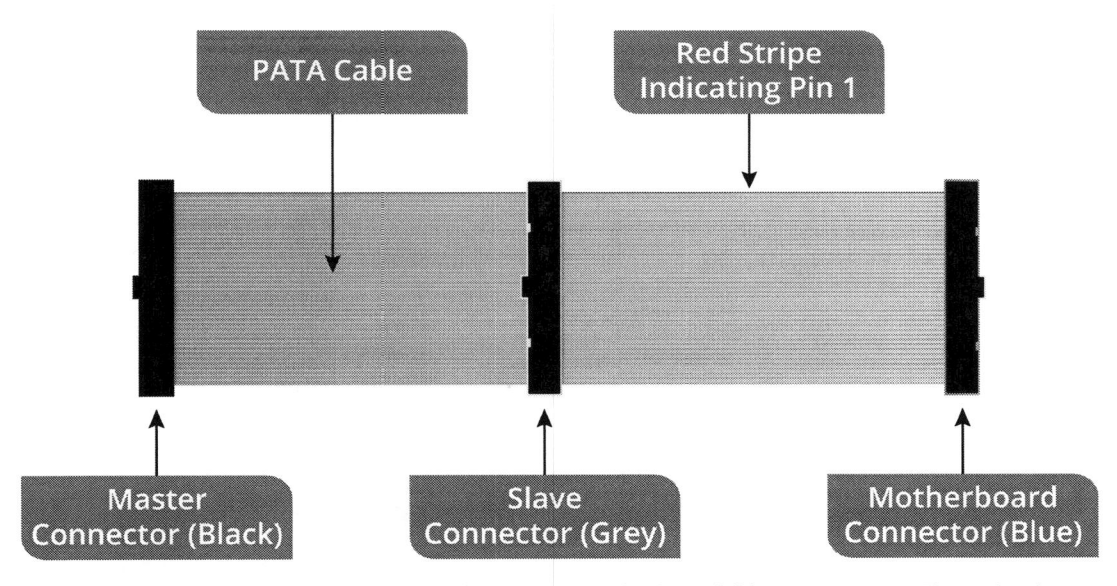

PATA cable with master (black), slave (grey), and motherboard (blue) connectors. The red strip indicates pin 1 on the cable. Note: There is currently a movement to generally rename the "master/slave" terminology to combinations like "parent/child" or "leader/follower." (Image © 123RF.com.)

PATA standards have evolved over the years. This table lists some of the later ATA standards.

Interface Standard	DMA Mode	Max. Transfer Rate (MBps)	Special Features
ATA/ATAPI-4	UDMA 2 (Ultra ATA/33)	33	Ultra DMA, 80-conductor cable, and cyclic redundancy checking
ATA/ATAPI-5	UDMA 4 (Ultra ATA/66)	66	

Interface Standard	DMA Mode	Max. Transfer Rate (MBps)	Special Features
ATA/ATAPI-6	UDMA 5 (Ultra ATA/100)	100	48-bit LBA expansion, and disk noise reduction
ATA/ATAPI-7	UDMA 6 (Ultra ATA/133)	133	Multimedia streaming

Table notes:

- ATAPI stands for ATA Packet Interface and is an extension to ATA to support CD/DVD drives and tape drives.
- DMA (Direct Memory Access) mode refers to the way that data is transferred to and from system memory.
- In the early days of the EIDE interface, BIOS versions severely restricted maximum drive capacity. Driver software in the OS now handles drive addressing. Logical Block Addressing (LBA) is a method of telling the drive how to address a particular place on the disk surface. 48-bit LBA supports drives up to a (theoretical) 144 Petabytes.

SCSI

Small Computer Systems Interface (SCSI) is another parallel bus. One SCSI Host Bus Adapter (HBA) can control multiple devices, attached by internal ribbon cables or external SCSI cables. The SCSI standard also defines a command language that allows the host adapter to identify which devices are connected to the bus and how they are accessed.

SCSI was used to connect peripherals of different types but is now only associated with the connection of storage devices. As with IDE, you will not find SCSI on new systems, but should know how to configure it in case you encounter any legacy systems still depending on it. A SCSI port is denoted by the following symbol: ⟡

The main SCSI standards are described in this table.

Interface Protocol	Standard	Bandwidth (MBps)	Bus Width (bits)	Max. Cable Length (meters)
SCSI-1	SCSI-1	5	8	• SE: 6 • LVD: NA • HVD: 25
Fast SCSI	SCSI-2	10	8	• SE: 3 • LVD: NA • HVD: 25
Fast-Wide SCSI	SCSI-2	20	16	• SE: 3 • LVD: NA • HVD: 25
Ultra SCSI	SCSI-3	20	8	• SE: 1.5 • LVD: NA • HVD: 25
Ultra Wide SCSI	SCSI-3	40	16	• SE: NA • LVD: NA • HVD: 25

Interface Protocol	Standard	Bandwidth (MBps)	Bus Width (bits)	Max. Cable Length (meters)
Ultra2 SCSI	SCSI-3	40	8	• SE: NA • LVD: 12 • HVD: 25
Ultra2 Wide SCSI	SCSI-3	80	16	• SE: NA • LVD: 12 • HVD: 25
Ultra3 SCSI (Ultra160 SCSI)	SCSI-3	160	16	• SE: NA • LVD: 12 • HVD: NA
Ultra 320 SCSI	SCSI-3	320	16	• SE: NA • LVD: 12 • HVD: NA

Given the number of different versions of the standard, SCSI configuration is relatively complex. SCSI devices were typically used on server-class hardware rather than on desktop PCs.

- Host adapter—the SCSI host adapter must be installed and recognized by the system for devices to be detected. A third-party driver might have to be installed for the host adapter to be recognized.
- Bus width—SCSI originally supported 8 devices (the host adapter counts as a device). Wide SCSI supports up to 16 devices.
- Signaling—SCSI specifies three signaling methods. Most buses and devices use Low Voltage Differential (LVD). Single Ended (SE) devices can be added to an LVD bus, but it reduces the performance of the whole bus. H(igh)VD is incompatible with the other two and must not be mixed.
- Termination—a SCSI bus must be terminated at both ends, usually by enabling termination on the first and last devices in the chain. Termination may either be enabled internally on the device by setting a switch or by physically connecting a terminator pack to a device or the host adapter.

  Note: There are passive and active terminators. Passive terminators are generally used with older devices (pre-Ultra SCSI). When installing a terminator pack, the terminator must match the signaling type (SE, LVD, HVD, or SE/LVD). Termination is also made more complex if there is a mix of narrow (8-bit) and wide (16-bit) devices on the bus.

- ID—each SCSI device must be allocated a unique ID, from 0 to 7 (or 15 for wide SCSI). IDs may be allocated automatically or by setting a jumper or click-wheel on the device itself. The order of SCSI ID priorities (from highest to lowest) is 7 through to 0 then 15 through to 8.

  Note: The host adapter is usually set to 7 or 15. A bootable hard disk is usually allocated ID 0.

There were numerous SCSI connectors. Some of the most common were:

- HD68—68-pin connectors used for internal and external ports. 68-pin adapters support Wide SCSI.
- Single Connector Attachment (SCA)—an 80-pin connector that incorporates both a power connector and configuration wires, allowing for hot swappable drives.

GUIDELINES FOR INSTALLING MASS STORAGE DEVICES

*Note: All of the Guidelines for this lesson are available as checklists from the **Checklist** tile on the CHOICE Course screen.*

Consider these guidelines when installing mass storage devices.

INSTALL MASS STORAGE DEVICES

There are several things to consider when you are installing an internal storage device in a computer system. It is not as simple as just plugging the device into the slot inside the case. Make sure you consider each factor before installation:

- **Does the computer have existing internal storage devices?** Do you need to plan for the addition of another controller for an additional device? You might need to purchase an additional SATA controller before you can add another SATA device. In addition, make sure that the computer has an available slot for the controller.
- **Does the device need additional drivers installed?** Make sure that you have the appropriate operating system device drivers to install the new storage device on the computer. If necessary, download the device drivers from the device manufacturer's website.
- **Does the computer have an available power supply cable to supply power to the device?** If not, you can purchase splitters to enable two (or more) devices to be connected to a single power connection, but be aware of power consumption. The number of connectors approximates the available power, so make sure that the storage device will not cause the computer to exceed the capacity of its power supply.
- **Does the computer have an available drive bay for the storage device?** Most hard drives require a 3.5-inch drive bay; most tape drives and optical drives require a 5.25-inch drive bay. If you want to install a hard drive in a 5.25-inch drive bay, you will need drive rails. Make sure you place the storage device where it will get good air flow to avoid overheating the device. Consider the placement of the drives inside the bays with the cable configurations. You may need to adjust the placement of the drives to match the order of cable connectors.
- **Do you have the necessary data cables to connect the storage device to the controller?** You will need a SATA data cable for each hard drive in the PC. Other types of storage devices might require different types of data cables.
- **Does the placement of the device interrupt the air flow of the case?** Make sure there is enough total air flow to handle whatever heat the new storage device will add to the computer.

Note: When adding or removing storage devices (or performing any type of work inside the PC case), make sure that you take a backup of any data stored on local drives.

*Note: To learn more, check the **Video** tile on the CHOICE Course screen for any videos that supplement the content for this lesson.*

Access the Checklist tile on your CHOICE Course screen for reference information and job aids on How to Install and Configure Mass Storage Devices.

Activity 3-3
Discussing Mass Storage Device Installation and Configuration

SCENARIO
Answer these questions to check your understanding of the content presented in this topic.

1. True or false? The read/write heads on an HDD require regular cleaning to obtain optimum performance from the disk.

2. What basic factor might you look at in selecting a high-performance drive?

3. What is a S.M.A.R.T. hard disk?

4. True or false? SATA is an interface for hard drives only.

5. How many storage devices can be attached to a single SATA port?

6. In what two ways could a PC be configured to use an SSD cache?

7. You are upgrading a drive. You have removed the main panel from the PC, disconnected the data and power cables, and removed the screws holding the drive to the cage, but it will not slide out. What is your next step?

Activity 3-4
Installing Storage Devices

BEFORE YOU BEGIN
To complete this activity, you will need the following hardware components for your workbench PC. If you do not have these available, you can remove and reinstall the existing hardware:
- A second hard drive or an optical drive and an empty drive bay.
- An available power connection for the device you are adding to the system.
- Optionally, rails to allow smaller drives to fit into larger drive bays.

You will perform this activity on your WORKBENCH PC.

SCENARIO
In this activity, you will install an additional disk drive into your system. The type of disk you install will depend on the components available, so check with your instructor to see which of the following steps you should complete and for any additional instructions.

---

1. List the type of removable storage devices in your PC and details such as model name or slot types.

Drive Type	Details
_____ Drive	
_____ Drive	
_____ Drive	
_____ Memory Card Reader	
_____ Memory Card Reader	

   > **Note:** You're likely to have an optical drive, one or more memory card readers, and one or more USB drives, as well as possible eSATA ports. Revise the left column as needed to distinctly identify each drive.

2. Add a SATA hard drive and/or optical drive to your system. Depending on the motherboard, you may also need to install a host adapter.
   a) Power off the system, unplug all the peripherals and power cord, and open the computer case.
   b) Examine the motherboard to determine whether there are any SATA ports.
   c) If there are no SATA ports, locate a free adapter slot, and remove the blanking plate. Install the SATA host adapter and screw it down.
   d) Locate an available drive bay, and determine if the bay is the same form factor as the drive. Secure the drive to it, using a caddy and rails if necessary.
   e) Connect the drive to an available SATA port using a SATA cable.

f) Attach a power connector to the drive. You may need to obtain a Molex-SATA power converter from your instructor.
g) Replace the cover on your PC and reboot it.
h) Observe startup messages to check that the drive is detected. If the drive is not detected, check either that the onboard controller is enabled (through system setup) or that the host adapter has been recognized.

3. If you installed a hard disk, complete the following steps to make a partition and format it so that the disk is usable. If you installed a removable storage device, just check that you can read some removable media using it.
   a) Reboot the PC into Windows and log on. Press the **Windows+X** keys and select **Computer Management**. Select the **Disk Management** tool.

   Your new disk should appear as Disk 1.
   b) In the **Initialize Disk** dialog box, select **GPT** and then select **OK**.
   c) Right-click the area of **Unallocated Space** and select **New Simple Volume**.
   d) Select **Next**.
   e) Select **Primary Partition** and select **Next**.
   f) Use the maximum amount of disk space. Select **Next**.
   g) Assign drive letter **H**. Select **Next**.
   h) Select the **NTFS** file system and use the partition label *HOME*. Check the box to perform a **quick format.** Select **Next**, and then select **Finish**.
   i) After the format is complete and the partition is marked healthy, test that it is accessible by copying some files to it from your **C:** drive.
   j) In **Disk Management**, right-click the volume and select **Delete Volume**. Select **Yes** to confirm.

4. Reverse the steps above to uninstall the extra drive(s) plus any adapter cards that you installed and return them to your instructor.

   Note: Your instructor will let you know if you need to perform this step.

Topic C
Install and Configure Removable Storage

EXAM OBJECTIVES COVERED
1001-3.4 Given a scenario, select, install, and configure storage devices.
1001-3.6 Explain the purposes and uses of various peripheral types.

Sometimes, the needs of the user are such that providing additional system memory and mass storage devices is not enough. Consider a situation where raw data is supplied to a user via a DVD, thumb drive, or flash memory card. How will the user get the information off the media and into their PC where they can work with it? In this topic, you will install and configure removable storage.

REMOVABLE STORAGE

Removable storage can refer to either a storage device that can be removed, or storage media that is removable.

Internal hard drives and Solid State Drives provide persistent storage for the computer's OS files, software applications, and user data files. Other types of persistent storage can be used as removable media. A removable disk or drive can be attached to a different computer to move or copy data files. Removable media is also used to make a backup.

OPTICAL MEDIA

Compact discs (CDs) and **digital versatile discs (DVDs)** are mainstream storage formats for consumer multimedia, such as music and video. Both formats have been adapted for data storage with PC systems. The CD/DVD drives used with PCs can also play consumer versions of the discs.

- The data version of the **CD-ROM (CD)** became ubiquitous on PC systems as it has sufficient capacity (700 MB) to deliver most software applications.
- DVD is an improvement on CD technology and delivers substantially more capacity (up to about 17 GB). DVDs are used for software installs and for games and multimedia.

COMPACT DISCS

A CD is a layer of aluminum foil encased in protective plastic, which can also incorporate a label or screen-printed image on the non-playing side. The foil layer contains a series of **pits** and spaces in-between (called **lands**) arranged in a spiral. The changes between pits and lands are used to encode each bit. A standard CD is 120 mm in diameter and 1.2 mm thick. There are also 80 mm discs, which are playable in most CD-ROM drives.

A recordable version of the CD **(CD-R)** was developed in 1999. Rather than a premastered layer of foil with pits and lands, CD-Rs feature a layer of photosensitive dye. A special laser is used to transform the dye, mimicking the pits and lands of a normal CD, in a process called **burning**. Most ordinary CD players and drives can read CD-Rs but they may not play back properly on older equipment. CD-R is a type of Write Once Read Many (WORM) media. Data areas once written cannot be overwritten. If there is space, a new session can be started on the disc. However, this makes the disc unreadable in older CD-ROM drives.

A rewritable (or multisession) disc format (**CD-RW**) has also been developed. This uses a heat sensitive compound whose properties can be changed between crystalline and amorphous by a special laser. There is some concern over the longevity of recordable CD (and DVD) media. Cheaply manufactured discs have shown a tendency to degrade and become unusable (sometimes over the space of just a few years).

> *Note: While the regular capacity of a CD is 700 MB, there are high capacity 800 MB (90 minute) and 860 MB (99 minute) discs that can be used with a CD writer that supports overburning. Note that overburning is more likely to produce disks with data or playback errors.*

DIGITAL VERSATILE DISCS

Compared to CDs, DVDs have higher densities. DVDs are also thinner and can be dual-layer (DVD DL) and/or double-sided (DVD DS). Double-sided discs need to be turned over to play or record to the second side.

DVDs also feature a higher transfer rate, with multiples of 1.32 MBps (equivalent to 9x CD speed). The fastest models feature 24x read and write speeds.

Like CDs, there are recordable and rewritable versions of DVDs, some of which support dual layer recording. There are two slightly different standards for recordable and rewritable DVDs, referred to as DVD-R/DVD-RW versus DVD+R/DVD+RW. Most drives can read all formats but write in either + or - format. Many consumer DVD players can play DVD±R discs. An additional format, Panasonic's DVD-RAM, is not widely supported by computer DVD drives but is optimized for multiple write operations and so well suited to data storage. DVD±R supports dual layer and double-sided media, whereas DVD±RW supports double-sided media only.

BLU-RAY DISCS

Blu-ray Discs (BDs) have emerged as the next generation format for distributing consumer multimedia and can be used to distribute large applications, such as video games. Blu-ray is principally required to cope with the demands of High Definition video recording and playback. HD requires more bandwidth and storage space because it uses a much higher resolution picture (1920x1080 compared to 720x480 [NTSC] or 720x576 [PAL]) and better quality audio (digital surround sound).

A Blu-ray Disc works on fundamentally the same principle as DVD but with a shorter wavelength laser (a 405 nm blue laser compared to DVD's 650 nm red laser). This means discs can be higher density, although the cost of components to make the drives is greater. The base speed for Blu-ray is 4.5 MBps and the maximum theoretical rate is 16x (72 MBps). 2x is the minimum required for movie playback.

A standard BD has a capacity of 25 GB per layer; mini-discs (8 cm) can store 7.8 GB per layer. Dual-layer discs can store up to 50 GB and are readable in ordinary BD drives. Triple-layer 100 GB and quad-layer 128 GB (not currently re-recordable) discs are defined in the BD-XL specification. These require BD-XL compatible drives for writing and reading. There are currently no double-sided formats.

STANDARDS

Standards for the different types of CDs are published by Phillips and Sony as differently colored books.

Standard	CD Type
Red book	Audio CDs (16-bit sampled at 44.1 Hz).

Standard	CD Type
Yellow book	Data CDs with error correction (Mode 1) or without (Mode 2). Mode 2 makes more space available but is only suitable for use with audio and video where small errors can be tolerated.
Orange book	Defines the unused CD-MO and the more popular CD-R and CD-RW.

Standards for DVDs include the following.

Standard	Capacity (GB)	Description
DVD-5	4.7	Single layer, single-sided.
DVD-9	8.5	Dual layer, single-sided.
DVD-10	9.4	Single layer, double-sided.
DVD-18	17.1	Dual layer, double-sided.
DVD-Video	Up to 17.1	Commercially produced DVDs using mpeg encoding and chapters for navigation (can be single or dual layer and single or double-sided).
DVD-Audio	8.5	Format for high quality audio (superior sampling rates and 5.1 surround sound, for instance).

DRM AND REGION CODING

Consumer DVDs feature copy protection mechanisms such as Digital Rights Management (DRM) and region coding. Region coding, if enforced, means that a disc can only be used on a player from the same region.

Here are the DVD region codes in use:
- Region 0: No coding (playback is not restricted).
- Region 1: Canada and the US.
- Region 2: Europe, the Middle East, Japan, South Africa, and Egypt.
- Region 3: SE Asia.
- Region 4: South America, Australia, and New Zealand.
- Region 5: Russia, parts of Africa, and parts of Asia.
- Region 6: China.

Note: The DVD drive region can be set via Device Manager.

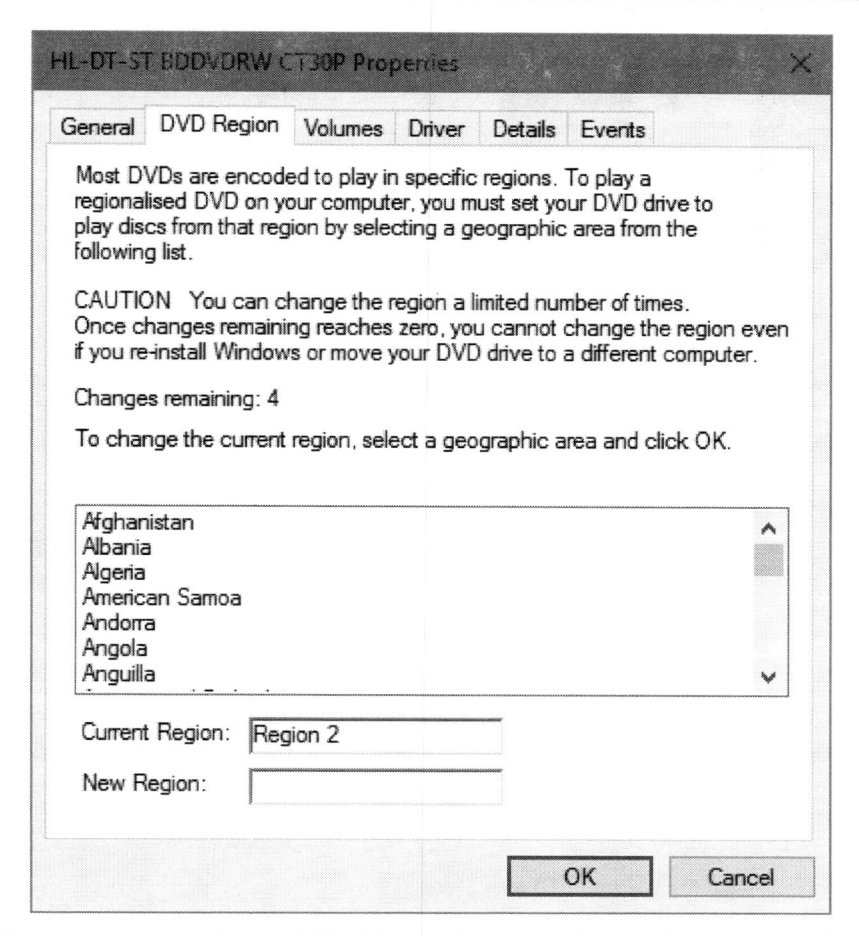

The DVD region supported by a PC DVD drive can be changed via Device Manager—though the firmware only permits a limited number of changes. (Screenshot used with permission from Microsoft.)

Some DVD players are multi-region, but some discs feature protection mechanisms to disable playback in such machines. PC software is not usually region coded, with the exception of some PC game discs.

Like DVDs, consumer Blu-ray Discs (BD-ROMs) are likely to be DRM-protected and may be region coded:

- Region A: America, Japan, and SE Asia.
- Region B: EMEA, Africa, Australia, and New Zealand.
- Region C: Russia and Central Asia (including China).

OPTICAL DRIVES

Optical drives include CD drives, DVD drives, and Blu-ray drives.

Optical drives are considerably larger than hard disks (5.25" form factor). An internal unit would be installed to a 5.25" drive bay and connected to the motherboard via SATA data and power connectors. An external unit would be connected via USB (or possibly eSATA or Thunderbolt). External optical drives typically require their own power supply, provided via a supplied AC adapter. CD drives are rated according to their data transfer speed. The original drives had a data transfer rate of 150 KBps. Subsequently, drives have been available that offer multiples of the original rate; this would be around 52x for new models, offering transfer rates in excess of 7 MBps.

Optical disc drive. (Image © 123RF.com.)

Many optical drives also function as recordable/rewritable CD burners (or writers). Such drives feature three speeds, always expressed as the Record/Rewrite/Read speed (for example, 24x/16x/52x). One feature to look out for on such drives is BURN-proof technology, which prevents discs being ruined by buffer under-run errors (where the software cannot supply the drive the data to write quickly enough).

A **CD drive** consists of a spindle motor (to spin the disc), a laser and lens (to read the disc), and a tracking system to move the laser and lens assembly. The mechanism for inserting a CD is either tray or slot based. Slot-loading mechanisms have rollers that grab the disc. Sometimes, these cannot handle non-standard disc sizes. A drive may feature audio play and volume controls and a headphone jack.

> **Note:** *Drives also feature a small hole that accesses a disc eject mechanism (insert a paper clip to activate the mechanism). This is useful if the standard eject button will not work or if the drive does not have power.*

A **DVD drive** is similar to a CD drive, but with a different encoding method and a shorter wavelength laser. DVD drives also feature a higher transfer rate, with multiples of 1.32 MBps (equivalent to 9x CD speed). The fastest models feature 24x read and write speeds.

> **Note:** *Most DVD drives can read and burn both DVD and CD media. When DVD was first introduced, drives that could burn CDs but only read DVDs were referred to as combo drives.*

Generally speaking, **Blu-ray drives** are also capable of CD and DVD playback and burning. Recordable (BD-R) and re-recordable (BD-RE) drives and discs are also available. BD-R is often available at the same speed as playback while BD-RE is usually half playback speed.

FLASH MEMORY DEVICES

Solid state storage is any type of persistent digital storage technology that does not use mechanical parts. Most solid state devices used with modern PCs are based on **flash memory**. Flash memory is a type of non-volatile Electrically Erasable Programmable Read-Only Memory (EEPROM), also referred to as NAND flash. Flash memory is non-volatile because it does not need a power source to retain information.

Compared to other types of storage, flash memory is very small and light. Mass manufacturing has seen prices fall to affordable levels. Storage capacity ranges from 512 MB to 256 GB. Larger drives than this are available but (at the time of writing) are prohibitively expensive.

As the costs of producing flash memory have fallen, it has become a very popular removable storage technology.

USB thumb drive (left) and SD memory card (right). (Image © 123RF.com.)

There are many ways of packaging flash memory for external storage use. One of the most popular is the USB drive (or thumb or pen drive). This type of drive simply plugs into any spare USB port.

Another popular type of packaging is the **memory card**, used extensively in consumer digital imaging products, such as digital still and video cameras. There are several proprietary types of memory card.

- Secure Digital (SD)—this full-size card comes in three capacity variants. The original SD cards have a 2 GB maximum capacity, whereas SDHC is up to 32 GB and SDXC is up to 2 TB. There are also four speed variants. The original specification is up to 25 MBps, UHS allows up to 108 MBps, UHS-II is rated at up to 156 MBps full duplex or 312 MBps half duplex, while UHS-III specifies two full duplex rates of 312 MBps (FD312) and 624 MBps (FD624).
- Mini-SD—this is a smaller version of the SD card, using the same capacity and speed designations.
- Micro-SD—this is the smallest version of the SD card, using the same capacity and speed designations.
- Compact Flash (CF)—nominally supports 512 GB, though no cards larger than 256 GB were ever made. The speed of CF cards is rated on the same system as CDs, using multiples of 150 KBps. The fastest devices work at up to 1066x read speeds (or 160 MBps).
- xD—this format was used on Olympus cameras but has been discontinued.

> *Note: The speeds quoted are "max burst speed." Sustained read and write speeds will be much lower. Cards also have a speed class rating indicating their minimum write speed capability.*

> *Note: The smaller form factors can be used with regular size readers using a caddy to hold the card.*

MEMORY CARD READERS

Many PCs are fitted with **memory card readers** with slots that will accommodate most of the sticks on the market.

A memory card reader is usually designed to fit in a front-facing 3.5" drive bay, though some can be fitted to a 5.25" bay.

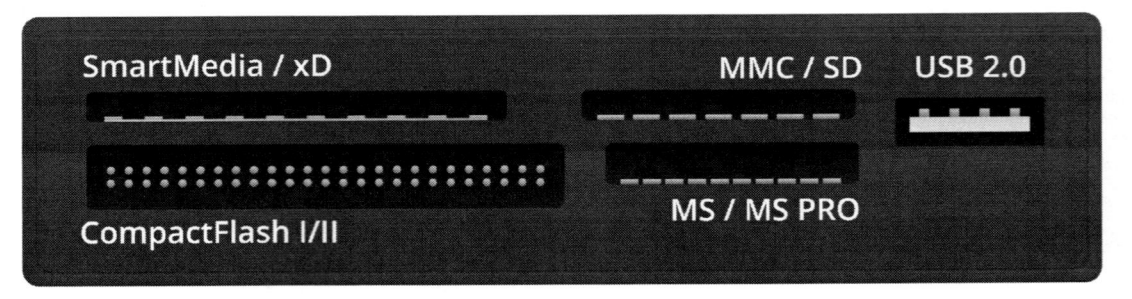

Multi-card reader. (Image © 123RF.com.)

The reader then needs to be connected to a USB hub. Most motherboards have at least one spare 9-pin USB header for making internal connections, or the reader may come with an expansion card (as with the HP model shown below). Alternatively, you may be able to run a USB converter cable from the reader to one of the external USB ports.

> **Note:** *To support the fast speeds of modern card types, the reader must be connected to a USB 3 port.*

Another option is an external USB memory card reader.

EXTERNAL STORAGE DRIVES

External hard disks and portable SSDs have become very popular for backup, additional storage, and as a means of transferring files. External drives are packaged in a **drive enclosure**. The drive enclosure usually provides USB, Thunderbolt, and/or eSATAp ports. The enclosure also provides for an external power supply, if the drive is too large to be powered over USB, and the casing protects the drive from damage.

External storage device. (Image © 123RF.com.)

Some enclosures support Ethernet network connections, referred to as **Network Attached Storage (NAS)**. Advanced enclosures are designed to host multiple disk units, possibly configured in a RAID array to provide better data security.

Activity 3-5
Discussing Removable Storage Device Installation and Configuration

SCENARIO
Answer the following questions to check your understanding of the topic.

1. What is the primary benefit of using removable solid state storage?

2. Which two media types allow you to write to an optical disc only once?
   - ☐ CD-ROM
   - ☐ CD-R
   - ☐ CD+RW
   - ☐ DVD+R
   - ☐ DVD-RW

3. If a CD writer is 12x8x32x, what is the maximum transfer rate when creating a CD-R?

4. True or false? DVD-RW media allows double-layer recording.

5. What is the transfer rate of a 10x DVD drive?

6. What is the capacity of a single Blu-ray dual-layer recordable disc?

7. True or false? A memory card reader is needed to attach a USB flash memory drive to a PC.

8. **Name the two main specifications for currently available memory card formats.**

Topic D
Configure RAID

EXAM OBJECTIVES COVERED
1001-3.4 Given a scenario, select, install and configure storage devices.

Whether it is the system files required to run the OS or data files generated by users, an HDD or SSD stores critical data. If a boot drive fails, the system will crash, and if a data drive fails, users will lose access to files and there may be permanent data loss if those files have not been backed up. To mitigate these risks, the drives that underpin critical systems can be provisioned in a redundant configuration. Redundancy sacrifices some disk capacity but provides fault tolerance for the mission-critical volume. As a PC technician, you will have to configure and support such systems very often, so it is important that you understand the types of redundant drive configurations available.

RAID

With **Redundant Array of Independent Disks (RAID)**, many hard disks can act as backups for each other to increase reliability and fault tolerance, or they can act together as one very large drive.

> **Note:** RAID can also be said to stand for "Redundant Array of Inexpensive Disks" and the "D" can also stand for "devices."

RAID LEVELS

The RAID advisory board defines RAID levels. The most common levels are numbered from 0 to 6, where each level corresponds to a specific type of fault tolerance. Only levels 0, 1, and 5 are of much relevance at the desktop, however.

- **RAID 0 (Striping without Parity). Disk striping** is a technique where data is divided into blocks and spread in a fixed order among all the disks in the array. RAID 0 requires at least two disks. Its principal advantage is to improve performance by spreading disk I/O over multiple drives.

  The logical volume size is the combined total of the smallest capacity physical disk in the array. When building a RAID array, all the disks should normally be identical in terms of capacity and ideally in terms of type and performance, though this is not mandatory. If disks are different sizes, the size of the smallest disk in the array determines the maximum amount of space that can be used on the larger drives. RAID 0 adds no storage overhead and is a means of obtaining a large logical volume from multiple, low capacity disks.

  However, because it provides no redundancy, this method cannot be said to be a true RAID implementation. If any physical disk in the array fails, the whole logical volume will fail, causing the computer to crash and requiring data to be recovered from backup. Consequently, RAID 0 would never be used for live data storage.

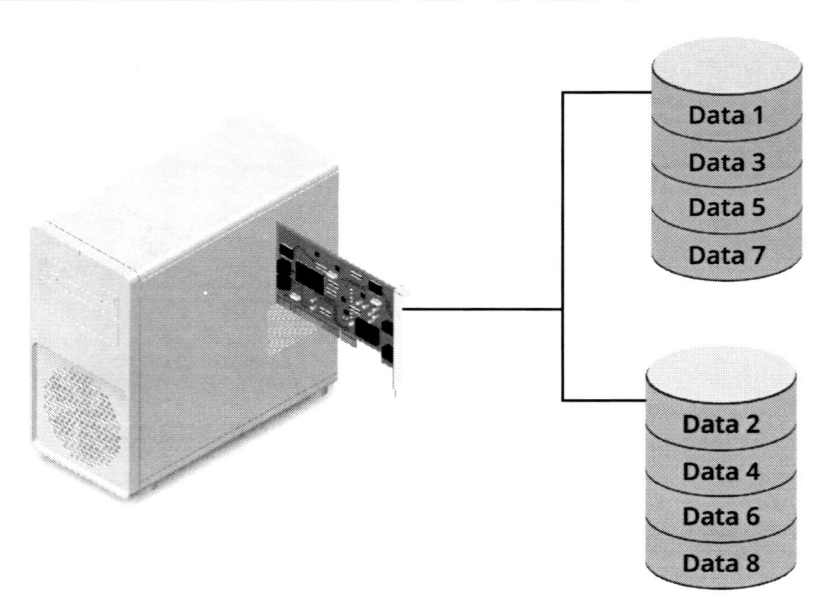

RAID 0 (striping) - data is spread across the array. (Image © 123RF.com.)

- **RAID 1 (Mirroring). Mirroring** requires two hard disks. The mirror disk is a duplicate of the data disk. Each write operation is duplicated on the second disk in the set, introducing a small performance overhead. A read operation can use either disk, boosting performance somewhat.

    This strategy is the simplest way of protecting a single disk against failure. If one disk fails (degrading the array), the other takes over. There is little impact on performance during this time (obviously the boost of having two drives available for read operations is lost), so availability remains good, but the failed disk should be replaced as quickly as possible as there is no longer any redundancy. When the disk is replaced, it must be populated with data from the other disk (resynching). Performance while rebuilding is reduced, though RAID 1 is better than other levels in that respect and the rebuilding process is generally shorter than parity-based RAID.

    In terms of cost per gigabyte, disk mirroring is more expensive than other forms of fault tolerance because disk space utilization is only 50 percent. Also the total volume size cannot exceed the available capacity of the physical disks. However, disk mirroring usually has a lower entry cost because it requires only two disks and a relatively cheap RAID controller (or software RAID). The availability of cheap, large HDDs makes the 50% overhead less of a drawback.

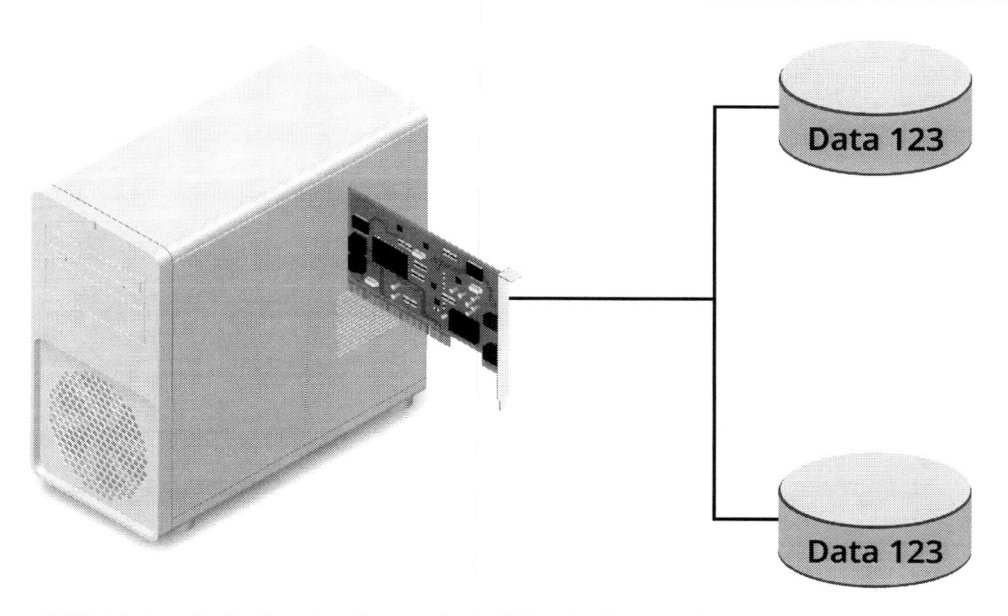

RAID 1 (mirroring) - data is written to both disks simultaneously. (Image © 123RF.com.)

- **RAID 5 (Striping with Distributed Parity)** Striping with distributed parity (RAID 5) writes error checking information across all the disks in the array. The data and parity information is managed so that the two are always on different disks. If a single disk fails, enough information is spread across the remaining disks to allow the data to be completely reconstructed. Stripe sets with parity offer the best performance for read operations. However, when a disk has failed, the read performance is degraded by the need to recover the data using the parity information. Also, all normal write operations suffer reduced performance due to the parity calculation.

  RAID 5 requires a minimum of three drives but can be configured with more. This allows more flexibility in determining the overall capacity of the array than is possible with RAID 1. A "hard" maximum number of devices is set by the controller or OS support, but the number of drives used is more likely to be determined by practicalities such as cost and risk. Remember that adding more disks increases the chance of failure.

  The level of fault tolerance and available disk space is inverse. As you add disks to the set, fault tolerance decreases but usable disk space increases. If you configure a RAID 5 set using 3 disks, a third of each disk is set aside for parity. If four are used, one quarter is reserved on each disk. Using a three 80 GB disk configuration, you would have a 160 GB usable volume.

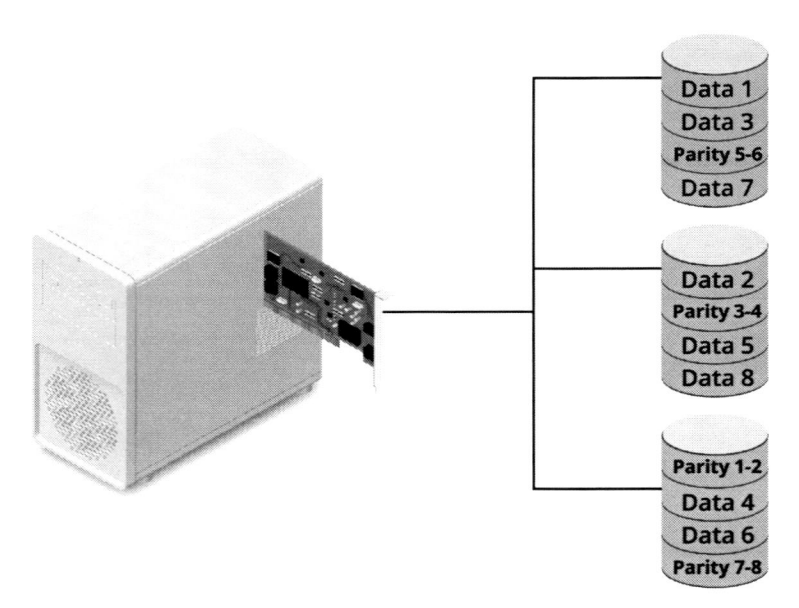

RAID 5 (striping with parity). (Image © 123RF.com.)

> **Note:** If the disks are different sizes, the size used is that of the smallest disk. Extra disk space on larger drives is wasted.

- **RAID 1+0 (RAID 10).** As described previously, RAID 0 is striping with no parity (that is, no fault tolerance is provided). This provides high throughput, but leaves the volume at risk. RAID 1 provides mirroring; the highest achievable disk fault tolerance. RAID 1+0 (also called RAID 10) is a combination of both these configurations (nested RAID). A logical striped volume is configured with two mirrored arrays. This configuration offers excellent fault tolerance as one disk in each mirror can fail and the array will still function.

  You will need at least four disks to create this configuration and there must be an even number of disks. Note that it carries the same 50% disk overhead that mirroring does.

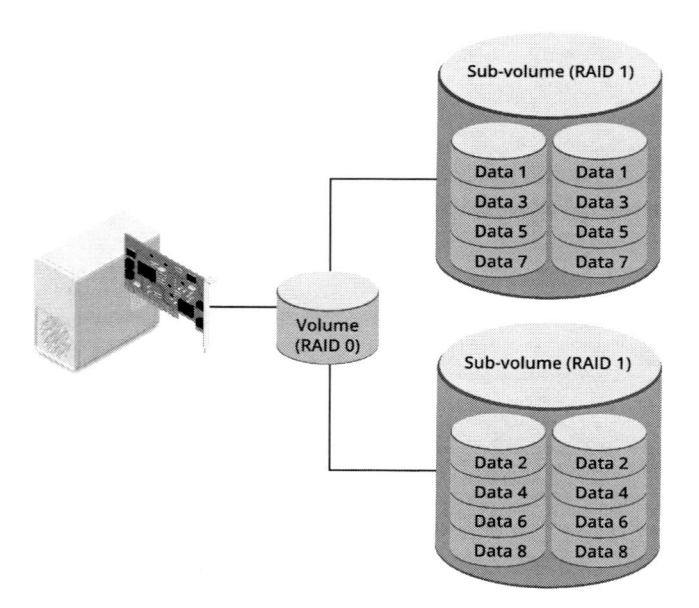

RAID 10 - either disk in each of the sub-volumes can fail without bringing down the mail volume. (Image © 123RF.com.)

RAID CONFIGURATION OPTIONS

It is possible to implement RAID using either hardware or software.

HARDWARE RAID

A **hardware RAID solution** means that creating volumes from an array of physical disks is an operation supported by a plug-in controller card or by the motherboard, independently of the installed operating system. Hardware solutions are principally differentiated by their support for RAID levels. Entry-level controllers might support only RAID 0 or RAID 1, whereas mid-level controllers might add support for RAID 5 and RAID 10.

In addition, hardware RAID is often able to hot swap a damaged disk (replace the failed unit without shutting down Windows), thereby keeping the system operational all the time. Hot swapping is a feature of high-end hardware RAID solutions and requires a compatible controller and disk units. When the new disk is installed, the RAID controller transparently synchronizes it with the remaining disks in the set.

On the downside, hardware RAID is more expensive than a software solution and may lock you into a single vendor solution.

Modern low cost RAID solutions may use the SATA interface whereas Serial Attached SCSI (SAS) is a popular technology for server-class machines.

The array is normally configured by launching the firmware configuration utility by pressing the appropriate key combination during startup. Sometimes a RAID controller configuration tool is available from within the OS, too.

Configuring a volume using RAID controller firmware.

SOFTWARE RAID

Windows provides the option to set up software-based RAID using standard disks and controllers. Windows Server and Windows client Professional/Enterprise editions support fault tolerant mirroring (RAID 1) and striping with parity (RAID 5) arrays. In a software solution, internal disks using different types of interface can be combined in an array but USB- or Thunderbolt-connected external drives are usually not supported. All editions of Windows 10, however, come with the Storage Spaces feature, which provides mirroring and parity-based RAID-like functionality with USB-connected and other external drive types. Linux® can use the Logical Volume Manager (LVM) to implement most RAID levels.

HOT SWAP

A system configured for RAID might support **hot swappable** drives. While this is usually a server-level feature, it might be implemented on high-end workstations. Rather than using cabled connectors, hot swappable drives plug (or "mate") into a combined data and power port on the enclosure. This means that drives can be easily added and removed from the front of the case without having to open the chassis. The drives are secured and released from the enclosure using a latch.

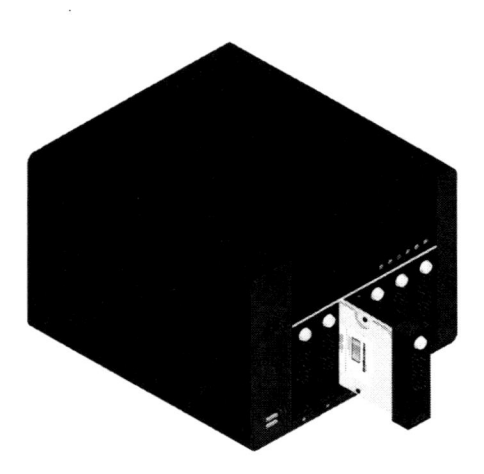

Media server with hot swappable hard drives. (Image © 123RF.com.)

Activity 3-6
Discussing RAID Configuration

SCENARIO
Answer the following questions to check your understanding of the topic.

1. **If you have a computer with three hard disks, what type of RAID fault-tolerant configuration will make best use of them?**

2. You are configuring four 120 GB drives in a RAID 5 array.

    How much space will be available?

3. **What is the minimum number of disks required to implement RAID 10 and how much of the disks' total capacity will be available for the volume?**

Topic E
Troubleshoot Storage Devices

EXAM OBJECTIVES COVERED
1001-5.3 Given a scenario, troubleshoot hard drives and RAID arrays.

End users rely on the hard drives in their PCs to store important system information and personal or professional data and files. Without a hard drive that works properly, the computer system is essentially worthless. As a CompTIA A+ technician, you will likely be called upon to fix or troubleshoot common problems with hard drives and other storage devices.

DISK FAILURES

Hard disk drives are most likely to fail due to mechanical problems either in the first few months of operation or after a few years, when they begin to reach the end of their useful life. Sudden loss of power can also damage a disk, especially if it is in the middle of a read/write operation.

A hard drive that is failing might display the following symptoms:

- **Read/write failure**. When you are trying to open or save a file, an error message such as "Cannot read from the source disk" is displayed.
- **Blue Screen of Death (BSoD)**. A failing hard disk and file corruption may cause a particularly severe read/write failure, resulting in system STOP errors (a crash screen).
- **Bad sectors**. When you run the `chkdsk /r` program it can test the surface of the hard disk. If more bad sectors are located each time the test is run, it is a sure sign that the disk is about to fail.

    Note: Use the Check Disk utility regularly to check that the drive is in good condition. `chkdsk /f` will fix file system errors but will not identify bad sectors.

- **Constant LED activity**. **Disk thrashing** can be a sign that there is not enough system RAM as data is continually moved between RAM and the pagefile.
- **Noise**. A healthy hard disk makes a certain low-level noise when accessing the platters. A loud or grinding noise or any sort of clicking is a sign of a problem.

When experiencing any of these symptoms, replace the disk as soon as possible to minimize the risk of data loss.

DISK INTEGRITY TESTING

You can use the Windows `chkdsk` utility to verify the integrity of a formatted disk. Most hard drives run a self-diagnostic program called **S.M.A.R.T (Self-Monitoring, Analysis, and Reporting Technology)** that can alert the operating system if reliability is compromised. In Windows, you can run the following command to perform a S.M.A.R.T check:

```
wmic /node:localhost diskdrive get status
```

If you suspect that a drive is failing, you should try to run more advanced diagnostic tests on the drive. Most hard drive vendors supply utilities for testing drives or there may be a system diagnostics program supplied with the computer system.

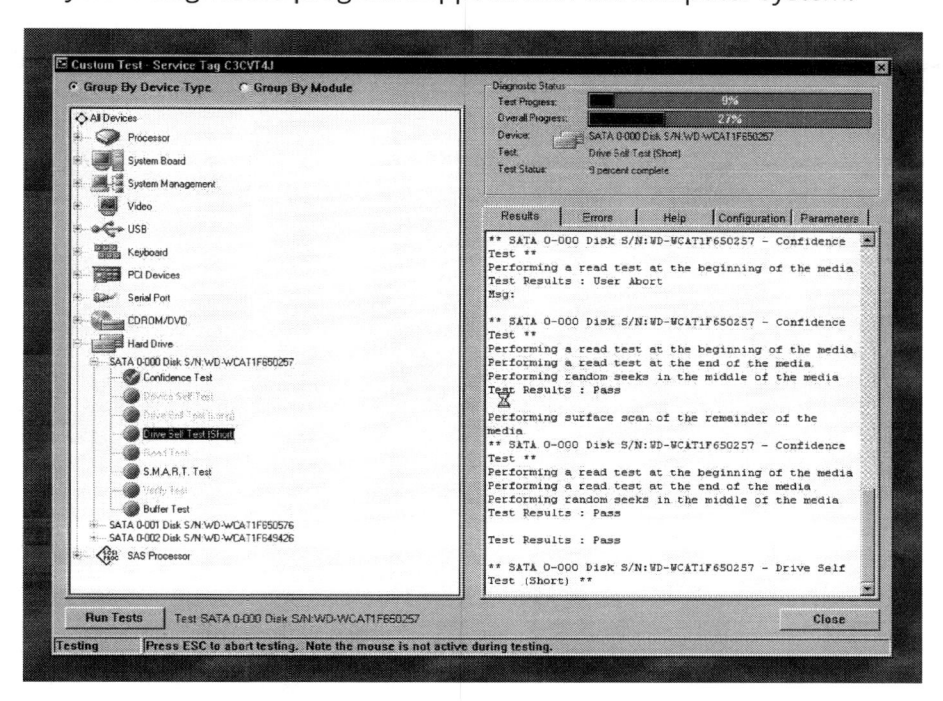

Using system diagnostics software to test a hard drive.

You can also use Windows utilities to query S.M.A.R.T. and run manual tests.

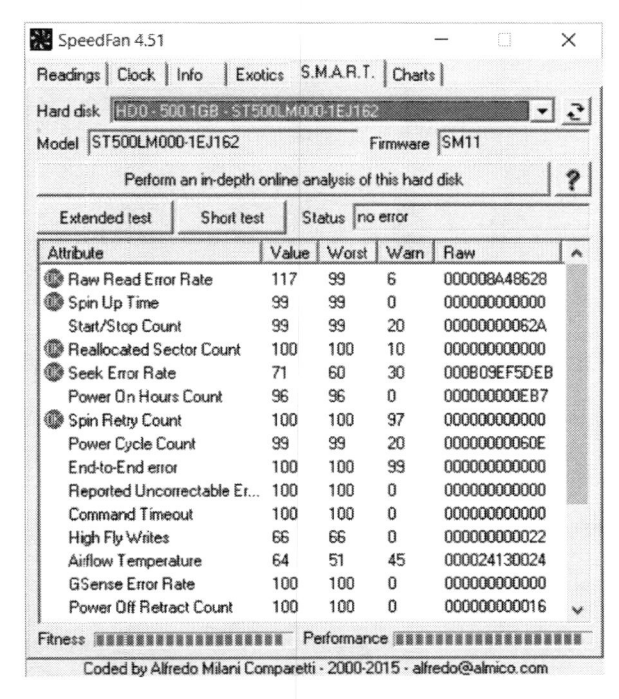

Viewing S.M.A.R.T. information via the SpeedFan utility.

BOOT FAILURES

If the hard drive is not detected at boot (or if a second hard drive is not shown under Windows), first check that it is powering up. Drive activity is usually indicated by an LED on the front panel of the system unit case. If this is inactive, check that the drive has a power connector attached. If the PC has no LEDs, or you suspect that they may be faulty, it is usually possible to hear the hard drive spinning up. Once you have determined that the drive is powering up, try the following:

- If the system is not booting correctly from the hard drive, check that the boot sequence is set correctly in the PC firmware system setup program and that there are no removable disks in floppy or optical drives.
- Check that data cables are not damaged and that they are correctly connected to the drive.
- If the drives are connected to a motherboard port, check that it has not been disabled by a jumper or via system setup.

Once you have determined that the drive configuration is correct, try the following. If a boot hard drive is detected by the firmware hardware check (**Power On Self-Test [POST]**) but not by Windows (for example, if you get an error such as "OS not found"), there is probably a problem with the file system. Boot into the recovery environment using the Windows setup disc and enter C: at the command prompt. If this produces the error message **Invalid media type**, the disk has no valid file system structure on it. This may be caused by surface errors or by a virus. You may be able to recover from this by running the `bootrec` tool at a boot command prompt or by reformatting the disk (at the expense of any data, of course).

If you enter C: at the command prompt and you see the error message **Invalid drive specification**, the drive may have an invalid partition structure. You can check the drive's partition structure with `diskpart`.

BOOT BLOCK REPAIR

One of the unwelcome actions that malware can perform is to damage the boot information on the hard drive. There are two ways of formatting the boot information: **MBR** and **GPT**.

- In the Master Boot Record (MBR) scheme, the MBR is located in the first sector of the first partition. It contains information about the partitions on the disk plus some code that points to the location of the active boot sector. The Boot Sector is located either on the sector after the MBR or the first sector of each other partition. It describes the partition file system and contains the code that points to the method of booting the OS (the Boot Configuration Data store for a Windows system, or GRUB or LILO Linux boot managers). Each primary partition can contain a boot sector, but only one of them can be marked active.
- With the Globally Unique ID (GUID) Partition Table (GPT) boot scheme, the boot information is not restricted to a single sector, but still serves the same basic purpose of identifying partitions and boot loaders. GPT is associated with UEFI firmware, but can also be used by most legacy BIOS firmware if supported by the OS (32-bit Windows has problems booting from a combination of GPT and BIOS). GPT is not subject to the restrictions on number and size of partitions that limit MBR; there are still limits, but not ones that are likely to be reached in practice.

Note: GPT often uses a "protective" MBR to prevent disk tools from overwriting the GPT.

Whether the disk is using an MBR or GPT partitioning scheme, damage to these records results in boot errors such as "OS not found" or "Invalid drive specification." If this problem has been caused by a virus (it can also occur due to disk corruption or installing operating systems with conflicting boot loaders in multiboot configurations), the best way to resolve it is to use the boot disk option in your antivirus software. This will include a basic antivirus scanner that may detect the virus that caused the problem in the first place.

If you don't have the option of using a recovery disk created by the antivirus software, you can try to use the repair options that come with the Windows product disk. Be aware that these may not work completely reliably if the system is still infected with a virus.

1. Boot from the product disk and select the **Repair** option.
2. First, try to use the **Startup Repair** option. If this does not work, select the **Command Prompt** option.
   - Enter `bootrec /fixmbr` to attempt repair of the MBR.
   - Enter `bootrec /fixboot` to attempt repair of the boot sector.
   - Enter `bootrec /rebuildbcd` to add missing Windows installations to the Boot Configuration Database (BCD).
3. Restart the PC.

Note: These tools may not be suitable for use with multiboot configurations if one of the other OSes has created a non-standard partition table.

FILE RECOVERY OPTIONS

If the computer will not boot from a hard disk, you may want to try to recover data from it. To do this, you will usually need to remove the drive from its internal enclosure and connect it to another PC. Use a driver that matches the type (flat, crosshead/crosspoint/Phillips, or star/Torx) and size of screw to avoid damaging the screw heads or threads.

External enclosure kits are available to provide the data and power connectors required. The enclosure will then generally be interfaced to the PC via a USB port and the disk can be mounted using **Disk Management** (if it is in a state to be recognized by Windows) or analyzed using file recovery software.

If a file is corrupted, it may be possible to use software to rebuild it (or at least, to recover some data from it). `chkdsk` restores file fragments from bad sectors to the root of the volume (as filennnn.chk files), but these are rarely directly usable. Third-party file recovery software is available and can be more successful.

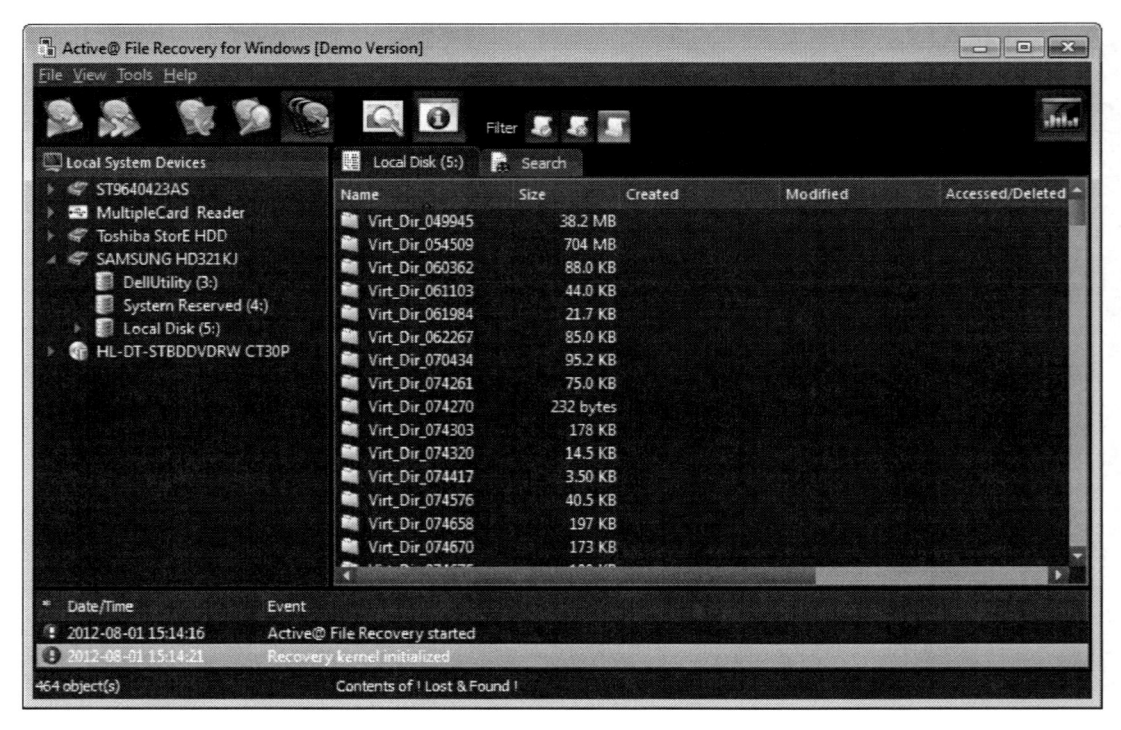

Using file recovery software to scan a disk.

DISK PERFORMANCE ISSUES

Slow disk performance is often a bottleneck for modern computer systems. In this case, the best solution may be to add more RAM rather than replace the disk or to upgrade the disk to an SSD or hybrid drive.

Disk performance can be improved by ensuring that file fragmentation is minimized. **Disk defragmentation** is a process whereby the contents of a disk are moved around to optimize disk access times. The components of a file (known as clusters) are placed adjacent on the disk surface (they are said to be contiguous). Windows normally tries to run the defragmenter periodically as a scheduled task, but this process can be interrupted by user file access requests. It may be necessary to run the tool manually during a "downtime" period.

Low disk capacity can also be a cause of slow performance. When a disk is 90% full, its capacity meter is shown in red in Explorer. Windows warns the user via the notification area when disk space is critically low (below 200 MB). If the disk continues to be filled up, system performance will be very severely impacted. You can use the Disk Cleanup program to free up space, but the user may have to take manual steps, such as moving or deleting files, uninstalling unnecessary applications, and so on.

GUIDELINES FOR TROUBLESHOOTING OPTICAL DRIVES

Consider these guidelines when troubleshooting optical drives.

GENERAL TROUBLESHOOTING TIPS FOR OPTICAL DRIVES

Here are some general guidelines for troubleshooting optical drives:

- Optical drives such as CD, DVD, and Blu-ray drives can generally go for a very long time between failures. This is because the part of the drive that reads the disc does not actually touch the disc. All reading (and writing with recordable and re-writable media) is done using lasers. This means that the read/write "heads" are not as likely to get dirty as with magnetic media drives such as floppy drives, where the read/

write heads commonly touch the disc. However, discs do get dirty and carry that dirt inside the optical drive. Special cleaning kits are available for cleaning optical drives if read/write problems are experienced. Most problems related to dirt, though, are caused by dirt on the disc itself.
- Support for CD drives is built into Windows. If your CD drive is not able to read CDs at all, it is likely to be a hardware problem.
- DVD-Video requires MPEG decoding hardware or software (codecs) to be installed for playback. This is supplied with Vista Home Premium and Ultimate editions and in each edition of Windows 7 except Starter and Home Basic. Windows 8 requires third-party software to be installed. Remember also that a DVD-ROM cannot be read from a CD-ROM drive.
- There is currently no native support for Blu-ray in any version of Windows, but the drive should be bundled with the appropriate codecs and software.

TROUBLESHOOTING CD/DVD/BD WRITING

Here are some guidelines for troubleshooting write errors on optical discs:
- Where Windows does not support a particular recordable or rewritable format directly, third-party software is required.
- Some writable media are not manufactured to the highest possible standards, so errors during CD or DVD write operations can be quite common. Check that you are using the write speed recommended for the brand of discs you have purchased. If the error is persistent, however, it is not due to the media.
- Most problems are connected to buffer underruns. On older devices, once the writing process starts, it cannot be paused. Therefore, if the OS does not supply data to the burner's buffer quickly enough, errors will be introduced into the disc's layout. The following solutions can usually be applied:
    - Try burning discs at a lower write speed.
    - Copy source files to the local hard disk (rather than removable or network drives).
    - Do not use other applications when burning a disc.
- The latest CD and DVD writers usually ship with buffer underrun protection.

COMMON RAID CONFIGURATION ISSUES

RAID is usually a means of protecting data against the risk of a hard disk drive failing. The data is either copied to a second drive (mirroring) or additional information is recorded on multiple drives to enable them to recover from a device failure (parity). RAID can be implemented using hardware controllers or features of the operating system. However, you might encounter the following issues with RAID systems:
- RAID not found.
- RAID stops working.

*Note: To learn more, check the **Video** tile on the CHOICE Course screen for any videos that supplement the content for this lesson.*

GUIDELINES FOR TROUBLESHOOTING RAID ISSUES

Here are some guidelines to consider when you are troubleshooting RAID issues.

TROUBLESHOOT RAID ISSUES

Consider these guidelines as you troubleshoot RAID issues:
- If Windows does not detect a RAID array during setup or at boot time:

- Check that the drivers for the RAID controller are installed and use the RAID configuration utility to verify its status.

```
                                                    F10 = System Services
                                                    F11 = BIOS Boot Manager
                                                    F12 = PXE Boot
One 2.40 GHz Quad-core Processor, Bus Speed:4.80 GT/s, L2/L3 Cache:1 MB/8 MB

System Memory Size: 4.0 GB, System Memory Speed: 1067 MHz


Broadcom NetXtreme II Ethernet Boot Agent v5.0.5
Copyright (C) 2000-2009 Broadcom Corporation
All rights reserved.
Press Ctrl-S to Configure Device (MAC Address - 842B2B19E291)


Dell PERC H200/6Gbps SAS HBA BIOS
MPTZBIOS-7.01.09.00 (2010.03.22)
Copyright 2000-2009 LSI Corporation.

Integrated RAID exception detected:
   Volume (Hd1:079) is currently in state INACTIVE/OPTIMAL
Enter the Dell PERC H200/HBA Configuration Utility to investigate!

Press Ctrl-C to start Dell PERC H200/HBA Configuration Utility..
```

Boot message indicating a problem with the RAID volume—press Ctrl+C to start the utility and troubleshoot.

- If you cannot access the configuration utility, then the controller itself could have failed.
- If RAID stops working:
  - One of the purposes of using RAID (or at least RAID 1/5/10) is that it is much less likely than a simple disk system to just "stop working." If one of the underlying disks fails, the volume will be listed as "degraded," but the data on the volume will still be accessible.

    Note: *RAID 0 has no redundancy, so if one of the disks fails, it will stop working. In this scenario, you had better hope that you have a recent data backup.*

  - The precise process for managing a disk failure with an array will be dependent on the vendor that supplied the array and the configuration being supported. All array controllers will be capable of generating an event to the OS system log and perhaps of generating an alert message for the administrator.

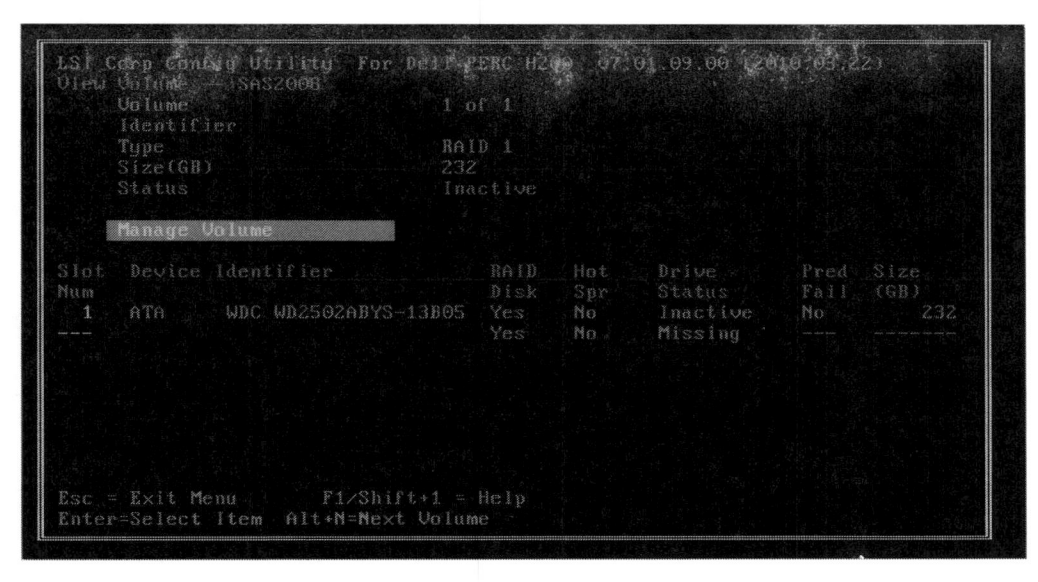

RAID errors using the configuration utility - this volume is missing one of its disks.

- Most desktop-level RAID solutions can tolerate the loss of only one disk, so it should be replaced as soon as possible. If the array supports hot swapping, then the new disk can simply be inserted into the chassis of the computer or disk chassis. Once this is done, the array can be rebuilt using the RAID configuration utility (if a hardware RAID controller is used) or Disk Management (if you are using dynamic disks to implement "software" RAID). Note that the rebuilding process is likely to severely affect performance as the controller is likely to be writing multiple gigabytes of data to the new disk.

    Note: *When hot swapping a faulty disk out, take extreme caution not to remove a healthy disk from the array as making a mistake could cause the array to fail, depending on the configuration. Disk failure is normally indicated by a red LED. Always make a backup beforehand.*

- If a volume is not available, either more than the tolerated number of disks has failed or the controller has failed. If the boot volume is affected, then the operating system will not start. If too many disks have failed, you will have to turn to the latest backup or try to use file recovery solutions. If the issue is controller failure, then data on the volume should be recoverable, though there may be file corruption if a write operation was interrupted by the failure. Either install a new controller or import the disks into another system.

    Note: *To learn more, check the **Video** tile on the CHOICE Course screen for any videos that supplement the content for this lesson.*

Activity 3-7
Discussing Storage Device Troubleshooting

SCENARIO
Answer the following questions to check your understanding of the topic.

1. A user complains that a "Buffer underrun" error keeps occurring when they try to write to recordable DVDs.

   What would you suggest?

2. You are trying to install Windows from the setup disc, but the computer will not boot from the CD.

   What should you do?

3. **If you experience an error such as "BCD missing" when booting the computer, what action could you take?**

4. **A user reports hearing noises from the hard disk—does this indicate it is failing and should be replaced?**

5. A PC displays the message "Invalid media type" when you try to access it from a command prompt.

   What is the likely cause and how might you attempt to fix it?

6. A user reports that there is a loud clicking noise when she tries to save a file.

   What should be your first troubleshooting step?

7. You are investigating a disk problem. The system can no longer access the C: drive.

   What command could you use to try to repair the error?

8. A RAID utility reports that the volume is degraded.

   What should you do?

Activity 3-8
Troubleshooting Storage Devices

BEFORE YOU BEGIN

To simulate the first issue, your instructor will introduce a drive problem on your system.

SCENARIO

In this activity, you will troubleshoot different issues relating to hard drives.

---

1. A user has reported that her computer cannot boot and is getting an error message at POST. Diagnose and correct the issue.
   a) Reproduce the problem by booting the computer and observing the error. Listen to determine if the drive is spinning up during POST.
   b) Access the firmware setup program to check that the drive port is enabled.
   c) Power off the computer, disconnect any cabling, and then open the case. Verify that the drive data cable and power cable are properly connected.
   d) If nothing else corrects the problem, replace the drive.

2. Another user has reported that there are grinding noises coming from her computer case. Once you take a closer look, you suspect that it is the hard drive.

   What is the possible cause and solution to this type of issue?

   ○ The hard drive is physically damaged, so the drive must be replaced.

   ○ A virus has attacked the hard drive, so you can use antivirus software to mitigate the issues.

   ○ Data is corrupt on the drive, and the PC has not been shut down correctly.

3. When a user tries to access the hard drive containing his data, the system locks up and makes a clicking sound. From the command prompt, he can change to drive D, but when he tries to access a file or list the files on the drive, it locks up and begins clicking again.

   What is the most likely cause of the problem?

4. **What steps might you take to attempt to resolve this problem?**

5. A user reports that some of his folders have begun disappearing and some folder and file names are scrambled with strange characters in their names.

   What is the most likely cause of the problem?

6. **What steps might you take to attempt to resolve this problem?**

Summary

In this lesson, you installed, configured, and performed troubleshooting on various types of storage devices. The ability to support users in their need to store and retrieve essential data is an integral part of an A+ technician's job duties.

Which types of storage devices have you worked with? Have you installed additional hard drives or replaced hard drives?

What sorts of issues have you experienced with storage devices? How will the troubleshooting tools and guidelines presented in this lesson help with future issues?

Practice Question: Additional practice questions are available on the CompTIA CHOICE platform within the **Assessments** tile.

Lesson 4

Installing, Configuring, and Troubleshooting Internal System Components

LESSON INTRODUCTION

As a CompTIA® A+® technician, you are not only responsible for the components outside the system unit, but all the internal components as well. On the job, you may be asked to connect peripheral components for a user, or you may be asked to swap out a motherboard.

Having the knowledge and skills to properly install and configure the internal system components is crucial because, in most cases, users will not have the knowledge or the experience to install the components themselves. It will be your professional responsibility to know the technical specifications for these components and how to manage them appropriately.

LESSON OBJECTIVES

In this lesson, you will:

- Select and install a CPU to upgrade or repair a computer system.
- Configure and update BIOS and UEFI.
- Install power supplies.
- Troubleshoot internal system components.
- Configure a custom PC.

Topic A
Install and Upgrade CPUs

EXAM OBJECTIVES COVERED
1001-3.5 Given a scenario, install and configure motherboards, CPUs, and add-on cards.

In this topic, you will examine the types and features of CPUs and cooling systems. Much like the motherboard, the CPU is another important component of the computer system that actually carries out all the tasks requested by the applications installed in the computer. The CPU is a heat generator, so part of understanding the CPU includes understanding how to manage heat inside the computer case by managing the airflow and temperature. Keeping the system cool is an easy but important way to maintain or even increase its productivity. A computer that runs too hot risks damaging its own components. As an A+ technician, you need to be familiar with these essential components of the computer system.

CPU

The **Central Processing Unit (CPU)**, or simply the **processor**, executes program instruction code, performs mathematical and logical calculations, and controls Input/Output (I/O) functions. The CPU is commonly described as the "brains" of a computer; in fact, it is better thought of as a very efficient sorting office. The CPU cannot think, but it can process simple instructions very, very quickly and efficiently. A computer is only as "clever" as its software.

PC processors are produced by Intel® or other manufacturers who use the Intel instruction set and whose processors are, therefore, IBM® PC (or x86) compatible. Currently, only AMD (Advanced Micro Devices) falls into this category.

CPU MANUFACTURING PROCESS

Note: This information is provided for reference; it is not part of the exam objectives.

A **microprocessor** is a programmable **integrated circuit (IC)**. An IC is a silicon chip embedded on a ceramic plate. A **silicon chip** is a wafer of purified silicon doped with a metal oxide (typically copper or aluminum). This doping process creates millions of transistors and signal pathways within an area called the **die**. These transistors provide the electrical on/off states that are the basis of binary computer systems.

The process used to create the transistors is referred to as an n-micron or n-nanometer (nm) process, reflecting the size of the features (a transistor for instance) that can be created. A micron is a millionth of a meter; a nanometer is a billionth of a meter. This process has developed from 1 micron (80486) to 0.014 micron (or 14 nm).

Scaling down the process allows reduced voltages and therefore more speed with less heat. It also allows more components to be added to the same package, which has enabled innovations such as on-die cache, multicore CPUs, and on-die graphics processors.

CPU ARCHITECTURES

The CPU is designed to run software programs. When a software program runs (whether it be an operating system, BIOS firmware, antivirus utility, or word processing application), it is assembled into instructions utilizing the fundamental **instruction set** of the CPU and loaded into system memory. The CPU then performs the following operations on these instructions:

1. The control unit fetches the next instruction in sequence from system memory to the pipeline.
2. The control unit decodes each instruction in turn and either executes it itself or passes it to the **Arithmetic Logic Unit (ALU)** or **Floating Point Unit (FPU)** for execution.
3. The result of the executed instruction is written back to a register or to system memory. A **register** is a temporary storage area available to the different units within the CPU.

This overview is grossly simplified, of course. Over the years, many different internal architectures have been developed to optimize the process of fetch, decode, execute, and writeback, while retaining compatibility with the basic x86 instruction set, which defines a CPU as IBM PC compatible.

INSTRUCTION SETS

The instruction set used by IBM PC compatible CPUs is called **x86-32** or **IA-32** (Intel Architecture). The way the instructions are processed internally has been modified and optimized by various different CPU architectures, but otherwise the same platform has been in use for the last 30 years (IA-32 updated the 16-bit x86 instruction set, first launched in 1978).

Up until a few years ago, CPUs were designed to run 32-bit code. This means that each instruction can be up to 32-bits in length. A 32-bit CPU's **General Purpose (GP) registers** are also 32-bits wide. However, since 2004, most desktop CPUs (and from 2006, most laptop CPUs) released to the market have been capable of running 64-bit code.

> *Note: 32-bit Pentium compatible CPUs feature additional larger registers for floating point calculations (80-bit) and SIMD processing (64- or 128-bit). They also feature a 64-bit data bus. It is the GP register size that makes a CPU 32- or 64-bit.*

Intel first developed a 64-bit instruction set for its Itanium server CPU platform in 2001. This platform (**IA-64**) has never gained acceptance in the PC market, however. AMD's 64-bit instruction set (**AMD64**) has proved more popular and was adopted by Intel for its 64-bit desktop and mobile line. Intel refers to it as EM64T or Intel 64. The same instruction set is also called **x86-64** or **x64**.

The utilization of 64-bit CPU features by installing 64-bit operating systems took some time to grow, principally because of the lack of 64-bit drivers for peripheral devices. However, at this point, it is estimated that well over half of the Windows install base is 64-bit.

ADDRESSING

The system bus between the CPU and memory consists of a data bus and an address bus. The width of the data bus (64-bit on all current CPUs) determines how much data can be transferred per clock cycle; the width of the address bus determines how many memory locations the PC can access.

> **Note:** In modern CPU designs, the bus is double or quad "pumped," meaning that there are two or four 64-bit transfers per clock cycle. Also, the memory architecture is likely to be multi-channel, meaning that there are two, three, or four 64-bit data paths operating simultaneously.

The address bus for most 32-bit CPUs is either 32- or 36-bits wide. A 32-bit address bus can access a 4 GB address space; 36-bit expands that to 64 GB. In theory, a 64-bit CPU could implement a 64-bit address space (16 Exabytes). In practice, the current generation of x64 CPUs are "restricted" to 48-bit address spaces (256 TB) to reduce the complexity in remaining compatible with 32-bit software.

CACHE

A computer stores the data for the programs and files currently open in *system memory*. The CPU has *registers* to store instructions and data that it is processing. Instructions are moved in and out of these registers to the system memory.

Cache is a small block of high-speed memory that enhances performance by pre-loading (caching) code and data from relatively slow system memory and passing it to the CPU on demand. Essentially, cache stores instructions and data that the CPU is using regularly.

In early CPU designs, cache was implemented as a separate chip on the motherboard, but almost all new CPUs incorporate most types of cache as features on the CPU itself (on die). Cache is designed in multiple levels. Level 1 cache is "closest" to the CPU and supports the fastest access. Level 2 cache is typically larger and a bit slower while Level 3 and Level 4 cache, if used, are larger and possibly a bit slower still.

HYPERTHREADING

One way to make instruction execution more efficient is to improve the way the pipeline works. The basic approach is to do the most amount of work possible in a single clock cycle (**multitasking**). There are various ways to achieve this goal, though.

- **Superpipelining.** CPUs process multiple instructions at the same time (for example, while one instruction is fetched, another is being decoded, another is being executed, and another is being written back to memory). This is referred to as a **superscalar architecture**, as multiple execution units are required. Superscalar architectures also feature longer pipelines with multiple stages but shorter actions (micro-ops) at each stage, referred to as **superpipelining**.

  The original Pentium® had a 5-stage pipeline; by contrast, the Pentium 4 has up to 31 stages (NetBurst® architecture). NetBurst actually proved relatively inefficient in terms of power and thermal performance, so Intel reverted to a modified form of the P6 architecture it used in Pentium IIs and IIIs for its "Core" brand CPUs (with around 14 stages).

- **Multithreading.** Another approach is **Simultaneous Multithreading (SMT)**, called **HyperThreading (HT)** or **HyperThreading Technology (HTT)** by Intel.

  A **thread** is a stream of instructions generated by a software application. Most applications run a single process in a single thread; software that runs multiple parallel threads within a process is said to be **multithreaded**. SMT allows the threads to run through the CPU at the same time. It duplicates many of the registers of the CPU. This reduces the amount of "idle time" the CPU spends waiting for new instructions to process. To the OS, it seems as though there are two or more CPUs installed.

  The main drawback of SMT is that it works best with multithreaded software. As this software is more difficult to design, it tends to be restricted to programs designed to run on servers. Desktop applications software often cannot take full advantage.

MULTIPROCESSING AND MULTICORE PROCESSORS

Yet another approach to making a computer system faster is to use two or more physical CPUs, referred to as **Symmetric Multiprocessing (SMP)**. An SMP-aware OS can then make efficient use of the processing resources available to run application processes on whichever CPU is "available." This approach is not dependent on software applications being multithreaded to deliver performance benefits. Traditionally, SMP was provided by physically installing two or more CPUs in a multi-socket motherboard. Obviously, this adds significantly to the cost and so is implemented more often on servers and high-end workstations.

However, improvements in CPU manufacturing techniques have led to another solution: dual-core CPUs, or **Chip Level Multiprocessing (CMP)**. A dual-core CPU is essentially two processors combined on the same die. The market has quickly moved beyond dual-core CPUs to multicore packages with 3, 4, 8, or more processors.

> *Note: Most mainstream CPU models are now multicore. Single-core CPUs are still produced for the lowest budget models but manufacturing volumes mean that multicore CPUs are at the point of being cheaper to produce than single-core ones.*

CLOCK SPEED

Despite the architectural features just discussed, the speed at which the CPU runs is generally seen as a key indicator of performance. This is certainly true when comparing CPUs with the same architecture but is not necessarily the case otherwise. Intel Core 2 CPUs run slower than Pentium 4s, but deliver better performance. Budget and low power models will work at around 1-2 GHz while premium models will run at 3-4 GHz.

The **core clock speed** is the speed at which the CPU runs internal processes and accesses L1 and L2 cache (L2 cache access speed actually depends on the CPU architecture, but full-speed access to L2 cache has been standard for some time). The Front Side Bus (FSB) speed is the interface between the CPU and system memory.

OVERCLOCKING

When a manufacturer releases a new chip, it sets an optimum clock speed based on systems testing. This clock speed will be set at a level where damage to the chip is not likely to occur during normal operation. Increasing this speed (**overclocking**) is done using the system setup firmware program by adjusting the **CPU Speed** or **Advanced Chipset Features** properties. You can either increase the core clock speed (multiplier) or the FSB speed (overclocking the memory chips) or both. Increasing the clock speed requires more power and generates more heat. Therefore, an overclocked system must have a suitable power supply and sufficient cooling. The operating environment (the warmth of the room and build-up of dust) must also be quite carefully controlled.

Overclocking is generally performed by hobbyists and games enthusiasts but it is also a means to build a PC more cheaply by specifying lower cost components, then boosting their performance.

Without cooling, overclocking increases the risk of thermal damage to components and may increase the frequency of system lockups. It also invalidates the warranty. Original Equipment Manufacturers (OEM) generally try to prevent overclocking in their PC systems by disabling custom settings in the computer's system setup program.

A CPU may also run at a lower actual speed than it is capable of if it is put in a power saving mode.

POWER MANAGEMENT (THROTTLING)

Rising energy costs and environmental legislation are placing power efficiency at the top of the agenda for IT buyers. In terms of CPU performance, more speed means greater power consumption and heat production. To deal with these issues, CPUs can implement power management to enter lower power states, referred to as **throttling**.

Another aspect of power management is protection for the CPU. If a processor runs too hot, the system can become unstable or damage can occur. CPUs provide routines to reduce performance to protect against overheating.

OTHER CPU FEATURES

Two other features of modern CPUs need to be covered here. These support the use of virtualization and power-efficient graphics capability.

- **Virtualization extensions.** Virtualization software allows a single computer to run multiple operating systems or **Virtual Machines (VM)**. Intel's Virtualization Technology (VT) and AMD's AMD-V provide processor extensions to support virtualization, also referred to as **hardware-assisted virtualization**. This makes the VMs run much more quickly. These extensions are usually features of premium models in a given processor range.

    There is also a second generation of virtualization extensions to support **Second Level Address Translation (SLAT)**, a feature of virtualization software designed to improve the management of virtual (paged) memory. These extensions are referred to as **Extended Page Table (EPT)** by Intel and **Rapid Virtualization Indexing (RVI)** by AMD.

- **Integrated GPU.** Most computer systems provide some sort of built-in graphics adapter. Initially, an **integrated GPU** would be implemented as part of the motherboard chipset; Intel's Graphics Media Accelerator, for instance. Nowadays, it is more likely that an integrated GPU, or Integrated Graphics Processor (IGP), will be part of the CPU (Intel HD Graphics, for example).

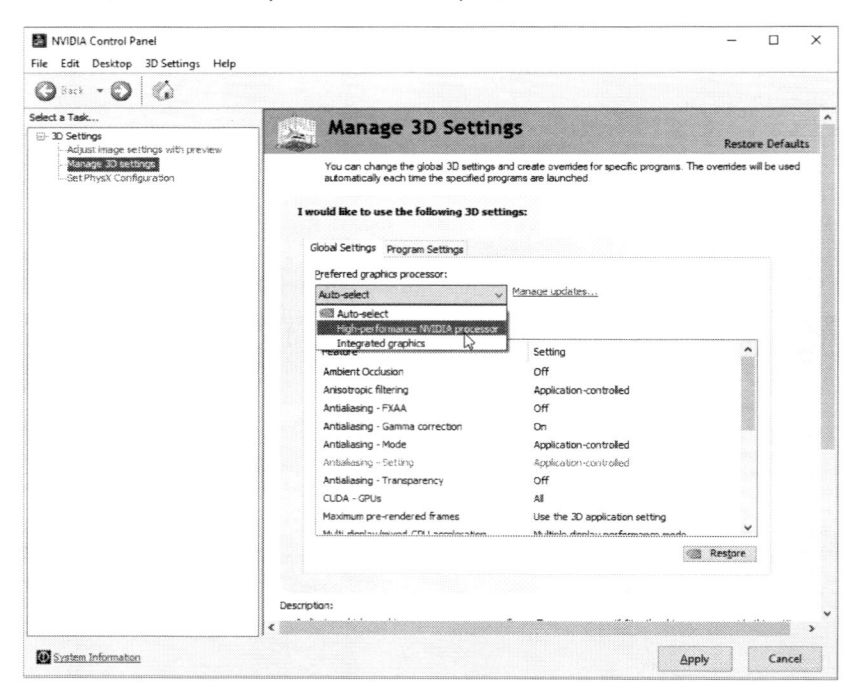

NVIDIA's control panel allows the system to select a graphics processor depending on application requirements.

Apart from cost, an IGP is more power-efficient than a dedicated card. Some laptop systems with both an IGP and a dedicated card are capable of switching automatically between them (NVIDIA Optimus and ATI Hybrid Graphics technologies), depending on whether an application requires advanced 3D performance or not, to conserve battery life.

CPU PACKAGING AND COMPATIBILITY

There have been numerous CPU architectures, and within each architecture, a number of different models, and for each set of models, a brand to position them within a particular market segment. CPU packaging refers to the **CPU's form factor** and how it is connected to the motherboard. Intel and AMD use different socket types so you will never be able to install an AMD CPU in a motherboard designed for an Intel CPU (and vice versa). Additionally, within Intel's and AMD's own ranges, a given CPU socket type will only be compatible with a fairly limited number of CPU models.

The following tables summarize some of the various CPU models and socket types that have been used over the years. Note that the supported desktop processors and memory are illustrative rather than definitive. For more up-to-date information, visit a site such as CPU World, Tom's Hardware, or AnandTech.

INTEL CPU RANGES AND SOCKET TYPES

Brand Name	Description
Core®	This is Intel's flagship desktop and mobile CPU series. The earliest models (Core Solo and Core Duo) were laptop-only chips. The Core 2 series introduced desktop versions plus 64-bit and multicore support. The current range is divided into Core i3, i5, and i7 brands, with i7 representing the best performing models. The Core iX range has been based on successive generations of microarchitectures, named Nehalem, Sandy Bridge, Ivy Bridge, Haswell, Broadwell, and Skylake.
Pentium®	The Pentium used to be Intel's premium 32-bit CPU brand and you may still find Pentium 4-based computers in use. The Pentium brand has been reintroduced to represent "mid-range" CPU models based on the Core microarchitecture
Celeron®	This has long been Intel's budget brand.
Atom®	This brand designates chips designed for low-power portable devices (smartphones and tablets).
Xeon®	This brand is aimed at the server/workstation market. Current Xeons are often differentiated from their Core counterparts by supporting n-way multiprocessing and ECC memory and coming with larger caches.

Intel uses **Land Grid Array (LGA)** form factor CPUs. In LGA, the pins that connect the CPU and socket are located on the socket. This reduces the likelihood of damage to the CPU but increases the chance of damaging the motherboard.

GIGA-BYTE Z97X Gaming motherboard with Intel Socket 1150. (Image © Gigabyte.)

AMD CPU RANGES AND SOCKET TYPES

Older AMD brands such as Athlon™, Phenom™, Sempron™, and Turion™ have been phased out over the last few years. The following brands represent the company's Zen microarchitecture in different segments:

- Ryzen™/Threadripper™ and Ryzen Mobile—this brand now represents AMD's pitch for the high-end enthusiast segment, replacing older AMD FX chips.
- Epyc™—AMD's server-class CPU brand, replacing its long-standing Opteron series of chips.

AMD uses **Pin Grid Array (PGA)** form factor chips, designed to fit in a **Zero Insertion Force (ZIF) socket** on the motherboard. As the name suggests, a PGA chip has a number of pins on the underside of the processor. These plug into corresponding holes in the socket. Care must be taken to orient the CPU correctly with the socket and to insert it so as not to bend or break any of the pins.

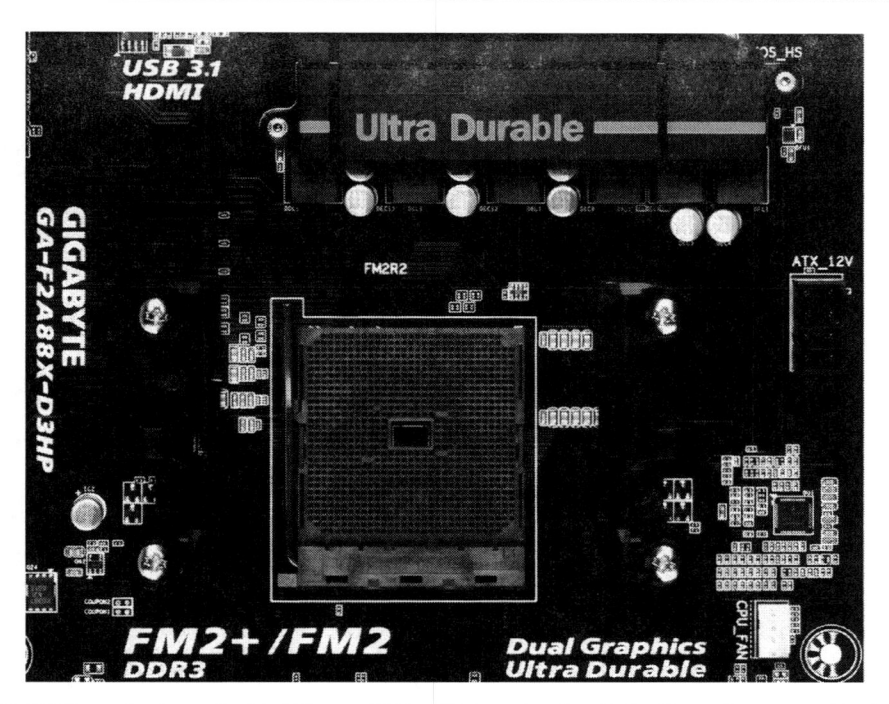

GIGA-BYTE motherboard with ZIF-type FM2+/FM2 socket for AMD CPUs. (Image © Gigabyte.)

COOLING MECHANISMS

Heat is a by-product of pushing electric current through the various electronic components in the computer. The faster the components work, the more heat is produced. Excessive temperatures can cause the components to malfunction or even damage them. One of the most significant problems with CPUs (and graphics cards) is their thermal output. While Intel and AMD are both focusing on making new CPU designs more thermally efficient, all CPUs require cooling. Also, a specific CPU model requires a specific cooling system as some run hotter than others (later Pentium 4s being a good example).

HEAT SINKS AND THERMAL PASTE

A **heat sink** is a block of copper or aluminum with fins. As the fins expose a larger surface area to the air around the component, a greater cooling effect by convection is achieved. Before attaching the heat sink, dots of **thermal paste** (also referred to as thermal grease or thermal compound) should be applied to the surface of the CPU so that placing the heat sink spreads the paste into a thin layer. At the microscopic level, when two solids touch, there are actually air gaps between them that act as insulation; the liquid thermally conductive compound gel fills these gaps to permit a more efficient transference of heat from the processor to the heat sink.

A heat sink is a **passive cooling device**. Passive cooling means that it does not require extra energy (electricity) to work. In order to work well, a heat sink requires good airflow around the PC. It is important to try to keep "cable clutter" to a minimum.

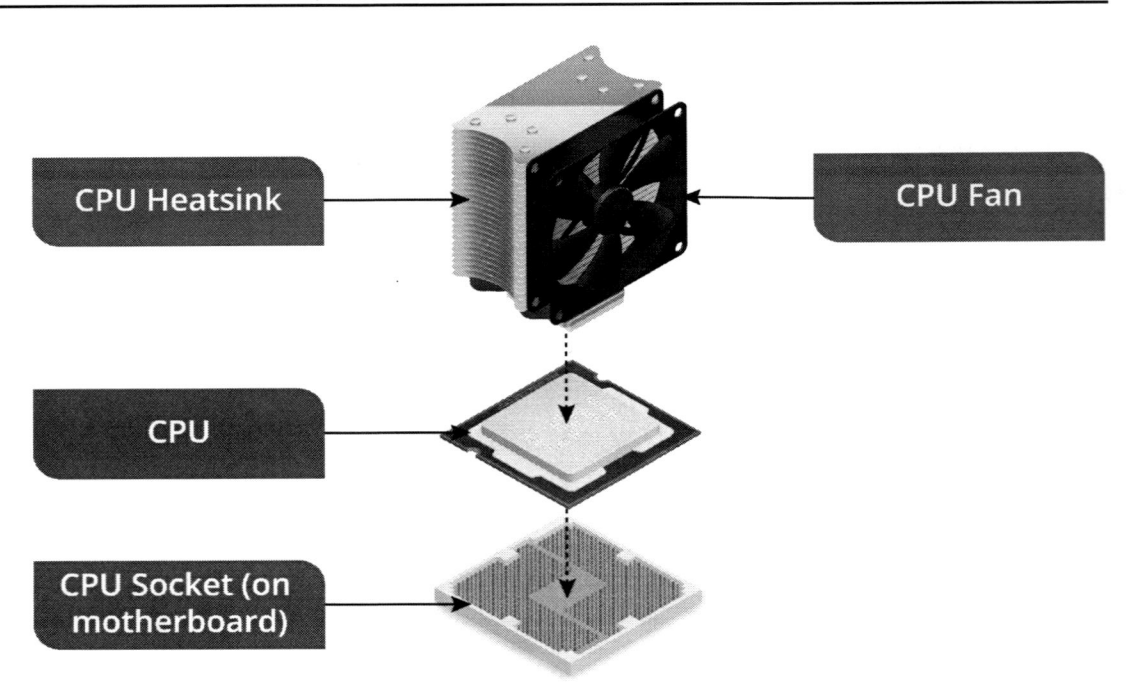

CPU heatsink and fan assembly. Note: When purchasing a CPU, most CPU fans included already have thermal paste applied to the bottom of the CPU fan. If there is no thermal paste applied or the CPU didn't come with a CPU fan, then you'll need to purchase a separate tube of thermal paste. (Image © 123RF.com.)

There are various mechanisms for clamping a CPU heat sink to the motherboard. There may be a retaining clip or push pins. Push pins can be released and reset for insertion by making a half turn with a screwdriver.

FANS

Many PCs have components that generate more heat than can be removed by passive cooling. A fan improves air flow and so helps to dissipate heat. Fans are used for the power supply and chassis exhaust points. The fan system will be designed to draw cool air from vents in the front of the case over the motherboard and expel warmed air from the back of the case.

> **Note:** *A common implementation is to include air vents near the bottom of the front of the case and to place a fan near the top of the rear of the case to pull cooler air through the system.*

Typically, the speed of the fan is varied according to the temperature, and sensors are used to detect whether a fan has failed. Smaller fans may be used to improve the performance of the heat sink on the CPU, GPUs, and even hard disks.

A fan is an active cooling device. It requires power to run.

The main problem with fans, especially at the lower end of the market, is that they generate noise. A fan also needs to be matched to the CPU model to ensure that it is powerful enough to cope with the processor's thermal output.

Most CPU fans are designed to be removed without the use of tools. Usually the fan assembly will have clips and a power connector.

Some chassis designs incorporate a plastic shroud or system of baffles to cover the CPU and channel the flow of air. The shroud is usually attached to the case using plastic clips.

HEAT PIPES AND SPREADERS

A **heat pipe** is a sealed tube containing some type of coolant (water or ethanol). The liquid close to the heat source evaporates then condenses at a cooler point in the pipe and flows back towards the heat source. The cool parts of the pipe are kept so by convection. This mechanism is more effective than a simple heat sink and fan assembly. It is necessary for a CPU that runs particularly hot or where there is not much space for airflow within the chassis. A **dual heat pipe** has two tubes, providing better cooling.

A **heat spreader** uses the same design but is a flat container rather than a pipe. This design is better suited to portable computers. If used without fans, heat pipes and spreaders are classed as passive cooling.

LIQUID-BASED COOLING SYSTEMS

PCs used for high-end gaming (those with twin graphics cards, for instance) and with overclocked components may generate more heat than basic thermal management can cope with. PCs used where the ambient temperature is very high may also require exceptional cooling measures.

A liquid-cooled PC. (Image by Olivér Svéd © 123RF.com.)

Liquid-based cooling refers to a system of pumping water around the chassis. Water is a much more effective coolant than air convection and a good pump can run more quietly than numerous fans. On the downside, liquid cooling makes maintenance and upgrades more difficult, requires comparatively more power to run, and is costly. Liquid cooling is an active cooling technology as the pump requires power to run.

FANS AND POWER

Power is supplied to a CPU or case fan by connecting its power connector to an appropriate header on the motherboard (make sure you plug the CPU fan into the header marked "CPU Fan" to ensure that the chipset can run the fan at an appropriate speed). Power connectors and headers for fans are 3-pin or 4-pin.

- 3-pin models control fan speed by varying the voltage.
- 4-pin models control fan speed by switching the voltage on and off (using a Pulse Width Module [PWM] signal carried by the fourth wire). This gives better control over fan speed.

Fans with a 3-pin connector can usually be used with 4-pin headers but the system may not be able to vary the fan speed (or may need special configuration to be able to do so). A fan with a 4-pin connector will usually work with a 3-pin header but will not be able to use PWM.

CPU INSTALLATION CONSIDERATIONS

Before you replace a processor, you need to make sure you select a processor that matches the type of socket on the system board. Not all processors that use a particular socket will be compatible with your system; this is just one of several items you will need to check for compatibility. Also, when it comes to removing the CPU, there are several cooling device designs and socket types to deal with.

If you are upgrading the CPU, check that the new model is supported by the motherboard. Use the motherboard manufacturer's website to get up-to-date information (for example, to find out about CPU models that were released after the motherboard's documentation was written).

Note: Just because a motherboard has the correct socket type does not mean that a CPU model will be compatible. The motherboard must have a compatible chipset and voltage regulators, too.

Pin 1 on the processor MUST match pin 1 on the processor socket. Both the processor and the socket carry distinguishing markings to indicate pin 1. On a processor, this may be:

- A beveled corner or a white dot printed in one corner of the processor.
- A square, rather than round, joint where one of the pins is connected to the underside of the processor.
- A "spur" on one corner of the gold patch on the underside of the processor.

On a processor socket, this may be:

- A difference in the pattern of pin holes in one corner.
- A "1" printed on the motherboard next to one corner.

*Note: To learn more, check the **Video** tile on the CHOICE Course screen for any videos that supplement the content for this lesson.*

Access the Checklist tile on your CHOICE Course screen for reference information and job aids on How to Install and Upgrade Processors.

Activity 4-1
Discussing CPU Upgrades

SCENARIO
Answer the following questions to check your understanding of the topic.

1. What limits upgrade potential for the system processor?

2. How can CPU performance be improved?

3. Why can cache improve performance?

4. What does SMP mean?

5. How is the heat sink and fan assembly attached, and what problems can occur releasing it?

6. What must you check when inserting a PGA CPU chip?

7. What is the difference between a heat sink and a heat pipe?

Activity 4-2
Planning for a CPU Upgrade

BEFORE YOU BEGIN
You will perform this activity at your WORKBENCH PC.

SCENARIO
You want to upgrade the CPU in your home PC. You need to make sure that the CPU you are installing will perform better than the one currently installed, and that it will work with the existing motherboard and other components.

1. Use the **Windows System Properties** page and the CPUID CPU-Z utility to report system information and configuration.
    a) Check **System Properties** to confirm the type of CPU currently installed.
    b) Run the **CPUID CPU-Z** utility using its desktop shortcut and click **Yes** when prompted by User Account Control (UAC).

    The first tab shows information about the CPU.

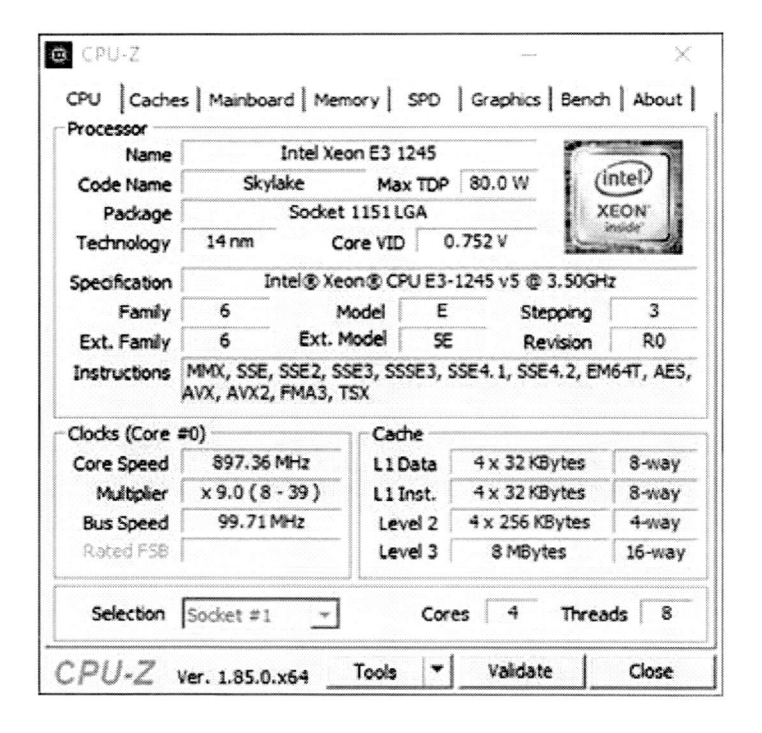

c) Select the **Caches** tab. Cache helps the CPU "smooth" the flow of instructions fetched from system memory and make processing more efficient. Different CPU models come with different amounts of cache, arranged in levels. Level 1 cache is the fastest and usually the smallest.

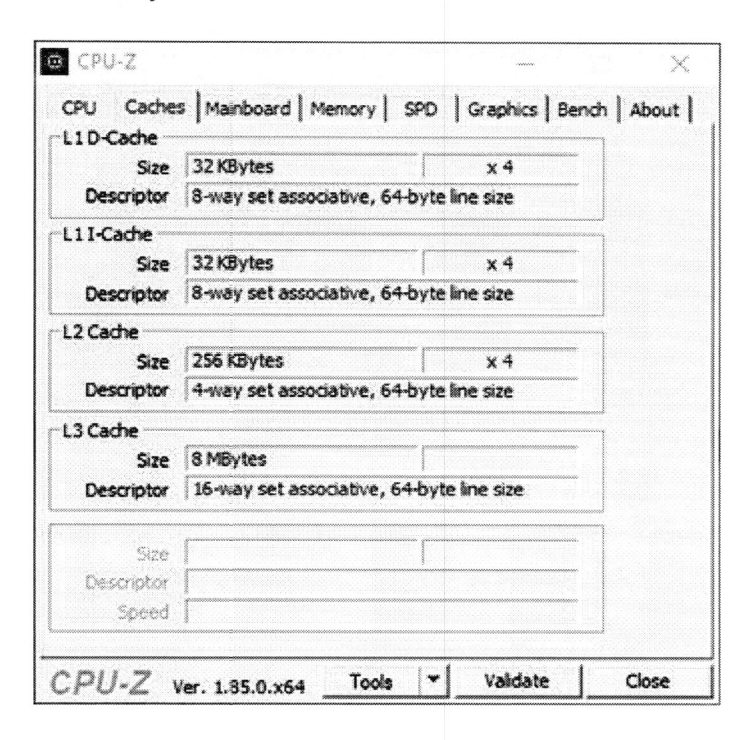

d) Select the **Mainboard** tab. This shows information about the motherboard and system firmware vendor and model.

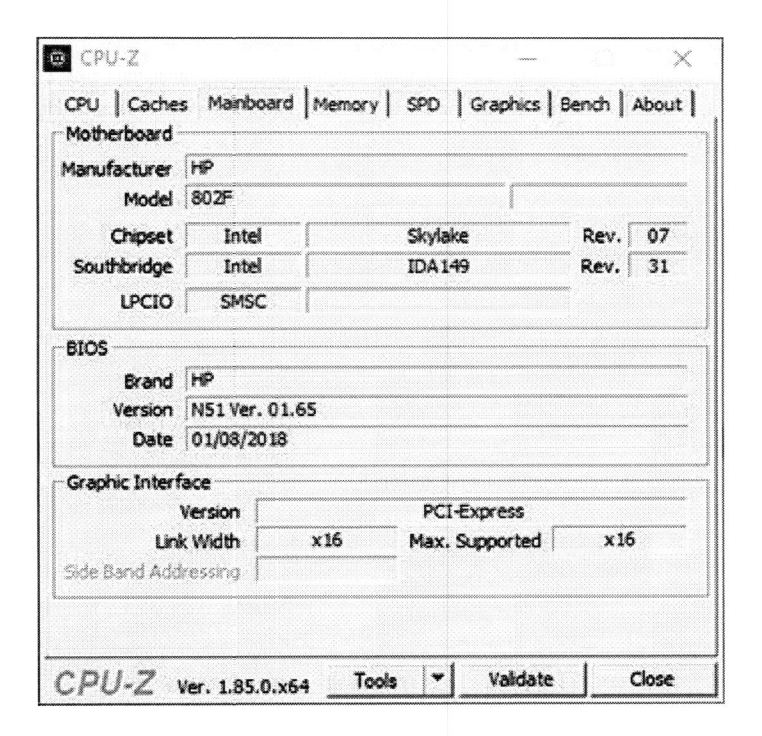

2. Determine which CPUs would provide better performance in the PC.

a) Using a vendor site such as **http://processormatch.intel.com/**, locate CPUs that are compatible with the motherboard and chipset.

b) If available, review installation instructions for the replacement CPU.

Topic B
Configure and Update BIOS/UEFI

EXAM OBJECTIVES COVERED
1001-3.5 Given a scenario, install and configure motherboards, CPUs, and add-on cards.

In PC support, you will often need to use the system setup program to check or modify firmware settings and to perform firmware updates.

SYSTEM FIRMWARE

Firmware straddles a gray area between hardware and software. Firmware is specialized software stored in memory chips that store information whether or not power to the computer is on. It is most often written on an electronically reprogrammable chip so that it can be updated with a special program to fix any errors that might be discovered after a computer is purchased, or to support updated hardware components.

System firmware provides low-level code to allow the computer components to be initialized and load the main operating system software.

BIOS

For many years, the system firmware for a PC was called the **BIOS** (Basic Input/Output System). BIOS provides the industry standard program code that initializes the essential components of the PC and ensures that the design of each manufacturer's motherboard is PC compatible.

UEFI

Newer motherboards may use a different kind of firmware called **Unified Extensible Firmware Interface (UEFI)**. UEFI provides support for 64-bit CPU operation at boot, a full GUI and mouse operation at boot, networking functionality at boot, and better boot security. A computer with UEFI may also support booting in a legacy BIOS mode.

SYSTEM FIRMWARE SETUP PROGRAMS

System settings can be configured via the system firmware setup program. This may also be referred to as **CMOS setup**, **BIOS setup**, or **UEFI setup**.

Note: The term CMOS Setup is still widely used, even though the setup configuration is no longer stored within the CMOS RAM component.

You can normally access the system setup program with a keystroke during the power-on (boot) process. The key combination used will vary from system to system; typical examples are **Esc**, **Del**, **F1**, **F2**, or **F10**. The PC's documentation will explain how to access the setup program; often a message with the required key is displayed when you boot the PC.

Bootup access to system firmware setup.

> **Note:** One issue with modern computers is that the boot process can be very quick. If this is the case, you can **Shift**-click the **Restart** button from the Windows logon screen to access UEFI boot options. Alternatively, the motherboard vendor may supply a tool for disabling fast boot or accessing the setup program.

You navigate a legacy BIOS setup program using the keyboard arrow keys. Pressing **Esc** generally returns to the previous screen. When closing setup, there will be an option to exit and discard changes or exit and save changes. Sometimes this is done with a key (**Esc** versus **F10**, for instance), but more often there is a prompt. There will also be an option for reloading the default settings, in case you want to discard any customizations you have made.

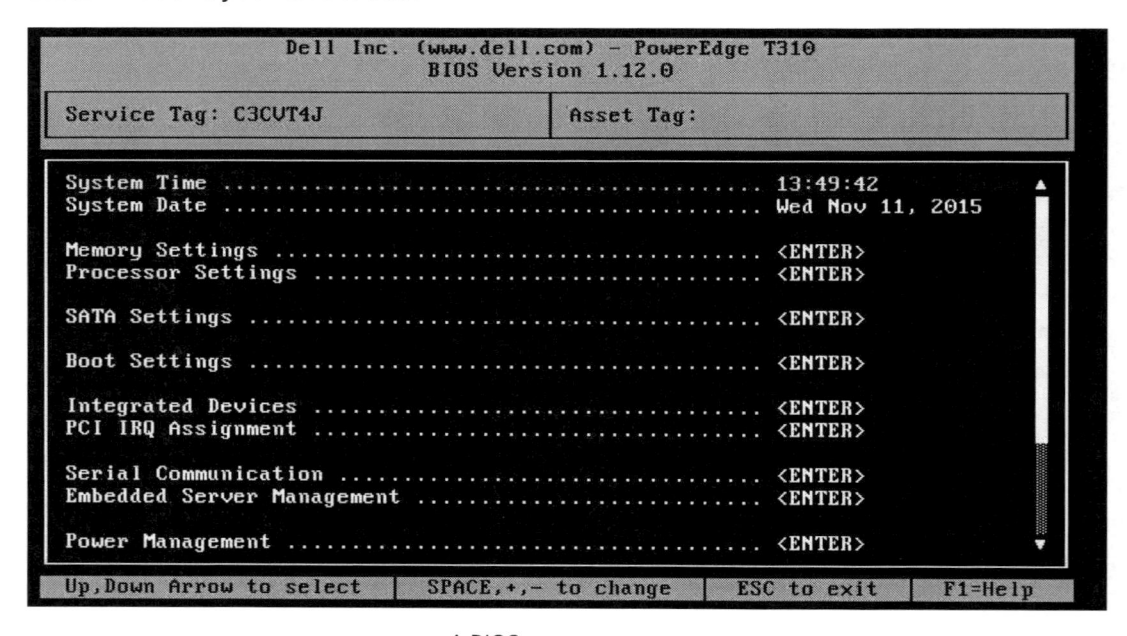

A BIOS setup program.

UEFI setup programs might feature a graphical interface and mouse support.

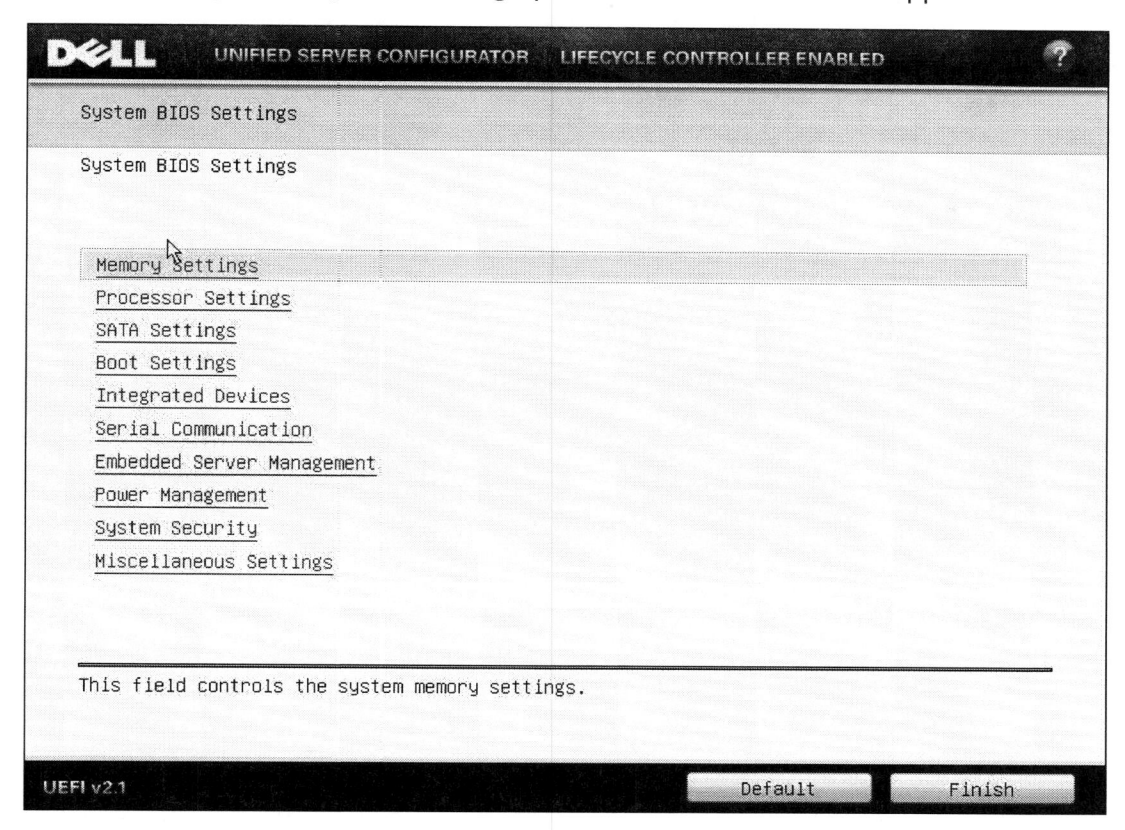

A UEFI setup program.

SYSTEM COMPONENT SETTINGS

The system firmware setup program will contain information about core components such as the CPU, chipset, RAM, hard drive(s), optical drive(s), and the battery (on a laptop).

CPU FEATURES

There will be options for configuring features of the CPU, such as number of cores, cache, power performance, support for instruction set extensions that speed up virtualization (running multiple guest operating systems in a hypervisor), and so on.

In most cases, these features will be detected and enabled by default. You may want to disable them to perform troubleshooting, however.

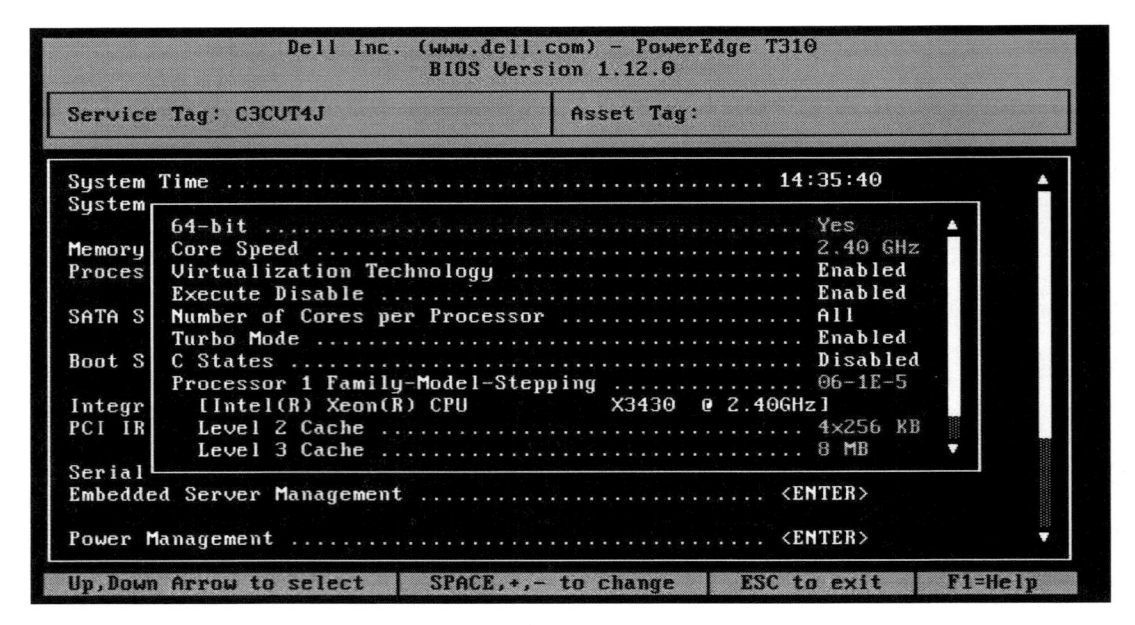

```
               Dell Inc. (www.dell.com) - PowerEdge T310
                         BIOS Version 1.12.0
 Service Tag: C3CUT4J                    Asset Tag:

 System Time ......................................... 14:35:40
 System ┌─────────────────────────────────────────────────────────┐
        │ 64-bit ......................................... Yes   │
 Memory │ Core Speed ..................................... 2.40 GHz│
 Proces │ Virtualization Technology ...................... Enabled│
        │ Execute Disable ................................ Enabled│
 SATA S │ Number of Cores per Processor .................. All   │
        │ Turbo Mode ..................................... Enabled│
 Boot S │ C States ....................................... Disabled│
        │ Processor 1 Family-Model-Stepping .............. 06-1E-5│
 Integr │     [Intel(R) Xeon(R) CPU       X3430  @ 2.40GHz]│
 PCI IR │     Level 2 Cache .............................. 4x256 KB│
        │     Level 3 Cache .............................. 8 MB   │
 Serial └─────────────────────────────────────────────────────────┘
 Embedded Server Management ........................... <ENTER>

 Power Management ..................................... <ENTER>

 Up,Down Arrow to select  │ SPACE,+,- to change │ ESC to exit │ F1=Help
```

CPU feature menu.

RAM

The system software detects installed memory modules via a Serial Presence Detect (SPD) chip in the modules. The system software will allow you to enable or disable a boot-time memory check. There may also be options for configuring multi-channel memory modes. There may also be the option to overclock system memory modules.

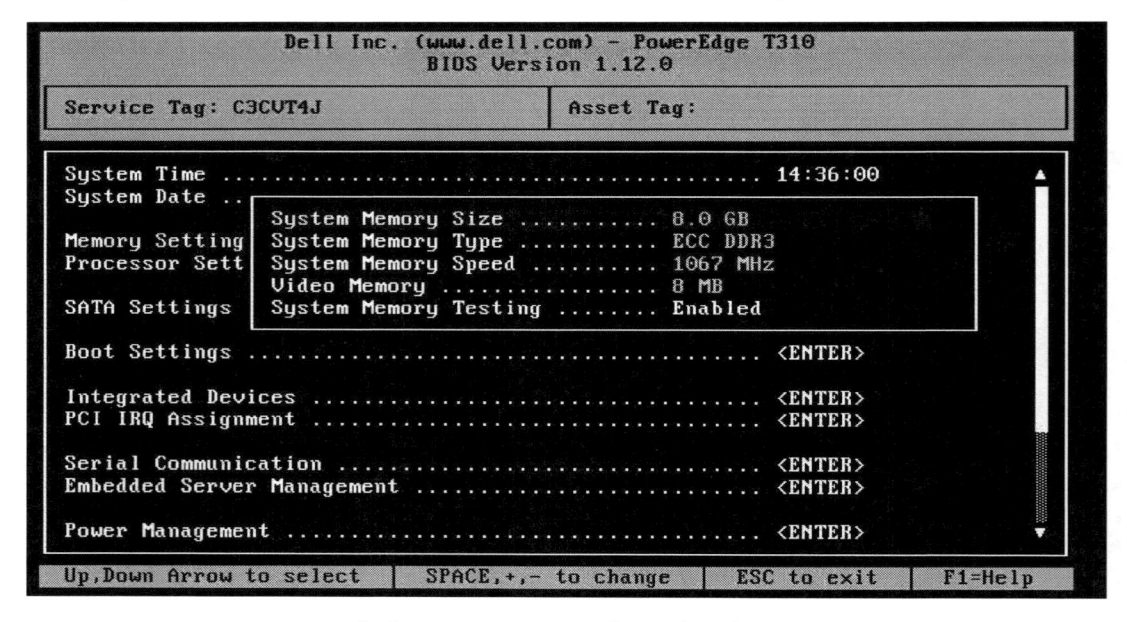

```
               Dell Inc. (www.dell.com) - PowerEdge T310
                         BIOS Version 1.12.0
 Service Tag: C3CUT4J                    Asset Tag:

 System Time ......................................... 14:36:00
 System Date ..
              ┌──────────────────────────────────────────────┐
              │ System Memory Size .......... 8.0 GB          │
 Memory Setting│ System Memory Type .......... ECC DDR3        │
 Processor Sett│ System Memory Speed ......... 1067 MHz        │
              │ Video Memory ................ 8 MB            │
 SATA Settings│ System Memory Testing ....... Enabled         │
              └──────────────────────────────────────────────┘
 Boot Settings ........................................ <ENTER>

 Integrated Devices ................................... <ENTER>
 PCI IRQ Assignment ................................... <ENTER>

 Serial Communication ................................. <ENTER>
 Embedded Server Management ........................... <ENTER>

 Power Management ..................................... <ENTER>

 Up,Down Arrow to select  │ SPACE,+,- to change │ ESC to exit │ F1=Help
```

System memory properties and settings.

POWER MANAGEMENT

Power management enables features such as soft power on/off (enabling the Windows Shut Down routine to power off the computer), power saving modes, hibernation, and so on. This option should normally be enabled.

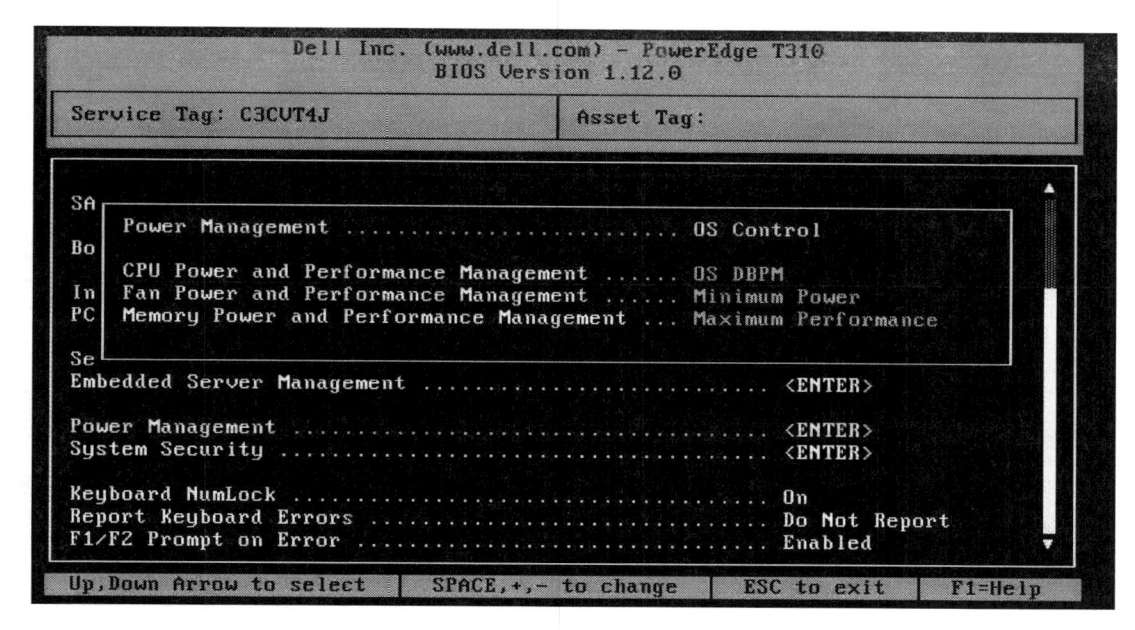

Power management profile configuration.

DATE, TIME, AND DAYLIGHT SAVINGS

Sometimes known as the **real time**, this is simply the calendar date and time. The PC's Real Time Clock (RTC) can be automatically adjusted back or forward one hour as appropriate, within the time zone under Windows. If the real time clock starts to lose the correct date or time, the RTC battery could be failing.

BOOT OPTIONS

One of the most important parameters in system setup is the **boot sequence** or **boot device priority**. This defines the sequence in which the system firmware searches devices for a boot manager. You will usually be able to set 3 or 4 options in priority order.

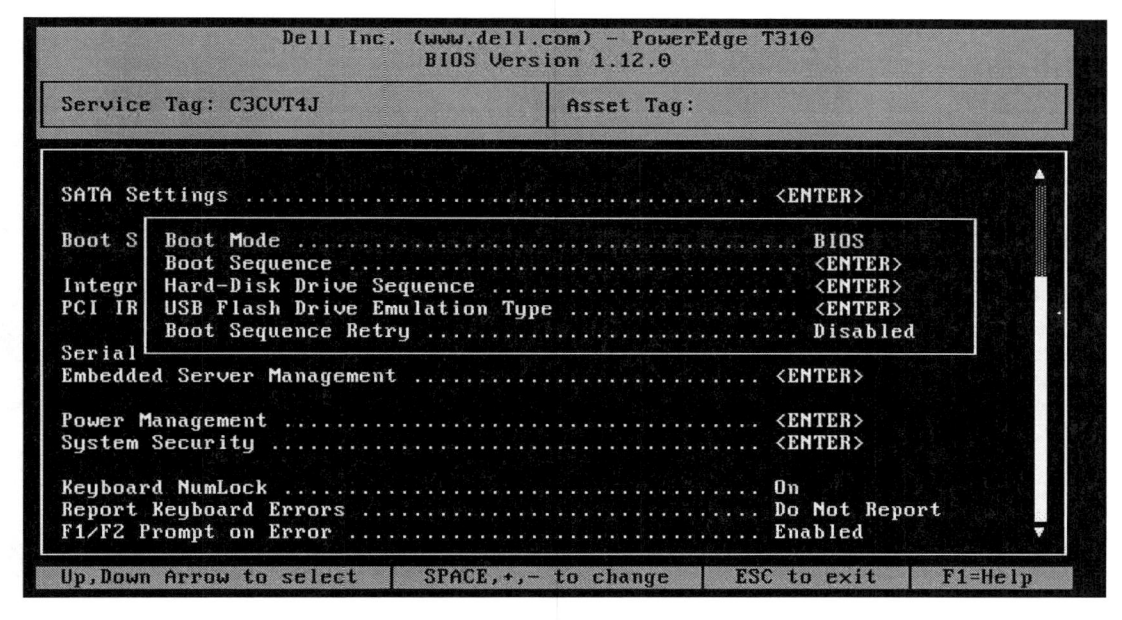

Boot parameters.

Typical choices include:

- **Hard drive.** A SATA boot disk should generally be connected to the lowest numbered port but it is usually possible to select the hard drive sequence if multiple fixed drives are installed.
- **Solid State Drive (SSD).** An SSD attached using SATA will be listed with other SATA/AHCI devices. An SSD installed as a PCIe Add-in Card (AIC) or on the M.2 interface can be used as a boot device if the firmware supports NVMe.
- **Optical drive (CD/DVD/Blu-ray).** If you are performing a repair install, you might need to make this device highest priority.
- **USB.** Most modern systems can boot from USB drives.
- **Network/PXE.** Uses the network adapter to obtain boot settings from a specially configured server.

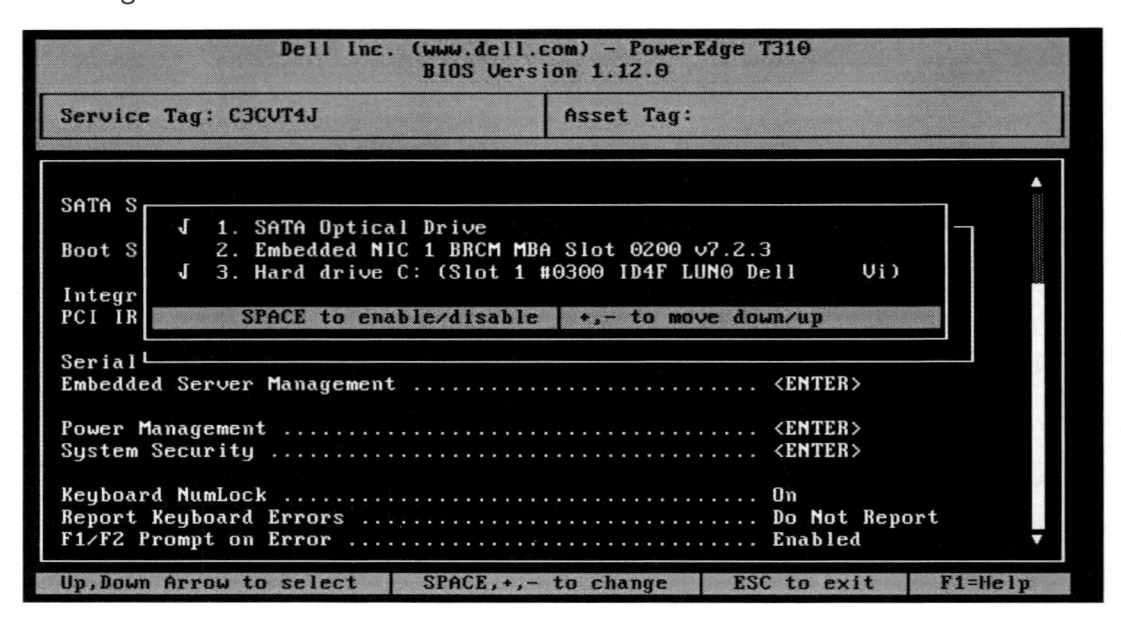

Boot order configuration.

INTERFACE CONFIGURATION SETTINGS

There will be options for enabling/disabling and configuring any controllers and adapters provided on the motherboard. This will certainly include storage adapters and possibly features such as USB, network adapter, graphics adapter, and sound adapter.

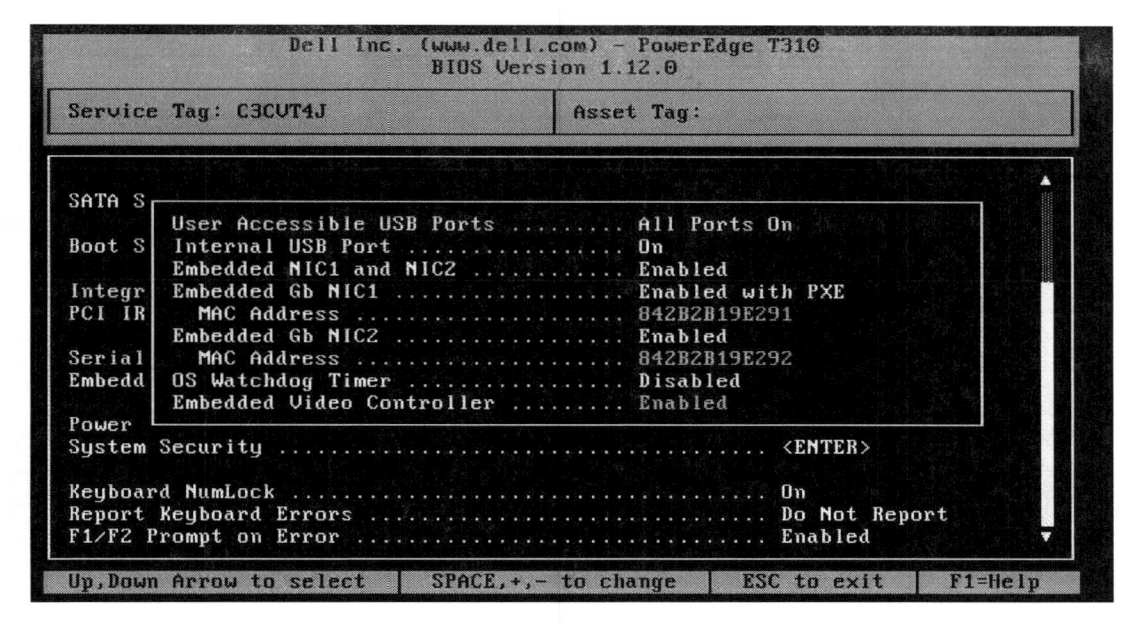

Onboard device configuration.

SECURITY SETTINGS

Several categories of security settings can be configured in system firmware setup programs.

AUTHENTICATION

Different system software will provide different support for authentication methods. There are usually at least two passwords, though some systems may allow for more:
- Supervisor/Administrator/Setup—protect access to the system setup program.
- User/System—lock access to the whole computer. This is a very secure way of protecting an entire PC as nothing can be done until the POST has taken place. The only real way of getting around this would be to open the PC and reset the system setup configuration, which isn't very easy to do.

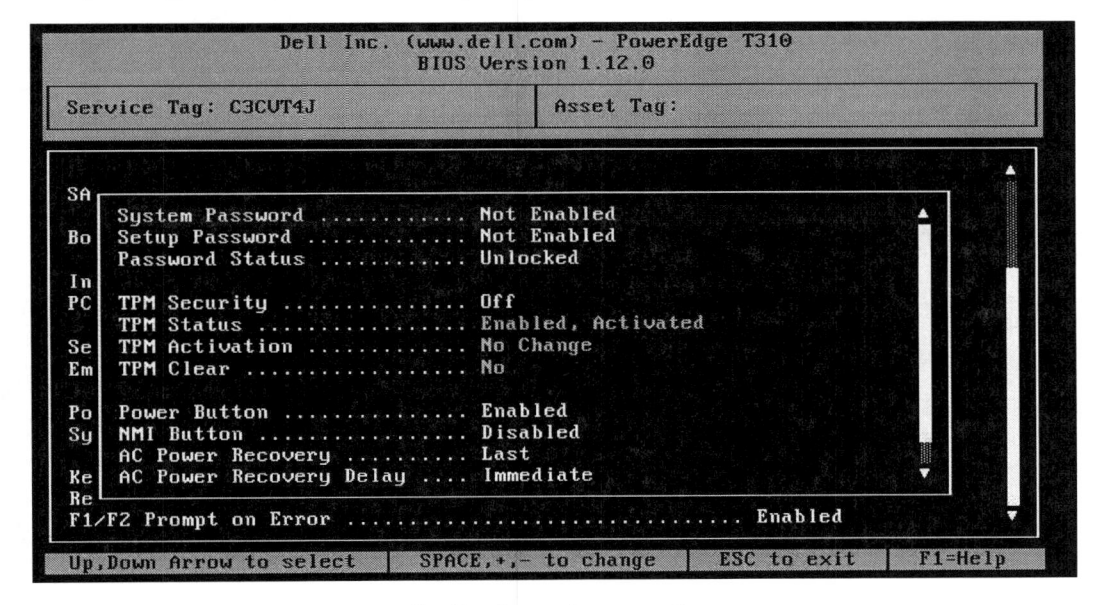

Configuring system security.

> **Note:** For user/system authentication, you have to tell everyone who uses the PC the password, which weakens the security considerably. This option would be used only on workstations and servers that aren't used for interactive logon (a computer running monitoring or management software, for instance).

DRIVE LOCKS

There are generally three options for securing access to the disk specifically (rather than the PC generally):

- Configure and store the password in the PC firmware; this means that the disk is unusable except with the designated computer.
- Store the password in the disk firmware; this is configured in conjunction with a compatible PC firmware and means that the disk is transferable between computers with a compatible firmware.
- Use **Full Disk Encryption (FDE)** to encode the contents of the drive as well as password-protecting it. The selected password is used as the basis of the encryption key. Again, this requires a hard drive and firmware compatible with the same FDE product.

> **Note:** In most cases, there is some sort of recovery mechanism. This might involve the supervisor password or a password recovery disk.

DRIVE ENCRYPTION

Drive encryption means that the entire contents of the drive (or volume), including system files and folders, are encrypted. OS security measures are quite simple to circumvent if you can get hold of the drive itself. Drive encryption allays this security concern by making the contents of the drive accessible only in combination with the correct encryption key.

Windows supports drive encryption in the BitLocker product, bundled with the Professional/Enterprise/Ultimate editions.

> **Note:** Third-party disk encryption products are available for other versions and editions of Windows.

TPM

BitLocker® requires the secure storage of the key used to encrypt the drive contents. Normally, this is stored in a **Trusted Platform Module (TPM)** chip on the computer motherboard. TPM is a specification for hardware-based storage of digital certificates, keys, hashed passwords, and other user and platform identification information. Essentially, it functions as an embedded smart card. Each TPM microprocessor is hard-coded with a unique, unchangeable key (the endorsement key). During the boot process, the TPM compares hashes of key system state data (system firmware, boot loader, and OS kernel) to ensure they have not been tampered with. The TPM chip has a secure storage area that a disk encryption program such as Windows BitLocker can write its keys to.

It is also possible to use a removable USB drive (if USB is a boot device option). As part of the setup process, you also create a recovery password or key. This can be used if the disk is moved to another computer or the TPM is damaged.

> **Note:** You may need to enable the TPM chip via the system setup before it can be used. Many vendors ship the computer with TPM disabled.

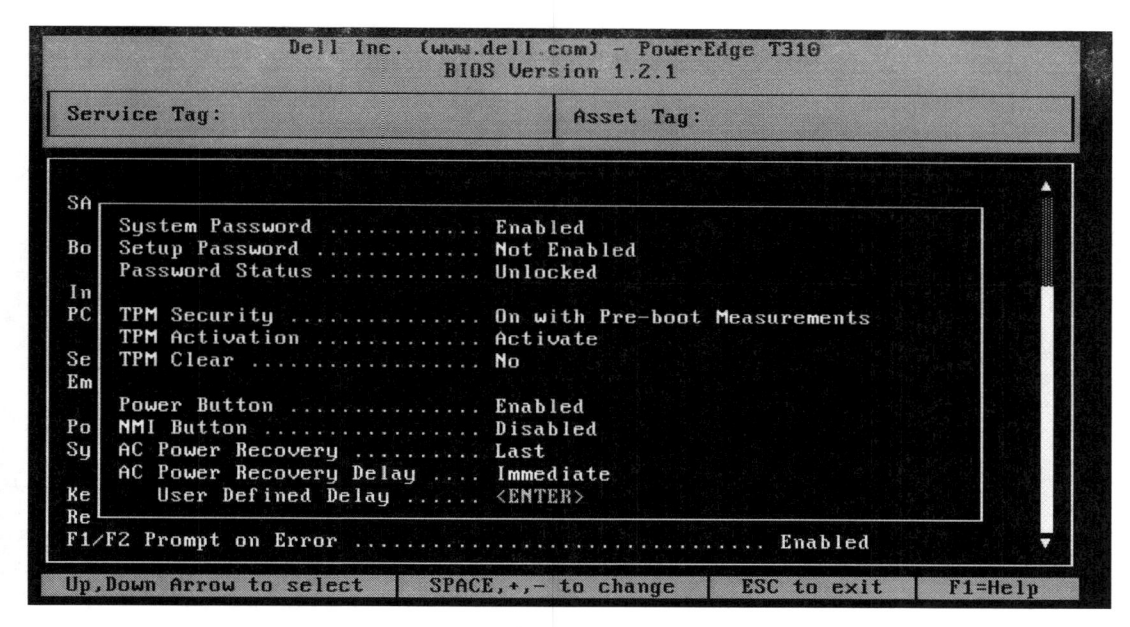

```
         Dell Inc. (www.dell.com) - PowerEdge T310
                      BIOS Version 1.2.1

 Service Tag:                          Asset Tag:


 SA
    ┌─────────────────────────────────────────────────┐
 Bo │  System Password ............. Enabled          │
    │  Setup Password  ............. Not Enabled      │
 In │  Password Status ............. Unlocked         │
 PC │                                                 │
    │  TPM Security   ............... On with Pre-boot Measurements│
    │  TPM Activation ............... Activate        │
 Se │  TPM Clear      ............... No              │
 Em │                                                 │
    │  Power Button   ............... Enabled         │
 Po │  NMI Button     ............... Disabled        │
 Sy │  AC Power Recovery ........... Last             │
    │  AC Power Recovery Delay ..... Immediate        │
 Ke │     User Defined Delay ...... <ENTER>           │
 Re └─────────────────────────────────────────────────┘
 F1/F2 Prompt on Error .............................. Enabled

 Up,Down Arrow to select  │ SPACE,+,- to change │ ESC to exit │ F1=Help
```

Configuring a TPM.

LoJack

Some laptop firmware is bundled with **LoJack tracking software** (developed by Absolute Software), essentially a security rootkit designed to prevent theft. If enabled (and the user has subscribed to LoJack®), a "dialer" is activated that attempts to contact Absolute Software's authorization servers each day. If the laptop is reported stolen, the authorization servers can force the laptop into a locked down mode (require a boot password or remotely wipe data, for instance). The software can also attempt to locate the laptop, either using GPS data if the laptop has a GPS chip or using information about nearby wireless networks. It can also try to identify the thief by installing forensic tools (a key logger and screen capture utility).

INTRUSION DETECTION

A computer chassis can be installed with sensors to report intrusion detection (if the chassis or lockable faceplate is opened) to management software or display an alert at boot time. Some setup programs can lock the workstation automatically if an intrusion is detected, requiring a supervisor to log on with the relevant password to unlock it again.

SECURE BOOT

Secure boot is a security system offered by UEFI. It is designed to prevent a computer from being hijacked by malware. Under secure boot, UEFI is configured with digital certificates from valid OS vendors. The system firmware checks the operating system boot loader using the stored certificate to ensure that it has been digitally signed by the OS vendor. This prevents a boot loader that has been modified by malware (or an OS installed without authorization) from being used.

> **Note:** *Certificates from vendors such as Microsoft (Windows 8/10 and Windows Server 2012 and later) and Linux distributions (Fedora, openSUSE, and Ubuntu) will be pre-loaded. Additional certificates for other boot loaders can be installed (or the pre-loaded ones removed) via the system setup software. It is also possible to disable secure boot.*

FIRMWARE UPDATES

System vendors and motherboard manufacturers may regularly update their system firmware in order to fix bugs, solve incompatibilities with operating systems, or to add new features. You should visit the relevant support website regularly to check whether upgrades are available. As upgrading the firmware is relatively risky (a failed motherboard update can leave the computer unbootable, for instance), it is only worth doing if the update fixes a specific problem that you are encountering or if it is regarded as a **critical update**.

Note: Performing a firmware update is often referred to as "flashing."

*Note: To learn more, check the **Video** tile on the CHOICE Course screen for any videos that supplement the content for this lesson.*

Access the Checklist tile on your CHOICE Course screen for reference information and job aids on How to Configure and Update System Firmware.

Activity 4-3
Discussing BIOS/UEFI Configuration and Updates

SCENARIO
Answer the following questions to check your understanding of the topic.

1. What advantages does UEFI have over BIOS?

2. Name three keys commonly used to run a PC's BIOS/UEFI system setup program.

3. What widely supported boot method is missing from the following list? HDD, FDD, Optical, USB.

4. Where should you launch a typical firmware upgrade utility—from system setup or from Windows?

5. If you want to enforce TPM system security, what other BIOS feature should you enable?

6. True or false? Processor extensions such as VT are set by the vendor depending on the CPU model and cannot be enabled or disabled by the user.

7. A user's computer was recently installed with a new optical drive. The user now reports a "chassis" error message after the POST sequence. What might be the cause?

8. When you are configuring BIOS security, what is the difference between a supervisor password and a user password?

9. What security system allows system boot to be disabled if the computer is reported stolen?

Topic C

Install Power Supplies

EXAM OBJECTIVES COVERED
1001-3.7 Summarize power supply types and features.

In this topic, you will take a closer look at the computer's power supply and its connections to the other system components. The computer's power supply is the main source of power for all components installed within the system unit. Understanding the power requirements of all the components and the maximum power supplied is crucial in managing the overall computer system power needs. Whether you are upgrading or replacing faulty components, you need to effectively manage the capacity of the current power supply.

ELECTRICAL CIRCUITS

Electricity is the flow of electrons through a conductor. The characteristics of the electricity supply are measured as voltage, current (amperage), resistance, and power.

- **Voltage**—the potential difference between two points (often likened to pressure in a water pipe) measured in Volts (V).
- **Current**—the actual flow of electrons, measured in Amps (I). A current flows in a circuit, which is made when conductors form a continuous path between the positive and negative terminals of a power source. The size of the current is determined by the conductivity of the circuit (for example, a higher current can flow in a thicker wire than can in a thinner one).
- **Resistance**—a degree of opposition to the current caused by characteristics of the conductor, measured in Ohms (Ω or R).
- **Power**—the rate at which electricity is drawn from the supply by the device using it, measured in Watts. Power is equal to the Voltage multiplied by the Current (W=V*I).
- **Energy**—the amount of power consumed by a device over time. This is measured in Watt-hours (or more typically, Kilowatt-hours [kWh]).

In a **Direct Current (DC)** circuit, the charge flows in one direction from the positive to negative terminals of the power source at a constant voltage. DC is used for electronic circuits, which require stable voltages. Grid power is supplied as **Alternating Current (AC)**, which means that the current flows in both directions around the circuit and the voltage alternates between low and high values. AC is a cheap way to distribute electrical power over long distances, but is incompatible with PC electronics. Transformers in the PC's power supply are used to convert AC to DC voltages.

In the US, grid power is supplied at 120 VAC with a tolerance of ±5 percent, giving a range of 114 VAC to 126 VAC. Historically, US grid power has been supplied at 110 VAC and 115 VAC, and these values are still widely referred to. In continental Europe and Ireland, mains electricity is supplied at 220 VAC, while in the UK it is 240 VAC; however, there are tolerances that mean most devices designed for IT use in the European market can work with a supply of 220-240 VAC.

Here are the electrical components used in a PC's electronic circuits:

- **Conductor**—a material that is good at conducting electricity, such as gold, copper, or tin. These are used for wires and contacts.

- **Insulator**—a material that does not conduct electricity, such as rubber or plastic. These are used as sheaths for wires to prevent short circuits or electric shocks.

  > **Note:** *Some materials are better conductors or insulators than others. Most materials have some degree of resistance, which creates heat as a current passes through it.*

- **Semiconductor**—a material that can act as both a conductor and an insulator. This provides switch-like functionality, where a circuit can be opened and closed, used to represent binary (on/off) digits.
- **Resistor**—these oppose the flow of current without blocking it completely and are used to manage electronic circuits.
- **Diode**—a valve, allowing current to flow in one direction only. These are used in a computer's power supply and as protection for components.
- **Fuse**—this is a safety device. The flow of electricity creates heat. A fuse is designed so that if the current is too high, the heat will cause the fuse wire to melt and break, breaking the circuit and shutting off the current.
- **Transistor**—in computers, these are semiconductor switches used to create logic devices. Typically, a type called a Field Effect Transistor (FET) is used to make components such as CPUs and memory.
- **Capacitor**—this stores electrical energy and is often used to regulate voltages. Note that a capacitor can hold a charge after the power is removed.

PSU

The **Power Supply Unit (PSU)** delivers Direct Current (DC) low voltage power to the PC components.

The PSU contains transformers (to step down to lower voltages), rectifiers (to convert AC to DC), and filters and regulators (to ensure a "clean" output or steady voltage). The other important component in the PSU is the fan, which dissipates the heat generated. Better quality models feature low noise fans.

PSU FORM FACTORS

The power supply's size and shape (or form factor) determines its compatibility with the system case, in terms of available room plus screw and fan locations. The form factor also determines compatibility with the motherboard, in terms of power connectors.

- Most PSUs are based on the ATX form factor. An ATX PSU should be 150 mm wide by 86 mm high by 140 mm deep. The "server-class" EPS12V specification allows PSUs to be 180 mm or 230 mm deep. These will usually fit ATX cases though obviously they protrude farther into the case so the available space should be measured first.
- For Small Form Factor (SFF) PCs such as those based on the Micro-ATX motherboard form factor, an ATX PSU may fit. If the case is a slimline type, a smaller form factor may be required. Although there is no definition of a Micro-ATX PSU, the standards documentation refers to the following:
  - SFX12V—100 mm wide by 50 mm high by 125 mm deep with a 40 mm fan or 63.5 mm high with a 60 mm fan. There is an option to use a top-mounted 80 mm fan, making the unit 80 mm high.
  - TFX12V (Thin Form Factor)—this is narrower and longer compared to the "boxy" ATX and SFX formats. It measures 85 mm wide by 65 mm high by 175 mm deep. The part that fits the case slot is 61 mm high but there is a 4 mm bevel to accommodate the top-mounted fan.

- SFF PSUs are rarely rated above 300 W. You can check **formfactors.org** for complete descriptions of the Intel specifications.

INPUT VOLTAGE

A PSU is plugged into an electrical outlet using a suitable power cable. The plug should always be fitted with a working fuse of the correct rating (typically 3 A or 5 A). The plug should suit the outlet type of the country you are in, though "travel plug" converters are commonly available.

A critical point to recognize if you are taking a computer to a different country is to ensure that the PSU is set to the correct **input voltage**. A PSU designed only for use in North America, with an input voltage of 115 V, will not work in the UK, where the voltage is 240 V. Some PSUs are dual voltage and are auto-switching (or auto-sensing); some have a switch to select the correct voltage; others can only accept one type of input voltage (fixed).

The input operating voltages should be clearly marked on the unit and accompanying documentation.

Autoswitching PSU (left) and PSU with manual voltage selector (between the power points).

PSU POWER RATINGS

A PSU must be able to supply adequate power to all the PC's components. The maximum power output (**power rating**) available from a PC power supply is measured in watts, calculated as voltage multiplied by current (V*I). This can be referred to as the power rating or wattage rating.

The PSU found in a standard desktop PC is typically rated at around 200-300 W. This is normally sufficient for a full range of expansion cards and peripherals. Slimline desktop PCs may be fitted with 100-200 W power supplies. Tower systems and servers often have units rated over 300 W; enough to power many more disk drives, tape units, and other storage devices than would be fitted in a desktop PC. Gaming PCs might require 500 W or better power supplies to cope with the high specification CPU and graphics card(s).

> **Note:** *The power requirement of different components varies widely (for example, CPUs can range from 17 W to over 100 W, depending on the model). If you are building or upgrading a system, the simplest way to work out the power requirement is to use an online calculator such as the one found at **outervision.com**.*

OUTPUT VOLTAGES

When specifying a PSU for a system that needs a lot of power, it is also important to look closely at the power distribution of each unit. Power distribution refers to how much power is supplied over each rail. A rail is a wire providing current at a particular voltage.

Output Rail (V)	Maximum Load (A)	Maximum Output (W)
+3.3	20	130
+5	20	130
+12	33	396
-12	0.8	9.6
+5 (standby)	2.5	12.5

The output of +3.3 V and +5 V has a combined limit. No combination of values actually adds up to 450 W, but PSU outputs are self-certified by the manufacturers, so this situation is not uncommon.

For a modern computer, the output rating of the +12 V rail (or rails) is the most important factor, as +12 V is the most heavily used. A PSU with two +12 V rails can be referred to as **dual rail**. Each rail has a safety feature called **Overcurrent Protection (OCP)**, which cuts the circuit if the current exceeds a safe limit. Some PSU vendors prefer single +12 V rail designs while others use multi-rail designs, and it is one factor in determining overall PSU performance and safety. The internal design of the PSU has no effect on the way you make the connections to the motherboard.

Also note that peak output is only achieved under optimum conditions; sustained (or continuous) power output represents "real world" performance.

The power output is not the same as the power the PSU draws from grid power. If a PSU works at around 75% efficiency, a 300 W supply would draw 400 W from the outlet. The extra energy is lost mainly as heat.

> *Note: As power becomes more expensive, power efficiency is an increasingly important criterion to use when selecting a PSU. An ENERGY STAR compliant PSU must be 80% efficient at 20-100% of load (many vendors only display the efficiency obtained under low load). 80 PLUS is a similar rating scheme.*

PSU ADAPTER TYPES

The power adapters supply various combinations of 3.3 V, 5 V, and 12 V positive and negative current. Not all components use power at precisely these voltages. **Voltage regulators** on the motherboard are used to correct the voltage supplied from the PSU to the voltage required by the component.

The ATX PSU standard has gone through several revisions, specifying different adapter types.

- **P1 adapter.** In the original ATX specification, the 20-pin P1 (2x10) adapter (also called the **main connector**) supplies power to the motherboard. Black wires are ground, yellow wires are +12 V, red wires are +5 V, and orange wires are +3.3 V.

    Most systems are now based on the ATX12V version 2 specification. This defines a 24-pin (2x12) P1 adapter to replace the 20-pin one. This is sometimes implemented as 20+4-pin P1 cable for compatibility with older ATX motherboards that have 20-pin adapters.

A 24-pin main motherboard power cable and port. (Image © 123RF.com.)

- **Molex and SATA connectors.** The 4-pin (1x4) **Molex connectors** and 15-pin (1x15) SATA (Serial ATA) connectors supply +12 V and +5 V power for peripheral devices housed within the system case. The number of connectors determines the number and type of devices (such as hard drives and optical drives) that can be supported.

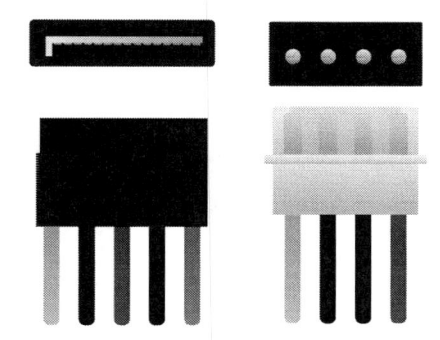

From left to right, SATA and Molex power adapters. (Image © 123RF.com.)

> **Note:** *Modular PSUs have cables that are detachable from the PSU unit, allowing only the connectors actually required to be used. This reduces clutter within the chassis, improving air flow and cooling.*

If there are insufficient adapters, it is possible to obtain splitters (also called y-adapters) so that two devices can be connected to the same cable. You can also obtain conversion adapters (Molex to SATA, for instance).

- **PCIe connectors.** A 6-pin (2x3) connector is used to supply an extra 75 W power (+12 V) to PCIe graphics cards. This was updated to an 8-pin (2x4) connector delivering 150 W in the ATX12V v2.2 specification. Some adapters or dual-card systems will require the use of multiple PCIe auxiliary power connectors.

A PCIe 6-pin power adapter. (Image © 123RF.com.)

P4 and EPS 12V connectors. The ATX12V standard specifies an additional 4-pin (2x2) +12 V connector (often labeled P4) to support the operation of the CPU.

You may also come across 8-pin +12 V connectors. The **Entry-level Power Supply (EPS) specification** was developed initially for server-class hardware. Many of its features were incorporated in ATX12V. EPS12V defines an 8-pin +12 V connector. This is often wired as two 2x2-pin connectors so that an EPS12V PSU can be connected to an ATX motherboard with a 4-pin +12 V port.

An EPS 12V connector. (Image © 123RF.com.)

POWER NEEDS CALCULATION

Calculating the amount of power needed for a PC helps ensure that you have enough power available for all the devices on the PC. The process is fairly simple:

1. List the devices that need to have power served by the PSU. Be sure to include the following:
    - Motherboard
    - CPU
    - RAM
    - Hard drives
    - CD drives
    - DVD drives
    - Floppy drives (if any)
    - Expansion cards

2. Determine the power requirements for each device.
3. Add up the power requirements for the existing total power load.
4. Consider adding a buffer of 20 to 30 percent for future power needs.
5. Examine the details on the PSU currently installed, paying particular attention to the maximum output.
    - If you have not exceeded the power available, you do not need to upgrade the PSU.
    - If you have, you will need to obtain a PSU with a higher output and install it.

*Note: To learn more, check the **Video** tile on the CHOICE Course screen for any videos that supplement the content for this lesson.*

Access the Checklist tile on your CHOICE Course screen for reference information and job aids on How to Install a Power Supply Unit.

Activity 4-4
Discussing Power Supply Installation

SCENARIO
Answer the following questions to check your understanding of the topic.

1. How would you calculate the power used by a component?

2. What causes a fuse to blow—excessive voltage or excessive current?

3. What is the significance of a PSU's power output when you are designing a custom build PC?

4. Are you able to use a standard ATX12V PSU with a Mini-ITX motherboard?

5. You have a power supply with an 8-pin connector on it. What is this for?

6. You are connecting a new PSU. The PSU has a square 4-pin P4 cable but there is no square 4-pin receptacle on the motherboard. Should you leave the cable disconnected?

7. What setting should you check before installing a PSU?

8. Another technician replaced the PSU on a PC. Later the same day the PC's owner contacts you to say that the system has been displaying numerous alerts about high temperature.

   What do you think might be the cause?

Activity 4-5
Calculating Power Requirements and Installing a PSU

BEFORE YOU BEGIN
You will perform this activity at your WORKBENCH PC.

SCENARIO
In the first part of this activity, you will calculate the power required by your workbench PC. As a guide, you can refer to the following table that includes common component types, example specifications, and required wattages.

Component Type	Example Specification	Example Wattage Required
CPU	Intel Core i7-970, 3.2 GHz	130
Memory	4 GB DDR3-1600	8
Video card	NVIDIA GeForce 8800 GTS	220
Motherboard	ASUS P6X58D Premium LGA	36
Hard drive	1 TB SATAII 7200 RPM	6
Optical drive	6x Blu-ray	32
NIC	10/100/1000 Mbps PCI-Express	14
Sound card	SoundBlaster X-Fi Titanium	23
USB wired keyboard	Yes/No	4
USB wired mouse	Yes/No	4
USB flash drive	Yes/No	5
Other external devices	External DVD+R drive	5

1. Examine your PC, and complete the **Specification** column of the following table. If you have different or additional components in your PC, revise the table accordingly.

Component Type	Specification	Wattage Required
CPU		
Memory		
Video card		
Motherboard		
Hard drive		
Optical drive		
NIC		
Sound card		
USB wired keyboard		

Component Type	Specification	Wattage Required
USB wired mouse		
USB flash drive		
Other external devices		

2. If you can, determine the power required by each component, and complete the table. Again, example values have been provided for your reference.

3. Calculate the total wattage required for your PC. Compare this value with the maximum wattage output listed on the power supply. Does this power supply need to be upgraded?

4. Add a buffer of 30 percent to the total wattage required for your PC. Will the existing power supply continue to supply enough power if additional components are added to the system?

5. After calculating the power load for all the components and future needs, you have determined that it exceeds the capacity of the installed power supply. Remove the existing power supply.
   a) Shut down the computer.
   b) Unplug the power cord from the electrical outlet.
   c) On ATX systems, to discharge any remaining electricity stored in the computer's capacitors, toggle the power switch on the computer on and off.
   d) Remove any components necessary in order to access the power supply and its connection to the system board.
   e) Unplug all power connections from devices, marking where each connection went to as you go.
   f) Unplug the power supply from the motherboard.
   g) Unscrew the power supply from the case.
   h) Remove the power supply from the case.

6. Install the replacement power supply.

   Note: If you don't have another power supply, reinstall the power supply you just removed.

   a) Insert the power supply into the case. Align the guides on the base of the supply with the base.
   b) Secure the power supply to the case.
   c) Plug all power connections into the devices.
   d) Plug the power supply into the system board.
   e) Reinstall any components you removed to access the power supply.
   f) Plug the power cord from the power supply to the electrical outlet.

7. Test the power supply.
   a) Turn on the system.
   b) Test all components.

Topic D
Troubleshoot Internal System Components

EXAM OBJECTIVES COVERED
1001-5.2 Given a scenario, troubleshoot problems related to motherboards, RAM, CPUs, and power.

As a CompTIA A+ technician, it is essential for you to be comfortable working with system components, whether you are installing them, configuring them, or trying to figure out how to resolve issues with them. It is only a matter of time before a personal computer's internal system hardware components experience problems, and generally these are problems users themselves cannot fix. As a CompTIA A+ technician, many of the service calls that you respond to will involve troubleshooting system hardware components, and your ability to quickly and effectively diagnose and solve the problems will be essential in maintaining the satisfaction level of the users you support.

BASIC HARDWARE PROBLEMS

When you are troubleshooting suspected problems, look for simple solutions first.
- Find out if anything has changed.
- Eliminate hardware issues as a cause first.
- Try one thing at a time.
- Take care to ensure that a user's data is backed up before proceeding.

There are several externally observable symptoms that may help you to diagnose a hardware problem without having to open the computer chassis.

INDICATOR LIGHTS

Most devices have a status **Light Emitting Diode (LED)** to indicate that the device is switched on and receiving power.

Some devices may have additional status indicators or show other functions. For example, a hard drive LED shows activity; normally this should flicker periodically. If a hard drive LED is solid for extended periods it can indicate a problem, especially if the PC is not doing any obvious processing.

Similarly, network adapters often have LEDs to indicate the connection speed and activity on the network.

ALERTS

Most PC systems now have quite good internal monitoring systems (such as the internal thermometers). When these systems detect problems, they can display an administrative alert, either on the local system or to some sort of network management system. The operating system may also be able to detect some kinds of hardware failure and display an appropriate alert.

OVERHEATING

Excessive heat damages the sensitive circuitry of a computer very easily. If a system feels hot to the touch you should check that the fans are operating and are not clogged by dirt or dust.

> **Note:** *PCs and laptops can get very warm without there being a specific problem.*

As mentioned above, many systems now come with internal temperature sensors that you can check via driver or management software. Use the vendor documentation to confirm that the system is operating within acceptable limits.

Unusual odors, such as a burning smell, or smoke will almost always indicate something (probably the power supply) overheating. The system should be shut down immediately and the problem investigated.

Thermal problems are also likely to cause symptoms such as spontaneous reboots, blue screens, lockups, and so on. These will typically be cyclic—if you turn the system off and allow it to cool, the problem will only reappear once it has been running long enough for heat to build up again.

LOUD NOISES

Devices may also start to fail over time. Drives of most types are most prone to failure, but sensitive chips such as memory and graphics adapters can also develop problems (often caused by some underlying thermal issue).

Loud or unusual noises can often indicate that a device such as a fan or hard drive is failing. Note that these may not be caused by hardware problems alone. For example, a fan that sounds noisy may be spinning too fast because its driver software is not controlling it properly.

You also need to be able to distinguish between "healthy" noises and "unhealthy" ones. For example, a hard disk may make a certain "whirring whine" when first spinning up and a "chattering" noise when data is being written, but clicking, squealing, loud noise, or continual noise can all indicate problems.

> **Note:** *Newer and more expensive models make very little noise. There may also be a setting in system setup to optimize disk performance to reduce noise.*

VISIBLE DAMAGE

If a system has had liquid spilled on it or if fans or the keyboard are clogged by dust or dirt, there may be visible signs of this.

Actual physical damage to a computer system is usually caused to peripherals, ports, and cables. Damage to other components is only really likely if the unit has been in transit somewhere. Inspect a unit closely for damage to the case; even a small crack or dent may indicate a fall or knock that could have caused worse damage to the internal components than is obvious from outside.

If a peripheral device does not work, examine the port and the end of the cable closely for bent, broken, or dirty pins and connectors. Examine the length of the cable for damage.

POWER PROBLEMS

PC components need a constant, stable supply of power to run. If the computer will not start, it is likely to be due to a power problem. If the PC suddenly turns off or restarts, power problems are also likely.

In the normal course of operations, the PSU converts the AC mains supply to DC voltages. DC voltage is used to power the internal drives and motherboard components. The PSU continually draws standby power from the mains (unless the PSU has its own on/off switch and it has been switched off). When the PC is switched on, the PSU starts supplying 12 V power and fans and disks should spin up. The PSU tests its 5 V and 3.3 V supplies, and when it is sure that it is providing a stable supply, it sends a "Power Good" signal to the processor.

The processor then begins to run the Power On Self-Test (POST) program. POST will not run without a CPU. Some motherboards may be able to sound an alert or light a status LED if the CPU is not present or not working.

If none of the LEDs on the front panel of the system case are lit up and you cannot hear the fans or hard drives spinning, the computer is not getting power. This is likely to be a fault in the PSU, incoming mains electricity supply, power cables/connectors, or fuses.

To isolate the cause of no power, try the following tests:

- Check that other equipment in the area is working; there may be a blackout.
- Check that the PSU cabling is connected to the PC and the wall socket correctly and that all switches are in the "on" position.
- Try another power cable—there may be a problem with the plug or fuse. Check that all of the wires are connected to the correct terminals in the plug. Check the fuse resistance with a multimeter.
- Try plugging another piece of "known-good" equipment (such as a lamp) into the wall socket. If it does not work, the wall socket is faulty. Use another socket and get an electrician to investigate the fault.
- Try disconnecting extra devices, such as optical drives. If this solves the problem, the PSU is underpowered and you need to fit one with a higher power rating.

MULTIMETER USE

A **multimeter** can be used to measure voltage, current, and resistance. Voltage readings can be used to determine whether, for example, a power supply unit is functioning correctly. Resistance readings can be used to determine whether a fuse or network cable is functioning correctly.

- To test a fuse, set the multimeter to measure resistance and touch the probes to each end of the fuse. A good fuse should have virtually zero Ohms of resistance; a blown fuse will have virtually infinite resistance.
- Power supply problems can be indicated by otherwise inexplicable system lockups or unprompted reboots.

> *Caution:* PC power supplies are NOT user-serviceable. Do NOT attempt any maintenance beyond the simple tests described. Never remove the cover of a power supply.

- When you measure the voltage for each pin in a connector, be aware that a degree of tolerance is allowed:

Supply Line	Color Code	Tolerance	Minimum Voltage	Maximum Voltage
+5 V	Red	±5%	+4.75 V	+5.25 V
+12 V	Yellow	±5%	+11.4 V	+12.6 V
-12 V	Blue	±10%	-10.8 V	-13.2 V
+3.3 V	Orange	±5%	+3.135 V	+3.465 V
+5 V Standby	Purple	±5%	+4.75 V	+5.25 V

Supply Line	Color Code	Tolerance	Minimum Voltage	Maximum Voltage
PSU On	Green	Higher than +3 V when PC is off; less than 0.9 V when the PC is on.		
Power Good	Gray	Less than 0.9 V when the PC is off; higher than 2.5 V when the PC is on.		
Ground	Black	-	-	-

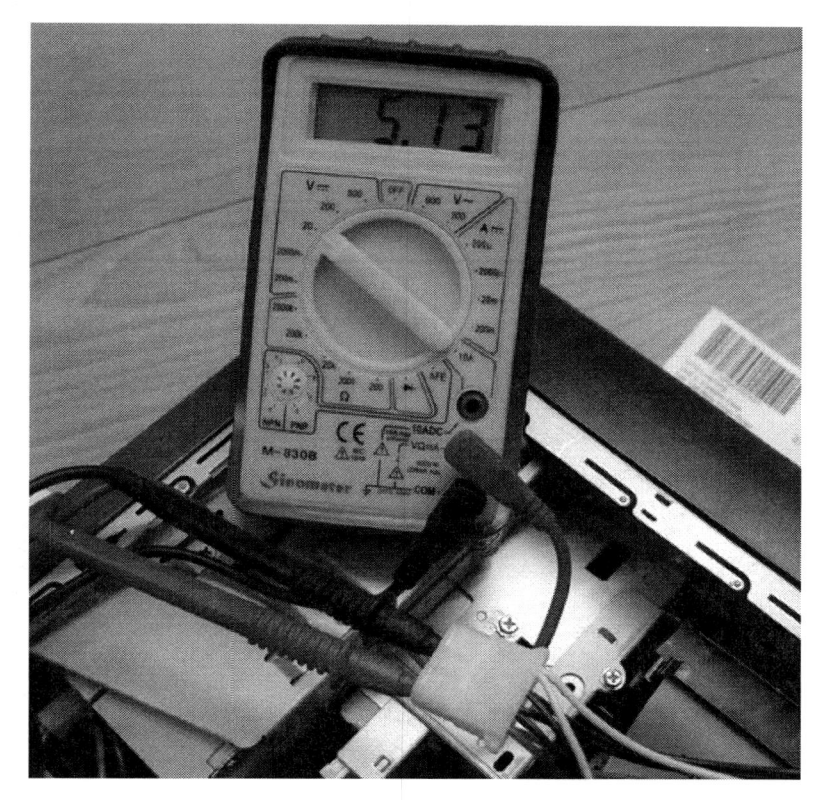

Testing a Molex connector with a multimeter.

If it seems that the PSU voltages are correct and that all power connectors are properly in place, then there may be a fault or overload on one of the peripheral devices (for example, the optical drive or the hard disk). Remove one peripheral device at a time (turn OFF when removing and reconnecting devices) to confirm whether the fault lies with one of these units. If you still cannot identify the fault, then the problem is likely to be a faulty motherboard or adapter card.

If you suspect that a power supply is faulty, do not leave it turned on for longer than absolutely necessary and do not leave it unattended. Keep an eye out for external signs of a problem (for example, smoke or fire). Turn off immediately if there are any unusual sights, smells, or noises.

> **Note:** It is usually easier (and safer) to test the power supply by substitution (install a known good PSU) than to test with a multimeter.

POWER SUPPLY TESTER

A **Power Supply Tester** is a device designed (unsurprisingly) with the sole purpose of testing PSUs. It is much simpler to use than a multimeter as you do not have to test each pin in turn.

Typical models come with ports for the 20/24-pin P1, Molex, SATA, plus 8-pin, 6-pin, and 4-pin connectors found on different models of PSU. Usually each pin on each port has an LED to indicate whether the voltage supplied is good or (in more advanced models) a reading of the voltage supplied.

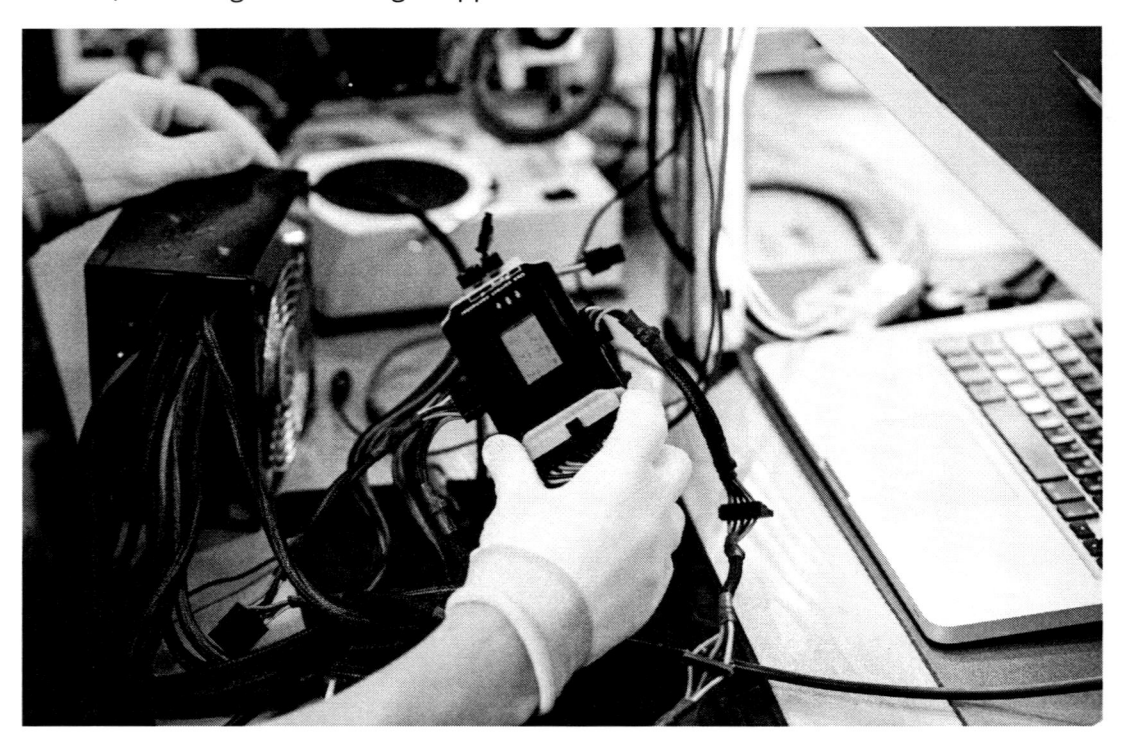

Technician working with a power supply tester. (Image by Konstantin Malkov © 123RF.com.)

POST AND BOOT PROBLEMS

Once the CPU has been given the power good signal, the system firmware performs the **Power On Self Test (POST)**. The POST is a built-in diagnostic program that checks the hardware to ensure the components required to boot the PC are present and functioning correctly. This is the general process for the POST:

1. The POST starts by locating video card firmware at the address C000 in memory. If found, the video card is initialized from its own firmware. Information from the card manufacturer may also be displayed at this point.
2. A startup screen is displayed. More tests on the system, including counting through system RAM, are performed. If any errors are found, a text error message is displayed. Explanations of these messages are usually found in the system guide. Once numeric codes, these messages now tend to be descriptive, such as "key stuck."
3. You should be able to access the system setup routine from this point. This allows you to reconfigure the settings stored in system setup. The key used to invoke system setup varies according to the firmware, but is usually **Delete**, **F2**, **Esc**, **F10**, or **F1**.
4. Some PCs indicate that system checks have been successfully completed at this point with a single short beep, but the trend for modern computers is to boot silently.
5. A search is made for further interfaces that may have firmware chips on them. This could include storage adapters and network cards. Further information about these cards may be displayed at this point and their memory addresses reserved.

6. The firmware may display a summary screen about the system configuration. This may scroll by quite quickly. Use the **Pause** key if you want to analyze it.
7. The operating system load sequence starts.

> **Note:** *On modern computers, the POST happens very quickly to improve boot times so you are unlikely to see any POST messages. A modern POST is unlikely to perform thorough checks such as a memory count.*

POST NOT RUNNING

If power is present (for example, if you can hear the fans spinning) but the computer does not start or the screen is blank and there are no beeps from the speaker, it is likely that the POST procedure is not executing.

If the screen is blank, check that the monitor cable is connected and undamaged and that the monitor is powered on. If the monitor has separate inputs (for example, HDMI and DVI), make sure it is switched to the correct one. If possible, test with another monitor to confirm that there is no problem with the display.

If you can rule out a problem with the display itself, other likely causes are faulty cabling or a damaged or mis-seated CPU or other motherboard component. To troubleshoot, try the following tests and solutions:

- Ask what has changed—if the system firmware has been flashed and the PC has not booted since, the system firmware update may have failed. Use the reset procedure.
- Check cabling and connections, especially if maintenance work has just been performed on the PC. An incorrectly oriented storage adapter cable or a badly seated adapter card can stop the POST from running. Correct any errors, reset adapter cards, and then reboot the PC.
- Check for faulty interfaces and devices—it is possible that a faulty adapter card or device is halting the POST. Try removing one device at a time to see if this solves the problem (or remove all non-essential devices then add them back one-by-one).
- Check the PSU—even though the fans are receiving power, there may be a fault that is preventing the Power Good signal from being sent to the CPU, preventing POST.
- Check for a faulty CPU or system firmware. If possible, replace the CPU chip with a known good one or update the system firmware.
- Some motherboards have jumpers to configure modes (such as firmware recovery) or processor settings. If the jumpers are set incorrectly it could cause the computer not to boot. If a computer will not work after being serviced, check that the jumpers have not been changed.

> **Note:** *Remember to ask "What has changed" when troubleshooting. For example, it is best practice to check that a system works properly after performing any sort of servicing work (such as updating the firmware) but not all technicians are so diligent. If a user complains that their previously working PC will not boot, find out what happened to it in the intervening period.*

POST BEEP CODES

If POST detects a problem, it generates an error message. As the error may prevent the computer from displaying anything on the screen, the error is often indicated by a series of beeps.

For a beep code, you must decode the pattern of beeps and take the appropriate action. Use resources such as the manufacturer's website to determine the meaning of the beep code. Examples of manufacturer websites include **ami.com**, **phoenix.com** (Award), **compaq.com**, and **dell.com**. Websites such as **bioscentral.com** provide a good summary and can be located easily through Internet search engines.

The codes for the original IBM PC are listed in this table.

Code	Meaning
1 short beep	Normal POST—system is OK.
2 short beeps	POST error—error code shown on screen.
No beep	Power supply or motherboard problem (use a multimeter to check the onboard speaker is functioning).
Continuous beep	Power supply, motherboard, or system memory problem.
Repeating short beeps	Power supply, motherboard, or keyboard problem.
1 long, 1 short beep	Motherboard problem.
1 long, 2 or 3 short beeps	Display adapter error.
3 long beeps	3270 keyboard card.

Error messages on the screen are usually descriptive of the problem. In each case, take the appropriate action.

Note: *If the screen is blank on bootup but you hear a single beep, check the monitor is turned on and connected properly. Try testing the monitor with a different computer. If the monitor is OK, try replacing the graphics adapter.*

BIOS TIME AND SETTINGS RESET

While modern computers do not rely on the CMOS battery to store system settings, if the computer is losing the correct time, it can be a sign that the Real Time Clock battery is failing. On older computers, the failure of the battery may lead to system setup settings being lost or corrupted. You may see a "CMOS Checksum" error or similar. To replace the CMOS battery:

1. Obtain a coin cell battery that is compatible with your motherboard.
2. Unclip the existing battery and take it out.
3. Plug in the new battery.
4. Switch the computer back on.

OPERATING SYSTEM SEARCH/BOOTS TO INCORRECT DEVICE

Once the POST tests are complete, the firmware searches the devices as specified in the boot sequence. If the first drive in the sequence is not found, it then moves on to the next. For example, if there is no fixed disk, the boot sequence checks for a USB-attached drive. If no disk-based boot device is found, the system might attempt to boot from the network. If no boot device is found, the system displays an error message and halts the boot process.

If the system attempts to boot to an incorrect device, check that the removable drives do not contain media that are interfering with the boot process and that the boot device order is correctly configured.

OS BOOT TROUBLESHOOTING AND LOG ENTRIES

If a boot device is located, the code from the boot sector on the selected device is loaded into memory and takes over from the system firmware. The boot sector code loads the rest of the operating system files into system memory. Error messages received after this point can usually be attributed to software (or driver) problems rather than issues with hardware devices.

Viewing startup messages on a Linux server.

> **Note:** In Windows 7, you can use the Startup Configuration utility (`msconfig`) to show boot messages (select OS boot information on the Boot tab). In Windows 10, this setting does not work and you need to enable verbose boot messages via the registry.

If no error message is displayed at startup, issues with the operating system can often be diagnosed by checking for log entries.

- In Windows, boot messages are written to the C:\Windows\ntbtlog.txt file. You should also use Event Viewer to analyze the **System** and **Application** logs for any errors.
- In Linux, you can review the boot messages using the `dmesg | less` command.

MOTHERBOARD COMPONENT PROBLEMS

Few problems are actually caused by the motherboard itself, but there are a few things to be aware of.

- The motherboard does contain soldered chips and components, which could be damaged by Electrostatic Discharge (ESD), electrical spikes, or overheating.
- The pins on integrated connectors can also be damaged by careless insertion of plugs.
- In some cases, errors may be caused by dirt (clean the contacts on connectors) or **chip creep**, where an adapter works loose from its socket over time, perhaps because of temperature changes.

> **Note:** Remember to ask "What has changed?" Check job logs to find out whether any maintenance or upgrades were carried out recently.

- **Unstable operation.** Symptoms of intermittent device failure such as the system locking up, unexpected shutdown, displaying a Blue Screen of Death (BSoD) crash screen, or continuous rebooting are difficult to diagnose with a specific cause, especially if you are not able to witness the events directly. The most likely causes are software, disk problems, or malware.

    > **Note:** A blue screen is a system crash screen proprietary to Windows. A macOS system that suffers catastrophic process failure shows a spinning pinwheel (of death), also called a spinning wait cursor.

    If you can discount these, try to establish whether the problem is truly intermittent or whether there is a pattern to the errors. If they occur when the PC has been running for some time, it could be a thermal problem.

    Next, check that the power supply is providing good, stable voltages to the system. If you can discount the power supply, you must start to suspect a problem with memory, CPU, or motherboard.

- **Visual inspection.** Inspect the motherboard for any sign of damage. If a component has "blown" it can leave scorch marks. You could also look for **distended capacitors**. The capacitors are barrel-like components that regulate the flow of electricity to the system chips. If they are swollen or bulging or emitting any kind of residue they could have been damaged or could have failed due to a manufacturing defect.

    If there is physical damage to the motherboard you will almost certainly need diagnostic software to run tests to confirm whether there is a problem. Testing by substituting "known good" components would be too time consuming and expensive. The most likely causes of physical damage are heat, ESD, or a power surge or spike. It is worth investigating any environmental problems or maintenance procedures that could be the "root cause" of the error.

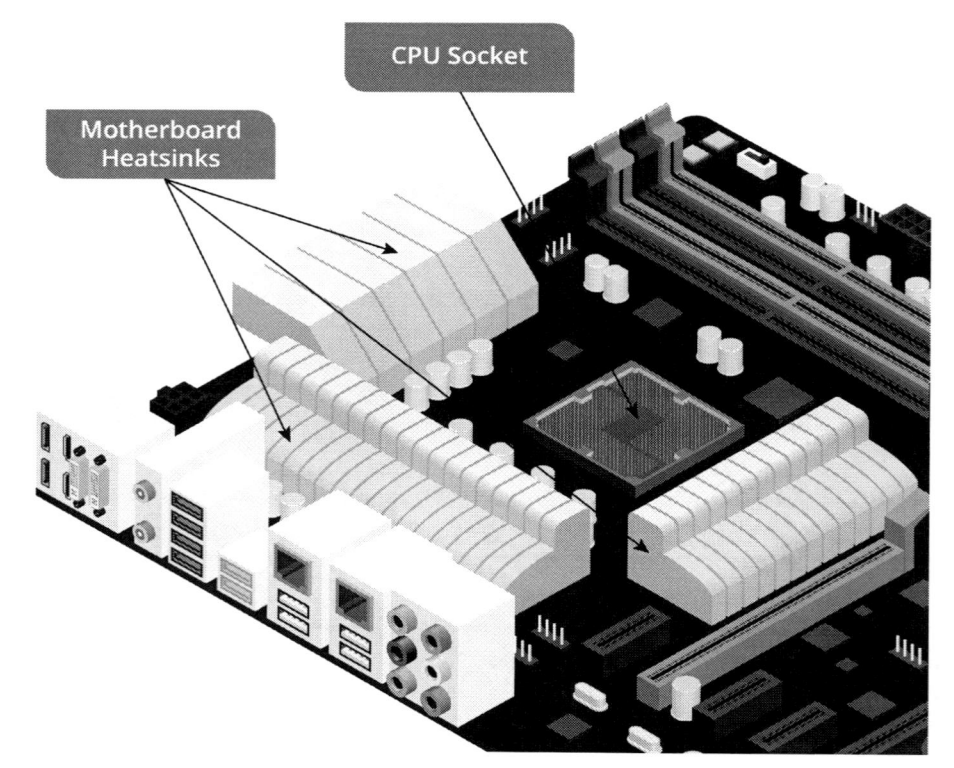

    Motherboard CPU socket and heatsinks surrounded by healthy capacitors. (Image © 123RF.com.)

- **Overheating.** Insufficient cooling is the main cause of processor, memory, and motherboard problems. Thermal faults are normally cyclic: a system works for some time, crashes, and then works again later because powering down allows the processor to cool. To check for overheating issues:

- Ensure that the CPU fan is working. Proper cooling is vital to the lifespan and performance of the processor. If the processor is running too hot, it can decrease performance. A processor that is overheating can cause crashes or reboot the machine.

  Is the fan's power cable properly connected? Is the fan jammed, clogged, or too small? If a processor upgrade is installed, the fan from the original CPU may not be suitable for the new device.

  > **Note:** *Pro-actively optimize the existing cooling system by clearing dust from chips, heat sinks, and fans. Also verify that there is sufficient space around the PC's vents to allow for adequate air flow. If the PC is positioned too closely to a wall, it might prevent effective cooling.*

- Make sure the heatsink is properly fitted. It should be snug against the processor. Heatsinks are usually "stuck" to the processor using a special heat conductive paste. Some manufacturers use lower quality paste. In these cases, it is possible to clean away the old paste and replace it with better paste, which will help the processor to run at a lower temperature.
- Always use blanking plates to cover up holes in the back or front of the PC. Holes can disrupt the airflow and decrease the effectiveness of the cooling systems.
- Speed—is the processor running at the correct speed? Running a processor at a higher clock speed can cause overheating. Double-check the voltage and timing settings in CMOS Setup.
- Environment—is the room unusually warm or dusty or is the PC positioned near a radiator or in direct sunlight?

Thermal problems may also affect system operation by causing loose connectors to drift apart, components to move in their sockets, or circuit board defects such as hairline cracks to widen and break connections. Some of these faults can be detected by visual inspection.

> **Note:** *CPUs and other system components heat up while running. Take care not to burn yourself when handling internal components.*

Activity 4-6
Discussing System Component Troubleshooting

SCENARIO
Answer the following questions to check your understanding of the topic.

1. What cause might you suspect if a PC experiences intermittent lockups?

2. How might you diagnose a thermal problem?

3. What measurement would you expect from a multimeter if a fuse is good?

4. What might stop a POST from executing?

Activity 4-7
Diagnosing Power Problems

BEFORE YOU BEGIN
Your instructor will provide you with a multimeter or power supply tester to use to test the output voltages from the PSU. This involves working with a live system. Follow the instructions carefully and do not touch parts of the computer when it is switched on.

You will perform this activity at your WORKBENCH PC.

SCENARIO
You have been assigned several power problems to solve.

---

1. **Problem #1** When the user turns on the PC, it does not always come on and sometimes it just shuts itself down abruptly, with no warning. When she turns on the system again, there is no fan noise. She is using a legacy database application and the data is being corrupted during the improper shutdowns.

    What would you do to resolve this problem?

2. **Problem #2** A user is reporting an odor coming out of his computer. You have serviced this machine recently and replaced the computer's power supply unit.

    What would you do to resolve this problem?

3. **Problem #3** One of the other hardware technicians has been trying to troubleshoot a power problem. The system will not come on when the user turns on the power switch. He determined that the user has an ATX motherboard and power supply. You have been assigned to take over this trouble ticket.
    a) You will be using a multimeter to measure 5 and 12 Volts DC. Set your multimeter accordingly and attach its probes if required.
    b) Remove the PC from the electrical supply, then remove the case cover.

c) Find a spare Molex connector, or remove a Molex connector from a optical drive or hard disk drive.
d) Insert the black (REF) probe into a black cable connector and the other probe into the yellow cable connector in the Molex.
e) Turn on your multimeter.
f) Reconnect the power cord to your PC and to building power, and turn it on.
g) Take a reading and record the results here.

   _____

h) Turn off your PC and repeat the above process for the red cable and write the result here:

   _____

i) Are these recordings acceptable?

4. **Problem #4** The user turns on the power switch, but the PC does not come on. He does not hear the fan, there is no power light on, and he hears no beeps or other sounds coming from the system. His system is plugged into a surge protector.

   What would you do to resolve this problem?

5. You also need to perform some routine testing of safety equipment. Using your multimeter, measure the resistance of your ESD kit's wrist strap cable, connecting the crocodile clip to the black probe and touching the red probe to the metal plate that makes contact with your skin.

   Why is it so high?

6. Using your multimeter, measure the resistance of a fuse—your instructor will provide you with these.

   What does it mean if the reading is zero or over range?

Activity 4-8
Diagnosing System Errors

BEFORE YOU BEGIN
You will perform this activity at your WORKBENCH PC.

SCENARIO
You are attempting to resolve problems for a user who has been reporting intermittent but severe system errors, such as frequent unexpected shutdowns. The problems have been getting more frequent, and you have been unable to pinpoint a cause within the system software, power supply, memory, or any adapter cards. You are starting to suspect that there is a bad CPU, and you need to proceed accordingly to get the user back to work with as little downtime and cost as possible.

1. **What initial steps should you take to identify and resolve a potential CPU problem?**

    ☐ Replace the CPU with a known-good processor.

    ☐ Verify that the CPU fan and other cooling systems are installed and functional.

    ☐ Replace the motherboard.

    ☐ If the CPU is overclocked, throttle it down to the manufacturer-rated clock speed.

2. **All other diagnostic and corrective steps have failed. You need to verify that it is the CPU itself that is defective. What should you do?**

    ○ Replace the CPU with a known-good chip.

    ○ Remove all the adapter cards.

    ○ Reinstall the operating system.

    ○ Replace the motherboard.

3. A colleague suggests that you might want to view the symptoms of some different system errors. For each following components:
    1. Prepare to work inside the computer case.
    2. Remove or alter the component as described in the following steps.
    3. Restore power to the PC.
    4. Examine and record what happens. You can use Notepad or a separate sheet of paper if you like.
    5. Shut down and cut power to the PC.
    6. Reinstall or otherwise restore the component.

4. Remove the system RAM from the motherboard. What happens?

5. Disconnect the hard disk drive from the motherboard. What happens?

6. Rearrange the memory cards by putting them in different slots or removing one of them. What happens?

7. Your instructor will now create a problem on your PC. Use your troubleshooting skills to try and solve it. Record what you found during the troubleshooting process.

Topic E
Configure a Custom PC

EXAM OBJECTIVES COVERED
1001-3.8 Given a scenario, select and configure appropriate components for a custom PC configuration to meet customer specifications or needs.
1001-3.9 Given a scenario, install and configure common devices.

As a CompTIA A+ technician, you must be knowledgeable in many different areas of information technology. This may include supporting a wide variety of client configurations, such as gaming or audio and video workstations. You must be prepared to fully support any type of environment, including more specialized hardware and software configurations based on job roles and tasks.

CLIENT PERSONAL COMPUTERS

When installing and configuring user workstations, it is important to identify what the specific needs are of the user that will be using the workstation to perform job tasks. Standard clients are a good starting point for any installation and must be examined to verify that they fit the requirements of the job function.

Standard business client computers are end-user computers that are administered and managed centrally by a server.

You might be called on to set up or service any of the following client types:

- **Standard (thick) clients.** A **standard client** (sometimes referred to as **thick client** to distinguish it from a thin client) is an ordinary office PC. It will be used to run locally installed desktop applications, such as office productivity (word processor, spreadsheet, and presentation) plus Line of Business software, email/calendaring/contact management, and a web browser.

  When you are configuring a standard client, it is important to pay attention to the *recommended* Windows or Linux system requirements and to the software application requirements. Using the minimum OS requirements is likely to lead to poor performance.

  A standard client might be configured with multiple user accounts. These user accounts might be defined locally on each computer (a workgroup) or on a network directory server (a domain). Windows 10 also supports the use of Microsoft accounts, which use cloud services to synchronize settings and data across each of the Windows-based devices that a user signs in to. Each standard user account is allocated its own private data storage folders. Each account can be configured with different desktop settings and (if applicable) network permissions and privileges.

  If data is stored locally, then access to storage locations is required with a consistent pathway to data. Similarly, if data is stored on a network, then a consistent path should be established to the storage location with proper security implementations.

- **Thin clients.** A **thin client** is a PC or appliance designed to act as an interface to applications that run on a network server. The client may be interfacing with particular software applications or with an entire Windows Desktop. This is referred to as **Virtual Desktop Infrastructure (VDI)**. In this scenario, the only really important performance criteria for the thin client is the network link. The client PC does no application processing. It just transfers mouse and keyboard input to the server and processes video and audio output coming back. The applications do not get installed on the computer and do not use up any hard drive space. RAM is used to run the application from the server.

> **Note:** Virtualization is covered in greater detail later in the course.

The client may be interfacing with particular software applications or with an entire Windows or Linux desktop. The client will have to meet the minimum requirements for installing the selected OS, but that is all. The computer might require specialized software in order to access the applications hosted by the server. The computer may also require a specific browser or browser version in order to run any web-based applications.

> **Note:** Microsoft has a Thin Client version of Windows 7 but its minimum spec is actually the same as any other Windows 7 edition. It's worth noting that Microsoft stopped distinguishing between "minimum" and "recommended" system requirements.

When the thin client starts, it boots a minimal OS, allowing the user to log on to a **Virtual Machine (VM)** stored on the company server infrastructure. The user makes a connection to the VM using some sort of remote desktop protocol (Microsoft Remote Desktop or Citrix ICA, for instance). The thin client has to find the correct image and use an appropriate authentication mechanism. There may be a 1:1 mapping based on machine name or IP address or the process of finding an image may be handled by a connection broker. Consequently, to configure a thin client you need only install the thin client OS and configure the connection manager/broker. User accounts are created on the server rather than directly on the thin client itself.

BUSINESS WORKSTATIONS

The term **workstation** is sometimes used to describe a computer that runs more demanding applications than standard office suites. These systems typically have faster processors, more memory, and faster and larger drives than standard desktop systems.

Most computers deployed for business use will fit one of the following profiles.

- **Programming, development, and virtualization workstations.** A workstation used to develop software or games will run one or more **Integrated Development Environments (IDEs)**. It may also run a local database server application for testing. Consequently, these workstations require fast CPUs and mass storage access, plus plenty of system memory.

  Development work is also likely to require virtualization, so that the developer has access to multiple operating system environments for testing. Virtualization requires a lot of system memory. Each guest OS would typically need at least 1—2 GB even for average performance. It also benefits from multiple CPU cores and multi-channel memory as well as a large, fast disk subsystem.

- **Graphics and CAD/CAM design workstations.** Media design workstations are configured to support the needs of graphic designers, engineers, architects, 3D media developers, and other design-driven job roles. A workstation used for different types of design will have to support applications with high CPU, GPU, and memory requirements. Such workstations also need a fast storage subsystem and are typically provisioned with Solid State Drives (SSDs), rather than older hard disks.

  Typical design applications include:
  - Image editing and illustration tools.

- **Desktop Publishing (DTP)** and web design.
- **Computer Aided Design (CAD)**.
- **Computer Aided Manufacturing (CAM)**.

> **Note:** CAM workstations can control machine tools found in manufacturing environments. Specialized controller cards may be required as well as specialized connections and software. CAM machines may be installed in harsh environments —such as manufacturing buildings and automotive factories—so the workstations may need to be hardened machines that will not be adversely affected by their working environments.

Design work will also often require specialist peripherals, such as a digitizer and styluses. Vendors often produce graphics adapters specially designed for use with CAD software.

- **Audio/Video editing workstations.** A workstation used to edit Audio/Video (A/V) files, create animations, or produce music will have high performance requirements. These computers must be able to support the demanding editing programs that audio/video technicians use in post-production editing functions. Most professional videos taken today include special effects and CGI (computer generated imagery) that is all applied after the digital video is taken.

Again, it is important not to overlook the disk subsystem, which can become a performance bottleneck as media files will often have to be streamed from the disk. Workstations will generally need 10 K or 15 K disks to perform well. Multimedia files are also extremely large, so the disk subsystem will have to be very high capacity. This means that the best performing Solid State Drive (SSD) storage may not be affordable at the capacities required.

These workstations require specialized adapters to capture audio and video from a variety of sources.

- An input/output (I/O) card allows audio/video input to be sampled and saved as a digital file. As with a consumer-level video capture card, an I/O card can use an HDMI or Thunderbolt connection to a recording device, but Serial Data Interface (SDI) over 75 ohm coax cabling is a more likely option for broadcast-quality equipment.
- For music recording and production, professional-level sound cards, referred to as audio interfaces, feature numerous inputs, including ¼" phone plugs to connect microphone and amplifier equipment, S/PDIF ports, and 5-pin DIN ports for MIDI equipment. Audio interfaces are usually provisioned as external units, connected to the PC over USB or Thunderbolt, to avoid the problem of electrical interference from PC components when making recordings.

OTHER REQUIREMENTS

You will also find other equipment might be required, such as:

- **Dual monitors.** With all types of workstation, screen "real estate" is often at a premium. This means that they are often provisioned with two or more monitors.
- **RAID.** As they are used to process critical data, where losing even an hour's work might represent a huge loss to the business, most workstations will be configured with a RAID disk system, to provide insurance against disk failure.

COMPUTERS FOR HOME USE

When not used solely for school homework, web browsing, and email, home computers are often specified as **media centers** or **gaming rigs**. When used for media streaming or gaming, these systems often require fast video, storage, and network connections. A home network might also have network attached storage or servers from which files can be shared.

Most media center or gaming computers deployed for home use will fit one of the following profiles.

- **Home theater PCs, home server PCs, and NAS.**
    - A **home theater PC (HTPC)** can be used in place of consumer appliances such as **personal video recorders (PVR)** to watch and record TV broadcasts and play movies and music, either from local files or from streaming Internet services. The PC will need to be equipped with an appropriate TV tuner card to process the incoming TV signal (broadcast, cable, or satellite) and usually comes with a remote control (and peripherals such as the mouse and keyboard would normally be wireless). The HTPC is usually equipped with specific entertainment software that can be used to manage the music and video files stored on the computer. The PCs are generally located near the TV and other home entertainment devices and have a HTPC form factor, which is aesthetically appealing and designed to look similar to other home entertainment devices. They are also designed to be less noisy than a traditional PC, with more compact quieter cooling methods and the addition of sound dampening foam or padding to limit excessive noise generated by the fan and hard drive.
    - A **home server PC** is either an HTPC with a slightly expanded role or a repurposed desktop or low-end PC server used primarily for file storage, media streaming, and printer sharing. Such PCs do not need to be particularly powerful in terms of CPU and memory, but they will need a good network link. Most would also be configured with RAID storage to reduce the risk of losing valuable movie and audio files, even though there should be a backup system in place to protect against theft, fire, or accidental deletion.
    - There are also purpose-built devices to fill a home server role. A **Network Attached Storage (NAS)** appliance is a hard drive (or RAID array) with a cut-down server board, usually running some form of Linux, that provides network access, various file sharing protocols, and a web management interface. The appliance is accessed over the network, either using a wired Ethernet port or Wi-Fi. In a SOHO network you would plug the NAS device into an Ethernet port on the Internet router.

        Note: Most network adapters (or Network Interface Cards [NIC]) in machines from the last few years will be Gigabit Ethernet capable. It may be worth upgrading the adapter on an older machine but you need to bear in mind that many of the SOHO Internet router appliances come with Fast Ethernet switch ports (100 Mbps) rather than Gigabit ones. It will usually make more sense to install two adapters and bond them. The vast majority of homes will be using Wi-Fi streaming in any case and the most useful upgrade will be to 802.11n or 802.11ac.

As well as sharing the disk resource, a NAS box will usually be able to share a printer. It will also be able to make files available over the Internet, using HTTP or FTP. Care needs to be taken to secure the device and the router/firewall properly if this is the case.

Some NAS devices and home server PCs can stream media files to wireless speakers or an IP-enabled TV (or various other types of media player). A streaming media server will have higher demand for CPU, memory, and bandwidth than an ordinary file server.

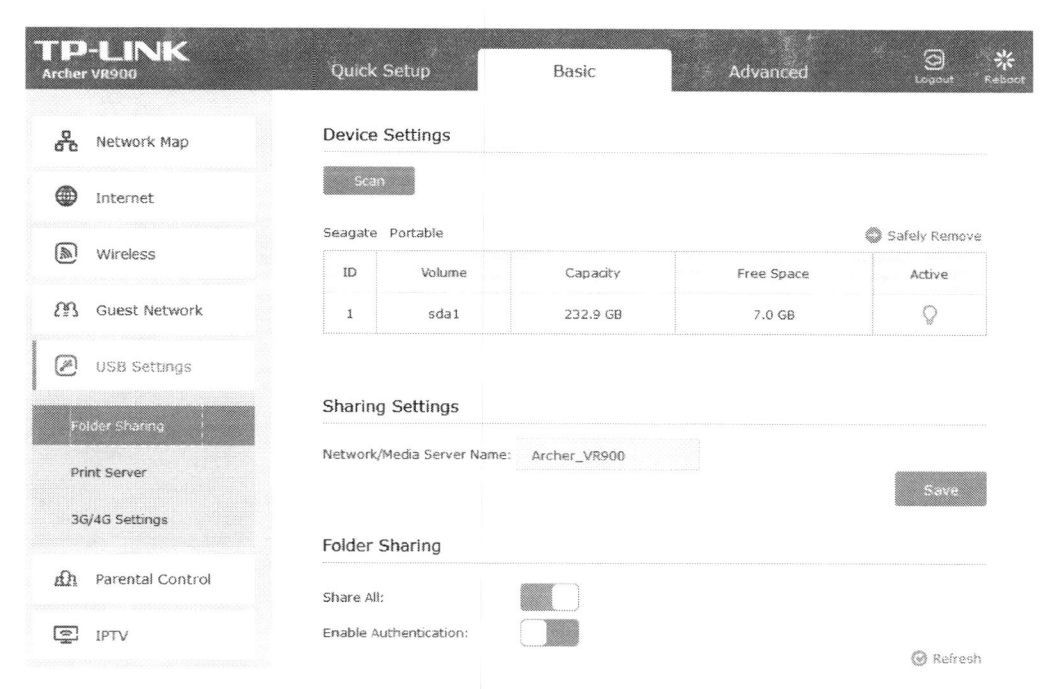

Most SOHO Internet router appliances can perform a basic file and printer sharing function, using USB-attached storage. (Screenshot courtesy of TP-Link.)

- **Gaming PCs.**
  - A PC built for gaming is almost always based around the latest graphics adapter technology. Of course, the latest games tend to be able to make the latest graphics technology obsolete within a few months of release, so upgrade potential is a key characteristic of these systems. PC games feature lots of media assets that must be loaded from permanent storage so a fast drive technology such as a Solid State Drive (SSD) is preferable to slower hard disks (HDD).

    Gaming PCs will share some of the traits of a home theater PC: surround sound audio and a high quality display. There are also gaming-oriented peripherals, such as keyboards and mice. Many games also benefit from headsets, so that players can bark instructions at one another as they eliminate enemies over the Internet. Low-latency, high bandwidth Internet access is almost as important to the average gamer as the frame rate the system's GPU can achieve.

    The addictive nature of PC games means that the processors are very highly utilized, or **thrashed** for considerable periods of time. Some gamers are also fond of overclocking components to obtain better performance. All this means that a gaming PC will generate more heat than most other types of computer. It is not unusual for them to use more powerful fans (which must run silently of course) or liquid cooling.
- There are many different peripherals used within the gaming world. The most common ones include the mouse and keyboard, but there are others that may be used depending on the type of game played. These might include:
  - Gaming mice that are either wired or wireless and include many buttons and different ergonomic form factors.
  - Customized keypads, with moveable keys.
  - Steering wheels used for auto racing games.
  - 3D glasses.
  - Specialized gaming mouse pads.
  - Specialized audio system.
  - PC video camera.

GUIDELINES FOR SELECTING COMPONENTS FOR A CUSTOM PERSONAL COMPUTER

*Note: All of the Guidelines for this lesson are available as checklists from the **Checklist** tile on the CHOICE Course screen.*

Here are some guidelines to consider when selecting components for custom personal computers.

SELECT COMPONENTS FOR A CUSTOM COMPUTER
Follow these guidelines when selecting components for a custom computer:
- Verify that the computer meets or exceeds the operating system and application requirements. This should include the fastest and most reliable:
    - RAM
    - CPU
    - Storage subsystem
    - Video subsystem, including a fast refresh rate on the monitor
- Verify you know what the main intention of the computer will be for. It might be for CAD/CAM, A/V editing, watching TV and movies, or gaming. While each of these types of custom computers require better performance than the average PC, each will likely have specific requirements that should be verified with the end user.
- Consider installing additional cooling mechanisms to keep the system from overheating.
- Verify that the network card, the router, and the network cabling or Wi-Fi signal are all capable of the highest possible speed.
- Consider purchasing specialized devices for the work that will be performed on the custom computer. This might include specialized keyboards, mice, or other adapters to connect specific devices such as MIDI instruments, video cameras, or manufacturing machines, to name just a few.
- Implement a RAID system to help ensure data is not lost. This should be in addition to performing regular backups that are securely stored off site.

*Note: To learn more, check the **Video** tile on the CHOICE Course screen for any videos that supplement the content for this lesson.*

Access the Checklist tile on your CHOICE Course screen for reference information and job aids on How to Configure Thick and Thin Client Personal Computers.

Activity 4-9
Discussing Custom PC Configuration

SCENARIO
Answer the following questions to check your understanding of the topic.

1. **Which component is likely to be a performance bottleneck on a workstation used to edit digital movies?**

2. **For what type of workstation is a CPU with 4 or more cores particularly well suited?**

3. **You are specifying a PC to act as a home theater. What multimedia outputs should it support?**

4. **Which factors are most likely to make a PC used for gaming require high-end cooling?**

5. **On a thin client, which component is more important: NIC or HDD?**

6. **Why might high-spec components (CPU, memory, RAID) not be a good idea in a home theater PC?**

Activity 4-10
Selecting Components for Custom Workstations

SCENARIO
You have been asked by your manager to evaluate the hardware and software needs for all the clients within the Human Resources (HR) department of your organization. There was a recent reorganization of the department, and some of the job roles and functions have changed. Based on the recent changes, you need to review the job functions and identify what type of client workstation will meet those needs.

1. **A user needs to be able to access the central employee data repository to run reports, but does not need access to any local applications used to create, edit, and manage the employee data. The employee data is managed on a server that can be accessed with a log in. What type of client is best in this case?**

    ○ Thin client

    ○ Virtualization workstation

    ○ Thick client

2. **June has recently been put in charge of making updates to the Human Resource employee benefits website. She will be publishing a monthly newsletter and posting company-wide announcements, among other small updates and changes, on a regular basis. All changes to the website must be tested on a number of platforms and web browsers to verify that the changes are correct regardless of the operating system and browser. What type of client setup would you suggest for her?**

3. **In order to properly support the HR employee benefits website, a new server running client VMs has been installed so that the environment that the application requires can be strictly administered by IT staff. Current PCs will be used to access the Client VM environment that is configured on the VM Server. What needs to be present at all PCs that will be accessing this new server and application?**

    ☐ Appropriately configured VM Client.

    ☐ Fast network connection to server hosting the VM environment.

    ☐ Upgrade to video cards.

4. **True or False? The HR manager's client computer must meet the recommended requirements to run Windows 10 so that she can access and use all of the HR-related applications used by the organization. In this case, the best client option is a thick client.**

Activity 4-11
Selecting Components for Custom Personal Computers

SCENARIO
You are a support technician for a local business that specializes in consulting, purchasing, and installing home computing solutions for consumers. You are responsible for fulfilling all the orders that have come in overnight through the business' website.

1. Customer 1 is using a desktop PC to play home movies and to set up slide shows to show his family their vacation photos and is having difficulty with the computer freezing during the movies. He is looking for a solution that will allow him to store and play his movies seamlessly through a computer. He also wants his wife to be able to access the pictures and movies from her laptop within the house.

   What type of computer setup would you suggest for this customer? What specific questions might you ask this customer about additional component needs?

2. Customer 2 is from a small real estate office who has recently hired a graphic designer to produce informational pamphlets and other marketing materials for the agency, such as property drop sheets and circular layout designs. The office manager has asked your company to determine the hardware and software needs for the designer's workstation so that it can be ordered and set up before their scheduled start date in two weeks.

   What hardware and software requirements would you suggest for the graphic designer's workstation?

3. Customer 3 is looking to make the switch from a traditional TV cable box and DVD player to a home theater PC, so that she can stream Netflix and record shows and movies from her TV. She already purchased a computer from a local home entertainment store but cannot figure out why she cannot connect the cable TV wire into the computer.

   What would you check for first?

Summary

In this lesson, you installed, configured, and performed troubleshooting on internal system components such as CPUs, system firmware, and power supplies, You also examined the requirements for configuring custom PCs for specific uses. Your ability and comfort level in performing these types of hardware support will make you a valuable asset to your IT team.

Which system firmware have you worked with, if any? What types of configuration did you perform?

What types of custom client setups do you think you will encounter the most in your role as an A+ technician?

Practice Question: Additional practice questions are available on the CompTIA CHOICE platform within the **Assessments** tile.

Lesson 5
Network Infrastructure Concepts

LESSON INTRODUCTION

In this lesson, you will learn about the technologies underpinning networking infrastructure, such as network cables, wireless standards, switches, routers, and protocols. Having a basic background in networking fundamentals is a vital prerequisite for providing IT support. In today's environment, standalone computing is a rarity. Just about every digital device on the planet today is connected to external resources via some kind of network, whether it is a small office/home office network, a corporate Wide Area Network (WAN), or directly to the Internet itself.

The ability to connect, share, and communicate using a network is crucial for running a business and staying connected to everything in the world, so as a CompTIA® A+® support technician, you will need to understand the technologies that underlie both local and global network communications to ensure that the organization you support stays connected.

LESSON OBJECTIVES

In this lesson, you will:

- Use appropriate tools to select, install, and test network cabling for a given network type.
- Compare and contrast the functions and features of networking hardware devices.
- Compare and contrast wireless networking protocols.
- Compare and contrast Internet connection types.
- Describe the properties and characteristics of Internet Protocol (IP) addressing and network configuration.
- Identify the protocols and ports underpinning Internet applications and local network services.

Topic A
Wired Networks

EXAM OBJECTIVES COVERED
1001-2.2 Compare and contrast common networking hardware devices.
1001-2.7 Compare and contrast Internet connection types, network types, and their features.
1001-2.8 Given a scenario, use appropriate networking tools.
1001-3.1 Explain basic cable types, features, and their purposes.
1001-3.2 Identify common connector types.

In this topic, you will identify types of wired networks. Recognizing network types and suitable cabling options for them will help you determine the best approach for customer needs. In order to properly and safely work with networking components, you must also understand how networking tools are used and how they can be used to fix common issues found in networks.

NETWORK TYPES

A **network** is two or more computer systems linked together by some form of transmission medium that enables them to share information. The network technology is what connects the computers, but the purpose of the network is to provide services or resources to its users. Historically, these services have included access to shared files, folders, and printers plus email and database applications. Modern networks are evolving to provide more diverse services, including web applications, social networking, Voice over IP, multimedia conferencing, and Internet of Things connectivity for household devices and appliances.

To categorize the size and nature of individual networks, the industry has developed terms that broadly define the scope of different types of network.

LOCAL AREA NETWORKS

One basic distinction between types of network is between **Local Area Networks (LANs)** and Wide Area Networks (WANs). A LAN is a self-contained network that spans a small area, such as a single building, floor, or room. In a LAN, all the nodes or hosts participating in the network are directly connected with cables or short-range wireless media. A LAN is typically a single site or possibly several sites in close proximity connected by high-speed backbones. The term **campus area network (CAN)** is sometimes used for a LAN that spans multiple nearby buildings. Any network where the nodes are within about 1 or 2 km (or about 1 mile) of one another can be thought of as "local."

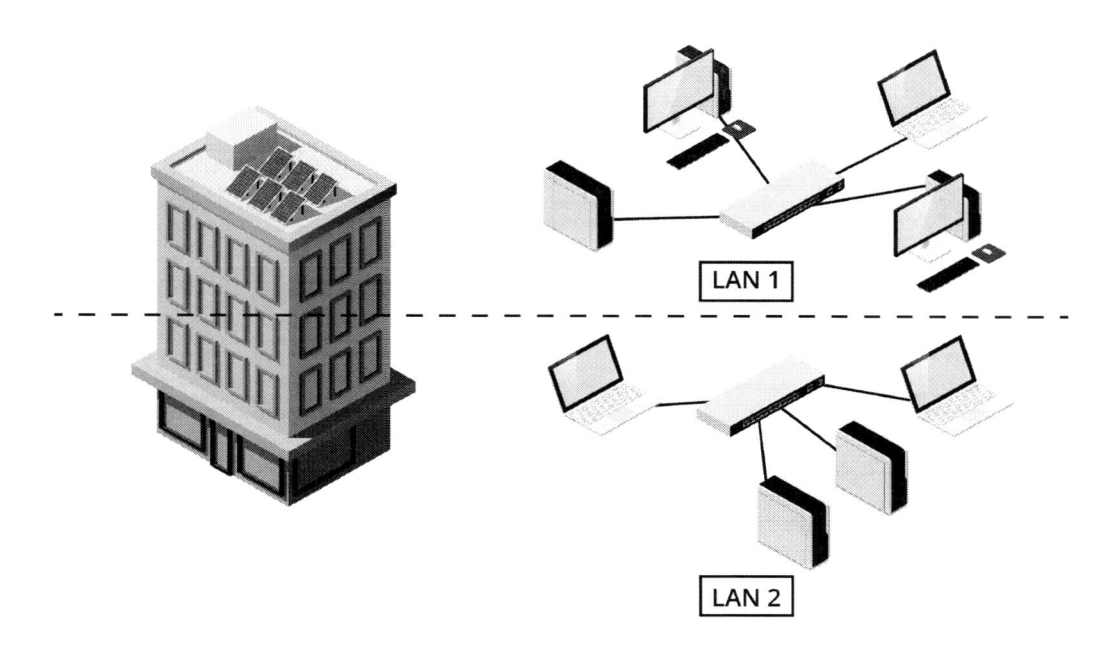

LANs within a building. (Image © 123RF.com.)

WIDE AREA NETWORKS

A **Wide Area Network (WAN)** spans multiple geographic locations. WANs typically connect multiple LANs using long-range transmission media. WANs are usually thought of as relying on some intermediate network, such as the Internet or phone system, to connect geographically diverse LANs. A network where remote users "dial-in" is also a type of WAN.

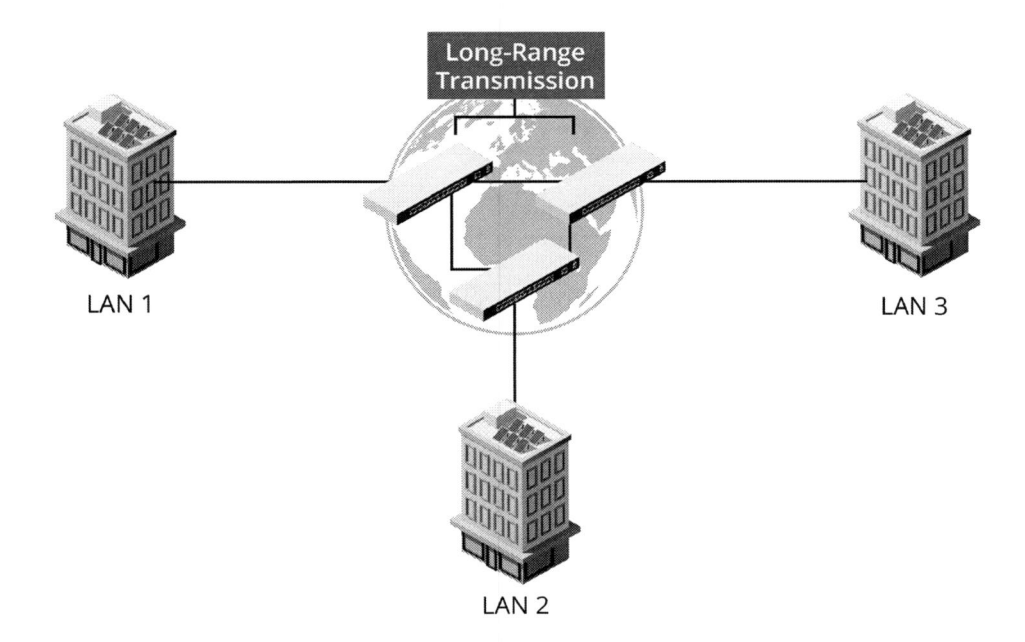

Wide Area Network (WAN). (Image © 123RF.com.)

METROPOLITAN AREA NETWORKS

The term Metropolitan Area Network (MAN) is sometimes used, though it doesn't really have a clear definition other than an area equivalent to a city or other municipality. It could mean a company with multiple connected networks within the same metropolitan area—so, larger than a LAN but smaller than a WAN.

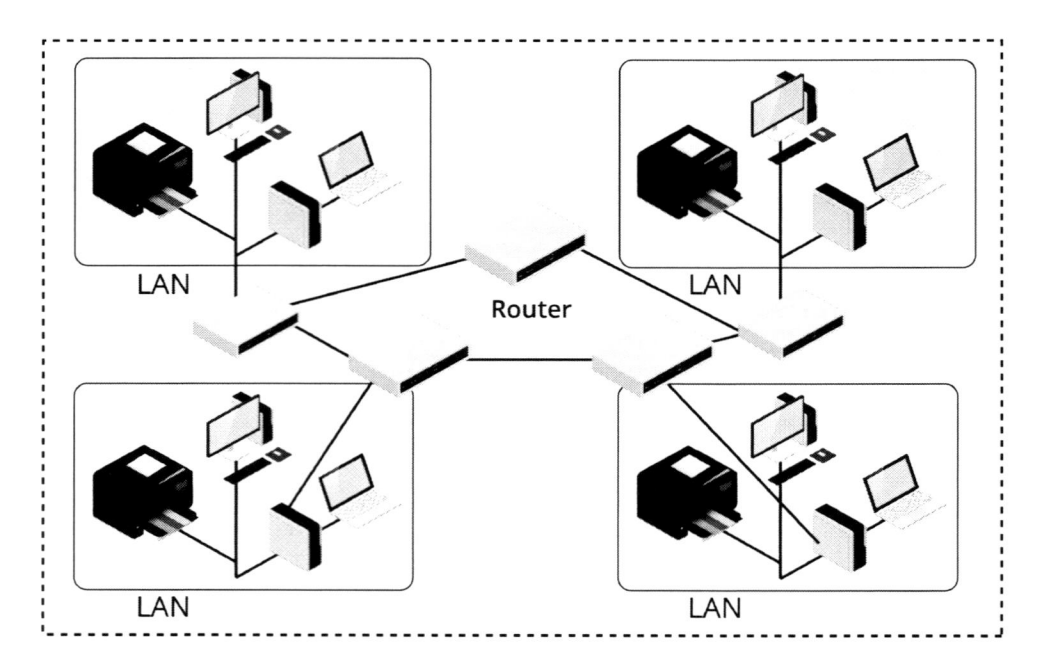

Metropolitan Area Network (MAN). (Image © 123RF.com.)

ETHERNET TYPES AND STANDARDS

Most cabled LANs are based on the **Ethernet** networking product, developed by the DIX consortium (Digital Equipment Corporation [DEC], Intel, and Xerox). Ethernet standards are now maintained by the Institute of Electrical and Electronics Engineers (IEEE). Ethernet is technically known by the series of standards produced by the IEEE 802.3 working group. Although the product name is not used in 802.3 standards documentation, it is otherwise universally referred to as Ethernet.

There are four broad "types" of Ethernet:

- 10 Mbps (10BASE-)—this is the original standard, specifying cabling and connectors for copper wire and fiber optic products.
- Fast Ethernet (100BASE-)—copper wire and fiber optic implementations of 100 Mbps LANs.
- Gigabit Ethernet (1000BASE-)—1000 Mbps LANs. This has replaced Fast Ethernet as the "standard" for a typical LAN.
- 10G Ethernet (10GBASE-)—10 Gbps links for LANs and WANs, mostly using fiber optic media. 10G Ethernet is widely used in data centers.

The **IEEE 802.11** series of standards (Wi-Fi) are used to implement Wireless Local Area Networks (WLAN) so the technologies complement one another and are often used together in the same network.

Ethernet is a very flexible technology. It can support a wide range of different types and sizes of LAN. While a LAN is self-contained, that does not mean that it has to be small. LANs can range from networks with three or four nodes to networks with thousands of nodes. We are going to focus on two particular classes of LAN: SOHO and enterprise.

COMMON ETHERNET NETWORK IMPLEMENTATIONS

Networks can range in size from just a few connected devices in a home environment, to thousands of devices in a large worldwide enterprise.

SOHO NETWORKS

A **SOHO** (Small Office Home Office) LAN is a business-oriented network possibly using a centralized server in addition to client devices and printers, but often using a single Internet appliance to provide connectivity. Home and residential networks may also be classed as SOHO.

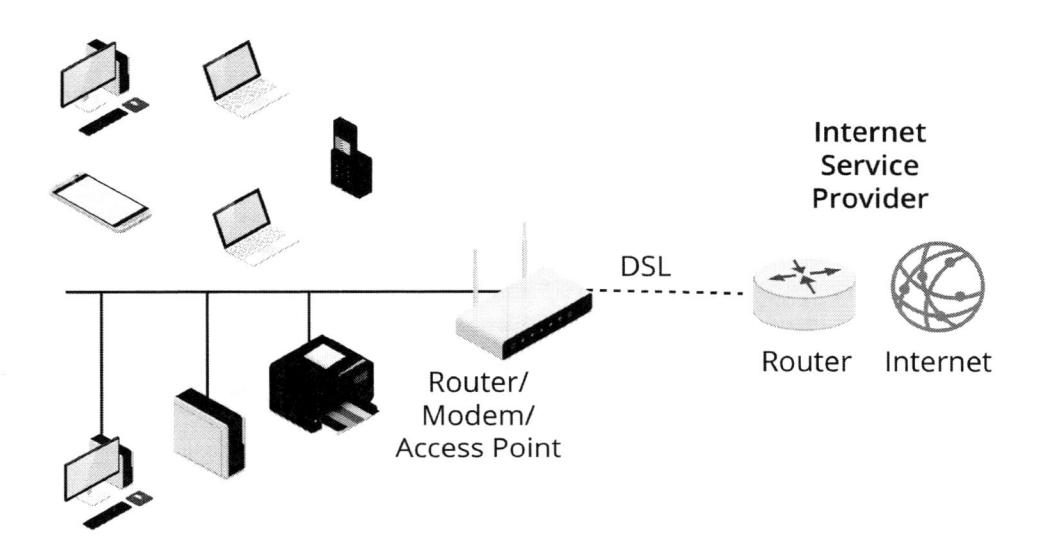

A typical SOHO network layout. (Image © 123RF.com.)

These Internet appliances provide the following functions:

- Access point—allows clients with wireless radio adapters to connect to the network.
- Ethernet switch—connects wired client devices and printers with RJ-45 cables.
- Internet modem—interfaces with the physical link to the ISP's routers (DSL or cable, for instance).
- Internet router—forwards communications to and from the Internet Service Provider (ISP) routers to provide Internet access.

ENTERPRISE NETWORK ARCHITECTURE

Networks supporting larger businesses or academic institutions use the same switch, access point, router, and modem functions as are present in SOHO networks, but because they must support more clients with a greater degree of reliability, each function is performed by a separate network device. You could think of these larger networks as falling into two categories:

- **SME (Small and Medium Sized Enterprise)**—A network supporting tens of users. Such networks would use structured cabling and multiple switches, access points, and routers to provide connectivity.
- **Enterprise LAN**—A larger network with hundreds or thousands of servers and clients. Such networks would require multiple enterprise-class switch, access point, and router appliances to maintain performance levels.

The term Campus Area Network (CAN) is sometimes used for a LAN that spans multiple nearby buildings.

The following graphic illustrates how network appliances might be positioned in an enterprise LAN. Client devices are located in work areas, which are connected to the network by cabling running through wall conduit and patch panel or by wireless access points. Workgroup switches connect these devices to core/distribution switches and routers, which provide access to network servers, printers, and Internet services. Internet services run in protected Demilitarized Zones (DMZ) to provide Internet access for employees, email and communications, remote access via Virtual Private Networks (VPNs), and web services for external clients and customers.

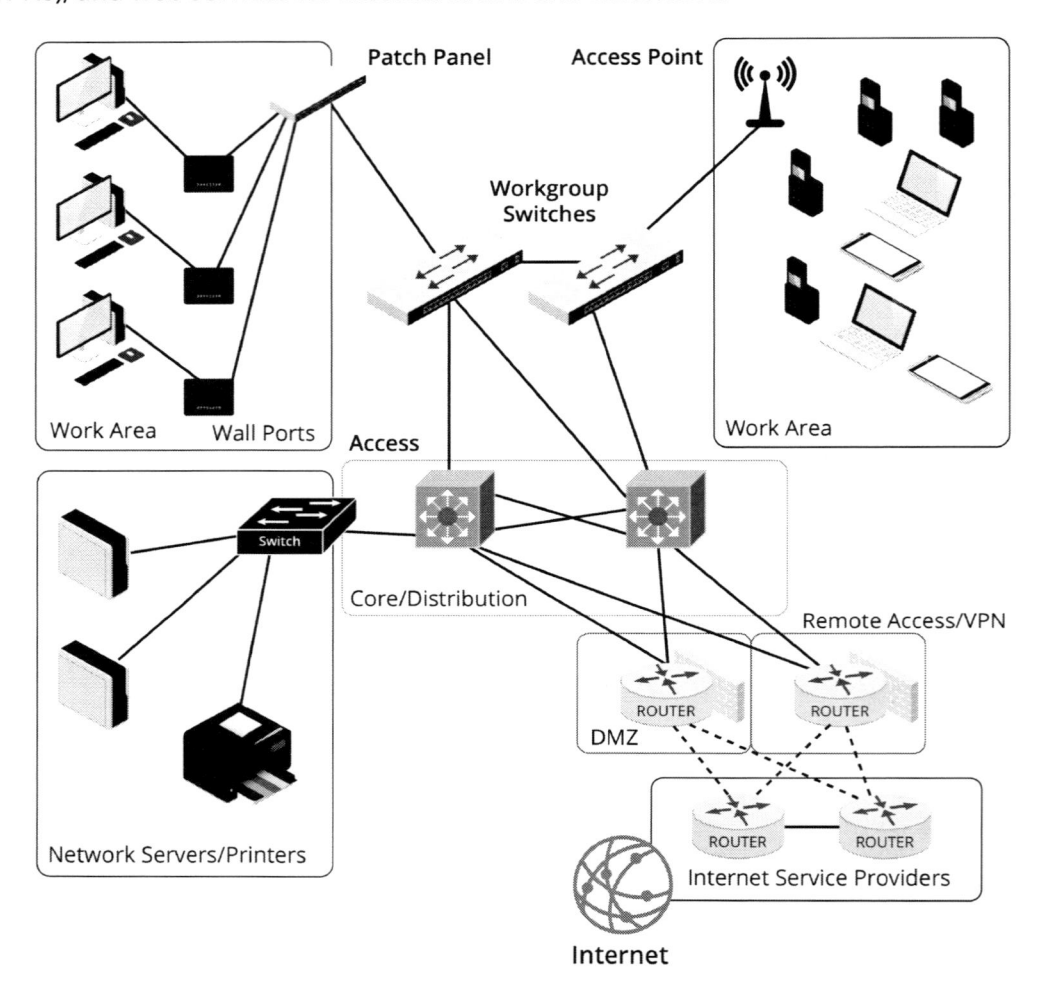

Positioning network components. (Image © 123RF.com.)

TWISTED PAIR CABLING AND CONNECTORS

Most cabled LANs use a type of copper wire called twisted pair as transmission media.

UNSHIELDED TWISTED PAIR (UTP) CABLE

Unshielded Twisted Pair (UTP) is the type of cabling most widely used for computer networking. With the type of UTP used for Ethernet, the cable contains four copper conductor "pairs." Each conductor has an insulating sheath. Each pair of conductors is twisted, which reduces interference between the wires (crosstalk) and interference from other electromagnetic sources, referred to as Electromagnetic Interference (EMI). Each pair is twisted at a different rate to further reduce interference. The signals sent over each pair are balanced. This means that each wire carries an equal but opposite signal to its pair. This is another factor helping to identify the signal more strongly against any source of interference.

The four pairs are covered by a protective outer jacket. The insulation sheaths and jacket are usually made of (PVC).

UTP works well where there are no powerful interference sources, but the electrical signaling method has limited range. The signal is said to suffer from attenuation, meaning that it loses power quickly over long ranges (above 100 m).

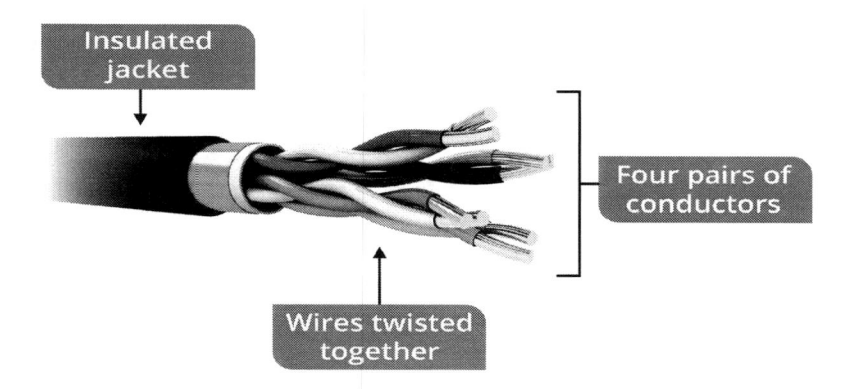

UTP cable. (Image © 123RF.com.)

CAT STANDARDS

The number of twists is one factor in determining the speed and transmission limitations of the cable. Twisted pair cable is rated for different Ethernet applications according to "Cat" specifications, defined in the TIA/EIA-568-C Commercial Building Telecommunications Cabling Standards.

Cat	Frequency	Capacity	Max. Distance	Network Application
5	100 MHz	100 Mbps	100 m (328 ft)	100BASE-TX
5e	100 MHz	1 Gbps	100 m (328 ft)	1000BASE-T
6	250 MHz	1 Gbps	100 m (328 ft)	1000BASE-T
6	250 MHz	10 Gbps	55 m (180 ft)	10GBASE-T
6A	500 MHz	10 Gbps	100 m (328 ft)	10GBASE-T

> **Note:** Vendors sometimes label Cat 6A cable as "Cat 6e" because Cat 5e followed Cat 5. The "A" stands for "augmented."

Cat 5 cable is no longer available. Cat 5e is tested at 100 MHz—as Cat 5 was—but to higher overall specifications for attenuation and crosstalk, meaning that the cable is rated to handle Gigabit Ethernet throughput. Cat 5e would still be an acceptable choice for providing network links for workstations. Cat 6 can support 10 Gbps, but over shorter distances. Cat 6A is an improved specification cable with the ability to support 10 Gbps over 100 m. It is mostly deployed in data centers or as backbone cabling between servers and network appliances.

> **Note:** Cabling is not the only part of the wiring system that must be rated to the appropriate category. For faster network applications (Gigabit Ethernet and better), the performance of connectors becomes increasingly critical. For example, if you are installing Cat 6A wiring, you must also install Cat 6A patch panels, wall plates, and connectors.

SHIELDED TWISTED PAIR (STP)

When twisted pair cabling was first used in networks based on IBM's Token Ring product, it was usually shielded to make it less susceptible to interference and crosstalk. Each pair was surrounded by a braided shield. This cable construction is referred to as **Shielded Twisted Pair (STP)**. STP is bulky and difficult to install, so where a degree of protection from interference is required, modern twisted pair cabling installations use screened cables, meaning a shield positioned around all pairs. There are many different ways of designating different types of shielding. Most Cat 5e/6/6A cable is available in shielded variants, notably F/UTP and U/FTP:

- F/UTP—with a foil screen around all pairs, often also designated ScTP.
- U/FTP—with foil shielding for each pair.

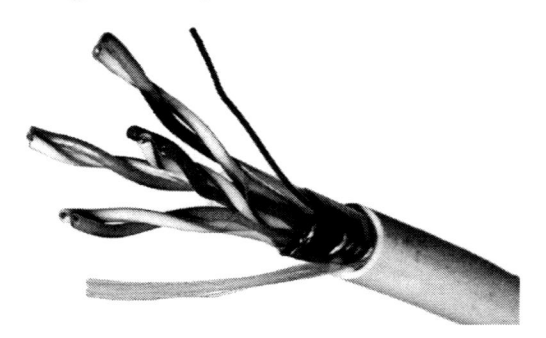

F/UTP cable with a foil screen surrounding unshielded pairs. (Image by Baran Ivo and released to public domain.)

Legacy STP cable could be more complex to install as it required bonding each element to ground manually but modern screened and shielded solutions (using appropriate cable, connectors, jacks, and patch panels) reduce this complexity by incorporating grounding within the design of each element.

PLENUM CABLE

A **plenum** space is a void in a building designed to carry Heating, Ventilation, and Air Conditioning (**HVAC**) systems. Plenum space is typically a false ceiling, though it could also be constructed as a raised floor. As it makes installation simpler, this space has also been used for communications wiring in some building designs. Plenum space is an effective conduit for fire, as there is plenty of airflow and no fire breaks, such as walls and doors. If the plenum space is used for heating, there may also be higher temperatures. Therefore, building regulations require the use of fire-retardant plenum cable in such spaces. **Plenum cable** must not emit large amounts of smoke when burned, be self-extinguishing, and meet other strict fire safety standards.

General purpose (non-plenum) cabling uses PVC (polyvinyl chloride) jackets and insulation. Plenum-rated cable uses treated PVC or Fluorinated Ethylene Polymer (FEP). This can make the cable less flexible but the different materials used have no effect on bandwidth. Data cable rated for plenum use under the US National Electrical Code (NEC) is marked CMP/MMP. General purpose cables are marked CMG/MMG or CM/MP.

WIRING STANDARDS FOR TWISTED PAIR

Twisted pair cabling for Ethernet is terminated using modular **RJ-45** connectors. RJ-45 connectors are also referred to as 8P8C, standing for 8-position/8-contact. Each conductor in 4-pair Ethernet cable is color-coded. Each pair is assigned a color (Blue, Orange, Green, or Brown). The first conductor in each pair has a predominantly white insulator with stripes of the color; the second conductor has an insulator with the solid color.

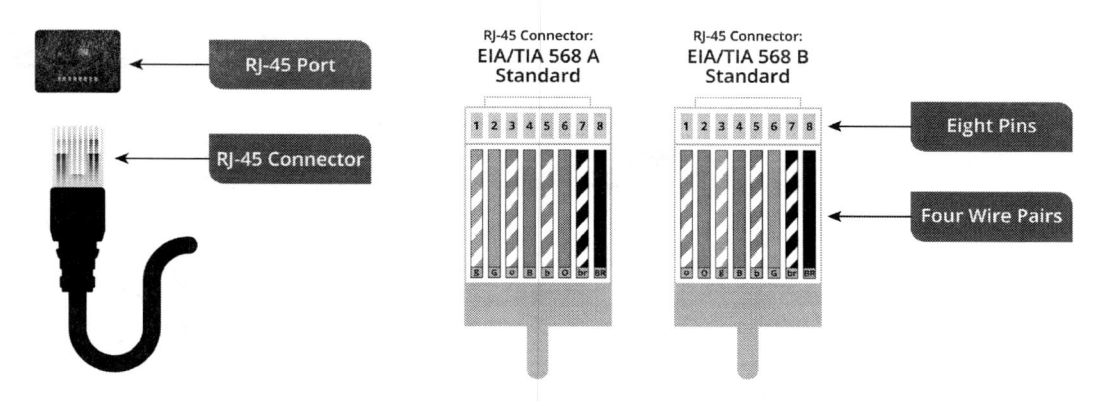

Twisted pair RJ-45 connectors. (Image © 123RF.com.)

The ANSI/TIA/EIA 568 standard defines two methods for terminating RJ-45 connectors: **T568A** and **T568B**. The wiring for T568A is shown in the previous figure. In T568B, pin 1 is wired to Orange/White, pin 2 is wired to Orange, pin 3 is wired to Green/White, and pin 6 is wired to Green or, put another way, the orange and green pairs are swapped over.

A normal—or straight through—Ethernet cable is wired with the same type of termination at both ends. Using T568A at one end and T568B at the other creates a **crossover cable**. Crossover cables were once used to connect computers directly, but Gigabit Ethernet interfaces can perform the crossover automatically, even if standard cable is used.

Organizations should try to avoid using a mixture of the two standards. It is difficult to say whether one is more prevalent than the other. T568A is mandated for US government premises and by the residential cabling standard (TIA 570).

PATCH PANELS AND STRUCTURED CABLING

A Gigabit Ethernet link using twisted pair cabling can be up to 100 m (328 feet) long. This means there must be no more than 100 m of cabling between the switch and the computer. There is also a distinction between solid and stranded cabling.

Solid cabling uses a single thick wire for each conductor. Solid cable is used for "permanent" links, such as cable running through walls. This is often also called **drop cable**, as the installer drops the cable through the wall void to the hole cut out for the port. This cable links the RJ-45 port on a wall plate with a patch panel. Rather than using modular RJ-45 connectors, solid cable terminates in Insulation Displacement Connectors (IDC) at the back of the wall plate and patch panel, as shown here.

The other side of the patch panel has pre-wired RJ-45 ports. A patch cord is used to connect a port on the patch panel to a port on the switch. A patch cord is made using stranded cable, which comprises lots of very thin wires twisted to make a single conductor. This makes the cable much more flexible but less efficient. A patch cord is not supposed to be longer than 5 m.

Patch panel with prewired RJ-45 ports. (Image by Svetlana Kurochkina © 123RF.com.)

A second patch cord is used between the computer's network adapter and the wall port. This use of patch cords, permanent links, and patch panels is referred to as a **structured cabling system**.

> **Note:** It is vital to use an effective labeling system when installing this type of network so that you know which patch panel port is connected to which wall port.

CABLE INSTALLATION AND TESTING TOOLS

You could fill a small van and spend a not-so-small fortune on the various tools available for installing and maintaining data cabling. The range of tools you require will of course depend on the cabling work you do, but the following can be considered typical.

WIRE STRIPPER/CUTTER

Electrician's scissors (snips) are designed for cutting copper wire and stripping insulation and cable jackets. Alternatively, there are dedicated tools or tools that have replaceable blades for different data cable types. Cable cutting blades should be rounded to preserve the wire geometry. Stripping tools should have the correct diameter to score a cable jacket without damaging the insulation around each wire.

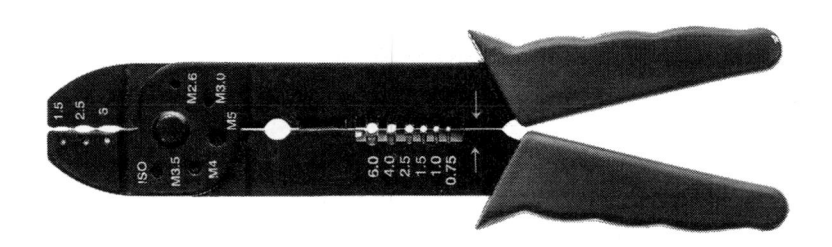

A cable stripper. (Image by gasparij © 123RF.com.)

PUNCH-DOWN TOOL

These tools fix conductors into an IDC. The wire pairs are untwisted and laid in the terminals in the IDC in the appropriate termination order (T568A or T568B). It is important not to untwist the pairs too much, however. The punch-down tool then presses the wire into the terminal, cutting through the insulation to make an electrical contact. There are different IDC formats (66, 110, and Krone) and these require different blades. Many punch-down tools have replaceable blades.

A punch-down tool. (Image by gasparij © 123RF.com.)

CRIMPERS

These tools fix a jack to a cable. As with an IDC, the wires are laid in the appropriate terminals in the jack and the crimper tool then closes and seals the jack. The tools are specific to a particular type of connector and cable, though some may have modular dies to support a range of RJ-type jacks.

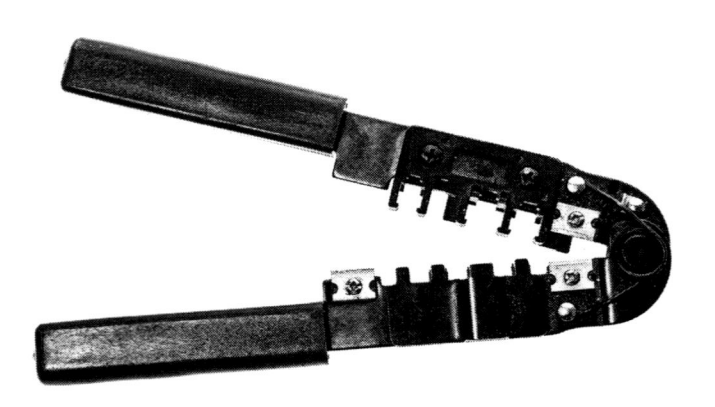

A wire crimper. (Image by gasparij © 123RF.com.)

Note: *It is best to use prefabricated patch cords where possible. These are far less likely to create problems.*

CABLE TESTING TOOLS

The best time to verify wiring installation and termination is just after you have made all the connections. This means you should still have access to the cable runs. Identifying and correcting errors at this point will be much simpler than when you are trying to set up end user devices. When troubleshooting a cabled network link, you may need to consider:

- The patch cord between the PC and the wall port.
- The wall port and the cabling in the wall.
- The port on the patch panel and the patch cord to the switch port.

Test patch cords by substitution with a "known good" one. If the problem is not caused by the patch cord and you can rule out configuration errors, you need to start testing the structured links. There are a number of network cabling and infrastructure troubleshooting devices to assist with this process.

A **multimeter** can be used as a basic cable testing tool. The primary purpose of a multimeter is for testing electrical circuits, but you can use one to test for the continuity of any sort of copper wire, the existence of a short, and the integrity of a terminator. To perform useful tests, you need to know the readings that are expected from a particular test. For example, if the resistance measured across UTP Ethernet cable is found to be 100 ohms, then the cable is OK, but if the resistance between the two ends of a cable is infinity, then the cable has a break. Many multimeters designed for ICT use incorporate the function of a wire map tester. These are also available as dedicated devices. Wire map testers can identify wiring problems that a simple continuity test will not detect, such as transpositions and reversed pairs.

Multimeter. (Image by Norasit Kaewsai © 123RF.com.)

More advanced cable testers provide detailed information on the physical and electrical properties of the cable. For example, they test and report on cable conditions, crosstalk, attenuation, noise, resistance, and other characteristics of a cable run. Devices classed as certifiers can be used to test and certify cable installations to a particular performance category (for example, that a network is TIA/EIA 568-C Category 6 compliant). They use defined transport performance specifications to ensure an installation exceeds the required performance characteristics for parameters such as attenuation and crosstalk.

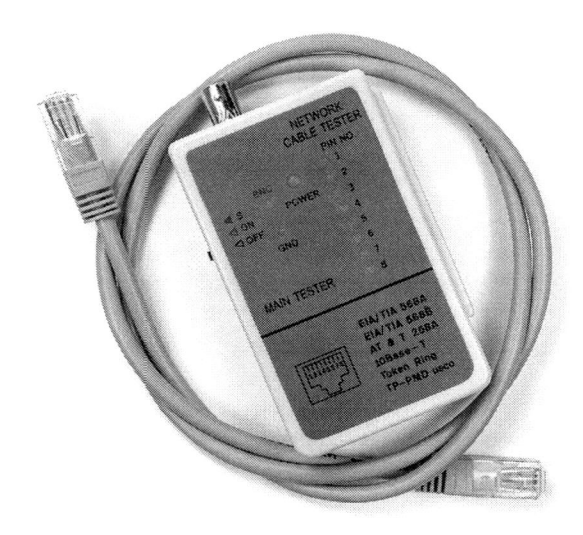

A cable tester. (Image by Vladimir Zhupanenko © 123RF.com.)

TONE GENERATOR AND PROBE

A **tone generator and probe** tool is used to trace a cable from one end to the other. This may be necessary when the cables are bundled and have not been labeled properly. This device is also known as a "Fox and Hound" or "toner and probe." The tone generator is used to apply a signal on the cable. The probe is used to detect the signal and follow the cable over ceilings and through ducts or identify it from within the rest of the bundle.

To locate a cable in a group of cables, connect the tone generator to the copper ends of the wires, then move the tone locator over the group of cables. A soft beeping tone indicates that you are close to the correct wire set; when the beeping is loudest, you have found the cable.

> **Note:** Do not connect a tone generator to a cable that is connected to a NIC. The signal sent by the tone generator can destroy network equipment.

LOOPBACK PLUGS

A **loopback plug** is used to test a port. It involves connecting pin 1 to pin 3 and pin 2 to pin 6. You can do this either by rewiring the jack or twisting the relevant pairs together on a cable stub. Alternatively, you can purchase a prefabricated loopback plug. When you connect a loopback plug to a port, you should see a solid connection LED. You can also use the plug in conjunction with diagnostic software.

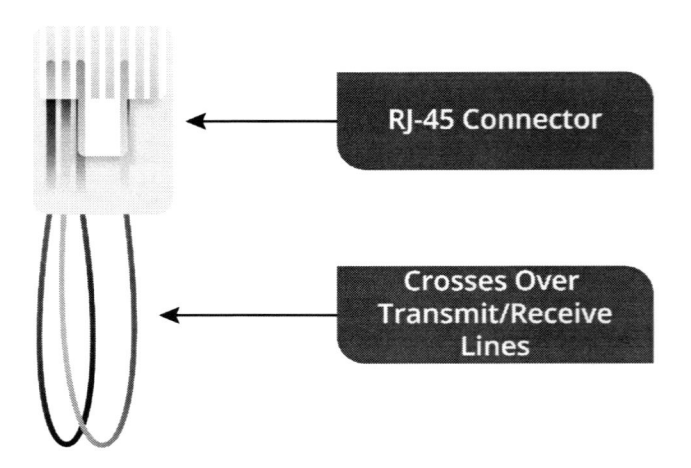

A loopback plug. (Image © 123RF.com.)

FIBER OPTIC CABLING AND CONNECTORS

Copper wire carries electrical signals, which are subject to interference and attenuation. Light signals are not susceptible to interference, cannot easily be intercepted (eavesdropped), and suffer less from attenuation. Consequently, fiber optic cabling can support much higher bandwidth, measured in multiple gigabits or terabits per second, and longer cable runs, measured in miles rather than feet.

A fiber optic strand. (Image by artush © 123RF.com.)

An optical fiber consists of an ultra-fine core of glass to carry the light signals surrounded by glass or plastic cladding, which guides the light pulses along the core, and a protective coating called the buffer. The fiber optic cable is contained in a protective jacket and terminated by a connector.

Fiber optic cables fall into two broad categories: single-mode and multi-mode:

- **Single-Mode Fiber (SMF)** has a small core (8-10 microns) and is designed to carry a long wavelength, near infrared (1310 or 1550 nm) light signal, generated by a laser. Single-mode cables support data rates up to 10 Gbps or better and cable runs of many kilometers, depending on the quality of the cable and optics.
- **Multi-mode (MMF)** has a larger core (62.5 or 50 microns) and is designed to carry a shorter wavelength light (850 nm or 1300 nm) transmitted in multiple waves of varying length. MMF uses less expensive optics and consequently is less expensive to deploy than SMF. However, it does not support such high signaling speeds or long distances as single-mode and so is more suitable for LANs than WANs.

A number of connectors have been designed for use with fiber optic cabling. Some types are more popular for multi-mode and some for single-mode. Connectors for MMF are usually color-coded beige while those for SMF are blue. The core of each connector is a ceramic or plastic ferrule that ensures continuous reception of the light signals.

- **Straight Tip (ST)**—A bayonet-style connector that uses a push-and-twist locking mechanism; used mostly for multi-mode networks.
- **Subscriber Connector (SC)**—Connector with a push/pull design that allows for simpler insertion and removal than FC. There are simplex and duplex versions, though the duplex version is just two connectors clipped together. It can be used for single- or multi-mode.
- Lucent or **Local Connector (LC)**—A small form factor connector with a tabbed push/pull design. LC is similar to SC but the smaller size allows for higher port density.

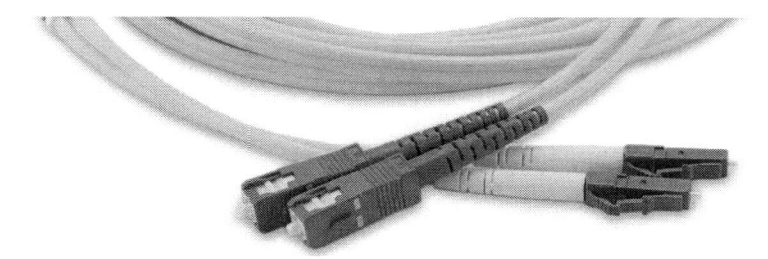

Patch cord with duplex SC format connectors (left) and LC connectors (right). (Image by YANAWUT SUNTORNKIJ © 123RF.com.)

Patch cords for fiber optic can come with the same connector on each end (ST-ST, for instance) or a mix of connectors (ST-SC, for instance). Fiber optic connectors are quite easy to damage and should not be repeatedly plugged in and unplugged.

Note: *To protect your eyesight, do not look directly into a fiber optic port.*

COAXIAL CABLING AND CONNECTORS

Coaxial, or **coax cable** is a different type of copper cabling, also carrying electrical signals. Where twisted pair uses balancing to cancel out interference, coax uses two conductors that share the same axis. The core signal conductor is enclosed by plastic insulation (dielectric) then a second wire mesh conductor serves both as shielding from EMI and as a ground.

Detailed layers of a coaxial cable. (Image by destinacigdem © 123RF.com.)

Coax cables are categorized using the Radio Grade (RG) "standard." The Radio Grade (or Radio Guide) classifications were developed by the US military but are no longer actively maintained by any sort of standards body. They do not prescribe the quality of coax cabling but categorize it by the thickness of the core conductor and the cable's characteristic impedance.

- RG-6 cable has a thicker core conductor for better signal quality and is often used as a drop/patch cable for modern Cable Access TV (CATV) and broadband cable modems.
- RG-59 cable has a thinner core conductor and was used as a drop cable for older CATV/cable modem installs and is also used for CCTV cabling.

Coax cabling is also available with tri- or quad-shielding for better resistance to EMI and eavesdropping.

In most cases, BNC (alternately Bayonet-Neill-Concelman, British Naval Connector, or Barrel Nut Connector) connectors are crimped to the ends of the cable. The impedance of the connector must match the cable type (50 or 75 ohm).

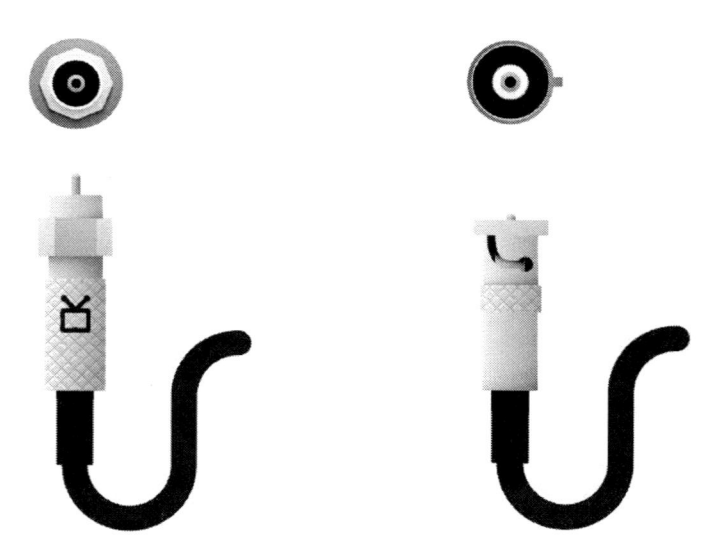

An example of a coaxial F-connector (left) and a BNC connector (right). (Image © 123RF.com.)

Coax installations also use screw-down F-connectors. A broadband cable service, for example, is likely to use the F-connector for drop cables.

As an Ethernet LAN media product (10BASE-5/Thicknet and 10BASE-2/Thinnet), coax could support 10 Mbps with cable lengths of up to 500 m and 185 m, respectively. Coax is considered obsolete in terms of LAN applications but is still widely used for CCTV networks and as drop cables for cable TV (CATV) and Internet access, where it can support higher bandwidths but at reduced range. In a Hybrid Fiber Coax (HFC) network, coax cable links the fiber optic trunk serving the whole street to the cable "modem" installed in the customer's premises. Coax suffers less from attenuation than twisted pair but is generally bulkier and more difficult to install.

Activity 5-1
Discussing Wired Networks

SCENARIO
Answer the following questions to check your understanding of the topic.

1. Your company has a global presence, and all locations can communicate. At each site, there is a network, and that network connects to the overall organizational network. In some locations, there are multiple sites within a city.

   Identify each type of network described here.

2. You are performing a wiring job, but the company wants to purchase the media and components from another preferred supplier. The plan is to install a network using copper cabling that will support Gigabit Ethernet. The customer is about to purchase Cat5e cable spools.

   Is this the best choice?

3. **What is the significance of network cabling marked "CMP/MMP"?**

4. You need to connect cable wires to a patch panel.

   Which networking tool might help you?

5. **What type of tool provides comprehensive information about the properties of a network cable installation?**

6. What features of fiber optic cable make it more suitable for WANs than copper cabling?

7. What types of connector are often used with coaxial cable?

Topic B
Network Hardware Devices

EXAM OBJECTIVES COVERED
1001-2.2 Compare and contrast common networking hardware devices.

In this topic, you will identify several types of network devices and other components. Network adapters, Internet modems, switches, and routers are fundamental network connectivity devices, and you will often encounter them in the network environments that you support. Understanding the functions and capabilities of these devices will prepare you to support a wide variety of network environments.

NETWORK INTERFACE CARDS

Communications are transported over an Ethernet cable by electrical signaling in the case of twisted pair, or light signaling in the case of fiber optic. The physical connection to the network media is made using a port in the computer's network adapter or **Network Interface Card (NIC)**. For the NIC to be able to transmit and receive the signals and process them as digital data, they must be divided into regular units with a consistent format. There must also be a means for each node on the local network to address communications to another node. Ethernet provides a data link protocol to perform these framing and addressing functions.

The signaling mechanism uses various encoding methods to represent the 1s and 0s of computer data as electrical or light pulses. The transceiver in the NIC is responsible for transmitting and receiving these pulses in the agreed frame format.

FRAMES

Each frame is identified by a preamble sequence, which is basically a warning to the NIC to expect a new frame. A frame is formatted with control information in the form of header fields, each of a fixed size and presented in a fixed order. The most important fields are the destination and source addresses of the adapter to which the frame is being directed and the adapter from which it was sent. Other information (not shown in the following simplified figure) includes the frame length and network layer protocol identifier.

Following these fields comes the payload. This is the data that is being transported over the network. It will normally consist of a network packet, such as an Internet Protocol (IP) packet, with its own headers and payload. Putting layers of packets within one another like this is called encapsulation.

The frame finishes with a checksum. The receiving computer can calculate its own checksum and compare it to this value. If they do not match, the receiving host rejects the frame as damaged.

| Pre-amble | Destination Address | Source Address | Payload | Error Checking |

Construction of a frame.

ETHERNET NIC FEATURES

Most motherboards come with an onboard Ethernet network adapter. An additional or replacement NIC could also be installed as a PCIe expansion card if the onboard adapter is not suitable for a particular network implementation.

All onboard cards support copper-based Ethernet with RJ-45 ports. You might use an add-in card to support other types of Ethernet, notably fiber optic. Some cards support more than one type of connector. You can also purchase cards with multiple ports of the same type—two or four Gigabit RJ-45 Ethernet ports, for instance. The multiple ports can be bonded to create a higher speed link. Four Gigabit Ethernet ports could be bonded to give a nominal link speed of 4 Gbps.

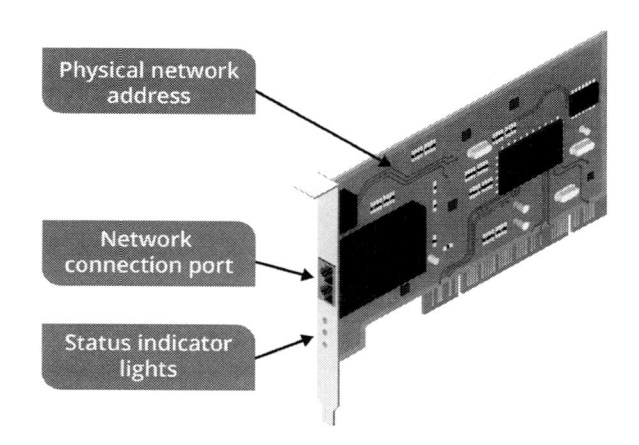

A network interface card. (Image © 123RF.com.)

MEDIA ACCESS CONTROL (MAC) ADDRESS

Each Ethernet network adapter port has a unique hardware or physical address known as the **Media Access Control (MAC)** address. MAC addresses provide the value used in a frame's source and destination address fields. A MAC address consists of 48 binary digits (6 bytes). This is typically represented as 12 digits of hexadecimal with colon or hyphen separators or no separators at all—for example, 00:60:8c:12:3a:bc or 00608c123abc.

NIC LED STATUS DIODES

Network adapters typically have one or more Light Emitting Diode (LED) status lights that can provide information on the state of the network connection.

- Most adapters have a link light that indicates if there is a signal from the network. If the link light is not lit, there is generally a problem with the cable or the physical connection.
- Most adapters also have an activity light that flickers when packets are received or sent. If the light flickers constantly, the network might be overused or there might be a device generating network noise.
- Some multi-speed adapters have a speed light to show whether the adapter is operating at 10 Mbps (Ethernet), 100 Mbps (Fast Ethernet), or 1000 Mbps (Gigabit Ethernet).
- Some types of equipment combine the functions of more than one light into dual-color LEDs. For example, a green flickering light might indicate normal activity, whereas an orange flickering light indicates network traffic collisions.

LEGACY NETWORKING DEVICES

In a structured cabling system, the computer is connected to a wall port and—via cabling running through the walls—to some sort of patch panel. The port on the patch panel is then connected to a port on the switch. The switch is the network appliance that "ties" the whole local network together. However, while switches are the appliances at the core of most modern Ethernet networks, you should also be aware of the basic function of legacy appliances, such as hubs and bridges.

HUBS AND REPEATERS

A **hub** is an early type of device used to implement the Ethernet cabling design, referred to as a star topology. The hub contains a number of ports—typically between 4 and 48—to provide connections for network devices. A hub simply ensures that all devices receive signals put on the network, working as a **multiport repeater**.

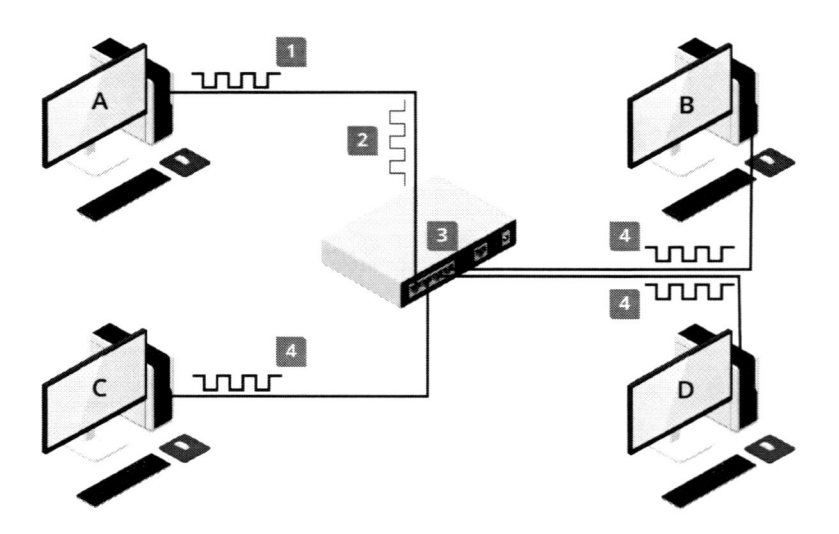

Using a hub to implement a physical star topology. Node A transmits a signal, which is received by the hub and forwarded out of each other port for reception by all the other nodes. (Image © 123RF.com.)

A **repeater** is a device used to overcome the distance limitations imposed by network cabling. It receives a transmission arriving over one cable segment and then regenerates and retransmits it at the original strength over another cable segment.

> **Note:** Standalone repeater devices are still widely used. On fiber optic networks it is often necessary to use repeaters on long-distance communications cabling.

BRIDGES

A **bridge** is a device that divides a local network into two or more segments. Hosts on one segment are able to communicate with those on another segment only via the bridge. **Contention** arises in hub-based Ethernet because all communications are received by all computers connected to the hub. The hub just repeats all transmissions across all ports. A lot of the communications are unnecessary and a lot of them "collide." When there is a collision, all the nodes have to stop and resend frames, slowing the network down. The network segment in which these collisions occur is called a **collision domain**. Any nodes attached to a hub are in a single collision domain.

A bridge can be used to divide an overloaded network into separate collision domains. The bridge keeps track of the MAC addresses attached to each segment. The bridge only passes signals from one segment to another if there is a match to the destination MAC address, reducing traffic loads in any one segment. The network should be designed so that relatively little traffic actually needs to pass over the bridge.

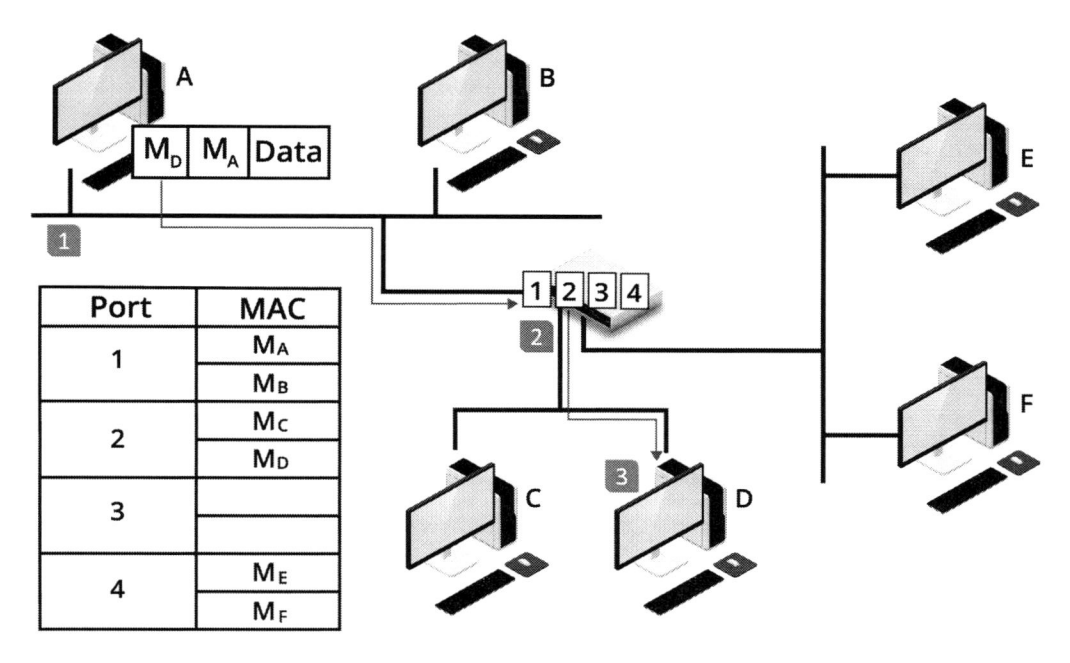

Bridge operation—the bridge tracks MAC addresses associated with each port and only forwards communications out of the port associated with the destination MAC address. (Image © 123RF.com.)

SWITCHES

Neither hub nor bridge appliances are widely used on networks anymore. Their functions have been replaced by Ethernet **switches**. Like hubs, switches can connect nodes together in a single network, repeating and regenerating signals over multiple ports. Like bridges, switches are used to reduce the effect of contention on network performance.

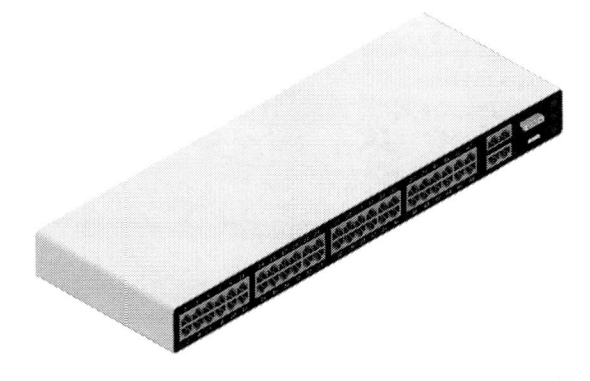

A workgroup switch. (Image © 123RF.com.)

MICROSEGMENTATION

An Ethernet switch performs the same sort of function as a bridge but can provide many more ports. Bridges only came with up to 4 ports. A single switch might have up to 48 ports and multiple switches can be connected together to create a switched fabric with thousands of ports. Each switch port is a separate collision domain. In effect, the switch establishes a point-to-point link called a virtual circuit between any two network nodes. This is referred to as **microsegmentation**. It works as follows:

1. Computer A transmits a frame intended for Computer B.
2. The switch receives the frame into a port buffer and reads the destination MAC address from the Ethernet frame.
3. The switch uses its MAC address table to look up the port connected to the destination MAC address.
4. The switch uses its high speed backplane to send the frame out on port 3 for computer B to receive.
5. None of the other connected devices, such as host C, observe any activity on the network while this process takes place. Therefore, these other devices are able to transmit and receive at the same time.

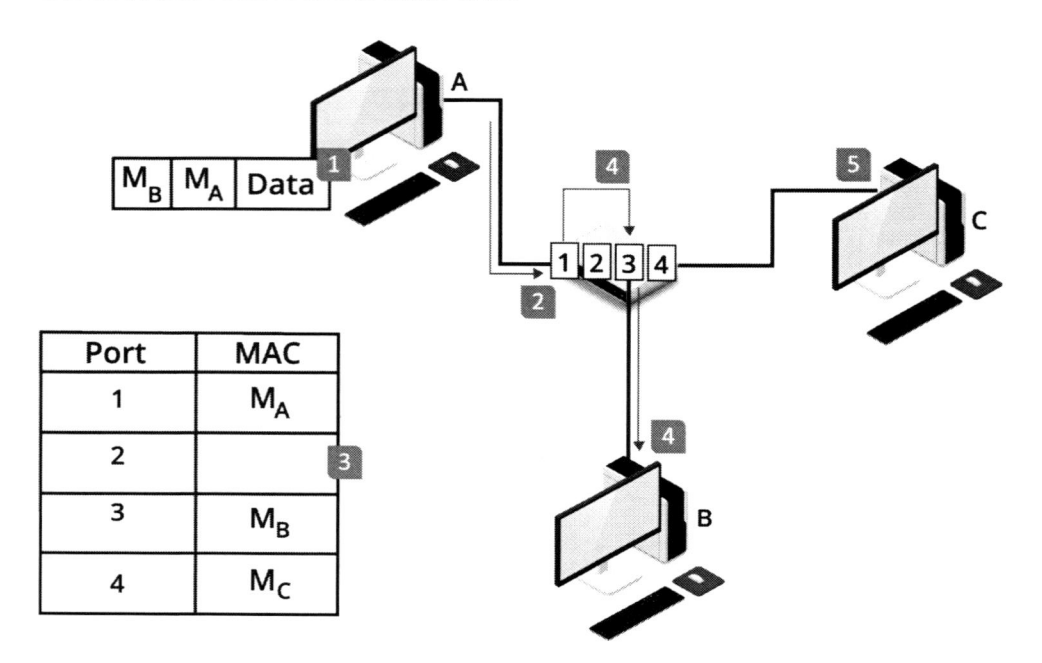

Switch operation. (Image © 123RF.com.)

Because each port is in a separate collision domain, collisions can only occur if the port is operating in half-duplex mode. This would only occur if a legacy network card or a hub is attached to it. Even then, collisions only affect the segment between the port and that adapter—they do not slow down the whole network. For other devices, the network appears free, so they are able to send communications at the same time using the full bandwidth of the network media.

> **Note:** Half duplex means that a port can either send or receive but cannot do both at the same time. Ports supporting Gigabit Ethernet can send and receive at the same time (full duplex).

> **Note:** You are very unlikely to come across hub or bridge appliances. The vast majority of Ethernet networks are implemented using switches. Gigabit Ethernet can only run using switches. Note that the function of a bridge is still an important one, though. For example, a PC might use a software bridge between network adapters (for network connectivity when the host is running virtualization software, for instance).

MANAGED AND UNMANAGED SWITCHES

An **unmanaged switch** performs the microsegmentation function described previously without requiring any sort of configuration. You just power it on, connect some hosts to it, and it works without any more intervention. You might find unmanaged switches with four or eight ports used in small networks. There is also an unmanaged switch embedded in most of the Internet router/modems supplied by Internet Service Providers (ISP) to connect to their networks.

Larger workgroups and corporate networks require additional functionality in their switches. Switches designed for larger LANs are called **managed switches**. A managed switch will work as an unmanaged switch out-of-the-box, but an administrator can connect to it over a management port, configure security settings, and then choose options for the switch's more advanced functionality.

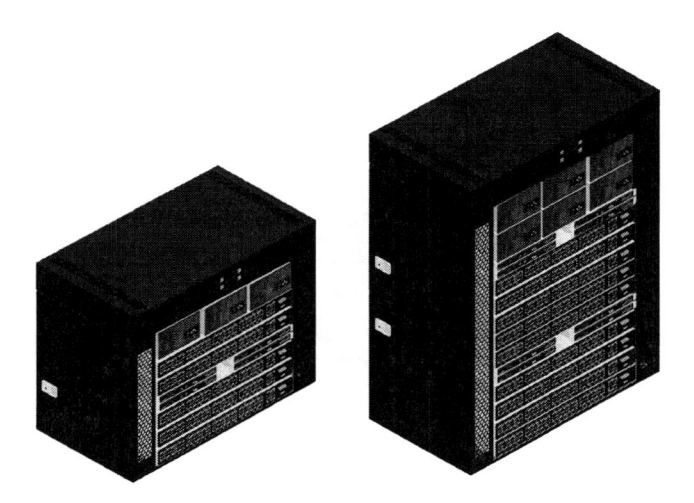

Modular chassis allows provisioning multiple access switches. (Image © 123RF.com.)

One of the main reasons for using managed switches is that enterprise networks might have to provide hundreds or thousands of access ports. This is accomplished by linking multiple switches together. Having that many ports on the same network creates its own performance and security issues, so managed switches support a method of dividing the ports into separate Virtual LANs (VLANs).

Configuration of a managed switch can either be performed over a web interface or some sort of command line.

```
FastEthernet1/0/1 is up, line protocol is up (connected)
  Hardware is Fast Ethernet, address is f41f.c253.7103 (bia f41f.c253.7103)
  MTU 1500 bytes, BW 100000 Kbit/sec, DLY 100 usec,
     reliability 255/255, txload 1/255, rxload 1/255
  Encapsulation ARPA, loopback not set
  Keepalive set (10 sec)
  Full-duplex, 100Mb/s, media type is 10/100BaseTX
  input flow-control is off, output flow-control is unsupported
  ARP type: ARPA, ARP Timeout 04:00:00
  Last input 00:00:51, output 00:00:00, output hang never
  Last clearing of "show interface" counters never
  Input queue: 0/75/0/0 (size/max/drops/flushes); Total output drops: 0
  Queueing strategy: fifo
  Output queue: 0/40 (size/max)
  5 minute input rate 0 bits/sec, 0 packets/sec
  5 minute output rate 0 bits/sec, 0 packets/sec
     18 packets input, 1758 bytes, 0 no buffer
     Received 4 broadcasts (2 multicasts)
     0 runts, 0 giants, 0 throttles
     0 input errors, 0 CRC, 0 frame, 0 overrun, 0 ignored
     0 watchdog, 2 multicast, 0 pause input
     0 input packets with dribble condition detected
     111 packets output, 13828 bytes, 0 underruns
     0 output errors, 0 collisions, 1 interface resets
     0 unknown protocol drops
```

Viewing interface configuration on a Cisco switch.

POWER OVER ETHERNET

Power over Ethernet (PoE) is a means of supplying electrical power from a switch port over Cat 5 or better data cabling to a connected powered device, such as a tablet computer, VoIP handset, security camera, or wireless access point. PoE is defined in two IEEE standards (now both rolled into 802.3-2012):

- **802.3af**—powered devices can draw up to about 13 W over the link. Power is supplied as 350mA@48V and limited to 15.4 W, but the voltage drop over the maximum 100 feet of cable results in usable power of around 13 W.
- **802.3at (PoE+)**—powered devices can draw up to about 25 W. PoE+ allows for a broader range of devices to be powered such as cameras with pan/tilt/zoom capabilities, door controllers, and thin client computers.

PoE-enabled switches are referred to as end-span (or end-point) **Power Sourcing Equipment (PSE)**. If an existing switch does not support PoE, a device called a **power injector** can be used. When a device is connected to a port on a PoE switch, the switch goes through a detection phase to determine whether the device is PoE-enabled. If not, it does not supply power over the port and therefore does not damage non-PoE devices. If so, it determines the device's power consumption and sets the supply voltage level appropriately.

Powering these devices through a switch is more efficient than using a wall-socket AC adapter for each appliance. It also allows network management software to control the devices and apply power schemes, such as making unused devices go into sleep states and power capping.

ETHERNET OVER POWER

SOHO networks are unlikely to use a structured cabling scheme, with cable conduit and patch panels. Many SOHO networks will be based around a single Internet router, server computer, and several workstations, possibly all located within the same room. A residential network might also require connectivity for smart appliances, such as

Smart TVs and game consoles. The main challenge is usually joining up the location selected for the majority of the equipment with the location of the Internet access line.

An obvious solution for connecting SOHO devices is wireless. For many SOHO networks, the bandwidth available for WLANs will be adequate. There may be interference issues, however, and some home appliances, such as set-top boxes, might not support Wi-Fi. As an alternative to installing new data cabling, Ethernet over Powerline products can make use of building power circuits. Power is typically delivered as a 50-60 Hz alternating current, at between 100-240 volts, varying from country to country. Powerline overlays a higher frequency carrier signal on the lines and uses this to transfer Ethernet frames.

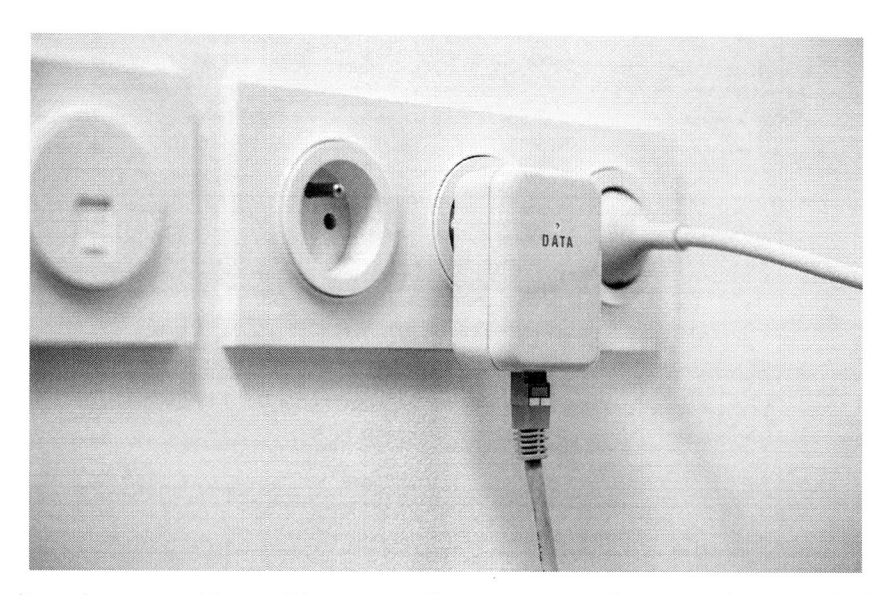

Powerline adapter provides an Ethernet port from a power outlet. (Image by Le Moal Olivier © 123RF.com.)

A network connection is established via a Powerline adapter plugged directly into an electrical outlet. Note that strip sockets are generally not supported. The adapter provides one or two Ethernet RJ-45 ports to connect network equipment. The adapters automatically detect and communicate with one another over the electrical wiring with no configuration needed, though optionally a security key can be enabled to encrypt transmissions. A pass-through adapter also features an electrical outlet, allowing continued use of the socket.

Standards for Ethernet over Powerline are defined by IEEE 1901 and products are managed by the HomePlug Powerline Alliance. Most products on the market conform to the HomePlug AV or AV2 standards, which are interoperable (older HomePlug 1.0 devices are not compatible). Within this, products are rated according to the maximum (theoretical) bandwidth, from AV200 (200 Mbps) to AV1200. If a mix of adapters is used, the network will operate only at the highest speed supported by all of the adapters.

> **Note:** Most Powerline installations will not achieve more than half the theoretical bandwidth.

Activity 5-2
Discussing Network Hardware Devices

SCENARIO
Answer the following questions to check your understanding of the topic.

1. **What is a MAC address?**

2. **What feature(s) should you check when ordering an Ethernet network card?**

3. A technician has discovered an 8-port Ethernet hub appliance in a store.
   Can this device be usefully deployed on a modern network?

4. Your manager is resisting the use of an unmanaged switch to support a network of up to a dozen computers at a branch office.
   What are the arguments for and against proceeding?

5. You are assisting a customer looking to purchase switches that support powering VoIP handset devices directly. The customer is confused between Power over Ethernet and Ethernet over Power.

   Can you explain the difference and identify which technology the customer needs?

Topic C
Wireless Networks

EXAM OBJECTIVES COVERED
1001-2.2 Compare and contrast common networking hardware devices.
1001-2.4 Compare and contrast wireless networking protocols.
1001-2.7 Compare and contrast Internet connection types, network types, and their features.

Wireless technologies can now achieve sufficient bandwidth to replace wired ports for many types of clients in a typical office. It is also more convenient for SOHO networks to use wireless as the primary access method for computers, laptops, smartphones, and tablets. Wireless can provide connectivity for desktops or even servers in places where it is difficult or expensive to run network cabling. As a CompTIA A+ technician, you will often be called upon to install, configure, and troubleshoot wireless technologies, so it is imperative that you understand the basics.

WHAT IS WIRELESS NETWORKING?

"Wireless" encompasses a whole range of connectivity products and technologies, from personal area networking to Internet connectivity. Most wireless technologies use radio waves as transmission media. Radio systems use transmission and reception antennas tuned to a specific frequency for the transfer of signals.

WIRELESS FREQUENCIES AND CHANNELS

The range of broadcast radio frequencies (RF) extends from 3 KHz to 300 GHz. Frequencies are subdivided into bands such as very low and ultra high. FM radio and television signals are broadcast in the Very High Frequency (VHF) band (30-300 MHz).

The use of the radio spectrum is regulated by national governments and (to some extent) standardized internationally by the International Telecommunications Union (ITU). Use of a frequency usually requires a license from the relevant government agency. The license ensures no one else can transmit that frequency within a particular area.

There are however, unregulated frequencies—Industrial, Scientific, and Medical (ISM) bands—that do not require a license, such as the 2.4 GHz and 5 GHz bands. The wireless networking products operate in these unregulated ultra high frequencies. There is a limit on power output, which means range is restricted.

802.11 (WIRELESS LAN STANDARDS)

When talking about "wireless networking" for desktops, laptops, smartphones, and tablets, the term is generally understood to mean the IEEE's 802.11 standards for Wireless LANs (WLANs), also called **Wi-Fi**. There are five main versions of the standard, as summarized here:

Standard	Maximum Transfer Rate	Band
802.11a (1999)	54 Mbps	5 GHz
802.11b (1999)	11 Mbps	2.4 GHz
802.11g (2003)	54 Mbps	2.4 GHz

Standard	Maximum Transfer Rate	Band
802.11n (2009)	288.8 Mbps/stream (Single Channel)	2.4/5 GHz
	600 Mbps/stream (Bonded Channels)	
802.11ac (2013)	1.7 Gbps (at time of writing)	5 GHz

Note that the transfer rates quoted are illustrative of an optimal installation and are heavily dependent on the quality of the access point, the number of clients connecting simultaneously, and interference and obstructions in the environment. The frequencies used by Wi-Fi lack penetrating power and there can be interference from nearby unregulated devices, such as baby monitors and cordless phones. Microwave ovens can also cause interference.

The actual data rate will drop with distance and in the presence of interference, with the preference being for a slower, stable connection over a faster, error-prone one.

FREQUENCIES

Every wireless device operates on a specific radio frequency within an overall frequency band. It is important to understand the difference between the two most common frequency bands in the IEEE 802.11 standards: 2.4 GHz and 5.0 GHz.

- 2.4 GHz is the longer wavelength, which gives it longer range (given the same power output) and makes it better at propagating through solid surfaces. However, the 2.4 GHz band does not support a high number of individual channels and is often congested, both with other Wi-Fi networks and other types of wireless technology, such as Bluetooth. Consequently, with the 2.4 GHz band there is increased risk of interference and the maximum achievable data rates are typically lower than with a 5 GHz channel.
- 5 GHz is less effective at penetrating solid surfaces and so does not support the maximum ranges achieved with 2.4 GHz standards. Nonetheless, the band supports more individual channels and suffers less from congestion and interference, meaning it supports higher data rates.

RANGE

Products working in the 2.4 GHz band can be quoted as having a maximum indoor range of anywhere from 30 to 45 m (100 - 150 feet). Products using 5 GHz are usually quoted as having a maximum range of about one third less (up to about 30 m, say). For most wireless networks, however, absolute range is less important than the number of clients that have to be supported and the construction of walls and ceilings.

CHANNELS

The 2. band is subdivided into up to 14 channels, spaced at 5 MHz intervals from 2412 MHz up to 2484 MHz. Wi-Fi requires bandwidth of approximately 20 MHz, not 5 MHz. Consequently, a site designer needs to choose the channels that do not overlap. On a WLAN where only the first 11 channels are available, channels 1, 6, and 11 can be selected as non-overlapping.

> **Note:** In the Americas, regulations permit the use of channels 1-11 only, while in Europe, channels 1-13 are permitted. In Japan, all 14 channels are permitted.

The limited number of non-overlapping channels means that co-channel interference is a real possibility. Special codes embedded in the signal give each transmitting node a distinguishing pattern, so that nearby networks can share the same channel at once. At some point, however, the channel becomes saturated with too many WLANs.

The 5 GHz band is subdivided into 23 non-overlapping channels each ~20 MHz-wide. The greater number of non-overlapping channels means that co-channel interference is less of a problem for the 5 GHz band. This means that more WLANs can occupy the same area or that you can provision more access points closer together to support a greater density of client devices.

> **Note:** Initially there were 11 channels in the 5 GHz band, but the subsequent 802.11h standard added another 12. 802.11h also adds the Dynamic Frequency Selection (DFS) method to prevent access points working in the 5 GHz band from interfering with radar and satellite signals. The exact use of channels can be subject to different regulations in different countries.

WIRELESS NETWORK STANDARDS

Use of the legacy standards—802.11a/b/g—is now limited to quite old equipment. You are relatively unlikely to come across networks still supporting them. As 802.11nb and g both worked at 2.4 GHz, 802.11g provided an upgrade path for 802.11b WLANs. Working in the 5 GHz band, 802.11a is incompatible with the other two and was not as widely adopted.

IEEE 802.11n

The 802.11n standard provides substantially more bandwidth than the legacy standards. It multiplexes the signals from 2-4 separate antennas in a process called **Multiple-Input-Multiple-Output (MIMO)**. The configuration of 802.11n devices is identified by AxB:C notation, where A is the number of transmit antennas, B is the number of receive antennas, and C is the number of simultaneous transmit and receive streams. The maximum possible is 4x4:4 but common configurations are 2x2:2, 3x3:2, or 3x3:3. Both the transmitter and receiver must support the same number of streams.

802.11n can deliver even more bandwidth with the option to use two adjacent 20 MHz channels as a single 40 MHz channel (channel bonding). 802.11n products can use channels in the 2.4 GHz band or the 5 GHz band. The 5 GHz band is preferred for optimal bandwidth and to avoid interference with existing 2.4 GHz networks and devices. Channel bonding is only a practical option in the 5 GHz band. Assuming the maximum number of spatial streams and optimum conditions, the nominal data rates for 802.11n are 288.8 Mbps for a single channel and 600 Mbps for bonded channels.

> **Note:** Cheaper adapters may only support the 2.4 GHz band. Many smartphone models only support 2.4 GHz. An access point or adapter that can support both is referred to as dual band. A dual band access point can support both 2.4 GHz and 5 GHz bands simultaneously. This allows legacy clients to be allocated to the 2.4 GHz band.

IEEE 802.11ac

The 802.11ac standard continues the development of 802.11n technologies. The main distinction is that 802.11ac works only in the 5 GHz band. The 2.4 GHz band can be used for legacy standards (802.11b/g/n) in mixed mode. The aim for 802.11ac is to get throughput similar to that of Gigabit Ethernet or better. It supports more channel bonding (up to 80 or 160 MHz channels), up to 8 spatial streams rather than 4, and denser modulation (at close ranges).

As with 802.11n, only high-end equipment will be equipped with sufficient antennas to make use of up to 8 streams. At the time of writing, no devices actually support more than 4x4:4 streams. The maximum theoretical data rate with 8 streams and 160 MHz channel bonding is about 6.93 Gbps. Cisco's Aironet 1850e 4x4:4 access points support up to 1.7 Gbps with 80 MHz channels.

ACCESS POINTS AND WIRELESS NETWORK MODES

Most Wi-Fi networks are configured in what is technically referred to as **infrastructure mode**. Infrastructure mode means that each client device (or station) is configured to connect to the network via an **Access Point (AP)**. In 802.11 documentation, this is referred to as a Basic Service Set (BSS). The MAC address of the AP is used as the **Basic Service Set Identifier (BSSID)**. More than one BSS can be grouped together in an **Extended Service Set (ESS)**.

The access point works as a bridge, forwarding communications between the wireless stations and the wired network, referred to as a Distribution System (DS). The access point will be joined to the network in much the same way as a host computer is—via a wall port and cabling to an Ethernet switch.

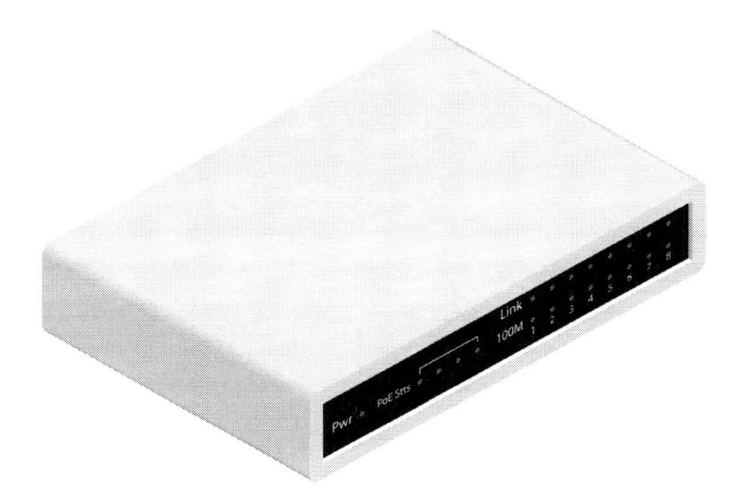

An access point. (Image © 123RF.com.)

Access Points can also be configured to forward frames between one another, functioning in a Wireless Distribution System (WDS) to extend the network without using a cabled backbone. A WDS can be configured in bridge mode, where the access points only forward communications between one another, and repeater mode, where they also communicate with stations.

A WDS can be complex to set up and can suffer from compatibility problems when devices from multiple vendors are used. For residential users, a **range extender** is a simpler device for regenerating a signal from an access point to a more remote location, such as an upstairs room. Another option is a range extender that works with a powerline adapter to communicate with the access point over the electrical wiring.

AD-HOC AND WI-FI DIRECT

Stations can also be configured to connect directly to one another. With older network standards, this is referred to as **ad-hoc mode**. Such peer-to-peer connections are now more likely to be implemented as Wi-Fi Direct, which has the advantage of automatically configuring a secure link between the stations.

WIRELESS MESH NETWORK (WMN) TOPOLOGY

The 802.11s standard defines a **Wireless Mesh Network (WMN)**. Unlike an ad-hoc network, nodes in a WMN (called Mesh Stations) are capable of discovering one another and peering, forming a Mesh Basic Service Set (MBSS). The mesh stations can perform path discovery and forwarding between peers, using a routing protocol, such as the Hybrid Wireless Mesh Protocol (HWMP).

PERSONAL AREA NETWORKS

The concept of a **Personal Area Network (PAN)** has gained some currency with the profusion of wireless and cellular connection technologies in the last few years. A PAN refers to using wireless connectivity to connect to devices within a few meters—printers, smartphones, headsets, speakers, video displays, and so on.

WIRELESS NETWORK CARDS

Each station in a Wi-Fi network needs to be installed with a Wi-Fi adapter supporting the 802.11 standard(s) used on the network. A Wi-Fi adapter can be installed if the function is not available on the motherboard. Both internally installed adapter cards and USB-connected adapters are available. A Wi-Fi card may also need to be installed to support the latest standard (upgrading from 802.11g to 802.11n or 802.11ac, for instance). Like an Ethernet card, a Wi-Fi adapter is identified at the data link layer by a MAC address.

Activity 5-3
Discussing Wireless Networks

SCENARIO
Answer the following questions to check your understanding of the topic.

1. What is the maximum transfer rate of an 802.11g Wi-Fi adapter?

2. Why are 2.4 GHz networks more susceptible to interference than 5 GHz networks?

3. How does 802.11n achieve greater speeds than previous Wi-Fi standards?

4. Can 802.11ac achieve higher throughput by multiplexing the signals from both 2.4 and 5 GHz frequency bands? Why or why not?

5. Why might a wireless mesh network topology be used?

Topic D

Internet Connection Types

EXAM OBJECTIVES COVERED
1001-2.2 Compare and contrast common networking hardware devices.
1001-2.4 Compare and contrast wireless networking protocols.
1001-2.7 Compare and contrast Internet connection types, network types, and their features.

In the previous topics, you identified the network cabling and devices used to implement different types of Local Area Networks (LANs). A key component of any network is the ability to communicate with remote hosts over the Internet. In this topic, you will learn to compare and contrasts methods of Internet access, as provided for typical SOHO network types.

INTERNET CONNECTIONS

The major infrastructure of the Internet, also referred to as the **Internet backbone**, consists of very high bandwidth trunks connecting **Internet eXchange Points (IXPs)**. These trunks and IXPs are mostly created by telecommunications companies and academic institutions. They are typically organized on national and international levels. Within the data center supporting any given IXP, **Internet Service Providers (ISPs)** establish high-speed links between their networks, using transit and peering arrangements to carry traffic to and from parts of the Internet they do not physically own. There is a tiered hierarchy of ISPs that reflects to what extent they depend on transit arrangements with other ISPs.

Customers connect to an ISP's network via a local **Point of Presence (PoP)**. The ISP uses a **backhaul** link (or a transit arrangement with another ISP) to connect each POP to their core network infrastructure and one or more IXPs.

INTERNET SERVICE PROVIDERS

Most home users and businesses rely on an Internet Service Provider (ISP) to facilitate the link between their SOHO network and the Internet. Internet access is then a question of how you join your local network to the ISP's PoP.

The consumer and small business technologies for doing this are dial-up, "broadband" (DSL, FTTx, or cable), and wireless (radio or satellite). Each has its advantages and disadvantages depending on the type of access and frequency of use required.

Most SOHO Internet access methods makes use of the **Public Switched Telephone Network (PSTN)**. The PSTN is the national and global telecommunications network. The voice-grade copper wire part of this network (between subscribers and the telecom provider's switches) is sometimes referred to as the **Plain Old Telephone Service (POTS)**, "local loop," or "last mile."

The ISP handles the business of allocating one or more public Internet Protocol (IP) addresses that will work on the Internet and other services, such as domain name registration, web and email hosting, and so on.

Enterprise ISP solutions will offer much higher bandwidth links, often using fiber optic cabling.

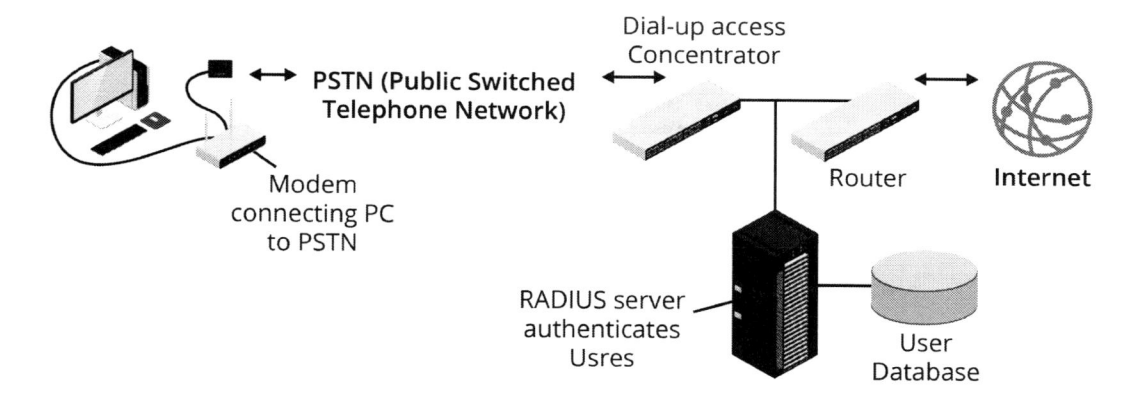

Internet access for a standalone PC via an ISP. (Image © 123RF.com.)

POINT-TO-POINT PROTOCOL

The **Point-to-Point Protocol (PPP)** is typically used to encapsulate the network protocol, which will usually be TCP/IP, over the link to the ISP. PPP also provides a mechanism to authenticate the user and manage the connection between the local computer or network and the ISP's router.

BROADBAND INTERNET ACCESS

Broadband covers a range of different connection technologies. The main characteristics are that they are "always-on" (that is, the connection does not need to be re-established for each session) and data transfer rates are (a lot) higher than analog dial-up.

DSL

Digital Subscriber Line (DSL) uses the higher frequencies available in a copper telephone line as a communications channel. The use of a filter prevents the DSL signals from contaminating voice traffic. The use of advanced modulation and echo cancelling techniques enable high bandwidth, full duplex transmissions.

A DSL "modem" makes the connection to the phone system. Typically, the modem function will be part of a DSL router/modem/access point appliance that can provide access to a small network of computers. The phone line makes the connection to a bank of DSL modems in the exchange, called a **DSL Access Multiplier (DSLAM)**. The DSLAM channels voice and data traffic to the appropriate network. Depending on the equipment used by the ISP, the data link protocol used for DSL may be **PPP over ATM (PPPoA)** or **PPP over Ethernet (PPPoE)**.

There are various "flavors" of DSL, notably asymmetrical and symmetrical types:

- **Asymmetrical DSL (ADSL)** is a "consumer" version of DSL that provides a fast downlink but a slow uplink. There are various iterations of ADSL, with the latest (ADSL2+) offering downlink rates up to about 24 Mbps and uplink rates up to 1.4 Mbps, or 3.3 Mbps upstream if the provider supports Annex M/ADSL2+ M.

    Often service providers impose usage restrictions to limit the amount of data downloaded per month. Actual speed may be affected by the quality of the cabling in the consumer's premises and between the premises and the exchange and also by the number of users connected to the same DSLAM (contention). The maximum range of an ADSL modem is typically about 10,000 feet (2 miles or 3 km), but the longer the connection, the greater the deterioration in data rate.

- Symmetric versions of DSL offer the same uplink and downlink speeds. These are of more use to businesses and for branch office links, where more data is transferred upstream than with normal Internet use.
- **Very High Bitrate DSL (VDSL)** achieves higher bit rates at the expense of range. It allows for both symmetric and asymmetric modes. Over 300 m (1000 feet), an asymmetric link supports 52 Mbps downstream and 6 Mbps upstream, whereas a symmetric link supports 26 Mbps in both directions. VDSL2 also specifies a very short range (100 m/300 feet) rate of 100 Mbps (bi-directional).

FIBER OPTIC INTERNET ACCESS

Fiber optic cabling supports much higher bandwidth and lower distance limitations than copper cabling. Fiber optic cabling has replaced copper cabling within the "core" of telecommunications networks. Extending fiber optic cabling to individual subscriber homes and businesses is slowly taking place. There are two principal types of businesses operating fiber optic networks for SOHO Internet access—companies with their roots in cable TV on one hand and the telecommunications providers with their roots in telephone services on the other.

HYBRID FIBER COAX (HFC)/CABLE

A cable Internet connection is usually available along with a **Cable Access TV (CATV)** service. These networks are often described as **Hybrid Fiber Coax (HFC)** as they combine a fiber optic core network with coax links to customer premises equipment, but are more simply just described as "broadband cable" or just as "cable."

The cable modem is interfaced to the local network or computer through an Ethernet adapter and with the cable network by a short segment of coax. More coax then links all the premises in a street with a **Cable Modem Termination System (CMTS)**, which routes data traffic via the fiber backbone to the ISP's Point of Presence (PoP) and from there to the Internet. Cable based on the **Data Over Cable Service Interface Specification (DOCSIS)** supports downlink speeds of up to 38 Mbps (North America) or 50 Mbps (Europe) and uplinks of up to 27 Mbps. DOCSIS version 3 allows the use of multiplexed channels to achieve higher bandwidth.

FIBER TO THE CURB (FTTC)

For the telecommunications companies, the major obstacle to providing really high bandwidth to consumers and small businesses is in the last mile of the telephone network. Copper cabling infrastructure in the last mile is often of poor quality as it was only designed to service a telephone line. The projects to update this wiring to use fiber optic links are referred to by the umbrella term "Fiber to the X" (FTTx).

The most expensive solution is **Fiber to the Premises (FTTP)** or its domestic variant **Fiber to the Home (FTTH)**. The essential point about both these implementations is that the fiber link is terminated on customer premises equipment. Such "pure" fiber solutions are not widespread and generally carry a price premium above other types of Internet access.

Other solutions can variously be described as **Fiber to the Node (FTTN)** or **Fiber to the Curb/Cabinet (FTTC)**. These extend the fiber link to a communications cabinet in the street servicing multiple subscribers. This is similar model to HFC, but instead of the coax segment, each subscriber is linked to the fiber service by running Very High Bitrate DSL (VDSL) over the existing telephone wiring.

DIAL-UP INTERNET ACCESS

Dial-up is simply a telephone conversation between two computers. Whereas with DSL this "conversation" is pushed to the higher frequency parts of the phone line, with dial-up it occupies the whole frequency range, but not very efficiently. Ordinary telephone charges apply for the duration of each session and the phone line cannot be used for voice calls at the same time. A dial-up link is very low bandwidth.

A dial-up connection is facilitated by analog modems on each end of the line. A dial-up modem converts digital signals to an analog carrier signal (modulation) and transmits it over the telephone cable, making a distinctive screeching noise. The modem at the other end converts the analog signal back to digital (demodulation) and processes the data.

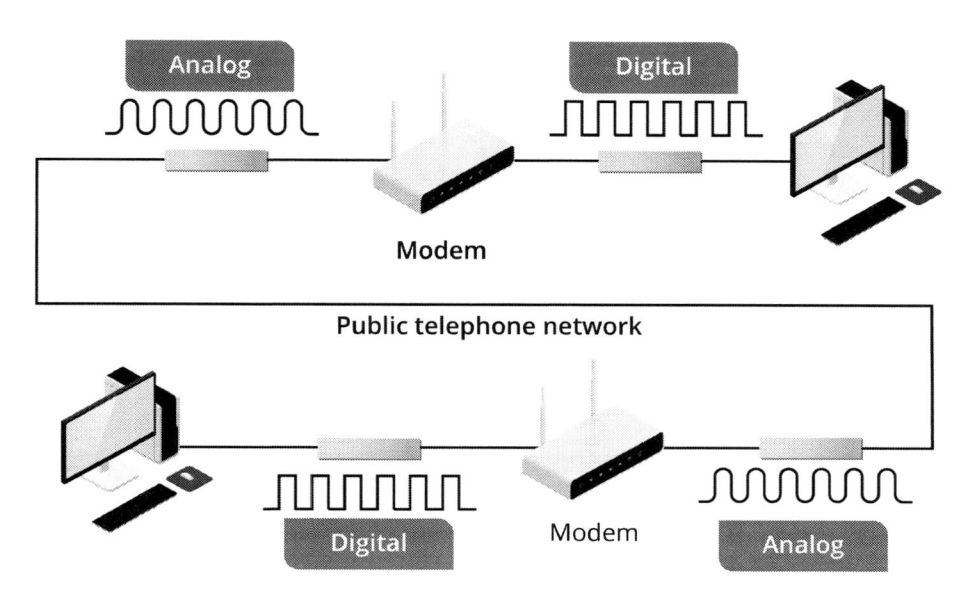

Dial-up modems. (Image © 123RF.com.)

The main disadvantages of this system are the low data transfer rates, the time it takes for the connection to be established, and error prone links. The fastest modems can only usually work at 33.6 Kbps (V.34+) and this speed is reaching the limitations of analog lines. Using the V.90 or V.92 digital signaling protocol, a downlink speed of up to 56 Kbps is possible in theory, though rarely achieved in practice. The use of compression can also improve the data transfer throughput, though as many of the files being transferred are likely to be compressed already (image files, for instance), the improvement will be variable.

Consequently, dial-up has been almost completely superseded by other technologies and would only be used as a backup method or in areas where no other access methods are supported.

ISDN INTERNET ACCESS

Integrated Services Digital Network (ISDN) is a digital circuit-switched technology for voice, video, and data (hence "integrated services"). ISDN makes use of existing copper telephone wiring, if the wiring is of sufficient quality. Unlike dial-up, however, it uses the line to transmit digital signatures for both voice and data. This means that there are no inefficient analog-to-digital conversions and so higher speeds can be supported.

ISDN is a dial-up service billed for by line rental and per-minute usage. Although it is a dial-up technology, it is capable of establishing a circuit connection in less than 1 second—much faster than an analog modem.

The most common uses of ISDN are for interconnection of LANs and remote users (teleworkers) to businesses. There are two classes of ISDN:

- **Basic Rate Interface (BRI)** provides two 64 Kbps "B" channels for data and one 16 Kbps "D" channel for link management control signals. It is sometimes called 2B+D. One option is to use one B channel for data and leave the other for voice or fax; another is to provide a 128 Kbps link by concatenating the two B channels. This form of ISDN is intended for SOHO use.
- **Primary Rate Interface (PRI)** provides 23 or 30 "B" channels (or between about 1.5 and 2 Mbps), depending on location in the world, and one 64 Kbps D channel. This form of ISDN is intended for larger companies and is commonly used to provide a link between two company locations.

Much of the switching technology of ISDN remains in use in terms of the telecommunications core network, but as an Internet access method for subscribers, it has largely been superseded by DSL and cable. It remains a good solution outside metropolitan areas where these other services may not be available.

An ISDN connection would typically be facilitated through a **Terminal Adapter (TA)**. The TA may be an external appliance or a plug-in card for a PC or compatible router. The TA is connected to the ISDN network via an NT1 device (Network Terminator). The ISDN-enabled router may then either be connected to a switch or support direct connections from ISDN devices.

FIXED WIRELESS INTERNET ACCESS

Wired broadband Internet access is not always available, especially in rural areas or in older building developments, where running new cable capable of supporting DSL or FTTC is problematic. In this scenario, some sort of fixed wireless Internet access might be an option.

SATELLITE INTERNET ACCESS

Satellite systems provide far bigger areas of coverage than can be achieved using other technologies. A **Very Small Aperture Terminal (VSAT)** microwave antenna is aligned to an orbital satellite that can either relay signals between sites directly or via another satellite. Satellites use frequency bands in the Super High Frequency range (3-30 GHz). The widespread use of satellite television receivers allows for domestic Internet connectivity services over satellite connections. Satellite services for business are also expanding, especially in rural areas where DSL or cable services are less likely to be available. The transfer rates available vary between providers and access packages, but 2 or 6 Mbps up and 15-20 Mbps down would be typical. There are also likely to be quite restrictive usage limits.

Satellite connections experience quite severe **latency** problems as the signal has to travel over thousands of miles more than terrestrial connections, introducing a delay of many times what might be expected over a land link. For example, if accessing a site over DSL involves a 15-50 ms delay on the link, accessing the same site over a satellite link could involve a 1000 ms delay. This is an issue for real-time applications, such as video-conferencing, VoIP, and multi-player gaming.

To create a satellite Internet connection, the ISP installs a satellite dish (antenna) at the customer's premises and aligns it with the orbital satellite. The satellites are in geostationary orbit above the equator, so in the northern hemisphere the dish will be pointing south. Because the satellite does not move relative to the dish, there should be no need for any realignment. The antenna is connected via coaxial cabling to a DVB-S (Digital Video Broadcast Satellite) modem. This can be installed in the PC as an adapter card or as an external box connected via a USB or Ethernet port.

LINE OF SIGHT WIRELESS INTERNET SERVICE PROVIDER (WISP)

Line of Sight (LoS) is a wireless connection method using ground-based microwave antennas aligned with one another. Endpoints can transmit signals to one another as long as they are unobstructed by physical objects. The antennas themselves are typically affixed to the top of tall buildings in order to reduce this interference. A line of sight service can cover great distances that typical wireless signals cannot, while at the same time saving the service provider from having to install cabling infrastructure. Additionally, the connection in an LoS service is often low latency, or at least, lower latency than satellite.

A disadvantage of LoS is that the actual unobstructed sight line can be difficult to maintain, especially if the area between the two endpoints is not owned by the client or the provider. Likewise, LoS services are usually more expensive than other methods.

A company specializing in LoS networks is referred to as a **Wireless Internet Service Provider (WISP)**. A WISP might use Wi-Fi type networking or proprietary equipment. The services can operate over a range of frequencies. The use of certain frequencies may be impacted by the deployment of 5G cellular services, which may involve changes to the way some frequency bands are licensed for use.

CELLULAR RADIO NETWORKS

The 2.4 GHz and 5 GHz frequency bands used by Wi-Fi have quite severely restricted range while fixed wireless Internet requires a large dish antenna. Cellular radio wireless networking facilitates communications over much larger distances using portable equipment like smartphones. Cellular networking is also used by some Internet of Things (IoT) devices, such as smart energy meters.

CELLULAR RADIO (GSM/TDMA AND CDMA)

A cellular radio makes a connection using the nearest available transmitter (cell or base station). Each base station has an effective range of up to 5 miles (8 km). The transmitter connects the phone to the mobile and landline telephone networks. Transmitter coverage in many countries is now very good, with the exception of remote rural areas. Cellular radio works in the 850 and 1900 MHz frequency bands (mostly in the Americas) and the 900 and 1800 MHz bands (rest of the world).

Cellular digital communications standards are described as belonging to a particular generation. For 2G, there were two competing formats, established in different markets:

- **Global System for Mobile Communication (GSM)**-based phones. GSM allows subscribers to use a **Subscriber Identity Module (SIM)** card to use an unlocked handset with their chosen network provider. GSM is adopted internationally and by AT&T and T-Mobile in the US.
- TIA/EIA IS-95 (cdmaOne)-based handsets. With **Code Division Multiple Access (CDMA)**, the handset is managed by the provider, not the SIM. CDMA adoption is largely restricted to the telecom providers Sprint® and Verizon.

In both cases, the cell network was built primarily to support voice calls, so 2G data access was provided on top, using Circuit Switched Data (CSD). CSD is somewhat similar to a dial-up modem, though no analog transmissions are involved. CSD requires a data connection to be established to the base station (incurring call charges) and is only capable of around 14.4 Kbps at best.

3G

The transition from 2G to 3G saw various packet-switched technologies deployed to mobiles:

- General Packet Radio Services/Enhanced Data Rates for GSM Evolution (GPRS/EDGE) is a precursor to 3G (2.5G) with GPRS offering up to about 48 Kbps and EDGE about 3-4 times that. Unlike CSD, GPRS and EDGE allow "always on" data connections, with usage billed by bandwidth consumption rather than connection time.

- Evolved High Speed Packet Access (HSPA+) is a 3G standard developed via several iterations from the Universal Mobile Telecommunications System (UMTS) used on GSM networks. HSPA+ nominally supports download speeds up to 168 Mbps and upload speeds up to 34 Mbps. HSPA+-based services are often marketed as 4G if the nominal data rate is better than about 20 Mbps.
- CDMA2000/Evolution Data Optimized (EV-DO) are the main 3G standards deployed by CDMA network providers. EV-DO can support a 3.1 Mbps downlink and 1.8 Mbps uplink.

4G

Long Term Evolution (LTE) is a converged 4G standard supported by all network providers. Any device using a 4G connection needs a SIM card. LTE has a maximum downlink of 150 Mbps in theory, but no provider networks can deliver that sort of speed at the time of writing. Around 20 Mbps is more typical of real-word performance.

LTE Advanced (LTE-A) is intended to provide a 300 Mbps downlink, but again this aspiration is not matched by real-world performance. Current typical performance for LTE-A is around 40 Mbps.

5G

According to the original specification, a 4G service was supposed to deliver 1 Gbps for stationary or slow-moving users (including pedestrians) and 100 Mbps for access from a fast-moving vehicle. Those data rates are now the minimum hoped-for standards for 5G. 5G is currently only available in trial areas. Speeds of up to 70 Gbps have been achieved under test conditions, but commercial products and service standards are not likely to appear until 2020.

Activity 5-4
Discussing Internet Connection Types

SCENARIO
Answer the following questions to check your understanding of the topic.

1. If you have remote employees who need to connect to the corporate network but they are located in a remote area with no access to high-speed Internet service, what do you think is the best Internet connection method to use?

2. True or false? Analog modems are required for dial-up and ISDN Internet access services.

3. What type of SOHO Internet access method offers the best bandwidth?

4. Which protocol enables a dial-up user to exchange frames of data with an ISP's access server?

5. What type of cabling is used with the WAN port of a cable modem?

6. What Internet access method would be suitable for a business requiring a high bandwidth connection where no cabled options exist?

Topic E
Network Configuration Concepts

EXAM OBJECTIVES COVERED
1001-2.2 Compare and contrast common networking hardware devices.
1001-2.6 Explain common network configuration concepts.

Now that you are familiar with the basic components that make up a network, you can start to take a look at Transmission Control Protocol/Internet Protocol (TCP/IP) addressing and data delivery. In this topic, you will identify the properties and characteristics of TCP/IP.

As a CompTIA A+ technician, you must be able to identify how protocols work together and with the network hardware to provide services. Understanding how everything is connected and functioning within the network will allow you to properly support TCP/IP within a network.

ROUTERS

Ethernet switches connect nodes on the basis of local or hardware (MAC) addresses. Everything connected to an unmanaged switch is part of the same physical and logical network. When you want to connect such a network to the Internet or when you want to divide a large local network into logical subnetworks, you need to use one or more routers.

A **router** is responsible for moving data around a network of networks, known as an internetwork or internet. While a switch forwards frames using hardware (MAC) addresses within a single network segment, a router forwards packets around an internetwork using logical network and host IDs.

A router. (Image © 123RF.com.)

There are many different types and uses of routers, but on an enterprise network, a router tends to perform one of the following two tasks:

- LAN router—divide a single physical network into multiple logical networks. This is useful for security and performance reasons.

- WAN or edge/border router—join a network using one type of media with a network using different media. A typical example is to join a LAN to a WAN, such as the Internet.

Selection of the path or route to the destination network is determined dynamically or statically. The packet moves, hop by hop, through the internetwork to the target network. Once it has reached the destination network, the hardware address can be used to move the packet to the target node. This process requires each logically separate network to have a unique network address.

ROUTERS VERSUS MODEMS

Make sure you understand the separate functions of modems and routers when connecting to the Internet. A **modem** works at the same level as a switch, making a physical network link with the ISP's network. The type of modem must be matched to the type of link (dial-up, DSL, cable, and so on). A router makes decisions about forwarding between the two logical networks. For SOHO networks, this is usually a simple choice between the local network and the Internet. On a SOHO network, the modem and the router are typically bundled in the same appliance.

VIRTUAL LAN (VLAN)

The switches on an enterprise network can provide thousands of ports. It is inefficient to have that many connections to the same "logical" network. The ports are divided into groups using a feature of managed switches called **Virtual LAN (VLAN)**. Each VLAN is associated with a different logical subnetwork address. Communications between different VLANs therefore have to go through a router. As well as improving performance, this is a security benefit too. Traffic passing between VLANs can be easily filtered and monitored to ensure it meets security policies.

THE TCP/IP PROTOCOL SUITE

Protocols are procedures or rules used by networked hosts to communicate. For communication to take place, the two hosts must have a protocol in common. Often, several protocols used for networking are designed to work together. This collection of protocols is known as a **protocol suite**.

A number of protocol suites have been used for LAN and WAN communications over the years. However, the overwhelming majority of networks have now converged on the use of the **Transmission Control Protocol/Internet Protocol (TCP/IP)** suite. Most network implementations you will be required to install and support will depend on the use of TCP/IP.

TCP/IP was originally developed by the US Department of Defense but is now an open standard to which anyone may contribute. Developments are implemented through the Internet Engineering Task Force (IETF), which is split into a number of working groups. Standards are published as Request For Comments (RFCs). The official repository for RFCs is at **www.rfc-editor.org** and they are also published in HTML format at **tools.ietf.org/html**.

TCP/IP protocols are packet-based. This means that rather than sending a data message as a single large whole, it is split into numerous small packets. Smaller packets have a better chance of being delivered successfully and are easier to resend if lost or damaged.

Routers choose the paths that packets take around the network from source to destination.

TCP/IP PROTOCOLS

The main protocols in the suite provide addressing and transport services. The function of these protocols can be better understood by dividing them into layers. The TCP/IP suite uses a model with four distinct layers.

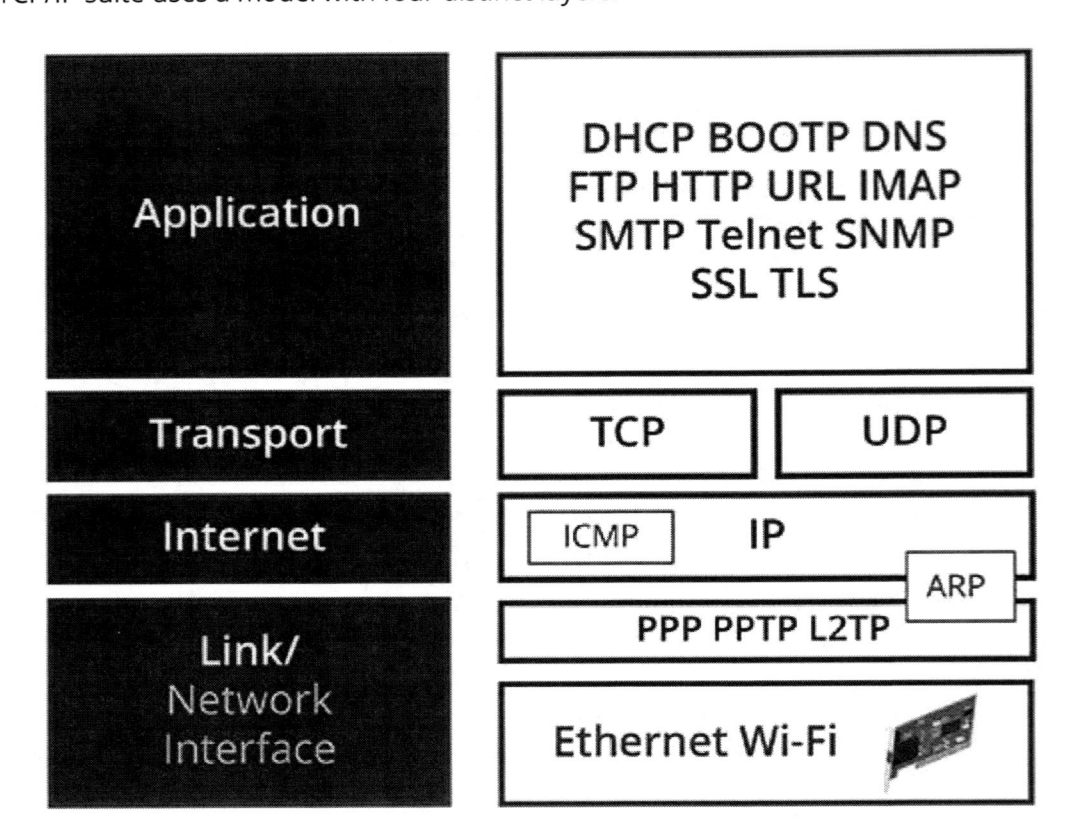

TCP/IP model. (Image © 123RF.com.)

The layers and main protocols working at each layer are as follows:

- **Link or Network Interface layer**—responsible for putting frames onto the physical network. This layer does not contain TCP/IP protocols as such. At this layer, different networking products and media can be used, such as Ethernet or Wi-Fi. Communications on this layer take place only on a local network segment and not between different networks. Data at the link layer is packaged in a unit called a frame and nodes are identified by a MAC address (assuming Ethernet or Wi-Fi).
- **Internet Protocol (IP)**—provides packet addressing and routing at the network layer. IP provides best effort delivery of an unreliable and connectionless nature. A packet might be lost, delivered out of sequence, duplicated, or delayed.
- **Transmission Control Protocol (TCP)**—guarantees orderly transmission of packets at the transport layer. TCP can identify and recover from lost or out-of-order packets. This is used by most TCP/IP application protocols as failing to receive a packet or processing it incorrectly can cause serious data errors.
- **User Datagram Protocol (UDP)**—provides unreliable, non-guaranteed transfer of packets. UDP is an alternative way of implementing the transport layer to TCP. UDP is faster and comes with less of a transmission overhead because it does not need to send extra information to establish reliable connections. It is used in time-sensitive applications, such as speech or video, where a few missing or out-of-order packets can be tolerated. Rather than causing the application to crash, they would just manifest as a glitch in video or a squeak in audio.

- **Application protocols**—there are numerous protocols used for network configuration, management, and services. Application protocols use a TCP or UDP port to connect the client and server.

ADDRESS RESOLUTION PROTOCOL (ARP)

When IP is being used with a physical/data link specification such as Ethernet or Wi-Fi, there must be a mechanism to deliver messages from IP at the network layer to computers addressed at the link layer. **Address Resolution Protocol (ARP)** finds the MAC (network adapter) address associated with an IP address.

ICMP

Additionally, you should be aware of the **Internet Control Message Protocol (ICMP)**, which works at the network layer. ICMP delivers status and error messages and is used by diagnostic utilities such as **ping** and **tracert**.

INTERNET PROTOCOL AND IP ADDRESSING

The core protocol in TCP/IP is the Internet Protocol (IP), which provides network and host addressing and packet forwarding between networks.

IPv4 PACKET STRUCTURE

As with a frame, an IP packet adds some headers to whatever transport/application layer data it is carrying in its payload. There are two versions of IP: IPv4 and IPv6. We will discuss IPv6 later. The main IPv4 headers are as follows:

Field	Description
Source IP address	Identifies the sender of the datagram by IP address.
Destination IP address	Identifies the destination of the datagram by IP address.
Protocol	Indicates whether the data should be passed to UDP or TCP at the destination host.
Checksum	Verifies the packet's integrity upon arrival at the destination.
Time to Live	The number of hops a datagram is allowed to stay on the network before being discarded, otherwise packets could endlessly loop around an internet. A router will decrease the TTL by at least one when it handles the packet.

IPv4 ADDRESS FORMAT

An IPv4 address is 32 bits long and is used within an IPv4 packet to define the source and destination of the packet. In its raw form it appears as:

```
11000110001010010001000000001001
```

The 32 bits are subdivided into four groups of 8 bits (1 byte) known as **octets**. The above IP address could therefore be rearranged as:

```
11000110   00101001   00010000   00001001
```

This representation of an IP address makes human memorizing of the number almost impossible (much less entering it correctly into configuration dialogs). To make IP addresses easier to use, they are usually displayed in **dotted decimal notation**. This notation requires each octet to be converted to a decimal value. The decimal numbers are separated using a period. Converting the previous number to this notation gives:

```
198 . 41 . 16 . 9
```

CONVERTING BETWEEN BINARY AND DECIMAL FORMAT

The following examples demonstrate the process of converting between binary and decimal notation. The base of any number system tells us two things: how many different values any given digit can have and the factor by which the value of a digit increases as we move from right to left in a number. Thus, in normal base 10 (or decimal) numbers, a digit can take any one of ten different values (0 through 9), and the values of the different place positions within a number, moving from right to left, are units (ones), tens, hundreds, thousands, and so on.

In base 2 (binary), digits can only take one of two different values (0 and 1). The place values are powers of 2 ($2^1=2$, $2^2=4$, $2^3=8$, $2^4=16$, and so on). Consider the octet "11101101" represented in base 2. The following figure shows the place value of each digit in the octet:

```
128      64      32      16      8       4       2       1
1        1       1       0       1       1       0       1
128*1    64*1    32*1    16*0    8*1     4*1     2*0     1*1
```

Therefore, the decimal equivalent is:

```
128  +  64  +  32  +  0  +  8  +  4  +  0  +  1  =  237
```

You can use the same sort of method to convert from decimal to binary. For example, the number 199 can be converted as follows:

```
199 =
128   +  64   +  0    +  0    +  0    +  4    +  2    +  1
128      64      32      16      8       4       2       1
128*1    64*1    32*0    16*0    8*0     4*1     2*1     1*1
1        1       0       0       0       1       1       1
```

If all the bits in an octet are set to 1, the number obtained is 255 (the maximum possible value). Similarly, if all the bits are set to 0, the number obtained is 0 (the minimum possible value). Therefore, theoretically an IPv4 address may be any value between 0.0.0.0 and 255.255.255.255. However, some addresses are not permitted or are reserved for special use.

SUBNET MASKS

An IP address provides two pieces of information encoded within the same value:
- The network number (**network ID**)—this number is common to all hosts on the same IP network.
- The host number (**host ID**)—this unique number identifies a host on a particular IP network.

A **subnet mask** (or netmask) is used to distinguish these two components within a single IP address. It is used to "mask" the host ID portion of the IP address and thereby reveal the network ID portion.

Where there is a binary 1 in the mask, the corresponding binary digit in the IP address is part of the network ID. The relative sizes of the network and host portions determines the number of networks and hosts per network a particular addressing scheme can support.

Many subnetting schemes use one of the **default masks**. These are masks comprising whole octets only. Each default mask is known by a particular "class."

Class	Dotted Decimal Mask	Network Prefix	Binary Mask
A	255.0.0.0	/8	11111111 00000000 00000000 00000000
B	255.255.0.0	/16	11111111 11111111 00000000 00000000

Class	Dotted Decimal Mask	Network Prefix	Binary Mask
C	255.255.255.0	/24	11111111 11111111 11111111 00000000

The mask can be expressed in dotted decimal format or as a network prefix. The network prefix is simply the number of ones that appear in the mask.

Note: The 1s in the mask are always contiguous. For example, a mask 11111111 11110000 00000000 00000000 is valid but 11111111 00000000 11110000 00000000 is not.

MASKING AN IP ADDRESS (ANDing)

The network ID portion of an IP address is revealed by "ANDing" the subnet mask to the IP address. When two 1s are ANDed together, the result is a 1. Any other combination produces a 0.

```
1  AND  1  =  1
1  AND  0  =  0
0  AND  1  =  0
0  AND  0  =  0
```

For example, to determine the network ID of the IP address 172.30.15.12 with a subnet mask of 255.255.0.0, the dotted decimal notation of the IP address and subnet mask must first be converted to binary notation. The next step is to AND the two binary numbers. The result can be converted back to dotted decimal notation to provide the network ID (172.30.0.0).

```
172. 30. 15. 12    10101100 00011110 00001111 00001100
255.255.  0.  0    11111111 11111111 00000000 00000000
172. 30.  0.  0    10101100 00011110 00000000 00000000
```

Instead of quoting the mask each time, you could express that network ID with a prefix instead: `172.30.0.0/16`.

ROUTING DECISION

A host can communicate directly on the local network segment with any other host that has the same network ID. Communications with a host that has a different network ID must be sent via a router.

When two hosts attempt to communicate via IPv4, the protocol compares the source and destination address in each packet against a subnet mask. If the masked portions of the source and destination IP addresses match, then the destination interface is assumed to be on the same IP network. For example:

```
172. 30. 15. 12    10101100 00011110 00001111 00001100
255.255.  0.  0    11111111 11111111 00000000 00000000
172. 30. 16.101    10101100 00011110 00010000 01100101
```

In the example, IP concludes the destination IPv4 address is on the same IP network and would try to deliver the packet locally.

If the masked portion does not match, IP assumes the packet must be routed to another IP network. For example:

```
172. 30. 15. 12    10101100 00011110 00001111 00001100
255.255.  0.  0    11111111 11111111 00000000 00000000
172. 31. 16.101    10101100 00011111 00010000 01100101
```

In this case, IP concludes the destination IPv4 address is on a different IP network and would forward the packet to a router rather than trying to deliver it locally.

> **Note:** This describes **unicast addressing**, where a single host is addressed. An address where the host bits are all "1"s is the **broadcast address** for a network. A message sent to a broadcast address is received by all hosts on the network. The broadcast address of the previous example would be 172.16.255.255.

HOST IP CONFIGURATION

Each host must be configured with an IP address and subnet mask at a minimum in order to communicate on an IPv4 network. This minimum configuration will not prove very usable, however. Several other parameters must be configured for a host to make full use of a modern network or the Internet.

IPv4 ADDRESS AND SUBNET MASK

An IPv4 address and subnet mask can be set manually (static address). The IP address is entered as four decimal numbers separated by periods (e.g., 172.30.15.12). The IP address identifies both the network to which the interface is attached and also its unique identity on that network. An interface must be configured with an IP address.

The subnet mask is used in conjunction with the IP address to determine whether another interface is located on a local or remote network. An interface must be configured with a subnet mask.

DEFAULT GATEWAY

The **default gateway** parameter is the IP address of a router to which packets destined for a remote network should be sent by default. This setting is not compulsory but failure to enter a gateway would limit the interface to communication on the local network only.

CLIENT-SIDE DNS

Another important part of IP configuration is specifying the IP address of one or more **Domain Name System (DNS)** servers. These servers provide resolution of host and domain names to their IP addresses and are essential for locating resources on the Internet. Most local networks also use DNS for name resolution. Typically, the DNS server would be the gateway address, though this may not be the case on all networks. Often two DNS server addresses (preferred and alternate) are specified for redundancy.

STATIC AND DYNAMIC IP ADDRESSES

Using static addressing requires that an administrator visit each computer to manually enter the configuration information for that host. If the host moves to a different subnet, the administrator must manually reconfigure it. The administrator must keep track of which IP addresses have been allocated to avoid issuing duplicates. In a large network, configuring IP statically on each node can be very time consuming and prone to errors that can potentially disrupt communication on the network.

Static addresses are typically only assigned to systems with a dedicated functionality, such as router interfaces, network-attached printers, or servers that host applications on a network.

DHCP

When an interface is given a static configuration manually, the installer may make a mistake with the address information—perhaps duplicating an existing IP address or entering the wrong subnet mask—or the configuration of the network may change, requiring the host to be manually configured with a new static address. To avoid these problems, a **Dynamic Host Configuration Protocol (DHCP)** Server can be used to allocate an IP address and subnet mask (plus other settings) dynamically.

The computer contacts the DHCP server as it starts up and is allocated a lease for an IP address. Settings such as default gateway and DNS server addresses may be passed to the computer at the same time. If the address information needs to change, this can be done on the DHCP server, and clients will update themselves automatically when they seek a new lease (or a new lease can be requested manually).

> **Note:** The DHCP client communicates with the server using broadcast communications so there is no need to configure a DHCP server address.

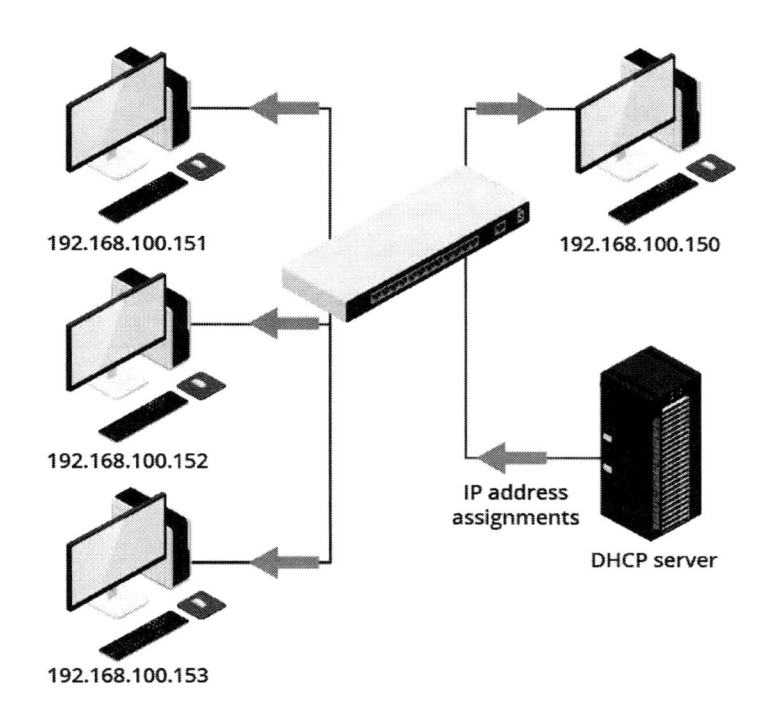

DHCP. (Image © 123RF.com.)

LINK LOCAL ADDRESSING/APIPA

Hosts also have a "fallback" mechanism for when the computer is configured to use a DHCP server but cannot contact one. In this scenario, the computer selects an address at random from the range 169.254.1.0 to 169.254.254.255. Microsoft calls this **Automatic Private IP Addressing (APIPA)**. When a host is using an APIPA address, it can communicate with other hosts on the same network that are using APIPA, but cannot reach other networks or communicate with hosts that have managed to obtain a valid DHCP lease.

> **Note:** "APIPA" is Microsoft's term. Other vendors and open source products use the term "link local" instead.

DHCP RESERVATIONS

It is often useful for a host to use the same IP address. Servers, routers, printers, and other network infrastructure can be easier to manage if their IP addresses are known. One option is to use static addressing for these appliances, but this is difficult to implement. Another option is to configure the DHCP server to **reserve** a particular IP address for that device. The DHCP server is configured with a list of the MAC addresses of hosts that should receive the same IP address. When it is contacted by a host with one of the listed MAC addresses, it issues a lease for the reserved IP address.

Note: The main drawback of this method is that if the DHCP server fails, then critical network devices might fail to obtain IP addresses.

PUBLIC AND PRIVATE IP ADDRESSES

To communicate on the Internet, a host must obtain a unique public IP address. Typically this is allocated by an Internet Service Provider. Relatively few companies can obtain sufficient public IP addresses for all their computers to communicate over the Internet, however. There are various mechanisms to work around this issue.

PRIVATE ADDRESSING

The IP address scheme defines certain ranges as **private addresses**. These ranges are defined by RFC 1918 and are sometimes referred to as RFC 1918 addresses. Hosts with IP addresses from these ranges are not allowed to route traffic over the Internet. Use of the addresses is confined to private LANs. There are three private address ranges, each associated with one of the default subnet masks:

- 10.0.0.0 to 10.255.255.255 (Class A private address range).
- 172.16.0.0 to 172.31.255.255 (Class B private address range).
- 192.168.0.0 to 192.168.255.255 (Class C private address range).
- 169.254.0.0 to 169.254.255.255 (APIPA/link-local autoconfiguration). As discussed earlier, this range is used by hosts for autoconfiguration when a DHCP server cannot be contacted (selecting a link-local address).

Internet access can be facilitated for hosts using the private addressing scheme in two ways:

- Through a router configured with a single or block of valid public addresses; the router translates between the private and public addresses using Network Address Translation (NAT).
- Through a proxy server that fulfills requests for Internet resources on behalf of clients.

NETWORK ADDRESS TRANSLATION

Most hosts on private networks are not configured with IP addresses that can communicate directly to the Internet. Instead, when clients on the local network connect via a router, the router converts the client's private IP address into a valid public address using **Network Address Translation (NAT)**.

A NAT address pool supports multiple simultaneous connections but is still limited by the number of available public IP addresses. Smaller companies may only be allocated a single or small block of addresses by their ISP. In this case, a means for multiple private IP addresses to be mapped onto a single public address would be useful, and this is exactly what is provided by **Network Address Port Translation (NAPT)**, which is also referred to as Port Address Translation (PAT) or as NAT overloading.

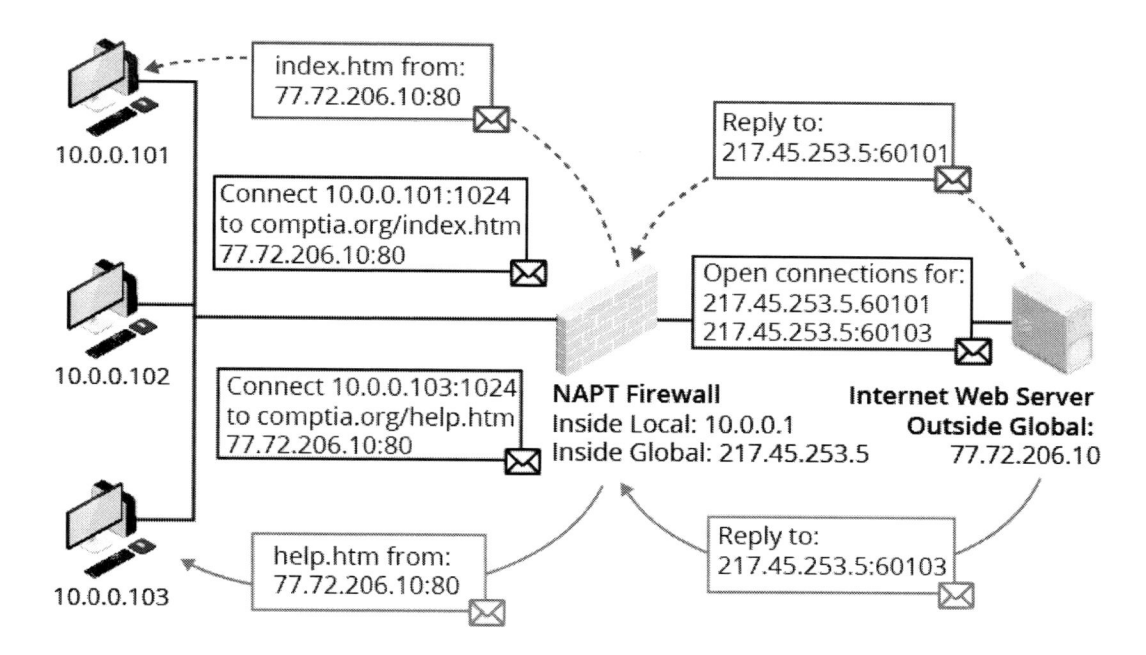

NAT overloading. (Image © 123RF.com.)

NAPT works by allocating each new connection a high level TCP or UDP port. For example, say two hosts (10.0.0.101 and 10.0.0.103) initiate a web connection at the same time, requesting responses on the client (or source) port 1024. The NAPT service creates two new client port mappings for these requests (10.0.0.101:60101 and 10.0.0.103:60103). It then substitutes the private source IPs for a single public source IP (217.45.253.5) and forwards the requests to the public Internet. It performs a reverse mapping on any traffic returned to those client ports, inserting the original private IP address and client port number, and forwarding the packets to the internal hosts.

VIRTUAL PRIVATE NETWORKS

A **Virtual Private Network (VPN)** connects the components and resources of two (private) networks over another (public) network. The Internet provides a cost effective way of connecting both users to networks and networks to networks. Rather than a user direct-dialing your server, which is private but expensive, the user connects to an ISP, which is cheap, but public.

A VPN is a "tunnel" through the Internet (or any other public network). It uses special connection protocols and encryption technology to ensure that the tunnel is secure and the user is properly authenticated. Once the connection has been established, to all intents and purposes, the remote computer becomes part of the local network (though it is still restricted by the bandwidth available over the WAN link).

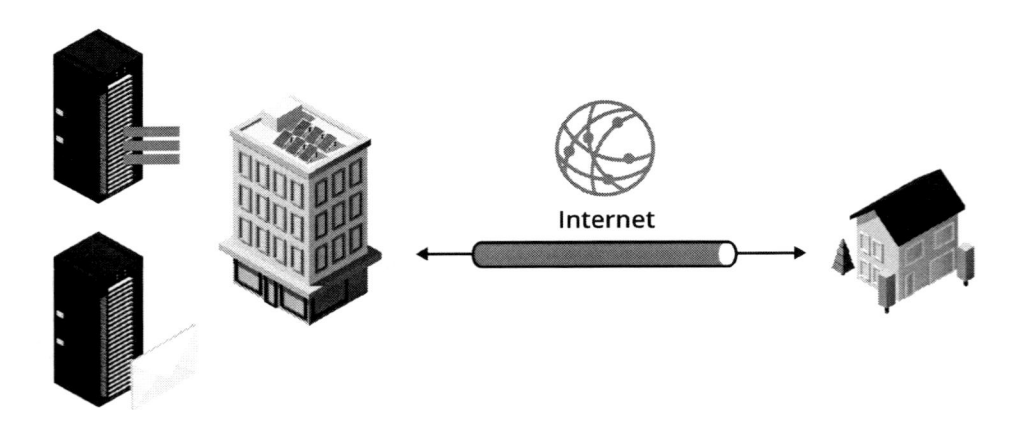

A typical VPN configuration. (Image © 123RF.com.)

IPv6

The addressing scheme discussed earlier is for IP version 4. Because it is feared the global supply of IPv4 addresses will run out, a new version of IP addressing, IP Version 6, has been developed. An IPv6 address is a 128-bit number (contrast with the 32-bit number used in v4). This massively increases the available pool of available addresses compared to IPv4.

IPv6 also includes new efficiency features, such as simplified address headers, hierarchical addressing, support for time-sensitive network traffic, and a new structure for unicast addressing.

BINARY AND HEXADECIMAL NOTATION

Network addresses are represented as binary values when processed by the computer but because binary has only two values for each position and the values for IPv6 addresses are very large, this would require a long string of characters to write out. This is difficult enough to read but even harder to type accurately into configuration dialogs.

Binary values are converted to decimal for IPv4 addresses but as IPv6 addresses are so much longer, hexadecimal notation is used. Hexadecimal has 16 characters (0...9 plus A, B, C, D, E, F). Therefore, it only takes 1 hexadecimal character to represent 4 binary characters. The following table summarizes the equivalent representations of decimal values from 0-15 in binary and hex.

Decimal	Hexadecimal	Binary
0	0	0000
1	1	0001
2	2	0010
3	3	0011
4	4	0100
5	5	0101
6	6	0110
7	7	0111
8	8	1000
9	9	1001

Decimal	Hexadecimal	Binary
10	A	1010
11	B	1011
12	C	1100
13	D	1101
14	E	1110
15	F	1111

IPv6 ADDRESS NOTATION

To express a 128-bit IPv6 address in hexadecimal notation, the binary address is divided into eight double-byte (16-bit) values delimited by colons. For example:

`2001:0db8:0000:0000:0abc:0000:def0:1234`

Even this is quite cumbersome, so where a double-byte contains leading zeros, they can be ignored. In addition, one contiguous series of zeroes can be replaced by a double colon place marker. Thus, the address above would become:

`2001:db8::abc:0:def0:1234`

IPv6 ADDRESSING SCHEMES

An IPv6 address is divided into two main parts: the first 64 bits are used as a network ID while the second 64 bits designate a specific interface.

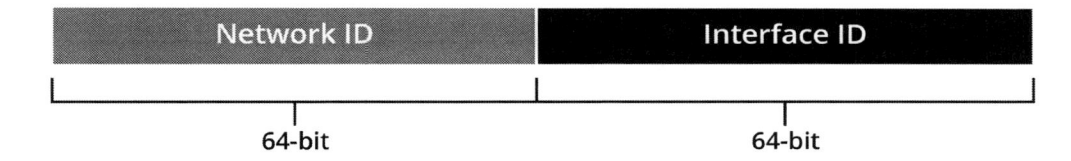

In IPv6, the interface identifier is always the last 64 bits; the first 64 bits are used for network addressing. (Image © 123RF.com.)

As the network and host portions are fixed size, there is no need for a subnet mask. Network addresses are written using prefix notation, where /nn is the length of the routing prefix in bits. Within the 64-bit network ID, the length of any given network prefix is used to determine whether two addresses belong to the same IP network.

GLOBALLY UNIQUE UNICAST ADDRESSING

As with IPv4, a unicast address identifies a single network interface. The main types of unicast addressing are global and link-local. A **global address** is one that is unique on the Internet (equivalent to public addresses in IPv4). Global unicast addresses have the following format:

- The first 3 bits indicate that the address is within the global scope. In hex notation, a global unicast address will start with either "2" or "3."
- The next 45 bits are allocated in a hierarchical manner to regional registries and from them to ISPs and end users.
- The next 16 bits identity site-specific subnet addresses.
- The final 64 bits are the interface ID. The interface ID is either generated from the adapter's MAC address (padded with extra bits to make it 64 bits in length) or is randomly generated.

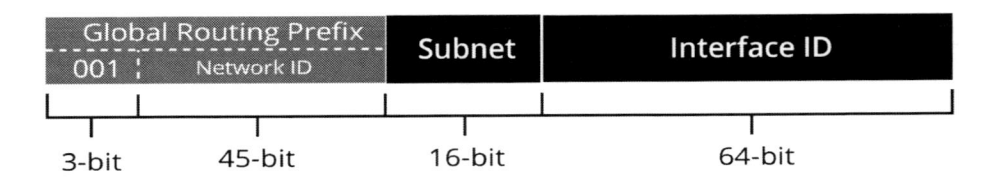

IPv6 global unicast address format. (Image © 123RF.com.)

In IPv6, address blocks are automatically assigned hierarchically by routers. Top-level routers have top-level address blocks, which are automatically divided and assigned as routers and segments are added. This divides the address space as a logical hierarchy, compared to the ad-hoc address-space management procedures that were developed for IPv4, making it easier to manage.

LINK-LOCAL ADDRESSING

Link-local addresses are used by IPv6 for network housekeeping traffic. Link-local addresses span a single subnet (they are not forwarded by routers). Nodes on the same link are referred to as neighbors. In hex notation, link-local addresses start with `fe80::`

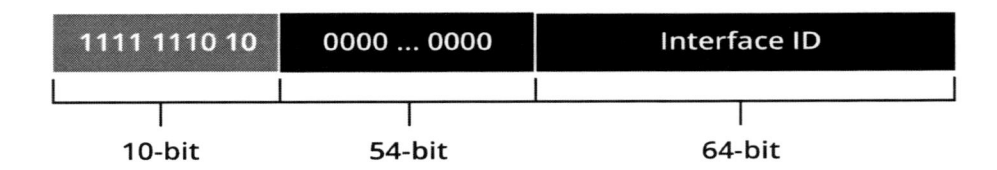

IPv6 link-local unicast address format. (Image © 123RF.com.)

The equivalent in IPv4 is Automatic Private IP Addressing (APIPA) and its 169.254.0.0 addresses. However, unlike IPv4, an IPv6 host is always configured with link-local addresses (one for each link), even if it also has a globally unique address.

Activity 5-5
Discussing Network Configuration Concepts

SCENARIO
Answer the following questions to check your understanding of the topic.

1. What is the difference between a router and a modem?

2. Protocols within the TCP/IP suite (and products supporting TCP/IP networks) are conceived as working at one of four layers.

   What are those four layers called?

3. What is meant by dotted decimal notation?

4. When is a default gateway required?

5. A host is configured with the IP address 192.168.1.10/24.

   What is the host's subnet mask?

6. What is the purpose of a DHCP server?

7. What is special about an IP address that starts 169.254?

8. A host is configured with the IP address 172.29.0.101.
   What is significant about this address?

9. What is the function of NAT?

10. Apart from its length, what is the main difference between the structure of an IPv4 address and an IPv6 address?

Topic F
Network Services

EXAM OBJECTIVES COVERED
1001-2.1 Compare and contrast TCP and UDP ports, protocols, and their purposes.
1001-2.5 Summarize the properties and purposes of services provided by networked hosts.

In the previous topics, you explored the network hardware and protocols that facilitate the process of making connections between hosts and networks, including Internet connections. In this topic, you will move on to examine the various ports and protocols that are used to provide application services.

Properly configuring the ports of a network device and selecting the right protocol will ensure that data gets transmitted over the network. As a CompTIA A+ technician, you must understand how ports and protocols are implemented within a network and how they function to provide the right level of data transmission while keeping data secure.

TCP AND UDP PORTS

The protocols we have looked at so far are primarily concerned with moving frames and packets between nodes and networks. At the link/physical layer, Ethernet allows nodes to send one another frames of data using MAC addresses. These frames would typically be transporting IP packets. At the network layer, IP provides addressing and routing functionality for a network of networks (or internetwork).

Protocols at the transport layer, one up from the network layer, are concerned with effective delivery. At the transport layer, the content of the packets starts to become significant.

Any given host on a network will be communicating with many other hosts using many different types of networking data. One of the critical functions of the transport layer is to identify each type of network application. It does this by assigning each application a **port number** between 0 and 65535. For example, data addressed to the HTTP web browsing application can be identified as port 80 while data requesting an email application service can be identified as port 143. At the transport layer, on the sending host, data from the upper layers is packaged as a series of segments and each segment is tagged with the application's port number. The segment is then passed to the network layer for delivery. The host could be transmitting multiple HTTP and email segments at the same time. These are multiplexed using the port numbers onto the same network link.

> **Note:** *In fact, each host assigns two port numbers. On the client, the destination port number is mapped to the service that the client is requesting (HTTP on port 80, for instance). The client also assigns a random source port number (47747, for instance). The server uses this client-assigned port number (47747) as the destination port number for its replies and its application port number (80 for HTTP) as its source port. This allows the hosts to track multiple "conversations" for the same application protocol.*

At the network and data link layers, the port number is not significant—it becomes part of the data payload and is "invisible" to routers and switches working at the network and data link layers. At the receiving host, each segment is extracted from its frame and then identified by its port number and passed up to the relevant handler at the application layer.

TCP VERSUS UDP

The transport layer is also responsible for ensuring reliable data delivery so that packets arrive error-free and without loss. The transport layer can overcome lack of reliability in the lower level protocols. This reliability is achieved by the **Transport Control Protocol (TCP)** using acknowledgement messages that inform the sender the data was successfully received.

The kinds of problems that may occur during the delivery of the data are non-delivery and delivery in a damaged state. In the first case, the lack of acknowledgement results in the retransmission of the data and, in the second case, a **Negative Acknowledgement (NACK)** forces retransmission. TCP is described as connection-oriented, because it ensures the reliability and sequencing of messages passing over the connection.

On the other hand, sometimes it is more important that communications be faster than they are reliable. The acknowledgements process of TCP adds a lot of overhead. The **User Datagram Protocol (UDP)** is a connectionless, non-guaranteed method of communication with no sequencing or flow control. There is no guarantee regarding the delivery of messages or the sequence in which packets are received. UDP is suitable for applications that do not require acknowledgement of receipt and can tolerate missing or out-of-order packets. It may be used for applications that transfer time-sensitive data but do not require complete reliability, such as voice or video. The reduced overhead means that delivery is faster. If necessary, the application layer can be used to control delivery reliability.

WELL-KNOWN PORTS

Any application or process that uses TCP or UDP for its transport, such as HTTP for web services or POP3 for email, is assigned a unique identification number called a port. The server and client applications use different ports. For example, a client may contact an HTTP server at IP address 77.72.206.10 on port 80 (77.72.206.10:80). The HTTP server would respond to the client on a temporary (or ephemeral) port number that the client has opened for that purpose (47747, for instance).

Server port numbers are assigned by the Internet Assigned Numbers Authority (IANA). Some of the "well-known" port numbers are listed in the following table.

Port #	TCP/UDP	Process	Description
20	TCP	ftp-data	File Transfer Protocol - Data
21	TCP	ftp	File Transfer Protocol - Control
22	TCP	ssh	Secure Shell
23	TCP	telnet	Telnet
25	TCP	smtp	Simple Mail Transfer Protocol
53	TCP/UDP	domain	Domain Name System
67	UDP	bootps	BOOTP/DHCP Server
68	UDP	bootpc	BOOTP/DHCP Client
80	TCP	http	HTTP
110	TCP	pop3	Post Office Protocol
123	UDP	ntp	Network Time Protocol
137-139	UDP/TCP	netbt	NetBIOS over TCP/IP
143	TCP	imap4	Internet Mail Access Protocol

Port #	TCP/UDP	Process	Description
161	UDP	snmp	Simple Network Management Protocol
162	UDP	snmp-trap	Simple Network Management Protocol Trap
389	TCP	ldap	Lightweight Directory Access Protocol
427	TCP	slp	Service Location Protocol
443	TCP	https	HTTP Secure
445	TCP	smb	Server Message Block/Common Internet File System
548	TCP	afp	Apple Filing Protocol
3389	TCP	rdp	Remote Desktop Protocol

IANA defines the ephemeral port range as 49152 to 65535, but some operating systems use different values.

Enabling and disabling ports is an important part of configuring a firewall, to ensure that only valid application protocols are allowed.

The TCP/IP suite encompasses a large number and wide range of protocols. Some of the principal protocols amongst these are discussed in the following sections.

DNS

The **Domain Name System (DNS)** is a hierarchical system for resolving names to IP addresses. It uses a distributed database that contains information on domains and hosts within those domains. The information is distributed among many name servers, each of which holds part of the database. The distributed nature of the system has the twin advantages that maintenance of the system is delegated and loss of one DNS server does not prevent name resolution from being performed.

At the top of the DNS hierarchy is the root, which is often represented by a period (.). There are 13 root level servers (A to M). Immediately below the root lie the **Top Level Domains (TLDs)**. There are several types of top level domain, but the most prevalent are generic (.com, .org, .net, .info, .biz), sponsored (.gov, .edu), and country code (.uk, .ca, .de).

The domain name system is operated by ICANN (**icann.org**), who also manage the generic top level domains. Country codes are generally managed by an organization appointed by the relevant government. Each domain name has to be registered with a Domain Name Registry for the appropriate top level domain.

Information about a domain is found by tracing records from the root down through the hierarchy. The root servers have complete information about the top level domain servers. In turn, these servers have information relating to servers for the second level domains.

No name server has complete information about all domains. Records within the DNS tell them where the missing information is found.

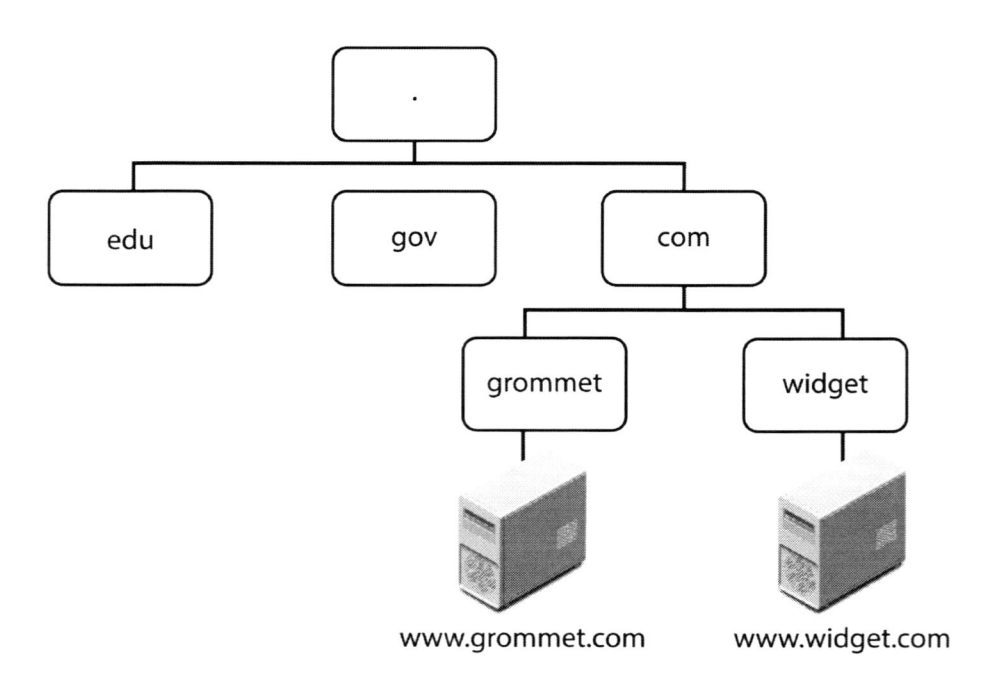

DNS hierarchy. (Image © 123RF.com.)

FULLY QUALIFIED DOMAIN NAME

The full name of any host is called its **Fully Qualified Domain Name (FQDN)**. FQDNs reflect the hierarchy, from most specific (the host) to least specific (the top level domain followed by the root). For example: www.widget.com.

The structure of a FQDN follows a fixed hierarchy, with the top level of the hierarchy shown to the right of the name. Each part of the name (a label) is separated by period characters (full stops). Any given label can consist of letters, numbers, and hyphens (though it cannot start with a hyphen).

The **domain name** identifies a company, organization, or even an individual. The name has to be unique and officially registered (a process that is normally handled by your ISP).

Host names and local domains are specified within the organization (for example, to identify a server located in the sales department of a company). The www host name is a common alias to indicate that the resource is a web server.

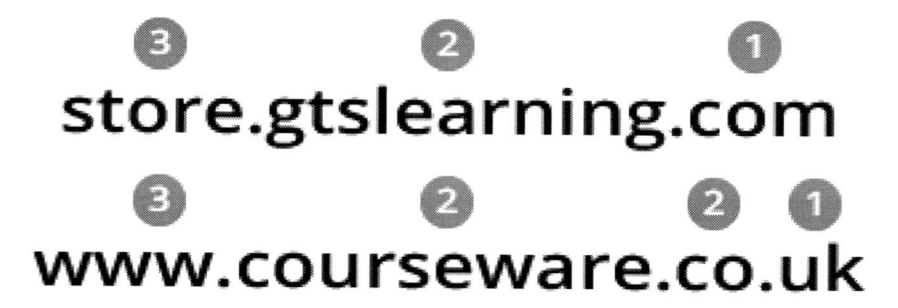

Parts of two FQDNs with 1) Top level domain; 2) Subdomain; 3) Host name. (Image © 123RF.com.)

DNS SERVERS

Different types of DNS servers are used by private organizations:

- **Authoritative name server**—this type of DNS server holds domain records and can respond authoritatively to requests for information about hosts in the domain(s) it manages. On a private network, such as an Active Directory (AD) domain, a name server must be running to host the AD DNS records. These records would not be made publicly available outside the LAN. On the Internet, public information about a domain, such as the location of its web and email servers, will be published to a name server. These are usually hosted by ISPs.
- **Recursive resolver**—when a client application wants to resolve a name or FQDN, it uses a recursive resolver to perform the query. The resolver contacts name servers in the DNS hierarchy until it either locates the requested record or times out. When you configure a DNS server on a client, it is usually the address of a resolver that you are entering.

> **Note:** On a private network, the same DNS server is likely to be identified for both functions. For example, an AD DNS server might both host the DNS records and provide name resolution for other Internet domain requests (typically by forwarding them to another server). Alternatively, the network might use client-facing forwarding-only servers whose only purpose is to select the best DNS server to answer a particular request and forward it on.

A DNS server is usually configured to listen for queries on UDP port 53.

WEB SERVERS AND HTTP/HTTPS

A **web server** is one that provides client access using the HyperText Transfer Protocol (HTTP) or its secure version (HTTPS).

HTTP AND HTML

HyperText Transfer Protocol (HTTP) is the basis of the World Wide Web. HTTP enables clients (typically web browsers) to request resources from an HTTP server. A client connects to the HTTP server using its TCP port (the default is port 80) and submits a request for a resource, using a **Uniform Resource Locator (URL)**. The server acknowledges the request and returns the data.

Typically, an organization will lease a server or space on a server from an ISP. Larger organizations with their own Internet Point-of-Presence may host websites themselves. Web servers are not only used on the Internet, however. Private networks using web technologies are described as **intranets** (if they permit only local access) or **extranets** (if they permit remote access).

HTTP is usually used to serve HyperText Markup Language (HTML) web pages, which are plain text files with coded tags describing how the page should be formatted. A web browser can interpret the tags and display the text and other resources associated with the page (such as picture or sound files). Another powerful feature is its ability to provide hyperlinks to other related documents. HTTP also features forms mechanisms (GET and POST) whereby a user can submit data from the client to the server.

The functionality of HTTP servers is often extended by support for scripting and programmable features (web applications).

UNIFORM RESOURCE LOCATOR

Resources on the Internet are accessed using an addressing scheme known as a Uniform Resource Locator (URL). A URL contains all the information necessary to identify and access an item. For example, a URL for an HTTP resource might contain the following elements:

- The protocol describes the access method or service type being used.
- The host location is usually represented by a Fully Qualified Domain Name (FQDN). The FQDN is not case sensitive. The host location can also be an IP address; an IPv6 address must be enclosed in square brackets.
- The file path specifies the directory and file name location of the resource (if required). The file path may or may not be case-sensitive, depending on how the server is configured.

http://store.gtslearning.com/comptia/index.htm

URL with 1) Protocol; 2) FQDN; 3) File path. (Image © 123RF.com.)

SSL/TLS

One of the critical problems for the provision of early e-commerce sites was the lack of security in HTTP. Under HTTP, all data is sent unencrypted and there is no authentication of client or server. **Secure Sockets Layer (SSL)** was developed by Netscape and released as version 3.0 in 1996 to address these problems. SSL proved very popular with the industry and is still in widespread use. **Transport Layer Security (TLS)** was developed from SSL and ratified as a standard by IETF. TLS is now the product in active development, with 1.2 as the latest version.

SSL/TLS is typically used with the HTTP application (referred to as **HTTPS** or HTTP Over SSL or HTTP Secure) but can also be used to secure other TCP/IP application protocols. TLS can also be used with UDP applications, referred to as **Datagram Transport Layer Security (DTLS)**. Some VPN solutions depend on the use of DTLS.

Note: HTTPS operates over port 443 by default. HTTPS operation is indicated by using https:// for the URL and by a padlock icon shown in the browser.

The basic function of TLS is:

1. A server is assigned a digital certificate by some trusted Certificate Authority.
2. The certificate proves the identity of the server (assuming that the client trusts the Certificate Authority).
3. The server uses the digital certificate and the SSL/TLS protocol to encrypt communications between it and the client.

This means that the communications cannot be read or changed by a third party.

Note: It is also possible to install a certificate on the client so that the server can trust the client. This is not often used on the web but is a feature of VPNs.

MAIL SERVERS

Email is a messaging system that can be used to transmit text messages and binary file attachments encoded using **Multipurpose Internet Mail Extensions (MIME)**. Email can involve the use of multiple protocols. The following process illustrates how an email message is sent from a typical corporate mail gateway (using the Microsoft Exchange mail server) to a recipient with subscriber Internet access:

1. The email client software on the sender's computer (sender@515support.com) sends the message to the Exchange email server using Microsoft's **Message Application Programming Interface (MAPI)** protocol. The mail server puts the message in a queue, waiting for the next **Simple Mail Transfer Protocol (SMTP)** session to be started. SMTP uses TCP port 25 by default.

2. When the Exchange SMTP server starts to process the queue, it first contacts a DNS server to resolve the recipient's address (for example, recipient@othercompany.com) to an IP address for the othercompany.com email server, listed as a Mail Exchanger (MX) record in DNS.
3. It then uses SMTP to deliver the message to this email server. The delivery usually requires several "hops"; for example, from the mail gateway to the sender's ISP, then to the recipient's ISP. The hops taken by a message as it is delivered over the Internet are recorded in the message header.
4. The message is put in the message store on the recipient's mail server. To retrieve it, the recipient uses his or her mail client software to connect with the mailbox on the server, using the **Post Office Protocol (POP3)** on TCP port 110 or **Internet Message Access Protocol (IMAP)** on TCP port 143. POP3 is more widely implemented, but IMAP provides extra features, such as support for mail folders other than inbox on the server and calendar functionality.

Note: Email communications between a client and server would normally be protected with SSL/TLS security. The default port numbers for these are 587 (SMTPS), 993 (IMAPS), and 995 (POP3S).

To configure an email account, you need the username, password, and default email address, plus incoming and outgoing server addresses and protocol types from the ISP.

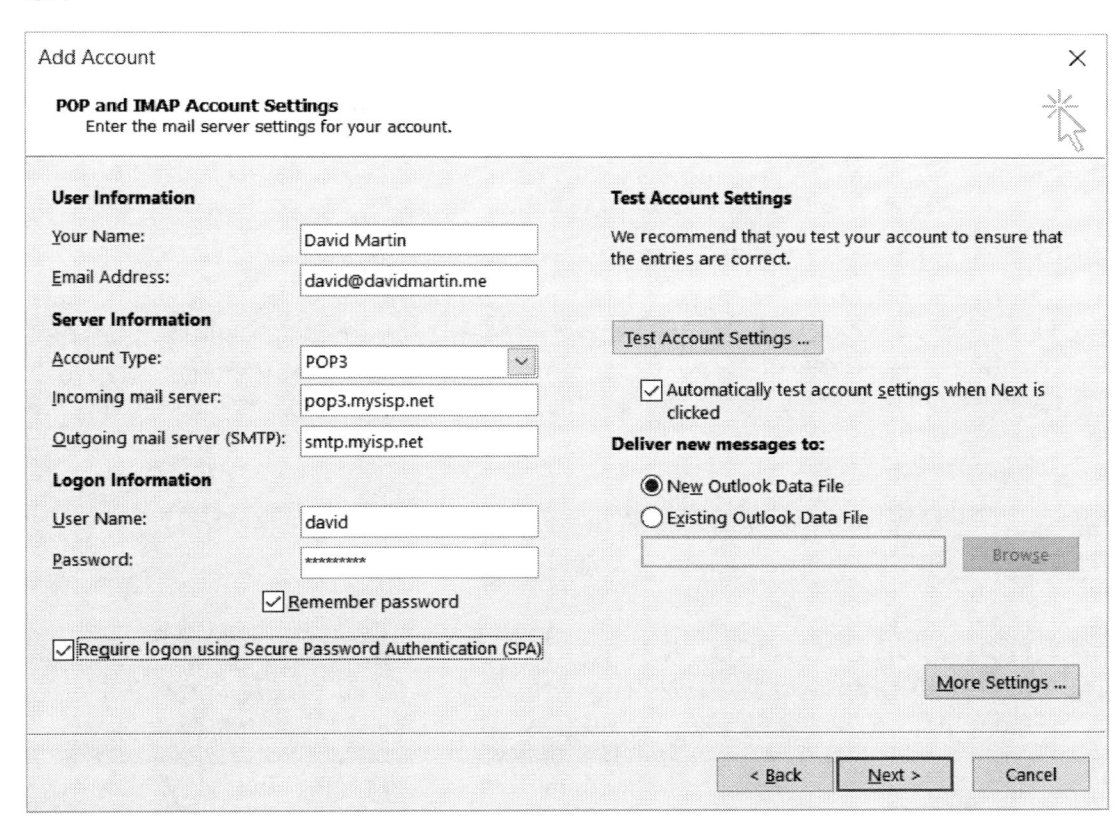

Configuring an email account. The incoming server is either POP3 or IMAP while the outgoing server is SMTP. (Screenshot used with permission from Microsoft.)

Internet email addresses follow the mailto URL scheme. An Internet email address comprises two parts—the username (local part) and the domain name, separated by an @ symbol. The domain name may refer to a company or an ISP; for example, david.martin@comptia.org or david.martin@aol.com.

Different mail systems have different requirements for allowed and disallowed characters in the local part. The local part is supposed to be case-sensitive, but most mail systems do not treat it as such. An incorrectly addressed email will be returned with a message notifying that it was undeliverable. Mail may also be rejected if it is identified as spam or if there is some other problem with the user mailbox (such as the mailbox being full).

Of course, there are many more network communication types than email. Network services are equally likely to support Voice over IP, videoconferencing, messaging, and integration with social media.

FILE AND PRINTER SHARING

One of the core network functions is to provide shared access to disk and print resources. These services may be performed using proprietary protocols, such as File and Print Services for Windows Networks. A file server could also be implemented using standard protocols, such as File Transfer Protocol (FTP), though this lacks a lot of the functionality of Windows file services.

SERVER MESSAGE BLOCK (SMB)/COMMON INTERNET FILE SYSTEM (CIFS)

Server Message Block (SMB) is the application protocol underpinning file and printer sharing on Windows networks. In all supported versions of Windows, version 2 of the protocol is used (SMB2), though there is support for legacy Windows clients. SMB usually runs directly over TCP on port 445 but can also run as part of NetBIOS over TCP/IP, over UDP and TCP in the port range 137-139. The Samba software package implements the protocol for Linux computers, enabling them to share and access resources on an otherwise Windows-based network. SMB is also sometimes referred to as the **Common Internet File System (CIFS)**.

APPLE FILING PROTOCOL (AFP)

The **Apple Filing Protocol (AFP)** performs a similar file sharing function to SMB but for Apple networks running Mac OS. AFP is associated with the use of two ports:

- UDP or TCP port 427—this is a port running the Service Location Protocol, used to advertise the availability of file shares. It is not required by later versions of OS X (10.2 and up).
- TCP port 548—this is the main port used by AFP.

> **Note:** *Apple is phasing out support for AFP in favor of its own version of SMB2 (SMBX).*

FILE TRANSFER PROTOCOL (FTP)

The **File Transfer Protocol (FTP)** was one of the earliest protocols used on TCP/IP networks and the Internet. As its name suggests, it allows a client to upload and download files from a remote server. It is widely used to upload files to websites. Also, if you have existing files that you want to make available to remote users, FTP is a simple service to install and maintain. Files made available through FTP can be in any format, including document, multimedia, or application files.

FTP is associated with the use of TCP port 21 to establish a connection and either TCP port 20 to transfer data in "active" mode or a server-assigned port in "passive" mode.

The FTP client may take a number of forms:

- Most installations of TCP/IP include a command-line client interface. The commands `put` and `get` are used to upload and download files, respectively.

- Dedicated GUI clients allow you to connect to servers, browse directories, and upload and download files.
- Internet browsers allow you to connect to an FTP service and download files. You use another type of URL to connect to an FTP server; for example, ***ftp://ftp.microsoft.com/***.

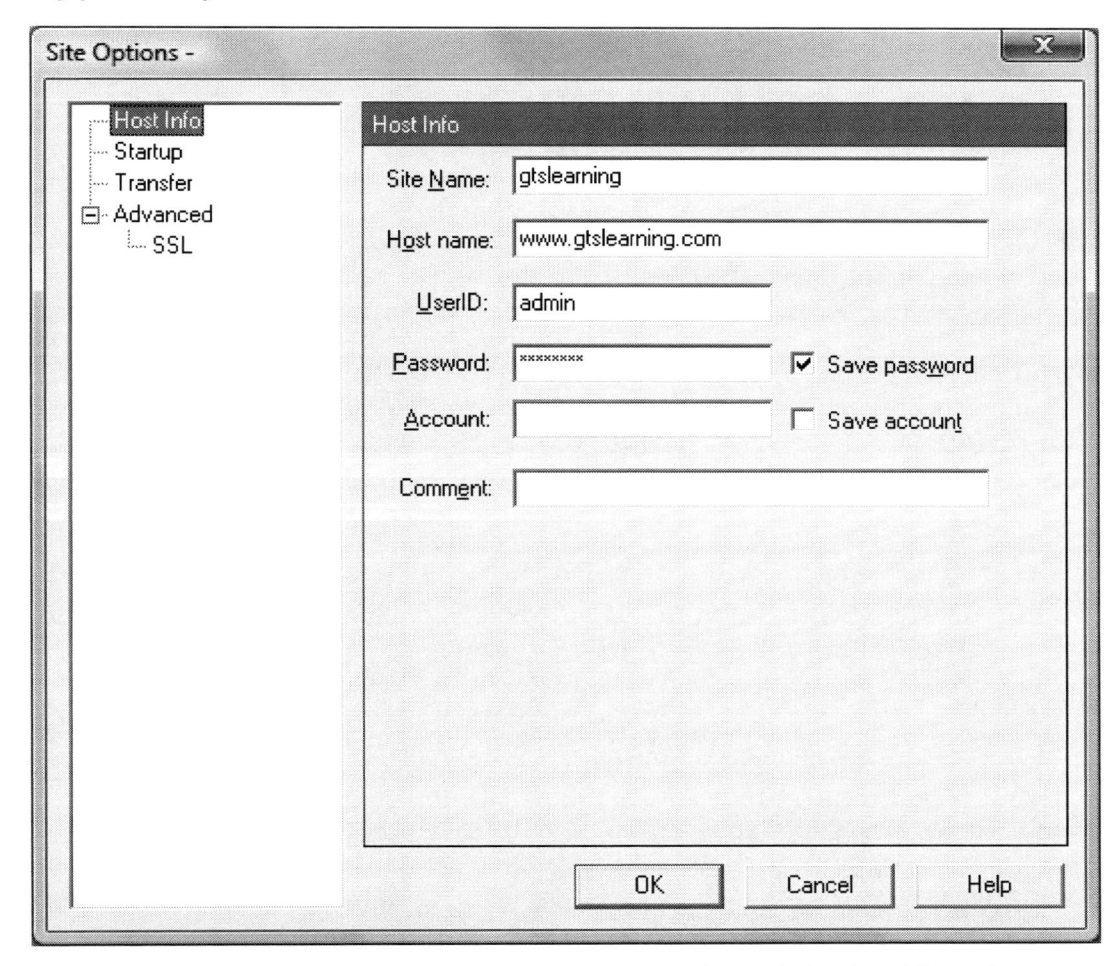

Configuring a site in an FTP client. (Screenshot used with permission from Microsoft.)

> **Note:** Plain FTP is unencrypted and so poses a high security risk. Passwords for sites are submitted in plaintext. There are ways of encrypting FTP sessions (FTPS and SFTP), however, and it is the encrypted services that are most widely used now.

NETWORK HOST SERVICES

The purpose of a network is to make host services available. There are many categories of network service, but some of the most important roles are described here.

AUTHENTICATION SERVER

Most networks have some sort of access control system to prevent unauthorized users (and devices) from connecting. In a Windows homegroup, for example, the access control method is a simple password, shared with all authorized users. Enterprise networks use authentication servers to configure user accounts and authenticate the subjects trying to use those accounts. On a Windows domain, the user database and authentication service is provided by Active Directory, using a mechanism based on the Kerberos protocol.

You are also likely to come across the terms AAA server and RADIUS server. An Authentication, Authorization, and Accounting (AAA) server is one that consolidates authentication services across multiple access devices, such as switches, routers, and access points. Remote Authentication Dial-in User Service (RADIUS) is an example of an AAA protocol.

DHCP AND DNS SERVERS

Authentication is just one part of providing network access. Hosts must also receive a suitable network configuration to be able to communicate on the network. DHCP and DNS are two of the services that facilitate this:

- Dynamic Host Configuration Protocol (DHCP) servers assign IP address information to host automatically when they connect to the network.
- Domain Name System (DNS) servers allow users to access resources using host names and Fully Qualified Domain Names (FQDN) by resolving those names to IP addresses.

LIGHTWEIGHT DIRECTORY ACCESS PROTOCOL (LDAP)

Network resources can be recorded as objects within a directory. A directory is like a database, where an object is like a record and things that you know about the object (attributes) are like fields. In order for products from different vendors to be interoperable, most directories are based on the same standard.

The main directory standard is the X.500 series of standards, developed by the International Telecommunications Union (ITU) in the 1980s.

The problem with X.500 is that the full set of standards specified the use of a complex protocol stack as a means of network access, at a time when most organizations were already opting to use TCP/IP. Researchers developed a means for clients to connect to an X.500 server over TCP/IP and this was standardized by the IETF as the **Lightweight Directory Access Protocol (LDAP)**. LDAP is a protocol used to query and update an X.500 directory, or any type of directory that can present itself as an X.500 directory. It is widely supported in current directory products—Windows Active Directory, Apple OpenDirectory, or the open source OpenLDAP, for instance.

LDAP uses TCP and UDP port 389 by default.

A **Distinguished Name** is a unique identifier for any given resource within the directory. A distinguished name is made up of attribute-value pairs, separated by commas. Examples of attributes include Common Name (CN), Organizational Unit (OU), and Domain Component (DC). The most specific attribute is listed first and successive attributes become progressively broader. This most specific attribute is also referred to as the **Relative Distinguished Name**, as it uniquely identifies the object within the context of successive (parent) attribute values.

NetBIOS/NetBT

The very earliest Windows networks used network software called the **Network Basic Input/Output System (NetBIOS)**. NetBIOS allowed computers to address one another by name and establish sessions. As the TCP/IP suite became the standard for local networks, NetBIOS was re-engineered to work over the TCP and UDP protocols, referred to as **NetBIOS over TCP/IP (NetBT)**:

- Name service (UDP port 137).
- Datagram transmission service (UDP port 138).
- Session service (TCP port 139).

As you know, modern networks use IP, TCP/UDP, and DNS for these functions. NetBT should be disabled on most networks. It is only required if the network has to support pre-Windows 2000 legacy systems (plus some network applications).

INVENTORY MANAGEMENT SERVERS

Inventory management refers to keeping a record of the systems running on your network. This is not a simple task to try to perform manually, so a number of protocols have been developed to assist.

SIMPLE NETWORK MANAGEMENT PROTOCOL (SNMP)

The **Simple Network Management Protocol (SNMP)** is a framework for management and monitoring network devices. SNMP consists of a management system and agents.

The **agent** is a process running on a switch, router, server, or other SNMP-compatible network device. This agent maintains a database called a **Management Information Base (MIB)** that holds statistics relating to the activity of the device. An example of such a statistic is the number of frames per second handled by a switch. The agent is also capable of initiating a trap operation where it informs the management system of a notable event (port failure, for instance). The threshold for triggering traps can be set for each value.

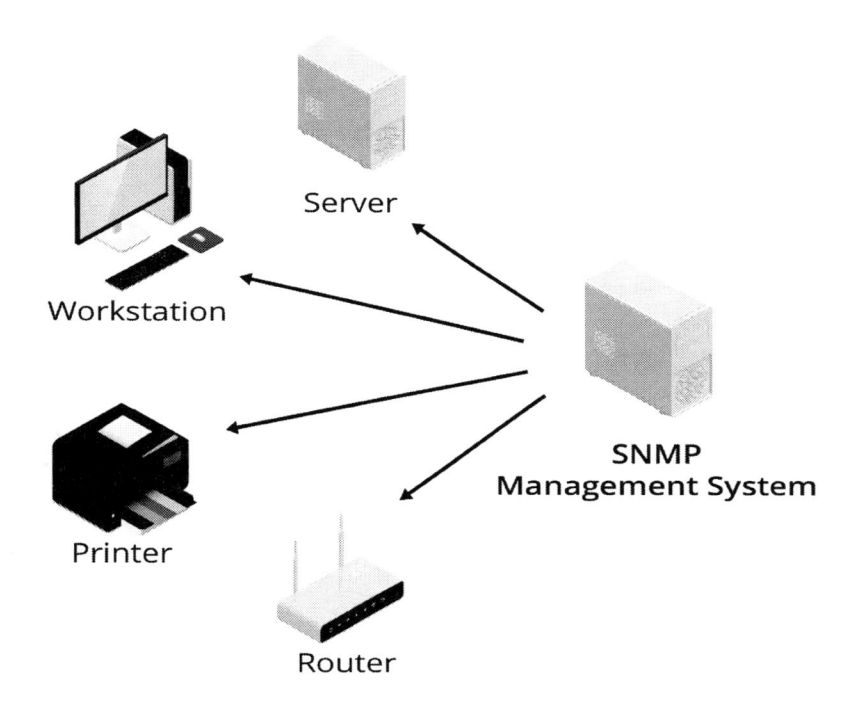

SNMP agents and management system. (Image © 123RF.com.)

The management system (a software program) provides a location from which network activity can be overseen. It monitors all agents by polling them at regular intervals for information from their MIBs and displays the information for review. It also displays any trap operations as alerts for the network administrator to assess and act upon as necessary.

SNMP device queries take place over UDP port 161; traps are communicated over UDP port 162.

ENDPOINT MANAGEMENT SERVER

Modern security models recognize that networks must not just apply security controls at the perimeter or border. A security principle called **defense in depth** calls for policies such as workstation hardening to ensure they cannot be compromised and used to attack the network from within. Of course, modern networks do not just consist of computer workstations—any type of endpoint computing device must be protected too, including laptops, smartphones, tablets, printers, and "smart" appliances.

An **Endpoint Management Server** facilitates this process by identifying computing devices running on the network and ensuring that they are securely configured. This might mean applying OS and antivirus updates automatically, cataloging software applications installed on each device, applying security policies, retrieving and analyzing log files, and monitoring performance and other status alerts.

Microsoft has the System Center and Configuration Manager (SCCM) for Windows (plus support for other device types). There are many other product examples.

syslog

Effective network management often entails capturing logs from different devices. It is much easier to review logs and respond to alerts if the logs are consolidated on a single system.

Prior to Windows 7, one limitation of Windows logs was that they only logged local events. This meant that third party tools were required in order to gain an overall view of messaging for the entire network. However, the development of event subscriptions allows logging to be configured to forward all events to a single computer, enabling a holistic view of network events.

The equivalent system in UNIX and Linux is usually **syslog**. This was designed to follow a client-server model and so allows for centralized collection of events from multiple sources. It also provides an open format for event logging messages and as such, has become a de facto standard for logging events from distributed systems. For example, syslog messages can be generated by Cisco routers and switches, as well as servers and workstations, and collected in a central database for viewing and analysis.

LEGACY AND EMBEDDED SYSTEMS

An **embedded system** is a computer system that is designed to perform a specific, dedicated function. These systems can be as small and simple as a microcontroller in an intravenous drip-rate meter or as large and complex as an industrial control system managing a water treatment plant. Embedded systems might typically have been designed to operate within a **closed network**; that is one where the elements of the network are all known to the system vendor and there is no connectivity to wider computer data networks. Where embedded systems need to interact within a computer data network, there are special considerations to make in terms of the network design, especially as regards security.

A **legacy system** is one that is no longer directly supported by its vendor. Networks often need to retain hosts running DOS or legacy versions of Windows (XP and earlier) or old-style mainframe computers to run services that are too complex or expensive to migrate to a more modern platform. Legacy systems usually work well for what they do (which is why they don't get prioritized for replacement) but they represent very severe risks in terms of security vulnerabilities. It is important to isolate them as far as possible from the rest of the network and ensure any network channels linking them are carefully protected and monitored.

Both legacy and embedded systems represent a risk in terms of maintenance and troubleshooting too, as they tend to require more specialist knowledge than modern, off-the-shelf, computing systems. Consultants with expertise in such systems can become highly sought after.

INTERNET SECURITY APPLIANCES AND SOFTWARE

Networks connected to the Internet need to be protected against malicious hosts and applications by a firewall and anti-malware scanners. Networks also need to scan for "unusual" host behavior or network traffic, using Intrusion Detection Systems (IDS) and Intrusion Prevention Systems (IPS). These services can be implemented on servers but enterprise networks are likely to use dedicated Internet security appliances.

INTRUSION DETECTION SYSTEM (IDS)

A network-based **Intrusion Detection System (IDS)** comprises a sensor plus an analysis engine that scans network traffic for signs of threats or other violations of security policy. The IDS can be programmed with signatures of known intrusion attempts. Like antivirus software, these intrusion signatures (usually called plug-ins in the context of IDS) must be kept up to date. Also like antivirus, IDS can use behavioral or **heuristic** techniques to identify potential threats. In contrast to a basic packet-filtering firewall, which can be configured with rules about IP addresses and application protocol ports, a network-based IDS examines the contents of the application layer payload in the packet.

When an IDS detects an intrusion event, it creates a log entry and can also send an alert to an administrator, if the event is considered important enough. One of the major drawbacks of IDS is the detection of too many innocuous events (false positives).

There are many vendors supplying IDS software and appliances. The underlying detection engine for most of these products is based either on **Snort** or on **Suricata**. Each IDS solution adds its own connectivity (options for sensor placement), configuration, and reporting tools.

INTRUSION PROTECTION SYSTEM (IPS)

An **Intrusion Protection System (IPS)** adds some sort of real-time blocking (or shunning) functionality on top of the basic IDS. An IPS may drop packets, reset connections, or run a script to trigger a response on another server or network device (firewall, switch, or router).

UNIFIED THREAT MANAGEMENT (UTM)

Network security applications include antivirus scanners, intrusion detection/prevention, and firewalls. These might be deployed as separate appliances or server applications, each with its own configuration and logging/reporting system. A **Unified Threat Management (UTM)** appliance is one that enforces a variety of security-related measures, combining the work of a firewall, malware scanner, and intrusion detection/prevention. A UTM centralizes the threat management service, providing simpler configuration and reporting compared to isolated applications spread across several servers or devices. Some of the major UTM vendors and products include Barracuda, Sophos, Check Point, Fortinet, Cisco Meraki, Juniper SRVX, and Dell SonicWall.

There are two basic ways of implementing network connectivity for IDS and IPS or UTM server services and appliances:

- **Install the appliance inline with the network**—this means that all network traffic passes through the server or appliance. This allows the appliance to block suspect traffic easily. The drawback is that a single appliance would represent a critical point of failure. If the forwarding function of the appliance were to fail, no traffic would be able to pass into or out of the network. This can be mitigated by using two or more appliances for redundancy.
- **Install the appliance as a sensor**—this means that the appliance has a tap or mirror that enables it to view the traffic passing over a network link or switch. This makes prevention slower and more complex as the appliance must trigger a script for the preventive action to be enacted by another device (switch, router, or firewall).

In both cases, the ability to deal with high traffic volumes is critical. If the device is overwhelmed by the traffic volume, it will not be inspecting all of that traffic and could be allowing malicious traffic to pass undetected. A dedicated security appliance should be able to perform better in this respect than running the security service on a server or router.

PROXY SERVER

On a SOHO network, devices on the LAN access the Internet via the router using a type of Network Address Translation (NAT), specifically Port-based Network Address Translation. This type of NAT device translates between the private IP addresses used on the LAN and the publicly addressable IP addresses used on the Internet.

Many enterprise networks use some sort of NAT too but another option is to use a proxy server. A **proxy server** does not just translate IP addresses. It takes a whole HTTP request from a client, checks it, then forwards it to the destination computer on the Internet. When the reply comes back, it checks it, and then shuttles it back to the LAN computer. A proxy can be used for other types of traffic too (email, for instance).

A proxy server can usually operate either as a transparent service, in which case the client requires no special configuration, or as non-transparent. For a non-transparent proxy, the client must be configured with the IP address and service port (often 8080 by convention) of the proxy server.

Activity 5-6
Discussing Network Services

SCENARIO
Answer the following questions to check your understanding of the topic.

1. If a network application cannot tolerate a missing packet, what type of transport protocol should it use?

2. True or false? Protocols that stream video and audio over the Internet are likely to be based on UDP.

3. What is DNS?

4. What configuration parameter must be entered to enable a client to use DNS?

5. True or false? An HTTP application secured using the SSL/TLS protocol should use a different port to unencrypted HTTP.

6. What protocol would a mail client use to access the message store on a remote mail server?

7. A firewall filters applications based on their port number.

   If you want to configure a firewall on the mail server to allow clients to download email messages, which port(s) might you have to open?

8. You are configuring a Network Attached Storage (NAS) appliance.

   What file sharing protocol(s) could you use to allow access to Windows, Linux, and Apple macOS clients?

9. **What is the difference between SNMP and syslog?**

10. You are advising a customer about types of security appliance.

    What are the principal types and configuration options?

Summary

In this lesson, you identified many different network concepts and technologies. Networking is at the heart of any type of business. Without it, a business simply cannot function in today's world. It is your job to help ensure that the networks behind the business are running properly and managed correctly.

What do you think are the most important network concepts covered in this lesson?

What experience do you have with any of the technologies discussed in this lesson?

Practice Question: *Additional practice questions are available on the CompTIA CHOICE platform within the **Assessments** tile.*

Lesson 6
Configuring and Troubleshooting Networks

LESSON INTRODUCTION

In a previous lesson, you identified networking technologies. With that knowledge, you are now prepared to implement those technologies. In this lesson, you will install and configure networking capabilities.

As a CompTIA® A+® technician, your duties will include setting up and configuring computers so that they can connect to a network. By installing, configuring, and troubleshooting networking capabilities, you will be able to provide users with the connectivity they need to be able to perform their job duties.

LESSON OBJECTIVES

In this lesson, you will:

- Configure Windows settings for different types of Internet and VPN connections.
- Install and configure SOHO router/modems and set up secure wireless access.
- Configure firewall settings and browser options to ensure safe Internet use on a SOHO network.
- Use remote access technologies to connect to hosts over a network.
- Troubleshoot wired and wireless problems plus IP configuration issues using command-line tools.
- Select, install, and configure Internet of Things (IoT) home automation devices.

Topic A
Configure Network Connection Settings

EXAM OBJECTIVES COVERED
1001-2.3 Given a scenario, install and configure a basic wired/wireless SOHO network.
1002-1.8 Given a scenario, configure Microsoft Windows networking on a client/desktop.
1002-1.6 Given a scenario, use Microsoft Windows Control Panel utilities.

Once all the hardware connections are made in a networking environment, you will need to make sure that the operating system is configured to use the hardware successfully. It is important to fully understand not only the hardware and the connections within a network, but also how Windows will need to be setup and configured to accomplish connectivity with the resources of a network.

NIC PROPERTIES

A computer joins a network by connecting the network adapter—or Network Interface Card (NIC)—to a switch or wireless access point. For proper end user device configuration, the card settings should be configured to match the capabilities of the network appliance.

WIRED NETWORK CARDS

Almost all wired network adapters are based on some type of Ethernet. The adapter's media type must match that of the switch it is connected to. Most use copper wire cable (RJ-45 connectors), though installations in some corporate networks may use fiber optic connections. The adapter and switch must also use the same Ethernet settings. The main parameters are:

- **Signaling speed**—most devices you will see will support Gigabit Ethernet, working at a nominal data rate of 1 Gbps. Older standards include Fast Ethernet (100 Mbps) and "plain" Ethernet (10 Mbps). Most network adapters will work at all three speeds. There is also a 10 Gbps standard, though this is not often used for desktop machines as the adapters and switches are expensive.
- **Half or full duplex**—this determines whether the connection transfers data in both directions simultaneously (full duplex) or not (half duplex). The overwhelming majority of devices use full duplex. Gigabit Ethernet requires full duplex to work.

Most wired network adapters will autonegotiate network settings such as signaling speed and half- or full duplex operation with the switch. For this to work, both the port on the switch and the network adapter should be configured to use the "Autonegotiate" setting, which should be the default.

If these settings do need to be configured manually, locate the adapter in **Device Manager**, right-click and select **Properties**, then update settings using the **Advanced** tab.

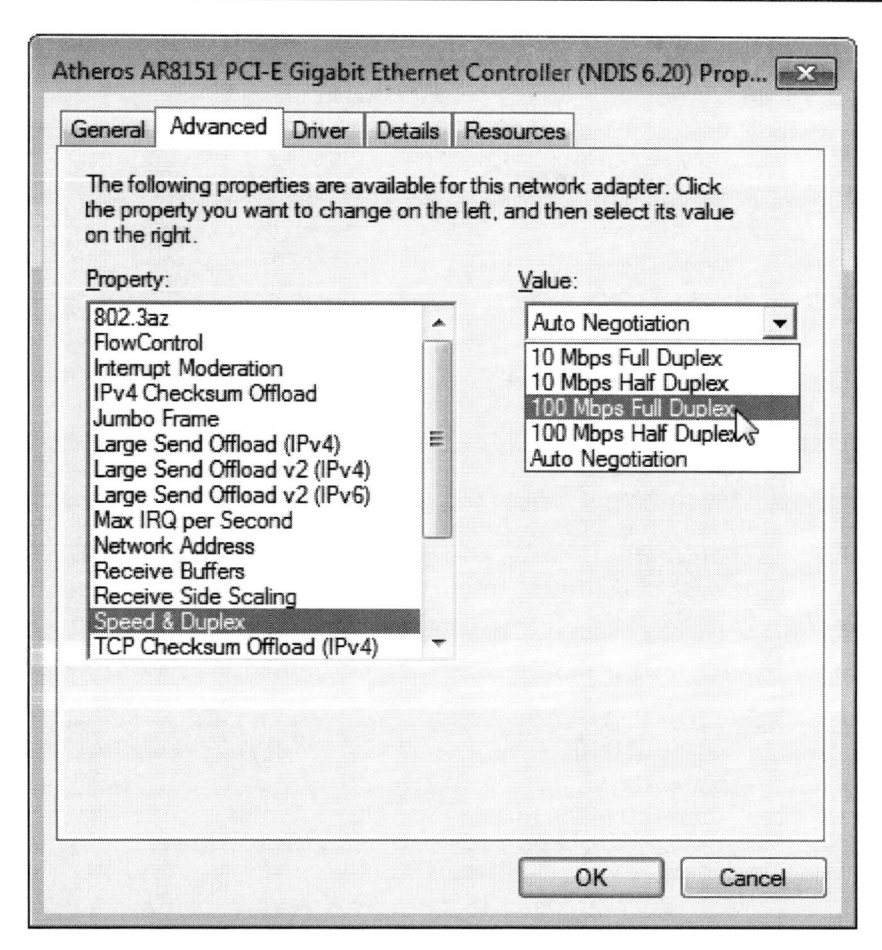

Ethernet adapter properties in Device Manager. (Screenshot used with permission from Microsoft.)

Most of the other settings can be left to the default. In some circumstances, you may be able to improve performance or troubleshoot connectivity problems by enabling or disabling or tweaking the parameters for settings such as jumbo frames, buffers, scaling, and offloads.

QOS

Quality of Service (QoS) means using a network protocol to prioritize certain types of traffic over others. Enterprise networks can use QoS protocols to make sure traffic such as Voice over IP calling or video conferencing is given higher priority than traffic where the timing of packets is less important, such as ordinary file downloads.

QoS parameters are usually configured on a managed switch. In the network adapter properties, you may need to enable the QoS protocol ("802.1p" or "QoS Packet Tagging," for instance). It is possible that QoS may also be controlled by a higher level protocol, which would be configured via the QoS Packet Scheduler client software installed by default on the OS's logical adapter.

ONBOARD NETWORK CARDS

Most computers come with an onboard Gigabit Ethernet network adapter as part of the system chipset. The port will be an RJ-45 type for use with twisted-pair cabling. If there is any issue with the onboard NIC, the first step should be to use the BIOS/UEFI system setup program to find out whether it is enabled (look in the "Integrated Peripherals" or "Onboard Devices" section). You might disable the onboard adapter if installing a plug-in card.

WIRELESS NETWORK CARDS

The most important setting on a wireless card is support for the 802.11 standard supported by the access point. Most cards are set to support any standard available. This means that a card that supports 802.11n will also be able to connect to 802.11g and 802.11b networks.

With the card shown in the following figure, for instance, you can enable or disable 802.11n Mode and select either mixed support for 802.11b/g or force use of either. For 802.11.n, you can also configure whether to use channel bonding.

Note: *Making a network work in compatibility mode can reduce the performance of the whole network.*

A couple of other settings are of interest:
- **Roaming Aggressiveness**—when the adapter starts to move out of range of one access point, it might try to connect to another one with a better signal. Roaming aggressiveness determines how tolerant the adapter is of weak signals. If you use multiple APs, tweaking this setting up or down might result in better performance.
- **Transmit Power**—this sets the radio power level. It is typically set to the highest possible by default.

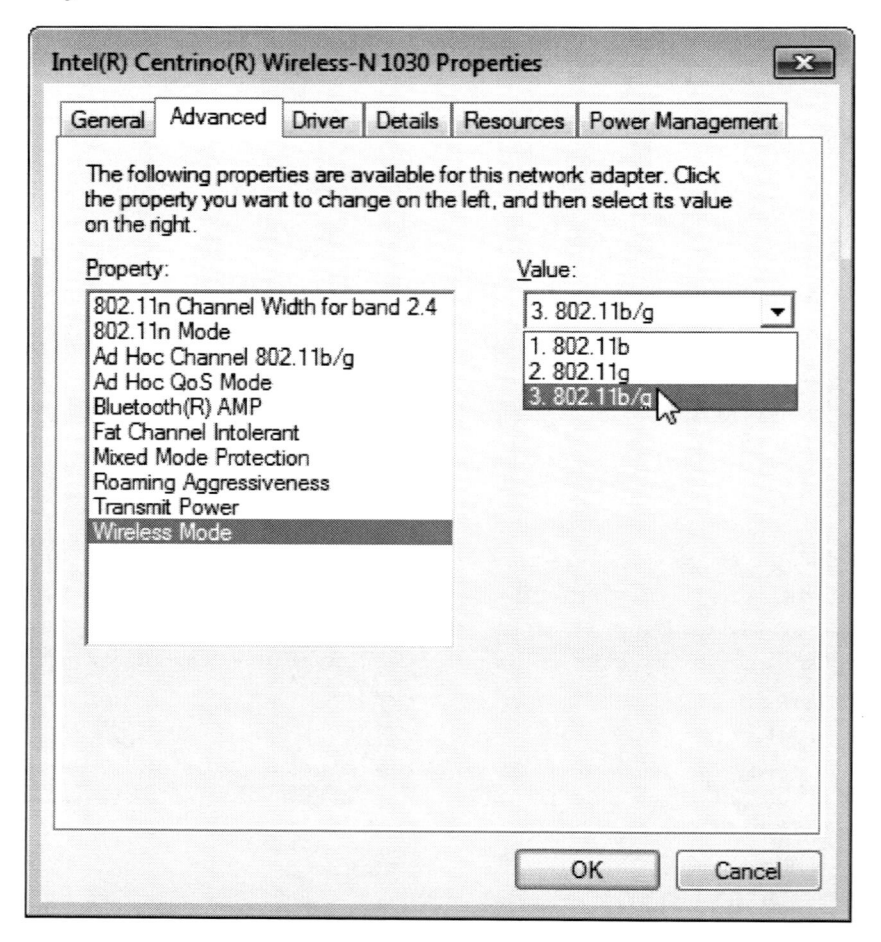

Wireless network adapter properties in Device Manager. (Screenshot used with permission from Microsoft.)

> **Note:** You might see a setting for "Ad hoc QoS Mode" on a wireless adapter. This enables Wireless Multimedia (WMM), which is a Wi-Fi specification for delivering QoS over wireless networks.

WAKE ON LAN

Wake on LAN (WoL) allows you to start up a computer remotely. When the computer is switched off (but not unplugged), the network card can be kept active using standby power. The administrator would use network software to broadcast a "magic packet" to the NIC; when it receives it, the NIC initiates the computer's boot process.

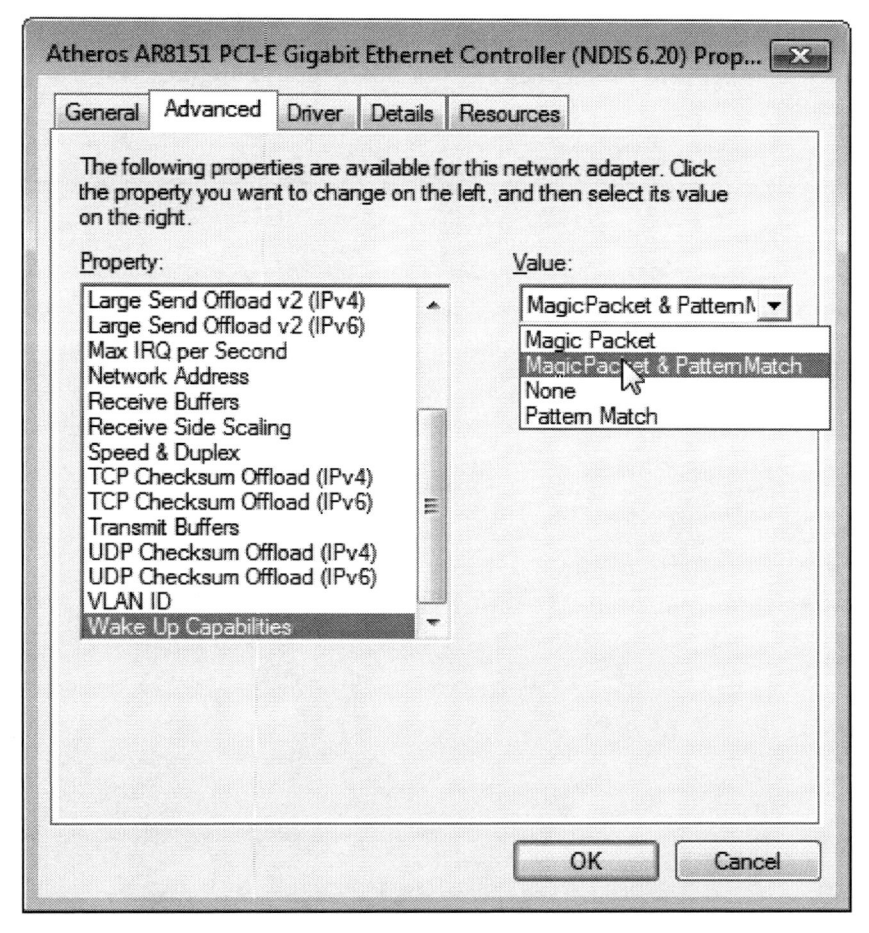

WoL settings for a network adapter. (Screenshot used with permission from Microsoft.)

Some devices with wireless chipsets come with **Wake-on-Wireless LAN (WoWLAN)**, but the technology is not so widely supported.

> **Note:** To learn more, check the **Video** tile on the CHOICE Course screen for any videos that supplement the content for this lesson.

> **Access the Checklist tile on your CHOICE Course screen for reference information and job aids on How to Set Up Wake on LAN.**

NETWORK CONNECTIONS IN WINDOWS 7 AND WINDOWS 8

Having verified connection properties of the Ethernet or Wi-Fi interface, you must also configure the card with the appropriate network client software and protocol, including addressing information relevant to the protocol.

Most Ethernet and Wi-Fi networks use the Internet Protocol (IP) with a DHCP server, which means that the card receives address parameters automatically.

NETWORK AND SHARING CENTER

In Windows® 7 and Windows 8, the Network and Sharing Center is used to provide an overview of network availability and configuration. Right-click the network status icon in the notification area and select **Open Network and Sharing Center** or open the applet via Control Panel.

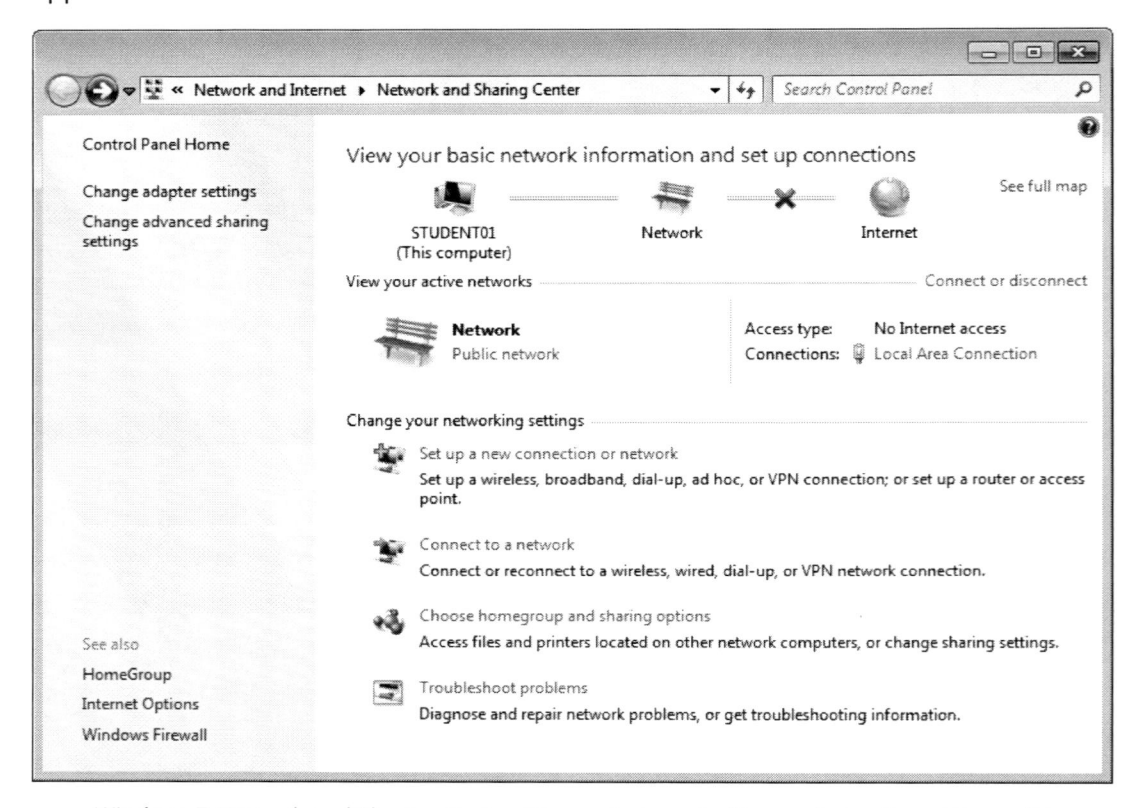

Windows 7 Network and Sharing Center. (Screenshot used with permission from Microsoft.)

WIRED NETWORK CONNECTIONS

To access the adapter property sheets, select **Change adapter settings**. In Windows 8, the option is labeled **Manage network connections**.

> **Note:** Alternatively, run `ncpa.cpl` from the **Instant Search** box or **Run** dialog box.

In Windows 7, the wired network adapter will be listed as **Local Area Connection** (though you can rename it if you prefer), whereas a wireless adapter will be listed as **Wireless Network Connection**. In Windows 8, the adapters are named **Ethernet** and **WiFi**.

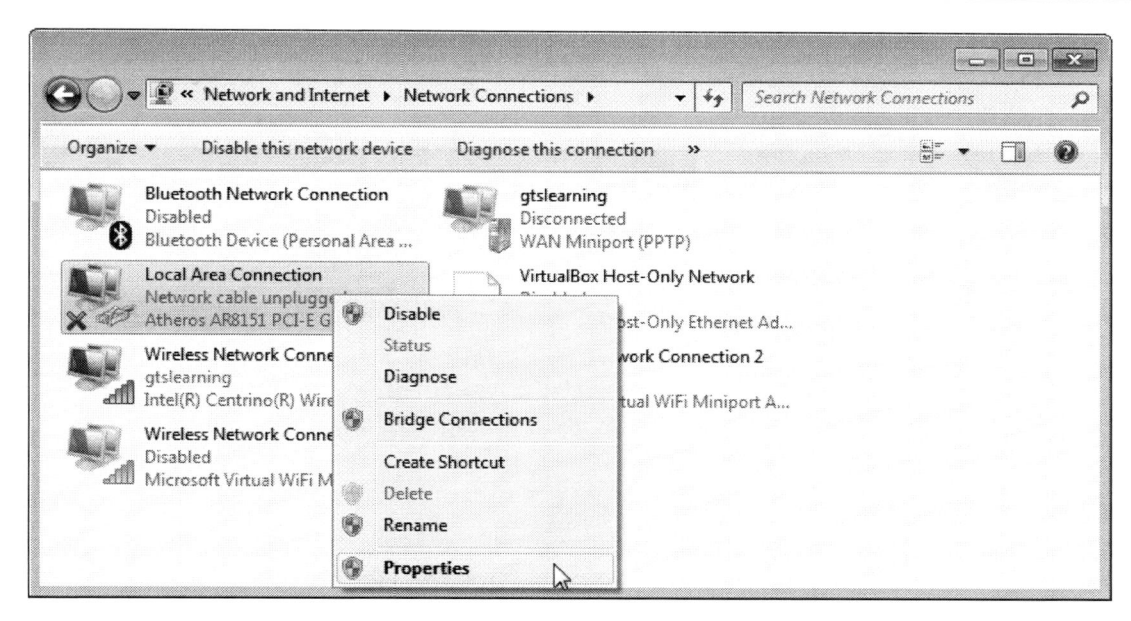

Network Connections in Windows 7. (Screenshot used with permission from Microsoft.)

ADAPTER PROPERTIES

Right-click an adapter and select **Properties** to configure settings or **Status** to view information about the connection. From the **Properties** dialog box, you can add or configure the appropriate service, protocol, or client.

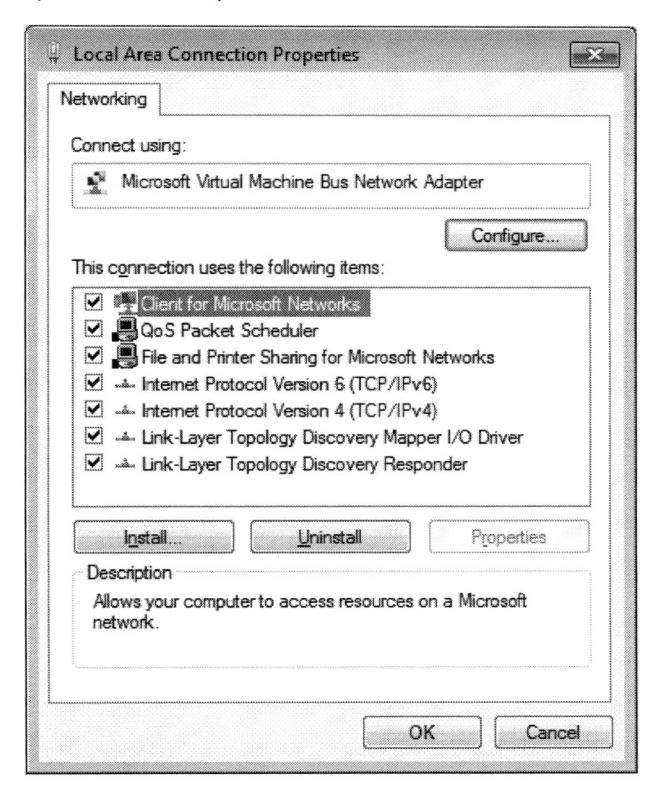

Local Area Network Adapter properties. (Screenshot used with permission from Microsoft.)

- **Clients** provide connections to types of file servers, such as Linux/UNIX or Windows.
- **Protocols** provide the format for addressing and delivering data messages between systems, the most widely adopted being TCP/IP.

- **Services** allow your machine to provide network functionality to other machines.

By default, the following clients, protocols, and services are installed on the default Ethernet adapter:

- Client for Microsoft Networks.
- File and Print Sharing for Microsoft Networks.
- Internet Protocol—both IP version 4 and IP version 6 will be installed. The network adapter automatically uses the appropriate version of the protocol depending on the network it is connected to.
- Link-layer Topology Discovery—provides the network mapping and discovery functions in the Network and Sharing Center.

Checked items are described as being "bound" to an adapter. When installing a new protocol or service, check that it is only bound to adapters that should be using that protocol or service.

WIRELESS NETWORK CONNECTIONS

To join a WLAN, click the network status icon in the notification area and select from the list of displayed networks. If the access point is set to broadcast the network name or Service Set ID (SSID), then the network will appear in the list of available networks. The bars show the strength of the signal and the lock icon indicates whether the network uses encryption. To connect, select the network then enter the pre-shared key (or log on in the specified way if using a network authentication server).

If you choose the **Connect automatically** option, Windows will use the network without prompting whenever it is in range.

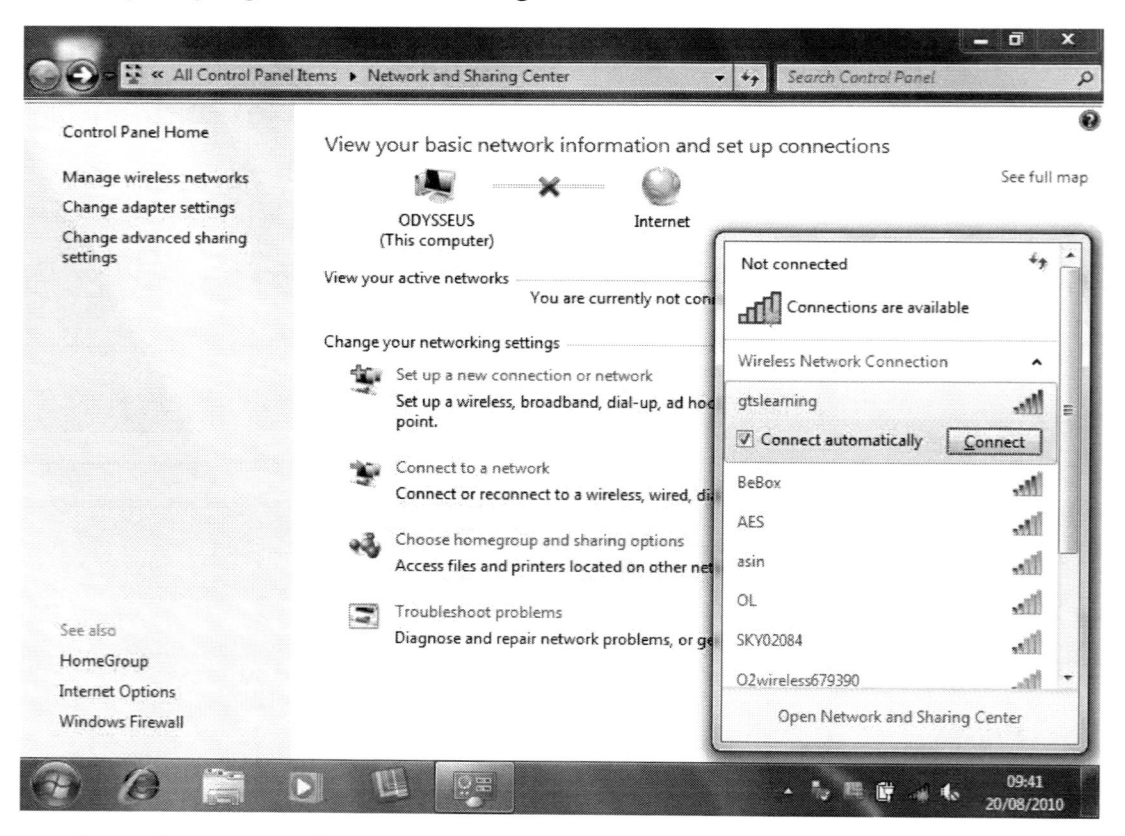

Connecting to a network using Windows 7. (Screenshot used with permission from Microsoft.)

If the WLAN is not shown (if SSID broadcast is disabled), click **Open Network and Sharing Center** then **Set up a new connection or network** and proceed by entering the network SSID, security information, and network location type.

NETWORK CONNECTIONS IN WINDOWS 10

Windows 10 manages network settings via the **Network & Internet** section in the Settings app. Use the **Status** page to monitor the current network connection. There are links to the **Network and Sharing Center** and **Network Connections** applets (via **Change adapter options**) from there.

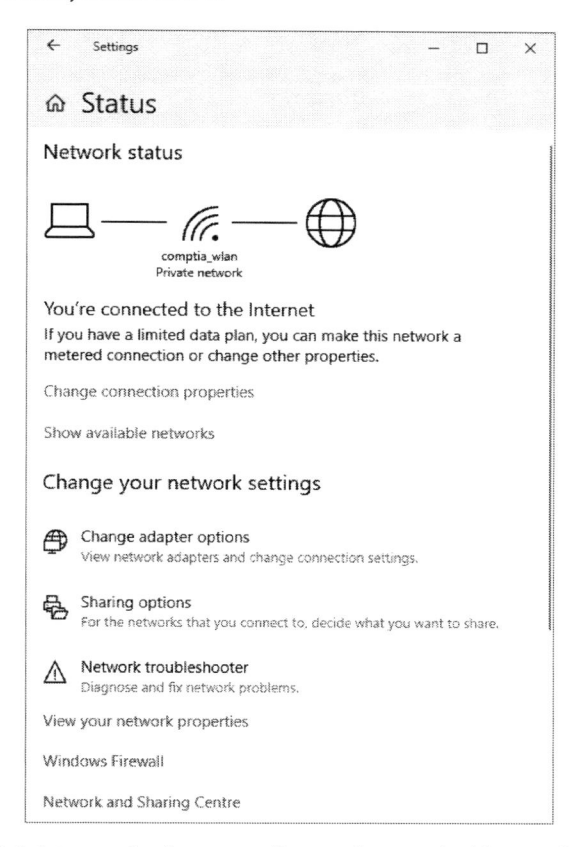

Windows 10 Network & Internet Settings app. (Screenshot used with permission from Microsoft.)

You can join a wireless network using the network status icon in the notification area. If you need to input WLAN settings manually, from the **Network & internet** page, select **WiFi→Manage known networks→Add a new network**.

IP ADDRESS CONFIGURATION

IP address properties can be configured through the network connection's **Properties** dialog box. Both wired and wireless adapters are configured in the same way. By default, Windows machines obtain an IP address dynamically, but you can configure a static IP address and other settings, such as DNS servers.

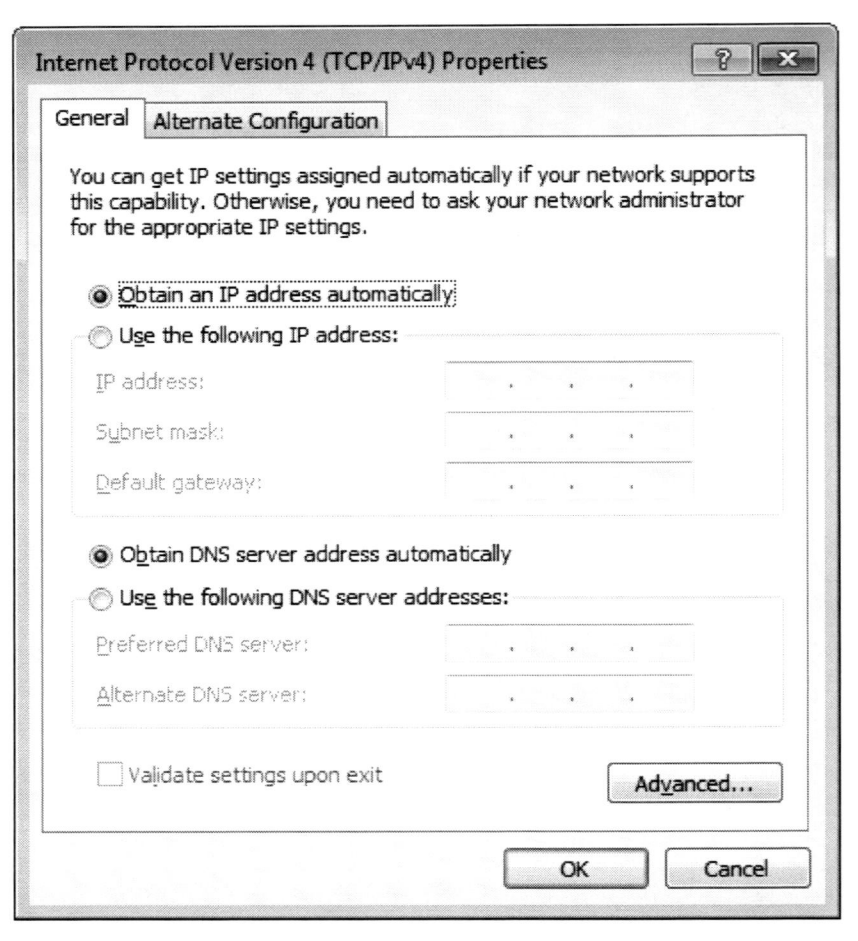

Internet Protocol version 4 (TCP/IP/v4) Properties dialog box. (Screenshot used with permission from Microsoft.)

Note: A machine can communicate with local hosts with a valid IP address and subnet mask but cannot communicate with other networks unless a default gateway is specified.

Note: A machine that cannot access a DNS server will not be able to resolve host names or web addresses. As DNS is a critical service, two server addresses are usually specified for redundancy.

Note: In Windows 10, you can also configure IP via the Settings interface. Select **Network & Internet** then **Ethernet** or **WiFi** as appropriate. Click the adapter or WLAN SSID. Under "IP Settings," click the **Edit** button.

AUTOMATIC IP CONFIGURATION AND DHCP

Configuring IP addresses and other TCP/IP network information manually raises many difficult administrative issues and makes misconfiguration of one or more hosts more likely. A Dynamic Host Configuration Protocol (DHCP) service can be provided by a Windows Server or by a device such as a switch or router. DHCP can allocate an IP address to a new machine joining the network. To use DHCP, select the **Obtain an IP address automatically** option. If a Windows machine fails to obtain an IP address dynamically, it will utilize an Automatic Private IP Addressing (APIPA) address from a reserved range (169.254.x.y).

ALTERNATE CONFIGURATION

Windows allows you to define an alternative IP address configuration for a machine if it cannot contact a DHCP server and using APIPA is unsuitable. This is useful in the scenario where you have a laptop computer connecting to DHCP in a corporate network but that requires a static IP address on the user's home network.

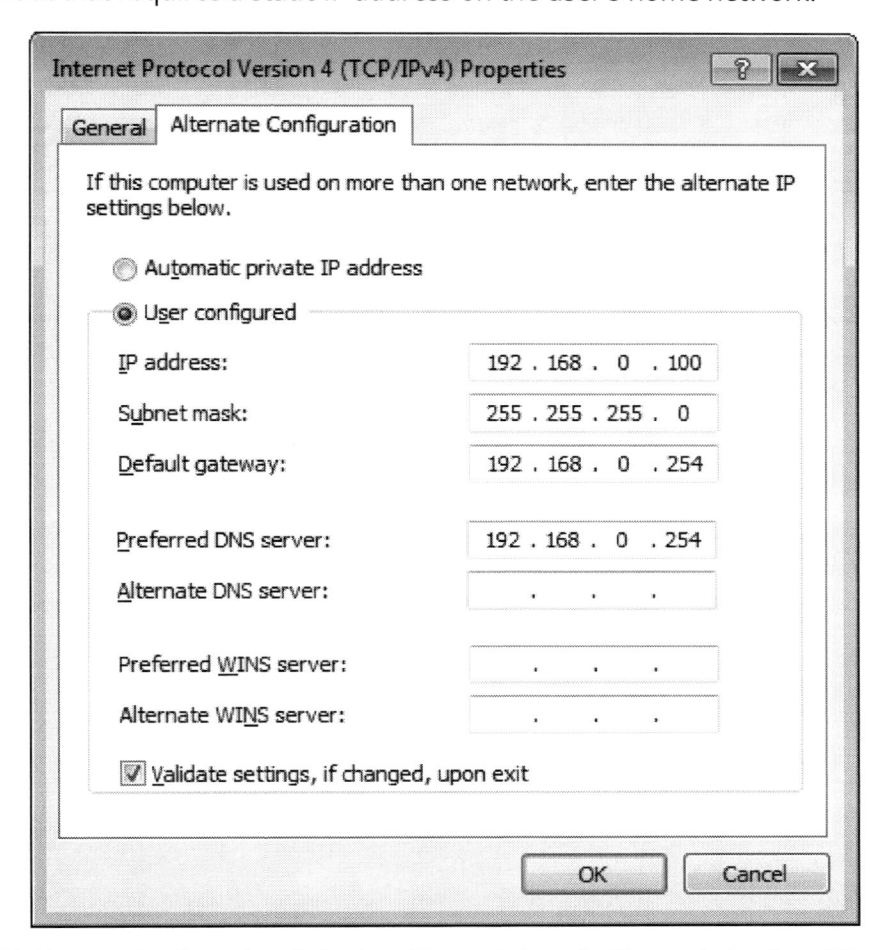

TCP/IP Alternate Configuration dialog box. (Screenshot used with permission from Microsoft.)

> **Note:** The **Alternate Configuration** tab is not displayed unless the **Obtain an IP address automatically** option is selected.

> **Note:** To learn more, check the **Video** tile on the CHOICE Course screen for any videos that supplement the content for this lesson.

> Access the Checklist tile on your CHOICE Course screen for reference information and job aids on How to Configure IP Addresses.

OTHER NETWORK CONNECTIONS

Most residential and small office networks connect to the Internet via a SOHO "router." These Internet appliances combine a 4-port switch and wireless access point with a router/modem that can connect to the ISP's network over DSL or Hybrid Fiber Coax (HFC) lines. The computers connect to the router by using the switch ports or access point and are assigned an IP configuration by a DHCP server running in the appliance. Correctly configuring the Ethernet or Wi-Fi adapter in Network Connections will allow the computer to join this type of network.

There are a number of other ways of connecting to the Internet and other remote networks, however.

DIAL-UP

A **dial-up connection** uses an analog modem to dial another modem on the ISP's remote access server, which then transfers the data onto the ISP's network and to and from the wider Internet. The call is placed in the same way as a voice call and may incur connection charges. The maximum link speed is just 56 Kbps.

> **Note:** *Given perfect line conditions, modems can work at up to 56 Kbps downlink and 48 Kbps uplink. Line conditions are rarely perfect, however, and actual speeds may be a lot lower.*

To create a dial-up connection, a modem must be installed in the computer or an external modem can be connected via USB. The dial-up port on the modem should then be connected to the phone socket. This is typically done using a silver satin cable with an RJ-11 connector for the modem and a suitable connector for the phone point, depending on region. For example, in the US an RJ-11 connector is used, but in the UK, a BT connector is often required. Regardless of the physical interface, the modem must be installed to one of the computer's software COM ports. The modem must also be configured with the local dialing properties, such as access prefix for an outside line, area code, and so on.

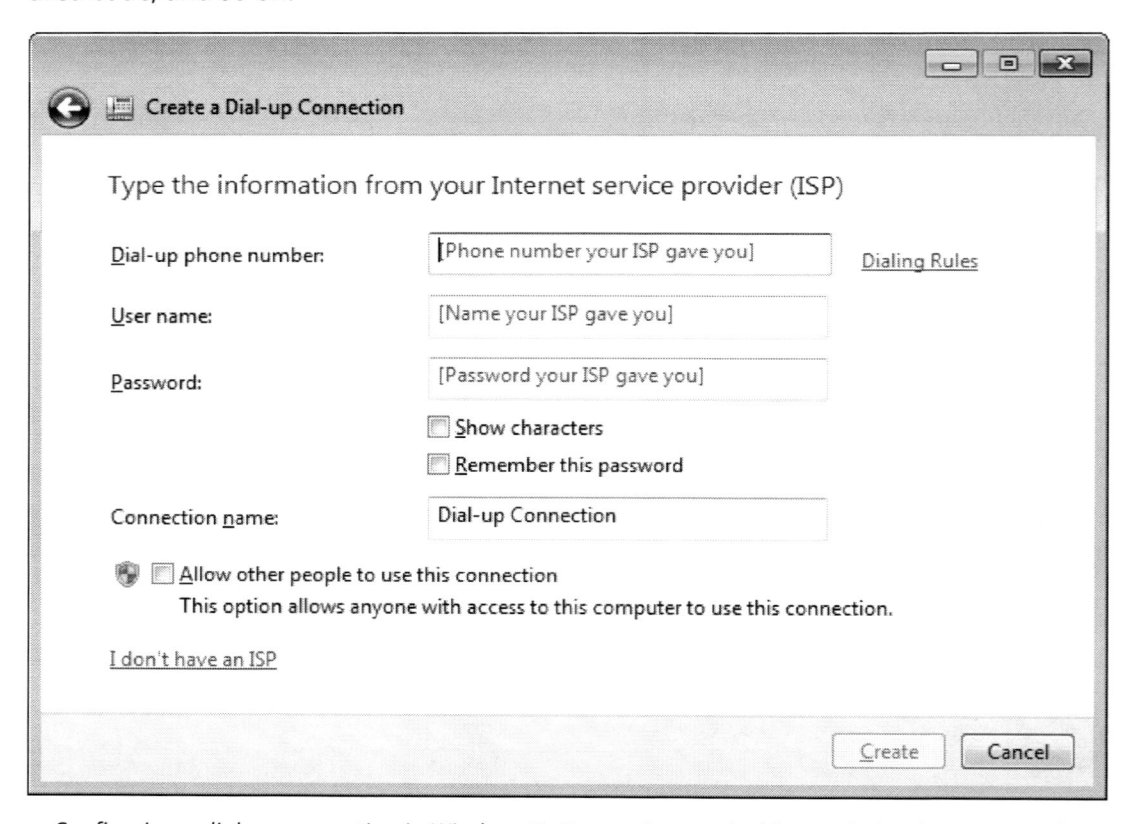

Configuring a dial-up connection in Windows 7. (Screenshot used with permission from Microsoft.)

You can use the **Set Up a Connection or Network** wizard to configure a link to the ISP's server.

You can connect or disconnect the link or reconfigure it using the network status icon.

WIRELESS WAN (CELLULAR)

Wireless Wide Area Network (WWAN or cellular) Internet access refers to using an adapter to link to a cellular phone provider's network via the nearest available transmitter (base station). The bandwidth depends on the technologies supported by the adapter and by the transmitter (3G or 4G, for instance).

The WWAN adapter can be fitted as a USB device or (on laptops) as an internal adapter. The advantage of the latter is that they do not protrude from the chassis; USB adapters are quite unwieldy.

Once the vendor's software has been installed, plug in the adapter and it will be detected and configured automatically. You can then use the software to open a connection, check signal strength, view usage, and so on.

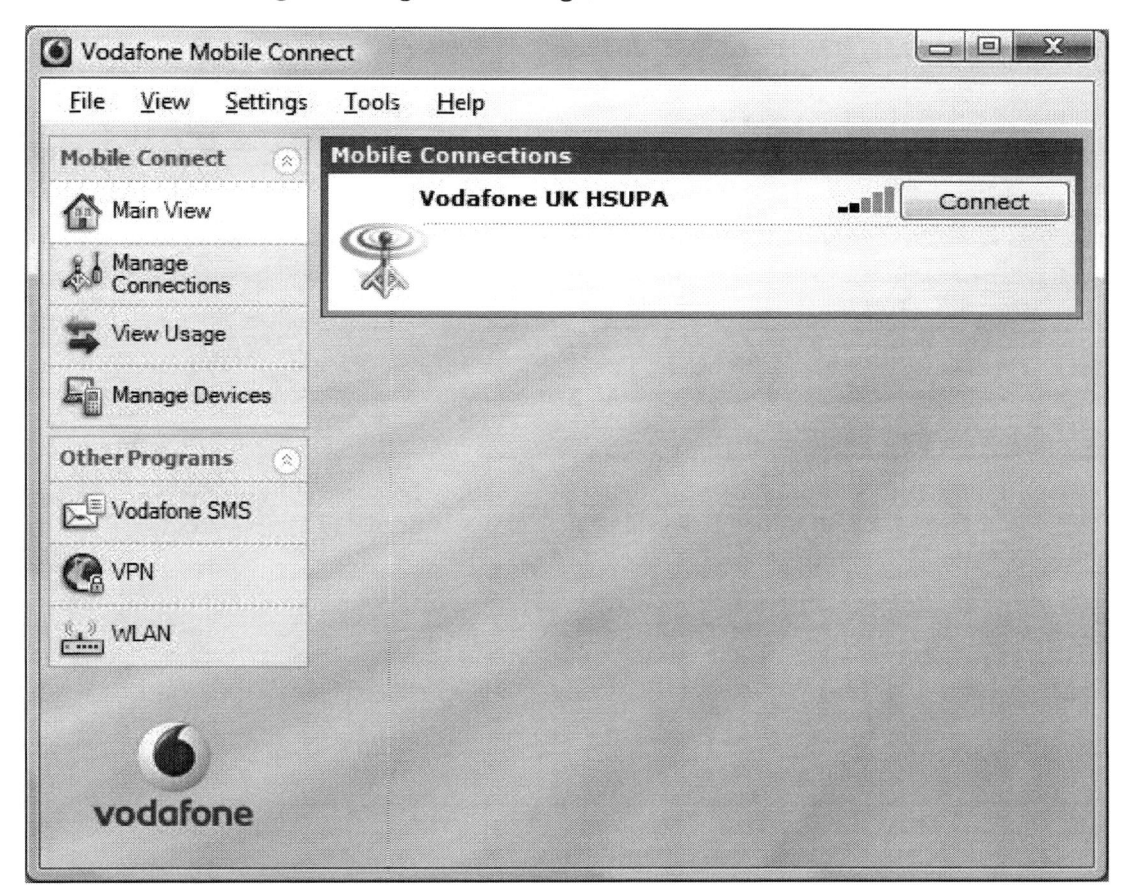

Vodafone Mobile Connect management software.

VIRTUAL PRIVATE NETWORK (VPN)

A Virtual Private Network (VPN) is a "tunnel" through the Internet. It allows a remote computer to join the local network securely. Windows supports a number of VPN types but you may need to obtain third-party software.

If the VPN type is supported, you can configure a connection using the Windows client from Network Connections.

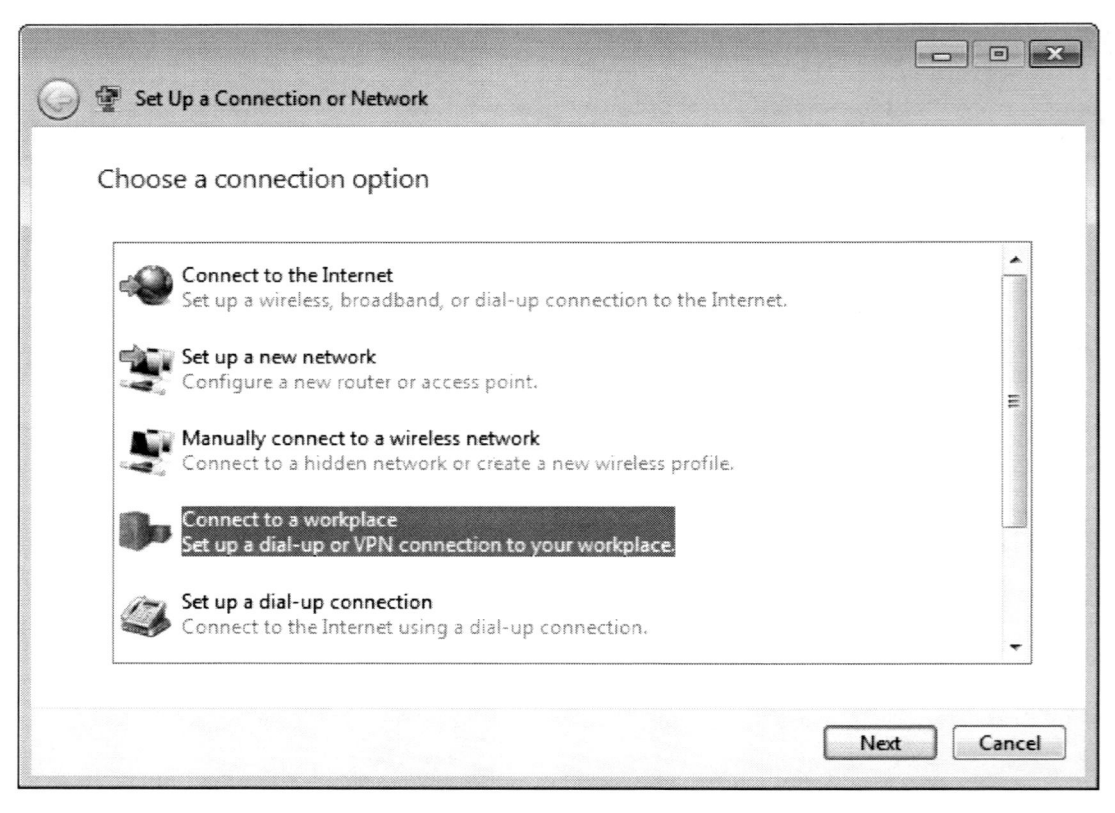

Set Up a Connection or Network wizard. (Screenshot used with permission from Microsoft.)

Subsequently, the network connection will be available by clicking the network status icon. Right-click the icon under "Dial-up and VPN" to **Connect** or **Disconnect** or modify the connection's Properties.

Accessing a VPN connection from the network status icon in Windows 7. (Screenshot used with permission from Microsoft.)

Note: To learn more, check the **Video** tile on the CHOICE Course screen for any videos that supplement the content for this lesson.

Access the Checklist tile on your CHOICE Course screen for reference information and job aids on How to Configure Other Network Connection Settings.

Activity 6-1
Discussing Network Connection Configuration Settings

SCENARIO
Answer the following questions to check your understanding of the topic.

1. You need to configure duplex settings on a network adapter manually.

   What steps do you need to follow?

2. **True or false? If you want a computer to be available through Wake-on-LAN, you can disconnect it from the power supply but must leave it connected to the network data port.**

3. A Windows computer is configured to use DHCP, but no DHCP server is available. The computer is not using an APIPA address either.

   Why is this?

4. **Why are IP addresses entered under DNS, and why should there be two of them?**

5. **What parameters do you need to specify to connect to a VPN?**

Topic B

Install and Configure SOHO Networks

EXAM OBJECTIVES COVERED
1001-2.3 Given a scenario, install and configure a basic wired/wireless SOHO network.
1002-2.3 Compare and contrast wireless security protocols and authentication methods.
1002-2.10 Given a scenario, configure security on SOHO wireless and wired networks.

Previously in this course, you covered basic networking concepts, the Transmission Control Protocol/Internet Protocol (TCP/IP) addressing scheme, and how networks are connected. In this topic, you will use that knowledge to install and configure a SOHO network.

No matter what the size or location of the network, you are still responsible for understanding how it is structured and configured. A+ technicians must understand the needs and complexities of SOHO wired and wireless networks.

SOHO NETWORKS

A Small Office Home Office (SOHO) LAN is a business-oriented network, possibly using a centralized server in addition to client devices and printers, but often using a single Internet appliance to provide connectivity. Home and residential networks may also be classed as SOHO.

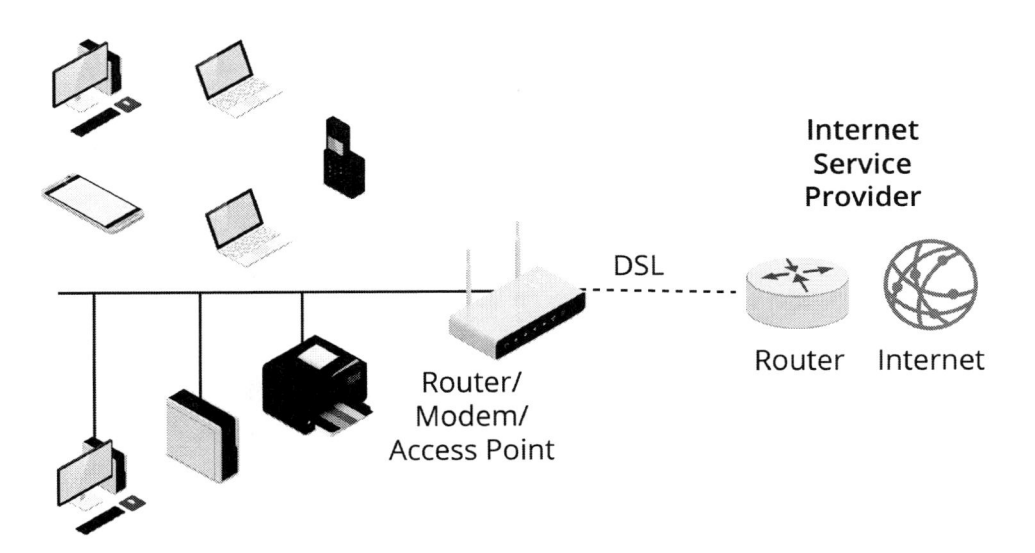

A typical SOHO network layout.

COMMON SOHO NETWORK HARDWARE

A DSL/cable modem is installed as Customer Premises Equipment (CPE), typically as some sort of combined router/modem. Make sure you understand the functions of the separate device types bundled within these appliances:

- **Modem**—connects to the service provider cabling and transfers frames over the link. The modem type must be matched to the network type (ADSL, VDSL, or cable).
- **Router**—forwards packets over the WAN (Internet) interface if they do not have a local destination IP address. Some appliances may provide the ability to configure local subnets, though this is not typical of the device's supplied by the service providers.
- **Switch**—allows local computers and other host types to connect to the network via RJ-45 ports. This will be an unmanaged switch so no configuration is necessary.
- **Access point**—allows hosts to connect to the network over Wi-Fi.

On a DSL modem, the RJ-11 port on the modem connects to the phone point. A microfilter (splitter) must be installed to separate voice and data signals. These can be self-installed on each phone point by the customer. Modern sockets are likely to feature a built-in splitter.

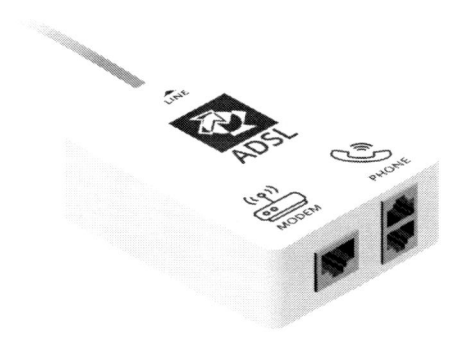

A self-installed DSL splitter.

> **Note:** The modem might be provided as a separate device. If this is the case, it will provide an RJ-45 port to connect to the RJ-45 WAN port on the router.

> **Note:** The steps for most cable modems are the same except that you will be connecting to the provider network using a coax cable. Make sure the coax connector is secure (but do not overtighten it).

SOHO NETWORK CONFIGURATION

You need to connect a computer (PC or laptop) to the device's built-in unmanaged switch so that you can configure the appliance. Make sure the computer is set to obtain an IP address automatically. Connect the computer to one of the RJ-45 LAN ports on the router/modem. These are usually color-coded yellow. Wait for the Dynamic Host Configuration Protocol (DHCP) server running on the router/modem to allocate a valid IP address to the computer.

Use a browser to open the device's management URL, as listed in the documentation. This could be an IP address or a host/domain name:

```
http://192.168.0.1
http://www.routerlogin.com
```

It might use HTTPS rather than unencrypted HTTP: If you cannot connect, check that the computer's IP address is in the same range as the device IP.

The management software will prompt you to choose a new administrator password. Enter the default password (as listed in the documentation or printed on a sticker accompanying the router/modem). Choose a long password (12 characters or more) with a mix of alphanumeric and symbol characters. If there is also an option to change the default username of the administrator account, this is also a little bit more secure than leaving the default configured.

CONFIGURING INTERNET ACCESS

Most appliances will use a wizard-based setup to connect to the Internet via the service provider's network. The DSL/cable link parameters are normally self-configuring. You might need to supply a username and password. If manual configuration is required, obtain the settings from your ISP.

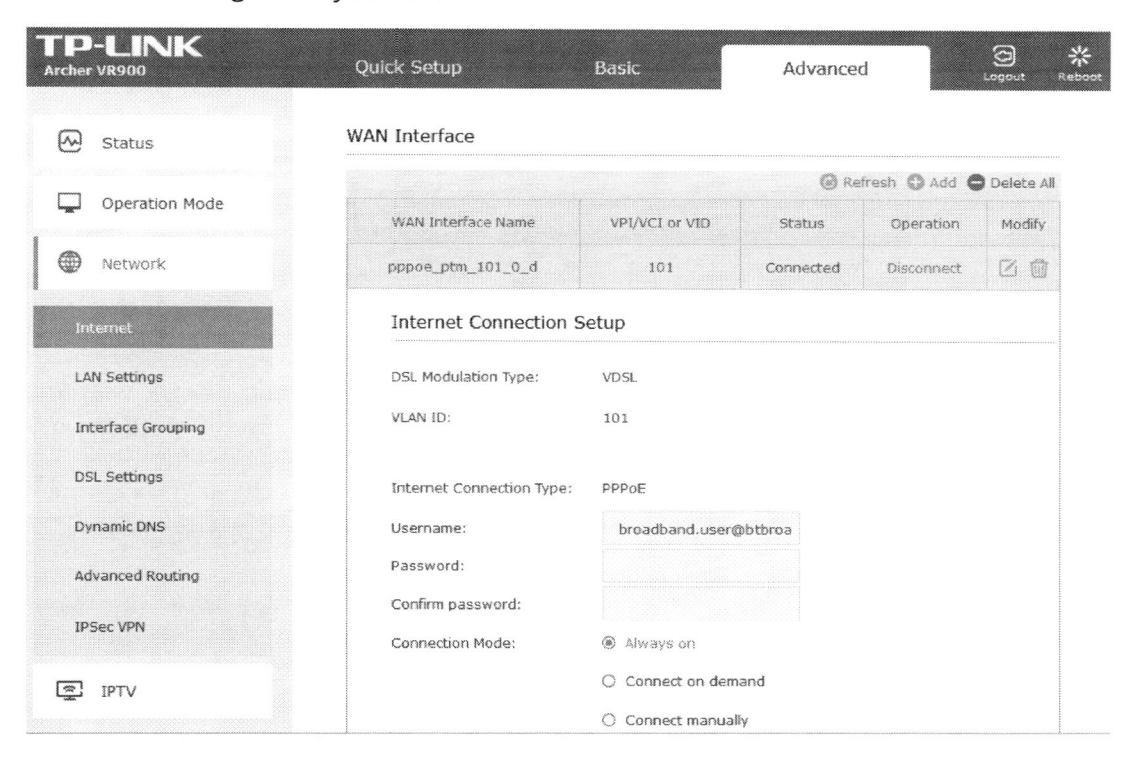

Configuring DSL modem settings. Note that this VDSL modem is connecting to a Fiber to the Curb (FTTC) service. The DSL segment only runs between the premises and the service provider's cabinet, located in a nearby street. From the cabinet, there is a fiber optic cable running back to the local exchange. (Screenshot courtesy of TP-Link.)

You can also use the management console to view line status and the system log. These might be required by the ISP to troubleshoot any issues with the connection.

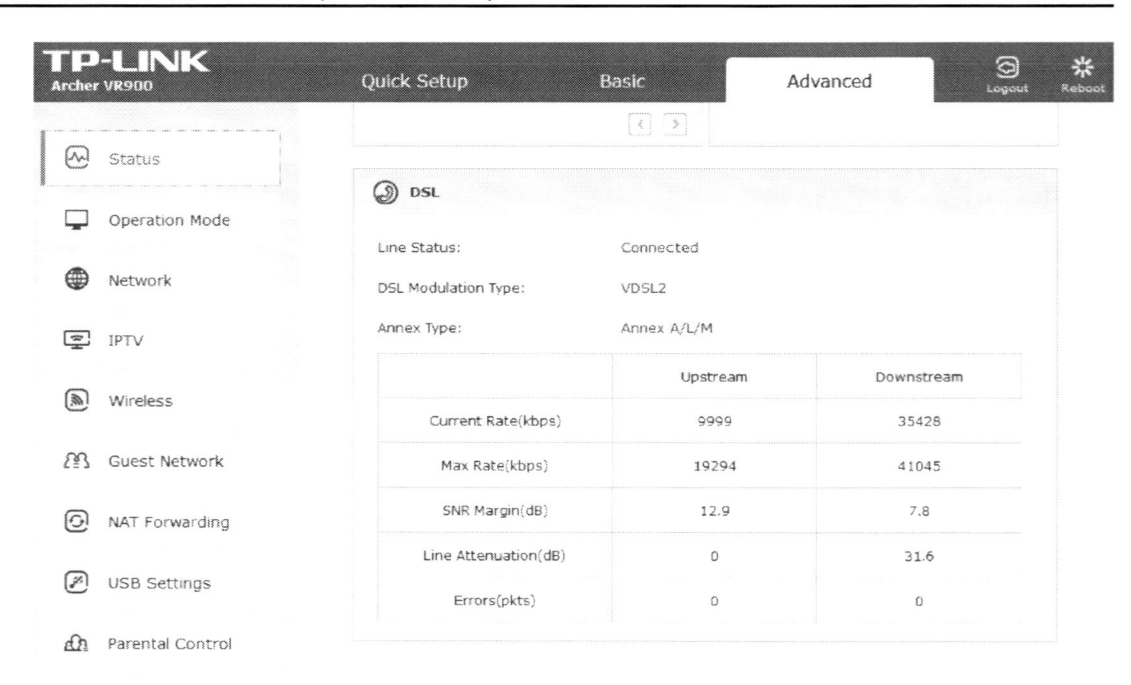

Viewing DSL line status. (Screenshot courtesy of TP-Link.)

WIRELESS SETTINGS

Having set up Internet access, the next step is to configure wireless settings. The majority of hosts will connect to the network wirelessly. Initial configuration is likely to be part of the device's setup wizard, but if you skipped that or need to reconfigure settings, the management software will have a separate page or section for wireless configuration.

Having checked the box to enable wireless communications, you can adjust the following settings from the default.

- Frequency band (2.4 GHz or 5 GHz)—on an 802.11ac access point, you can use the same network settings over both bands. Clients will connect to any supported frequency. Alternatively, you can configure different network names for each frequency. You might want to use one frequency but not the other, depending on the range of devices you have using the wireless network.

    Note: It is best practice not to enable services you do not need, especially on a multifunction device such as this. Most devices are now shipped in "security-enabled" configurations, meaning that you explicitly have to choose to enable services that you want to run.

- SSID (Service Set ID)—a name for the WLAN. This can be up to 32 characters and must be different to any other networks nearby.
- Security version and encryption type—always choose the highest mode supported by your wireless clients (WPA2 with AES). Note that WEP provides very weak security and should not be relied upon for confidentiality.
- Password (Pre-Shared Key)—on a SOHO network you will choose a password for use by all client devices to connect to the network. The password generates the encryption key. The same key must be configured on client adapters to enable them to connect.

    Note: Choose a strong passphrase and keep it secret. In order to generate a strong key, use a longer phrase than you would for a normal password.

- Mode—enable compatibility for different 802.11 devices. Performance may be improved if you disable support for unnecessary legacy standards. The typical configuration is to use the 2.4 GHz band for legacy b/g/n stations and the 5 GHz band for ac stations.
- Channel and channel width—the access point will try to auto-detect the best channel at boot time. You might adjust the settings manually if you subsequently experience a weak connection caused by interference from other devices. For 802.11n/ac access points, you may be able to configure the use of wide channels (bonding) for more bandwidth. This may only be practical in the 5 GHz band, depending on the wireless site design.

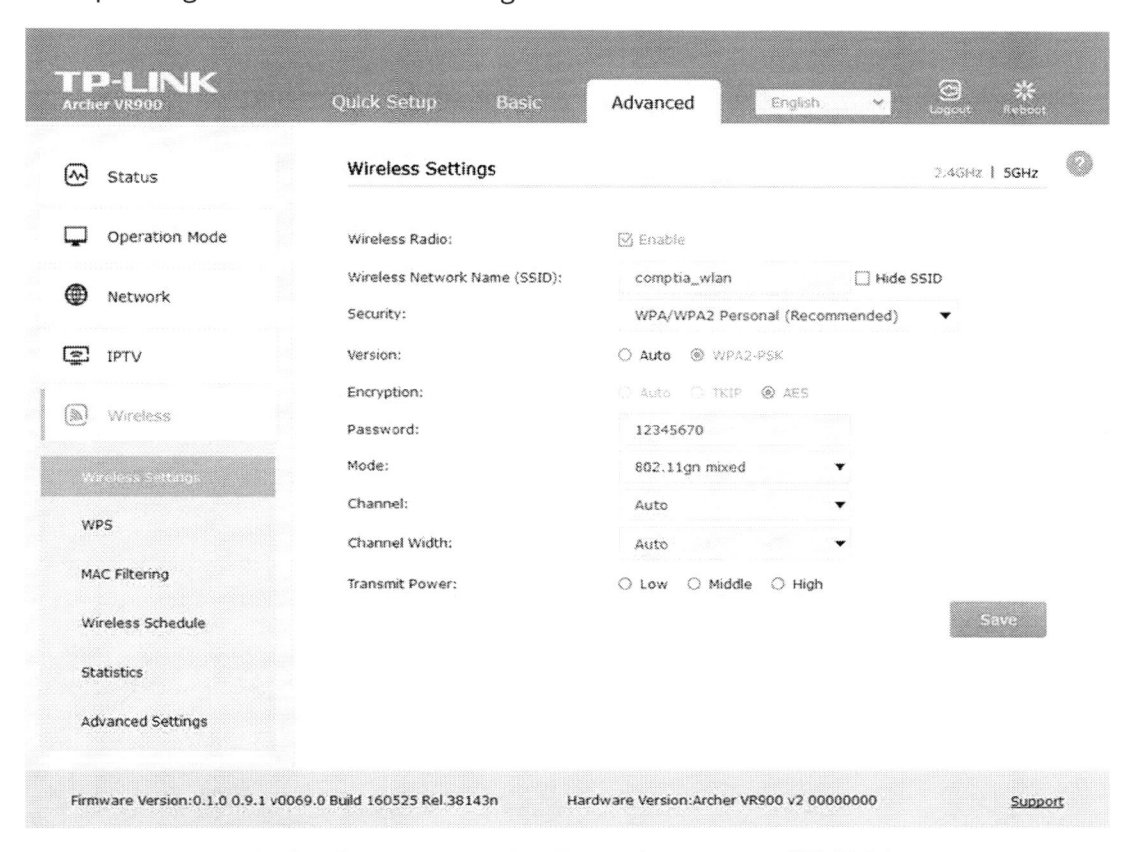

Configuring an access point. (Screenshot courtesy of TP-Link.)

DHCP AND IP ADDRESS CONFIGURATION

You may want to adjust the settings for the DHCP server. This assigns wired and wireless clients an appropriate IP addressing configuration. It is always enabled "out of the box" to allow users to connect to the configuration page easily. If you disable DHCP, IP settings have to be allocated and configured manually on client devices. This adds a lot of administrative overhead and introduces the possibility of configuration errors. Also, it is not difficult for a determined attacker to identify the IP scope in use.

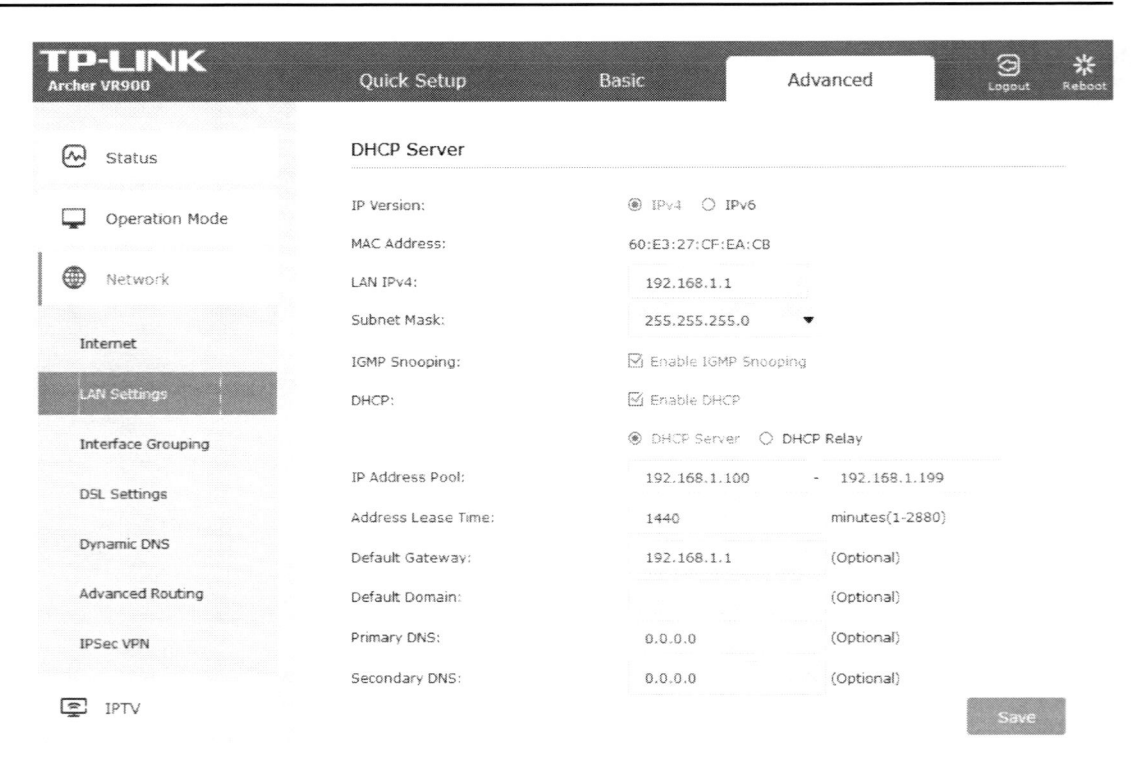

Configuring the DHCP server. (Screenshot courtesy of TP-Link.)

WPS

As setting up an access point securely is relatively complex, vendors have developed a system to automate the process called **Wi-Fi Protected Setup (WPS)**. To use WPS, all the wireless devices (access point and wireless adapters) must be WPS-capable. Typically, the devices will have a push-button. Activating this on the access point and the adapter simultaneously will associate the device with the access point using WPA2. The system generates a random SSID and passphrase.

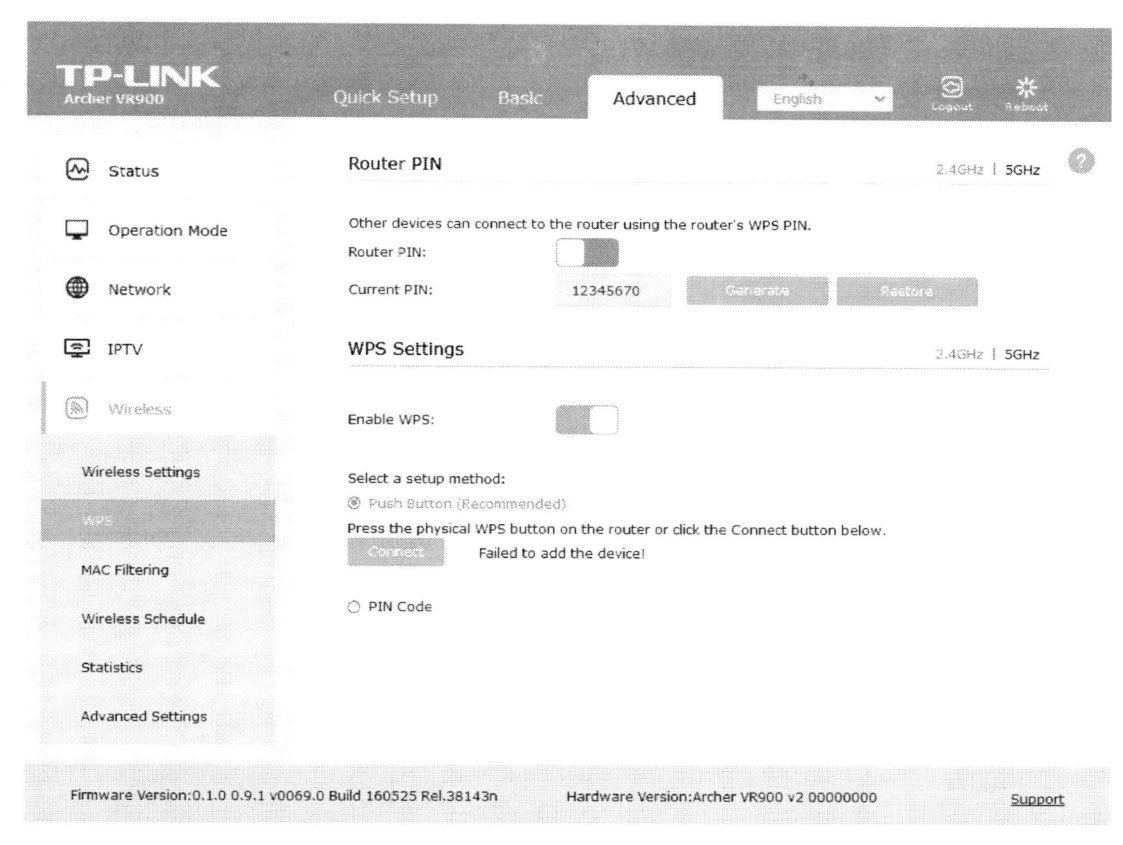

If you use WPS, disable the PIN configuration method if possible. (Screenshot courtesy of TP-Link.)

Note: There is a WPS PIN method too but this is vulnerable to "brute force" attacks, where someone tries to guess the passphrase to get access to the networks. It is advisable to disable this method if possible.

ACCESS POINT PLACEMENT

Antenna and access point placement is important for ensuring a robust network—one that clients can connect to wherever they are in the building. In a SOHO network, with an integrated router/modem/access point, placement of the access point is likely to be constrained by the location of the service provider's cabling. If this does not provide sufficient coverage, the typical solution is to use extenders to repeat and boost the wireless signal in locations where it is not strong enough.

A site survey can be performed with wireless signal measuring software (such as inSSIDer) to identify "dead zones."

CHANNEL SELECTION

The 2.4 GHz band for 802.11b/g/n is subdivided into 11 channels (in the US), spaced at 5 MHz intervals. However, the recommendation is to allow 25 MHz spacing between channels in active use. In practice, therefore, no more than three nearby 802.11b/g/n access points can have non-overlapping channels. This could be implemented, for example, by selecting channel 1 for AP1, channel 6 for AP2, and channel 11 for AP3. When using the 5 GHz band, more non-overlapping channels are available.

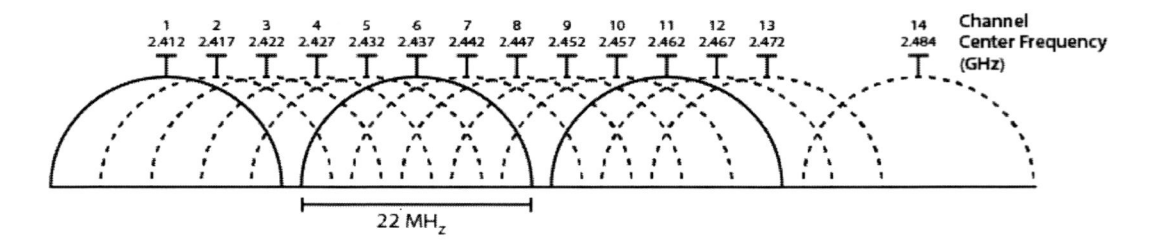

Frequencies and overlap of wireless channels.

Newer access points will auto-detect the channel that seems least congested at boot time. As the environment changes, you may find that this channel selection is not the optimum one. You can use a wireless spectrum analyzer to find which channels in your area are actually the least busy.

RADIO POWER LEVELS

You may want to turn the power output on an AP down to prevent "war driving." War driving is the practice of driving around with a wireless-enabled laptop scanning for unsecure WLANs. The main problem with this approach is that it requires careful configuration to ensure that there is acceptable coverage for legitimate users. You also expose yourself slightly to "**evil twin**" attacks, as users may expect to find the network at a given location and assume that a rogue AP is legitimate.

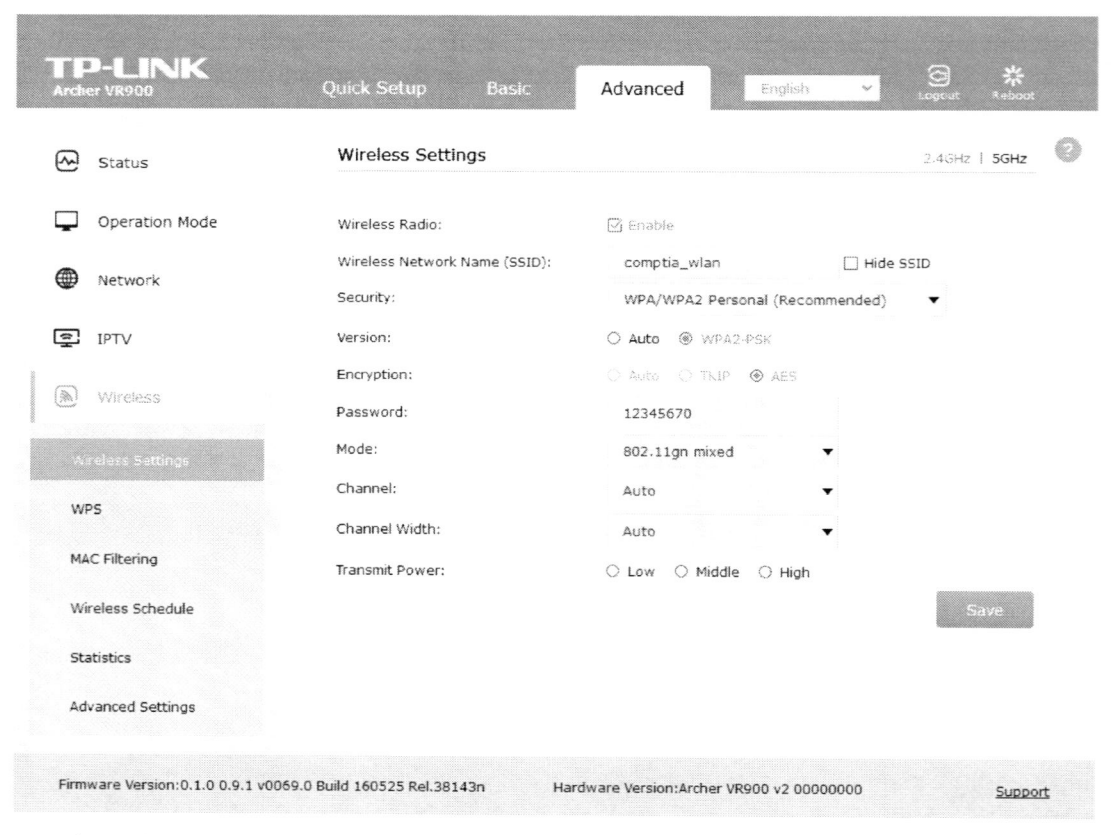

You have the option to set the Transmit Power level when configuring wireless settings on this access point. (Screenshot courtesy of TP-Link.)

Increasing power output to boost a signal is not always reliable. As you increase power, you also increase the chance of the signal bouncing, causing more interference, especially if there are multiple access points. Also, the client radio power levels should match those of the access point or they may be able to receive signals but not transmit back. Consequently, power levels are best set to autonegotiate. You should also be aware of legal restrictions on power output—these vary from country-to-country.

WI-FI SECURITY PROTOCOLS

Wireless LANs require careful configuration to make the connection and transmissions over the connection secure. The main problem with wireless is that because it is "unguided," there is no way to contain the signal. Anyone with a suitably equipped laptop or RF (Radio Frequency) scanner can intercept the signals. If the proper security has not been put in place, this could allow the interception of data or the unauthorized use of the network.

The crucial step in enforcing wireless security is to enable **encryption**. Encryption scrambles the messages being sent over the WLAN so that anyone intercepting them is not able to capture any valuable information. An encryption system consists of a cipher, which is the process used to scramble the message, and a key. The key is a unique value that allows the recipient to decrypt a message that has been encrypted using the same cipher and key. Obviously, the key must be known only to valid recipients or the encryption system will offer no protection.

WIRED EQUIVALENT PRIVACY (WEP)

The **Wired Equivalent Privacy (WEP)** encryption system is based on the RC4 cipher. RC stands for Ron's Cipher, after its inventor, Ron Rivest. Under WEP version 1, you can select from different key sizes (64-bit or 128-bit). A larger key makes it more difficult to attack the security system.

Although WEP might sound like a good solution at first, it is not as secure as it should be. The problem stems from the way WEP produces keys. Because of a flaw in the method, attackers can quite easily generate their own keys by using a wireless network capture tool to analyze network data and crack WEP in a short period of time.

Consequently, WEP is deprecated and should not be used to secure a wireless network.

WI-FI PROTECTED ACCESS (WPA)

Wi-Fi Protected Access (WPA) fixes most of the security problems with WEP. WPA still uses the RC4 cipher but adds a mechanism called **Temporal Key Integrity Protocol (TKIP)** to fix the issues with key generation.

The original version of WPA was introduced as an upgrade for equipment supporting WEP. The continued reliance on WEP meant that the protocol did not meet the requirements of the IEEE 802.11i security standard. An update, known as WPA2, was developed as a fully compliant 802.11i security protocol. The main difference to WPA is the use of the **Advanced Encryption Standard (AES)** cipher for encryption. AES is much stronger than RC4/TKIP.

The only reason not to use WPA2 is if it is not supported by adapters, APs, or operating systems on the network. WPA2 is very well-established now and most devices should support it. WPA is an acceptable fallback, especially on home networks, where the risk of intrusion is quite low.

> **Note:** *WPA/WPA2 can still depend on the use of a passphrase to generate the key. If the passphrase is an easy-to-guess word or phrase, the key can be discovered and the encryption system cracked.*

WI-FI AUTHENTICATION

It is possible to configure a WLAN as open, meaning that anyone can connect to it. In order to secure the WLAN, however, you need to be able to confirm that only valid users are connecting to it by authenticating them. WLAN authentication comes in two types.

PERSONAL

The personal authentication mode is based on a **Pre-shared Key (PSK)**. This is the key that is used to encrypt communications. A PSK is generated from a passphrase, which is like a long password. In WPA-PSK, the router administrator defines a passphrase of between 8 and 63 ASCII characters. This is converted into a 256-bit cryptographic hash, expressed as a 64-digit hex value where each hex digit represents 4 bits.

> *Note:* It is critical that PSK passphrases be long (12 characters or more) and complex. This means that it should contain a mixture of upper- and lower-case letters and digits and no dictionary words or common names.

The main problem is that distribution of the key or passphrase cannot be secured properly, and on a home network, the user acting as the administrator may choose an unsecure phrase. It also fails to provide accounting, as all users share the same key. The advantage is that it is simple to set up. Conversely, changing the key periodically (as would be good security practice) is difficult as the new key must be communicated to all users and updated on all their devices.

PSK is the only type of authentication available for WLANs that use WEP encryption technology. It is also suitable for SOHO networks and workgroups that use WPA or WPA2 encryption.

ENTERPRISE

WPA and WPA2 can implement enterprise mode authentication, where the access point passes authentication information to a **Remote Authentication Dial-in User Service (RADIUS)** server for validation. This type of authentication is suitable for server-/domain-based networks.

COMMON SOHO SECURITY ISSUES

Although encryption and setting a strong passphrase are the most important factors in configuring effective Wi-Fi security, there are other configuration changes you may want to make. Here are some additional security problems and solutions.

SERVICE SET ID (SSID)

The **Service Set ID (SSID)** is a simple name (case sensitive 32-bit alphanumeric string) for users to identify the WLAN by. Vendors use default SSIDs for their products based on the device brand or model. You should change it to something that your users will recognize and will not get confused between nearby networks. Given that, on a residential network, you should not use an SSID that reveals personal information, such as an address or surname. Similarly, on a business network, you may not want to use a meaningful name. For example, an SSID like "Accounts" could prove tempting to would-be attackers.

Disabling broadcast of the SSID prevents any adapters not manually configured to connect to the name you specify from finding the network. This provides a margin of privacy.

> *Note:* Hiding the SSID does not secure the network; you must enable encryption. Even when broadcast is disabled, the SSID can still be detected using packet sniffing tools.

PHYSICAL SECURITY

On a business network, physical access to important network infrastructure like switches and routers should be restricted to administrators and technicians. Most devices are stored in a locked equipment room and may also be protected by lockable cabinets. Many devices can be reset to the factory configuration with physical access. This could allow someone to disrupt the network or gain access to administrative settings (though probably not without being noticed).

UPDATING FIRMWARE

You should keep the firmware and driver for the Internet appliance up-to-date with the latest patches. This is important to fix security holes and to support the latest security standards, such as WPA2. To perform a firmware update, download the update from the vendor's website, taking care to select the correct patch for your device make and model. Select the **Firmware Upgrade** option and browse for the firmware file you downloaded.

Make sure that power to the device is not interrupted during the update process.

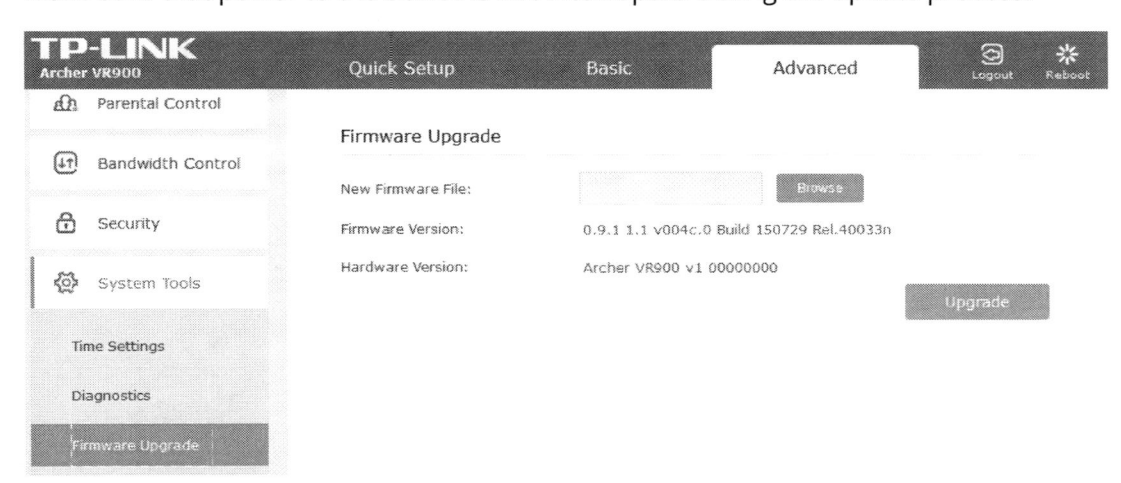

Upgrading device firmware. (Screenshot courtesy of TP-Link.)

ASSIGNING STATIC IP ADDRESSES

Assigning static IP addresses means that the DHCP server is disabled and clients must be configured manually to join the network properly. It would be trivial for an attacker to identify the appropriate subnet so this is not something that would deter a determined attack.

Note that devices such as the router/modem must be configured with a static address because it acts as a DHCP server, and client devices need to use it as the default gateway.

LATENCY AND JITTER

Quality of Service (QoS) means using a network protocol to prioritize certain types of traffic over others.

Many networks are now being pressed into service to provide two-way communications, with applications such as Voice over IP (VoIP), video conferencing, and multiplayer gaming. Applications such as voice and video that carry real-time data have different network requirements to the sort of data represented by file transfer. With "ordinary" data, it might be beneficial to transfer a file as quickly as possible, but the sequence in which the packets are delivered and variable intervals between packets arriving do not materially affect the application. This type of data transfer is described as "bursty." Network protocols such as HTTP, FTP, or email are very sensitive to packet loss but are tolerant to delays in delivery. The reverse is applicable to real-time applications; they can compensate for some amount of packet loss, but are very sensitive toward delays in data delivery.

Problems with the timing and sequence of packet delivery are defined as latency and jitter:

- **Latency** (Delay)—the time it takes for a signal to reach the recipient. A video application can support a latency of about 80 ms, while typical latency on the Internet can reach 1000 ms at peak times. Latency is a particular problem for 2-way applications, such as VoIP (telephone), online conferencing, and multiplayer gaming.
- **Jitter**—variation in the delay; often caused by congestion at routers and other internetwork devices or by configuration errors.

Real-time applications are sensitive to the effects of latency and jitter because they manifest as echo, delay, and video slow down. End users are generally very intolerant of these kinds of errors.

It is difficult to guarantee Quality of Service (QoS) over a public network such as the Internet. Enterprise networks can deploy sophisticated QoS and traffic engineering protocols on managed switches and routers. On a SOHO network, you may be able to configure a QoS or bandwidth control feature on the router/modem to prioritize the port used by a VoIP application over any other type of protocol. This will help to mitigate issues if, for example, one computer is trying to download a Windows 10 feature update at the same time as another set of computers are trying to host a video conference.

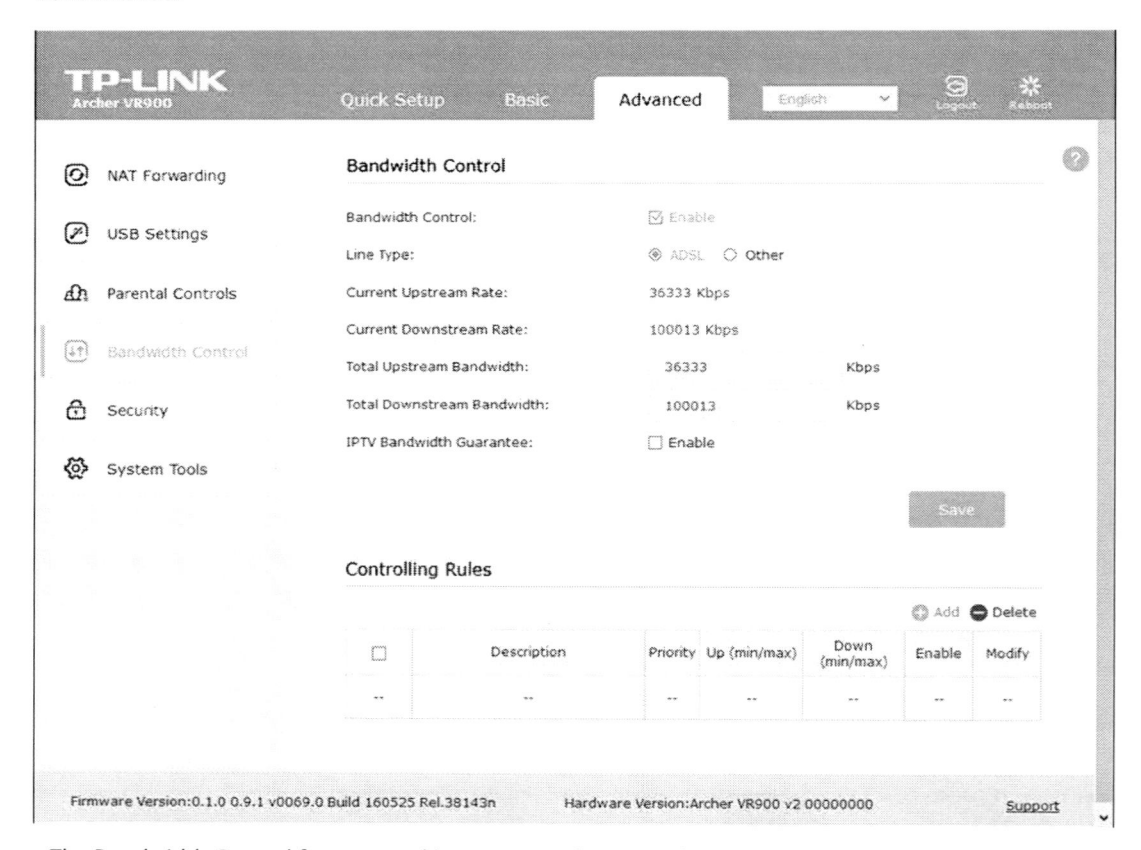

The Bandwidth Control feature on this router/modem provides a basic QoS mechanism. (Screenshot courtesy of TP-Link.)

Activity 6-2
Discussing SOHO Network Installation and Configuration

SCENARIO
Answer the following questions to check your understanding of the topic.

1. What type of cable and connectors are used to connect a modem to a phone port?

2. What is the function of a microfilter?

3. To configure a router/modem, what type of IP interface configuration should you apply to the computer you are using to access the device administration web app?

4. What is the effect of reducing transmit power when you are configuring an access point?

5. Which standard represents the best available wireless network security?

6. How can QoS improve performance for SOHO Internet access?

Activity 6-3
Installing and Configuring SOHO Networks

BEFORE YOU BEGIN

Ideally, you would set up a mix of networks with different modes and frequencies. Experiment with using the same network name for 2.4 GHz and 5 GHz bands. Try setting up clashing network channels to see if there is any adverse effect.

If you do not have physical access points to use, consider asking learners to connect to an emulator, such as

- https://www.cisco.com/assets/sol/sb/AP541N_GUI/AP541N_1_9_2/Getting_Started.htm,
- http://ui.linksys.com/, http://support.dlink.ca/emulators/wbr2310/index.htm,
- https://tools.netgear.com/landing/gui/wireless/wg102/simulators/wg102_v_1_0_31/start.htm, or
- https://www.tp-link.com/us/support/emulators.

If the equipment is available, you will join a wireless network set up by your instructor, or you will configure your own wireless network as part of a group. Depending on the equipment available, you may receive either a dedicated access point or a multifunction router/modem/access point, or you might be asked to connect to a wireless access point emulator.

Use this table to record the wireless settings that your group will configure, or that your instructor will configure for you to connect to.

Option	2.4 GHz Band Settings	5 GHz Band Settings
SSID		
Mode/Compatibility		
Channel		
Security/Authentication Type		
Preshared Key/Password		

SCENARIO

In this activity, you will connect computers together in a wireless network, depending on the devices available in your learning environment.

1. If you have a physical wireless access point, reset it to the factory configuration, and then connect to the management interface.
    a) Connect the access point to a power source and switch it on.
    b) Unless you are advised otherwise by your instructor, press the access point's reset switch and hold for about 20 seconds (or as instructed) to apply the default configuration.

The reset switch will be a recessed button on the back of the access point. You might need to use a paper clip to press it.

c) Verify that the network adapter on your HOST computer is set to obtain an IP address automatically.

d) Disconnect the network cable from your HOST computer's network adapter. Connect an RJ-45 patch cable from the HOST computer's network adapter to one of the **LAN** or **Ethernet** ports on the access point.

e) If the network location banner appears prompting you to trust the network, select **Yes**.

f) Start a web browser, and open the device's management URL.

This may be printed on a sticker on the device.

g) If prompted, log in using the default user name and password.

Again, this may be printed on a sticker on the device.

h) If you are prompted to change the default user name and password, set the user name to *admin* and password to *Pa$$w0rd*

2. Configure the access point to use the settings suggested by your instructor (the ones you recorded in the table).

a) Locate the menu option for manual or advanced wireless settings.

In the environment shown in the following figure, you would select **Advanced→Wireless→Basic Settings**.

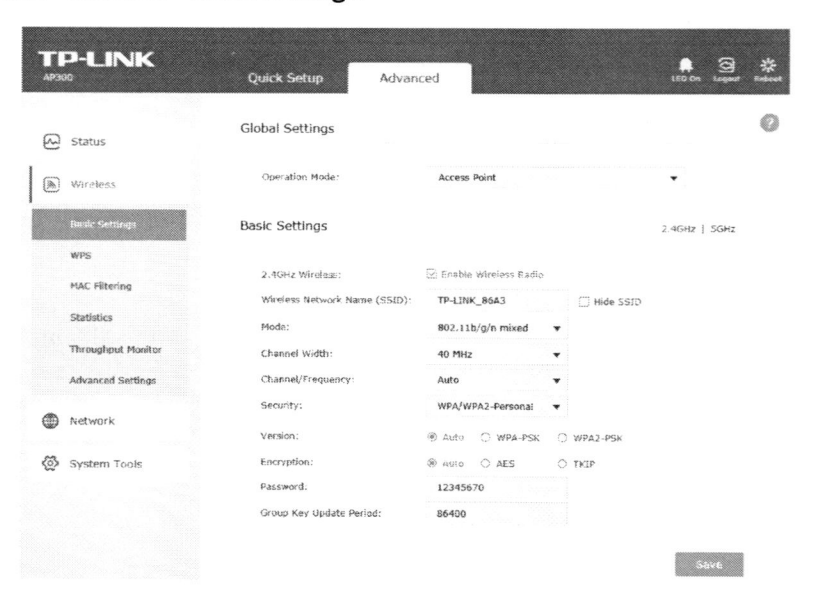

Access point configuration. (Screenshot courtesy of TP-Link.)

Note: *Your instructor will guide you through this activity if you are using a different wireless router than the one depicted in the previous screenshot.*

b) If there is an **Operation mode** option (as shown above), set it to **Access Point**.

The device may also support being configured as a repeater or bridge.

c) Enter the settings you recorded in the table, and then save the settings using the options appropriate for your configuration page. This might be a **Save** button, **Apply Changes** button, or something similar.

3. Install a wireless network adapter in your HOST computer.

Your instructor will provide you with a wireless network adapter. This may be a plug-in card or a USB device.

a) If your adapter has a setup-based install, run the **Setup** program to install the adapter driver software.
b) Physically connect the wireless adapter to the HOST computer.
   - If you have a USB wireless adapter, connect it to a USB port.
   - If you have a plug-in card, power off the PC, and remove all the cables. Follow instructions from your instructor to add the card to a spare slot, and then reassemble and restart the computer.
c) When the adapter is installed, restart Windows if necessary and wait for the adapter to be detected or for the **Device Setup** wizard to start.
d) If necessary, point to the location of the driver files, and follow any other prompts required to install the device and drivers.

4. When the adapter is physically installed, connect to the access point configured by the instructor or by your group.
   a) In the notification area, select the network status icon.
   b) If more than one network is detected, select the SSID associated with your access point, and select **Connect**.
   c) Enter the network key and select **Next**.
   d) If prompted, select **No** to set the network location as **Public**.
   e) Open **File Explorer** and browse the **Network** object.

   You should not see any computers listed, as the firewall settings for public networks prevent discovery.

   f) Select the yellow **Network discovery is turned off** bar and select **Turn on network discovery and file sharing**.

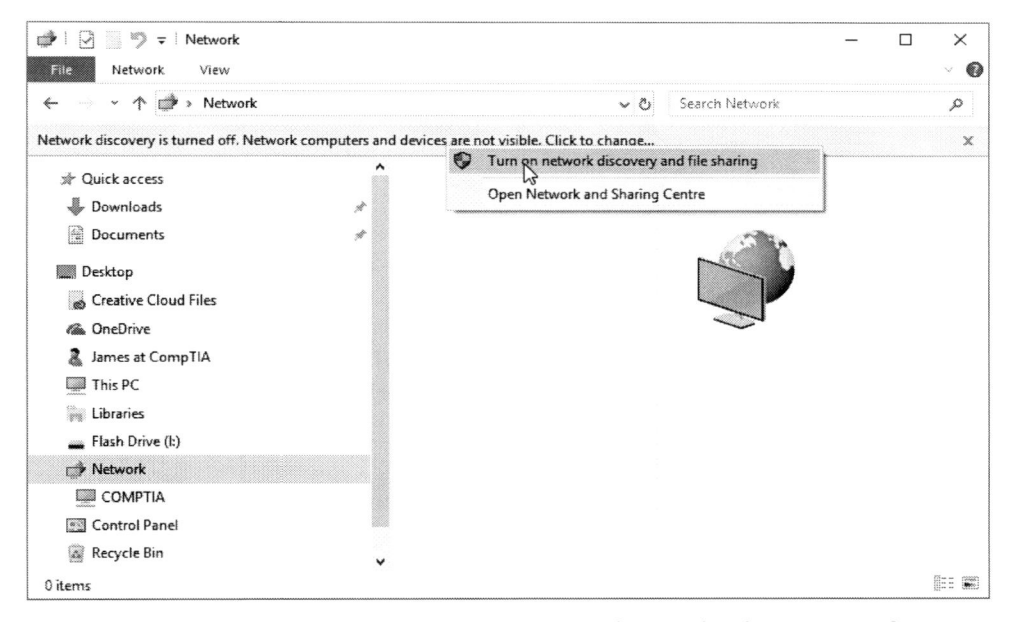

Click the bar to enable network discovery. (Screenshot used with permission from Microsoft.)

   g) At the prompt, select **No, make the network that I am connected to a private network**.

h) Browse for other computers again.

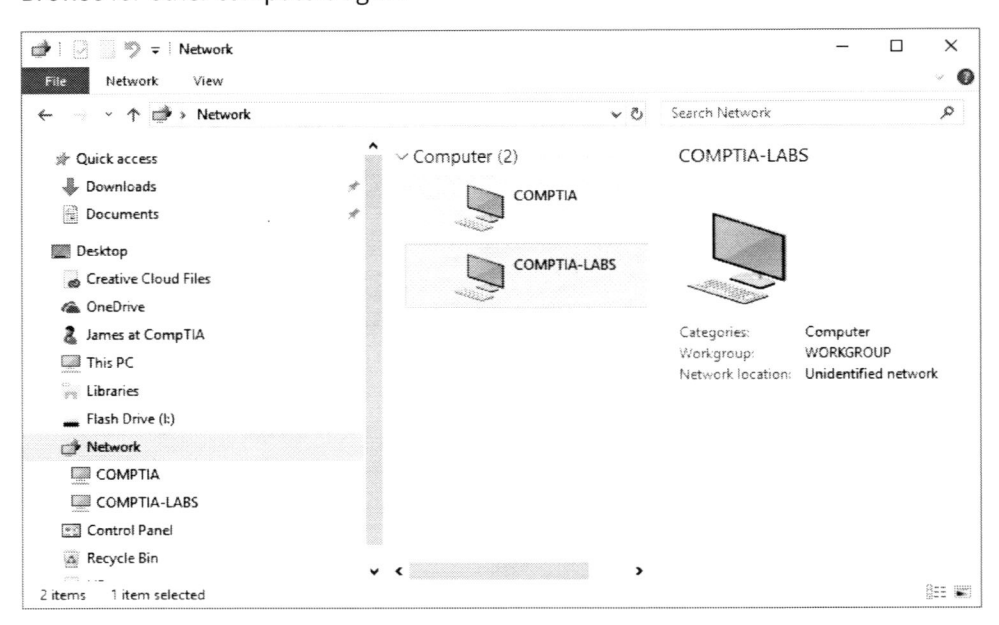

Browsing the network—two computers have joined this network (COMPTIA and COMPTIA-LABS). (Screenshot used with permission from Microsoft.)

5. View the network properties using the **Settings** app.
    a) Select the network status icon and select **Network & Internet Settings**.
    b) In the **Settings** app, select **Wi-Fi**.
    c) Select the network name.
        You can change the network location type here.
    d) Scroll down the page to view the IP settings and connection properties, including the network band and channel.
    e) Record the **Physical address (MAC)**.
    f) Close the Settings app.

6. View the Wi-Fi adapter's driver properties in Device Manager.
    a) Right-click **Start** and select **Device Manager**.
    b) Expand **Network adapters** and then right-click the wireless adapter and select **Properties**.
    c) Select the **Advanced** tab.
    d) Locate settings for preferred wireless mode and frequency. Are there options to set any of the following: **Transmit Power**, **QoS**, or **Wake-on-Wireless LAN**?
        Answers will vary depending on the wireless adapter.
    e) Select **Cancel**.

7. If you are managing an access point in your group, change the settings on the AP to use a different SSID, and ensure that it is not broadcast.

Option	2.4 GHz Band Settings	5 GHz Band Settings
SSID		
Mode/Compatibility		
Channel		
Security/Authentication Type		

| Option | 2.4 GHz Band Settings | 5 GHz Band Settings |

Preshared Key/Password

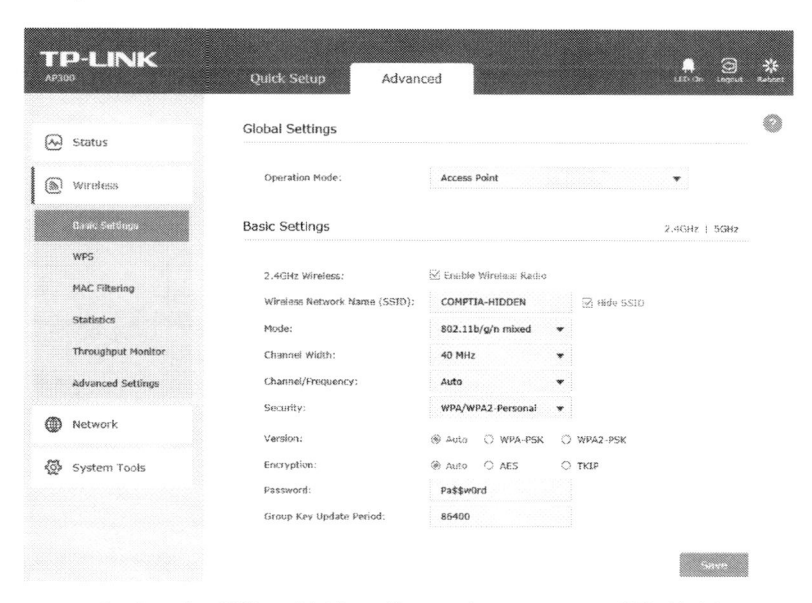

Setting the SSID to hidden. (Screenshot courtesy of TP-Link.)

8. When the AP has been reconfigured, manually connect to the wireless network.
   a) Select the network status icon and select **Network & Internet Settings**.
   b) In the **Settings** app, select **Wi-Fi**.
   c) Select the **Manage known networks** link.
   d) Select **Add a new network**.
   e) Enter the network connection details. Make sure you check **Connect automatically** and **Connect even if this network is not broadcasting.**

Configuring a wireless network connection manually.

f) Select **Save**.
g) If you are prompted to enable discovery and file sharing, select **Yes**. If no prompt appears, enable network discovery via Explorer as you did before.
h) In Explorer, browse the network, and verify that other computers are visible.

9. Optionally, configure MAC filtering to prevent one of the stations in your group from connecting.

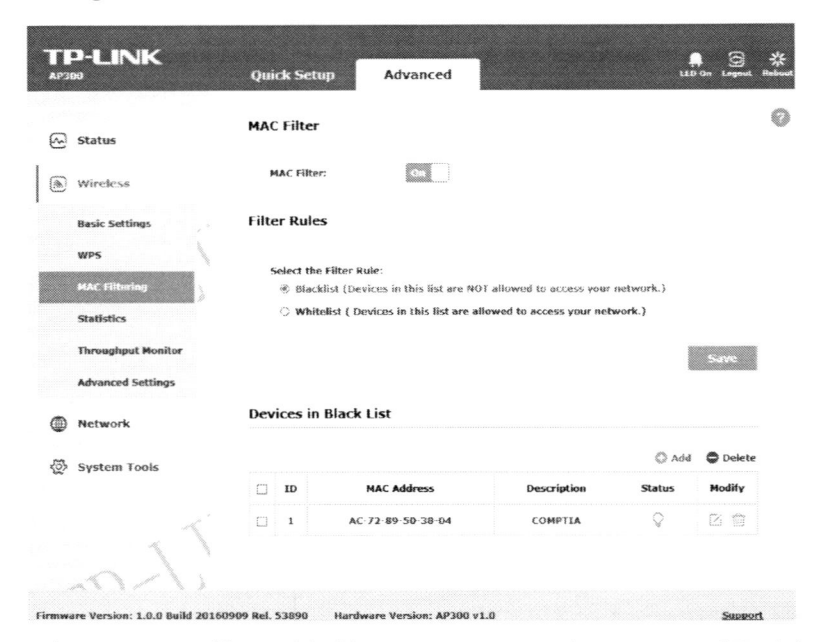

Configuring a MAC filter to blacklist stations. (Screenshot courtesy of TP-Link.)

10. At the end of the activity, if requested, uninstall the wireless adapter and return it to your instructor. Reconnect your computer to the classroom network.

Topic C
Configure SOHO Network Security

EXAM OBJECTIVES COVERED
1001-2.2 Compare and contrast common networking hardware devices.
1001-2.3 Given a scenario, install and configure a basic wired/wireless SOHO network.
1002-1.5 Given a scenario, use Microsoft operating system features and tools.
1002-1.6 Given a scenario, use Microsoft Windows Control Panel utilities.
1002-1.8 Given a scenario, configure Microsoft Windows networking on a client/desktop.
1002-2.10 Given a scenario, configure security on SOHO wireless and wired networks.

Although security models stress the importance of defense in depth, the network edge must still be closely guarded. As a CompTIA A+ technician, you must be able to configure firewall settings and other types of access controls to ensure safe Internet use. In this topic, you will learn how to configure common security features of SOHO router/modems, use the Windows Firewall, and set browser options.

FIREWALLS

There are many types of **firewalls** and many ways of implementing them. One distinction can be made between network and host firewalls:

- **Network firewall**—placed inline in the network and inspects all traffic that passes through it.
- **Host firewall**—installed on the host and only inspects traffic addressed to that host.

Another distinction is what parts of a packet a firewall can inspect and operate on.

PACKET FILTERING FIREWALL

Packet filtering describes the earliest type of firewall. All firewalls can still perform this basic function. A **packet filtering** firewall can inspect the headers of IP packets. This means that rules can be based on the information found in those headers:

- IP filtering—accepting or blocking traffic on the basis of its source and/or destination IP address.
- Protocol ID/type—TCP, UDP, ICMP, and so on.
- Port filtering/security—accepting or blocking a packet on the basis of source and destination port numbers (TCP or UDP application type).

This configuration is referred to as an **Access Control List (ACL)**. The firewall may provide the option to accept all packets except for those on the reject list or, alternatively, it may provide the option to reject all packets except for those on the accept list. Generally, the latter is the best choice, since it is more secure and involves less configuration.

HOST FIREWALL

A host (or software or **personal firewall**) is one that is implemented as software on the individual host PC or server. This might be deployed instead of or in addition to the network firewall. As well as being able to filter traffic based on data in network packets (IP address and port number, for instance), a host-based firewall can be defined with rules for whether particular software programs and services (processes) or user accounts are allowed or denied access.

Having two firewalls is more secure; if one firewall is not working or is misconfigured, the other firewall might prevent an intrusion. The downside is complexity; you must configure rules in two places, and there are two things that could be blocking communications when you come to troubleshoot connections.

> **Note:** Using both a network firewall to secure the "perimeter" and a host firewall provides defense in depth. This is the concept that multiple, well-coordinated layers of defensive controls make a system harder to compromise than a single defensive barrier.

FIREWALL SETTINGS

Most Internet router/modems come with a basic firewall product; some come with quite sophisticated firewalls. On a SOHO network, it is more typical to filter incoming traffic than outgoing traffic. Some router/modems may not support outbound filtering at all.

DISABLING PORTS

One of the basic principles of secure configuration is only to enable services that must be enabled. If a service is unused, then it should not be accessible in any way. The most secure way of doing this is to remove the service on each host. There may be circumstances in which you want a service port to be available on the local network but not on the Internet. This is where a firewall is useful. If you configure an ACL to block the port, or if the port is blocked by the default rule, then Internet hosts will not be able to access it.

MAC FILTERING

The MAC is the hardware address of a network card, in the format aa:bb:cc:dd:ee:ff. Firewalls, switches, and access points can be configured either with whitelists of allowed MACs or blacklists of prohibited MACs. This can be time-consuming to set up and it is easy for malicious actors to spoof a MAC address. On a SOHO network, the security advantages are unlikely to outweigh configuration and troubleshooting issues.

CONTENT FILTERING/PARENTAL CONTROLS

Most Internet appliances also support the configuration of filters to block websites and services on the basis of keywords or site rating and classification services. Another option is to restrict the times at which the Internet is accessible. These are configured in conjunction with services offered by the ISP.

One issue for ISP-enforced parental controls is that the filters are not usually able to distinguish account types, so the filters apply to all Internet access unless the filtering is manually disabled, which requires the ISP account holder's password. Parental controls can also be enforced at the OS level in Windows 10, where different filters can be applied based on the account type.

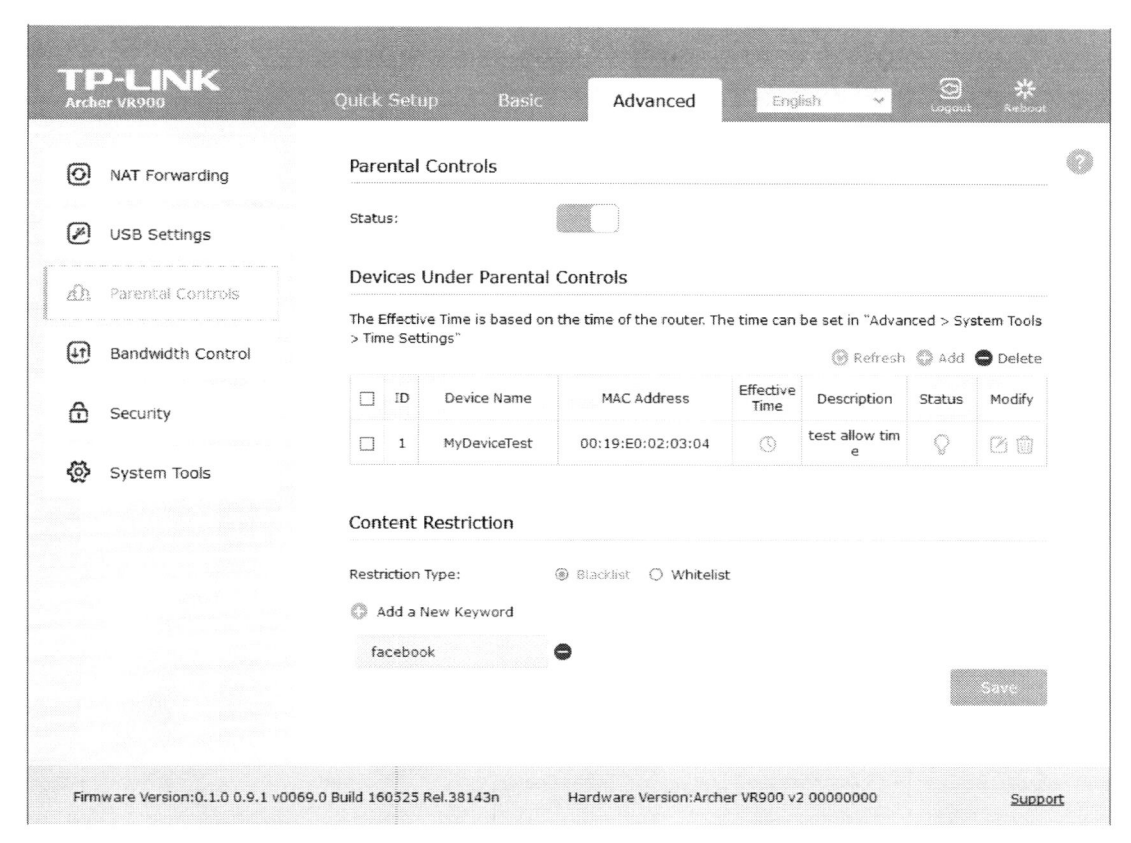

Configuring parental controls to restrict when certain devices can access the network. (Screenshot courtesy of TP-Link.)

WHITELISTS/BLACKLISTS

Content filtering works on the basis of **blacklists** of URLs that are known to harbor a particular type of content. There will be separate blacklists for different types of content that users might want to block. There are also blacklists of sites known to host malware. The firewall will block any IP address or domain name appearing on a blacklist for which a filter has been configured.

Conversely, **whitelisting** a site means that it will be accessible even if a filter is applied. If you want to lock down Internet usage very tightly, it should be possible to configure a filter so that only whitelisted sites are accessible.

NAT

All router/modems implement **Network Address Translation (NAT)**. More specifically, they implement **Network Address Port Translation (NAPT)**, which is also referred to as NAT overloading or **Port Address Translation (PAT)**. The router/modem is issued with a single public IP address by the ISP. Some ISPs might allocate a static address, but it is more common for it to be dynamic (issued by the ISP's DHCP server).

Hosts connected to the router/modem's switch or access point are configured with local (private) addresses, typically in the range 192.168.0.0/24 or 192.168.1.0/24. When one of these devices tries to contact a host on the Internet, the router identifies the connection using an ephemeral port number, adds the original private IP address and port number to a NAT table, and sends the transmission to the Internet host, using its public IP address and the new port number. When (or if) an Internet host replies to that port, the router looks up the port number in the NAT table, locates the original IP address and port, and forwards the response to the local device.

NAT overloading on a SOHO router/modem generally works without any configuration. There might be an option to configure an Application Layer Gateway (ALG) for one or more protocols. NAT can pose problems for some types of protocol. ALG mitigates these problems by opening ports dynamically to allow connections.

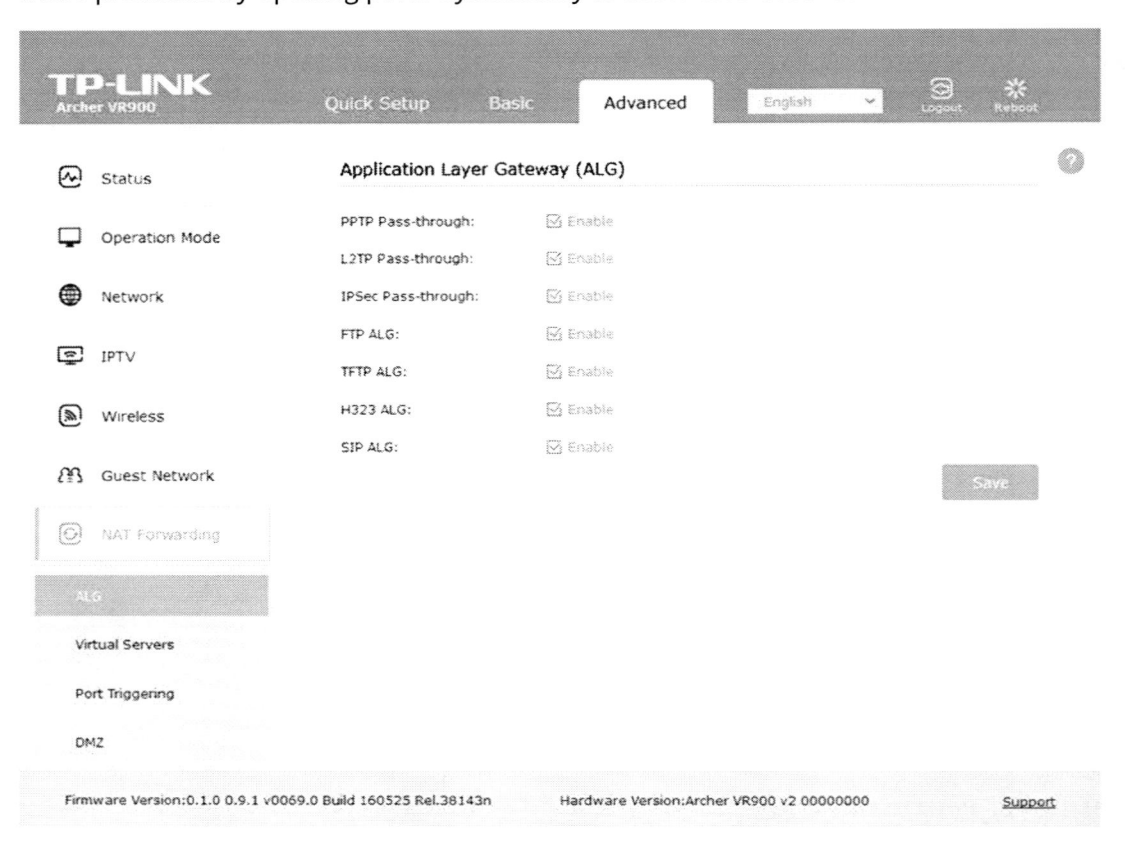

Configuring ALGs for NAT. (Screenshot courtesy of TP-Link.)

PORT FORWARDING AND PORT TRIGGERING

When NAT overloading is deployed, hosts on the Internet can only "see" the router and its public IP address. If you want to run some sort of server application from your network and make it accessible to the Internet, you need to set up port forwarding or Destination NAT (DNAT).

Port forwarding means that the router takes requests from the Internet for a particular protocol (say, HTTP/port 80) and sends them to a designated host on the LAN. The request could also be sent to a different port, so this feature is often also called port mapping. For example, the Internet host could request HTTP on port 80, but the LAN server might run its HTTP server on port 8080 instead.

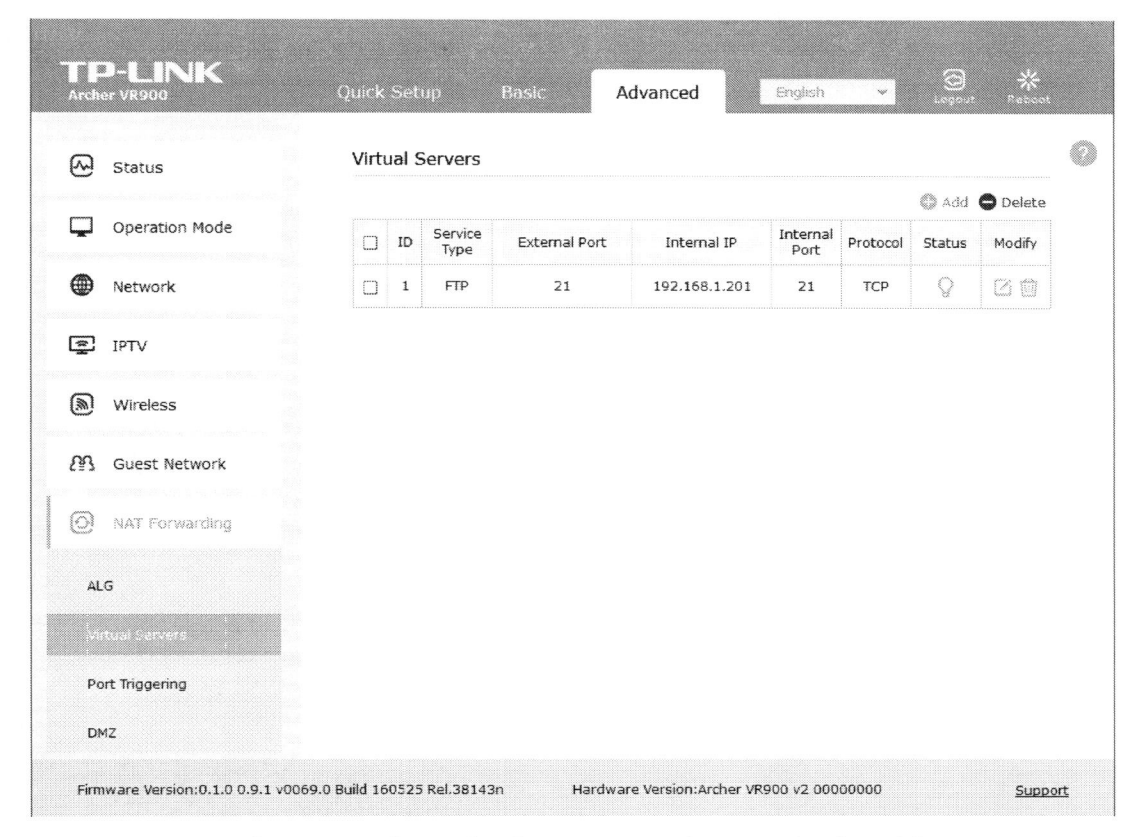

Configuring port forwarding for FTP. (Screenshot courtesy of TP-Link.)

Port triggering is used to set up applications that require more than one port. Basically, when the firewall detects activity on outbound port A destined for a given external IP address, it opens inbound access for the external IP address on port B for a set period.

DMZ

When making a server accessible on the Internet, careful thought needs to be given to the security of the local network. A simple firewall with port forwarding will only support servers on the local network. There can only be one set of access rules. If a server is compromised, because it is on the local network there is the possibility that other LAN hosts can be attacked from it or that the attacker could examine traffic passing over the LAN.

In an enterprise network, a **Demilitarized Zone (DMZ)** is a means of establishing a more secure configuration. The idea of a DMZ is that hosts placed within it are untrusted by the local network zone. Some traffic may be allowed to pass between the DMZ and the local network, but no traffic is allowed to pass from the Internet to the local network through the DMZ.

Most SOHO routers come with only basic firewall functionality. The firewall in a typical SOHO router screens the local network, rather than establishing a DMZ.

However, you should note that many SOHO router/modem vendors use the term "DMZ" or "DMZ host" to refer to a computer on the LAN that is configured to receive communications for any ports that have not been forwarded to other hosts. When DMZ is used in this sense, it means "not protected by the firewall" as the host is fully accessible to other Internet hosts (though it could be installed with a host firewall instead). This also means that the LAN is still exposed to the risks described previously.

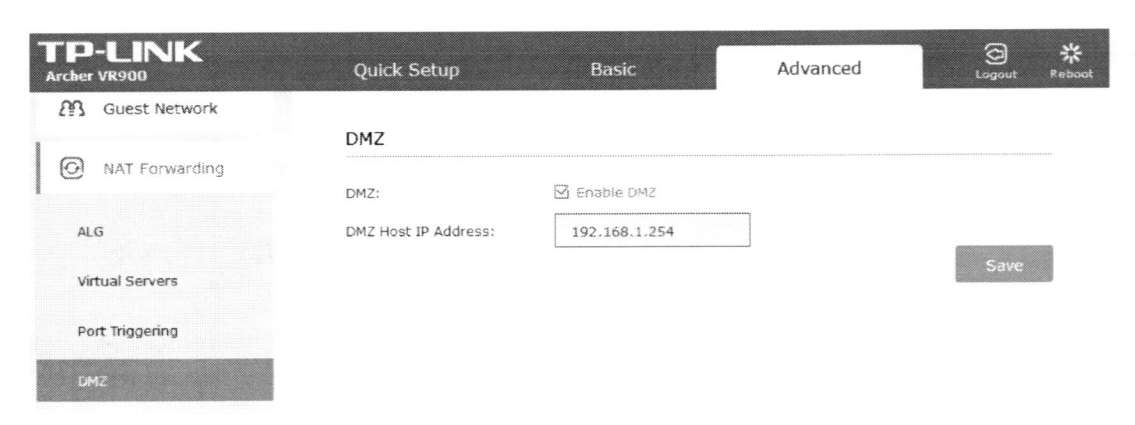

Configuring a SOHO router version of a DMZ—the host 192.168.1.254 will not be protected by the firewall. (Screenshot courtesy of TP-Link.)

UNIVERSAL PLUG-AND-PLAY

ACLs and port forwarding/port triggering are challenging for end users to configure correctly. Many users would simply resort to turning the firewall off in order to get a particular application to work. As a means of mitigating this attitude, services that require complex firewall configuration can use the **Universal Plug-and-Play (UPnP)** framework to send instructions to the firewall with the correct configuration parameters.

On the firewall, check the box to enable UPnP. A client UPnP device, such as an Xbox, PlayStation, or Voice-over-IP handset, will be able to configure the firewall automatically to open the IP addresses and ports necessary to play an online game or place and receive VoIP calls.

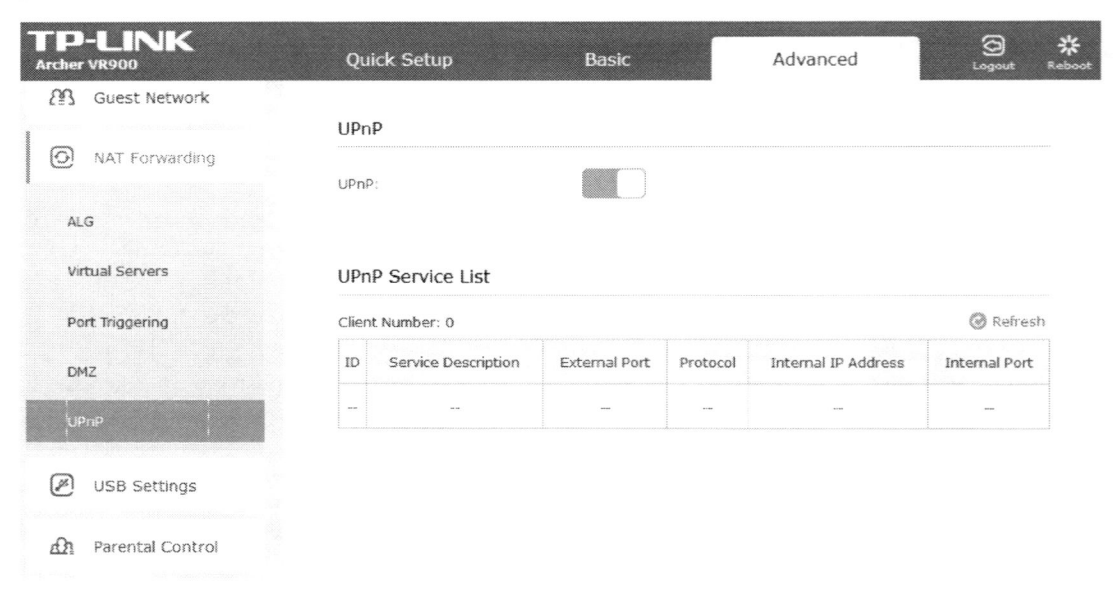

Enabling UPnP—there is nothing to configure, but when client devices use the service, the rules they have configured on the firewall are shown in the service list. (Screenshot courtesy of TP-Link.)

UPnP is associated with a number of security vulnerabilities and is best disabled if not required. You should ensure that the router does not accept UPnP configuration requests from the external (Internet) interface. If using UPnP, keep up-to-date with any security advisories or firmware updates from the router manufacturer.

> **Note:** Also make sure that UPnP is disabled on client devices, unless you have confirmed that the implementation is secure. As well as game consoles, vulnerabilities have been found in UPnP running on devices such as printers and web cams.

WINDOWS FIREWALL

As well as configuring the network firewall, you may want to configure a personal firewall on each host. Windows ships with bundled firewall software.

> **Note:** There are also third-party firewalls. If you install another firewall product, it should disable Windows Firewall. Do not try to run two host firewalls at the same time. The products may interfere with one another and attempting to keep the ACLs synchronized between them will be extremely challenging.

CONFIGURING WINDOWS FIREWALL

To configure the firewall in Windows 7, open **Windows Firewall** in Control Panel to view a status page, then click **Turn Windows Firewall on or off**. The Windows Firewall can be turned on or off depending on whether the network location is private (home/work) or public or domain. For example, you could have an Internet connection through an open access point set to public with a VPN to your corporate network running over the link, but set to domain.

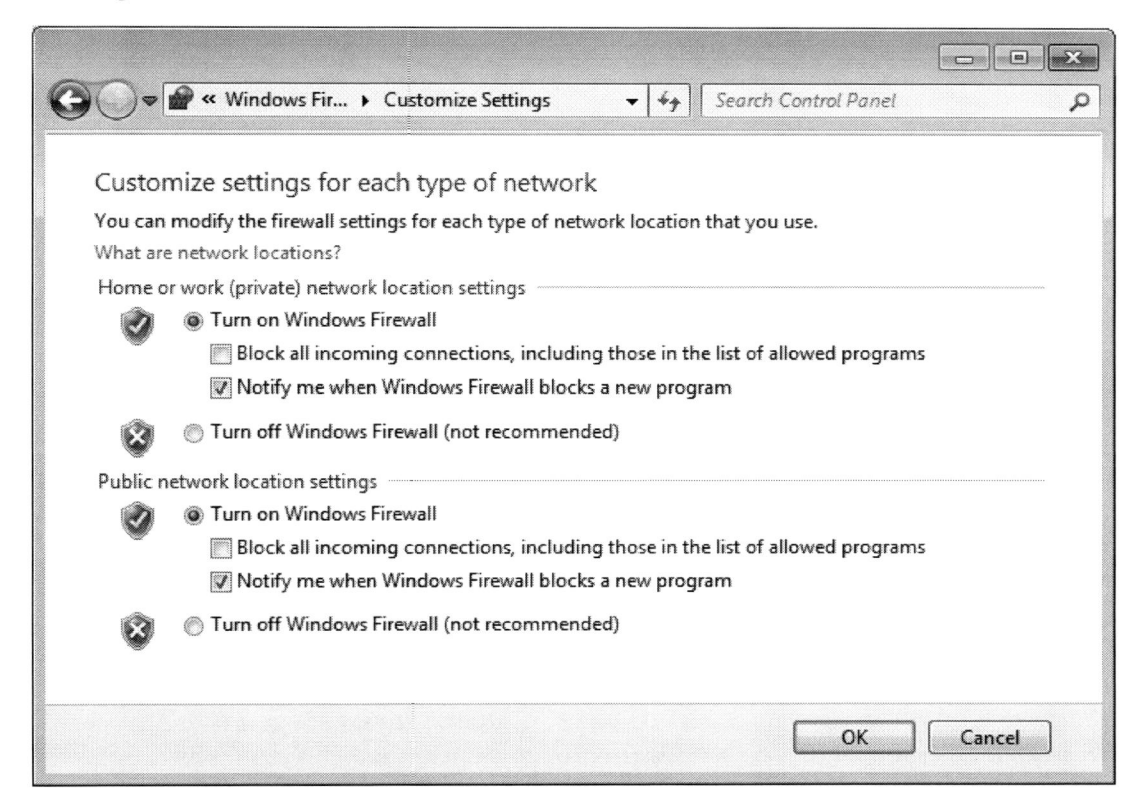

Customizing Windows Firewall settings in Windows 7. (Screenshot used with permission from Microsoft.)

CONFIGURING EXCEPTIONS

To allow or block programs (configure exceptions), from the **Windows Firewall** status page, click **Allow a program or feature through the Windows Firewall**. Check the box for either or both network type or use **Allow another program** to locate its executable file and add it to the list.

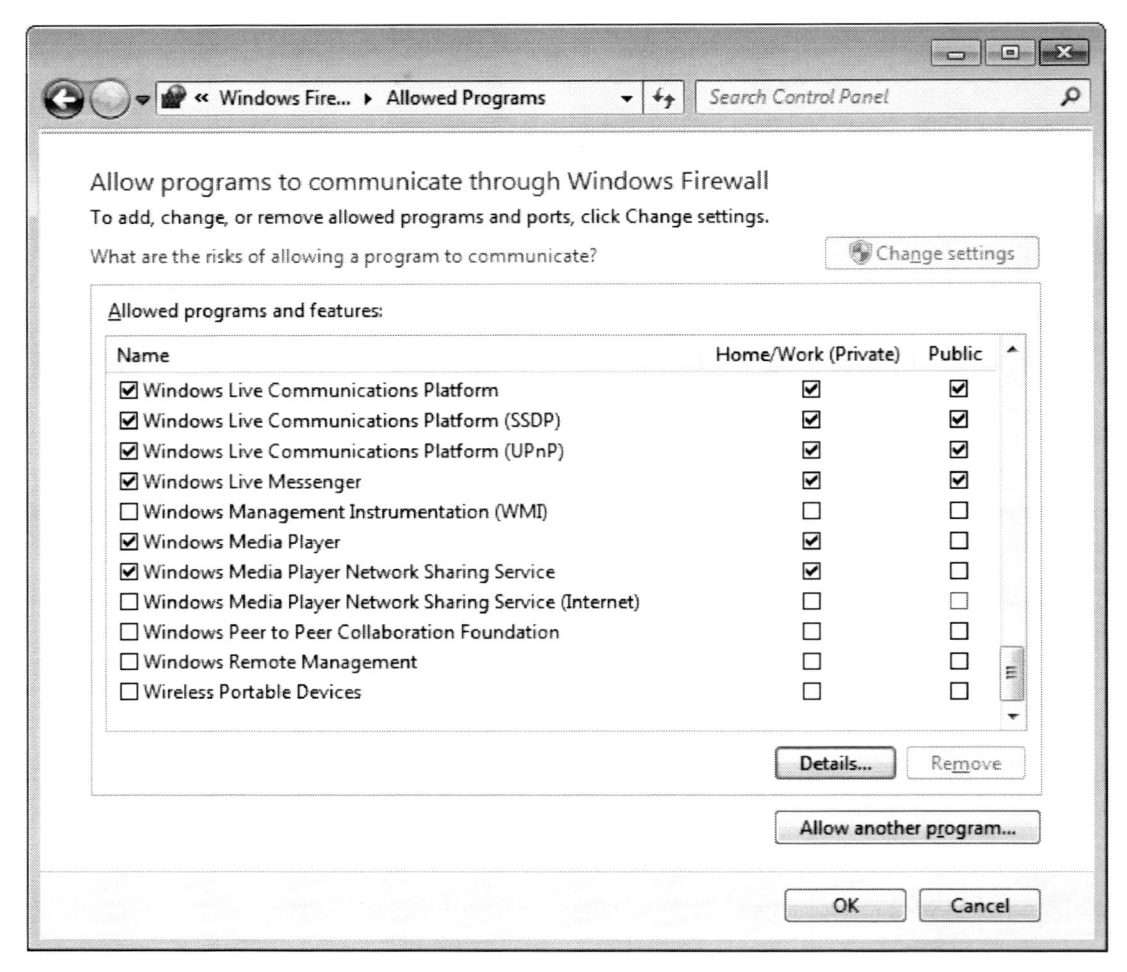

Windows Firewall Allowed Programs. (Screenshot used with permission from Microsoft.)

WINDOWS DEFENDER SECURITY CENTER

In Windows 10, you can turn the firewall on or off and access the configuration applets shown previously via the **Firewall & network protection** page in the Windows Defender Security Center.

WINDOWS FIREWALL WITH ADVANCED SECURITY

An add-in to the basic firewall (Windows Firewall with Advanced Security) allows configuration of outbound filtering, as well as IPsec connection security and additional monitoring tools.

The Advanced Firewall can be configured through group policy on a domain; on a standalone PC or workgroup, open the `wf.msc` management console (or enter "firewall" at the Search box or use the **Advanced settings** link in the Windows Firewall Control Panel applet). On the status page, you can click **Windows Firewall properties** to configure each profile. The firewall can be turned on or off and you can switch the default rule for inbound and outbound traffic between **Block** and **Allow**.

You can also set which network adapters are linked to a profile and configure logging.

Windows Firewall with Advanced Security—Profile Settings. (Screenshot used with permission from Microsoft.)

> **Note: Block** stops traffic unless a specific rule allows it. Conversely, **Allow** accepts all traffic unless a specific rule blocks it. You can also use **Block all connections** to stop inbound connections regardless of the rules set up.

Back in the main Advanced Firewall console, you enable, disable, and configure rules by clicking in the **Inbound Rules** or **Outbound Rules** folder as appropriate. Rules can be based on a number of triggers, including program, Windows Feature, service, protocol type, network port, and IP address range.

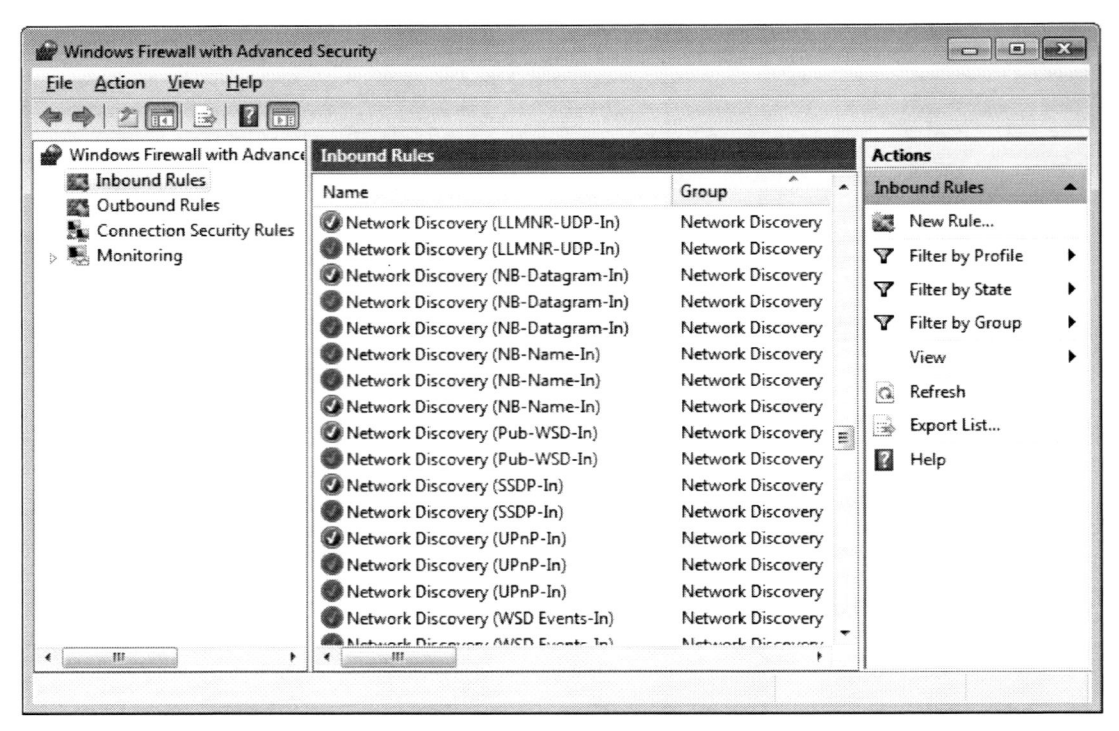

Configuring Windows Firewall with Advanced Security. (Screenshot used with permission from Microsoft.)

LOCATION AWARENESS

Different Windows Firewall settings can be applied depending on the network to which the PC is connected. When Windows 7 detects a new network (wired, wireless, dial-up, or VPN), the **Set Network Location** dialog box is displayed.

You can make the following choices:

- **Home**—enables network discovery (the ability to contact other computers on the network) and the use of homegroups.
- **Work**—enables network discovery.
- **Public**—disables network discovery and file sharing.
- **Domain**—you cannot choose this option, but if the computer is joined to a domain, then the firewall policy will be configured via Group Policy.

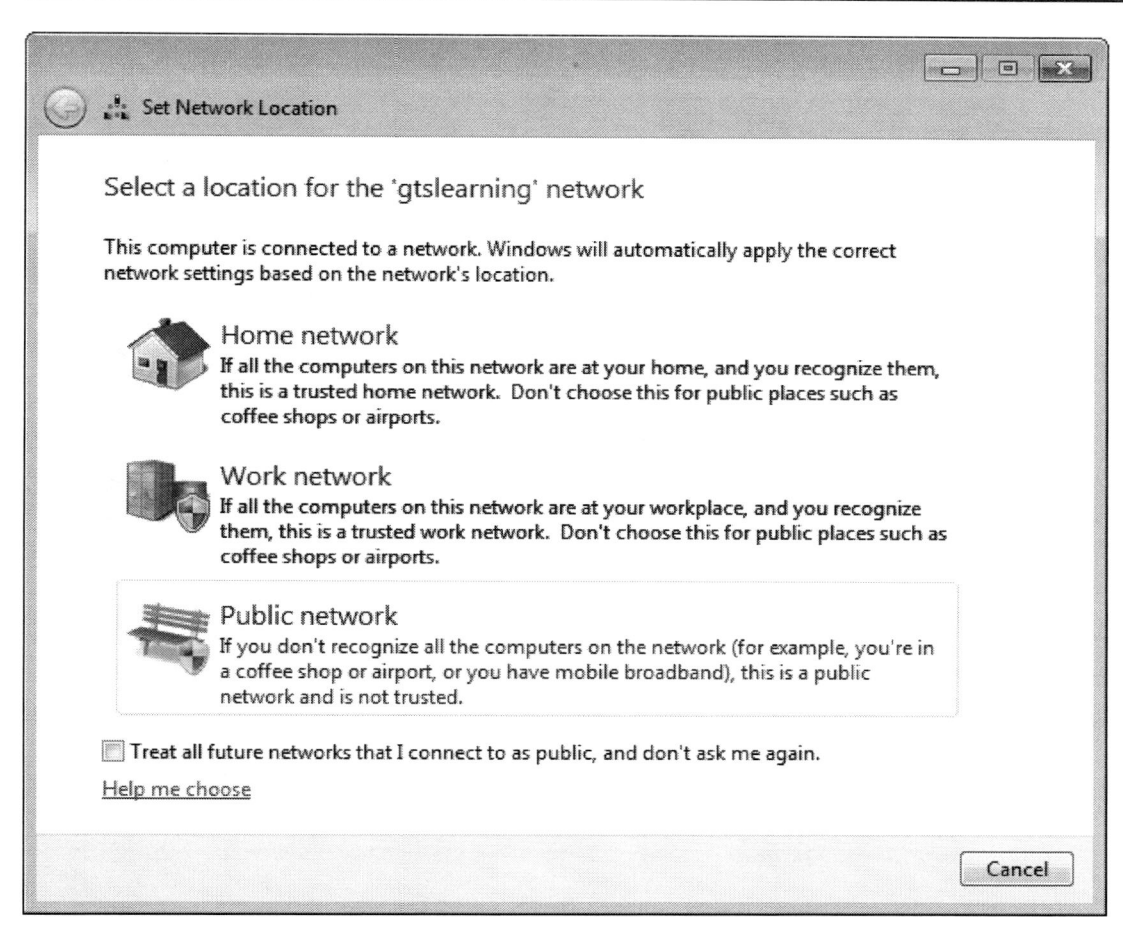

Set Network Location dialog box. (Screenshot used with permission from Microsoft.)

To change the location defined for a network, open the **Network and Sharing Center**. Click the network location label under the network name.

In Windows 8 and Windows 10, the concept of home and work networks has been discarded. Networks are either public or private depending on whether you choose to enable discovery and file sharing or not. If the computer is joined to a domain, then the network type will be set to domain.

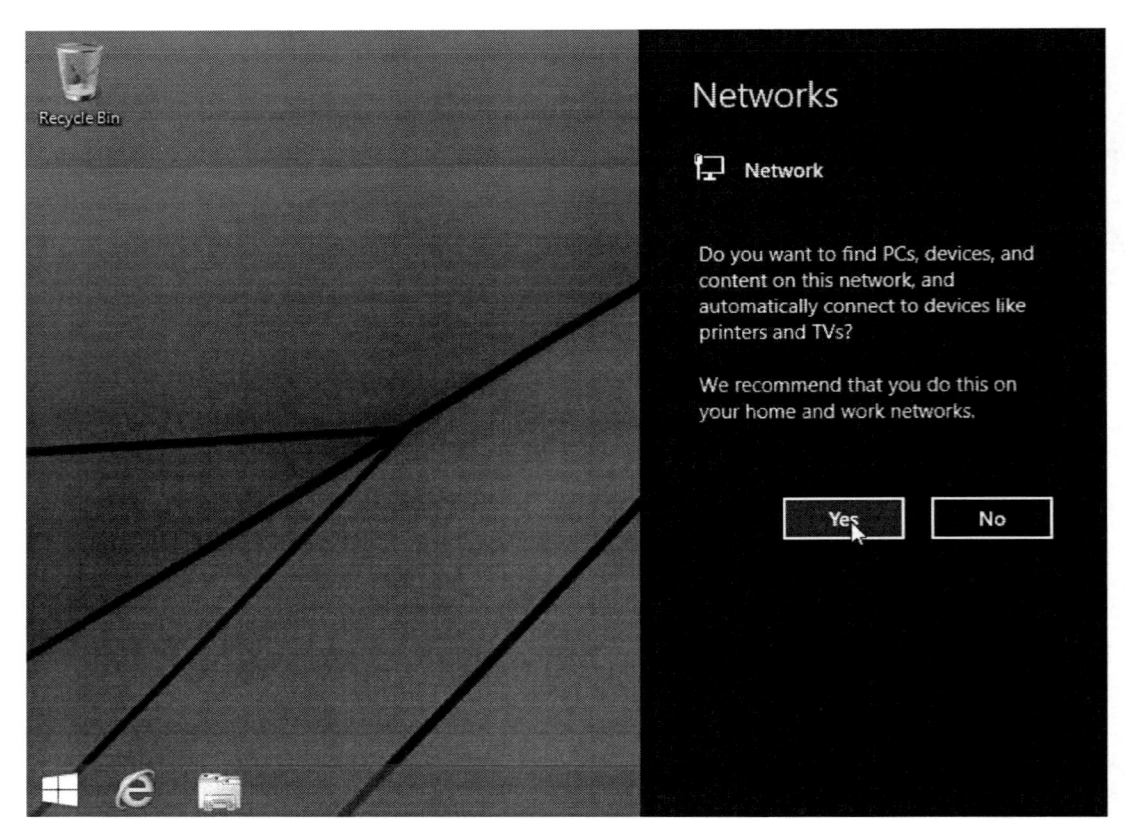

Setting network location type in Windows 8. (Screenshot used with permission from Microsoft.)

You can subsequently change the setting via the **Settings** app.

BROWSER CONFIGURATION

The browser has become one of the most important bits of software on a computer. As well as actual web browsing, it is frequently used as the interface for many types of web applications. The basic browser is also often extended by plug-ins that run other types of content. Internet Explorer (IE) used to be completely dominant in the browser market, but alternatives such as Google's Chrome™ and Mozilla's Firefox® now have substantial market share. This section describes the **Internet Options** applet for Internet Explorer®, but similar settings can be configured for other versions and browsers.

> **Note:** *In fact, in Windows 10, the Internet Explorer browser is replaced by the Edge browser. IE is still available in Windows 10, but its use is deprecated.*

GENERAL TAB

The main functions of the **General** tab are to configure home pages (pages that load when the browser is started) and manage browsing history. On a public computer, it is best practice to clear the browsing history at the end of a session. You can configure the browser to do this automatically.

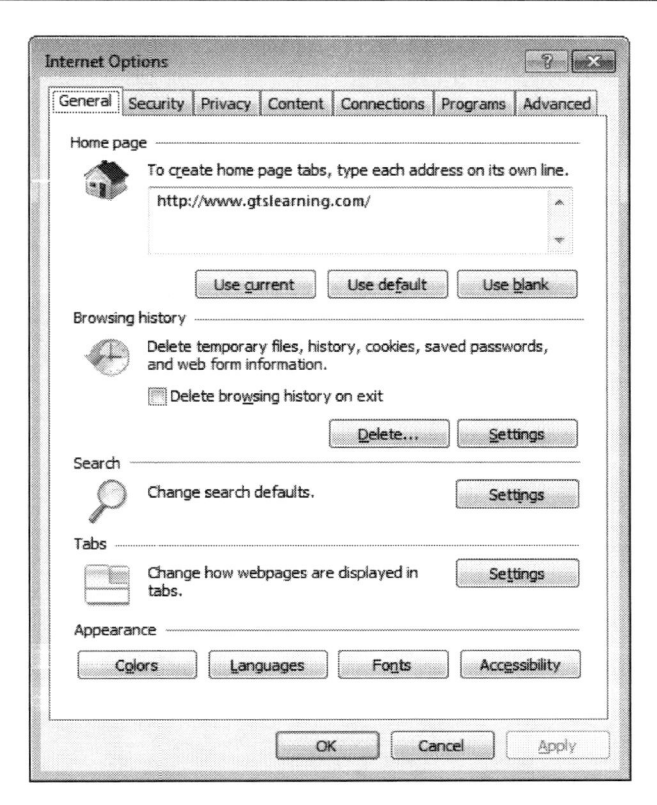

Internet Options—General tab. (Screenshot used with permission from Microsoft.)

> **Note:** You can also start an "In Private" mode session by pressing **Ctrl+Shift+P**. This mode disables browsing history, cookies, and browser toolbars and extensions.

CONNECTIONS TAB AND PROXY SETTINGS

The **Connections** tab sets the method Internet Explorer uses to connect to the Internet.

- To use a dial-up connection, select either **Dial whenever a network connection is not present** or **Always dial my default connection**. You would typically select the former option for a laptop computer that connects via the LAN in the office but a modem elsewhere. If the connection selected in the **Dial-up Settings** box is not the default, click **Set Default**.
- To use a router, you simply need to configure the Default gateway and DNS server parameters in TCP/IP properties for the local network adapter (though more typically, this would be configured automatically using DHCP). The browser will use this connection when you select **Never dial a connection** or **Dial whenever a network connection is not present**.

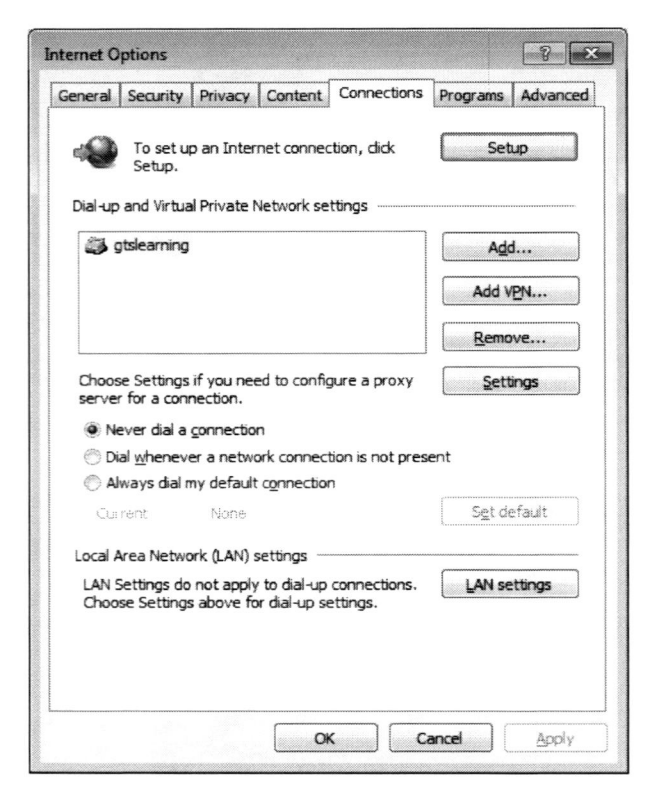

Internet Options—Connections tab. (Screenshot used with permission from Microsoft.)

On some networks, a proxy may be used to provide network connectivity. A proxy server can be used to improve both performance and security. User machines pass Internet requests to the proxy server, which forwards them to the Internet. The proxy may also cache pages and content that is requested by multiple clients, reducing bandwidth. The proxy may be able to autoconfigure the browser but if not, its address must be configured manually. Select the **LAN Settings** button to do this.

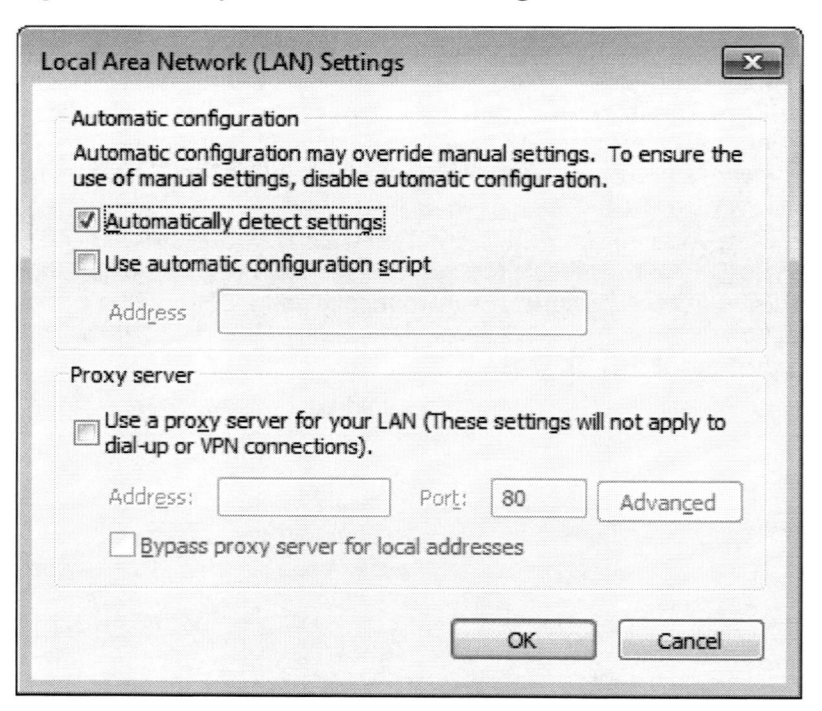

Local Area Network (LAN) Settings dialog box. (Screenshot used with permission from Microsoft.)

> **Note:** In Windows 10, use the **Settings→Network & Internet→Proxy** configuration page.

SECURITY TAB

The **Security** tab is designed to prevent malicious content hosted on web pages from infecting the computer or stealing personal information.

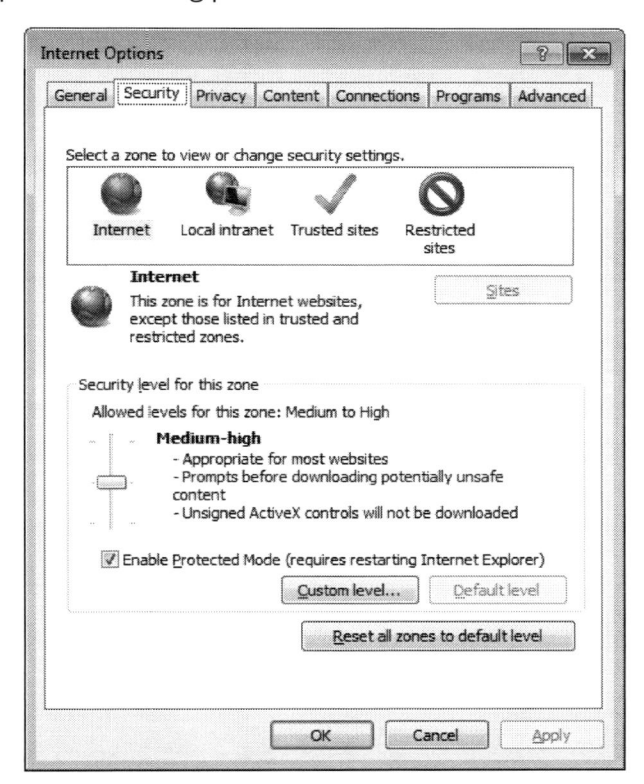

Internet Options—Security tab. (Screenshot used with permission from Microsoft.)

There are lots of security settings, configuring things such as whether scripts and plug-ins are allowed to run or install, files to download, and so on.

Internet Explorer operates a system of zones, each with different security settings. Everything off the local subnet is in the Internet zone by default; the user (or a domain's group policy) can add particular sites to the **Trusted** and **Restricted** zones as appropriate. The settings for a particular zone can also be changed using the **Custom Level** button.

PRIVACY TAB

The main function of the **Privacy** tab is to control sites' use of cookies. A cookie is a text file used to store session data. For example, if you log on to a site, the site might use a cookie to remember who you are. If the site is prevented from setting these cookies, it may not work correctly. On the other hand, a modern website might host components from many different domains. These components might try to set third-party cookies, most often to track pages you have been visiting and display relevant advertising at you.

You can use the slider to set the default policy for the Internet zone and use the **Sites** button to always block or allow cookies from particular domains.

The **Privacy** tab also allows you to configure the Pop-up Blocker, which prevents sites from spawning new windows through scripting.

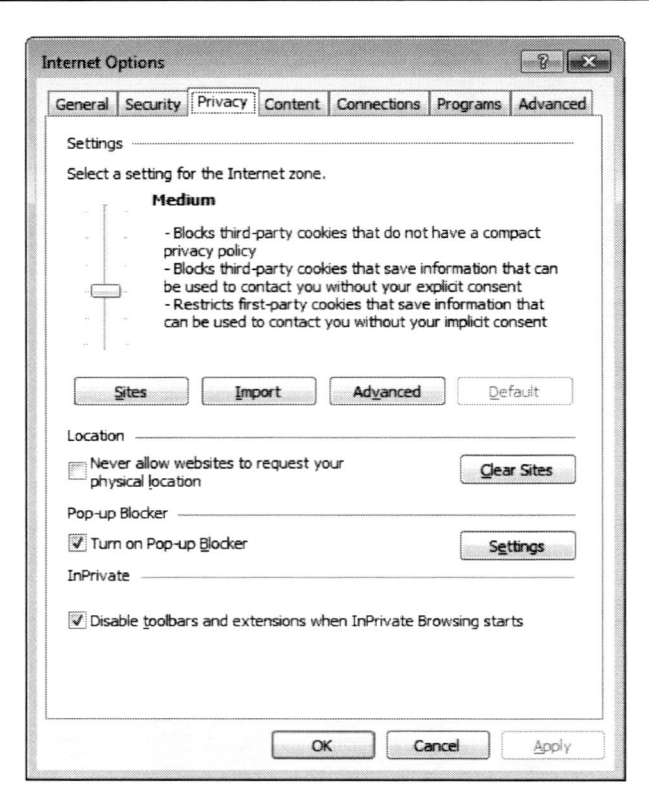

Internet Options—Privacy tab. (Screenshot used with permission from Microsoft.)

PROGRAMS TAB

You can use the **Programs** tab to check whether IE is the default browser.

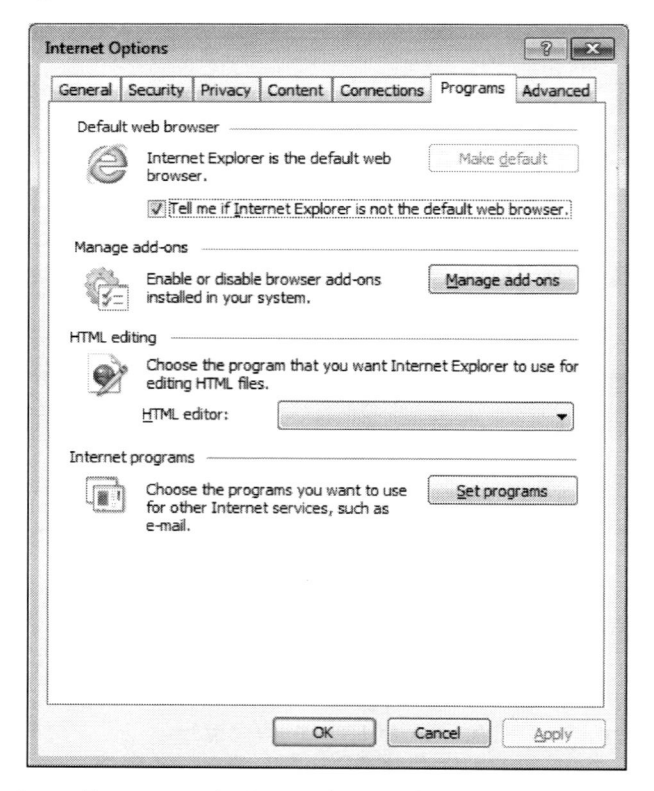

Internet Options—Programs tab. (Screenshot used with permission from Microsoft.)

Click **Set programs** to open the **Default Programs** applet to make another browser the default. You can also manage add-ons from here. Add-ons are code objects that extend the functionality of the browser. Examples include toolbars, malware scanners, content players (such as Adobe® Flash® player), and document readers (such as PDF viewers). **Manage add-ons** lets you disable or uninstall these objects.

ADVANCED TAB

The **Advanced** tab contains settings that do not fit under any of the other tabs.

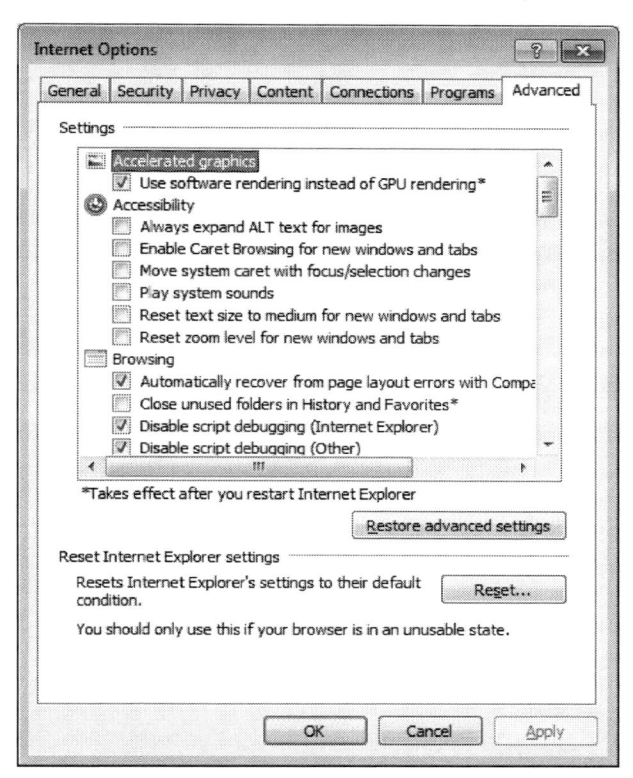

Internet Options—Advanced tab. (Screenshot used with permission from Microsoft.)

Some notable options include:

- Disable certain types of content (pictures, for instance).
- Enable a script debugger.
- Enable or disable passive FTP.
- Allow or prevent active content from running on local computer drives.

You can also use this tab to completely reset the browser.

Activity 6-4
Discussing SOHO Network Security

SCENARIO
Answer the following questions to check your understanding of the topic.

1. True or false? A firewall can be configured to block hosts with selected IP address ranges from connecting to a particular TCP port on a server that is available to hosts in other IP address ranges.

2. What sort of configuration options are available to apply parental controls, as opposed to packet filtering via a firewall?

3. What security method could you use to allow only specific hosts to connect to a SOHO router/modem?

4. A user wants to be able to access an FTP server installed on a computer on their home network from the Internet. The home network is connected to the Internet by a DSL router.

   How would you enable access?

5. You are setting up a games console on a home network.

   What feature on the router will simplify configuration of online multiplayer gaming?

6. True or false? To allow a PC game to accept incoming connections over a custom port you need to configure the Advanced Security Firewall.

7. What option on the General tab of the Internet Options dialog box is most relevant to user privacy?

8. How would you configure a Windows 7 computer to use a proxy server for web browsing?

Topic D
Configure Remote Access

EXAM OBJECTIVES COVERED
1001-2.1 Compare and contrast TCP and UDP ports, protocols, and their purposes.
1002-1.5 Given a scenario, use Microsoft operating system features and tools.
1002-1.8 Given a scenario, configure Microsoft Windows networking on a client/desktop.
1002-4.9 Given a scenario, use remote access technologies.

A remote access utility allows you to establish a session on another computer on the network. There are command-line and GUI remote access tools. These are very useful for technical support and troubleshooting. The fact that remote access is so useful shows how important it is that such tools be used securely. In this topic, you will learn about the features of different remote access tools and security considerations of using each one.

WINDOWS REMOTE ACCESS TOOLS

Windows comes with several remote access features. Two of the GUI remote tools are Remote Desktop and Remote Assistance. These use some of the same underlying technologies but suit different purposes.

REMOTE DESKTOP

Remote Desktop allows a remote user to connect to their desktop machine. The desktop machine functions as a terminal server and the dial-in machine as a Windows terminal. This allows the user to work as if physically connected to their workstation.

This would ideally suit laptop users working from home with a slow link. Having gained access to the corporate network (via the Internet using a VPN, for example) they could then establish a remote desktop connection to their own office-based system. A technician can also use Remote Desktop to configure or troubleshoot a computer.

Remote Desktop runs on TCP port 3389.

> **Note:** *Windows Home editions do not include the Remote Desktop server so you cannot connect to them, but they do include the client so you can connect to other computers from them.*

REMOTE ASSISTANCE

Remote Assistance allows a user to ask for help from a technician or co-worker. The "helper" can then connect and join the session with the user. This session can include an interactive desktop, whereby the helper can control the system of the user.

Remote Assistance assigns a port dynamically from the ephemeral range (49152 to 65535). This makes it difficult to configure through firewalls, but remote assistance is designed more for local network support anyway.

REMOTE SETTINGS CONFIGURATION

By default, Remote Assistance connections are allowed but Remote Desktop ones are not. To change these settings, open **System Properties** then click **Remote settings**.

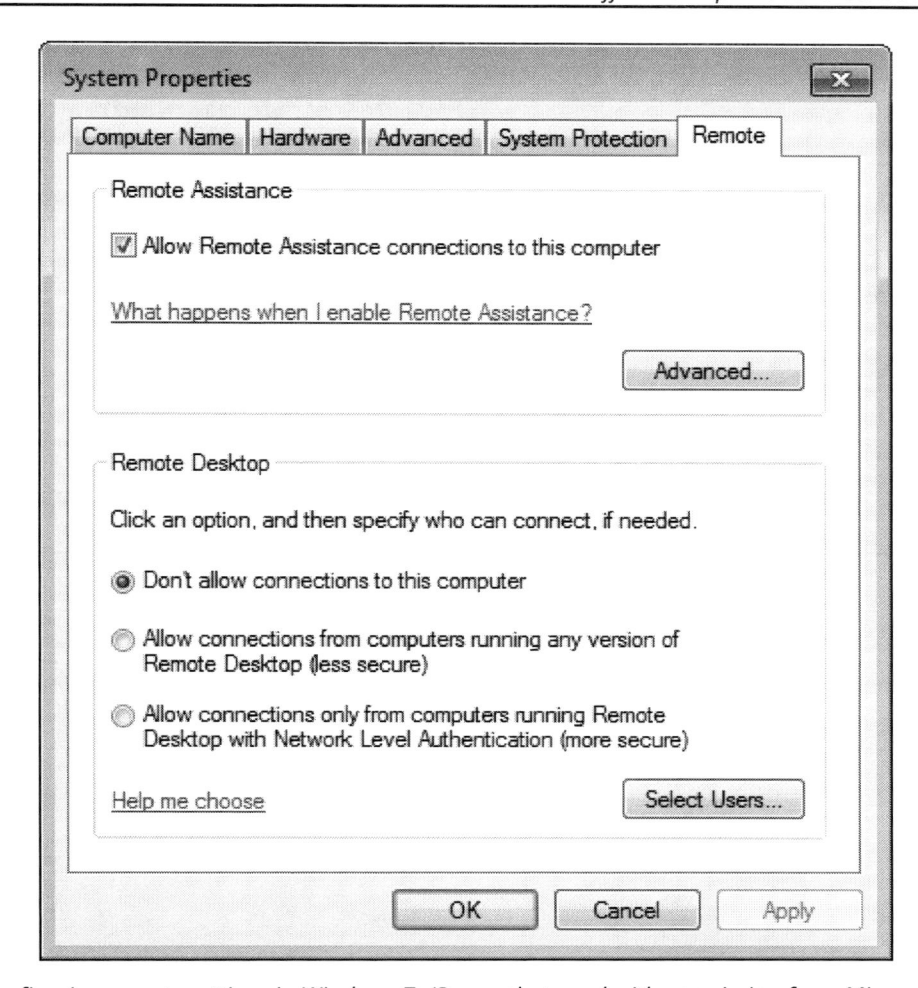

Configuring remote settings in Windows 7. (Screenshot used with permission from Microsoft.)

You can choose between allowing older RDP clients to connect and requiring RDP clients that support **Network Level Authentication (NLA)**. NLA protects the computer against Denial of Service attacks. Without NLA, the system configures a desktop before the user logs on. A malicious user can create multiple pending connections in an attempt to crash the system. NLA authenticates the user before committing any resources to the session.

RDP authentication and session data is always encrypted. This means that a malicious user with access to the same network cannot intercept credentials or interfere or capture anything transmitted during the session.

Click the **Select (Remote) Users** button to define which users can connect remotely. Users in the local administrators group already have this property. You can select from members of the local accounts database or from the domain of which your machine is a member.

> **Note:** *The biggest limitation of Remote Desktop on Windows is that only one person can be logged in to the machine at once, so once you log in using Remote Desktop, the monitor at the local computer will go to the login screen. If a local user logs in, the remote user will be disconnected. Remote Desktop is not really a remote diagnostic and troubleshooting tool as much as a management tool.*

REMOTE CREDENTIAL GUARD

If Remote Desktop is used to connect to a machine that has been compromised by malware, the credentials of the user account used to make the connection become highly vulnerable. **RDP Restricted Admin (RDPRA) Mode** and **Remote Credential Guard** are means of mitigating this risk. You can read more about these technologies at **docs.microsoft.com/en-us/windows/security/identity-protection/remote-credential-guard**.

THE REMOTE ASSISTANCE PROCESS

A request for remote assistance is made using the **Windows Remote Assistance** tool. You can send an invitation as a file, via email, or using Easy Connect. The tool will generate a password and a connection file for you to transmit to the helper.

To provide assistance, open the invitation file and enter the password and wait for the user to accept the offer of assistance. When the offer is accepted, a remote desktop window is opened with an additional chat tool that you can use to communicate with the user.

Remote Assistance sessions are encrypted using the same technologies as RDP.

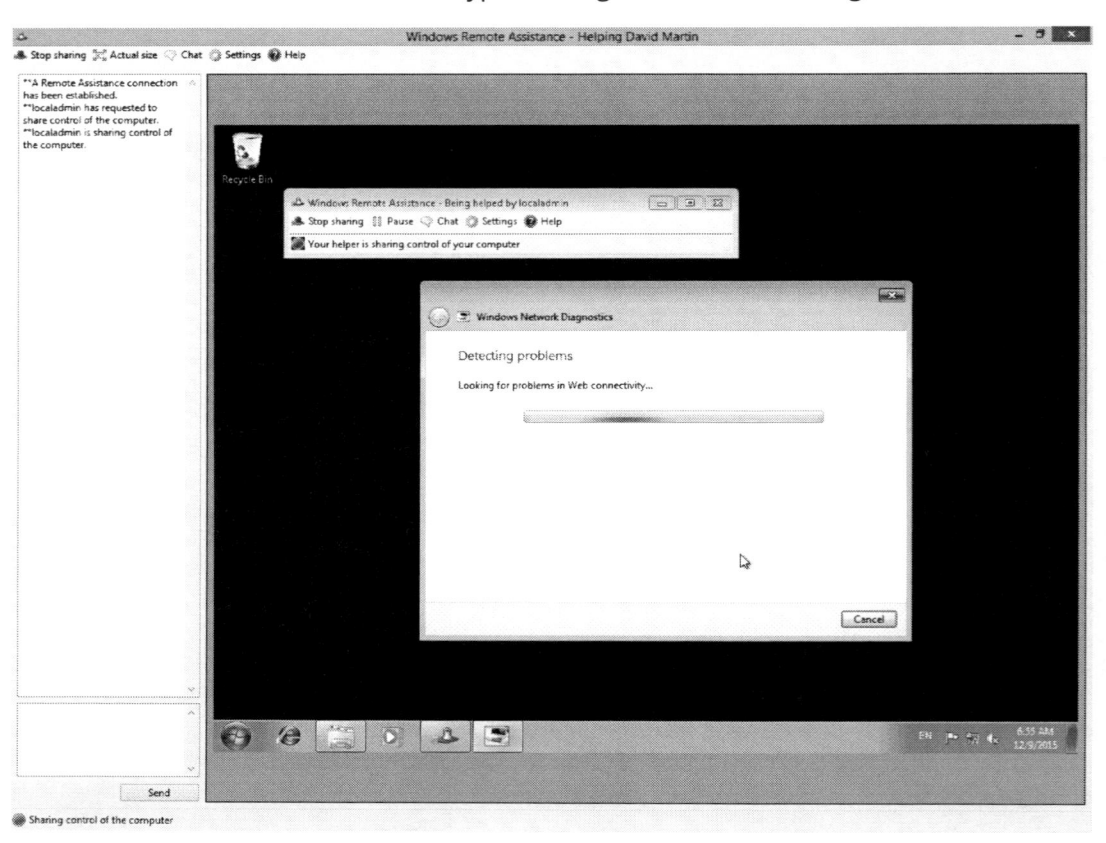

Using Remote Assistance. (Screenshot used with permission from Microsoft.)

REMOTE DESKTOP

To connect to a server via Remote Desktop, from the **Communications** menu in **Accessories**, open the **Remote Desktop Connection** shortcut, or run `mstsc` at a command prompt or the **Run** dialog box or **Instant Search** box. Enter the server's computer name or IP address to connect. The server can be installed with a certificate to identify it securely.

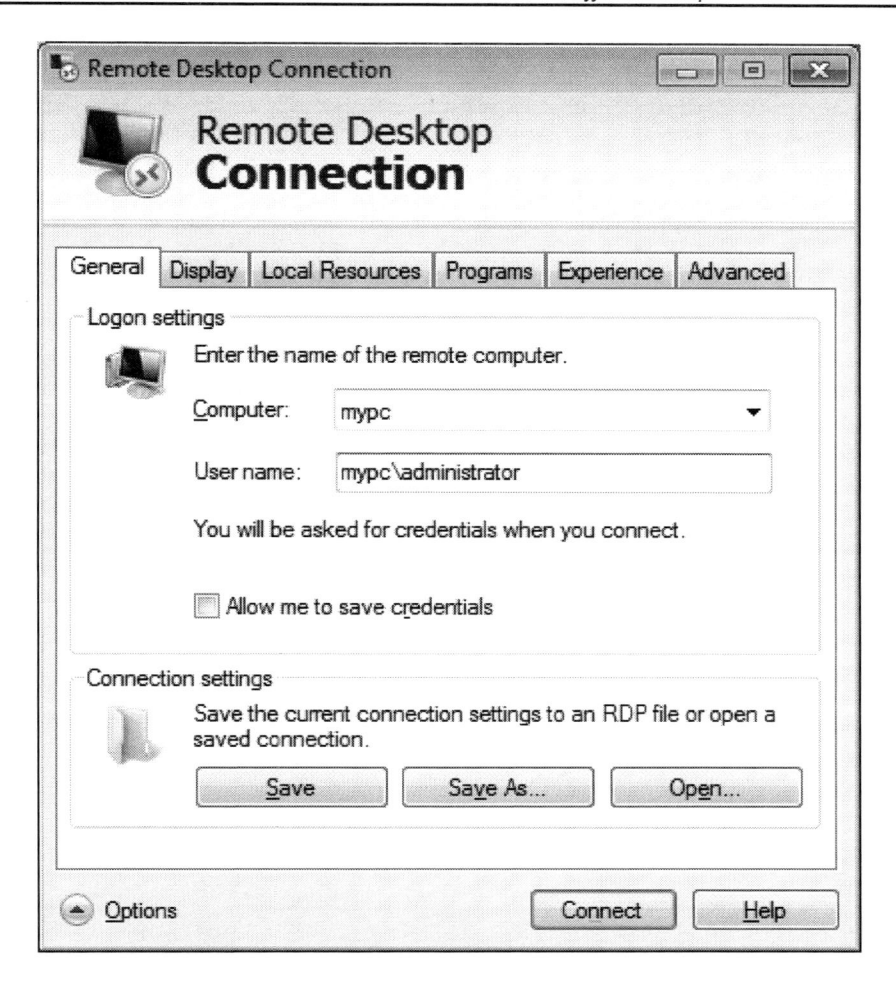

Remote Desktop Connection client. (Screenshot used with permission from Microsoft.)

You will need to define logon credentials. To specify a domain or computer account, use the format *ComputerOrDomainName\UserName*. In addition, you might need to define display properties. You can use either full screen or some windowed display. Also, you can configure the quality of the color scheme. The **Local Resources** tab allows you to define how key combinations (such as **Alt+Tab**) function—that is, will they affect the local computer, the remote computer, or the remote computer in full screen mode. Because the connection may be over a slow link, such as dial-up, you can configure optimization based on the line speeds (modem, LAN, and so on). This affects bitmap caching and video options.

Once you have your remote desktop connection established, you can work quite normally, as if physically adjacent to the target machine—but be aware that no one else can use the target system while in remote mode. The system becomes locked and can be unlocked by the administrator or the remotely connected user only.

REMOTE ACCESS TECHNOLOGIES

Remote Desktop and Remote Assistance are technologies for Windows networks. There are versions of the `mstsc` client software for Linux®, macOS®, iOS®, and Android™ so you can use devices running those operating systems to connect to an RDP server running on a Windows machine.

Other protocols and software tools are available for accepting incoming connections to non-Windows devices.

TELNET

Telnet is a command-line terminal emulation protocol and program. The host server runs a Telnet daemon listening for connections on TCP port 23. The client system runs a Telnet program to send commands to the daemon. When you connect, your computer acts as if your keyboard is attached to the remote computer and you can use the same commands as a local user.

> **Note:** Telnet sends all messages in clear text. Anyone able to intercept ("sniff") network traffic would be able to see the passwords for accounts.

If you enter `telnet` at a command prompt, some of the basic commands you can use are listed in the following table.

Command	Use
`open HostPort`	Starts a session with the host on that port. Host can be a host name, FQDN, or IP address.
`?`	Displays help.
`status`	Check session status.
`close`	Ends the current session.
`quit`	Exits the telnet prompt.

Telnet is sometimes still used for troubleshooting services such as SMTP or HTTP. For example, to connect to an SMTP server at the IP address 192.168.1.2, you would enter `telnet 192.168.1.2 25`.

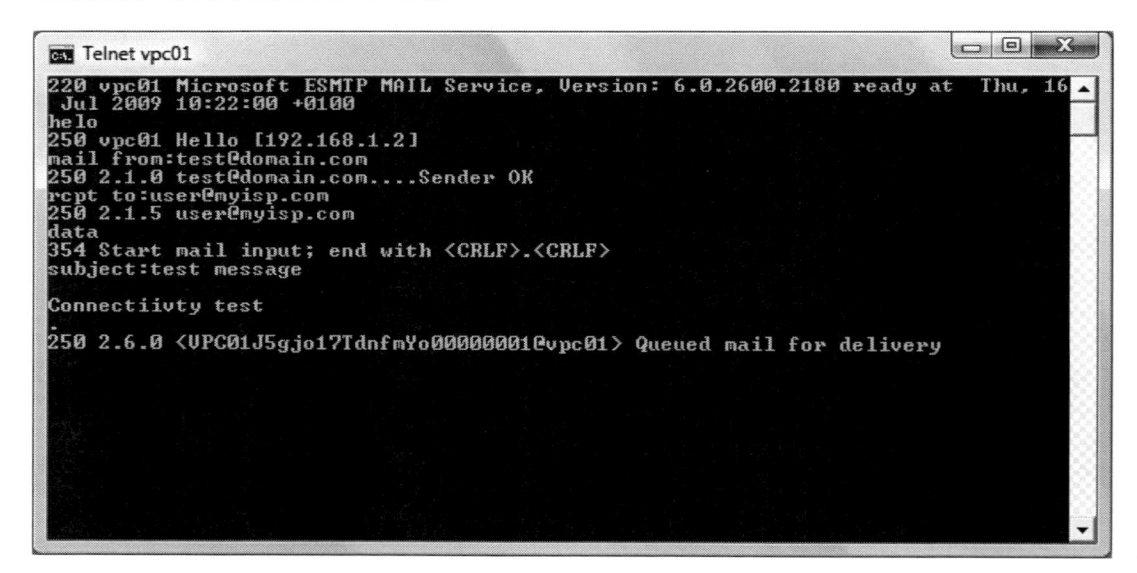

Telnet session with an SMTP server. (Screenshot used with permission from Microsoft.)

Another application of Telnet is router or switch configuration. The Telnet application is used to connect to the Telnet Daemon on the router and then command-line instructions can be issued to configure it.

> **Note:** Telnet is not installed by default in Windows. You can add it using Programs and Features. On a Windows network, you are more likely to use Windows Remote Shell (WinRS), which has better functionality and security features.

SSH

Secure Shell (SSH) is designed to replace unsecure administration and file copy programs such as Telnet and FTP. SSH uses TCP port 22 (by default). SSH uses encryption to protect each session. There are numerous commercial and open source SSH products available for all the major OS platforms (UNIX, Linux, Windows, and macOS).

SSH servers are identified by a public/private key pair (the host key). A mapping of host names to public keys can be kept manually by each SSH client or there are various enterprise software products designed for SSH key management.

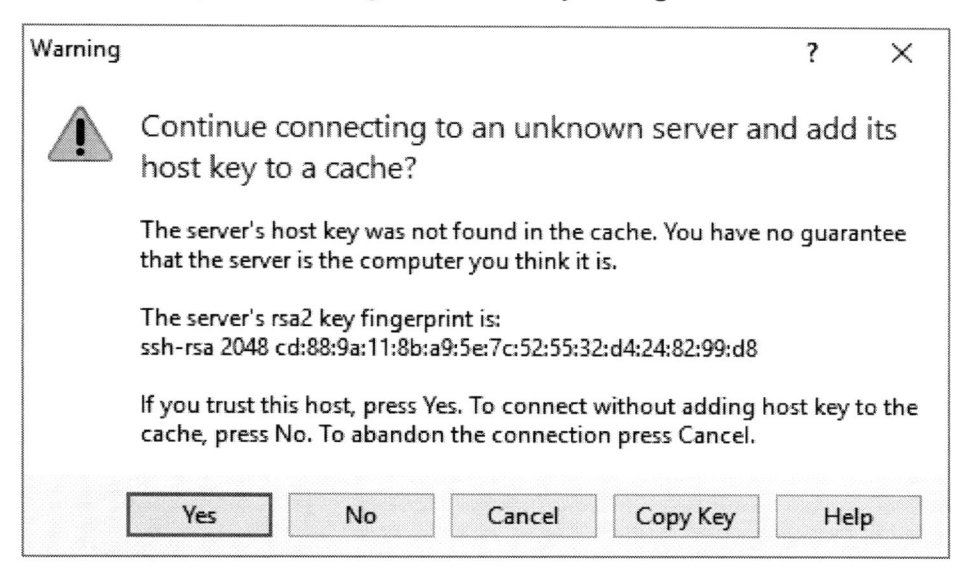

Confirming the SSH server's host key. (Screenshot used with permission from Microsoft.)

SSH CLIENT AUTHENTICATION

The server's host key is used to set up a secure channel to use for the client to submit authentication credentials. SSH allows various methods for the client to authenticate to the SSH server. Each of these methods can be enabled or disabled as required on the server:

- Username/password—the client submits credentials that are verified by the SSH server either against a local user database or using an authentication server.
- Kerberos—this allows Single Sign On (SSO) on a network that runs the Kerberos authentication protocol. Windows Active Directory domain networks use Kerberos.
- Host-based authentication—the server is configured with a list of authorized client public keys. The client requests authentication using one of these keys and the server generates a challenge with the public key. The client must use the matching private key it holds to decrypt the challenge and complete the authentication process. This provides non-interactive login but there is considerable risk from intrusion if a client host's private key is compromised.

  Note: With host-based authentication, managing valid client public keys is a critical security task. Many recent attacks on web servers have exploited poor key management.

- Public key authentication—host-based authentication cannot be used with fine-grained access controls as the access is granted to a single user account. The same sort of public key authentication method can be used for each user account. The user's private key can be configured with a passphrase that must be input to access the key, providing an additional measure of protection compared to host-based authentication.

SCREEN SHARING AND VNC

In macOS, you can use the Screen Sharing feature for remote desktop functionality. Screen Sharing is based on **Virtual Network Computing (VNC)**. You can use any VNC client to connect to a Screen Sharing server.

VNC itself is a freeware product with similar functionality to RDP. It works over TCP port 5900. Freeware versions of VNC provide no connection security and so should only be used over a secure connection, such as a VPN. However, there are commercial products packaged with encryption solutions. macOS Screen Sharing is encrypted.

FILE SHARE

Setting up a network file share can be relatively complex. You need to select a file sharing protocol that all the connecting hosts can use, configure permissions on the share, and provision user accounts that both the server and client recognize. Consequently OS vendors have developed other mechanisms for simple file sharing between devices.

- AirDrop®—supported by Apple iOS and macOS, this uses Bluetooth® to establish a Wi-Fi Direct connection between the devices for the duration of the file transfer. The connection is secured by the Bluetooth pairing mechanism and Wi-Fi encryption.
- Near Share—Microsoft's version of AirDrop. Near Share was introduced in Windows 10 (1803), partly replacing the previous Homegroup feature.

There are plenty of third-party and open source alternatives to AirDrop.

Although the products have security mechanisms, there is the potential for misuse of features such as this. Users accepting connections from any source could receive unsolicited transfer requests. It is best only to accept requests from known contacts. The products can be subject to security vulnerabilities that allow unsolicited transfers.

Activity 6-5
Discussing Remote Access Configuration

SCENARIO
Answer the following questions to check your understanding of the topic.

1. Which edition(s) of Windows support connecting to the local machine over Remote Desktop?

2. What is the goal of RDP Restricted Admin (RDPRA) Mode and Remote Credential Guard?

3. True or false? SSH is not available for use with Windows.

4. How can you confirm that you are connecting to a legitimate SSH server?

Topic E
Troubleshoot Network Connections

EXAM OBJECTIVES COVERED
1001-2.8 Given a scenario, use appropriate networking tools.
1001-5.7 Given a scenario, troubleshoot common wired and wireless network problems.
1002-1.4 Given a scenario, use appropriate Microsoft command line tools.
1002-3.1 Given a scenario, troubleshoot Microsoft Windows OS problems.

As a CompTIA A+ technician, you will be expected to be able to troubleshoot basic network connectivity issues. At this support level, you will be focusing on client issues. As you have learned, networks are complex and involve many different hardware devices, protocols, and applications, meaning that there are lots of things that can go wrong! In this topic you will learn how to identify and diagnose the causes of some common wired and wireless network issues.

COMMON WIRED NETWORK CONNECTIVITY ISSUES

When troubleshooting a network issue, it is often a good idea to rule out any problem with connectivity at the hardware layer. If a single host is unable to connect to the network, the first thing you should check is whether the network cable is properly connected. If the problem is not that obvious, then there are a few other tools you can use to diagnose a problem with network hardware (adapters and cabling).

TROUBLESHOOTING WIRED CONNECTIVITY

To diagnose a cable problem, perform a basic local connectivity test using the `ping` utility (discussed later) with a known working system on the local subnet. If you can ping another local system, the problem is not in the cabling (at least, not this cable).

If you can't ping anything then, assuming you've physically checked the back of the machine for the cable's presence, verify that the patch cord is good. The easiest thing to do is swap the patch cord to the wall socket with another—known working—cable.

Can you ping anything now? If not, verify the patch cord between the patch panel and the switch. Swap with another known good cable and test again. If this still fails, try connecting a different host to the network port. If the other host connects, suspect a problem with network adapter in the original host. Use Device Manager to verify that the adapter's link properties are set correctly (typically to autonegotiate). If there is no configuration issue, swap the network adapter with a known good one and re-test.

> **Note:** The link LEDs on network adapter and switch ports will indicate whether the link is active and possibly at what speed the link is working. The LEDs typically flicker to show network activity.

If you still haven't isolated the problem, try plugging the problem computer into a different network port. By testing from different ports, you should be able to establish the scope of the problem and the likely location of the fault. Eventually, through the process of substituting working components for suspect components, you should resolve the cable problem. Remember that if several users have the problem, you should check the switch in this way too.

Note: If you have suitable tools, you can use them in place of substituting and transposing devices. For example, a loopback plug can be used to test whether a port is working (and therefore indicate that the problem is with the cable).

Problems with patch cords are simple as you can just throw the broken one away and plug in a new one. If the problem is in the structured cabling, however, you will want to use cable testing tools to determine its cause, especially if the problem is intermittent (that is, if the problem comes and goes). The solution may involve installing a new permanent link, but there could also be a termination or external interference problem.

TROUBLESHOOTING SLOW TRANSFER SPEEDS

The transfer speed of a cabled link could be reduced if the network equipment is not all working to the highest available standard. Check the configuration of the network adapter driver (via Device Manager) and the setting for the switch port (via the switch's management software). Slow transfer speeds can be caused by a variety of other problems and can be very difficult to diagnose.

- There may be congestion at a switch or router or some other network-wide problem. This might be caused by a fault or by user behavior, such as transferring a very large amount of data over the network.
- There could be a problem with the network adapter driver.
- The computer could be infected with malware.
- The network cabling could be affected by interference. This could be from an external source but check the ends of cables for excessive untwisting of the wire pairs as poor termination is a common cause of problems.

COMMON WIRELESS NETWORK CONNECTIVITY ISSUES

When troubleshooting wireless networks, as with cabled links, you need to consider problems with the physical media, such as interference and configuration issues.

The **Radio Frequency (RF)** signal from radio-based devices weakens considerably as the distance between the devices increases. If you experience slow transfer speeds or you cannot establish a connection, try moving the devices closer together. If you still cannot obtain a connection, check that the security and authentication parameters are correctly configured on both devices.

TROUBLESHOOTING WIRELESS CONFIGURATION ISSUES

If a user is looking for a network name that is not shown in the list of available wireless networks (**SSID not found**), the user could be out of range or broadcast of the SSID name might be suppressed. In the latter scenario, the connection to the network name must be configured manually.

Another factor to consider is **standards mismatch**. Choosing a compatibility mode for an access point will reduce the features available (no WPA for 802.11b compatibility, for instance). If an access point is not operating in compatibility mode, it will not be able to communicate with devices that only support older standards. Also, when an older device joins the network, the performance of the whole network can be affected. To support 802.11b clients, an 802.11b/n access point must transmit legacy frame preamble and collision avoidance frames, adding overhead. If at all possible, upgrade 802.11b devices rather than letting them join the WLAN. 802.11g and 802.11n are more compatible in terms of negotiating collision avoidance. In a mixed 802.11g/n WLAN, performance of the 802.11n devices operating in the 2.4 GHz band is only likely to be severely impacted when 802.11g devices perform large file transfers. As these take longer to complete, there is less "airtime" available for the 802.11n clients.

> *Note: With 802.11n dual-band APs operating in mixed mode or with 802.11ac, it is typical to assign the 2.4 GHz band to support legacy clients. The 5 GHz band can be reserved for 802.11n or 802.11ac clients and bonded channels can be configured.*

Also consider that not all clients supporting 802.11n have dual band radios. If a client cannot connect to a network operating on the 5 GHz band, check whether its radio is 2.4 GHz-capable only.

LOW RF SIGNAL/RSSI

A wireless adapter will be configured to drop the connection speed if the **Received Signal Strength Indicator (RSSI)** is not at a minimum required level. The RSSI is an index level calculated from the signal strength level. For example, an 802.11n adapter might be capable of a 144 Mbps data rate with an optimum signal, but if the signal is weak it might drop to a 54 Mbps or 11 Mbps rate to make the connection more reliable. If the RSSI is too low, the adapter will drop the connection entirely and try to use a different network. If there are two fairly weak networks, the adapter might "flap" between them. Try moving to a location with better reception.

TROUBLESHOOTING WIRELESS SIGNAL ISSUES

If a device is within the supported range but the signal is very weak or you can only get an **intermittent connection**, there is likely to be interference from another radio source broadcasting at the same frequency. If this is the case, try adjusting the channel that the devices use. Another possibility is interference from a powerful electromagnetic source, such as a motor or microwave oven. Finally, there might be something blocking the signal. Radio waves do not pass easily through metal or dense objects. Construction materials such as wire mesh, foil-backed plasterboard, concrete, and mirrors can block or degrade signals. Try angling or repositioning the device or antenna to try to get better reception.

> *Note: The ideal position for an access point is high up and in the center of the area it is supposed to serve.*

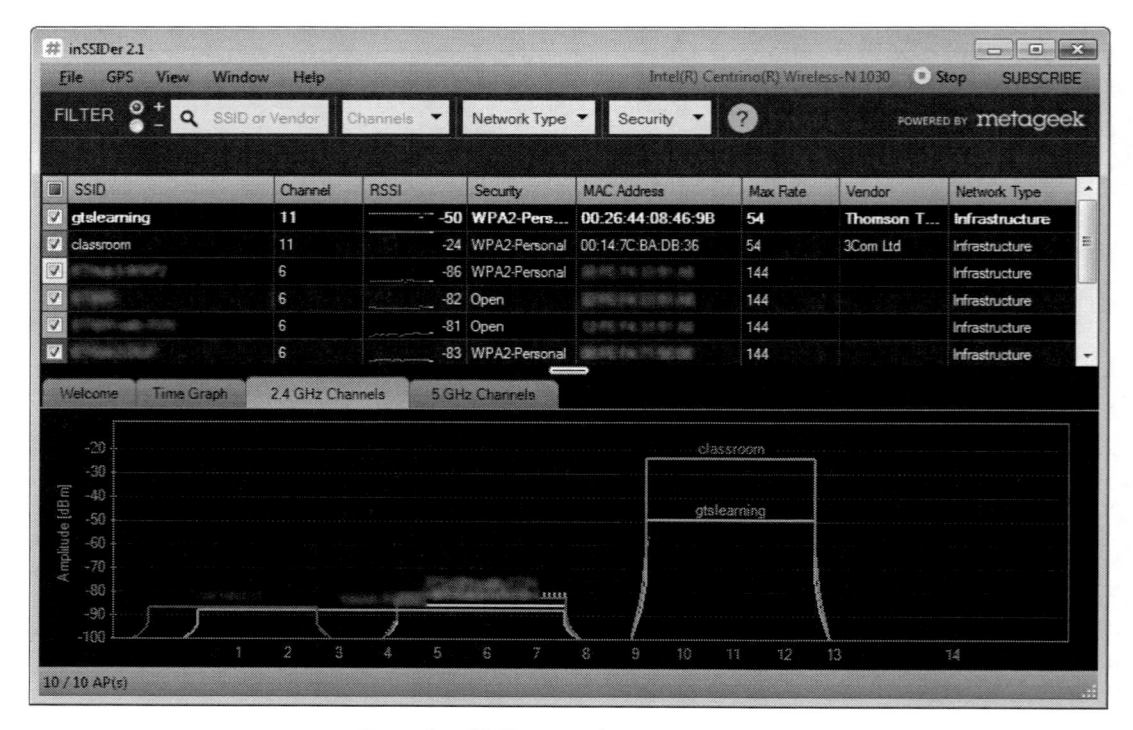

Surveying Wi-Fi networks using inSSIDer.

Wi-Fi Analyzer software, such as inSSIDer, is designed to support a site survey, to identify nearby networks that may be causing interference problems, and to measure signal strength. You can use a Wi-Fi Analyzer for troubleshooting, too. It shows the signal strength, measured in dBm. This can also be expressed as a percentage; for example, -35 dBm or better would represent the best possible signal at 100%, -90 dBm or worse would represent 1%, and -65 dBm would represent 50% signal strength.

The analyzer will also show how many networks are utilizing each channel. Setting the network to use a less congested channel can improve performance.

IP CONFIGURATION ISSUES

If a host does not have an appropriate IP configuration for the network that it is connected to, it will not be able to communicate with other hosts, even if the physical connection is sound. There are a number of command-line tools for testing and troubleshooting the IP configuration.

VIEWING IP CONFIGURATION (ipconfig)

In Windows, IP configuration information is displayed through the adapter's status dialog (Windows 7/8) or Windows Settings (Windows 10). You can also view this information at a command line using the `ipconfig` tool. Used without switches, `ipconfig` displays the IP address, subnet mask, and default gateway (router) for all network adapters to which TCP/IP is bound. Typical ipconfig switches and arguments are as follows.

Switch	Description
`ipconfig /all`	Displays detailed configuration, including DHCP and DNS servers, MAC address, and NetBIOS status.
`ipconfig /release AdapterName`	Releases the IP address obtained from a DHCP server so that the network adapter(s) will no longer have an IP address.
`ipconfig /renew AdapterName`	Forces a DHCP client to renew the lease it has for an IP address.
`ipconfig /displaydns`	Displays the DNS resolver cache. This contains host and domain names that have been queried recently. Caching the name-to-IP mappings reduces network traffic.
`ipconfig /flushdns`	Clears the DNS resolver cache.

Note that omitting the *AdapterName* argument releases or renews all adapters. If *AdapterName* contains spaces, use quotes around it (for example, `ipconfig /renew "Local Area Connection"`).

TROUBLESHOOTING WITH ipconfig

You would use `ipconfig` to determine whether the adapter has been correctly configured. `ipconfig` can resolve the following questions:

- Is the adapter configured with a static address? Are the parameters (IP address, subnet mask, default gateway, and DNS server correct)?
- Is the adapter configured by DHCP? If so:
  - An address in the range 169.254.x.y indicates that the client could not contact a DHCP server and is using Automatic Private IP Addressing (APIPA). If this is the

case, Windows will display a yellow alert icon and a notification that the adapter has only **Limited connectivity**.
- A DHCP lease can be static (always assigns the same IP address to the computer) or dynamic (assigns an IP address from a pool)—has the computer obtained a suitable address and subnet mask?
- Are other parameters assigned by DHCP correct (default gateway, DNS servers, and so on)?

```
C:\Users\Admin>ipconfig /all

Windows IP Configuration

   Host Name . . . . . . . . . . . . : ROGUE
   Primary Dns Suffix  . . . . . . . :
   Node Type . . . . . . . . . . . . : Hybrid
   IP Routing Enabled. . . . . . . . : No
   WINS Proxy Enabled. . . . . . . . : No
   DNS Suffix Search List. . . . . . : classroom.local

Ethernet adapter Ethernet:

   Connection-specific DNS Suffix  . : classroom.local
   Description . . . . . . . . . . . : Microsoft Hyper-V Network Adapter
   Physical Address. . . . . . . . . : 00-15-5D-01-CA-0E
   DHCP Enabled. . . . . . . . . . . : Yes
   Autoconfiguration Enabled . . . . : Yes
   IPv4 Address. . . . . . . . . . . : 10.1.0.131(Preferred)
   Subnet Mask . . . . . . . . . . . : 255.255.255.0
   Lease Obtained. . . . . . . . . . : Wednesday, January 4, 2017 2:40:05 AM
   Lease Expires . . . . . . . . . . : Thursday, January 12, 2017 2:40:03 AM
   Default Gateway . . . . . . . . . : 10.1.0.254
   DHCP Server . . . . . . . . . . . : 10.1.0.1
   DNS Servers . . . . . . . . . . . : 10.1.0.1
   NetBIOS over Tcpip. . . . . . . . : Enabled
```

Using ipconfig. (Screenshot used with permission from Microsoft.)

If any of these results are negative, you should investigate either communications between the client and the DHCP server, the configuration of the DHCP server, or whether multiple DHCP servers are running on the network (and the client has obtained the wrong configuration from one).

ifconfig

UNIX and Linux hosts provide a command called `ifconfig`, which provides similar output to Windows' ipconfig program. Note some differences between the Windows and Linux commands:

- `ifconfig` can also be used to bind an address to an adapter interface, set up communication parameters, and enable or disable the adapter.
- The Windows switches for configuring the adapter with DHCP and DNS are not supported by `ifconfig`.
- The `ifconfig` command output does not show the default gateway (use `route` instead). It does show traffic statistics, though.

```
administrator@lamp:~$ ifconfig
eth0      Link encap:Ethernet  HWaddr 00:15:5d:01:c0:9f
          inet addr:192.168.1.1  Bcast:192.168.1.255  Mask:255.255.255.0
          inet6 addr: fe80::215:5dff:fe01:c09f/64 Scope:Link
          UP BROADCAST RUNNING MULTICAST  MTU:1500  Metric:1
          RX packets:0 errors:0 dropped:0 overruns:0 frame:0
          TX packets:36 errors:0 dropped:0 overruns:0 carrier:0
          collisions:0 txqueuelen:1000
          RX bytes:0 (0.0 B)  TX bytes:1728 (1.7 KB)

lo        Link encap:Local Loopback
          inet addr:127.0.0.1  Mask:255.0.0.0
          inet6 addr: ::1/128 Scope:Host
          UP LOOPBACK RUNNING  MTU:16436  Metric:1
          RX packets:57 errors:0 dropped:0 overruns:0 frame:0
          TX packets:57 errors:0 dropped:0 overruns:0 carrier:0
          collisions:0 txqueuelen:0
          RX bytes:4153 (4.1 KB)  TX bytes:4153 (4.1 KB)

administrator@lamp:~$
```

Using ifconfig. (Screenshot used with permission from Microsoft.)

Note: Additionally, a separate command (`iwconfig`) is used to manage wireless interfaces. Note that both these commands are deprecated in favor of the newer `ip` and `iw` utilities.

IP CONNECTIVITY ISSUES

If the link and IP configuration both seem to be correct, the problem may not lie with the local machine but somewhere in the overall network topology. You can test connections to servers such as files shares, printers, or email by trying to use them. One drawback of this method is that there could be some sort of application fault rather than a network fault. Therefore, it is useful to have a low-level test of basic connectivity that does not have any dependencies other than a working link and IP configuration.

ping

The `ping` utility is a command-line diagnostic tool used to test whether a host can communicate with another host on the same network or on a remote network. It is the basic tool to use to establish that a link is working. `ping` uses the **Internet Control Message Protocol (ICMP)** to request status messages from hosts. The following steps outline the procedures for verifying a computer's configuration and for testing router connections:

1. Ping the loopback address to verify TCP/IP is installed and loaded correctly (`ping 127.0.0.1`)—the loopback address is a reserved IP address used for testing purposes.
2. Ping the IP address of your workstation to verify it was added correctly and to check for possible duplicate IP addresses.
3. Ping the IP address of the default gateway to verify it is up and running and that you can communicate with a host on the local network.
4. Ping the IP address of a remote host to verify you can communicate through the router. If no router is available, Windows will display a yellow alert icon and a notification that the adapter has **No Internet access**.

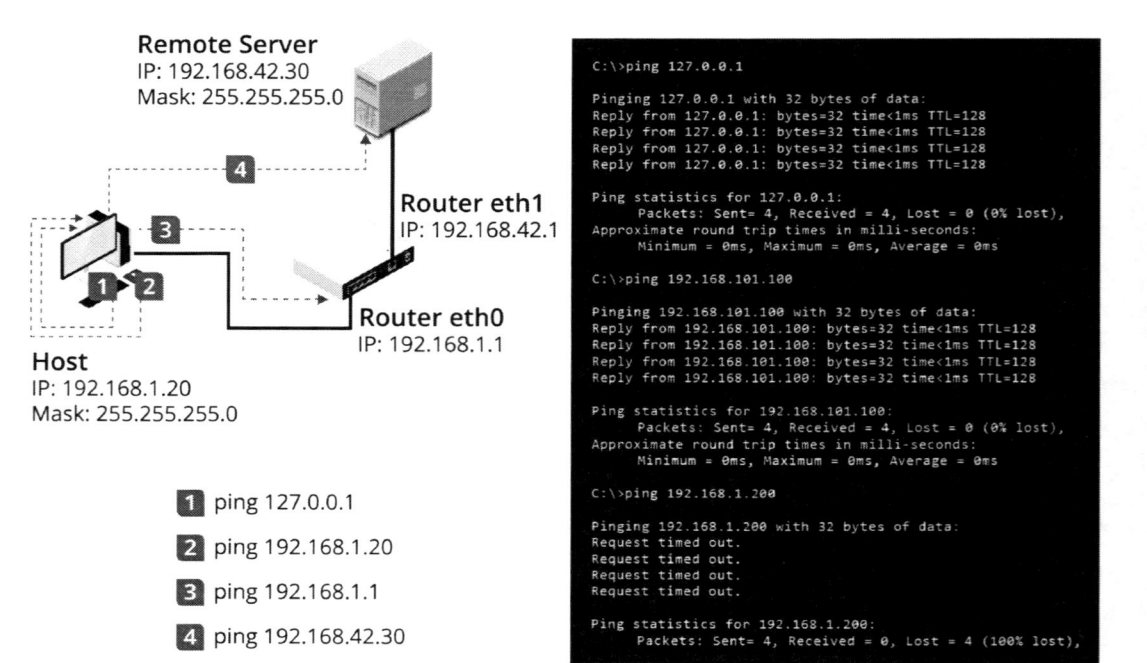

```
Remote Server
IP: 192.168.42.30
Mask: 255.255.255.0

Router eth1
IP: 192.168.42.1

Router eth0
IP: 192.168.1.1

Host
IP: 192.168.1.20
Mask: 255.255.255.0
```

1. ping 127.0.0.1
2. ping 192.168.1.20
3. ping 192.168.1.1
4. ping 192.168.42.30

```
C:\>ping 127.0.0.1

Pinging 127.0.0.1 with 32 bytes of data:
Reply from 127.0.0.1: bytes=32 time<1ms TTL=128
Reply from 127.0.0.1: bytes=32 time<1ms TTL=128
Reply from 127.0.0.1: bytes=32 time<1ms TTL=128
Reply from 127.0.0.1: bytes=32 time<1ms TTL=128

Ping statistics for 127.0.0.1:
    Packets: Sent= 4, Received = 4, Lost = 0 (0% lost),
Approximate round trip times in milli-seconds:
    Minimum = 0ms, Maximum = 0ms, Average = 0ms

C:\>ping 192.168.101.100

Pinging 192.168.101.100 with 32 bytes of data:
Reply from 192.168.101.100: bytes=32 time<1ms TTL=128
Reply from 192.168.101.100: bytes=32 time<1ms TTL=128
Reply from 192.168.101.100: bytes=32 time<1ms TTL=128
Reply from 192.168.101.100: bytes=32 time<1ms TTL=128

Ping statistics for 192.168.101.100:
    Packets: Sent= 4, Received = 4, Lost = 0 (0% lost),
Approximate round trip times in milli-seconds:
    Minimum = 0ms, Maximum = 0ms, Average = 0ms

C:\>ping 192.168.1.200

Pinging 192.168.1.200 with 32 bytes of data:
Request timed out.
Request timed out.
Request timed out.
Request timed out.

Ping statistics for 192.168.1.200:
    Packets: Sent= 4, Received = 0, Lost = 4 (100% lost),
```

Troubleshooting with ping.

If `ping` is successful, it responds with the message **Reply from IP Address** and the time it takes for the server's response to arrive. The millisecond measures of Round Trip Time (RTT) can be used to diagnose latency problems on a link.

If `ping` is unsuccessful, one of two messages are commonly received:

- **Destination unreachable**—there is no routing information (that is, the local computer or an intermediate router does not know how to get to that IP address). If the host is on the same network, check the local IP configuration—IP address, subnet mask, and so on. If you can discount any configuration error, then there may be a hardware or cabling problem. If the host is on another network, check the IP configuration and router.
- **No reply (Request timed out)**—the host is unavailable or cannot route a reply back to your computer. Check physical cabling and infrastructure devices such as the switch. If the host is on a remote network, try using `tracert` (described shortly).

> **Note:** *Be aware that ICMP traffic is often blocked by firewalls, making a response such as request timed out or destination unreachable inevitable. As well as network firewalls, consider that a host firewall, such as Windows Firewall, might be blocking ICMP.*

TESTING DNS

You can also ping DNS names (`ping comptia.org`, for example) or FQDNs (`ping sales.comptia.org`, for instance). This will not work if a DNS server is unavailable. Use the `-a` switch to perform a reverse lookup on an IP address to try to get the host name. For example, `ping -a 192.168.1.1` should return the message "Pinging *HostName* [192.168.1.1]."

TROUBLESHOOTING AN IP CONFLICT

Two systems could end up with the same IP address because of a configuration error; perhaps both addresses were statically assigned or one was assigned an address that was part of a DHCP scope by mistake. If Windows detects a duplicate IP address, it will display a warning and disable IP. If there are two systems with duplicate IPs, a sort of "race condition" will determine which receives traffic. Obviously, this is not a good way for the network to be configured and you should identify the machines and set them to use unique addresses.

ROUTING ISSUES

The `tracert` command-line utility is used to trace the route a packet of information takes to get to its target. Like `ping`, it uses ICMP status messages. For example, a user might type the following: `tracert 10.0.0.1`. This command would return details of the route taken to find the machine or device with the IP address of 10.0.0.1. `tracert` can also be used with a domain name or FQDN, such as: `tracert comptia.org`.

```
C:\Users\localadmin>tracert 10.0.0.1

Tracing route to 10.0.0.1 over a maximum of 30 hops

  1  HOST [192.168.1.110] reports: Destination host unreachable.

Trace complete.

C:\Users\localadmin>tracert gtslearning.com

Tracing route to gtslearning.com [185.41.10.123]
over a maximum of 30 hops:

  1    <1 ms    <1 ms    <1 ms  ARCHER_VR900 [192.168.1.1]
  2     *        *        *     Request timed out.
  3     *       11 ms    11 ms  31.55.187.181
  4    11 ms    11 ms    11 ms  31.55.187.188
  5    12 ms    11 ms    11 ms  core2-hu0-17-0-1.southbank.ukcore.bt.net [195.99
.127.188]
  6    12 ms    12 ms    12 ms  195.99.127.70
  7    13 ms    13 ms    13 ms  peer2-et-9-1-0.redbus.ukcore.bt.net [62.172.103.
43]
  8    13 ms    13 ms    18 ms  linx2.ixreach.com [195.66.236.217]
  9    20 ms    20 ms    20 ms  r1.tcw.man.ixreach.com [91.196.184.181]
 10    19 ms    23 ms    20 ms  rt1-tjh-ixr.as200083.net [46.18.174.222]
 11    20 ms    20 ms    20 ms  server1.gtslearning.com [185.41.10.123]

Trace complete.

C:\Users\localadmin>_
```

Using tracert—the first trace to a local private network has failed but the trace over the Internet to gtslearning.com's web server has succeeded, passing first through the SOHO router then through the routers belonging to the user's ISP, then the routers belonging to the web host. (Screenshot used with permission from Microsoft.)

If the host cannot be located, the command will eventually timeout but it will return every router that was attempted. The output shows the number of hops (when a packet is transferred from one router to another), the ingress interface of the router or host (that is, the interface from which the router receives the ICMP packet), and the time taken to respond to each probe in milliseconds (ms). If no acknowledgement is received within the timeout period, an asterisk is shown against the probe.

Note: `ping` and `tracert` use Internet Control Message Protocol (ICMP) traffic. A firewall may be configured to block this traffic to prevent network snooping.

UNAVAILABLE RESOURCES

If you cannot identify a problem with the cabling, switches/routers, or the IP configuration, you should start to suspect a problem at a higher layer of processing. There are three main additional "layers" where network services fail:

- Security—a firewall or other security software or hardware might be blocking the connection.
- Name resolution—if a service such as DNS is not working, you will be able to connect to file/print/email services by IP address but not by name.
- Application/OS—the software underpinning the service might have failed. If the OS has failed, there might not be any sort of connectivity to the host server. If the server can be contacted, but not a specific service, the service process might have crashed.

When troubleshooting Internet access or unavailable local network resources, such as file shares, network printers, and email, try to establish the scope of the problem. If you can connect to these services using a different host, the problem should lie with the first client. If other hosts cannot connect, the problem lies with the application server or print device or with network infrastructure between the client and the server.

TROUBLESHOOTING INTERNET AVAILABILITY

When Windows reports that a network adapter has "No Internet access," it means that the IP configuration is valid but that Windows cannot identify a working Internet connection. Windows tests Internet access by attempting a connection to `www.msftncsi.com` and checking that DNS resolves the IP address correctly.

If the local PC settings are correct, locate your ISP's service status page or support helpline to verify that there are no wider network issues or DNS problems that might make your Internet connection unavailable. If there are no ISP-wide issues, try restarting the router/modem.

Note: Do not restart a router without considering the impact on other users!

If these measures don't help, also consider that there might be some sort of security issue, such as a proxy configuration not working or a firewall blocking the host.

PERFORMING A NETWORK RESET

If there are persistent network problems with either a client or a server, one "stock" response is to try restarting the computer hardware. You can also try restarting just the application service.

Note: As before, do not restart a server without considering the impact on other users. A restart is probably only warranted if the problem is widespread.

In Windows, you can try running the network troubleshooter app to automatically diagnose and fix problems. Another option is to reset the network stack on the device. In Windows, this will clear any custom adapter configurations and network connections, including VPN connections. These will have to be reconfigured after the reset.

In Windows 10, there is a **Network reset** command on the **Settings→Network & Internet→Status** page. In Windows 7/8, you can use the Network Adapter troubleshooter or run the following commands (as administrator):

```
ipconfig /flushdns
netsh int ip reset resetlog.txt
netsh winsock reset
```

Use Device Manager to remove any network adapters. Reboot the computer and allow Windows to detect and install the adapter(s) again. Update network settings on all adapters to the appropriate configuration.

netstat

`netstat` can be used to investigate open ports and connections on the local host. In a troubleshooting context, you can use this tool to verify whether file sharing or email ports are open on a server and whether other clients are connecting to them.

```
C:\Windows\system32>netstat -b -n

Active Connections

  Proto  Local Address          Foreign Address        State
  TCP    192.168.1.110:5806     185.41.10.123:80       CLOSE_WAIT
 [IEXPLORE.EXE]
  TCP    192.168.1.110:5807     185.41.10.123:80       CLOSE_WAIT
 [IEXPLORE.EXE]
  TCP    192.168.1.110:5808     216.58.208.40:443      ESTABLISHED
 [IEXPLORE.EXE]
  TCP    192.168.1.110:5809     216.58.208.40:443      ESTABLISHED
 [IEXPLORE.EXE]
  TCP    192.168.1.110:5810     104.27.151.216:80      CLOSE_WAIT
 [IEXPLORE.EXE]
  TCP    192.168.1.110:5811     104.27.151.216:80      CLOSE_WAIT
 [IEXPLORE.EXE]
  TCP    192.168.1.110:5812     104.27.151.216:80      CLOSE_WAIT
 [IEXPLORE.EXE]
  TCP    192.168.1.110:5813     104.27.151.216:80      CLOSE_WAIT
 [IEXPLORE.EXE]
  TCP    192.168.1.110:5814     104.27.151.216:80      CLOSE_WAIT
 [IEXPLORE.EXE]
  TCP    192.168.1.110:5815     104.27.151.216:80      CLOSE_WAIT
 [IEXPLORE.EXE]
  TCP    192.168.1.110:5816     52.28.192.217:443      ESTABLISHED
 [IEXPLORE.EXE]
  TCP    [fe80::5c9e:8be5:bb3e:f341%4]:2179  [fe80::5c9e:8be5:bb3e:f341%4]:5519
 ESTABLISHED
 [vmms.exe]
  TCP    [fe80::5c9e:8be5:bb3e:f341%4]:3587  [fe80::5cf0:94fe:4f4:a8a%4]:57395
 ESTABLISHED
  p2psvc
 [svchost.exe]
  TCP    [fe80::5c9e:8be5:bb3e:f341%4]:5519  [fe80::5c9e:8be5:bb3e:f341%4]:2179
 ESTABLISHED
 [VmConnect.exe]

C:\Windows\system32>
```

Displaying open connections with netstat. (Screenshot used with permission from Microsoft.)

The following represent some of the main switches that can be used:

- `-a` displays all the connections and listening ports.
- `-b` shows the process that has opened the port.
- `-n` displays ports and addresses in numerical format. Skipping name resolution speeds up each query.

Linux supports a similar utility with slightly different switches.

nslookup

If you identify or suspect a problem with name resolution, you can troubleshoot DNS with the `nslookup` command, either interactively or from the command prompt:

`nslookup -Option Host Server`

`Host` can be either a host name/FQDN or an IP address. Server is the DNS server to query; the default DNS server is used if this argument is omitted. `-Option` specifies an nslookup subcommand. Typically, a subcommand is used to query a particular DNS record type.

For example, the following command queries Google's public DNS servers (8.8.8.8) for information about comptia.org's mail records:

`nslookup -type=mx comptia.org 8.8.8.8`

```
C:\Users\James>nslookup -type=mx comptia.org 8.8.8.8
Server:  google-public-dns-a.google.com
Address:  8.8.8.8

Non-authoritative answer:
comptia.org     MX preference = 10, mail exchanger = comptia-org.mail.protection.outlook.c
om
```

Using nslookup to query the mail server configured for the comptia.org domain name using Google's public DNS servers (8.8.8.8). (Screenshot used with permission from Microsoft.)

If you query a different name server, you can compare the results to those returned by your own name server. This might highlight configuration problems.

Note: *The* `dig` *utility is often used as a more up-to-date and flexible alternative to* `nslookup`. `dig` *allows you to query a name server directly and retrieve any of the information known about the domain name. It is helpful in determining if the server is running correctly and if the domain record is properly configured.*

Activity 6-6
Discussing Network Connection Troubleshooting

SCENARIO
Answer the following questions to check your understanding of the topic.

1. You are trying to add a computer to a wireless network but cannot detect the access point.

   What would you suspect the problem to be?

2. **What readings would you expect to gather with a Wi-Fi analyzer?**

3. You have restarted the DHCP server following a network problem.

   What command would you use to refresh the IP configuration on Windows 7 client workstations?

4. **What command can you use on a Linux computer to report the IP configuration?**

5. A single PC on a network cannot connect to the Internet.

   Where would you start troubleshooting?

6. A computer cannot connect to the network. The machine is configured to obtain a TCP/IP configuration automatically. You use ipconfig to determine the IP address and it returns 0.0.0.0.

   What does this tell you?

7. If a host has a firewall configured to block outgoing ICMP traffic, what result would you expect from pinging the host (assuming that the path to the host is otherwise OK)?

8. What Windows tool is used to test the end-to-end path between two IP hosts on different IP networks?

9. Which command produces the output shown in this graphic?

```
Active Connections

Proto  Local Address         Foreign Address        State           PID
TCP    0.0.0.0:135           0.0.0.0:0              LISTENING       652
TCP    0.0.0.0:445           0.0.0.0:0              LISTENING       4
TCP    0.0.0.0:5985          0.0.0.0:0              LISTENING       4
TCP    0.0.0.0:47001         0.0.0.0:0              LISTENING       4
TCP    0.0.0.0:49664         0.0.0.0:0              LISTENING       428
TCP    0.0.0.0:49665         0.0.0.0:0              LISTENING       912
TCP    0.0.0.0:49666         0.0.0.0:0              LISTENING       864
TCP    0.0.0.0:49669         0.0.0.0:0              LISTENING       1996
TCP    0.0.0.0:49670         0.0.0.0:0              LISTENING       524
TCP    0.0.0.0:49703         0.0.0.0:0              LISTENING       516
TCP    0.0.0.0:49706         0.0.0.0:0              LISTENING       524
TCP    10.1.0.100:139        0.0.0.0:0              LISTENING       4
TCP    10.1.0.100:49764      10.1.0.192:3000        ESTABLISHED     4280
TCP    [::]:135              [::]:0                 LISTENING       652
TCP    [::]:445              [::]:0                 LISTENING       4
TCP    [::]:5985             [::]:0                 LISTENING       4
TCP    [::]:47001            [::]:0                 LISTENING       4
```

Command output exhibit. (Screenshot used with permission from Microsoft.)

Topic F

Install and Configure IoT Devices

EXAM OBJECTIVES COVERED
1001-2.3 Given a scenario, install and configure a basic wired/wireless SOHO network.
1001-2.4 Compare and contrast wireless networking protocols.

As a CompTIA A+ technician, you should be alert to the need to stay up to date with new technologies. The market for home automation systems is expanding all the time, and these technologies are also starting to appear in office buildings. In this topic, you will learn about the main types of devices and networking standards plus basic procedures for setting up a smart hub and connecting devices to it.

INTERNET OF THINGS

Wi-Fi dominates wireless networking for devices like computers and laptops. It is also supported by smartphones and tablets. Wi-Fi requires quite powerful adapters with large antennas, however. Other wireless technologies support communications between smaller devices, where low weight, bulk, and power consumption are the primary requirements.

The term **Internet of Things (IoT)** is used to describe the global network of personal devices—such as phones, tablets, and fitness trackers, home appliances, home control systems, vehicles, and other items that have been equipped with sensors, software, and network connectivity. These features allow these types of objects to communicate and pass data between themselves and other traditional systems like computer servers. This is often referred to as **Machine to Machine (M2M)** communication.

Each "thing" is identified with some form of unique serial number or code embedded within its own operating or control system and is able to inter-operate within the existing Internet infrastructure either directly or via an intermediary.

IoT WIRELESS NETWORKING TECHNOLOGIES

When you work with IoT devices, you might encounter one or more of these network connection technologies.

BLUETOOTH AND BLUETOOTH LOW ENERGY

Bluetooth uses radio communications and supports speeds of up to 3 Mbps. Adapters supporting version 3 or 4 of the standard can achieve faster rates (up to 24 Mbps) through the ability to negotiate an 802.11 radio link for large file transfers (BT + HS [High Speed]).

Bluetooth does not require line-of-sight and supports a maximum range of 10 m (30 feet), though signal strength will be weak at this distance. Many portable devices, such as smartphones, tablets, wearable tech, audio speakers, and headphones now use Bluetooth connectivity. Bluetooth devices can use a pairing procedure to authenticate and exchange data securely.

Version 4 introduced a **Bluetooth Low Energy (BLE)** variant of the standard. BLE is designed for small battery-powered devices that transmit small amounts of data infrequently. A BLE device remains in a low power state until a monitor application initiates a connection. BLE is not backwards-compatible with "classic" Bluetooth, though a device can support both standards simultaneously.

Z-Wave

Z-Wave is a wireless communications protocol used primarily for home automation. It was developed in 2001 by Zensys, a Danish company, but with interest and investment from other technology and engineering companies such as Cisco, Intel, Panasonic, and Danfoss, the Z-Wave Alliance was formed. Z-Wave operates a certification program for devices and software.

Z-Wave creates a mesh network topology, using low-energy radio waves to communicate from one appliance to another. Devices can be configured to work as repeaters to extend the network but there is a limit of four "hops" between a controller device and an endpoint. This allows for wireless control of residential appliances and other devices, such as lighting control, security systems, thermostats, windows, locks, swimming pools, and garage door openers. Z-Wave has been registered in most countries worldwide and uses radio frequencies in the high 800 to low 900 MHz range. It is designed to run for long periods (years) on battery power.

Zigbee

Zigbee has similar uses to Z-Wave and is an open source competitor technology to it. The Zigbee Alliance operates a number of certification programs for its various technologies and standards.

Zigbee uses the 2.4 GHz frequency band. This higher frequency allows more data bandwidth at the expense of range compared to Z-Wave and the greater risk of interference from other 2.4 GHz radio communications. Zigbee supports more overall devices within a single network (65,000 compared to 232 for Z-wave) and there is no hop limit for communication between devices.

RFID AND NEAR FIELD COMMUNICATIONS (NFC)

Radio Frequency ID (RFID) is a means of tagging and tracking objects using specially encoded tags. When an RFID reader scans a tag, the tag responds with the information programmed into it. A tag can either be an unpowered, passive device that only responds when scanned at close range (up to about 25 m), or a powered, active device with a range of 100 m. Passive RFID tags can be embedded in stickers and labels to track parcels and equipment and are used in passive proximity smart cards.

Near Field Communications (NFC) is a peer-to-peer version of RFID; that is, an NFC device can work as both tag and reader to exchange information with other NFC devices. NFC normally works at up to 2 inches (6 cm) at data rates of 106, 212, and 424 Kbps. NFC sensors and functionality are starting to be incorporated into smartphones. NFC is mostly used for contactless payment readers, security ID tags, and shop shelf-edge labels for stock control. It can also be used to configure other types of connection (pairing Bluetooth devices, for instance).

IoT DEVICE CONFIGURATION

One of the applications of Internet of Things (IoT) functionality is the use of home automation devices, also called a smart home. A smart home essentially means that ordinary controls, such as the thermostat or lighting, can be controlled using a simple computer interface. The interface could be an app on your smartphone or a voice-enabled home automation hub (or both).

For consistency and the use of a single point-of-control, you ideally need to pick devices that are all compatible. There are two main compatibility considerations:

- That devices all share the same networking protocol, such as Z-Wave or Zigbee.
- That devices are all compatible with the same virtual assistant or hub.

ENDPOINT DEVICES

In home automation, endpoint devices are the things that physically interface with or implement the system you are controlling.

- Thermostat—operate heating and hot water controls and measure the current temperature.
- Light switches/bulbs—turn lights on or off or set to a particular dimmer level or color (in the case of smart bulbs).
- Security cameras—the main function is to record images to cloud storage, but these come with a very wide range of features, including intruder alerting/motion detection, face recognition, night vision, two-way microphone, zoom, and tracking.
- Door locks—a smart lock can be operated using voice or a tap and can be set to lock automatically if your smartphone is more than a certain distance away. Locks can also log events.

Depending on type, an endpoint device might need to be fitted by a qualified installer, such as an electrician or heating engineer. The next step is to register the device with some sort of controller. This could either be a smartphone app or some sort of smart hub.

SMARTPHONE CONTROL

Smartphones can only be used to control a device directly over Wi-Fi, Bluetooth, or NFC. There are no smartphones with Z-Wave or Zigbee radios (at the time of writing).

SMART HUB AND SMART SPEAKER CONTROL

Devices using Z-Wave or Zigbee can be controlled using a smart hub. Most of the major hub vendors support both technologies (as well as Wi-Fi and Bluetooth). You can then use a smartphone to operate the devices via the hub.

Most Z-Wave or Zigbee smart devices will come with their own dedicated hub or bridge. A dedicated hub can only usually control devices made by a single vendor. Dedicated hubs tend to be fairly limited devices that you can configure via a management URL or mobile app.

It may be possible to replace or supplement use of a dedicated hub with a more generic smart speaker/digital assistant-type hub. Examples of smart speaker brands include Samsung SmartThings, Amazon Echo, and Google Home™. Note that most of the brands include different models with different capabilities.

To set up a smart speaker, you usually install the product's app on a smartphone or tablet then use it to connect to the speaker. Configure the speaker to connect to your home Wi-Fi network. You should now be able to start configuring specific settings and integration features.

Integration with a digital assistant depends on the hub model and smart device. As an example, Amazon's Alexa digital assistant can be configured with "skill" shortcuts. A smart device vendor could create skills to allow Alexa to respond to commands to "Alexa, dim the lights" or "Alexa, turn the heating up" by sending appropriate commands to the relevant device.

*Note: In most cases, the dedicated hub will have to remain in place. When you issue a command to Alexa, Alexa sends a command to the dedicated hub, and the dedicated hub sends the command to the device. As smart device ecosystems evolve, the integration between devices and hubs is likely to become tighter. Another option is the Wink Hub (**wink.com/products/wink-hub**), which is specifically designed to act as a smart home systems integrator. The web platform If This Then That (**ifttt.com**) represents another means of integrating diverse technologies.*

When you connect a new smart device, you can use the hub to scan for it. The device will be allocated a node ID to register it on the network operated by the hub. If you have to register a number of similar devices, it is best to do so one-by-one, so that you can give them meaningful names. If you connect multiple devices of the same type at the same time, it can be tricky to distinguish them in the hub management app. If you have to do things this way, look for a unique serial number or code printed on the device. That value might be reported to the hub as a device property.

Note: *The node ID is assigned by the network controller rather than coded into the device. Zigbee devices have burned-in MAC addresses but Z-Wave devices do not.*

DIGITAL ASSISTANTS

A **digital assistant** (or **virtual assistant**) is a voice interface designed to respond to natural language commands and queries. Most smartphones and computers now support a voice assistant and they are also implemented on smart speaker hubs. The voice interface transfers requests for processing by a backend server, reducing processing demands on the device but raising privacy and security concerns.

The market is dominated by the major smartphone OS and smart hub vendors. Each voice assistant can be configured to respond to a wake word.

- Google Assistant™—"OK Google."
- Amazon Alexa—"Alexa."
- Apple® Siri®—"Hey Siri."
- Microsoft Cortana®—"Hey Cortana" or just "Cortana" (Microsoft is dropping the "Hey" requirement at the time of writing).

There are obviously considerable difficulties in providing a natural language interface that can cope with the diversity of languages, accents, and speaking styles used by people around the world. As vendors gather more voice data, however, they can make the assistants more accurate and more capable of providing a useful, individualized service.

To use a voice-based virtual assistant, the feature may first need to be enabled and then trained by completing a setup wizard to configure the assistant to recognize the user's voice.

Activity 6-7
Discussing IoT Devices

SCENARIO
Answer the following questions to check your understanding of the topic.

1. What type of network topology is used by protocols such as Zigbee and Z-Wave?

2. What types of home automation device might require specialist installer training?

3. What are the two main options for operating smart devices?

4. True or false? Voice processing by a smart speaker is performed internally so these devices can be used without an Internet connection.

Activity 6-8
Configuring IoT Devices

BEFORE YOU BEGIN
In addition to the actual IoT equipment, you will need a wireless network with an Internet connection and a computer with a wireless adapter to perform this activity.

SCENARIO
Depending on the equipment available, you might watch as your instructor sets up some home automation devices, or you might assist in setting them up yourself. This suggested activity requires an Echo Dot smart speaker, a Philips smart bulb kit, and one or more lamps.

You will configure the smart speaker so that it can respond to your voice queries. Then you will install the smart bulbs and configure the smart speaker to operate them.

1. Configure the smart speaker hub. The specific steps provided here are for configuring an Amazon Echo Dot smart speaker.
    a) Connect the smart speaker to the power supply.
    b) Unless you are instructed otherwise, reset it to factory settings. For example, with an Echo Dot, press and hold the **Microphone off** and **Volume down** buttons until the LED turns orange.
    c) Open **https://alexa.amazon.com**.
    d) If you do not already have an Amazon account, create one, and then sign in.
    e) If you are prompted to accept terms and conditions, select **Continue**.
    f) Select the model of smart speaker you are configuring.
    g) When you are prompted to connect your computer, use the network status icon (on the Windows taskbar) to connect to the **Amazon-XXX** wireless network, making sure to check the **Connect automatically** box.

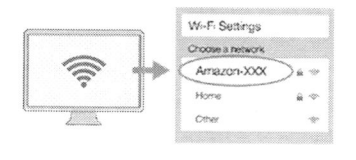

Connect to the built-in Echo access point when prompted to continue with setup.

h) Switch back to the browser setup app.

You should see a prompt to connect the smart hub to your own wireless network.

Echo Dot Setup

Select your Wi-Fi network

Previously Saved to Amazon.   Learn More

No Wi-Fi networks have been saved.

Other Networks

COMPTIA-WLAN

Cancel setup   Rescan

Your Echo Dot's MAC address is 5C:41:5A:56:E9:38

Join the smart hub to your own wireless network.

i) Select the appropriate wireless network to join the smart hub to (it must have an Internet connection).
j) Enter the PSK for the network.
k) Uncheck the **Save password to Amazon** box.
l) Select **Connect**.
m) Select **Use built-in speaker**.

Alexa should now be available to respond to your queries, though possibly not able to answer complex ones such as:

```
Alexa, how do I configure smart bulbs?
```

2. Use a Philips Hue account to set up the smart bulbs and bridge.

    The detailed steps are for a Philips Hue smart bulb kit (with bridge). Philips smart bulbs use Zigbee wireless networking. This means that you must install a Zigbee-capable hub to facilitate a connection to the Echo Dot smart speaker or allow control via a smartphone or computer with Wi-Fi. The hub must be connected to the cabled network (it does not support Wi-Fi itself).

    a) Connect the smart bulbs to lamps and switch them on.
    b) Connect the Hue bridge to the power supply.
    c) Unless you are instructed otherwise, reset it to factory settings, by using the button on the bottom of the device.
    d) Connect the Hue Bridge to a LAN port on the router/modem, or if you are using a standalone access point, connect it to a switch port on the same network.
    e) In the Alexa web app, select **Skills**.
    f) Search for the **Hue** skill by Philips Hue.

g) Select the **Enable** button.

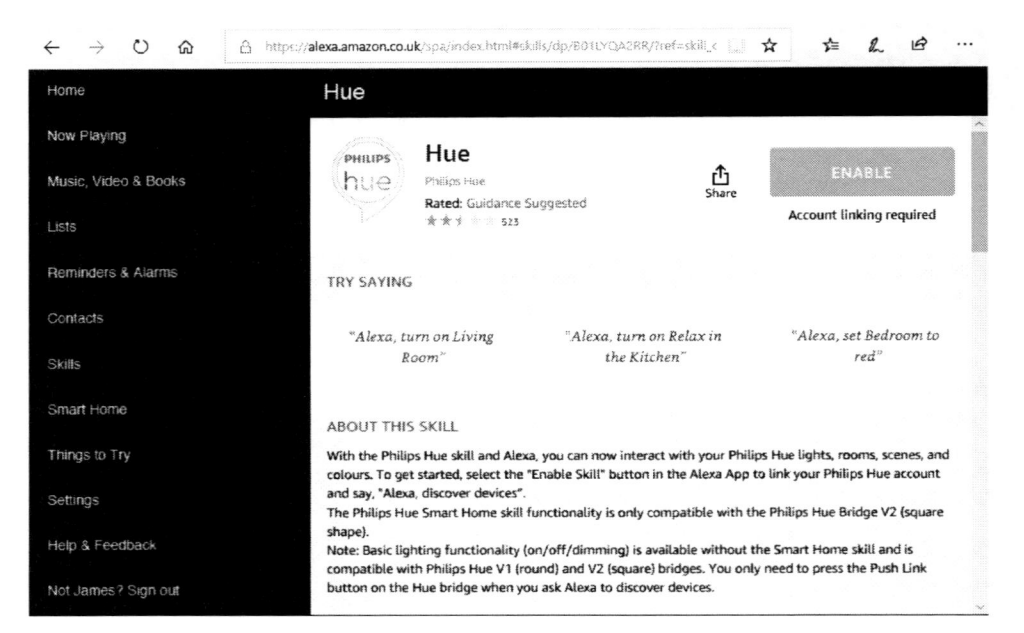

Installing the "skill" to use to control devices of a specific type.

h) When the separate browser window opens to **https://account.meethue.com/login**, either sign in or create an account and sign in.
i) When you are prompted, press the button on the Hue Bridge to allow the app to manage the bridge.
j) In the web app, select **Continue**.
k) When you are prompted, select **Yes** to trust Alexa.
l) Close the MeetHue browser tab.
m) In the Alexa app browser tab, select **Discover Devices**.

The device list should be populated with the smart bulbs (their names may vary). Note that "All lights" is treated as an independent device. This allows you to configure actions that operate on each light at the same time—"Alexa, turn off all lights" for example.

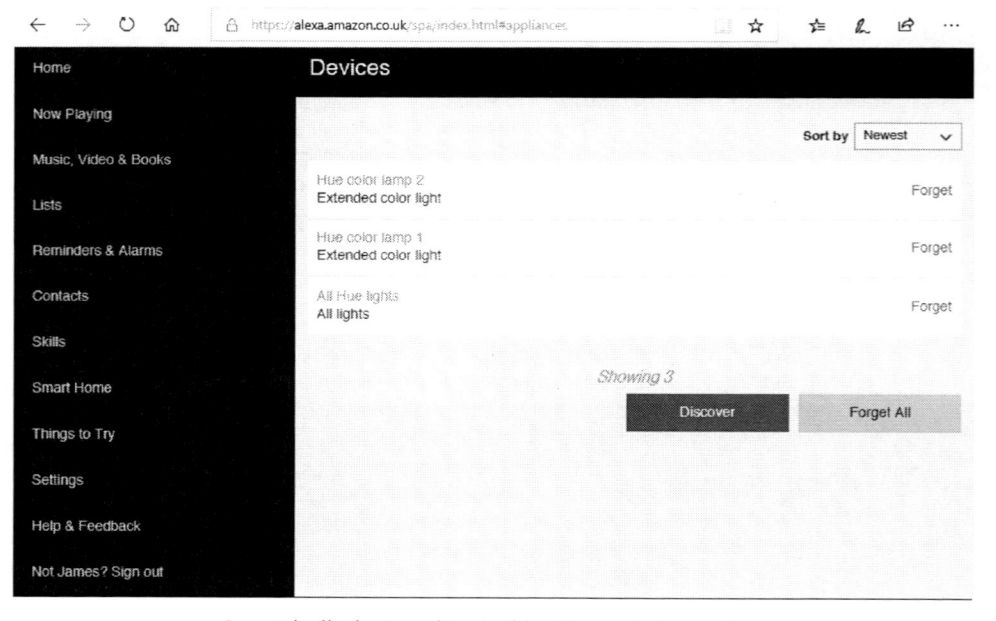

Smart bulb devices detected by Alexa via the bridge.

n) If necessary, refresh the view by selecting **Smart Home→Devices**.

o) When the bulbs are listed, you will be able to control the lamps with voice commands such as the following:

   ```
   Alexa, turn off hue color lamp one.
   Alexa, dim hue color lamp two.
   Alexa, make hue color lamp two blue.
   ```

3. Optionally, if you have time, explore other options for configuring the smart bulbs.

   Philips provides a management app only for Android and iOS. You can use a third-party app such as Huetro for Hue from Windows.

Summary

In this lesson, you configured and performed troubleshooting on SOHO and other networks. Ensuring consistent access to network resources is often an integral part of an A+ technician's day-to-day duties.

What experiences do you have in working with the networking technologies discussed in this lesson?

Do you have any experience working with SOHO networks? What do you expect to support in future job functions?

Practice Question: Additional practice questions are available on the CompTIA CHOICE platform within the **Assessments** tile.

Lesson 7
Implementing Client Virtualization and Cloud Computing

LESSON INTRODUCTION

As organizations grow in size and scope, there is an increased need for resources, especially when it comes to computing. Virtualization can help ease the growing pains of an organization by providing the opportunity to leverage one computer and one operating system for use over many systems, and save valuable time and resources when it comes to hardware, software, and personnel.

Virtualization is also the technology underpinning cloud computing; one of the dominant trends in networking. Many organizations are outsourcing parts of their IT infrastructure, platforms, storage, or services to a cloud service provider. Virtualization is at the core of cloud service provider networks. As a CompTIA® A+® technician, your customers will expect you to be able to advise on types of cloud deployments and identify some of the configuration issues involved in connecting to cloud services.

LESSON OBJECTIVES

In this lesson, you will:

- Set up and configure a hypervisor and virtual machine guests.
- Identify the purposes and types of cloud services.

Topic A
Configure Client-Side Virtualization

EXAM OBJECTIVES COVERED
1001-4.2 Given a scenario, set up and configure client-side virtualization.

Virtualization separates the elements of the computing environment—the applications, operating system, programs, documents, and more—from each other and from the physical hardware by using an additional software layer to mediate access. Virtualization can provide flexibility and scalability for organizations where the costs for hardware and software and the IT infrastructure needed to maintain them both continue to increase. It can increase resource utilization by allowing resources to be pooled and leveraged as part of a virtual infrastructure, and it can provide for centralized administration and management of all the resources being used throughout the organization.

As a CompTIA A+ technician, you will often be called upon to deploy, configure, and support Virtual Machines (VMs). You need to know about the types, capabilities, and uses of different virtualization technologies.

VIRTUALIZATION

When computers based on the microprocessor CPU were first produced, a single computer was designed to run a single operating system at any one time. This makes multiple applications available on that computer—whether it be a workstation or server—but the applications must all share a common OS environment. Some computers were configured with two or more operating systems and could choose the one to load at boot time (multiboot). The operating systems could not be used simultaneously, however.

Dramatic improvements and cost reductions in CPU and system memory technology mean that all but the cheapest computers are now capable of virtualization. **Virtualization** means that multiple operating systems can be installed and run simultaneously on a single computer.

There are many different ways of implementing this and many different reasons for doing it. In general terms, though, a virtual platform requires at least three components:

- Computer(s)—the platform or host for the virtual environment. Optionally, there may be multiple computers networked together.
- Hypervisor or Virtual Machine Monitor (VMM)—manages the virtual machine environment and facilitates interaction with the host hardware and network.
- Guest operating systems or Virtual Machines (VMs)—operating systems installed under the virtual environment. The number of operating systems is generally only restricted by hardware capacity. The type of guest operating systems might be restricted by the type of hypervisor.

The presence of other guest OSs can be completely transparent to any single OS. Each OS "thinks" it is working with a normal CPU, memory, hard disk, and network link. The guest OSs can be networked together or they may be able to share data directly through the hypervisor, though for security reasons this is not commonly implemented.

HYPERVISORS

As noted previously, a hypervisor manages the virtual machine environment and facilitates interaction with the host hardware and network.

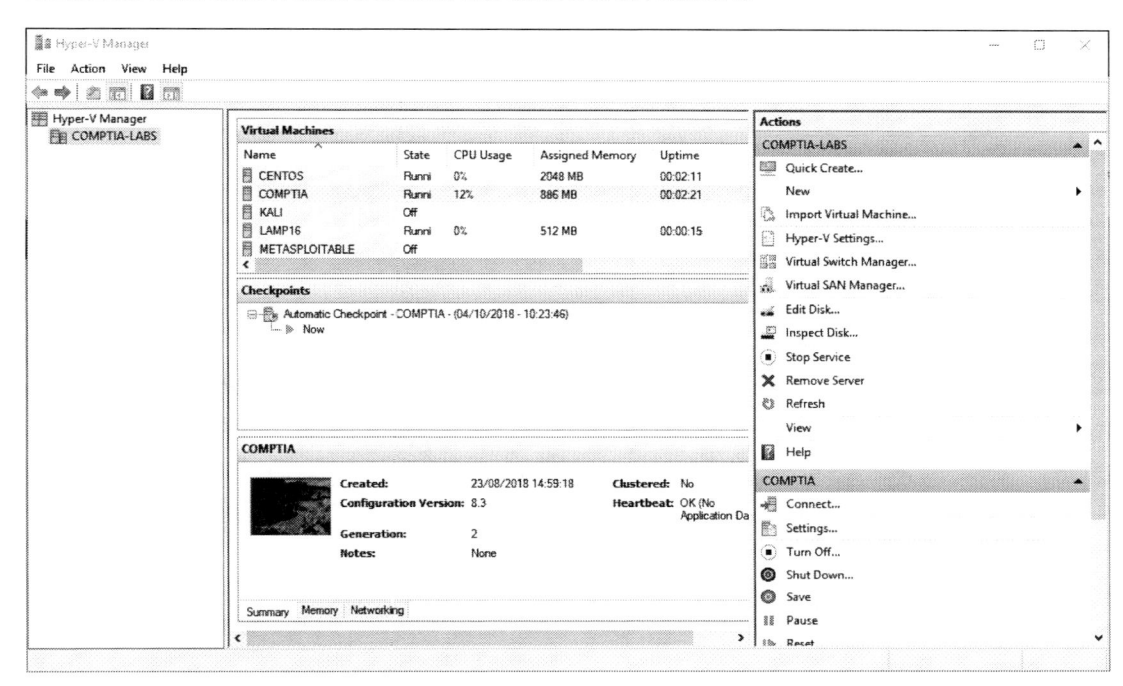

Microsoft Hyper-V hypervisor software. This machine is running several Windows and Linux guest operating systems. You can see each is allocated a portion of system memory to use. (Screenshot used with permission from Microsoft.)

Some of the main functions of the hypervisor include:

- Emulation—each guest OS expects exclusive access to resources such as the CPU, system memory, storage devices, and peripherals. The hypervisor emulates these resources and facilitates access to them to avoid conflicts between the guest OSs. The VMs must be provided with drivers for the emulated hardware components.
- Guest OS support—the hypervisor may be limited in terms of the different types of guest operating systems it can support. Virtualization is often used as a means of installing old OSs, such as MS-DOS or Windows 9x, as well as modern versions of Windows and Linux.

> **Note:** macOS can also be installed as a VM. This breaks the terms of Apple's EULA if the hardware platform is not itself an Apple PC.

- Assigning resources to each guest OS—for example, if the host computer has 4 GB memory, 1 GB might be required by the host OS, leaving 3 GB to assign to each guest OS. You could have three guests, each configured with 1 GB, for instance. Similarly, each guest OS will take up disk space on the host. Data is saved to virtual disk image files.
- Configuring networking—a hypervisor will be able to create a virtual network environment through which all the VMs can communicate. It will also be able to create a network shared by the host and by VMs on the same host and on other hosts. Enterprise virtual platforms allow the configuration of virtual switches and routers.

- Configuring security—ensures that guests are "contained" and cannot access other VMs or the host except through authorized mechanisms. This is important to prevent data "leaking" from one VM to another, to prevent one compromised VM from compromising others, and to prevent malware from spreading between VMs or from a VM to the host.

One basic distinction that can be made between virtual platforms is between host and bare metal methods of interacting with the computer hardware.

HOST-BASED HYPERVISOR

In a guest OS (or host-based) system, the hypervisor application, known as a **Type 2 hypervisor**, is itself installed onto a host operating system. Examples of host-based hypervisors include VMware Workstation™, Oracle® VirtualBox, and Parallels® Workstation. The hypervisor software must support the host OS. For example, Parallels Workstation is designed to run on macOS®. You cannot run it on a Windows® PC but you *can* use it to run a Windows VM on macOS.

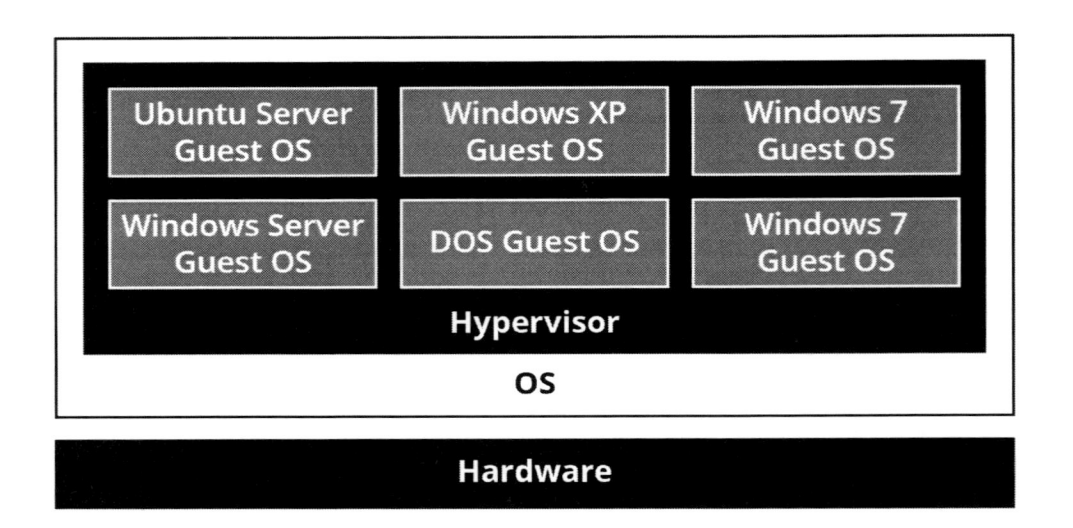

Guest OS virtualization (Type 2 Hypervisor). The hypervisor is an application running within a native OS and guest OSs are installed within the hypervisor.

BARE METAL HYPERVISOR

A bare metal virtual platform means that the hypervisor—called a **Type 1 hypervisor**—is installed directly onto the computer and manages access to the host hardware without going through a host OS. Examples include VMware ESX® Server, Microsoft's Hyper-V®, and Citrix's XEN Server. The hardware need only support the base system requirements for the hypervisor plus resources for the type and number of guest OSs that will be installed. Linux® also supports virtualization through Kernel-based Virtual Machine (KVM). KVM is embedded in the Linux kernel.

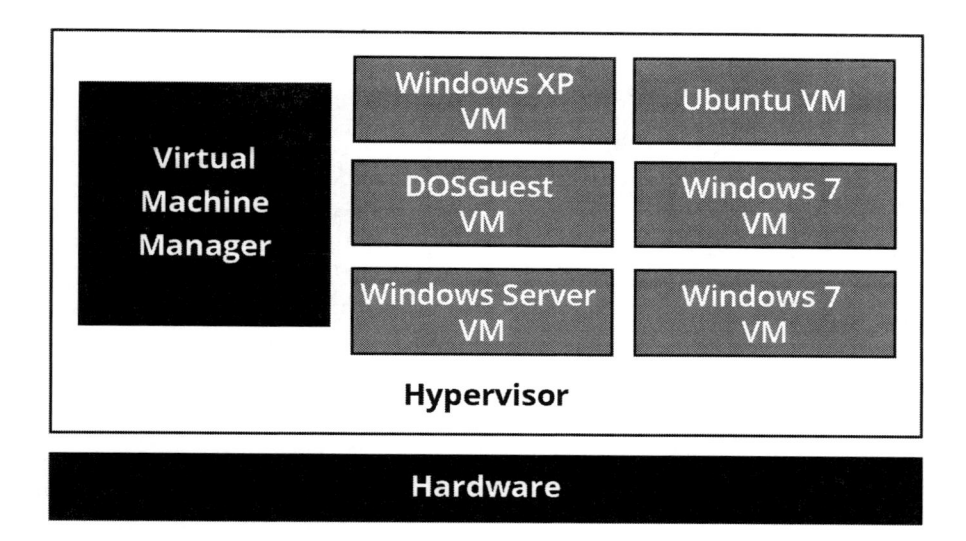

Type 1 "bare metal" hypervisor. The hypervisor is installed directly on the host hardware along with a management application, then VMs are installed within the hypervisor.

> **Note:** *If the hypervisor is running in a 64-bit environment, 32-bit guest OSs can still be installed, providing the hypervisor supports them. 32-bit hypervisors will not support 64-bit guest OSs, however.*

PROCESSOR SUPPORT AND RESOURCE REQUIREMENTS

CPU vendors have built special instruction set extensions to facilitate virtualization. The Intel technology for this is called **VT-x** (Virtualization Technology) while AMD calls it **AMD-V**. Most virtualization products also benefit from a processor feature called **Second Level Address Translations (SLAT)**, which improves the performance of virtual memory when multiple VMs are installed. Intel implements SLAT as a feature called Extended Page Table (EPT) and AMD calls it Rapid Virtualization Indexing (RVI).

Most virtualization software requires a CPU with virtualization support enabled and performance of the VMs will be impaired if virtualization is not supported in the hardware. Some cheaper CPU models ship without the feature and sometimes the feature is disabled in the system firmware. If specifying a computer that will be used for virtualization, check the CPU specification carefully to confirm that it supports Intel VT-x or AMD-V and SLAT, if necessary.

Multiple CPU resources—whether through **Symmetric Multiprocessing** (SMP) or multiple physical processors, multicore, or HyperThreading—will greatly benefit performance, especially if more than one guest OS is run concurrently.

As mentioned earlier, each guest OS requires sufficient system memory over and above what is required by the host. For example, it is recommended that Windows 7 be installed on a computer with at least 1 GB memory. This means that the host must have at least 2 GB and possibly more. As you can see, if you want to run multiple guest operating systems concurrently, the resource demands can quickly add up. If the VMs are only used for development and testing, then performance might not be critical and you may be able to specify less memory.

Each guest OS also takes up a substantial amount of disk space. The VM's "hard disk" is stored as an image file on the host. Most hypervisors use a "dynamically expanding" image format that only takes up space on the host as files are added to the guest OS. Even so, a typical Windows installation might require 20 GB. More space is required if you want to preserve snapshots. A snapshot is the state of a disk at a particular point-in-time. This is useful if you want to be able to roll back changes you make to the VM during a session.

> **Note:** In an enterprise environment, you need not be constrained by the local disk resources on the host. Disk images could be stored in a high-speed Storage Area Network (SAN).

Most hypervisors also allow guest VMs to use the host's adapters (sound card, for instance) and peripherals (input devices, printers, and USB devices, for instance).

VIRTUAL NETWORKS

Where multiple virtual machines are running on a single platform, virtualization provides a means for these VMs to communicate with each other and with other computers on the network—both physical and virtual—using standard networking protocols.

The guest operating system running in each virtual machine is presented with an emulation of a standard hardware platform. Among the hardware devices emulated will be one or more network adapters. The number of adapters and their connectivity can typically be configured within the hypervisor.

Within the virtual machine, the virtual adapter will look exactly like an ordinary NIC and will be configurable in exactly the same way. For example, protocols and services can be bound to it and it can be assigned an IP address.

Typically, a hypervisor will implement network connectivity by means of one or more **virtual switches** (or vSwitches using VMware's terminology). These perform exactly the same function as Ethernet switches, except that they are implemented in software rather than hardware.

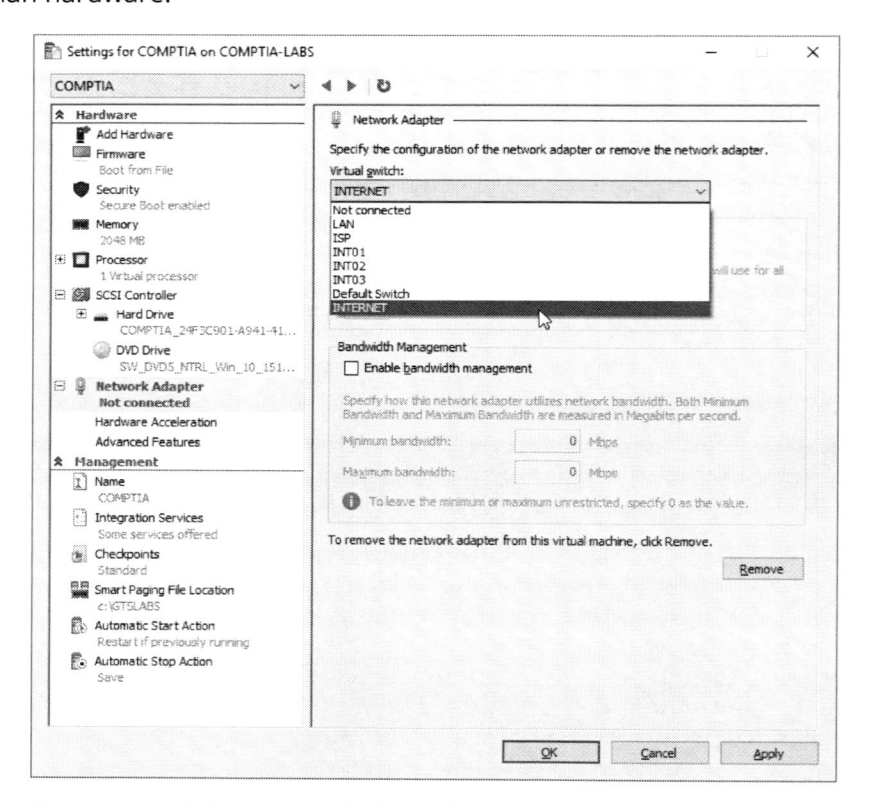

Selecting which virtual switch the network adapter in a VM is connected to. Note that there is also a "Not connected" option. (Screenshot used with permission from Microsoft.)

Connectivity between the virtual network adapters in the guest VMs and the virtual switches is configured via the hypervisor. This is analogous to connecting patch cables between real computers and real switches. Multiple virtual machines may be connected to the same virtual switch or to separate switches. The number of virtual switches supported varies from one hypervisor to another.

In this networking model, the virtual machines and the virtual switch can all be contained within a single hardware platform, so no actual network traffic is generated. Instead, data is moved from buffers in one virtual machine to another.

It is also possible to configure connectivity between the host computer's physical NIC and the virtual switches. This provides a bridge between the virtual switches within the host platform and the physical switches on the network, allowing frames to pass between physical and virtual machines and between the virtual machines and the host.

For example, in Microsoft's Hyper-V virtualization platform, three types of virtual switch can be created:

- **External**—binds to the host's NIC to allow the VM to communicate on the physical network.
- **Internal**—creates a switch that is usable only by VMs on the host and the host itself.
- **Private**—creates a switch that is usable only by the VMs. They cannot use the switch to communicate with the host.

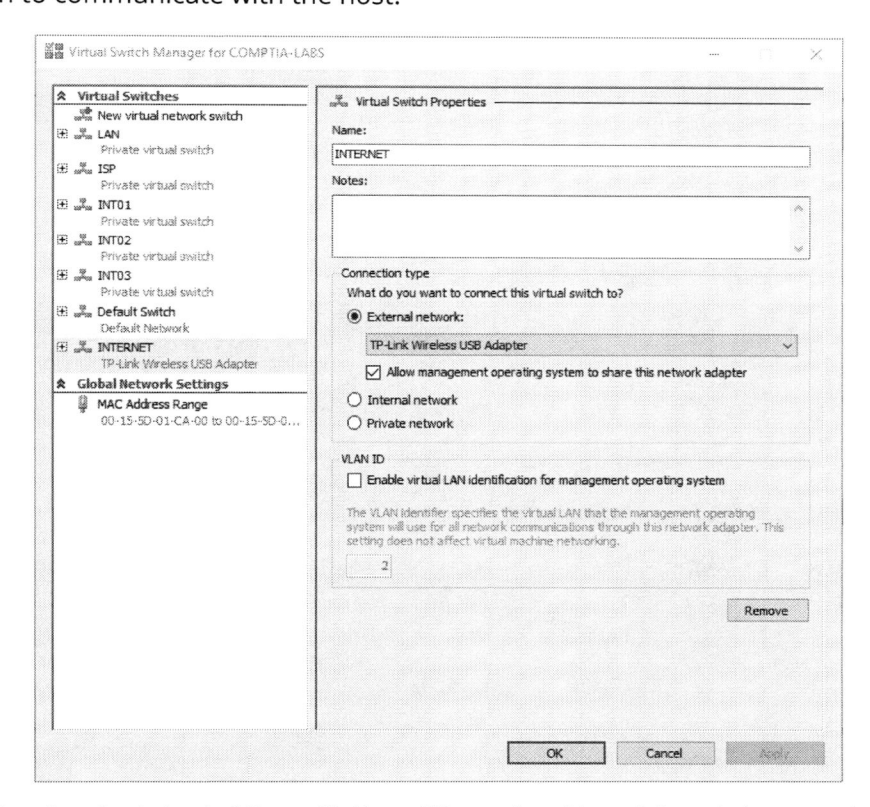

Configuring virtual switches in Microsoft's Hyper-V hypervisor. Most of the switches are private, which means that only the VMs can access them. The selected virtual switch can share the host network adapter, though, allowing communication between the VM and the host and allowing the VM to use the physical network to access the Internet. (Screenshot used with permission from Microsoft.)

Note: When the VMs are allowed to interact with a "real" network, the host must support a high bandwidth, high availability network link. Any failure of the physical link will affect multiple VMs.

VIRTUAL MACHINES

In principle, any type of operating system can be virtualized. This includes client OSs and server OSs. Note that some hypervisors have limited support for certain operating systems. For example, Hyper-V only provides support for particular distributions of Linux, though the situation is improving as the Hyper-V Linux Integration Services (LIS) drivers get added to the kernel of more Linux distributions.

There are also many different purposes for deploying a virtual platform. You can make a rough distinction between **client-side virtualization**, deployed to desktop-type machines, and **server-side virtualization.**

CLIENT-SIDE VIRTUALIZATION

Client-side virtualization refers to any solution designed to run on "ordinary" desktops or workstations. Each user will be interacting with the virtualization host directly. Desktop virtual platforms, usually based on some sort of guest OS hypervisor, are typically used for testing and development:

- Virtual labs—create a research lab to analyze viruses, worms, and Trojans. As the malware is contained within the guest OS, it cannot infect the researcher's computer or network.
- Support legacy software applications—if the host computers have been upgraded, software may not work well with the new operating system. In this scenario, the old OS can be installed as a VM and the application software accessed using the VM.
- Development environment—test software applications under different operating systems and/or resource constraints.
- Training—lab environments can be set up so that learners can practice using a live operating system and software without impacting the production environment. At the end of the lab, changes to the VM can be discarded so the original environment is available again for the next student to use.

SERVER-SIDE VIRTUALIZATION

For server computers and applications, the main use of virtualization is better hardware utilization through **server consolidation**. A typical hardware server may have resource utilization of about 10%. This implies that you could pack the server computer with another 8 or 9 server software instances and obtain the same performance.

SECURITY REQUIREMENTS

Like any computing technology, deploying a virtualization solution comes with security challenges.

GUEST OS SECURITY

Each guest OS must be patched and protected against viruses and Trojans like any other OS. Patching each VM individually has performance implications, so in most environments, a new image would be patched and tested then deployed to the production environment. Running security software (antivirus and intrusion prevention) on each guest OS can cause performance problems. Solutions for running security applications through the host or hypervisor are being developed.

> *Note: Ordinary antivirus software installed on the host will NOT detect viruses infecting the guest OS. Scanning the virtual disks of a guest OS from the host could cause serious performance problems.*

The process of developing, testing, and deploying images brings about the first major security concern with the virtual platform itself. This is the problem of rogue VMs. A **rogue VM** is one that has been installed without authorization. The uncontrolled deployment of more and more VMs is referred to as **VM sprawl**. It's a lot easier to add a guest image to a server than it is to plug a new hardware server into the network!

System management software can be deployed to detect rogue builds. More generally, the management procedures for developing and deploying machine images need to be tightly drafted and monitored. VMs should conform to an application-specific template with the minimum configuration needed to run that application (that is, not running unnecessary services). Images should not be developed or stored in any sort of environment where they could be infected by malware or have any sort of malicious code inserted. One of the biggest concerns here is of rogue developers or contractors installing backdoors or "logic bombs" within a machine image. The problem of criminal or disgruntled staff is obviously one that affects any sort of security environment, but concealing code within VM disk images is a bit easier to accomplish and has the potential to be much more destructive.

HOST SECURITY

Another key security vulnerability in a virtual platform is that the host represents a single point of failure for multiple guest OS instances. For example, if the CPU on the host crashes, three or four guest VMs and the application services they are running will suddenly go offline.

Another point is that running the host at a constantly high level of utilization could decrease the **Mean Time Between Failure (MTBF)** of its components. The MTBF is the number of hours the manufacturer expects that a component will run before experiencing some sort of hardware problem. If hardware is subjected to greater than expected loads, it may fail more often than expected.

A successful **Denial of Service (DoS)** attack on a host machine, host OS, or hypervisor will cause far more damage to the server infrastructure than a DoS on a single web server. As an example, most hypervisors support a disk snapshots feature. Snapshots allow the user to revert to the saved image after making changes. This can be misused to perform DoS by causing the undo files to grow to the point where they consume all the available disk space on the host.

HYPERVISOR SECURITY

Apart from ensuring the security of each guest OS and the host machine itself, a virtual platform introduces an additional layer for the attention of security analysts—that of the hypervisor. At the time of writing, there are few significant exploits, but hypervisor software is subject to patches and security advisories like any other software. As the use of virtual platforms grows, hypervisors will increasingly be the target of attacks.

Another issue is **VM escaping**. This refers to malware running on a guest OS jumping to another guest or to the host. As with any other type of software, it is vital to keep the hypervisor code up-to-date with patches for critical vulnerabilities.

Activity 7-1
Discussing Client-Side Virtualization Configuration

SCENARIO
Answer the following questions to check your understanding of the topic.

1. What is a Type 2 hypervisor?

2. What is a guest OS?

3. What system resources are most important on a system designed to host multiple virtual machines?

4. What might you need to install to a guest OS to make full use of a hypervisor's features?

5. True or false? VMs can be networked together by using a virtual switch, which is implemented in software by the hypervisor.

6. If users have access to virtualization tools, what network security controls might be required?

7. If you are using a normal antivirus product to protect a VM from malware, should you install the A-V product on the host to scan the VM disk image or on the VM itself?

Topic B
Cloud Computing Concepts

EXAM OBJECTIVES COVERED
1001-2.2 Compare and contrast common networking hardware devices.
1001-4.1 Compare and contrast cloud computing concepts.

One of the latest trends in networking is to outsource part of an organization's IT infrastructure, platforms, storage, or services to a cloud service provider. In this topic, you will identify basic cloud concepts.

CLOUD COMPUTING

The **cloud** has lots of different definitions but generally refers to any sort of IT infrastructure provided to the end user where the end user is not aware of or responsible for any details of the procurement, implementation, or management of the infrastructure. Its internal workings are a "cloud"; the end user is only interested in and pays for the services provided by the cloud.

The **National Institute of Standards and Technology (NIST)** created a standardized definition for cloud computing. This allows consumers to more easily compare services and deployment models from different vendors if they all use the same definition.

The NIST definition states: "Cloud computing is a model for enabling ubiquitous, convenient, on-demand network access to a shared pool of configurable computing resources (e.g., networks, servers, storage, applications, and services) that can be rapidly provisioned and released with minimal management effort or service provider interaction." (**https://nvlpubs.nist.gov/nistpubs/Legacy/SP/nistspecialpublication800-145.pdf**, section 2.)

NIST identifies five characteristics that are essential in defining something as being cloud computing. These are defined in the following table.

Characteristic	Description
On-demand self service	Consumers can provision services on the fly without interaction with service provider personnel.
Broad network access	Services are available over networks using standard clients, including workstations, laptops, tablets, and smart phones.
Resource pooling	Multiple customers share the service provider's resources in a multi-tenant model. Resources are dynamically assigned as they are needed without regard to where the customer or the resource are located. However, a customer can request resources from a specific location at the country, state, or data-center level. Resources include memory, storage, processing, and network bandwidth.
Rapid elasticity	Resources are automatically provisioned to scale up or down as resources are required by the customer.

Characteristic	Description
Measured service	Resources are measured through metering on a per use basis. The metering measurement is based on the type of resource such as storage, processing, bandwidth, or active users. The metering mechanism should be accessible to the customer via a reporting dashboard, providing complete transparency in usage and billing.

BENEFITS OF CLOUD COMPUTING

There are many benefits to using cloud computing. This includes savings in the cost of infrastructure and support, energy cost savings, rapid deployment, and allowing the customer to make the choices that make the most sense for their organization.

One of the most often cited benefits of implementing cloud computing is that the cloud provides **rapid elasticity**. This means that the cloud can scale quickly to meet peak demand. For example, a company may operate a single web server instance for most of the year, but provision additional instances for the busy Christmas period and then release them again in the New Year.

This example also illustrates the principles of on-demand and pay-per-use—key features of a cloud service (as opposed to a hosted service). On-demand implies that the customer can initiate service requests and that the cloud provider can respond to them immediately. This feature of cloud service is useful for project-based needs, giving the project members access to the cloud services for the duration of the project, and then releasing the cloud services back to the hosting provider when the project is finished. This way, the organization is only paying for the services for the duration of the project.

The provider's ability to control a customer's use of resources through metering is referred to as **measured service**. The customer is paying for the CPU, memory, disk, and network bandwidth resources they are actually consuming rather than paying a monthly fee for a particular service level.

In order to respond quickly to changing customer demands, cloud providers must be able to provision resources quickly. This is achieved through **resource pooling** and virtualization. Resource pooling means that the hardware making up the cloud provider's data center is not dedicated to or reserved for a particular customer account. The layers of virtualization used in the cloud architecture allow the provider to provision more CPU, memory, disk, or network resources using management software, rather than (for instance) having to go to the data center floor, unplug a server, add a memory module, and reboot.

Flexibility is a key advantage of cloud computing. However, the implications for data risk must be well understood when moving data between private and public storage environments. You need to be aware that any point from the server to the end user could be compromised if proper security measures are not taken and adhered to when transferring data over public and private networks.

COMMON CLOUD MODELS

In most cases, the cloud (that is, the hardware and/or software hosting the service) will be off-site relative to the organization's users, who will require an Internet link to access the cloud services. There can be different ownership and access arrangements for clouds, which can be broadly categorized as described in the following table.

Cloud Model	Description
Public or multi-tenant	This model is hosted by a third-party and shared with other subscribers. This is what many people understand by cloud computing. As a shared resource, there are risks regarding performance and security.
Hosted private	This model is hosted by a third-party for the exclusive use of one organization. This is more secure and can guarantee a better level of performance, but is correspondingly more expensive. The OpenStack project (**openstack.org**) is one example of a technology you could use to implement your own cloud computing infrastructure.
Private	In this model, the cloud infrastructure is completely private to and owned by the organization. In this case, there is likely to be one business unit dedicated to managing the cloud while other business units make use of it. This type of cloud could be on-site or off-site relative to the other business units. An on-site link can obviously deliver better performance and is less likely to be subject to outages (loss of an Internet link, for instance). On the other hand, a dedicated off-site facility may provide better shared access for multiple users in different locations.
Community	With this model, several organizations share the costs of either a hosted private or fully private cloud.
Hybrid	There will also be cloud computing solutions that implement some sort of hybrid public/private/community/hosted/on-site/off-site solution. For example, a travel organization may run a sales website for most of the year using a private cloud but "break out" the solution to a public cloud at times when much higher utilization is forecast. Google's **Gov Cloud** is another example. This cloud can be used by government branches within the U.S., but it is not available to consumers or businesses.

INTERNAL AND EXTERNAL SHARED RESOURCES

All networks provide a pool of shared resources for use by servers and clients. For example, file servers can provide disk storage resources to client computers in the form of shared folders. Servers themselves can use shared disk storage in the form of Storage Area Networks (SANs). Use of virtualization and hybrid cloud computing solutions allows these shared resources to be provisioned using a mixture of internally owned assets and externally provisioned assets.

CLOUD SERVICE OPTIONS

As well as the ownership model (public, private, hybrid, or community), cloud services are often differentiated on the level of sophistication provided. These models are referred to as **Something as a Service (*aaS)**, where the *something* can refer to infrastructure, network, platform, or software.

Service Type	Description
IaaS	**Infrastructure as a Service (IaaS)** is a means of provisioning IT resources such as servers, load balancers, and Storage Area Network (SAN) components quickly. Rather than purchase these components and the Internet links they require, you rent them on an as-needed basis from the service provider's data center. In an IaaS arrangement, you are typically billed based on the resources you consume, much like a utility company bills you for the amount of electricity you use. IaaS is a bare bones service offering. You will need to configure the components and build the platform on top. Examples of IaaS include Rackspace's CloudServers offering, in which you rent a virtual server running an operating system of your choice. You then install the applications you need onto that virtual server. Other examples include Amazon's Elastic Compute Cloud (EC2) service and Amazon's Simple Storage Service (S3).
SaaS	**Software as a Service (SaaS)** is a different model of provisioning software applications. Rather than purchasing software licenses for a given number of seats, a business would access software hosted on a supplier's servers on a pay-as-you-go or lease arrangement (on-demand). Virtual infrastructure allows developers to provision on-demand applications much more quickly than previously. The applications can be developed and tested within the cloud without the need to test and deploy on client computers. Perhaps the most well-known SaaS example is the Salesforce® Customer Relationship Management (**CRM**) service. Other notable SaaS examples are the Zoho suite of applications, Google's applications suite, and Microsoft's Office 365 suite.
PaaS	provides resources somewhere between SaaS and IaaS. A typical PaaS solution would provide servers and storage network infrastructure, but also provide a multi-tier web application/database platform on top, in contrast to Infrastructure as a Service. This platform might be based on Oracle® or MS SQL or PHP and MySQL™. As distinct from SaaS, though, this platform would not be configured to actually do anything. Your own developers would have to create the software, such as the CRM or e-commerce application, that runs using the platform. The service provider would be responsible for the integrity and availability of the platform components, but you would be responsible for the security of the application you created on the platform. An example is Rackspace's CloudSites offering, in which you rent a virtual web server and associated systems such as a database or email server. Amazon's Relational Database Service (RDS) enables you to rent fully configured MySQL and Oracle database servers.

Operating Systems and Software

Operating Systems

Amazon Machine Images (AMIs) are preconfigured with an ever-growing list of operating systems. We work with our partners and community to provide you with the most choice possible. You are also empowered to use our bundling tools to upload your own operating systems. The operating systems currently available to use with your Amazon EC2 instances include:

Operating Systems		
Red Hat Enterprise Linux	Windows Server	Oracle Enterprise Linux
OpenSolaris	Amazon Linux AMI	Ubuntu Linux
Fedora	Gentoo Linux	Debian
	SUSE Linux Enterprise	

Software

Amazon EC2 enables our partners and customers to build and customize Amazon Machine Images (AMIs) with software based on your needs. We have hundreds of free and paid AMIs available for you to use. A small sampling of the software available for use today within Amazon EC2 includes:

Databases	Batch Processing	Web Hosting
IBM DB2	Hadoop	Apache HTTP
IBM Informix Dynamic Server	Condor	IIS/Asp.Net
Microsoft SQL Server Standard	Open MPI	IBM Lotus Web Content Management
MySQL Enterprise		IBM WebSphere Portal Server
Oracle Database 11g		

Application Development Environments	Application Servers	Video Encoding & Streaming
IBM sMash	IBM WebSphere Application Server	Wowza Media Server Pro
JBoss Enterprise Application Platform	Java Application Server	Windows Media Server
Ruby on Rails	Oracle WebLogic Server	

Amazon's EC2 offers IaaS (Linux or Windows machine images) and PaaS (database and application development environments).

VIRTUAL DESKTOPS

Virtual Desktop Infrastructure (VDI) refers to using a VM as a means of provisioning corporate desktops. In a typical VDI, desktop computers are replaced by low-spec, low-power thin client computers.

When the thin client starts, it boots a minimal OS, allowing the user to log on to a VM stored on the company server or cloud infrastructure. The user makes a connection to the VM using some sort of remote desktop protocol (Microsoft Remote Desktop or Citrix ICA, for instance). The thin client has to find the correct image and use an appropriate authentication mechanism. There may be a 1:1 mapping based on machine name or IP address, or the process of finding an image may be handled by a connection broker.

All application processing and data storage in the **Virtual Desktop Environment (VDE)** or workspace is performed by the server. The thin client computer only has to be powerful enough to display the screen image, play audio, and transfer mouse, key commands and video, and audio information over the network.

All data is stored on the server or in the cloud so it is easier to back up and the desktop VMs are easier to support and troubleshoot. They are better locked against unsecure user practices because any changes to the VM can easily be overwritten from the template image. With VDI, it is also easier for a company to completely offload their IT infrastructure to a third-party services company.

The main disadvantage is that in the event of a failure in the server and network infrastructure, users have no local processing ability. This can mean that downtime events may be more costly in terms of lost productivity.

VIRTUAL NIC

A virtual machine includes a virtual NIC. However, there will also need to be a physical NIC to get the thin client computer onto the network. These adapters do not have to connect to the same network. The physical NIC might be isolated to a network provisioning the VDI solution. The virtual NIC available from the virtual desktop would connect to the corporate data network and (via the organization's routers) to the Internet.

CLOUD-BASED APPLICATIONS

Application virtualization is a more limited type of VDI. Rather than run the whole client desktop as a virtual platform, the client either accesses a particular application hosted on a server or streams the application from the server to the client for local processing. This enables programmers and application administrators to ensure that the application used by clients is always updated with the latest code.

Most application virtualization solutions are based on Citrix XenApp. Microsoft has developed an App-V product within its Windows Server range. VMware has the ThinApp product.

OFF-SITE EMAIL APPLICATIONS

Traditionally, most organizations set up and configured their own email server. With cloud computing, the email server can be another off-site service. It might be something like Gmail™ or Yahoo!® Mail. It also might be part of a Office 365 Business Premium, which includes the Exchange email server service. Using an off-site email application to access these off-site email services makes it easier for users to access their mail from multiple devices and locations such as their laptop, desktop, tablet, and smart phone. The mailbox is synchronized so that no matter which device the mail is accessed from, the account accurately indicates which messages have been read, unread, deleted, or moved to other folders.

CLOUD FILE STORAGE

A variety of cloud file storage services are available. These services might be integrated into the Windows File Explorer, or they might have their own dedicated synchronization app, or both. OneDrive® is one cloud file storage service. All Office 365 users receive dedicated storage space for their account. Personal and business OneDrive accounts are separate, but can be linked. OneDrive is integrated into the Windows File Explorer and also has a dedicated OneDrive app that can be installed. OneDrive can also be accessed through a browser. Dropbox™ is another file storage service that can be accessed in the same types of ways. Other cloud file storage services that can be synchronized between all of a user's devices include iCloud® from Apple® and Google Drive™.

In addition to allowing a single user to synchronize content between all of their own devices, the user can also share the cloud storage content with other users. In this case, multiple users can simultaneously access the content to work collaboratively, or they can access it at different times. Each user's changes are typically marked with a flag or color highlighting to indicate who made changes to what content.

VIRTUAL APPLICATION STREAMING

When **virtual application streaming** is implemented, a small piece of the application is typically installed on the end user device. This is just enough of the application for the system to recognize that the application is available to the user. When the user accesses the application, additional portions of the application code are downloaded to the device. Many users only use a small portion of the features available in an application. By downloading only the portions that are being used, the streaming goes quickly, making the user unaware in most cases that the application is being streamed. If additional features are accessed from the application menu, the supporting code for those features is then downloaded. The administrator can configure the streaming application to remove all of the downloaded code, or they can configure it to retain what has been downloaded so it will be faster to load the application the next time the user wants to use it.

CLIENT PLATFORMS

Cloud-based applications can often be deployed for smart cell phones and tablets as well as for laptops and desktops. Typically, the application uses the same base code for all of these platforms, but has additional features that are better supported on laptops and desktops that would be difficult to implement with small screen size, less RAM, and less storage space on a smart phone or tablet. In other instances, the features are the same across all client platforms; it all depends on the features and purpose of the application. By streaming an application or running it in the cloud, much of the memory and storage requirements are eliminated on the client.

CONTAINER VIRTUALIZATION

Container virtualization dispenses with the idea of a hypervisor and instead enforces resource separation at the operating system level. The OS defines isolated containers for each user instance to run in. Each container is allocated CPU and memory resources, but the processes all run through the native OS kernel.

These containers may run slightly different OS distributions but cannot run guest OSs of different types (you could not run Windows or Ubuntu® in a RedHat® Linux® container, for instance). Alternatively, the containers might run separate application processes, in which case the variables and libraries required by the application process are added to the container.

One of the best-known container virtualization products is Docker (**docker.com**). Containerization is also being widely used to implement corporate workspaces on mobile devices.

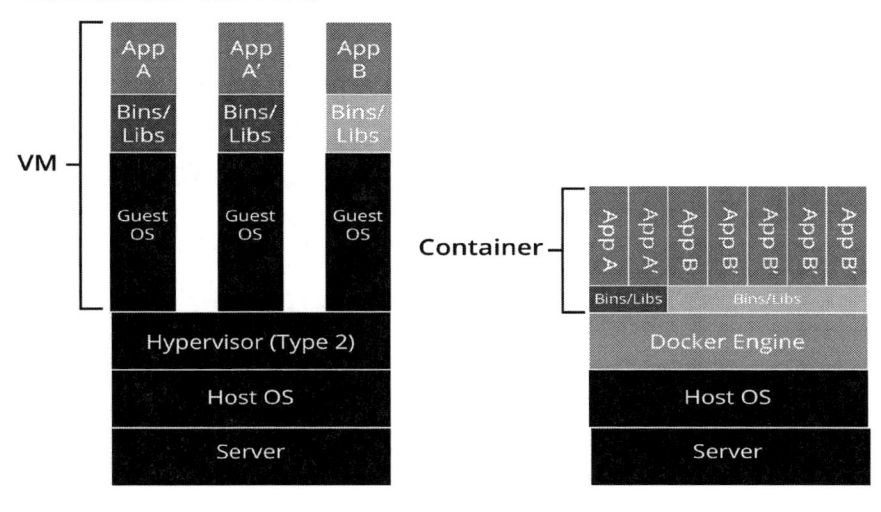

Comparison of Containers versus Virtual Machines.

CLOUD-BASED NETWORK CONTROLLERS

When you deploy a network using a mixture of local and cloud-based resources, potentially using different cloud providers, it can be difficult to obtain "visibility" of the whole network from a single management and monitoring interface. For example, you might have an overall network where clients are using multiple wired and wireless local networks to connect, there might be use of Virtual Private Networks (VPNs), some of the organization's servers might be privately controlled, but others might be hosted in the cloud, and so on.

A **cloud-based network controller** allows you to register and monitor some (or perhaps all) of these different component networks, clients, and servers. Cloud-based network controllers (and network controllers generally) depend on **Software Defined Networking (SDN)**. SDN means that network access devices—access points, switches, routers, and firewalls—can be configured using software programs and scripts.

Activity 7-2
Discussing Cloud Computing Concepts

SCENARIO
There has been a lot of talk around the office recently about cloud services. You have heard some other people touting this as the only way to go for storage. In order to be sure of yourself before you join in these conversations, you wrote down some questions and did a little research about them to make sure you know what you are talking about.

1. **How do the five components of cloud computing defined by the NIST work together to provide users with cloud computing services?**

2. **Which type of cloud would your organization be likely to use?**

3. A cloud service should exhibit rapid elasticity, allow users to access resources on-demand, and pay on a per-use basis.

   What type of service should the provider run to enable these features?

4. A company has contracted the use of a remote data center to offer exclusive access to Platform as a Service resources to its internal business users.

   How would such a cloud solution be classed?

5. When users connect to the network, they use a basic hardware terminal to access a desktop hosted on a virtualization server.

   What type of infrastructure is being deployed?

Summary

In this lesson, you examined implementation requirements for client virtualization and cloud computing. The ability to support these and other emerging technologies is very likely to have an impact on the day-to-day responsibilities of an A+ technician.

What types of client-side virtualization technologies does your organization use?

What type of cloud computing does your organization use? What other services might you recommend be implemented?

*Practice Question: Additional practice questions are available on the CompTIA CHOICE platform within the **Assessments** tile.*

Lesson 8
Supporting and Troubleshooting Laptops

LESSON INTRODUCTION

As a CompTIA® A+® technician, you will require a robust knowledge of portable computing principles. In this lesson, the focus will be on laptops and how they differ from desktop systems in terms of features, upgrade/repair procedures, and troubleshooting.

LESSON OBJECTIVES

In this lesson, you will:

- Use laptop features.
- Install and configure laptop hardware.
- Troubleshoot common laptop issues.

Topic A
Use Laptop Features

EXAM OBJECTIVES COVERED
1001-1.3 Given a scenario, use appropriate laptop features.
1001-3.1 Explain basic cable types, features, and their purposes.
1001-3.9 Given a scenario, install and configure common devices.

One of the most prevalent mobile devices in today's workplaces has to be the laptop computer. As a CompTIA A+ technician, you will be asked to select and configure laptops for different business and leisure uses. In this topic, you will focus on features that distinguish different laptop models and laptops from desktop computers.

LAPTOPS

A **laptop** is a complete portable computer system. Laptops have specialized hardware designed especially for use in a portable chassis and can run on battery or AC power. Laptops use the same sort of operating systems as desktop PCs, however, and have many upgradeable or replaceable components.

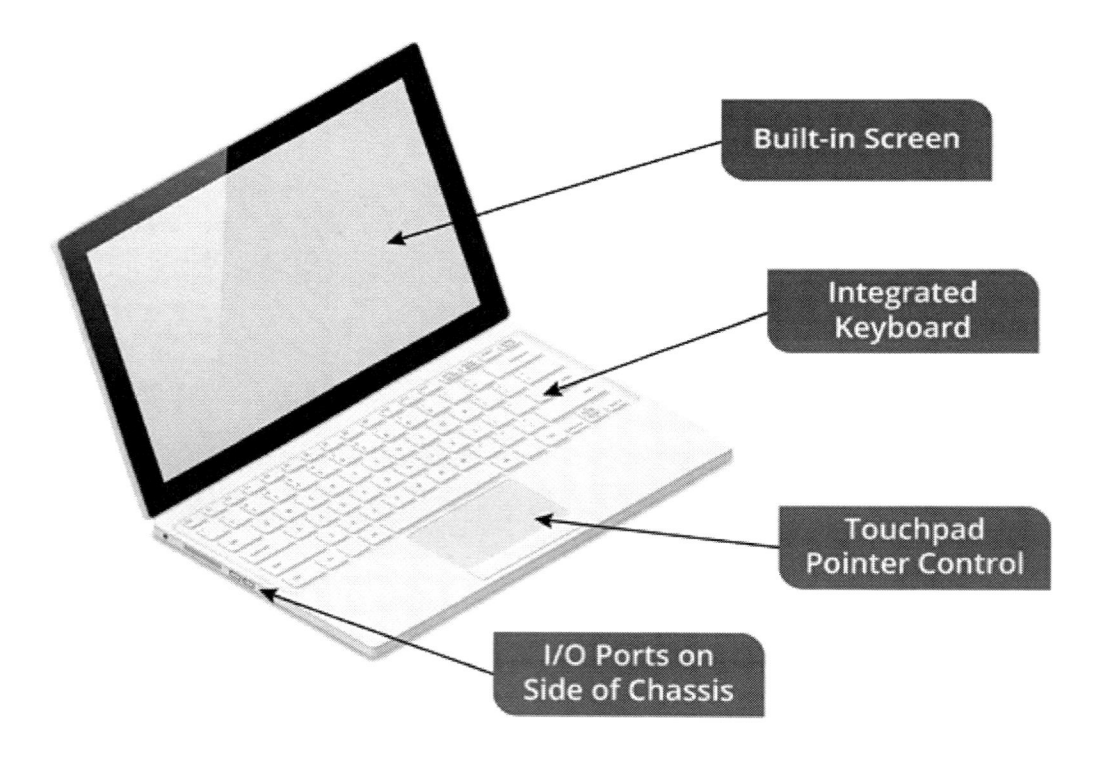

Distinctive features of a laptop computer, including the built-in screen, integrated keyboard, touchpad pointer control, and I/O ports (on both sides and rear of chassis). (Image © 123RF.com.)

Like desktops, laptops come in many different models and specifications. You could broadly categorize laptops as follows:

- **Entry Level/Budget**—basic model (often with home or business versions) featuring average components and a trade-off between features and portability.
- **Ultraportable**—very small and light machines offering extended operating time on battery power. The trade-off here is smaller screen size, lower capacity drives, and fewer peripherals.
- **Desktop Replacement**—a powerful machine with similar performance, capacity, and peripherals to a desktop PC. The trade-off is that these machines are less portable and less able to run for long on battery power.
- **Media Center**—portable home entertainment systems, featuring large screens, storage capacity, media features (such as TV tuner, video recording, and surround sound), and components capable of running the latest games.
- **Gaming Laptop**—an increasingly popular class of machine. ATI and NVIDIA are producing more graphics adapters designed for laptops, though they cannot quite match the power of desktops built for gaming.

Although laptops can use peripheral devices, the basic input and output devices are provided as integrated components.

TOUCHPADS

Almost all laptops use **touchpads** as the primary pointing device. Moving a finger over the touch-sensitive pad moves the cursor and tapping it issues a click. Touchpads also come with buttons and scroll areas to replicate the function of a mouse's scroll wheel. Most touchpads now support multi-touch or using gestures, such as a pinch to zoom the display.

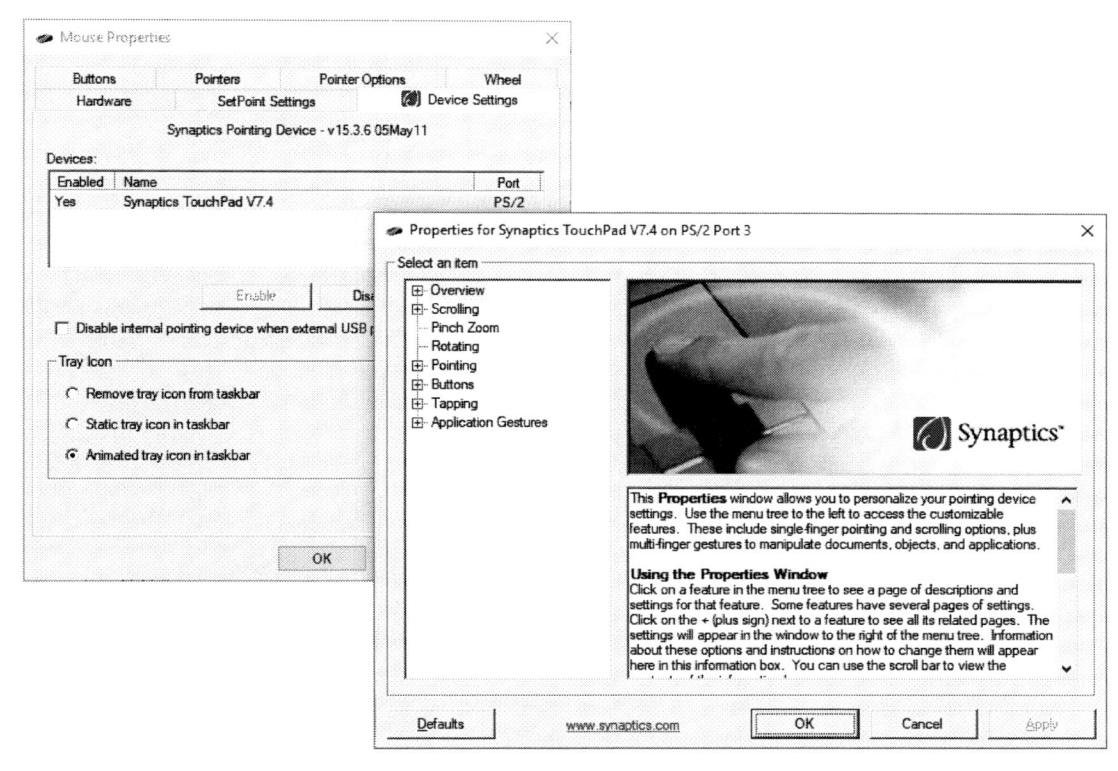

The Mouse applet in Control Panel allows you to configure both mice and touchpads—installing the vendor's driver makes extra configuration settings available.

In Windows®, the touchpad can be configured using the **Mouse** applet in Control Panel. Installing the manufacturer's driver will make the device-specific options available, such as configuring scroll areas or gesture support.

> **Note:** When you are using a touchpad, it is easy to brush the pad accidentally and for this to be interpreted as a click event. If this happens a lot, adjust the sensitivity setting or completely disable the **Tap to click** functionality.

KEYBOARDS

Apart from being flatter and more compact, a laptop keyboard is similar to a desktop keyboard. The main difference is the Function (Fn) keys operate using the **Fn** key with the top row of numerals.

> **Note:** Actually, many desktop keyboards also include function keys to support use as an external keyboard for a laptop. If not being used with a laptop, these keys can be mapped to perform different functions.

A laptop keyboard with function and media control keys across the top.

These Function (Fn) keys perform laptop-specific functions indicated by distinctive icons. Typical functions include:

- **Display**—toggle the video feed between the built-in laptop display, the built-in display and an external monitor (dual display), and an external monitor only.
- **Screen orientation**—some tablet/laptop hybrids have rotatable screens while others can be used in tablet mode and can switch the screen orientation automatically between portrait and landscape modes depending on how the device is being held. A screen orientation function key will allow you to choose whether to lock the screen in one orientation.
- **Wireless/Bluetooth/Cellular/GPS**—toggle the radio for Wi-Fi, Bluetooth®, cellular data, and/or Global Positioning System (GPS) on and off. Each of these settings might be separately configurable or be selectively disabled via different toggle states and indicators. There is often an airplane mode toggle to completely disable all wireless functions.
- **Volume**—adjust the sound up, down, or off (mute).
- **Screen brightness**—dim or brighten the built-in display.
- **Keyboard backlight**—illuminate the keys (useful for typing in low light).
- **Touchpad**—sometimes the touchpad can interfere with typing, causing the cursor to jump around. A touchpad toggle allows you to enable or disable it as required.
- **Media options**—this allows control over audio and video playback, such as stop, pause, fast forward, and rewind controls, or skipping between tracks.

Depending on the size of the chassis, a laptop keyboard may not support a numeric keypad. In this case, some of the ordinary keys may function as a keypad in conjunction with **NumLock** or the **Fn** key.

> **Note:** One issue to watch out for in laptop keyboards and chassis designs is flex, where the board buckles slightly when keys are pressed. None of the input devices on a laptop are really suitable for sustained use. An external keyboard and/or mouse can of course be connected using a USB or wireless port.

CONFIGURATION OF KEYBOARD SETTINGS

In Windows, you use the **Keyboard** applet in Control Panel or Windows Settings to configure options such as the repeat rate and sensitivity for keys. The vendor driver may make additional settings available for configuring function keys.

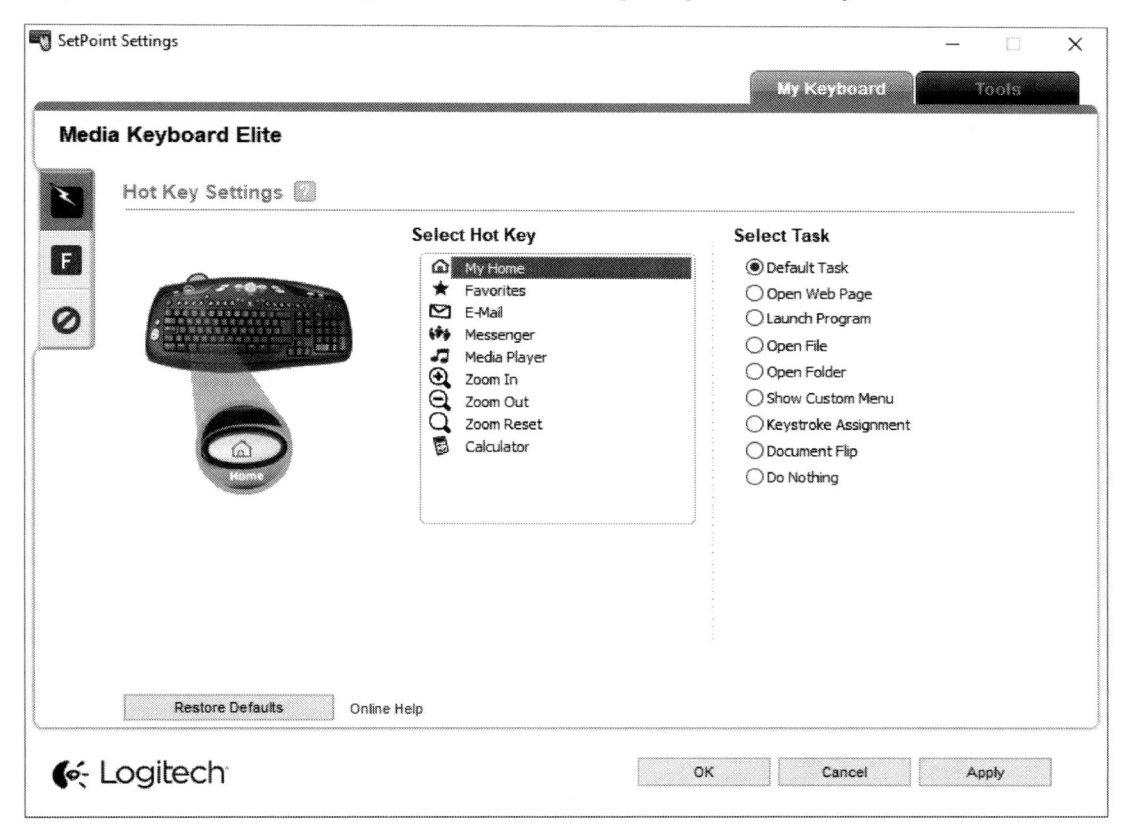

Logitech SetPoint software for configuring programmable keys and hot keys.

DISPLAYS AND TOUCHSCREENS

Most modern laptop displays are also **touchscreens** of one kind or another. Some can be used with a stylus as well as (or instead of) finger touch.

Another important point to note about the laptop display screen is that it holds the antenna wires for the Wi-Fi adapter. These are connected to the adapter via internal wiring.

ROTATING OR REMOVABLE SCREENS

Some laptops are based on tablet hybrid form factors where the touchscreen display can be fully flipped or rotated between portrait and landscape orientations. Another approach, used on Microsoft's Surface® tablets, is for the keyboard portion of the laptop to be detachable and for the screen to work independently as a tablet.

> **Note:** *In Windows 10, tablet mode for the Start Screen is selected automatically (by default) on hybrid devices. For example, removing the keyboard from a Microsoft Surface tablet or folding the screen of an HP X360 device over through 360 degrees puts Windows 10 into tablet mode. You can use Windows 10 settings to manually select tablet mode and to configure these automatic behaviors.*

TOUCHSCREEN CONFIGURATION

In Windows, touchscreen options are configured using the **Tablet PC Settings** and **Pen and Touch** applets.

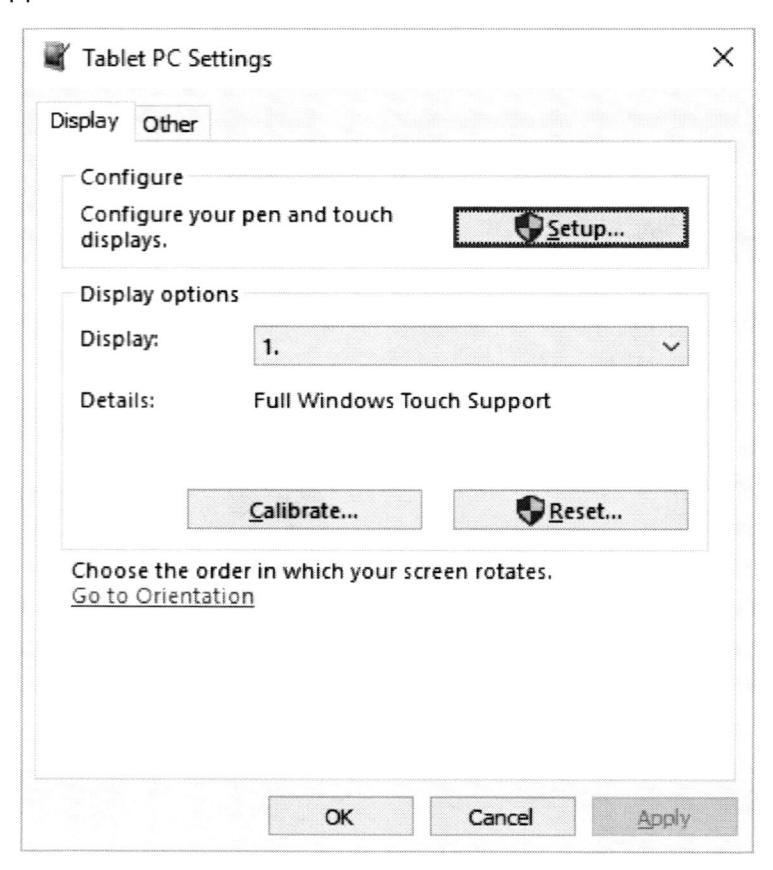

Use the Tablet PC Control Panel applet to set up or calibrate a touchscreen. (Screenshot used with permission from Microsoft.)

You can use **Tablet PC Settings** to calibrate the display and set options for orientation and left- or right-handed use, and you can use **Pen and Touch** to configure gesture settings, such as using tap-and-hold to trigger a right-mouse click event.

EXPANSION OPTIONS

Laptops ship with standard wired ports for connectivity. The ports are usually arranged on the left and right edges. Older laptops might have ports at the back of the chassis. There will be at least one video port for an external display device, typically HDMI or DisplayPort/Thunderbolt, but possibly VGA or DVI on older laptops. There will also be a number of USB Type A ports and one or more USB Type C ports on a modern laptop, one of which may also function as a Thunderbolt port.

Other standard ports include microphone and speaker jacks and RJ-45 (Ethernet) for networking. Finally, a laptop might come with a memory card reader.

USB provides a simple means of adding or upgrading an adapter without having to open the laptop chassis. USB adapters (or "dongles") can provide a wide range of functionality:

- **USB to RJ-45**—provide an Ethernet port for a laptop or mobile device. Ultrathin laptops often omit a built-in RJ-45 port as it is too tall to fit in the chassis.

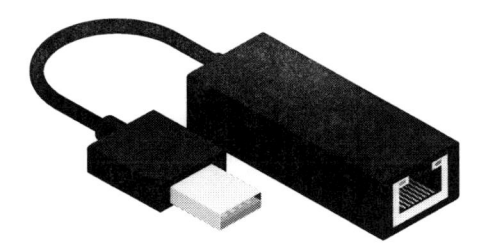

USB to Ethernet adapter. (Image © 123RF.com.)

- **USB to Wi-Fi/Bluetooth**—this might be used to upgrade to a better Wi-Fi standard than the laptop's built-in adapter. Most dongles will also function as a Bluetooth adapter. Some Wi-Fi dongles are compact but those lacking large antennas may not perform well; the drawback of large antennas is, of course, that they protrude significantly.
- **USB Optical Drive**—most ultraportable laptops no longer feature optical drives as they cannot fit within the ultrathin chassis.

PORT REPLICATORS

A **port replicator** usually attaches to a special connector on the back or underside of a portable computer. It provides a full complement of ports for devices such as keyboards, monitors, mice, and network connections. A replicator does not normally add any other functionality to the portable computer.

A port replicator. (Image by Elnur Amikishiyev © 123RF.com.)

DOCKING STATIONS

A **docking station** is a sophisticated port replicator that may support add-in cards or drives via a media bay. When docked, a portable computer can function like a desktop machine or use additional features, such as a full size expansion card.

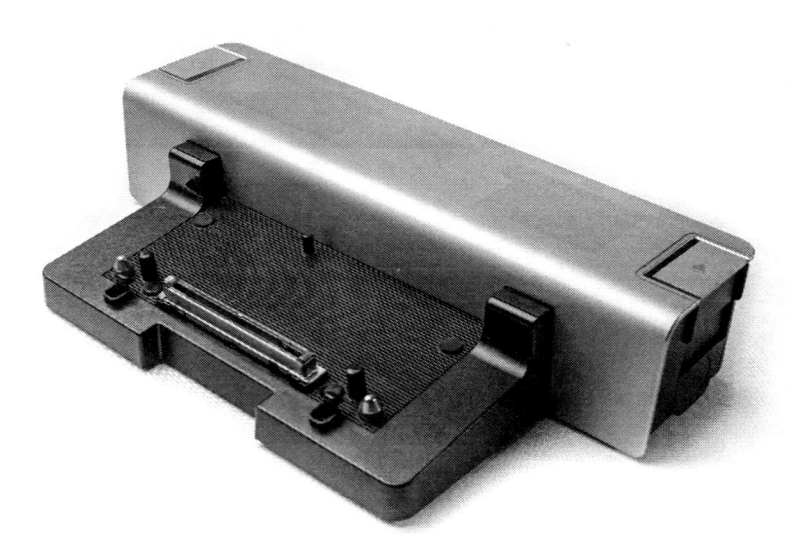

A laptop docking station. (Image by Luca Lorenzelli © 123RF.com.)

Note: *Most port replicators and docking stations use proprietary connectors. There are USB versions but their performance can be a bit erratic.*

PHYSICAL LOCKS

Being so portable makes laptops easy devices to steal. Many cable locks are available to chain the laptop to a desk. These are typically either key or combination operated. If key operated, make sure you record the key code in case you need to get a replacement.

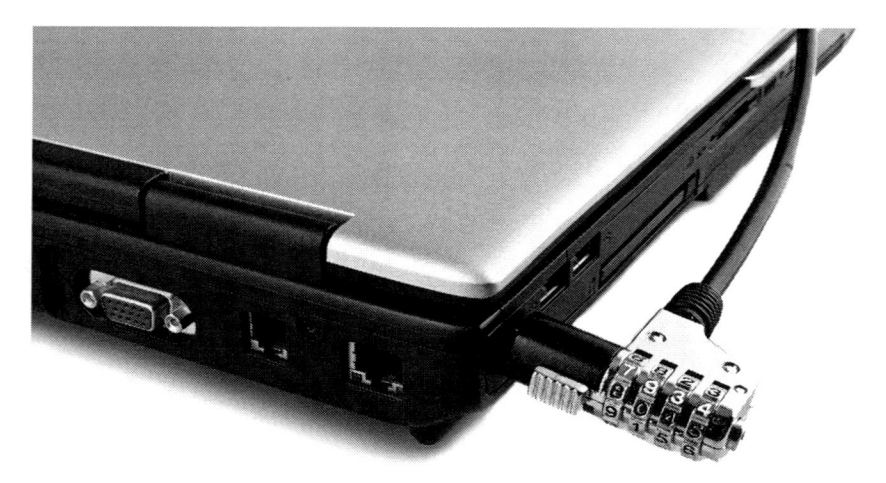

Kensington laptop locks. (Image by © 123RF.com.)

Most laptops come with a connection point for a Kensington lock in the chassis.

Activity 8-1
Discussing Laptop Features

SCENARIO
Answer the following questions to check your understanding of the topic.

1. What feature would you expect to find on a modern touchpad, compared to older models?

2. True or false? Touchpad settings would be configured via the Touch applet in Windows Control Panel.

3. What two display settings would you expect to be able to control via a laptop's Fn keys?

4. What device would you use to extend the functionality of a laptop while sitting at a desk?

5. What connectivity issue is resolved by providing a USB-to-RJ-45 dongle?

6. What is the brand name of the standard cable lock security system for laptops?

Topic B
Install and Configure Laptop Hardware

EXAM OBJECTIVES COVERED
1001-1.1 Given a scenario, install and configure laptop hardware and components.
1001-1.2 Given a scenario, install components within the display of a laptop.
1001-5.5 Given a scenario, troubleshoot common mobile device issues while adhering to the appropriate procedures.

There will be situations where dealing with external components won't completely address the issues or problems a user is having with his or her laptop. You will need to be able to install and configure internal laptop hardware components.

LAPTOP DISASSEMBLY PROCESSES

When it comes to performing upgrades or replacing parts, there are some issues specific to laptops that you should be aware of.

Note: Only open a laptop to access internal components if it is no longer under warranty or if you are an authorized technician for the laptop brand.

HAND TOOLS AND PARTS

Laptops use smaller screws than are found on desktops. You may find it useful to obtain a set of jeweler's screwdrivers and other appropriate hand tools. It is also much easier to strip the screws—remove the notch for the screwdriver—take care and use an appropriately sized screwdriver!

You need to document the location of screws of a specific size and the location and orientation of ribbon cables and other connectors. It can be very easy to remove them quickly during disassembly and then to face a puzzle during reassembly.

Note: A useful tip is to take a photo of the underside of the laptop and print it out. As you remove screws, tape them to the relevant point in your picture. This ensures you will not lose any and will know which screw goes where. Photograph each stage of disassembly so you know where to re-fit cables and connectors.

As with a desktop, organize parts that you remove or have ready for installation carefully. Keep the parts away from your main work area so that you do not damage them by mistake. Keep static-sensitive parts, such as the CPU, memory, and adapter cards, in anti-static packaging.

FORM FACTORS AND PLASTICS/FRAMES

Many laptops are built using proprietary components and scope for customization and upgrade is fairly limited. However, as laptops have become cheaper and more popular, there are more vendors offering "bare bones" laptops and compatible components.

The laptop chassis incorporates the motherboard, power supply, display screen, keypad, and touchpad. The plastics or aluminum frames are the hard surfaces that cover the internal components of the laptop. They are secured using either small screws or pressure tabs. Note that screws may be covered by rubber or plastic tabs.

Make sure you obtain the manufacturer's service documentation before commencing any upgrade or replacement work. This should explain how to disassemble the chassis and remove tricky items, such as plastic bezels, without damaging them. You should only perform this work if a warranty option is not available.

LAPTOP FRUs

Laptops have fewer field replaceable units (FRUs) than desktops. That said, laptop components and designs have become better standardized. Using components sourced from the laptop vendor is still recommended, but basic upgrade options, such as memory and disks, have become much simpler as it reduces warranty support costs for the vendors.

Some FRUs can be accessed easily by removing a screw plate on the back cover (underside) of the laptop. This method generally provides access to the disk drive, optical drive, memory modules, and possibly Mini PCIe adapters such as Wi-Fi cards and modems. The connectors can usually be flipped up and down to allow easy insertion and removal.

MASS STORAGE FOR LAPTOPS

Laptops use the same kind of mass storage devices as PCs:

- Hard Disk Drive (HDD)—magnetic disk technology offering low cost per gigabyte storage.
- Solid State Drive (SSD)—flash memory technology offering much faster performance and less weight and power consumption. SSDs are now the mainstream choice for laptops.
- Hybrid—an HDD with a large (8 GB+) cache of flash memory, offering a performance boost compared to basic HDDs.

A laptop typically supports one internal mass storage device only, with extra storage attached to an external port. The internal drive can usually be accessed via a panel, but you may have to open the chassis on some models.

Laptop mass storage drives are usually 2.5" form factor though sometimes the 1.8" form factor is used. Compared to 3.5" desktop versions, magnetic 2.5" HDDs tend to be slower (usually 5400 rpm models) and lower capacity. Within the 2.5" form factor, there are also reduced height units designed for ultraportable laptops. A standard 2.5" drive has a z-height of 9.5 mm; an ultraportable laptop might require a 7 mm (thin) or 5 mm (ultrathin) drive.

A laptop HDD with SATA interface. (Image © 123RF.com).

Magnetic and hybrid drives use ordinary SATA data and power connectors, though the connectors on the drive mate directly to a port in the drive bay, without the use of a cable. 1.8" drive bays might require the use of the Micro SATA (μSATA or uSATA) connector.

SSD flash storage devices can also use the SATA interface and connector form factors but could also use an adapter or memory card-like interface:

- mSATA—an SSD might be housed on a card with a Mini-SATA (mSATA) interface. These cards resemble Mini PCIe cards but are not physically compatible with Mini PCIe slots. mSATA uses the SATA bus, so the maximum transfer speed is 6 Gbps.
- M.2—this is a new set of form factors for mini card interfaces. An M.2 SSD usually interfaces with the PCI Express bus, allowing much higher bus speeds than SATA. M.2 adapters can be different lengths (42 mm, 60 mm, 80 mm, or 110 mm) so you should check that any given adapter will fit within the laptop chassis. 80 mm (M.2 2280) is the most popular length for laptop SSDs.

Note: The specific M.2 form factor is written as 22 nn, where nn is the length. "22" refers to the card width, all of which are 22 mm.

LAPTOP RAM

Laptop DDR SDRAM is packaged in small modules called **Small Outline DIMM (SODIMM)**. Both DDR and DDR2 use 200-pin packages, but the key position for DDR2 is slightly different to prevent insertion in a slot designed for DDR. DDR3 uses a 204-pin SODIMM module whereas DDR4 modules have 260 pins.

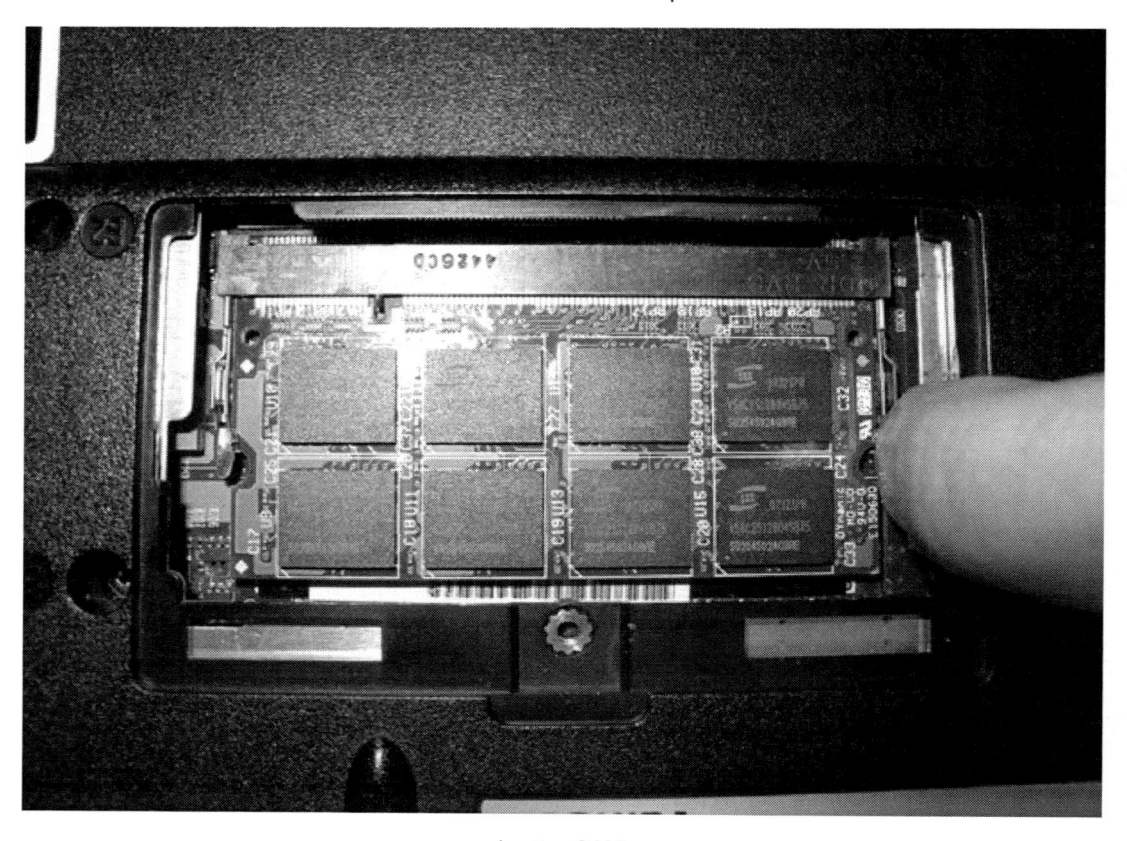

Laptop RAM.

The memory is typically fitted into slots that pop-up at a 45° angle to allow the chips to be inserted or removed. Sometimes one of the memory slots is easily accessible via a panel but another requires more extensive disassembly of the chassis to access.

> **Note:** There are a couple of other laptop memory module form factors, including Mini-DIMM and Micro-DIMM. These are smaller than SODIMM and used on some ultraportable models. Always check the vendor documentation before obtaining parts for upgrade or replacement.

ADAPTER CARDS FOR LAPTOPS

Depending on the design, adapters for modems, wireless cards, and SSD storage cards may be accessible and replaceable via screw-down panels. Note that there are a number of adapter formats, notably Mini PCIe, mSATA, and M.2, none of which are compatible with one another.

You can obtain "wireless" mini PCIe or M.2 adapters for laptops that will provide some combination of Wi-Fi, Bluetooth, and/or cellular data (4G LTE) connectivity. Remember that when upgrading this type of adapter, you need to re-connect the antenna wires used by the old adapter or install a new antenna kit. The antenna wires are usually routed around the screen in the laptop's lid. The antenna connections can be tricky and are quite delicate, so take care.

If installing an adapter with cellular functionality, remember to insert the SIM as well.

OPTICAL DRIVES FOR LAPTOPS

Laptops use slimline optical drive units. The unit is typically accessible from the bottom panel. As with a hard drive, the unit mates with a fixed SATA data and power connector at the back of the drive bay. You will typically need to replace the device with the same Original Equipment Manufacturer (OEM) part, or at least the same caddy design.

> **Note:** Optical drives are of decreasing relevance to mobile computing. It is more cost-effective to use an external drive as a replacement. You might want to consider replacing an optical drive with a second hard drive. The hard drive must be fitted to a caddy that fits the optical drive bay.

> **Note:** To learn more, check the **Video** tile on the CHOICE Course screen for any videos that supplement the content for this lesson.

Access the Checklist tile on your CHOICE Course screen for reference information and job aids on How to Upgrade Laptop System Components.

LAPTOP CPU AND MOTHERBOARD UPGRADES

The CPU is generally upgradeable as long as the new device is supported by the motherboard.

> **Note:** Some laptop CPUs—those that use Ball Grid Array (BGA) sockets—are soldered to the motherboard and, therefore, are not upgradeable.

The CPU is covered by a heatpipe, rather than a heat sink. This is a long, flat metal strip that conducts heat toward the fan. Otherwise, it is locked into place in much the same way as a desktop CPU.

There will be few occasions when it is economical to replace the system board itself. If you do need to do so, detach the stand-offs that hold the board to the chassis. If upgrading the system board, you will probably also need to update the chipset driver (or notebook system software) and allow Windows to discover the new device using Plug-and-Play.

LAPTOP VIDEO CARD UPGRADES

Laptops often use an integrated graphics adapter that is part of the system chipset or CPU, especially at the lower end of the market. Integrated graphics can be advantageous in terms of battery life and cooling. However, as laptops get used more and more as desktop replacements, particularly as game machines, dedicated graphics becomes important. Cheaper graphics adapters may also feature a limited amount of onboard memory (or none at all). In this scenario, they share system memory with the CPU. Obviously, this decreases the amount of system memory available.

Few laptop video cards are actually upgradeable, though they may be replaceable. This is because high-end cards tend to have specific power and cooling requirements and a modular approach is not possible given the limited space available.

LAPTOP COMPONENT REPLACEMENT

There are other components that you may need to replace to effect repairs. In most cases, you will need to source "like-for-like" replacements to ensure the proper fit.

LAPTOP DISPLAY AND DIGITIZER REPLACEMENT

A built-in laptop display will be one of three types:

- LCD (TFT) with fluorescent backlight—this has been the standard display technology for the last few years. The backlight is a fluorescent bulb that illuminates the image, making it bright and clear. An inverter supplies the correct AC voltage to the backlight from the laptop's DC power circuits.
- LCD with LED backlight—manufacturers are increasingly switching to this technology. LED backlights do not require an inverter.
- OLED—this technology is expensive at the screen size required by laptops and there are issues with power draw and battery life. Consequently, OLED has not really established itself as a mainstream choice for laptop displays.

When a laptop has a touchscreen display, it will also have a **digitizer** fitted. The digitizer is sandwiched between a layer of glass and the LCD display. Analog signals are created when you tap or swipe the surface of the display. The digitizer is connected to the laptop with a flexible digitizer cable. A grid of sensors is activated when you tap or swipe the screen. The information from the sensors is sent through the digitizer cable to a circuit that converts the analog signal to a digital signal.

If you need to replace a display, digitizer, or inverter, make a very careful record of how the existing unit is connected to the video card and system board, including the routing of any cables.

> *Note: Replacing these components is relatively tricky and upgrading them can be even more complex. Make sure you get specific information or advice for the model of laptop you are servicing.*

LAPTOP SPEAKER REPLACEMENT

To replace laptop speakers, you will need to disassemble the laptop to the system board. Make sure you obtain replacement speakers that are compatible with your laptop model. Remove the old speakers and fit the new ones, remembering to connect the audio cable.

LAPTOP INPUT DEVICE REPLACEMENT

Laptop input devices include keyboards, touchpads, webcams, microphones, and smart card readers.

KEYBOARDS AND TOUCHPADS

When you are replacing components like the keyboard and touchpad, you will almost always need to use the same parts. Each part connects to the motherboard via a data cable, typically a flat ribbon type. Accessing the parts for removal and replacement might require complete disassembly or might be relatively straightforward—check the service documentation.

> **Note:** *If you are upgrading the keyboard or touchpad (rather than replacing the same part), you may need to install a new driver and configure settings via the Mouse and Keyboard applets.*

WEBCAMS AND MICROPHONES

Almost all laptops come with built-in webcams and microphones. The webcam is normally positioned at the top of the display with an LED to show whether it is active.

> **Note:** *Laptop users are understandably worried about the privacy implications of built-in webcams. If the laptop is infected with malware, it is usually possible for the malware to enable the webcam without activating the LED.*

The microphone will be positioned somewhere on the laptop chassis. There will also be microphone and speaker 3.5 mm jacks for the connection of a headset or external speakers.

SMART CARD READERS

A smart card reader is a feature of enterprise laptops supporting authentication using digital smart cards. You will typically need to replace this with the same OEM part. The laptop will probably need to be completely disassembled to access the device. It is connected to the system board by a data cable.

LAPTOP POWER SUPPLIES

Portable computers can work off both building power and battery operation.

AC ADAPTERS

To operate from building power, the laptop needs a power supply that can convert from the AC (Alternating Current) supplied by the power company to the DC (Direct Current) voltages used by the laptop's components. The power supply is provided as an external **AC adapter**.

AC adapters are normally universal (or auto-switching) and can operate from any 110-240 VAC 50/60 Hz supply (check the label to confirm). Some adapters (notably some sold with US machines) are fixed-input (for instance, they only work with a 115 VAC supply or have to be manually switched to the correct input).

An AC adapter for an HP laptop. (Image by Olga Popova © 123RF.com.)

> **Note:** Plugging a fixed-input 240 V adapter into a 110 V supply won't cause any damage (though the laptop won't work), but plugging a fixed-input 110 V adapter into a 240 V supply will.

> **Note:** When you are using a laptop abroad, in addition to a universal AC adapter, you will also need a power plug adapter to fit the type of socket used in that country. It is also best to get a surge protector designed for the voltage used in the country too. This helps to protect the laptop from damage.

AC adapters are also rated for their power output (ranging from around 65-120 W). Again, this information will be printed on the adapter label. Output (W) is calculated by multiplying voltage (V) by current (I). A larger output will be able to power more peripheral devices.

The power output of adapters and batteries can vary, so using an adapter designed for an ultra-mobile model probably won't work with a desktop replacement, even if it's the same brand. A 90 W adapter should be sufficient for most uses, but always check the documentation carefully. If you need to replace the power supply, it is best to get the manufacturer's recommended model, though universal AC adapters are available. These typically ship with a number of DC power connectors, which vary quite widely in size. They also have variable voltage settings. You must set the voltage correctly before plugging it in.

> **Note:** Most laptops will display a message at boot time if an underpowered AC adapter or battery is present.

DC JACK REPLACEMENT

It is relatively common for the DC jack to fail. The port can become loose over time or the jack itself can become separated from the motherboard. Replacing a DC jack means disassembling the laptop, de-soldering and removing the old jack, then soldering the new jack into place. Most laptop DC jacks are specific to the manufacturer and even the laptop model.

Replacement DC jack—the part is soldered to the motherboard via the contact pin seen on the right. (Image by Sergey Kolesnikov © 123RF.com.)

BATTERY POWER

Laptop computers use removable, rechargeable Lithium ion (Li-ion) battery packs. Li-ion batteries have good storage capacity and hold their charge well. They are typically available in 6, 9, or 12 cell versions, with more cells providing for a longer charge.

Before inserting or removing the battery pack, you must always turn the machine off and unplug it from the AC wall outlet. A portable battery is usually removed by releasing catches on the back or underside of the laptop.

A removable laptop battery pack. (Image by cristi180884 © 123RF.com.)

A portable computer's battery can be charged in three ways:

- Plug the computer into an AC wall outlet with the computer turned off. This method is called a quick charge. It takes a couple of hours to fully charge a flat battery.
- Charge the battery while the computer is plugged into an AC wall outlet and turned on. This method is called a trickle charge. Trickle charging is slower because the primary use of power is for operating the PC, rather than for charging the battery. It can take several hours to charge a battery while the machine is turned on.
- Use a battery charger. This method charges the battery while it is not in the computer, but involves purchasing an extra charging unit.

To maximize battery life, different battery types require different charging regimes. Always consult the manufacturer's instructions for obtaining optimal battery life for a specific product. Modern Li-ion batteries should not be allowed to fully discharge, as this reduces battery life. They benefit from regular charging and have circuitry to prevent over-charging. However, some degree of caution should be exercised when leaving batteries to recharge unattended (for example, overnight) as this circuitry has been known to fail. Do not leave a battery charger close to flammable material and ensure there is plenty of ventilation around the unit.

Li-ion batteries are also sensitive to heat. If storing a Li-ion battery, reduce the charge to 40% and store at below 20° C.

Note: Li-ion batteries hold less charge as they age and typically have a maximum usable life of around 2-3 years. If you charge a battery and the run time is substantially decreased, you may need to purchase a new battery.

*Note: To learn more, check the **Video** tile on the CHOICE Course screen for any videos that supplement the content for this lesson.*

Activity 8-2
Discussing Laptop Hardware Installation and Configuration

SCENARIO
Answer the following questions to check your understanding of the topic.

1. **What is the process for installing memory in a laptop?**

2. **What type of standard adapter card might be used to connect internal FRU devices to the motherboard of a laptop?**

3. **What distinguishes a magnetic hard drive designed for a laptop from one designed for a PC?**

4. A user reports that when they plug in anything to a USB port on the laptop, the device is not recognized by the system.

    Is this something you can easily repair?

5. Several laptops need to be replaced in the next fiscal cycle, but that doesn't begin for several months. You want to improve functionality as much as possible by upgrading or replacing components in some of the laptops that are having problems.

   Which items are most easily replaced in a laptop?

Activity 8-3
Installing and Configuring Laptop Hardware

BEFORE YOU BEGIN
Read the following notes carefully before you start:
- Create a clean work environment with plenty of working space.
- Gather all necessary tools and equipment. A notepad and pen will be useful for making diagrams and notes.
- Implement anti-static and safety procedures.
- Make sure that the laptop is powered off and disconnected from building and battery power before proceeding.
- Always take time and care.
- Always place static-sensitive equipment such as processors and memory in anti-static bags.

SCENARIO
In the first part of the activity, you will disassemble a laptop using these steps as your guidelines. Check with your instructor for any extra instructions. Your instructor may not want you to completely disassemble the laptop due to the risk of breaking plastics, etc. If so, make a note now of which step you are to stop at.

In the second part of the activity, you will reassemble a laptop, working from the notes made by your partner.

---

1. Shut down Windows and turn off your laptop.

2. Disconnect all peripherals (keyboard, mouse, and monitor), removable storage (media bay or memory card), and power cables from the system unit. Place these in a tidy manner under your workbench (or wherever your instructor tells you to).

3. Remove the laptop battery and store it safely. Hold down the laptop power button for 30 seconds.

4. With the lid shut, flip the laptop and use your notepad and pen to make a diagram of the existing layout of cut-out panels and drives, plus their screw locations.
   Some screws may be covered by caps or rubber feet.

5. Remove each cut-out and its component, making a careful note of how to reconnect any wires and cables attached to adapter cards. Carefully put each component in an anti-static bag and the screws in a container, using a system to identify which screw is used at any given location.

6. If you are continuing from here, release the screws that secure the chassis and the plastics (palm rest and touchpad assembly). Carefully put the screws in a container, using a system to identify which screw is used at any given location.

7. Flip the laptop over again, and open the lid. Remove the plastic bezel at the top of the keyboard. This might be difficult but take care not to snap it. When lifting the bezel, take care to discover whether any cables are connected to it. If there are, unplug them and make a note of how they should be re-attached.

8. Remove the keyboard by releasing the screws that secure it, then unplugging the ribbon cable. Record how the cable should be reattached, then store the components.

9. Disconnect the LCD cable and LCD power connector connecting the display to the motherboard. There is also likely to be a cable connecting the radio antenna (running around the screen) to the wireless adapter. Again, make a careful note of how to reconnect these components.

10. Remove the LCD panel, taking care to handle and store it safely, as it is fragile.

11. Locate any remaining cables preventing disassembly of the top panel (touchpad, audio connectors, and power button, for instance) taking care to note how they should be reconnected.

12. Remove any internal drive cages or heat pipes covering the components you want to inspect. As with a desktop, make a careful note of how fan power connectors are attached.

    Note: This concludes the first part of the activity.

13. When you and your partner have completed the first part of the activity, swap places and completely reassemble your partner's laptop. Allow them to access any notes and diagrams you have made, and tell them of any particular difficulties you had during disassembly.

14. Reboot the laptop that you just reassembled. If it does not reboot, or if there are errors when you try to resolve the problem, ask your instructor for guidance.

Topic C
Troubleshoot Common Laptop Issues

EXAM OBJECTIVES COVERED
1001-5.5 Given a scenario, troubleshoot common mobile device issues while adhering to the appropriate procedures.

Part of your duties as a CompTIA A+ technician will be helping users when they encounter problems with their mobile devices. In this topic, you will troubleshoot issues with laptop hardware and associated mobile app issues.

COMMON LAPTOP ISSUES

The same basic approach to troubleshooting applies for laptops as it does for desktop PCs, though there are some issues specific to laptops and other portable devices that you should be aware of.

- Display issues, including problems with built-in display devices, touchscreens, and external displays.
- Power and cooling issues.
- Input and output device issues.
- Communication and connectivity issues.
- Issues with GPS and location services.
- OS and app issues, such as performance problems and unresponsive apps.

DISPLAY ISSUES

Display issues include:

- **Problems with a built-in display.** When you are troubleshooting a laptop display, you will often need to take into account the use of the integrated display and/or an external display and how to isolate a problem to a particular component, such as either display, the video card, or a display toggle.

  The components most likely to fail on an older LCD screen are the backlight and inverter. The backlight is a fluorescent bulb that illuminates the image, making it bright and clear. The inverter supplies the correct AC voltage to the backlight. If the display has been flickering or if the image is very dim, but still present, suspect a problem with the backlight or inverter rather than the LCD itself. As you may know if you have fluorescent lighting at home, the inverter is more likely to fail than the tube itself.

  Many laptops now use LED arrays for the backlight. As these work off DC power, there is no inverter.

  The LCD is only likely to need replacing if it gets physically damaged.

  > *Note: As well as the display itself, it is fairly common for the plastics around the case to get cracked or broken and for the hinges on the lid to wear out. The plastics are mostly cosmetic (though a bad break might expose the laptop's internal components to greater risks) but if the hinges no longer hold up the screen, they will have to be replaced.*

The backlight, inverter, or screen on a laptop can be replaced by unscrewing the plastic bezel (the screws will be concealed by rubber stoppers). Take care not to damage the connectors once the panel has been freed from its housing.
- **Problems with a touchscreen.** Common touchscreen issues include:
  - Touchscreen is not responsive.
  - Touchscreen doesn't act as expected.
- **Problems with an external display.** External display issues include:
  - No image on external display.
  - Wrong image on external display.
  - External display image is too large or too small.

GUIDELINES FOR TROUBLESHOOTING DISPLAY ISSUES

*Note: All of the Guidelines for this lesson are available as checklists from the **Checklist** tile on the CHOICE Course screen.*

Here are some guidelines for troubleshooting display issues.

TROUBLESHOOT BUILT-IN DISPLAY ISSUES
Consider these guidelines when you need to troubleshoot built-in display issues:
- Determine whether the source of the problem is the integrated display, an external display, or other component of the display subsystem.
  - First check that the video card is good by using an external monitor. Toggle the appropriate **Fn** key—usually **Fn+4** or **Fn+8**. Alternatively, there should be a very dim image on the LCD if the graphics adapter is functioning but the backlight/inverter has failed.
  - Ensure the laptop is switched to using the built-in display again. Check that power management settings are not set to an energy saving mode that disables or dims the backlight.
  - Check that a cutoff switch (a small plastic pin near the hinge connecting the LCD to the rest of the chassis) is not stuck. When it is depressed, power to the backlight is switched off.
  - If all these tests are negative, the backlight, inverter, or cable has failed. If the backlight flickers (or has been flickering before complete failure), there's more likely to be a problem with the inverter. An inverter can be tested using a bulb or multimeter, but at this point you will probably need to book the laptop in for repair or use it with an external monitor only.
- Check for physical damage. If the display is damaged (if it has been bent or dented, for example), this can cause pixelation problems—areas of the image break down with mis-coloring, blockiness, or jaggedness.
- Check the resolution. LCDs are best used at the native resolution. Any other resolution will produce some distortion in the image, which isn't a sign of a fault in the screen itself. Also, fast changing images (such as those produced by video playback) can produce artifacts on low quality screens.
- Check the driver. When updating the driver for a display adapter, check whether the laptop vendor has released their own driver. Laptops often contain OEM (Original Equipment Manufacturer) versions of graphics adapters and you need to use the system vendor's driver rather than the retail driver.

TROUBLESHOOT TOUCHSCREEN ISSUES
Consider these guidelines when you need to troubleshoot touchscreen issues such as unresponsive or misbehaving touchscreens:

- Verify that the touchscreen is clean.
- Look for evidence that the laptop might have been dropped or severely damaged.
- Try using the device in a different location in case some source of electromagnetic interference (EMI) is affecting the operation of the touchscreen.
- If the laptop has just been serviced, check that the right wires are still connected in the right places for the digitizer to function. Remember to ask "What has changed?"
- If you cannot identify an obvious physical problem, you should attempt to rule out a software problem before suspecting a more serious hardware problem.
  - In many cases, a restart may solve the problem.
  - In Windows, you can also try uninstalling the touchscreen driver and reinstalling the device, using the latest driver if possible.
  - You could also try running the calibration utility.

Note: Removing a faulty digitizer from an existing display can be tricky. It might be cheaper to replace the whole unit, depending on the cost of parts.

TROUBLESHOOT EXTERNAL DISPLAY ISSUES

Consider these guidelines as you troubleshoot external display issues such as no image or wrong image on an external display, or if the external display image is too large or too small:

- A keyboard toggle switch cuts the display between built-in only, both simultaneously, and external only. Verify this switch is set properly.
- Windows display settings control whether the external display duplicates or extends the built-in one. If there is no external image and the toggle button is set correctly, after checking other obvious things (Is the external display switched on? Is it in power-saving mode? Is it set to the correct input mode? Is the cable connected?), check that the resolution for the external display is appropriate.
- Look for updated drivers for the graphics adapter and laptop chipset (system software).
- Try a different display unit and/or cable to rule out hardware problems.

Note: If the external display is connected via a cable, try using a different (known good) cable. If the display is using a wireless connection, such as Miracast or Wi-Fi Direct, check that both device and display support the same standards.

POWER AND COOLING ISSUES

Power and cooling issues include battery issues, AC power issues, and overheating.

- **Battery issues.** If you are working from the battery, first check that it is inserted correctly and seated properly in its compartment. Also check whether the battery contacts are dirty. You can clean them by using alcohol preps or even just a dry cloth.

  An LED may be present to indicate when the laptop is running on battery power or an LED may simply show when a battery is being charged. If the battery is properly inserted and still does not work, it is most likely completely discharged. If the battery will not hold a charge, it could be at the end of its useful life. You can test this by using a "known good" battery; if this does not work, then there is something wrong with the power circuitry on the motherboard.

  Properly caring for the battery not only prolongs battery life, but also mitigates health and safety risks. Using an incorrect battery charging cable or exposing a battery to harsh environmental conditions, such as extreme heat, can result in an explosion.

- **Short battery life.** As batteries age, the maximum charge they can sustain decreases, so short battery life will usually indicate that the battery needs replacing. If the battery is not old or faulty, you could suspect that an app is putting excessive strain on the battery. In Windows 10, you can use the **Settings** app to identify whether an app is having an adverse effect on battery life.

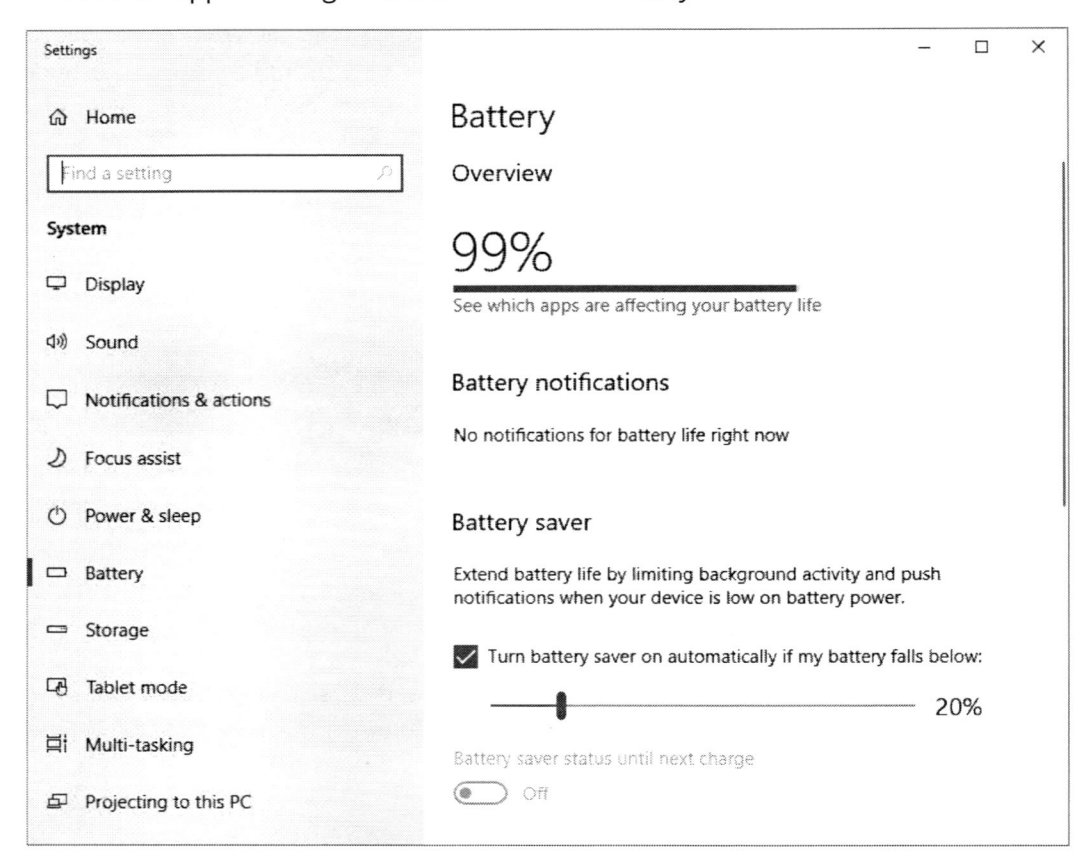

Battery status and notifications in Windows 10. (Screenshot used with permission from Microsoft.)

- **Swollen batteries.** If you notice any swelling from the battery compartment, discontinue use of the laptop immediately. Signs that the battery has swollen can include a device that wobbles when placed flat on a desk or a deformed touchpad or keyboard. A swollen battery is usually caused by overcharging, indicating some sort of problem with the battery's charging circuit, which is supposed to prevent overcharging. If a device is exposed to liquid, this could also have damaged the battery.

  Li-ion batteries are designed to swell to avoid bursting or exploding but great care must be taken when handling a swollen battery to avoid further damage that may cause it to burst or explode. It may also be a fire hazard and/or leaking hazardous chemicals—do not allow these to come into contact with your skin or your eyes. If the battery cannot be released safely and easily from its compartment, contact the manufacturer for advice. You should also contact the manufacturer for specific disposal instructions. A swollen battery should not be discarded via standard recycling points unless the facility confirms it can accept batteries in a potentially hazardous state.

  Note: Problems with batteries and AC adapters often occur in batches. Make sure you remain signed up to the vendor's alerting service so that you are informed about any product recalls or safety advisories.

- **AC power issues.** AC power issues usually surface as problems with a battery not charging, slow performance, devices not functioning. error messages, and spontaneous rebooting.
- **Overheating.** Overheating can be a considerable problem with laptops due to their compact size and integrated design. The components are all within close proximity and can generate and trap a lot of heat.

  Dust trapped in cooling passages acts as an insulator and can prevent proper cooling, possibly resulting in overheating. Excessive heat should be avoided in such devices as it can shorten the life of components.

  The bottom surface of the laptop gets quite hot when improperly ventilated. This can easily happen when laptops are put on soft surfaces, on people's laps, or in places where there is not enough room between the vents and a wall. Sometimes people will get careless and unwittingly cover the vents with books, mouse pads, etc.

  There are several cooling methods and considerations used to keep the devices within a safe heat range for operation:
  - Laptop CPUs are engineered to draw less power and thus run cooler than their similarly rated desktop counterparts.
  - Fans are used to move the hot air out from the inside of the laptop case.
  - Limit the use of the laptop battery as much as possible. The battery itself can be a heat source.
  - Laptop cooling (or chiller) pads are accessories that are designed to sit under the laptop to protect a user from getting a burn from a device overheating. The cooler is placed underneath the laptop to move the air away from the device.

*Note: To learn more, check the **Video** tile on the CHOICE Course screen for any videos that supplement the content for this lesson.*

GUIDELINES FOR TROUBLESHOOTING POWER AND COOLING ISSUES

Here are some guidelines for troubleshooting power and cooling issues.

TROUBLESHOOT BATTERY ISSUES

Some simple guidelines for acceptable battery maintenance include:
- Follow manufacturer instructions on the proper charging and discharging of the battery.
- Use the battery charger provided by the manufacturer or an approved replacement charger.
- Never expose the battery to fire or water or drop, throw, or jolt the battery.
- Only use the recommended battery for your device.
- Make use of power management features included with your device/OS to prolong battery life.

TROUBLESHOOT AC POWER ISSUES

Consider these guidelines as you troubleshoot AC power issues:
- If there is a power problem, first establish how the laptop should be operated and confirm that this procedure is being followed. For example, some laptops require that a battery be present, even on AC power.
- If you experience problems working from AC power, first test the outlet with a "known good" device (such as a lamp). Next check that an LED on the AC adapter is

green; if there is no LED, check the fuse on the plug and if available, try testing with a "known good" adapter.
- If this does not work, inspect the DC socket on the laptop for any sign of damage. You could also check the AC adapter using a multimeter.

> **Note:** Most adapters contain a circuit breaker to prevent overloads. If this trips, it will be a few minutes before the adapter will work again.

- Sometimes AC adapters can get mixed up. If an underpowered adapter is used—for example, a 65 W adapter is plugged into a 90 W system—the laptop BIOS will display a warning at boot time.
- As with desktops, spontaneous reboots may indicate a power problem, though a more likely cause is overheating. Another possibility is that peripherals are trying to draw down too much power.
- Try disconnecting drives from the media bays or USB then re-booting to see if the problem is fixed. Note that larger 3.5" hard drives and external CD/DVD writers will typically require their own power supply, even if connected via USB.

TROUBLESHOOT COOLING ISSUES

Consider these guidelines as you troubleshoot cooling issues:
- Because laptops do not have the air circulation that desktop PCs do, it is important to keep the device air ducts clean.
- In servicing laptops, it is a good practice to regularly blow dust from the cooling passages using compressed air or vacuum it with an electronics vacuum. When using compressed air to clean the inside of the laptop, you must be cautious of the internal components. It is easy to damage other components inside the laptop while cleaning.

INPUT AND OUTPUT DEVICE ISSUES

Here are some common issues you might encounter with laptop input and output devices:
- **Input devices.** The main problem with keypads tends to be stuck keys.

  Be aware that the Function (Fn) keys can often be used to disable devices, such as the wireless adapter. Each device will have an LED on the chassis showing whether it is enabled or not.

  If the laptop does not have a separate keypad, users may become confused when NumLock is active and the keys go to numeric input.

  Another issue is with using an external keyboard and experiencing problems with the Function key being locked. This can typically be solved by turning off NumLock on the external keyboard.

  Another problem is where the touchpad is configured to be too sensitive and typing causes vibrations that move the cursor. Examples include the pointer drifting across the screen without any input or a "ghost cursor" jumping about when typing.
- **Sound and speaker issues.** On a laptop, problems can arise with the onboard speakers and with external speakers, resulting in no sound or distorted sound.

> **Note:** To learn more, check the **Video** tile on the CHOICE Course screen for any videos that supplement the content for this lesson.

GUIDELINES FOR TROUBLESHOOTING INPUT AND OUTPUT DEVICE ISSUES

Here are some guidelines for troubleshooting input and output device issues.

TROUBLESHOOT INPUT AND OUTPUT DEVICE ISSUES

Consider these guidelines as you troubleshoot input and output device issues:

- If there is debris under a key, try cleaning with compressed air.
- If the laptop has been serviced recently and the keyboard has stopped working, check that the connector has not been dislodged as some service operations require the keyboard to be removed.

    Note: Removing a key on a laptop keyboard can be a risky proposition. They are typically not the type of key where the key cap is in a peg, which you find on full-sized keyboards. Laptop keys are usually floating on a dual-hinge mechanism, usually plastic, that will easily break if you attempt to remove it forcefully. Refer to the manufacturer's instructions when attempting to fix a key on the keyboard.

- If a device that is activated via a function key is not working, check that it has not been disabled by accident.
- If the wrong characters appear when you type, check the NumLock status indicator if available.
- For touchpad issues, install up-to-date drivers and configure input options to suit the user. Many laptops now come with a **Fn** key to disable the touchpad.

    Note: Conversely, mouse problems can often arise following the installation of updates or version upgrades. Try to identify "what changed?" when troubleshooting problems like this.

- If no sound is played from the onboard speakers:
    - Check that the volume controls have not been turned all the way down or that sound has not been muted. Remember that on a laptop there may be function or multimedia keys to control the volume.
    - Check that the correct playback device is configured in Windows (using the **Sound** applet in Control Panel). The applet includes a utility that can test the speaker setup.
    - If you cannot locate a configuration problem, try connecting external speakers or a headset to identify whether the problem may be with the internal speaker unit.
    - If there is no sound from either type of output, suspect a problem with the sound card or internal wiring.

    *Note: To learn more, check the **Video** tile on the CHOICE Course screen for any videos that supplement the content for this lesson.*

COMMUNICATION AND CONNECTIVITY ISSUES

Wi-Fi and Bluetooth connectivity issues on a laptop can be approached in much the same way as on a PC. Problems can generally be categorized as either relating to "physical" issues, such as interference, or to "software" configuration problems.

- Remember that wireless devices need power.
- Wireless devices can often experience difficulties following the laptop being put into sleep or hibernation mode.
- If there are intermittent connectivity problems, be aware that wireless input and communications devices can experience trouble with interference.

> **Note:** The radio antenna wire for a mobile will be built into the case (normally around the screen).

GPS AND LOCATION SERVICES

Here are some issues you might encounter with GPS and location services:

- GPS and other wireless functions do not seem to work at all, or they work only intermittently.
- GPS does not usually work well indoors as the satellite signals lack the power to penetrate dense construction material. Most devices use a combination of GPS and the **Indoor Positioning System (IPS)**, which uses information from nearby Wi-Fi hotspots, to provide location services.

GUIDELINES FOR TROUBLESHOOTING COMMUNICATION AND CONNECTIVITY ISSUES

Here are some guidelines for troubleshooting communication and connectivity issues.

TROUBLESHOOT COMMUNICATION AND CONNECTIVITY ISSUES

Consider these guidelines when you are troubleshooting issues with communication and connectivity:

- If there is a problem with wireless, Bluetooth, or cellular data/GPS:
  - Verify that the adapter is enabled.
  - Check the status of function key toggles on a laptop or use the notification shade toggles on a mobile device to check that something like airplane mode has not been enabled.
  - Different wireless functions may be toggled on or off selectively or collectively.
  - If the laptop has been serviced recently and wireless functions have stopped working, check that the antenna connector has not been dislodged or wrongly connected.
- If a wireless device such as a Bluetooth mouse or keyboard that has been working stops, it probably needs a new battery.
- If you experience problems restoring from hibernate or sleep mode, try cycling the power on the device or reconnecting it and check for updated drivers for the wireless controller and the devices.
- If you are experiencing intermittent connectivity issues:
  - Try moving the two devices closer together.
  - Try moving the devices from side-to-side or up-and-down.
  - Consider using a Wi-Fi analyzer to measure the signal strength in different locations to try to identify the source of interference.
- If there is a problem with the Global Positioning System (GPS):
  - Check that the GPS receiver is enabled and that the laptop is not in airplane mode.
  - Ensure that Location Services are enabled for the device.
  - Verify that each app has been granted permission to use the service. If the app does not prompt for permission if it has not been granted, try uninstalling and reinstalling the app.

> **Note:** To learn more, check the **Video** tile on the CHOICE Course screen for any videos that supplement the content for this lesson.

OS AND APP ISSUES

Although this topic covers common laptop hardware issues, you should also be aware of some problems that can arise from OS and app issues.

- Slow performance.
- Unresponsive devices and apps.
- Email issues. Users often want to send confidential email with the assurance that only the recipient can read it. To do this, the recipient sends the sender a digital certificate and the sender uses the public key in that certificate to encrypt the message. The recipient then uses another part of the certificate (the private key) to decrypt the message. If the certificate is missing or not recognized, the device will be unable to decrypt the email.

GUIDELINES FOR TROUBLESHOOTING OS AND APP ISSUES

Here are some guidelines for troubleshooting OS and app issues.

TROUBLESHOOT OS AND APP ISSUES

Consider these guidelines as you troubleshoot OS and app issues on a laptop:

- For slow performance issues:
    - A Windows laptop might suffer from slow performance for the same reasons as a PC and you should approach troubleshooting in the same way.

        Slow performance on a mobile device is likely either to be caused by an app that requires a higher system specification or by running too many apps. Mobile devices are designed to manage system requirements without intervention from the user, but it may be worth closing all apps in case there is a fault in one that has not been detected.

- For unresponsive apps and devices: If an app or the mobile device as a whole is not responding—for example, if the screen is frozen or if apps are not loading—or performing very slowly, the best solution is usually to perform a reset.
    - App reset: use this if a particular app is not responding. In iOS®, double-click **Home** twice to open the multitasking toolbar then tap-and-hold the app and click the **Stop** icon that appears when it starts jiggling. In Android™, you can manage an app's cached data and access a Force Stop option through **Settings→Applications→Manage Applications**.
    - Restart/"soft" reset/power cycle: essentially rebooting the device (without losing any settings or data). Holding the **Sleep/Wake/Power** button down for a few seconds brings up a menu prompting the user to turn off the device. When troubleshooting, leave the device powered off for a minute then restart by holding the **Sleep** button again.
    - Forced restart: if the touchscreen is not responding to input and you cannot perform a power cycle normally, you can force the device to turn off. On an Android device, hold down the **Sleep/Wake/Power** button for 10 seconds; in iOS, hold **Home+Sleep** for 10 seconds.
    - Factory reset/erase: this deletes any user data and settings and puts the device in its "vanilla" factory state. In iOS, use **Settings→General→Reset→Erase All Content and Settings**. In Android, select **Settings→Backup & reset→Factory data reset**.

        *Note: These procedures can vary from device-to-device so always check the instructions. If you cannot get an ordinary screen in Android, check the vendor documentation for the hardware buttons to use to get to a boot recovery screen (from a powered off state, **Power+Volume Down** is typical). iOS can be booted in recovery mode by holding the **Home** button when connecting the device to iTunes over USB.*

- For email issues, use the email client or encryption program's support documentation to find out how to install or locate the appropriate certificate.

*Note: To learn more, check the **Video** tile on the CHOICE Course screen for any videos that supplement the content for this lesson.*

Activity 8-4
Troubleshooting Common Laptop Issues

SCENARIO
Answer the following questions to check your understanding of the topic.

1. You are troubleshooting a laptop display.

   If the laptop can display an image on an external monitor but not the built-in one, which component do you know is working, and can you definitively say which is faulty?

2. You received a user complaint about a laptop being extremely hot to the touch.

   What actions should you take in response to this issue?

3. A user complains that their Bluetooth keyboard, which has worked for the last year, has stopped functioning.

   What would you suggest is the problem?

4. A user working in graphics design has just received a new laptop. The user phones to say that performance with the graphics program in the office is fine but dismal when he takes the laptop to client meetings.

   What could be the cause?

5. A laptop user reports that they are only getting about two hours of use out of the battery compared to about three hours when the laptop was first supplied to them.

   What do you suggest?

6. A laptop user is complaining about typing on their new laptop. They claim that the cursor jumps randomly from place-to-place.

   What might be the cause of this?

Summary

In this lesson, you performed support and troubleshooting routines on laptop computers. Familiarity with using various laptop features and technologies, as well as installing, configuring, and troubleshooting laptop components and behavior, will no doubt contribute to your success as an A+ support technician.

In your professional experience, have you supported laptop computers? If not, what kind of experience do you have with using them?

Of the common laptop issues discussed in this lesson, which do you expect to encounter most often? Briefly explain your response.

Practice Question: Additional practice questions are available on the CompTIA CHOICE platform within the **Assessments** tile.

Lesson 9
Supporting and Troubleshooting Mobile Devices

LESSON INTRODUCTION

Mobile devices are everywhere today. Because of their portability and powerful computing capabilities, they are prominent in most workplaces. So, as a certified CompTIA® A+® technician, you will be expected to configure, maintain, and troubleshoot mobile computing devices. With the proper information and the right skills, you will be ready to support these devices as efficiently as you support their desktop counterparts.

LESSON OBJECTIVES

In this lesson, you will:

- Describe characteristics of mobile devices.
- Connect and configure mobile device accessories.
- Configure network connectivity for mobile devices.
- Support mobile apps.

Topic A
Mobile Device Types

EXAM OBJECTIVES COVERED
1001-1.4 Compare and contrast characteristics of various types of other mobile devices.

Driven by the iPhone® and iPad®, the last few years have seen a huge uptake in the use of mobile devices. In some instances they have replaced traditional computer form factors (laptop and desktop) for day-to-day tasks, such as messaging/email and browsing the web. In this topic, you will learn about the smartphone and tablet form factors and about other types of portable computing technologies.

MOBILE DEVICES

As an A+ technician, your primary focus is likely to be on the more traditional system hardware components and laptop technologies. However, you might also be asked to support devices in the mobile computing realm. Not only has mobile technology reached a new level of performance and portability, but also the use of these devices is on the rise every day. As a certified A+ technician, you will be expected to understand how these devices work and how they should be deployed within the workplace.

Mobile devices such as smartphones and tablets are based on one of three operating systems (Apple® iOS®, Android™, or Windows Mobile®) and a store-based software ecosystem, which allows for third-party apps to be downloaded to add functionality to the device. The main distinction between a smartphone and tablet is the size of the device, rather than its functionality.

The major smartphone and tablet vendors are Apple and Samsung. Other vendors include LG, Google™, HTC, Huawei, Motorola/Lenovo, Microsoft®, Nokia, Sony, and Amazon™.

SMARTPHONES

A smartphone is a device with roughly the same functionality as a personal computer that can be operated with a single hand. Previous handheld computers, known as Personal Digital Assistants (PDA), and earlier types of mobile phones with some software functionality (feature phones), were hampered by clumsy user interfaces. Modern smartphones use touchscreen displays, making them much easier to operate.

Most smartphones have a screen size between 4.5" and 5.7". Leading smartphones provide high resolution screens. For example, the iPhone X has a resolution of 2436x1125.

Smartphones have fast multi core CPUs, anywhere between 2 and 6 GB system memory, and 16 GB+ flash memory storage. They come with features such as premium front and back digital cameras, input sensors like accelerometers, and Global Positioning System (GPS) chips. They can establish network links using Wi-Fi and a cellular data plan.

Typical smartphone form factor. (Image © 123RF.com.)

TABLETS

Prior to the iPad, tablet PCs were usually laptops with touchscreens. The iPad defined a new form factor; smaller than a laptop and with no physical keyboard. Tablets tend to be sized at around either 10" or 7" screens. Tablets use a range of screen resolutions, depending on the price. Microsoft's Surface® 4 tablet features a resolution of 2736x1824.

An example of a tablet. (Image © 123RF.com.)

Many Windows® mobile devices adopt a hybrid approach where a laptop can be converted into a tablet by flipping the screen. Microsoft's Surface Pro tablet is available with a detachable keyboard, which can also function as a cover for the screen. Other vendors are also producing hybrid devices that can function as both a laptop and a tablet.

Network links are mainly established using Wi-Fi, although some tablets come with a cellular data option, too.

PHABLET

Phablets sit between smartphones and tablets in terms of size and usability. The name is a portmanteau of Phone and Tablet. They were first popularized by Samsung with their successful Note devices. Phablets have screen sizes between 5.5" and 7". These devices often come with a stylus which can be used for note taking, sketching, and annotations.

Phablets always come with cellular data and a connection to the phone system, as well as Wi-Fi.

MOBILE DEVICES VS. LAPTOPS

Laptops and smartphones/tablets/hybrids are obviously all classes of portable or mobile devices, but you should be aware of the factors that distinguish them.

Factor	Description
Processors	CPUs and their chipsets for smartphones and tablets are often based on the ARM (Advanced RISC Machine) microarchitecture, such as the Apple A, Samsung Exynos, and NVIDIA Tegra derivatives. RISC stands for Reduced Instruction Set Computing. RISC microarchitectures use simple instructions processed very quickly. This contrasts with Complex (CISC) microarchitectures, which use more powerful instructions but process each one more slowly. Intel's PC/laptop CPU microarchitecture is CISC with RISC enhancements (micro-ops).
	As well as the computing power to keep up with increasingly complex apps and games available for these devices (many models are now dual- or quad-core and some use 64-bit CPUs), mobile CPUs must deliver power and thermal efficiency to maximize battery life to an even greater extent than laptops.
System memory	Tablet RAM (a low power DDR SDRAM variant) works much as it does in a PC or laptop to store instructions for the OS when it loads plus any apps the user starts.
Storage	Solid State Drives (flash memory) are used for mass storage rather than hard disks (though this is increasingly the case for laptops and PCs, too).
Component replacements/upgrades	Many of the hardware components of a laptop can be fixed and replaced when issues arise. There are few field-serviceable parts in a smartphone or tablet. What makes it difficult to repair a tablet is that the parts are soldered and not socketed. Many components are glued into place to keep them stable. When something breaks, in most cases, the entire device needs to be replaced. Similarly, components in a tablet are not upgradeable.
Operating System	Laptops can run a number of different operating systems, including versions from Microsoft®, Linux®, and UNIX®. Smartphones and tablets can only run the OS that the device was manufactured to run (iOS, Android, or Windows).

MOBILE DISPLAY/TOUCH INTERFACE

A **touchscreen** allows the user to control the OS directly by swiping or tapping with a finger (or with a stylus) rather than using navigation buttons or a scroll wheel.

Modern mobile devices use capacitive touchscreens. These capacitive displays support **multitouch**, meaning that gestures such as "sweeping" or "pinching" the screen can be interpreted as events and responded to by software in a particular way. Newer devices are also starting to provide **haptic feedback**, or touch responsiveness, making virtual key presses or gestures feel more "real" to the user. On the latest models, screens feature **light sensors** to dim and brighten displays based on ambient conditions. Some devices also feature an eye tracking display to scroll up and down based on where the user is looking.

The touchscreen itself is covered by a thin layer of scratch-resistant, shock-resistant tempered glass, such as Corning's Gorilla Glass. Some users may also apply an additional screen protector. If so, these need to be applied carefully (without bubbling) so as not to interfere with the touch capabilities of the screen.

Apple uses its own version of shatter resistant glass on its current models which is coupled with its branded Retina Display. Other manufacturers utilize Samsung-derived displays, whereas Samsung's flagship phone utilizes a *curved* **OLED** display.

Most mobile devices can be used either in portrait or landscape orientation. A component called an **accelerometer** can detect when the device is moved and change the screen orientation appropriately. There will actually be three accelerometers to measure movement along three axes. Newer devices may use both accelerometers and **gyroscopes** to deliver more accurate readings. As well as switching screen orientation, this can be used as a control mechanism (for example, a driving game could allow the tablet itself to function as a steering wheel).

On some devices, these sensors can be calibrated via a utility that uses a predetermined pattern of movement to calibrate the sensor.

MOBILE DEVICE FORM FACTORS

Mobile devices are even less likely than laptops to have field serviceable parts. The electronics will be densely packed and often soldered or glued together. Most will require return to the manufacturer to replace failed components such as a battery, display screen, or storage device.

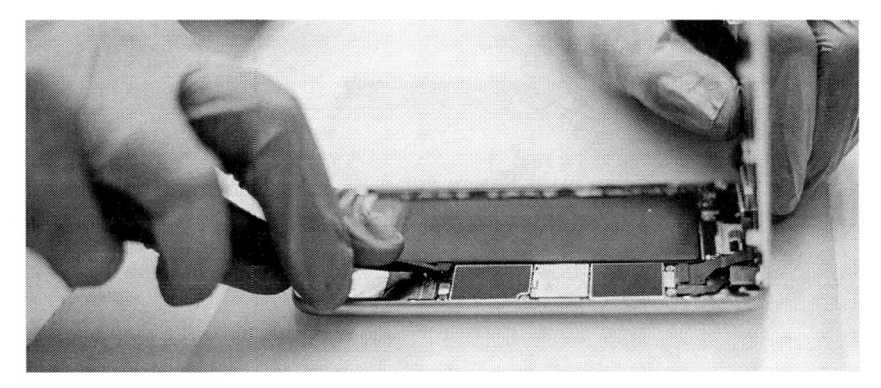

Mobile handset with cover removed—note the slot for the SIM card in the top-right and that the battery is accessible but not designated as user-removable. (Image by guruxox © 123RF.com.)

Some mobiles have a user-replaceable battery, accessed by removing the cover. There will also be a port for a Subscriber Identity Module (SIM) card for GSM-based or 4G LTE cellular access. This may also be fitted by removing the case. Refer to the device documentation for instructions on removing the case. Always power off the device before opening the case.

> **Caution:** While it would usually void the warranty to further disassemble the device, there may be some circumstances in which you want to replace a part yourself. The best guide to doing so is a website hosting gadget "teardown" videos and repair guides, such as *ifixit.com*.

E-READERS

Unlike a tablet, an **e-reader** is designed for the sole purpose of reading digital books and magazines (with perhaps the option to add annotations). E-readers use **electrophoretic ink (e-ink)** technology to create an **Electronic Paper Display (EPD)**. Compared to the LED or OLED display used on a tablet, an EPD has low power consumption but facilitates high contrast reading in a variety of ambient light conditions. In typical conditions, these screens do not need to use a backlight, saving power and extending battery life. It is not unusual to get several days of usage on a single charge for these devices. Like most tablets and smartphones, an e-reader is charged using a USB cable.

An example of an e-reader device. (Image © 123RF.com.)

E-readers are manufactured for major book retailers such as Amazon and Barnes and Noble. They have Wi-Fi connectivity to download e-books directly from the retailer's webstore.

WEARABLE TECHNOLOGY

Electronics manufacturing allows a great deal of computing power to be packed within a small space. Consequently, computing functionality is being added to wearable items, such as watches, bracelets, and eyeglasses.

SMART WATCHES

Smart watches have risen in popularity in recent years. Current competing technologies are based on the Android Wear OS, Samsung's Tizen OS, and Apple iOS, each with their own separate app ecosystems. A smart watch is likely to be customizable with different watch faces and wrist straps.

An example of a smart watch. (Image © 123RF.com.)

Most smart watches use Bluetooth® to pair with a smartphone. They are able to display key information at a glance (emails, messages, and social media status, for instance), allowing the user to better interact with the phone. Some newer smart watches are starting to appear with their own Wi-Fi connectivity, allowing use of the watch without proximity to a paired phone.

As well as helping with personal information management, many smart watches come with health features. Technologies bundled include heart rate monitors via Infrared (IR) sensors, accelerometers to measure sleeping patterns and movement for exercise, plus cameras and IR sensors to operate devices such as TVs.

FITNESS MONITORS

As the name suggests, fitness monitors focus on exercise and health uses rather than a range of computing tasks. This makes them cheaper devices than smart watches. They usually connect via Wi-Fi or Bluetooth to send data to a mobile app or PC software for analysis. Some feature a GPS tracker to allow runners to map their exercise accurately.

Example of a wearable fitness monitor. (Image © 123RF.com.)

Features of fitness monitors might include:
- Pedometer to count the steps taken during a specified period of time.
- Accelerometer to measure the intensity of the workout.
- Heart rate and blood pressure monitors.
- A calculation of the number of calories burned.

VR/AR HEADSETS AND SMART GLASSES

A Virtual Reality (VR) headset is designed to replace what you can see and hear in the real world with sights and sounds from a game or conferencing app generated by software. There are tethered VR headsets that connect to a computer as a peripheral device, but it is also possible to use a smartphone with a headset to get the VR experience.

Mobile VR headsets, such as Samsung Gear or Google Daydream View™, only work with selected (premium) smartphone models. These headsets contain lenses that split the smartphone display into a stereoscopic image, giving the illusion of depth. The headsets also come with a motion controller to allow you to interact with objects in the VR environment.

> **Note:** There are also standalone mobile VR headsets, such as the Oculus Go. This contains a basic smartphone (without cellular capability) embedded in the headset. Apple does not make a VR headset for the iPhone (at the time of writing), but there are third-party options.

Augmented Reality (AR) is a somewhat similar technology to VR. Rather than provide a completely simulated environment, AR projects digital artefacts onto "ordinary" reality. This could be as simple as providing context-sensitive notes, messages, or advertising or as complex as generating digital avatars within the real world. This latter technique is exploited by popular smartphone camera games, such as Pokémon Go, which enables you to locate collectible cartoon characters in unlikely real world locations through your smartphone camera. Another use case is an app like Samsung's AR Emoji, which transforms people captured in the viewfinder in various unsettling ways.

There are also some AR devices, though they have not gained a very large market yet. Smart glasses were pioneered by Google with their Google Glass range and Google is rumored to be working on a more sophisticated AR headset (codenamed Google A65 at time of writing). Other AR-like devices are made by Microsoft (HoloLens®) and AiR for industrial applications.

Example of smart glasses. (Image © 123RF.com.)

Network connectivity and pairing with other mobile devices is provided by Wi-Fi and/or Bluetooth. Most AR headsets or smart glasses also come with a camera, and there are issues arising due to the potential invasion of privacy or breach of confidentiality such a relatively concealed recording device could pose.

Input methods allowing the user to control the software running on the glasses include buttons, eye tracking, natural language voice input, plus gesture controls.

GPS NAVIGATION DEVICES

A **Global Positioning System (GPS)** chip is built into most smartphones and many tablets and other smart devices, but there are also dedicated GPS navigation devices (also called sat navs, for "satellite navigation"). These come in 5-6" models aimed both at in-vehicle use and smaller clip-on devices for walkers and cyclists. GPS devices combine providing an accurate geolocation system with map and local traffic information to allow users to plot routes and help them follow a route with turn-by-turn navigation advice. Some devices use over-the-air radio to provide live traffic information; other models have to be tethered to a smartphone to use its data plan. Most are touchscreen-operated with many models also supporting voice control.

Activity 9-1
Discussing Mobile Device Types

SCENARIO
Answer the following questions to check your understanding of the topic.

1. What are the principal characteristics of the phablet form factor?

2. What is the relevance of ARM to smartphones?

3. True or false? Smartphones use a type of memory technology that works both as system memory and as persistent storage.

4. What is meant by wearable technology?

5. What technology gives an e-Reader better battery life than a tablet?

Topic B
Connect and Configure Mobile Device Accessories

EXAM OBJECTIVES COVERED
1001-1.5 Given a scenario, connect and configure accessories and ports of other mobile devices.
1001-2.7 Compare and contrast Internet connection types, network types, and their features.

Mobile devices gain much of their functionality by being able to connect to the user's regular computer. By making the files available on the mobile device, they can continue working on the files from a mobile device. Being able to connect the mobile device back to the computer might require additional accessories. In this topic, you will examine the connection types and accessories used for mobile devices.

WIRED CONNECTIONS FOR ACCESSORIES

Although mobile devices are designed to be self-contained, there is the need to attach peripheral devices, connect to a computer, or attach a charging cable

APPLE DOCK AND LIGHTNING CONNECTORS

Older Apple devices use a proprietary 30-pin dock connector, enabling connections to various peripheral devices. The dock is also used to charge the battery. A dock-connector to USB cable facilitates connections to a USB bus (that is, to a PC), though not the connection of USB devices such as hard drives to the iPhone/iPad.

On the latest Apple devices, the 30-pin dock connector is replaced by an 8-pin Lightning® connector (also proprietary). The Lightning connector is reversible (can be inserted either way up). There are various Lightning converter cables to allow connections to interfaces such as HDMI, VGA, and SD card readers.

USB CONNECTORS

Android-based devices usually have a Micro-B USB port for charging and connectivity. You might find older devices using the Mini-B USB port. New devices are quickly adopting the USB-C connector. One issue for Android is that there is no standard way of positioning the connectors, so connections to devices such as speaker or charging docks tend to have to use a cable .

WIRELESS CONNECTIONS FOR ACCESSORIES

Short-range wireless connectivity is often a better option for mobile devices than wired connections.

BLUETOOTH

Bluetooth is used for so-called Personal Area Networks (PAN) to share data between devices and connect peripheral devices to hosts, such as smartphones and tablets. Bluetooth is a radio-based technology but it is designed to work only over close range. Bluetooth is quoted to work at distances of up to 10 meters (30 feet) for Class 2 devices or 1 meter (3 feet) for Class 3 devices. Devices supporting the Bluetooth 2.0—

Enhanced Data Rate (EDR)— standard have a maximum transfer rate of 3 Mbps; otherwise, the maximum rate is 1 Mbps.

> *Note:* Bluetooth 3 supports a 24 Mbps HighSpeed (HS) mode, but this uses a specially negotiated Wi-Fi link rather than the Bluetooth connection itself.

Bluetooth needs to be enabled for use via device settings. You may also want to change the device name—remember that this is displayed publicly. Opening the settings page makes the device discoverable to other Bluetooth-enabled devices.

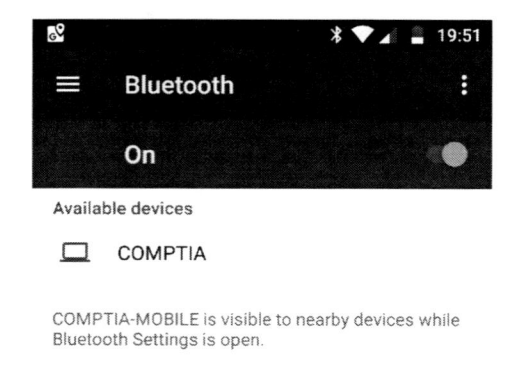

Enabling Bluetooth on an Android device. In this figure, the Android device is named "COMPTIA-MOBILE." "COMPTIA" is a nearby Windows PC with Bluetooth enabled.

NFC

An increasing range of smartphone models have **Near Field Communications (NFC)** chips built in. NFC allows for very short range data transmission (up to about 20 cm/8 in) to activate a receiver chip in the contactless credit card reader. The data rates achievable are very low but these transactions do not require exchanging large amounts of information.

NFC allows a mobile device to make payments via contactless Point-of-Sale (PoS) machines. To configure a payment service, the user enters their credit card information into a Mobile Wallet app on the device. The wallet app does not transmit the original credit card information, but a one-time token that is interpreted by the card merchant and linked backed to the relevant customer account. There are three major Mobile Wallet apps: Apple Pay, Android Pay, and Samsung Pay. Some PoS readers may only support a particular type of wallet app or apps.

As with Bluetooth, NFC can be enabled or disabled via settings. The device must be unlocked to initiate a transaction.

InfraRed (IR)

Many mobile devices are also equipped with an **infrared (IR)** sensor or **blaster**. This is not used for data connections as such but does allow the device to interact with appliances such as TVs and set-top boxes. An app on the device can be installed to allow the mobile device to be used as a remote control for the appliance.

TETHERING AND MOBILE HOTSPOTS

Tethering refers to using a mobile device's cellular data plan to get Internet access on a PC or laptop (or other device). Not all carriers allow tethering and some only allow it as a chargeable service add-on. Connect the device to the PC via USB or Bluetooth, then configure tethering settings through the **Settings→Network** menu.

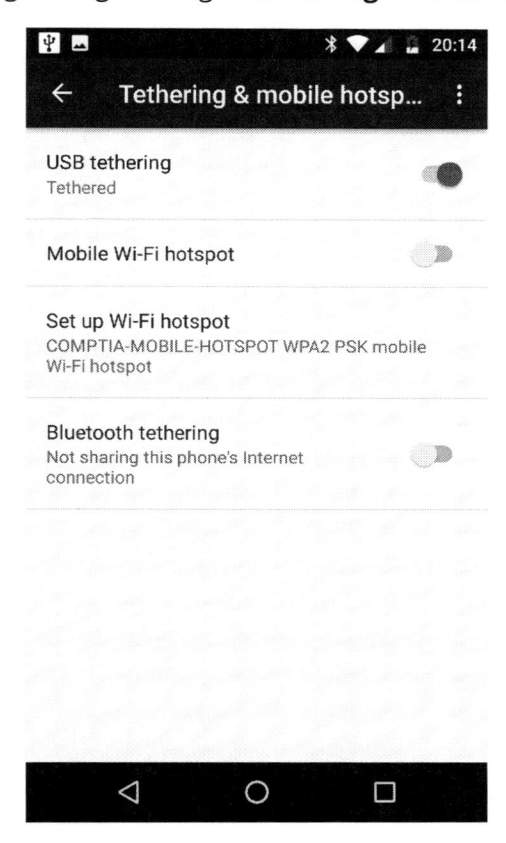

Configuring tethering on an Android phone. The device in this figure is connected to the PC over USB, but you could use Bluetooth too.

If you want to provide access to more than one device, you can enable the **Mobile Hotspot** setting. Configure the device with the usual settings for an access point (network name, security type, and passphrase) and then other devices can connect to it as they would any other WLAN.

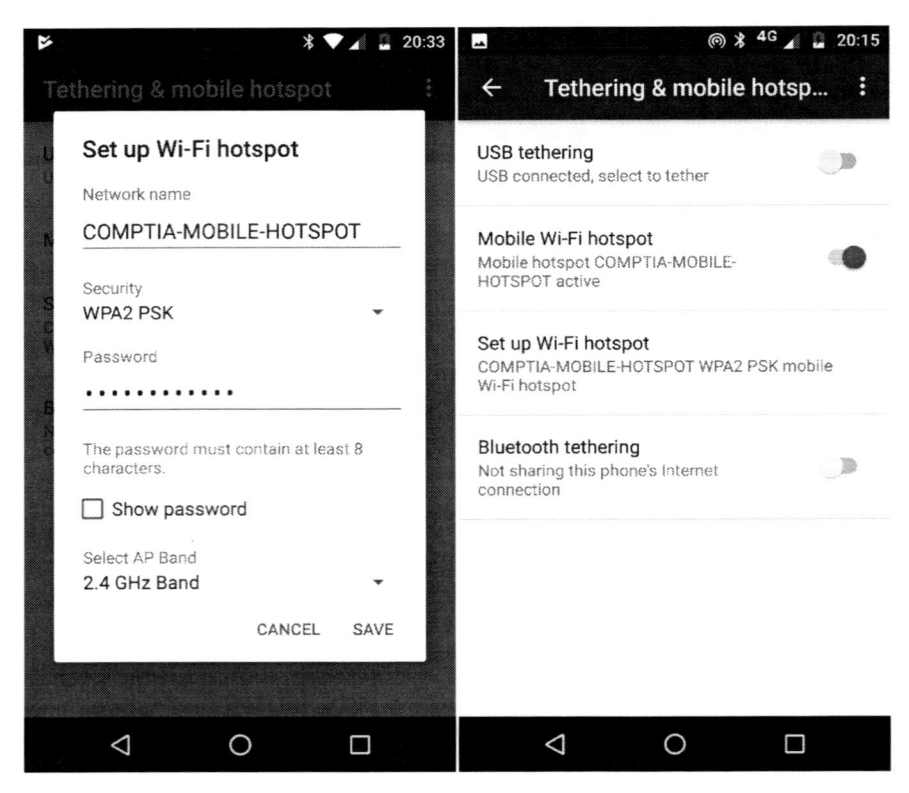

Configuring mobile hotspot settings (left) then enabling it (right). In this figure, hosts can connect to the "COMPTIA-MOBILE-HOTSPOT" network and use the device's cellular data plan to get Internet access.

COMMON MOBILE DEVICE ACCESSORIES

Some popular peripheral options for mobile devices include the following:

Peripheral	Description
External keyboard	As the touchscreen keyboards can be quite small and difficult to use, an external keyboard facilitates any extended typing work.
Headset	Provides audio input/output. As well as being useful for the phone function, some devices support voice recognition. There will usually be an audio connector for headsets or they can be connected via Bluetooth.
Speaker dock	Allows the device to play audio through external speakers. These can be connected either via the data port, the 3.5 mm audio jack, or more commonly through Bluetooth.
Game pad	Allows the use of a console-type controller (with joystick, cursor pad, and action buttons) with compatible mobile game apps. The game pad will come with some sort of clip to place the smartphone in. It must then be connected via USB or Lightning or paired with the device over Bluetooth. The functionality of the joystick and buttons is configured through each app individually.
Micro-SD (Secure Digital) slot	Allows the device's internal storage to be supplemented with a removable memory card.

DOCKING STATIONS

As modern smartphones develop, manufacturers have been able to include processing power to rival some desktops and sometimes even replace them altogether. A smartphone docking station connects the device to a monitor and input devices (keyboard and mouse).

Example of a smartphone dock. (Image © 123RF.com.)

PROTECTIVE COVERS AND WATERPROOFING

Although they are made from relatively tough components, mobiles are still prone to damage from dropping, crushing, scratching, or immersion. Rigid or rubber protective covers mitigate this risk a little. Covers can also often function as a stand so that the device can be placed upright on a desk. Many smartphone users also just like to personalize their phone with a cover.

A screen protector is a thin but tough film designed to provide extra protection for the display without compromising touch sensitivity.

Some cases are able to provide a degree of waterproofing. Some mobile devices are designed to be inherently waterproof. Waterproofing is rated on the **Ingress Protection (IP) scale**. A case or device will have two numbers, such as IP67. The first (6) is a rating for repelling solids, with a 5 or 6 representing devices that are dust protected and dust proof, respectively. The second value (7) is for liquids, with a 7 being protected from immersion in up to 1 m and 8 being protected from immersion beyond 1 m.

> **Note:** *If dust protection is unrated, the IP value will be IPX7 or IPX8.*

CREDIT CARD READERS

For devices with the appropriate port, a credit card reader can be added to a tablet or smartphone. This enables mobile vendors, such as those at festivals or street vendors, to take credit card payments without having a network cable or phone line connected to the credit card reader.

MOBILE POWER

Obviously, smartphones and tablets are primarily designed to work from battery power but can be plugged into building power via the charging cable and adapter. Some devices come with removable battery packs but these are very much the exception rather than the rule. Most vendors try to design their devices so that they will support "typical" usage for a full day without charging.

The charging speed that can be expected depends on what kind of USB connection is available:

- USB over Type A/B ports and power adapters can supply up to 2.5 W (500 mA at 5 V) for USB 2 or 4.5 W (900 mA at 5 V) for USB 3.
- **Quick Charge (QC)** adapters can deliver up to 18 W over USB Type A/B ports.
- Computer ports and charging adapters using USB-C can nominally supply up to 100 W (5 A at 20 V). Not all devices will be able to draw power at that level, though.
- Wireless charging (by induction) pads and stands can supply up to 15 W. Most wireless charging devices are based on the Qi standard developed by the Wireless

Power Consortium. Some chargers may be capable of charging multiple devices simultaneously.
- Portable charging banks provide a larger battery, such as 10,000 or 20,000 milliamp hours (mAh), than is found in a typical phone. This allows the phone to be charged from the power pack two or three times before the power pack itself needs recharging. The output of these devices ranges from 2.1 A to about 5 A.

> **Note:** If connected to a computer (or a laptop running on AC power) the device will **trickle charge**, which takes longer (try disconnecting other USB devices to improve charge times using this method). Also, the Quick Charge standard imposes a phased charging regime to protect battery lifetime (overcharging can reduce the maximum possible charge more quickly). If power is available, the battery is **fast-charged** to 80% and then trickle charged.

As the battery ages, it becomes less able to hold a full charge. If it is non-removable, the device will have to be returned to the vendor for battery replacement.

> **Note:** To learn more, check the **Video** tile on the CHOICE Course screen for any videos that supplement the content for this lesson.

> **Access the Checklist tile on your CHOICE Course screen for reference information and job aids on How to Connect and Configure Mobile Device Accessories.**

Activity 9-2
Discussing Mobile Device Accessory Connection and Configuration

SCENARIO
Answer the following questions to check your understanding of the topic.

1. What type of peripheral port would you expect to find on a current generation smartphone?

2. How would you upgrade storage capacity on a typical smartphone?

3. What technology do smartphones use to facilitate payment at points of sale?

4. True or false? An IP67-rated smartwatch could be considered risk-free for wear while swimming in an indoor pool.

Topic C

Configure Mobile Device Network Connectivity

EXAM OBJECTIVES COVERED
1001-1.6 Given a scenario, configure basic mobile device network connectivity and application support.
1001-2.7 Compare and contrast Internet connection types, network types, and their features.
1001-3.9 Given a scenario, install and configure common devices.

In this topic, you will examine some of the features and methods used to connect mobile devices to networks and the Internet.

CELLULAR DATA NETWORKS

Cellular data means connecting to the Internet via the device's cell phone radio and the handset's cellular network provider. The data rate depends on the technology supported by both the phone and the cell tower (3G or 4G, for instance). When a mobile device uses the cellular provider's network, there are likely to be charges based on the amount of data downloaded. These charges can be particularly high when the phone is used abroad (referred to as roaming) so it is often useful to be able to disable mobile data access.

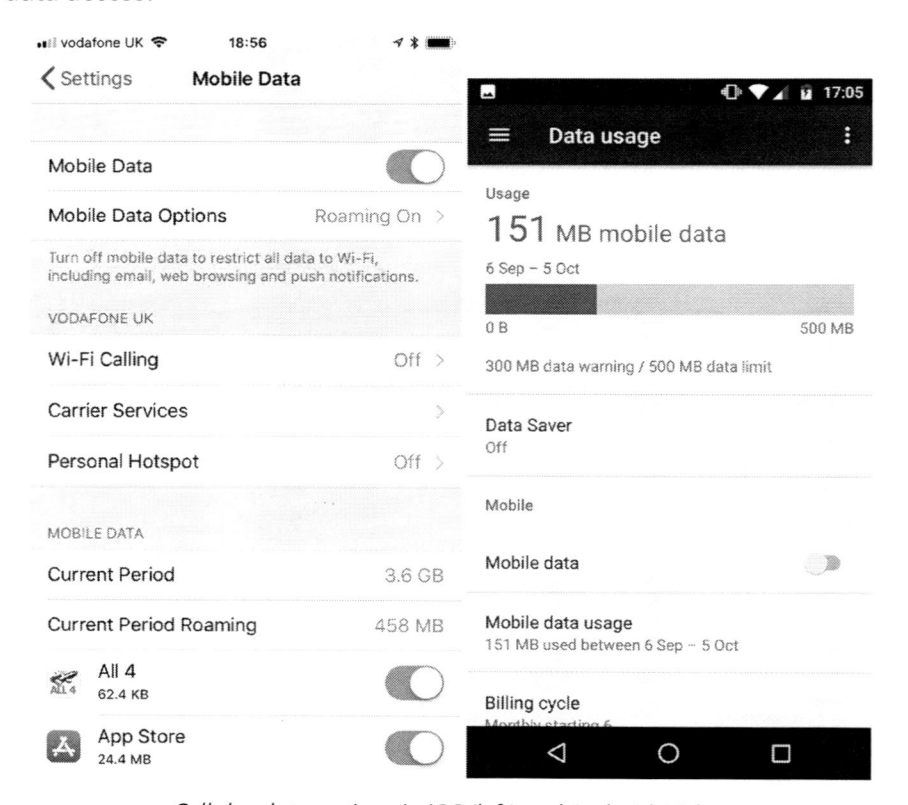

Cellular data options in iOS (left) and Android (right).

The indicator on the status bar at the top of the screen shows the data link in use. A device will usually default to Wi-Fi if present and show a signal strength icon. A device using a cellular data network may show a strength icon for a 4G network or the type of data network (H+ for HSPA+ for instance).

The cellular data connection can usually be enabled or disabled via the notification shade but there will also be additional configuration options via the **Settings** menu. You can usually set usage warnings and caps and prevent selected apps from using cellular data connections.

MOBILE HOTSPOTS AND TETHERING

As explained earlier, tethering means connecting another device to a smartphone or tablet via USB or Bluetooth so that it can share its cellular data connection. You can also share the link by configuring the smartphone or tablet as an access point, turning it into a personal or mobile hotspot.

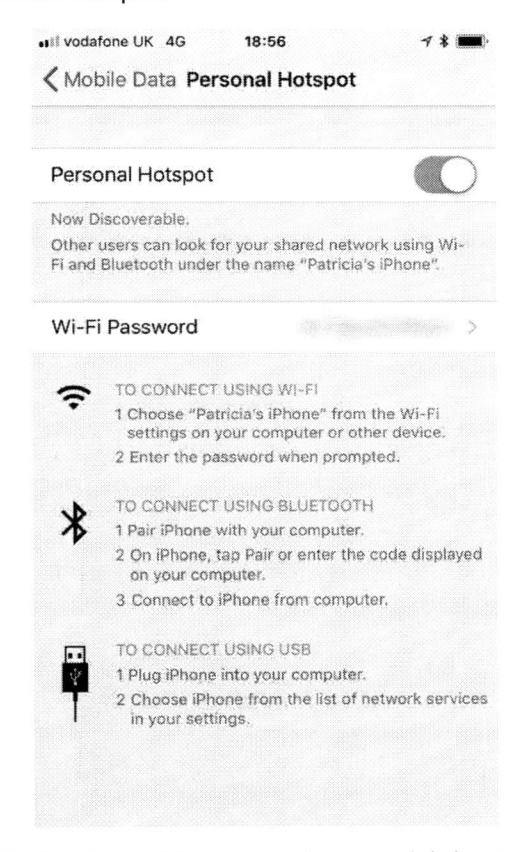

Configuring an iPhone to work as a mobile hotspot.

CELLULAR RADIOS

A **cellular radio** makes a connection using the nearest available transmitter (cell or base station). Each base station has an effective range of up to 5 miles (8 km). The transmitter connects the phone to the mobile and landline telephone networks. Cellular radio works in the 850 and 1900 MHz frequency bands (mostly in the Americas) and the 900 and 1800 MHz bands (rest of the world). There are two main cellular radio network types, each developing different standards for the "generations" of cellular data access (2G, 3G, and so on). **Global System for Mobile Communication (GSM)** is deployed worldwide while **Code Division Multiple Access (CDMA)** is adopted by carriers in the Americas.

Note: Just to confuse things, GSM radios now use a type of CDMA technology too. In its technical sense, CDMA is a means of exchanging radio signals, it's just that the term "CDMA" has become a handy label to distinguish these networks from GSM. Within the US, Sprint and Verizon use CDMA while AT&T and T-Mobile use GSM.

GSM NETWORKS AND SIM CARDS

GSM works with a **Subscriber Identity Module (SIM) card**. The user adds the card to the device and the card obtains all the information it needs to connect to the network, including a phone number, radio frequency bands to use, and information about how to connect when roaming in different countries. Updates to this information are "pushed" to the card by the network provider so there is never a need to perform a manual update.

Under GSM, a handset is identified by an **International Mobile Station Equipment Identity (IMEI)**. It is used by the GSM network to identify valid devices and can be used to stop stolen phones from accessing the network, regardless of the SIM used.

This number is usually printed on a label in the battery compartment on a mobile phone. If it is a sealed case, then the number will be found on the back or bottom of the device. You can also access the IMEI number by dialing ***#06#** and it will display the IMEI on the device screen. Any phone connected to a GSM network must have the IMEI number stored in the **Equipment Identity Register (EIR) database**. If a phone is reported as being lost or stolen, the IMEI number is marked to be invalid in the EIR.

A SIM card is registered to a particular user and can be transferred between devices. The user is identified by an **International Mobile Subscriber Identity (IMSI)** number. The number is stored on the SIM card in the format:

- Three-digit mobile country code.
- Two-digit mobile network code.
- Up to 10 digit mobile station identification number.

Note: The IMEI number identifies the device. The IMSI number identifies the subscriber.

An unlocked handset can be used with any type of SIM card from the user's chosen network provider; a locked handset is tied to a single network provider.

CDMA NETWORKS

CDMA locks the handset to the original provider and does not require any sort of SIM card. Handsets are identified by a **Mobile Equipment ID (MEID)**. Information that the cellular radio needs to connect to the network is provided as **Preferred Roaming Index (PRI)** and **Preferred Roaming List (PRL)** databases.

Note: Handsets from CDMA providers might come with a SIM card but the SIM card is to connect to 4G networks, which are all GSM-based. A handset might also have a SIM card to support roaming when traveling internationally as CDMA networks are not widespread outside the Americas.

*Note: To learn more, check the **Video** tile on the CHOICE Course screen for any videos that supplement the content for this lesson.*

Access the Checklist tile on your CHOICE Course screen for reference information and job aids on How to View IEMI and IMSI Numbers.

BASEBAND UPDATES AND RADIO FIRMWARE

A **baseband update** modifies the firmware of the radio modem used for cellular, Wi-Fi, Bluetooth, NFC, and GPS connectivity. **Radio firmware** in a mobile device contains an operating system that is separate from the end-user operating system (for example, Android or iOS). The modem uses its own baseband processor and memory, which boots a **Realtime Operating System (RTOS)**. An RTOS is often used for time-sensitive embedded controllers, of the sort required for the modulation and frequency shifts that underpin radio-based connectivity.

The procedures for establishing radio connections are complex and require strict compliance with regulatory certification schemes, so incorporating these functions in the main OS would make it far harder to bring OS updates to market. Unfortunately, baseband operating systems have been associated with several vulnerabilities over the years, so it is imperative to ensure that updates are applied promptly. These updates are usually pushed to the handset by the device vendor, often as part of OS upgrades. A handset that has been jailbroken or rooted might be able to be configured to prevent baseband updates or apply a particular version manually, but in the general course of things there is little reason to do so.

Note: **Jailbreaking** *and* **rooting** *mean circumventing the usual operation of the mobile OS to obtain super-user or root administrator permissions over the device.*

WI-FI NETWORKS AND HOTSPOTS

Not all mobile devices support cellular radios, but every smartphone and tablet supports a Wi-Fi radio.

In Android, you can use the notification shade to select a network or open the Wi-Fi settings menus.

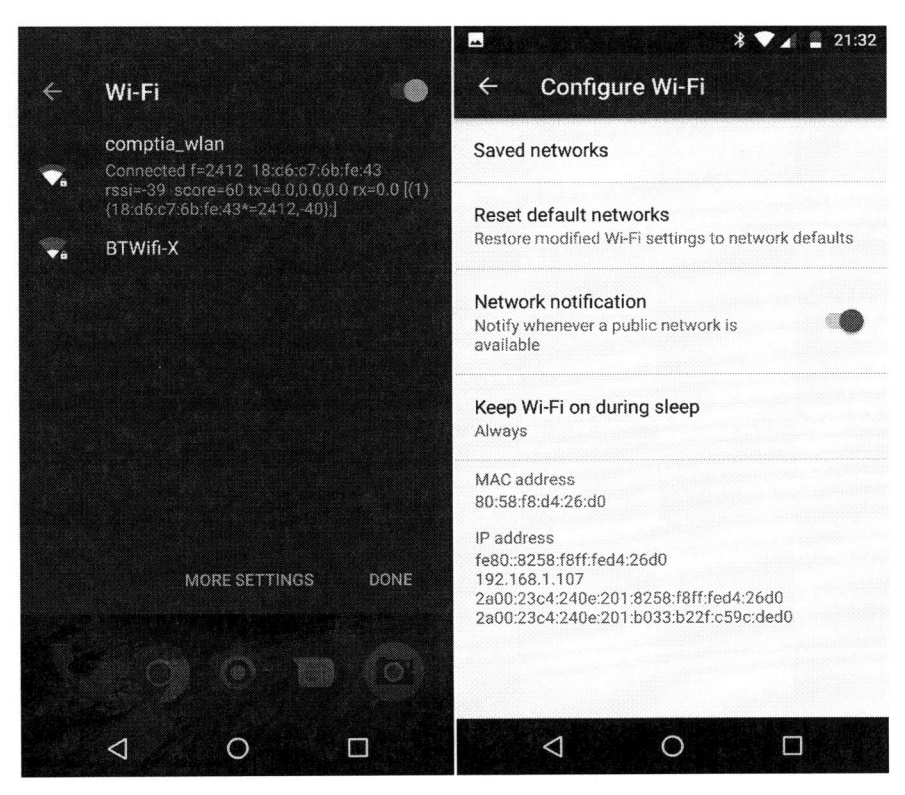

Using Android to join a Wi-Fi network (left). The device's network address can be checked using the Advanced Settings page (right).

In iOS, Wi-Fi networks can be setup via **Settings→Wi-Fi**. Either select the network name (if it is being broadcast) and credentials or manually configure the SSID and security level (WEP, WPA, or WPA2, for instance).

A **hotspot** is a location served by some sort of device offering Internet access via Wi-Fi. There are many ways to implement a hotspot:

- A business may set up an open access point to allow public access (or require payment via a captive portal).
- A smartphone or tablet might be configured to share its cellular data connection (a personal hotspot).
- A "Mi-Fi" mobile broadband device is one dedicated to providing a personal hotspot service.

When you are using a public hotspot, anyone else joined to the wireless network and the owner of the hotspot can easily intercept traffic passing over it. Consequently, users need to be careful to use SSL/TLS (with a valid digital certificate) to send confidential information to and from web servers and mail clients. Another option is to use a Virtual Private Network (VPN) to protect the browsing session.

Access the Checklist tile on your CHOICE Course screen for reference information and job aids on How to Enable or Disable Network Connections on Mobile Devices.

MOBILE VPN CONFIGURATION

A Virtual Private Network (VPN) uses a protocol such as **IPSec** or **Secure Sockets Tunneling Protocol (SSTP)** to create a **tunnel** through a carrier network. The contents of the tunnel can be encrypted so that no one with access to the carrier network (such as open access point) can intercept information passing through the VPN.

A **mobile VPN** is one that can maintain the VPN link across multiple carrier networks, where the IP address assigned to the mobile device may change often. The Mobile VPN app assigns a virtual IP address to connect to the VPN server, then uses any available carrier network to maintain the link. It is also capable of sustaining the link when the device is in sleep mode. Mobile VPNs are usually implemented as third party apps on both Android and iOS devices.

BLUETOOTH

Bluetooth is a short-range (up to about 10 m) radio link, working at a nominal rate of up to about 3 Mbps (for v2.0 + EDR). The latest versions of Bluetooth support a 24 Mbps data rate by negotiating a higher bandwidth link using the Wi-Fi radio. Bluetooth is used for so-called Personal Area Networks (PANs) to share data with a PC, connect to a printer, use a wireless headset, and so on.

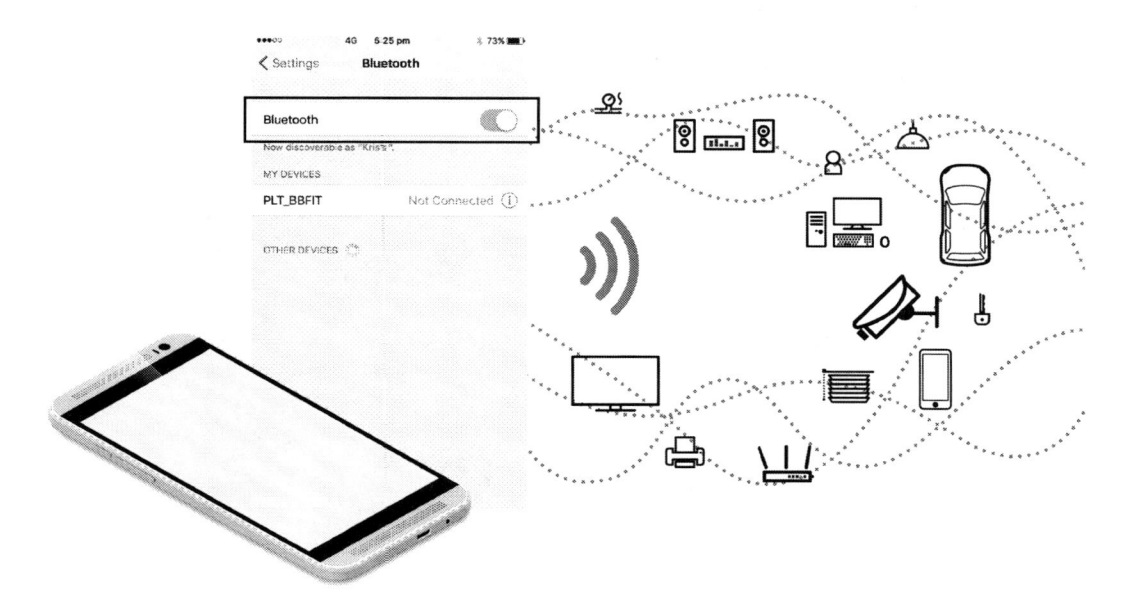

Bluetooth pairing.

In iOS, Bluetooth devices are configured via **Settings→General→Bluetooth**. Switch Bluetooth on to make the device discoverable and locate other nearby devices. In Android, you can access Bluetooth settings via the notification shade.

In Windows, you can manage Bluetooth Devices using the applet in Control Panel or Windows Settings and the Bluetooth icon in the notification area. The pairing system should automatically generate a passkey when a connection request is received. Input or confirm the key on the destination device and accept the connection.

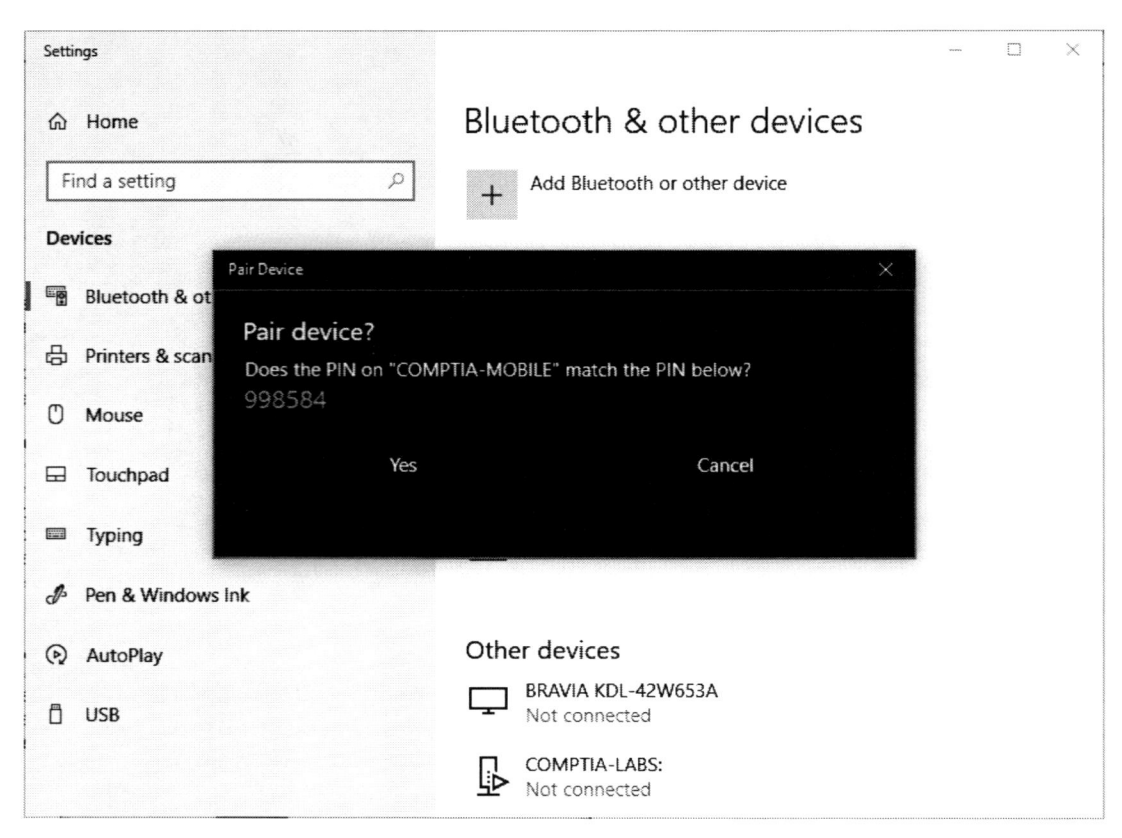

Pairing a Windows 10 computer with a smartphone. (Screenshot used with permission from Microsoft.)

To test the connection, you can simply try use the device—check that music plays through Bluetooth headphones, for example. If you are connecting a device and a Windows PC, you can use the Bluetooth icon 🔵 or `fsquirt` command to launch the Bluetooth File Transfer Wizard and enable sending or receiving of a file.

If you cannot connect a device, check that it has been made discoverable. Another option is to make the computer visible to Bluetooth devices (so that you can initiate a connection from the device rather than from Windows). You should also check that the PC is configured to allow connections (and that the Bluetooth radio is turned on).

If you make a computer discoverable, check the pairing list regularly to confirm that the devices listed are valid.

If you still cannot add or use Bluetooth devices, check that the **Bluetooth Support Service** is running. Also, consider using **Device Manager** to disable power management settings on the Bluetooth adapter and the problematic Bluetooth device.

*Note: To learn more, check the **Video** tile on the CHOICE Course screen for any videos that supplement the content for this lesson.*

Access the Checklist tile on your CHOICE Course screen for reference information and job aids on How to Enable Bluetooth.

AIRPLANE MODE

Each type of wireless radio link can be toggled on or off individually using the **Control Center** (swipe up from the bottom in iOS) or **notification shade** (swipe down from the top in Android). For example, you could disable the cellular data network while leaving Wi-Fi enabled to avoid incurring charges for data use over the cellular network. Most airlines prevent flyers from using radio-based devices while onboard a plane. A device can be put into **airplane mode** to comply with these restrictions, though some carriers insist that devices must be switched off completely at times such as take-off and landing. Airplane mode disables all wireless features (cellular data, Wi-Fi, GPS, Bluetooth, and NFC). On some devices, some services can selectively be re-enabled while still in airplane mode.

iOS iPhone (left) and Android phone (right) with Airplane (Aeroplane) mode enabled.

EMAIL CONFIGURATION OPTIONS

One of the most important features of mobile devices is the ability to receive and compose email. The settings are configured on the device in much the same way you would set up a mail account on a PC. For example, in iOS, open **Settings→Mail, Contacts, Calendars** then select **Add Account**.

COMMERCIAL PROVIDER EMAIL CONFIGURATION

Most mobile devices have integrated provider configurations that allow the OS to **autodiscover** connection settings. Autodiscover means that the mail service has published special Domain Name System (DNS) records that identify how the account for a particular domain should be configured. Many autodiscover-enabled providers will be listed on the device. Choose the mail provider (Exchange, Gmail™, Yahoo!®, Outlook®, iCloud®, and so on) then enter your email address and credentials and test the connection.

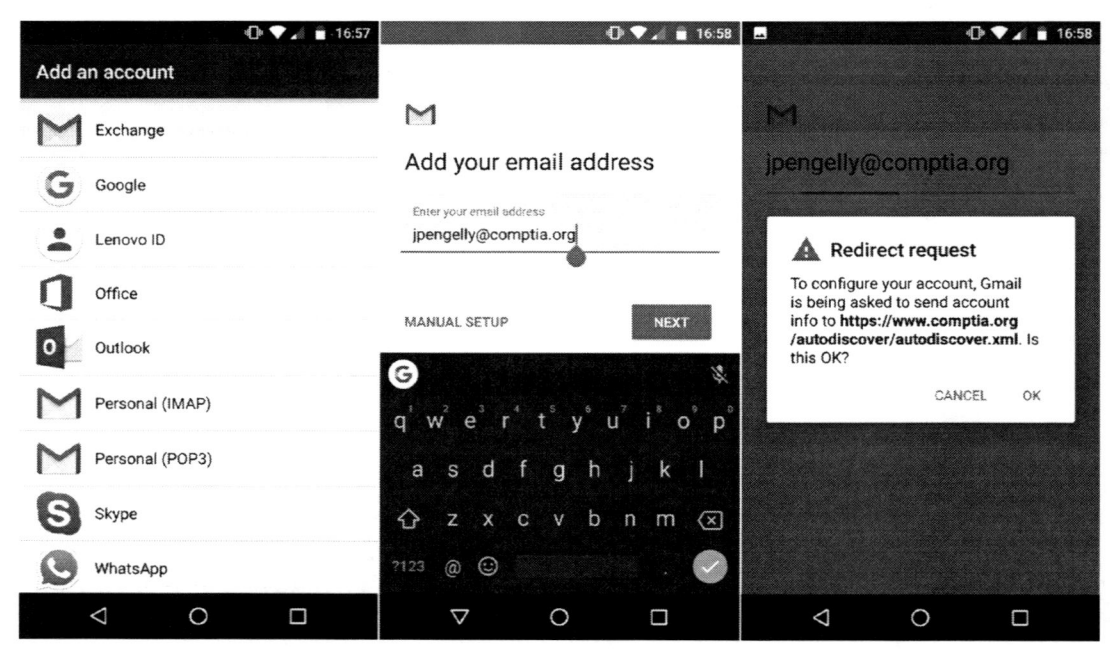

Configuring an autodiscover-enabled Exchange mail account in Android.

CORPORATE AND ISP EMAIL CONFIGURATION

Exchange is usually an integrated provider option and clients can autodiscover the correct settings. To manually configure an **Exchange ActiveSync** account you need to enter the email address and user name (usually the same thing) and a host address (obtain this from the Exchange administrator) as well as a password and the choice of whether to use **SSL** (most Exchange servers will require SSL). There is often also a field for domain but this is usually left blank.

Note: If there is a single "Domain\User Name" field, prefix the email address with a backslash: \me@company.com.

If you are connecting to an **Internet Service Provider (ISP)** or **corporate mail gateway** that does not support autodiscovery of configuration settings, you can enter the server address manually by selecting **Other**, then inputting the appropriate server addresses:

- Incoming mail server—**Internet Message Access Protocol (IMAP)** or **Post Office Protocol (POP3)**.

    *Note: Choose IMAP if you are viewing and accessing the mail from multiple devices. POP3 will download the mail to the device, removing it from the server mailbox. Note that Exchange doesn't use either POP3 or IMAP (though it can support them) but a proprietary protocol called **Messaging Application Programming Interface (MAPI)**.*

- Outgoing mail server—**Simple Mail Transfer Protocol (SMTP)**.
- Enable or disable **Secure Sockets Layer (SSL)**.

    Note: SSL protects confidential information such as the account password and is necessary if you connect to mail over a public link (such as an open Wi-Fi "hotspot"). Note that you can only enable SSL if the mail provider supports it.

- Ports—the secure (SSL enabled) or unsecure ports used for IMAP, POP3, and SMTP would normally be left to the default. If the email provider uses custom port settings, you would need to obtain those and enter them in the manual configuration.

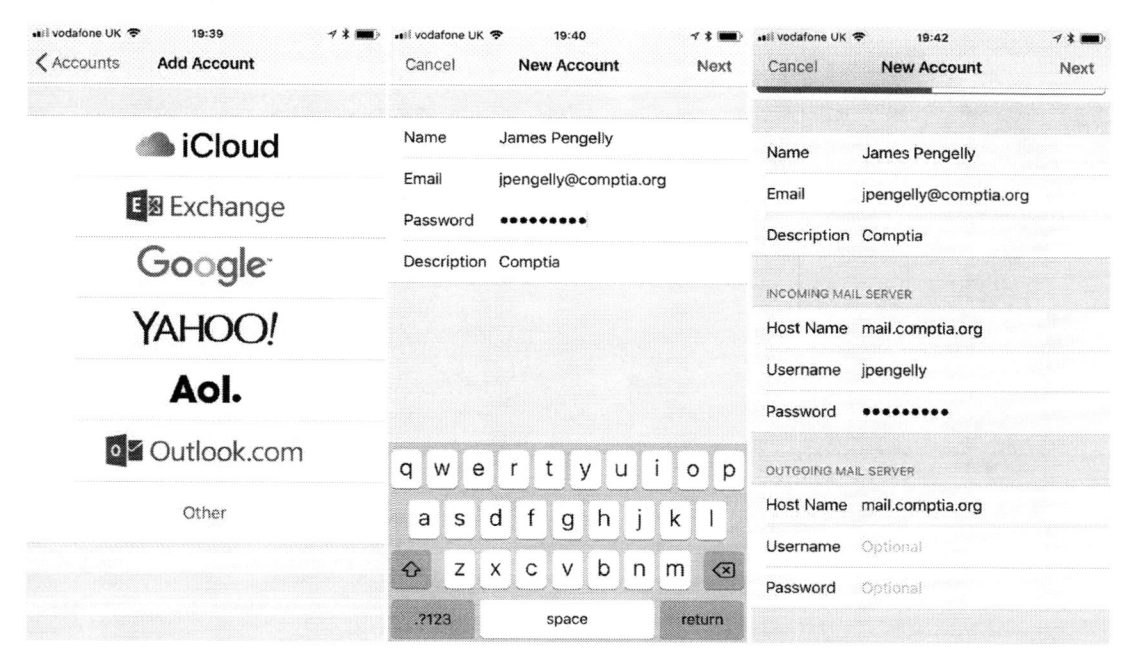

Configuring an email account manually in iOS.

S/MIME

Connecting to email servers by using secure ports ensures that the password you use to connect is protected by encryption. It does not provide "end-to-end" encryption of the messages you send, however. Encryption of an actual email message by using digital certificates and digital signatures ensures that a message can be read only by the intended recipient, that the identity of the sender is verified, and that the message has not been tampered with. The main difficulty is that both sender and recipient must agree to use the same (or compatible) encryption products. There are two main standards: **Pretty Good Privacy (PGP)** and **Secure Multipart Internet Mail Extensions (S/MIME)**. Both provide similar sorts of functions but use different mechanisms to trust digital identities.

Both PGP and S/MIME work with digital certificates and public/private key pairs. It is important to understand the two different ways these key pairs are used in an asymmetric encryption system:

- When you sign a message, you use your private key to validate who you are and give the public key related to that private key to anyone you want to communicate with. The public key allows the recipient to verify who you are.
- When you want people to send you messages that only you can read, your public key is used by the sender to encrypt the message. Once encrypted, only your private key can decrypt it (your public key cannot be used to reverse the encryption).

The **encryption keys** are stored and exchanged using digital certificates. Each mobile OS has a store for certificates, and for email encryption to work properly, the correct certificates and root certificates must be available to the application. In most scenarios, these would be added to the device using **Mobile Device Management (MDM)** software.

Note: To learn more, check the **Video** tile on the CHOICE Course screen for any videos that supplement the content for this lesson.

Access the Checklist tile on your CHOICE Course screen for reference information and job aids on How to Configure Email Accounts.

Activity 9-3
Discussing Mobile Device Network Connectivity Configuration

SCENARIO
Answer the following questions to check your understanding of the topic.

1. Why would a user be likely to disable cellular data access but leave Wi-Fi enabled?

2. What is tethering?

3. What serial number uniquely identifies a particular handset?

4. What is the function of a smartphone's baseband processor?

5. How do you configure an autodiscover-enabled email provider on a smartphone?

6. True or false? S/MIME is used to configure a secure connection to a mailbox server, so that your password cannot be intercepted when connecting over an open access point.

Activity 9-4
Configuring Bluetooth

SCENARIO
Personal Area Networks (PAN) are widely used to provide connectivity for wireless peripherals, as well as Internet connection tethering and personal hot spots. In this activity, you will practice using Bluetooth to configure a PAN.

1. Access the settings on the mobile device to determine which wireless connection methods are supported on your mobile device.

   Note: Your instructor will provide you with documentation or help guide you through this activity. As mobile devices vary widely, step-by-step directions would not necessarily apply to the devices available to you.

2. Create a Bluetooth connection between two Bluetooth capable devices.
   a) Enable Bluetooth on the mobile device by using the system settings.
   b) Enable pairing on the device.
   c) On your mobile device, find a device for pairing.
   d) Once the device is found, it will ask for a PIN code.
   Depending on the type of device, the PIN code will be sent via a text, or will be a standard code, such as "0000" used for wireless headsets.
   e) Verify that a connection message has been displayed.
   f) Test the connection by using the two devices together to either transfer data, answer or make a call, or play music.

Topic D
Support Mobile Apps

EXAM OBJECTIVES COVERED
1001-1.7 Given a scenario, use methods to perform mobile device synchronization.
1001-3.9 Given a scenario, install and configure common devices.

Data synchronization is the process of automatically merging and updating common data that is stored on multiple devices. For example, a user can access his or her email contacts list from both his or her mobile device and his or her laptop computer. Synchronization is established when the devices are either connected via a cable or wirelessly, or over a network connection. In this topic, you will identify methods and best practices for managing accounts and apps and synchronizing mobile devices.

MOBILE ACCOUNT SETUP

Most mobile devices have a single user account, configured when the device is used for the first time (or re-initialized). This account is used to manage the apps installed on the device by representing the user on the app store. iOS requires an Apple ID while an Android device requires either a **Google Account** or a similar vendor account, such as a **Samsung Account**. This type of account just requires you to select a unique ID (email address) and to configure your credentials (pattern lock, fingerprint, face ID, and so on). Accounts can also be linked to a cellphone number or alternative email address for verification and recovery functions.

> *Note: Multi-user capability is more useful on tablet devices (for use in the classroom, for instance) than on smartphones. Android has some multi-user functionality. Apple makes classroom deployment software available, but otherwise iOS is single user per device.*

As well as managing the app store, the account can be used to access various services, such as an email account and cloud storage.

The user can set up sub-accounts for services not represented by their Apple ID or Google Account, such as a corporate email account. Each app can set up a sub-account, too. For example, your device might have accounts for apps such as Facebook or LinkedIn®.

Account settings allow you to choose which features of a particular account type are enabled to synchronize data with the device. You can also add and delete accounts from here.

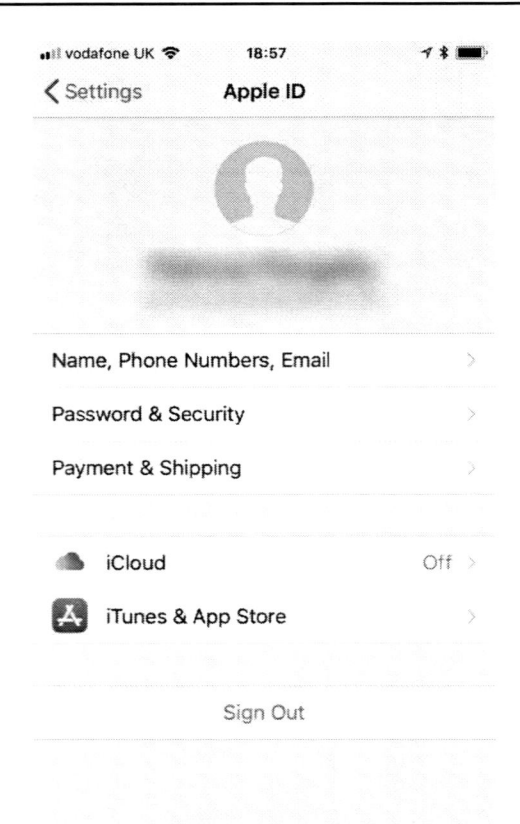

iOS supports a single Apple ID account per device. (Screenshot courtesy of Apple.)

MOBILE APPLICATIONS AND APP STORES

Apps are installable programs that extend the functionality of the mobile device. An app must be written and compiled for a particular mobile operating system (Apple iOS, Android, or Windows).

iOS APPS

Apps are made available for free or can be bought from the **App Store**. Apps have to be submitted to and approved by Apple before they are released to users. This is also referred as the **walled garden model** and is designed to prevent the spread of malware or code that could cause faults or crashes. Apps can use a variety of commercial models, including free to use, free with in-app purchases, or paid-for.

Third-party developers can create apps for iOS using Apple's **Software Development Kit (SDK) Xcode** and the programming language **Swift**. Xcode can only be installed and run on a computer using macOS®.

Note: There is also an Apple Developer Enterprise program allowing corporate apps to be distributed to employees without having to publish them in the App Store.

Apple's App Store and app permission settings. This app is already installed, but an update is available.

ANDROID APPS

Android's app model is more relaxed, with apps available from both Google Play™ and third-party sites, such as Amazon's app store. The Java-based SDK (Android Studio) is available on Linux, Windows, and macOS. Apps are supposed to run in a sandbox and have only the privileges granted by the user.

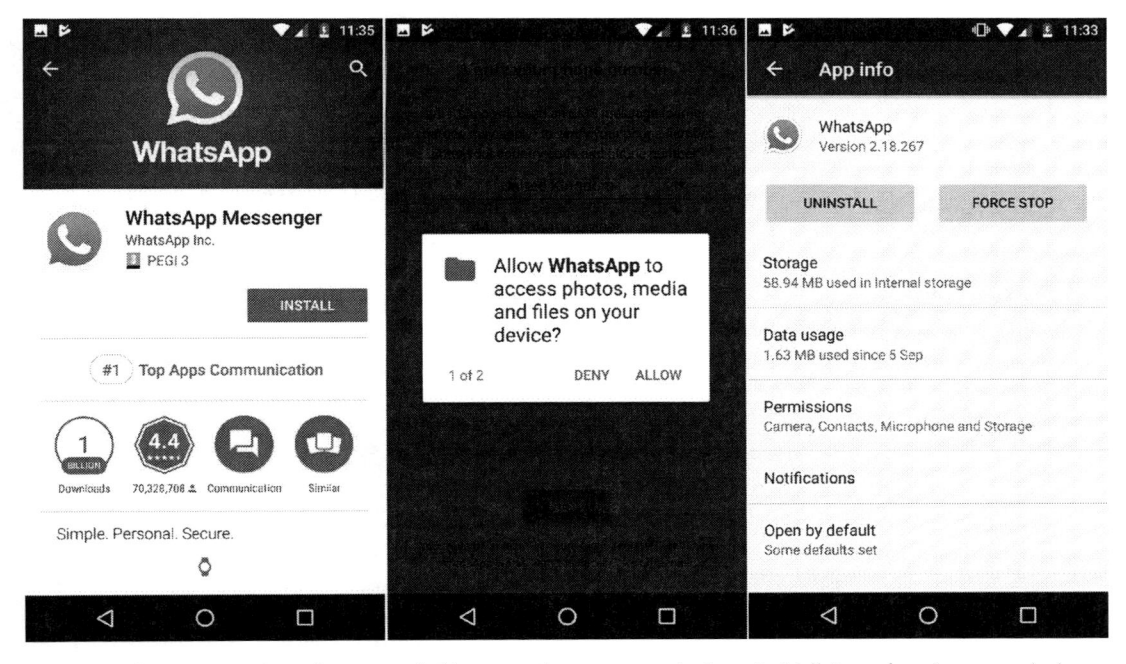

Use the Play Store to install an app (left), grant the app permissions (middle), and review permissions and other settings (right).

An app will normally prompt when it needs to obtain permissions. If these are not granted, or if they need to be revoked later, you can do this via the app's **Settings** page.

Android also allows third-party or custom programs to be installed directly via an **Android Application Package (apk)** file, giving users and businesses the flexibility to directly install apps (**sideload**) without going through the storefront interface. An APK file contains all of that program's code, including .dex files, resources, assets, certificates, and manifest files. Similar to other file formats, APK files can be named almost anything, as long as the file name ends in .apk.

TYPES OF DATA TO SYNCHRONIZE

Mobile device synchronization (sync) refers to copying data back and forth between different devices. This might mean between a PC and smartphone or between a smartphone, a tablet, and a PC. Many people have multiple devices and need to keep information up-to-date on all of them. If someone edits a contact record on a phone, they want the changes to appear when they next log into email on their PC.

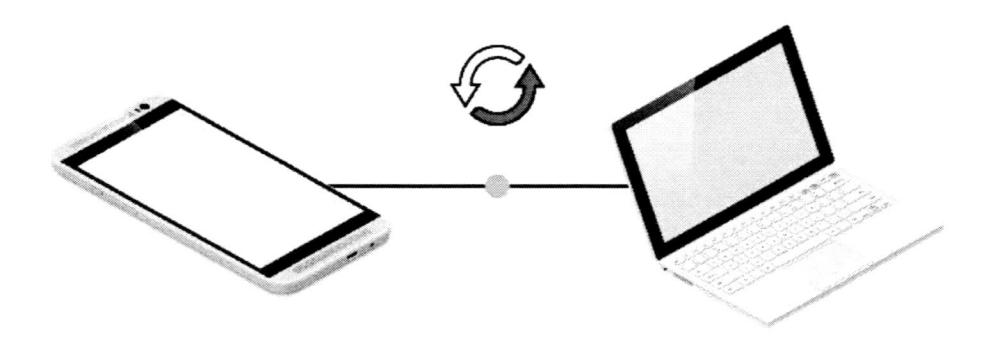

Data synchronization. (Image © 123RF.com.)

There are many different types of information that users might synchronize and many issues you might face dealing with synchronization problems.

CONTACTS

A **contact** is a record with fields for name, address, email address(es), phone numbers, notes, and so on. One issue with contacts is that people tend to create them on different systems and there can be issues matching fields or phone number formats when importing from one system to another using a file format such as **Comma Separated Values (CSV)**. **vCard** represents one standard format and is widely supported now. Maintaining a consistent, single set of contact records is challenging for most people, whatever the technology solutions available!

CALENDAR

A calendar item is a record with fields for appointment or task information, such as subject, date, location, and participants. Calendar records have the same sort of sync issues as contacts; people create appointments in different calendars and then have trouble managing them all. Calendar items can be exchanged between different services using the iCalendar format. Another (fairly minor) issue is that the reminders tend to go off on all devices at the same time.

EMAIL

Most email systems store messages on the server and the client device is used only to manage them (IMAP, Exchange, and web mail, for instance). There can often be sync issues, however, particularly with deletions, sent items, and draft compositions.

PICTURES, MUSIC, AND VIDEO

The main sync issue with media files tends to be the amount of space they take up. There might not be enough space on one device to sync all the files the user has stored. There can also be issues with file formats; not all devices can play or show all formats.

DOCUMENTS

As with media files, documents can use many different formats (Microsoft Word, PDF, plain text, Open XML, and so on). Users editing a document on different devices may have trouble with version history, unless the changes are saved directly to the copy stored in the cloud.

E-BOOKS

There are many apps for purchasing or borrowing **e-books** and **e-magazines** or **e-newspapers**. Often the formats used by different merchants are not interoperable, so multiple e-readers may be required. An e-reader will usually track where you have read to in an e-book, so if you open it on a different device, you can pick up on the page you left off. There are also often facilities for making annotations.

LOCATION DATA

Modern services add **geolocation** data to pretty much everything. If you use a map or travel planner while signed into the service, your location history is likely to have been recorded, unless you have selected an opt-out.

SOCIAL MEDIA DATA

The apps used to manage our **online social lives** store pretty much all information in the cloud, using local storage for cache only, so the view of your online life from your phone is likely to be pretty much the same as from your PC.

APPLICATIONS

When you purchase an app from a store, it will be available across all devices you sign in on, as long as they are the same platform. If you have a Windows PC and an Apple iPhone, you will find yourself managing two sets of apps. Most of them will share data seamlessly, however (the social media ones, for instance). Apple has introduced a family sharing feature to allow apps to be shared between different Apple IDs within the same family.

BOOKMARKS

A **bookmark** is a record of a website or web page that you visited. Browsers keep an automatic history of bookmarks and you can also create a shortcut (or favorite) manually.

PASSWORDS

Both iOS and Android will prompt you to save passwords when you sign in to apps and websites. These passwords are cached securely within the device file system and protected by the authentication and encryption mechanisms required to access the device via the lock screen.

These cached passwords can be synchronized across your devices using cloud services. You have to remember that anyone compromising your device/cloud account will be able to access any service that you have cached the password for.

SYNCHRONIZATION METHODS

Historically, data synchronization would most often take place between a single smartphone and desktop PC. You might use the PC to back up data stored on the smartphone, for instance, or to sync calendar and contact records. Nowadays, it is much more likely for all our devices to be connected via cloud services. If given permission, the device OS backs up data to the cloud service all the time. When you sign in to a new device, it syncs the data from the cloud seamlessly.

iOS SYNCHRONIZATION METHODS

iOS can synchronize with a Windows or Mac computer via the iTunes® program. As with any software, you need to ensure that the computer meets the requirements to install the sync software. The system requirements for these programs are not typically onerous, however. At the time of writing, the principal system requirements for iTunes are a 1 GHz PC with 512 MB RAM, 400 MB free disk space, and Windows 7 or later or any Mac running OS X® or macOS 10.8.5 or later.

The software may install background services and require these to be running to facilitate connections. For example, iTunes requires the Apple Mobile Device Service to communicate with devices and the Bonjour service to enable some features, such as sharing media libraries.

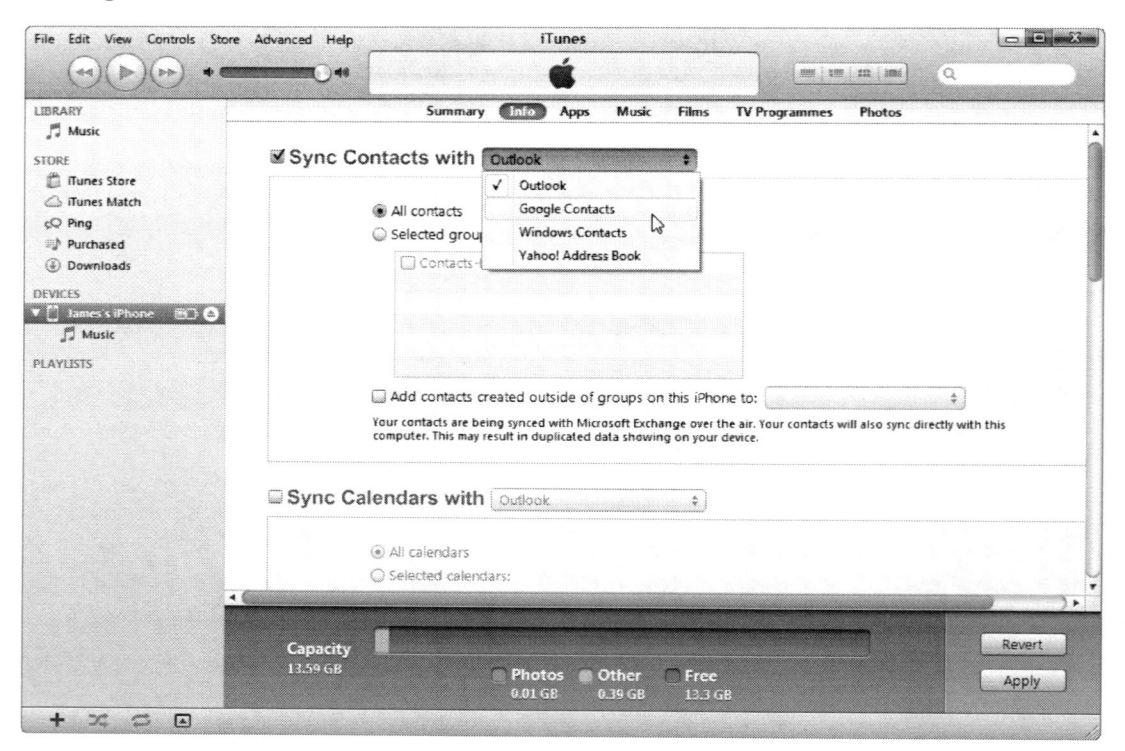

Using iTunes to sync data between an iPhone and a PC.

Once iTunes is installed, the device can be connected to the computer via a USB cable (with an Apple Dock or Lightning connector at the iPhone end) or via a Wi-Fi link.

The software allows the user to choose what to synchronize with the device. Users can also use iTunes as a means of purchasing apps to be sent to their mobile devices.

Another feature of iTunes is the ability to back up, recover, and reinstall firmware on the phone. It is also used to activate the device at the first use.

Apple has also the iCloud service, which allows synchronization of devices via a cloud storage facility so that all iOS devices owned by a user with the same ID can share data, photos, music, and contacts.

ANDROID SYNCHRONIZATION METHODS

Android-based phones are primarily set up to sync with Google's Gmail email and calendar/contact manager cloud services.

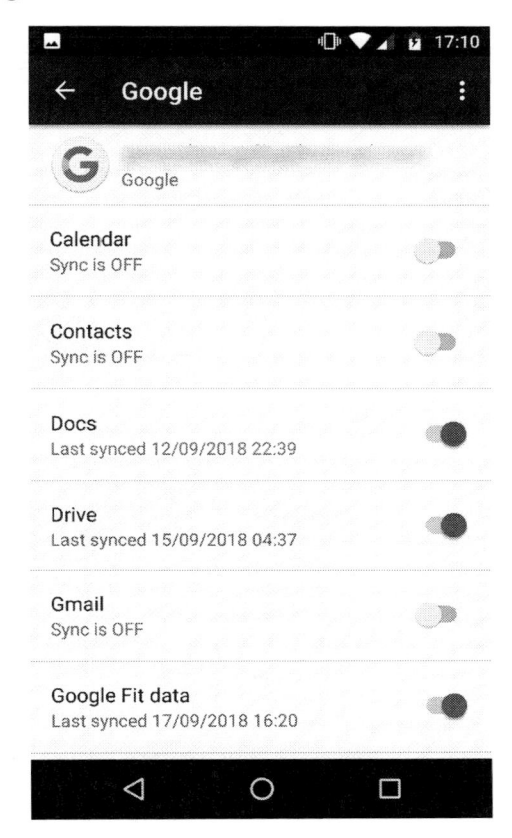

Account settings for the Google master account on an Android smartphone. This account is used for the Play Store and to sync data with other cloud services, but not email, contacts, or calendar.

You can usually view an Android phone or tablet from Windows over USB or Bluetooth and use drag-and-drop for file transfer (using the Media Transfer Protocol). Some Android vendors have utilities for synchronization similar to iTunes, such as Samsung Kies for Samsung phones.

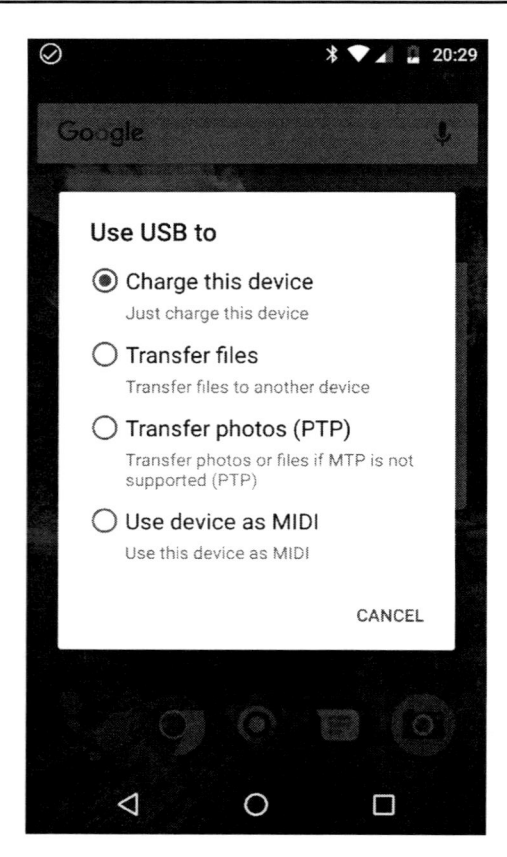

Connecting an Android smartphone to a Windows PC over USB. You can choose whether to allow some sort of data transfer as well as charge the battery. If you enable data transfer, the device's file system will be made available via File Explorer.

The app doubleTwist provides a means of synching with an iTunes library, and there are various other third-party apps for synching with other programs or using protocols such as File Transfer Protocol (FTP).

MICROSOFT AND THIRD-PARTY SYNCHRONIZATION METHODS

Microsoft makes a whole range of cloud services available with a Microsoft account, including free storage space on OneDrive and email/calendar/contact management on Outlook.com. There is also the cloud-based Office suite Office365 with word processing, spreadsheet, and presentation software (amongst others).

Apple, Google, and Microsoft obviously make it easy to use "their" cloud services on "their" devices, but all produce apps for the different platforms, so you can (for example) run OneDrive on an iPhone if you want. There are also third-party cloud sync and storage services, most notably Dropbox™. You should check the vendor's website for any software requirements for installing the desktop app. For example, Dropbox's desktop app runs on Windows 7 or later, macOS 10.9 or later, Ubuntu™ 14.04 or later, or Fedora 21 or later. There are additional requirements for a supported file system (NTFS, HFS/APFS, or ext4, respectively) and in Linux™, for the presence of various libraries and supporting packages.

SYNCHRONIZING TO AUTOMOBILES

Most new automobiles come with in-vehicle entertainment and navigation systems. The main part of this system is referred to as the **head unit**. If supported, a smartphone can be used to "drive" the head unit so the navigation features from your smartphone will appear on the display (simplified for safe use while driving) or you could play songs stored on your tablet via the vehicle's entertainment system. The technologies underpinning this are **Apple CarPlay** and **Android Auto**. Typically, the smartphone has to be connected via USB. Both CarPlay Wireless and Android Auto Wireless have been released, and at time of writing, are supported by a few in-vehicle systems.

MUTUAL AUTHENTICATION FOR MULTIPLE SERVICES

Most service providers want to obtain as much personal data as they can and are consequently hungry for us to register accounts with their apps and websites. Equally, though, many service providers recognize that users don't want to be continually creating multiple accounts on multiple apps or sites and that registration can be a barrier to a user choosing to continue to use the app.

What the CompTIA exam objectives describe as **Mutual authentication for multiple services (SSO [Single Sign On])** means that one service accepts the credentials from another service. This is more usually described as **federated identity management**. For example, you could sign into a popular newspaper app using your Facebook credentials. In this scenario, the newspaper does not process the sign in itself and your password is not passed to the newspaper app. Instead, the newspaper app relies on Facebook's web services to authenticate the account and provide authorization information, which the newspaper app then uses to identify you as a previous customer or user.

A true single sign-on environment means that you authenticate once to access many services. This model is typical of enterprise networks and their email, database, and document management applications. Mobile device apps supporting a true single sign-on environment would usually take the device credentials. For example, when you associate your iPhone with an Apple ID (say, david.martin@apple.com) and unlock it, an SSO newspaper app on that iPhone would identify that you are signed in as david.martin@apple.com and load the appropriate profile for you automatically, without requiring you to sign in again. Not many third party apps actually integrate with SSO in this way, but the vendor cloud services work on this basis. For example, when you sign in to Google, you are signing in to email, maps, YouTube, search, and so on.

*Note: To learn more, check the **Video** tile on the CHOICE Course screen for any videos that supplement the content for this lesson.*

Access the Checklist tile on your CHOICE Course screen for reference information and job aids on How to Support Mobile Apps.

Activity 9-5
Discussing Mobile App Support

SCENARIO
Answer the following questions to check your understanding of the topic.

1. Why must a vendor account usually be configured on a smartphone?

2. What is sideloading?

3. Which types of data might require mapping between fields when syncing between applications?

4. What software is used to synchronize data files between an iOS device and a PC and what connection methods can it use?

5. How might an app register users without implementing its own authentication process?

Summary

In this lesson, you worked with mobile computing devices. You examined mobile device technologies, including smartphones, tablets, wearable devices, and more. As an A+ technician, you will need to be able to expertly support and troubleshoot mobile devices.

In your professional experience, have you supported mobile devices? If not, what kind of experience do you have with them?

What type of technical support do you think will be expected of an A+ technician as mobile devices become even more prominent within the workplace?

Practice Question: Additional practice questions are available on the CompTIA CHOICE platform within the **Assessments** tile.

Lesson 10
Installing, Configuring, and Troubleshooting Print Devices

LESSON INTRODUCTION

Despite predictions that computers would bring about a paperless office environment, the need to transfer digital information to paper or back again remains as strong as ever. Therefore, printing is still among the most common tasks for users in almost every home or business environment. As a CompTIA® A+® certified professional, you will often be called upon to set up, configure, and troubleshoot printing environments, so you will need to understand printer technologies as well as know how to perform common printer support tasks.

As a professional support technician, you might be supporting the latest cutting-edge technology, or you might be responsible for ensuring that legacy systems continue to function adequately. So, you must be prepared for either situation and be able to provide the right level of support to users and clients. Having a working knowledge of the many printer technologies and components will help you to support users' needs in any technical environment.

LESSON OBJECTIVES

In this lesson, you will:

- Maintain laser printers.
- Maintain inkjet printers.
- Maintain impact, thermal, and 3D printers.
- Install and configure printers.
- Troubleshooting print device issues.
- Install and configure imaging devices.

Topic A
Maintain Laser Printers

EXAM OBJECTIVES COVERED
1001-3.6 Explain the purposes and uses of various peripheral types.
1001-3.11 Given a scenario, install and maintain various print technologies.

Before you can provide the right level of support, you must fully understand how these systems are used in a production environment. You need to understand how the various components work within a printer to provide the desired outputs. In this topic, you will identify components of, and the print process for, laser printer technologies.

PRINTER TYPES

A **printer** is a device that produces text and images from electronic data onto physical media such as paper, photo paper, and labels. A printer output of electronic documents is often referred to as **hard copy**. Printers employ a range of technologies; the quality of the print output varies with the printer type and generally in proportion to the printer cost.

A **printer type** or **printer technology** is the mechanism used to make images on the paper. The most common types for general home and office use are **inkjet** (or **ink dispersion**) and **laser**, though others are used for more specialist applications. Some of the major print device vendors include HP, Epson, Canon, Xerox, Brother, OKI, Konica/Minolta, Lexmark, Ricoh, and Samsung.

There are many types of printers. Each type of printer, and each printer from different manufacturers, implements the printing process slightly differently. All of the printers will have the following common components:

- A connection to computing devices.
- A mechanism for creating text and images.
- A paper feed mechanism.
- Paper input and output options.

Each of these will be discussed in detail throughout this lesson.

PRINTER FEATURES

The following criteria are used to select the best type and model of printer.

SPEED

The basic speed of a printer is measured in Pages Per Minute (ppm). You will see different speeds quoted for different types of output (for example, pages of monochrome text will print more quickly than color photos).

INTERFACES

Almost all printers support USB, but printer models designed for workgroups also support network connections, usually at a higher cost than standard models. Wireless connections may also carry a price premium.

IMAGE QUALITY

The basic measure of image quality is the maximum supported resolution, measured in dots per inch (dpi). Printer dots and screen image pixels are not equivalent. It requires multiple dots to reproduce one pixel at acceptable quality. Pixel dimensions are typically quoted in pixels per inch (ppi) to avoid confusion. Vertical and horizontal resolution are often different, so you may see figures such as 2400x600 quoted. The horizontal resolution is determined by the print engine (that is, either the laser scanning unit or inkjet print head); vertical resolution is determined by the paper handling mechanism.

The minimum resolution for a monochrome printer should be 600 dpi. Photo-quality printers start at 1200 dpi.

Resolution is not the only factor in determining overall print quality, however (especially with color output). When evaluating a printer, obtain samples to judge text and color performance.

> **Note:** *Image quality needs to be matched to use. The best quality will be correspondingly expensive. Always request sample sheets when evaluating a printer.*

PAPER HANDLING

Paper handling means the type of paper or media that can be loaded. It may be important that the printer can handle labels, envelopes, card stock, acetate, and so on. The amount of paper that can be loaded and output is also important in high volume environments. Overloaded output trays will cause paper jams. If the output tray is low capacity, this could happen quite quickly in a busy office.

TOTAL COST OF OWNERSHIP (TCO)

TCO is the cost of the printer over its lifetime, including the cost of replacement components and consumables. It is important to know how a printer will be used to work out TCO.

OPTIONS

Options might include additional memory, duplex (double-sided) printing, large format (A3 and greater), binding, and so on. These may be fitted by default or available for additional purchase as optional extras.

MULTI-FUNCTION DEVICE (MFD)

An **MFD** is a piece of office equipment that performs the functions of a number of other specialized devices. MFDs typically include the functions of a printer, scanner, fax machine, and copier. However, there are MFDs that do not include fax functions. Although the multifunction device might not equal the performance or feature sets of the dedicated devices it replaces, multi-function devices are very powerful and can perform most tasks adequately and are an economical and popular choice for most home or small-office needs.

LASER PRINTERS

A laser printer is a printer that uses a laser beam to project (or "draw") a latent image onto an electrically charged drum; toner adheres to the drum and is transferred onto the paper as the paper moves through the mechanism at the same speed the drum rotates. The toner is fixed using high heat and pressure, creating a durable printout that does not smear or fade.

Laser printers are one of the most popular printer technologies for office applications because they are cheap (both to buy and to run), quiet, and fast, and they produce high quality output. There are both grayscale and color models.

LASER PRINTER IMAGING PROCESS

In the laser printing process, laser printers print a page at a time using a combination of electrostatic charges, toner, and laser light. The laser print process follows the steps detailed in the following sections.

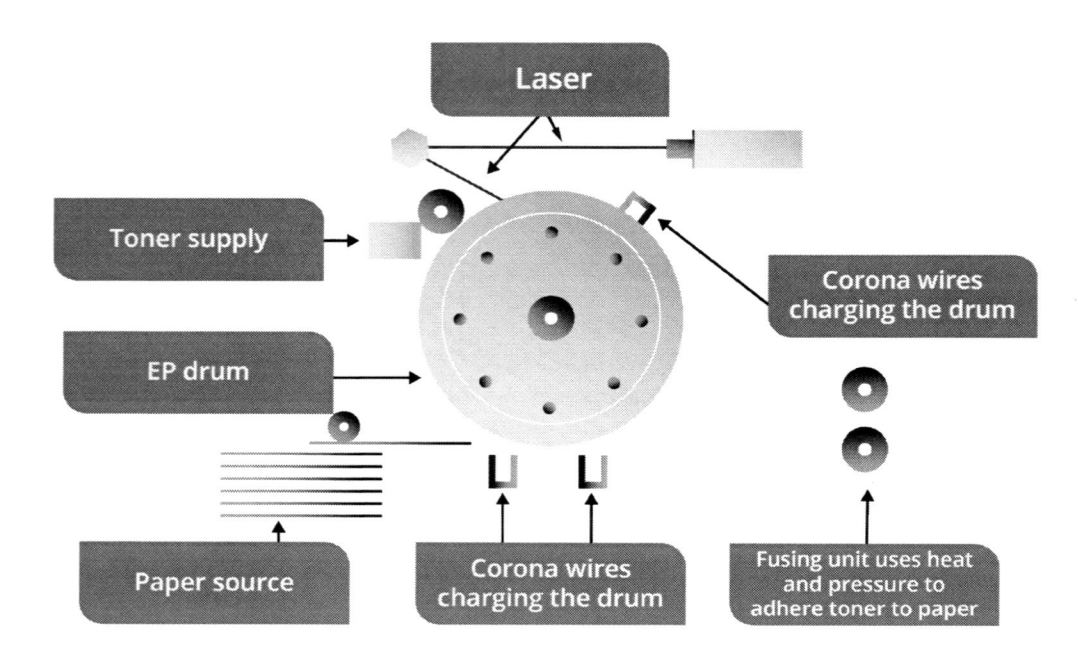

The laser print process.

PROCESSING

Like most printers, laser printers produce their printed output in a series of dots. The computer encodes the page in a printer language and sends it to the printer. The printer's formatter board processes the data to create a bitmap (or **raster**) of the page and stores it in the printer's RAM.

The entire laser printer cycle takes place in one smooth sequence but, since the circumference of the drum that processes the image is smaller than a sheet of paper, the process must be repeated 2-4 times (according to size) to process a single page.

CHARGING (CONDITIONING)

The **electrostatic photographic (EP) drum**, or **imaging drum** is conditioned by a corona wire powered by a high voltage power supply assembly. The corona wire applies a uniform -600 V electrical charge across the drum's surface. A laser printer has a power supply capable of generating very high voltages. It converts the supplied current to optimal AC and DC voltages for specific components, such as the corona wire.

> *Note: The charging corona is also referred to as the primary corona. On most modern printers, the function of the charging corona wire is actually performed by a metal roller with a rubber coating—the Primary Charge Roller (PCR).*

EXPOSING (WRITING)

The surface coating of the photosensitive drum loses its charge when exposed to light. A laser neutralizes the charge that was applied by the corona wire selectively, dot-by-dot and line-by-line, as the drum rotates. The laser-scanning assembly houses a small, low-power laser, similar to that used in an optical drive. As the laser receives the image information, it fires a short pulse of light for each dot in the raster. The pulsing light beam is reflected by a rotating polygonal mirror through a system of lenses onto the photosensitive drum. The drum ends up with a whole series of raster lines with charge/no-charge areas that represent an **electrostatic latent image** of the image to be printed.

DEVELOPING

Laser (and photocopier) toner is composed of a fine compound of dyestuff and either wax or plastic particles. The toner is fed evenly onto a magnetized roller (the **developer roller**) from a hopper.

The developer roller is located very close to the photosensitive drum. The toner carries the same negative charge polarity as the drum, which means that, under normal circumstances, there would be no interaction between the two parts. However, once areas of charge have been selectively removed from the photosensitive drum by the laser, the toner is attracted to them and sticks to those parts of its surface. The drum, now coated with toner in the image of the document, rotates until it reaches the paper.

TRANSFERRING

The paper transport mechanism includes components such as gears, pads, and rollers that move the paper through the printer. Paper loaded into a tray should be held by **media guides**. The printer uses sensors from the guides to detect the paper type. Different trays may support different types, sizes, and thicknesses of media. Pickup components lift a single sheet of paper from the selected input tray and feed it into the printer. To do this, a **pickup roller** turns once against the paper stack, pushing the paper into a **feed** and **separation roller** assembly (the manual feed tray uses a **separation pad** rather than rollers). This assembly is designed to allow only one sheet to pass through.

Pickup, feed, and separation rollers on an HP 5Si laser printer.

When the paper reaches the **registration roller**, a signal tells the printer to start the image development process. When the drum is ready, the paper is fed between the photosensitive drum and the high voltage **transfer roller** (or secondary corona). The transfer roller applies a positive charge to the underside of the paper. This causes the toner on the drum to be attracted to the paper. As the paper leaves the transfer assembly, a **static eliminator** strip (or **detac corona**) removes any remaining charge from the paper, which might otherwise cause it to stick to the drum or curl as it enters the fuser unit.

FUSING

From the drum and transfer assembly, the paper passes into the **fuser assembly**. The fuser unit squeezes the paper between a hot roller and a pressure roller so that the toner is fused, or melted, onto the surface of the paper. The hot roller is a metal tube containing a heat lamp; the pressure roller is typically silicon rubber. The heat roller has a Teflon coating to prevent toner from sticking to it.

CLEANING

To complete the printing cycle, the photosensitive drum is cleaned to remove any remaining toner particles using a **cleaning blade**, roller, or brush resting on the surface of the drum. Any residual electrical charge is removed using either a discharge (or **erase lamp**) or the **primary charge roller**.

DUPLEX PRINTING AND PAPER OUTPUT PATH

When the paper has passed through the fuser, if a **duplexing assembly** unit is installed, it is turned over and returned to the developer unit to print the second side. Otherwise, the paper is directed to the selected output bin using the exit rollers.

If there is no auto duplex unit, the user can manually flip the paper stack. When duplex mode is selected for the print job, the printer pauses after printing the first side of each sheet. The user must then take the printed pages and return them (without changing the orientation) to the same input paper tray. Once this is done, the user resumes the print job.

COLOR LASER PRINTERS

Color laser printers, once very highly priced and positioned at the top end of the market, are becoming more affordable, with medium quality, entry-level models priced competitively against inkjet equivalents. Color lasers use separate color toner cartridges (Cyan, Magenta, Yellow, and Black) but employ different processes to create the image. Some may use four passes to put down each color; others combine the colors on a **transfer belt** and print in one pass.

LED PRINTERS

A traditional laser printer uses a laser with a rotating mirror and prisms to scan across each raster line. An **LED printer** uses a fixed array of tiny Light Emitting Diodes (LED) to create the light pulses for each dot in each scan line. Vendors claim that with fewer moving parts, LED printers can be more reliable than lasers, but damage to the LED array is expensive to repair. LED printers are usually much lighter than laser printers, however, and print speeds can be a bit faster.

LASER PRINTER MAINTENANCE TASKS

As devices with moving parts and consumable items that deplete quickly, printers need more maintenance than most other computer devices. Printers generate a lot of dirt—principally paper dust and ink/toner spills—and consequently require regular cleaning. Consumable items also require replacing frequently under heavy use. To keep them working in good condition requires a regular maintenance schedule and user training.

One of the first steps in maximizing the lifetime of a printer is to train users to treat it with sufficient care and attention. Depending on the environment, users might be expected to perform basic maintenance tasks—such as reloading paper and changing cartridges. Typical problems include:

- Overloading input trays or output trays (not collecting completed jobs promptly).
- Using unsuitable media—for example, card stock or labels in an auto-feed tray.
- Using creased, folded, or dirty paper.
- Breaking trays or covers.
- Inserting ink or toner cartridges incorrectly.

It is also easy for users to be confused by settings such as default paper size, form-to-tray assignment, duplex printing, printing to labels or envelopes, collating multiple copies, and dealing with paper jams.

> **Note:** *For best results and to stay within warranty, use branded supplies designed for the specific model of printer.*

Most laser printers benefit from regular, routine maintenance to ensure optimum print quality.

LOADING PAPER

The printer will report when a tray runs out of paper. When loading new paper, remember the following guidelines:

- Use good quality paper designed for use with the model of printer that you have and the printing function.
- Do not overload a paper tray.
- Do not use creased, dirty, or damp paper.
- Refer to the instruction manual when loading non-standard print media, such as transparencies or envelopes. Make sure this type of material is oriented correctly to avoid wasting stocks.

You will also need to deal with paper jams. The printer's status panel will indicate what area of the printer is jammed. Check the instruction manual to find out how to remove any components that might prevent you from removing the paper.

> **Note: Do not allow a jammed page to rip!** *If a page is stuck in the fuser or developer unit, look for a release mechanism or lever.*

REPLACING THE TONER CARTRIDGE

Laser printer toner is a fine powder made of particles of iron, carbon, and resin. Laser printers require a toner cartridge, which is a single, replaceable unit that contains toner as well as additional components used in image production. You will need to maintain a supply of the proper toner cartridges for your printer model. Refill or recycle empty toner cartridges; do not dispose of them in regular trash.

Users can change toner cartridges, but everyone should follow proper handling procedures, which are usually printed right on the cartridge. When toner is low, the printer will display a status message advising you of the fact. Frugal departments may continue printing until the actual output starts to dip in quality. Removing the cartridge and rocking gently from front-to-back can help to get the most out of it.

To replace the toner cartridge, remove the old cartridge by opening the relevant service panel and pulling it out. Place the cartridge in a bag to avoid shedding toner everywhere. Color lasers will usually have four cartridges for the different colors, which can be replaced separately.

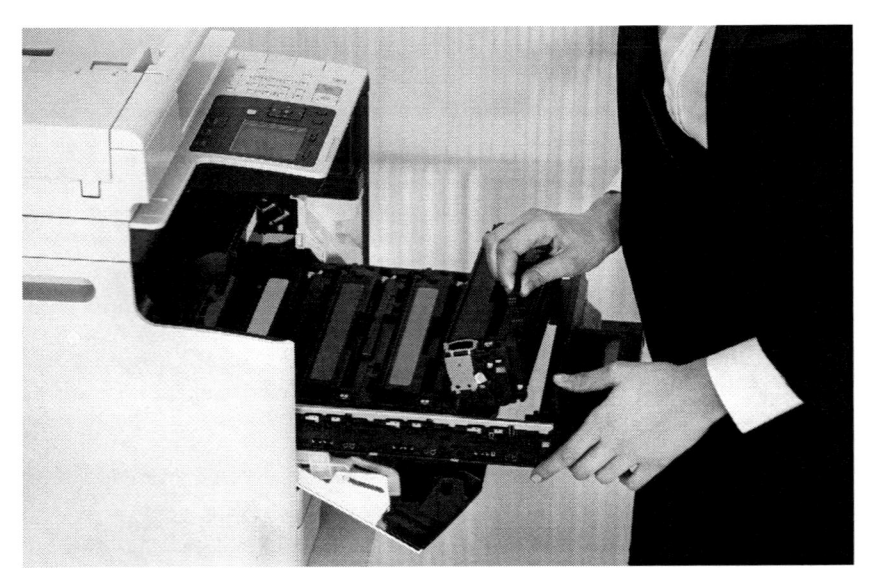

Accessing the toner cartridge on a printer. (Image by Andriy Popov © 123RF.com.)

Take the new cartridge and remove the packing strips as indicated by the instructions. Rock the cartridge gently from front-to-back to distribute the toner evenly. Insert the cartridge, close the service panel, turn on, and print a test page.

If possible, dispose of old cartridges by recycling them.

> **Note:** *The replacement cartridge often incorporates both toner and the photosensitive drum. An integrated toner cartridge/drum unit is light-sensitive. If you remove it, place it in its storage bag or in a dark area. Remove the cartridge for as short a time as possible.*

CLEANING A PRINTER

The manufacturer's recommendations for cleaning and maintenance must always be followed, but the following guidelines generally apply:

- Unplug the printer before cleaning or performing routine maintenance.
- Use a damp cloth to clean exterior surfaces.
- Do not use volatile liquids such as thinners or benzene to clean the interior or exterior of the printer. Use only approved cleaning solutions or solvents specifically designed for the job.
- The inside of the printer may be hot—take care.
- Wipe dust and toner away with a soft cloth. DO NOT use an ordinary domestic vacuum cleaner. Toner is conductive and can damage the motor. Toner is also so fine that it will pass straight through the dust collection bag and back into the room. Use an approved toner safe vacuum if necessary.

> **Note: Do not use compressed air or an air blaster to clean a laser printer!** *You risk blowing toner dust into the room, creating a health hazard. Compressed air should only be used in a controlled environment with appropriate safety masks and goggles.*

- If toner is spilt on skin or clothes, wash it off with COLD water. Hot water will open the skin's pores and push the toner into the skin.
- Use IPA (99% Isopropyl Alcohol solution) and non-scratch, lint-free swabs to clean rollers. Take care not to scratch a roller.
- Check the manufacturer's recommendations for replacing the printer's dust/ozone filters (if fitted).

CALIBRATING A PRINTER

Calibration is the process by which the printer determines the appropriate print density or color balance (basically, how much toner to use). Most printers calibrate themselves automatically. If print output is not as expected, you can often invoke the calibration routine from the printer's control panel or its software driver.

REPLACING THE MAINTENANCE KIT

A **maintenance kit** is a set of replacement feed rollers, new transfer roller, and a new fuser unit. The feed rollers guide paper through the printer assembly. When they begin to wear out, paper jams become more frequent. Wear on the fuser or rollers is also evidenced by consistent marks on print output or excess toner "blobs" appearing on sheets.

Replacement of the maintenance kit is guided by the printer's internal record of the number of pages that it has printed (copy count). The printer's status indicator will display the message "Maintenance Kit Replace" at this point.

Before replacing the kit, turn off the printer, disconnect from the power, open the service panels, and allow it to cool (the fuser unit becomes extremely hot and may cause burns). Remove the old fuser and rollers and clean the printer. Install the fuser and new rollers (don't forget to remove the packing strips), following the instructions carefully.

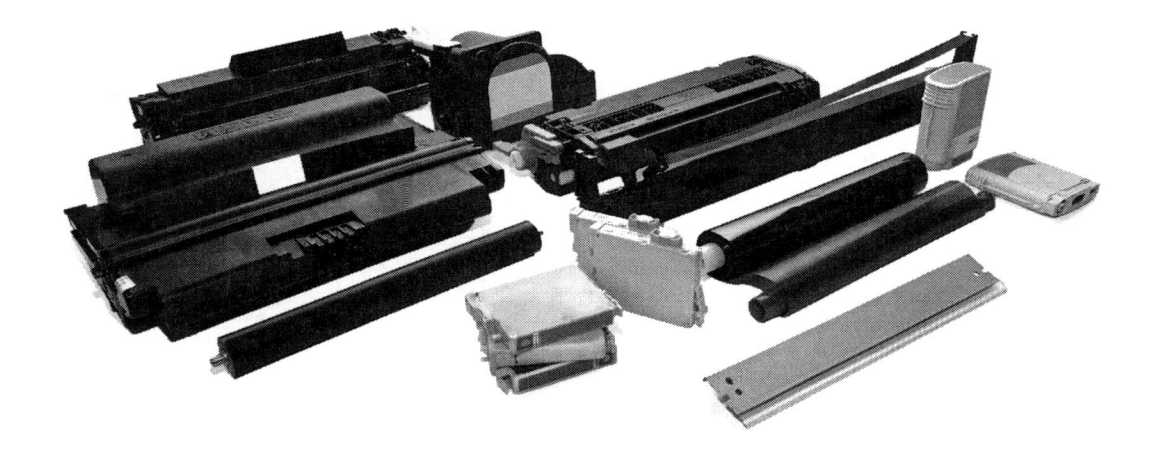

An example of a maintenance kit with feed rollers, new transfer rollers and a new fuser unit. (Image by Inga Tihonova © 123RF.com.)

Once you have replaced the maintenance kit, start the printer up and print a test page to check functionality. Use the property sheet or the printer's control panel menu (for example, the Configuration menu on an HP printer) to reset the page count to zero.

As with toner cartridges, try to use a recycling program to dispose of the fuser unit in an environmentally responsible manner.

Note: To learn more, check the **Video** tile on the CHOICE Course screen for any videos that supplement the content for this lesson.

Access the Checklist tile on your CHOICE Course screen for reference information and job aids on How to Maintain Laser Printers.

Activity 10-1
Discussing Laser Printer Maintenance

SCENARIO
Answer the following questions to check your understanding of the topic.

1. Why is a laser printer better suited to most office printing tasks than an inkjet?

2. What makes the power supply in a printer different to that used in a PC?

3. How is the imaging drum in a laser printer charged?

4. What is the removal of the charge from the photosensitive drum by a laser called?

5. What is the process of image transfer?

6. What must you do before installing a new toner cartridge into a printer?

7. Which components are provided as part of a laser printer maintenance kit?

Topic B
Maintain Inkjet Printers

EXAM OBJECTIVES COVERED
1001-3.11 Given a scenario, install and maintain various print technologies.

Inkjets are often used for good-quality color output and domestic use. Inkjets are typically cheap to buy but expensive to run, with high cost consumables such as ink cartridges and high-grade paper. Compared to laser printers, they are slower and often noisier, making them less popular in office environments, except as a cheap option for low volume, good quality color printing.

INKJET PRINTERS

An inkjet—or more generally ink dispersion—printer forms images by firing microscopic droplets of liquid ink out of nozzles mounted together on a carriage assembly that moves back and forth across the paper. The printer can use heat or vibrations to release the ink.

Color images are created by combining four inks, referred to as **CMYK** (Cyan, Magenta, Yellow, and Black [K]). The inks are stored in separate reservoirs, which may be supplied in single or multiple cartridges.

> *Note: The "K" in CMYK is usually explained as standing for "key," as in a key plate used to align the other plates in the sort of offset print press used for professional color printing in high volumes. It might be more helpful to think of it as "blacK," though.*

There are many types of inkjet printers, ranging from cheaper desktop models, through "prosumer" high quality photo printers, to large format, commercial print solutions. Higher quality printers feature additional ink colors (light magenta and light cyan). These help to produce a wider range of colors (gamut).

INKJET PRINTER IMAGING PROCESS

Inkjets work by firing microscopic droplets of ink (about 50 microns in size) at the paper. The process creates high quality images, especially when specially treated paper is used, but they can be prone to smearing and fading over time.

An inkjet print head is composed of a series of very small holes or nozzles, behind which can be found a reservoir of ink. Under normal conditions, the ink cannot flow though the nozzles because the gap is very small, and the ink reservoir is kept at a pressure slightly below that of the ambient pressure. Characters are formed when a small controlled amount of ink is forced through voltage-charged deflection plates and onto the paper. By synchronizing this action with the movement of the print head across the paper, text and images can be built up in a series of differently shaded or colored dots.

Inkjet printers are line printers—where laser printers are page printers—because they build up the image line-by-line (or at least, row-by-row). A stepper motor moves the print head across the page, advancing a tiny amount each time. On some types of printer, ink is applied when the print head moves in one direction only (unidirectional); on others, ink is applied on both the "outward" and "return" passes over the page (bidirectional). When a line or row has been completed, another stepper motor advances the page a little bit and the next line or row is printed.

If the printer has been idle for some time (or when it is first started up), it applies a cleaning cycle to the print head to remove any dried or clogged ink. This means pushing ink through all the print heads at once then wiping it away into a waste ink collector. The cleaning cycle can also be invoked manually through the printer control panel or driver.

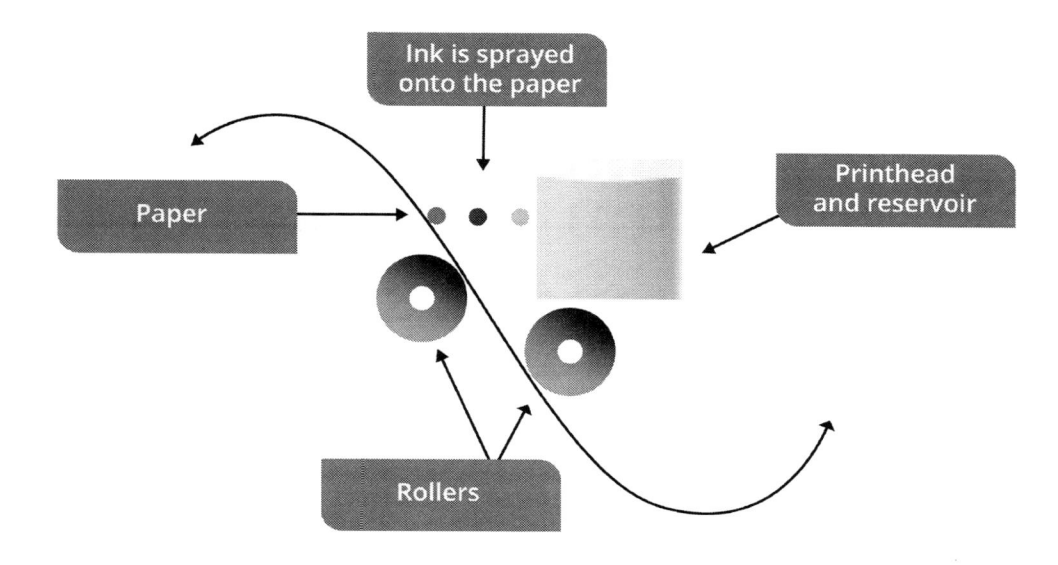

The inkjet printing process.

COMPONENTS OF INKJET PRINTERS

There are two main Ink Delivery Systems (IDS). The charge (or **piezoelectric**) method is used by Epson. The **thermal** method is used by HP, Canon (who refer to it as **Bubblejet**), and Lexmark. Each of these four vendors has licensed their inkjet technology to several other vendors or produce re-branded versions of their printers.

THERMAL PRINT HEADS

With the thermal method, the ink at the nozzle is heated, creating a bubble. When the bubble bursts, it sprays ink through the nozzle and draws more ink from the reservoir. In general, thermal inkjet print heads are cheaper and simpler to produce, but the heating elements have a relatively short life. Most thermal printers use a combined print head and ink reservoir. When the ink runs out, the print head is also replaced.

PIEZOELECTRIC PRINT HEADS

In the Epson design, the nozzle contains a piezoelectric element, which changes shape when a voltage is applied. This acts like a small pump, pushing ink through the nozzle and drawing ink from the reservoir.

INK CARTRIDGES

Inkjet print heads are often considered consumable items. Often this is unavoidable because the print head is built into the **ink cartridge**, as is the case with most (but not all) thermal print heads. Epson piezoelectric print heads are non-removable and designed to last as long as the rest of the printer components.

As well as containing ink, the ink reservoir has sensors to detect the level of ink remaining. A color printer has at least four ink reservoirs (Black, Cyan, Magenta, and Yellow). The four ink reservoirs may come in a single cartridge or there may be separate cartridges for black and colored ink or each ink may come in its own cartridge.

Ink cartridges. (Image by © 123RF.com.)

CARRIAGE SYSTEM

The print head is moved back and forth over the paper by a carriage system. This comprises a stepper motor (to drive the system), a pulley and belt (to move the print head), a guide shaft (to keep the print head stable), and sensors (to detect the position of the print head). A flat ribbon data cable connects the print head to the printer's circuit board.

There may also be a lever used to set the platen gap or the printer may adjust this automatically depending on driver settings. The platen gap is the distance between the print head and the paper. Having an adjustable platen gap allows the printer to use thicker media.

The carriage mechanism in an inkjet printer. (Image by Erik Bobeldijk © 123RF.com.)

PAPER HANDLING AND DUPLEXING ASSEMBLY

Most inkjets only support one paper path, with single input and output trays, though some have automatic duplexers, and some may have accessory trays. Printers are generally split between models that load from the top and output at the bottom and those that have both input and output bins at the bottom and turn the paper (an "up-and-over" path).

The paper pickup mechanism is quite similar to that of a laser printer. Paper is fed into the printer by an **AutoSheet Feeder (ASF)** mechanism. A **load roller** turns against the paper stack to move the top sheet while a **separation roller** prevents more than one sheet entering.

When the paper is sufficiently advanced, it is detected by a sensor. Feed rollers and sensors then ensure the paper is positioned correctly for printing to begin. The stepper motor controlling the paper feed mechanism advances the paper as the print head completes each pass until the print is complete.

The eject rollers then deliver the paper to the **duplexing assembly** (if installed and duplex printing has been selected) or the output bin. Some inkjets with a curved paper path may have a "straight-through" rear panel for bulkier media.

INKJET PRINTER MAINTENANCE TASKS

Inkjets do not usually handle such high print volumes as laser printers, so maintenance focuses on paper stocking and replacing or refilling ink cartridges, which always seem to run down very quickly. Manufacturers recommend not trying to clean inside the case as you are likely to do harm for no real benefit. The outside of the printer can be cleaned using a soft damp cloth.

LOADING PAPER

Inkjets tend to have smaller paper trays than laser printers and so can need restocking with paper more often. Most inkjets can use "regular" copier/laser printer paper but better results can be obtained by using less absorbent premium grades of paper stock, specifically designed for inkjet use. Often this type of paper is designed to be printed on one side only—make sure the paper is correctly oriented when loading the printer.

As with laser printers, you will also need to clear paper jams. With an inkjet, it is usually easy to see exactly where the paper has jammed. If the sheet will not come out easily, do not just try to pull it harder—check the instruction manual to find out how to release any components that might prevent you from removing the paper.

REPLACE INKJET CARTRIDGES

When the inkjet's driver software determines that a cartridge is empty, it will prompt you to replace it. Check the printer's instruction manual for the correct procedure.

OTHER INKJET MAINTENANCE OPERATIONS

Two other operations may be required periodically.

- **Print head alignment**—if output is not aligned correctly, use the print head alignment function from the printer's property sheet to calibrate the printer. This is typically done automatically when you replace the ink cartridges.
- **Print head cleaning**—a blocked or dirty nozzle will show up on output as a missing line. Use the printer's cleaning cycle (accessed via the property sheet or control panel) to try to fix the problem. If it does not work, there are various inkjet cleaning products on the market.

EPSON S22 Series Printing Preferences

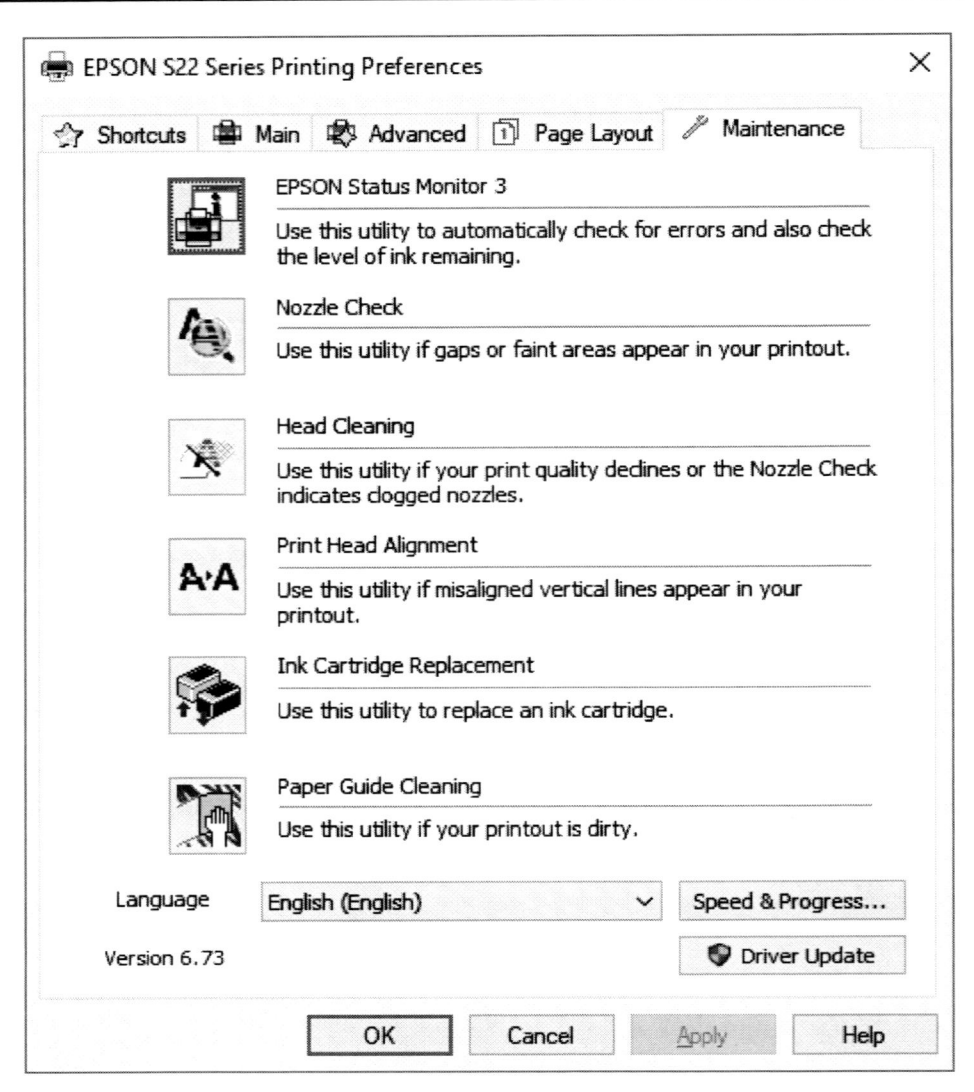

Tabs: Shortcuts | Main | Advanced | Page Layout | **Maintenance**

EPSON Status Monitor 3
Use this utility to automatically check for errors and also check the level of ink remaining.

Nozzle Check
Use this utility if gaps or faint areas appear in your printout.

Head Cleaning
Use this utility if your print quality declines or the Nozzle Check indicates clogged nozzles.

Print Head Alignment
Use this utility if misaligned vertical lines appear in your printout.

Ink Cartridge Replacement
Use this utility to replace an ink cartridge.

Paper Guide Cleaning
Use this utility if your printout is dirty.

Language: English (English)   Speed & Progress...
Version 6.73   Driver Update

[OK]   [Cancel]   [Apply]   [Help]

Use the Maintenance or Tools tab on an inkjet printer's property sheet to access cleaning routines and calibration utilities.

Note: To learn more, check the **Video** tile on the CHOICE Course screen for any videos that supplement the content for this lesson.

Access the Checklist tile on your CHOICE Course screen for reference information and job aids on How to Maintain Inkjet Printers.

Activity 10-2
Discussing Inkjet Printer Maintenance

SCENARIO
Answer the following questions to check your understanding of the topic.

1. Which inks are typically used in the color printing process?

2. What two types of print heads are used by inkjet printers?

3. You have been asked to perform basic maintenance on an inkjet printer. One of the users noticed that the colors are not printing correctly and that the bottom of some letters are not printing.

   What would you do?

4. Can inkjet printers use plain copy paper?

5. What is an ASF?

Topic C
Maintain Impact, Thermal, and 3D Printers

EXAM OBJECTIVES COVERED
1001-3.11 Given a scenario, install and maintain various print technologies.

Laser and inkjet printers are widely deployed but there are a number of other printer types that are better optimized for certain tasks. In this topic, you will learn about thermal, impact, and 3D printer types.

IMPACT PRINTERS

An **impact printer** strikes an inked ribbon against paper to leave marks. One common type is the **dot matrix** printer, which uses a column of pins (also called print wires) to strike the ribbon.

Desktop dot matrix printers are no longer very widely deployed, but they are still used for specialist functions such as printing invoices or pay slips, on continuous, tractor-fed paper. Portable models are still widely used for printing receipts.

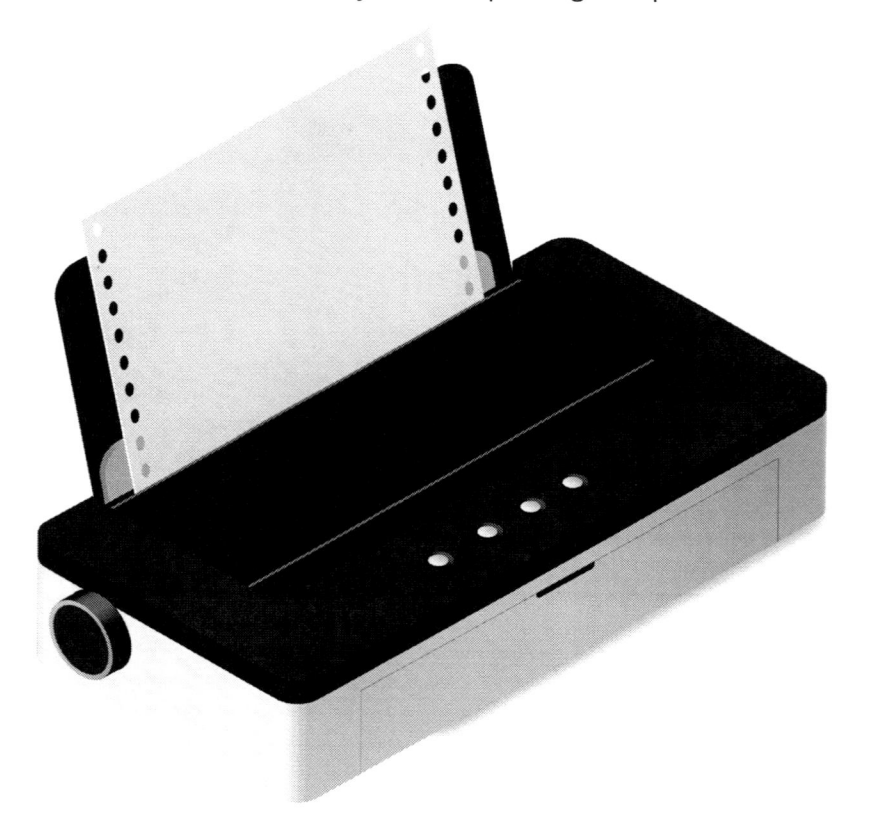

Example of a dot matrix printer. (Image © 123RF.com.)

COMPONENTS OF IMPACT PRINTERS

Impact printers are composed of a ribbon cartridge, rollers, and pins for moving paper through the printer, a printhead composed of a number of electromagnetic pins, and some optional components, which might include a paper tray, an output tray, and a support for sheet-fed paper.

IMPACT PRINTER CONSUMABLES

Impact printers can be used with either plain, carbon, or **tractor-fed** paper:

- **Plain paper** is held firmly against the moving roller (the platen) and pulled through the mechanism by friction as the platen rotates. A cut sheet feeder may be added to some printers to automate the process of providing the next page.
- **Carbon paper** (or **impact paper**) is used to make multiple copies of a document in the same pass (hence carbon copy, or "cc"). A sheet of carbon paper is inserted between each sheet of plain paper and when the print head strikes, the same mark is made on each sheet.
- **Tractor-fed** paper is fitted with removable, perforated side strips. The holes in these strips are secured over studded rollers at each end of the platen. This type of paper is more suitable for multi-part stationery as there is less chance of skewing or slippage since the end rollers fix the movement of the paper.

PAPER FEED MECHANISMS

Impact printers can use either tractor feed when printing on continuous-roll impact paper, or **friction feed** when printing on individually cut sheets of paper. Tractor feed uses pairs of wheels with pins evenly spaced around the circumference at a set spacing. Continuous-roll paper with matching holes in the edges fits over the pins. The wheels turn and pull the paper through the printer. There are usually just two wheels, but there might be additional wheels or pin guides that the paper is latched to. There is usually a lever or other setting on the printer that needs to be engaged in order to use the tractor feed.

Friction feed uses two rollers placed one on top of the other. The rollers turn to force individual cut sheets of paper or envelopes through the paper path. This is used to print on individual sheets of paper (cut-sheet paper) and envelopes. Be sure to set the printer lever or other setting to the cut-sheet mode when printing using friction feed.

IMPACT PRINTER RIBBONS

An impact printer will also have some form of replaceable ribbon. Older-style printers used to have a two-spool ribbon. However, most units now have a cartridge device that slots over or around the carriage of the print head. These integrated ribbons simplify the design of the printer because they can be made as a complete loop moving in one direction only. The two-spool design requires a sensor and reversing mechanism to change the direction of the ribbon when it reaches the end.

When the ribbon on an impact printer fails to produce sufficiently good print quality, the ribbon-holder and contents are normally replaced as a whole. Some printers can use a re-usable cartridge.

IMPACT PRINTER IMAGING PROCESS

In a dot matrix printer, the pins are contained in the **print head**, which is secured to a moving carriage that sweeps across the paper. The pins are fired by coils of wire called solenoids. When a coil is energized, it forms a strong electromagnet that causes the metal firing pin to move sharply forwards, striking the ink-bearing **ribbon** against the paper. A strong permanent magnet moves the pins back into their resting position immediately after firing.

> **Note:** Do not touch the print head after using the printer. The print head can become very hot, even after short periods of use.

The output quality of a dot-matrix printer is largely governed by the number of pins in the print head. Most modern printers use 9-pin or 24-pin print heads. The latter offer a much-improved print quality. More sophisticated printers may use 48-pin print heads, although if you require this level of quality, an inkjet or laser printer may be a better option.

A platen gap lever is often fitted to printers capable of printing on multi-part stationery. This lever adjusts the gap between the print head and the platen to accommodate different thickness of paper. Incorrect adjustment of the platen gap can cause faint printing (gap too wide) or smudging (too narrow). On more sophisticated printers, the platen gap is adjusted automatically.

IMPACT PRINTER MAINTENANCE TIPS

When you are loading a tractor-fed impact printer with paper, ensure that the holes in the paper are engaged in the sprockets and that the paper can enter the printer cleanly. Ensure that the lever is in the correct position for friction feed or tractor feed as appropriate for the media being used. Follow the manufacturer's instructions to replace the print head or ribbon cartridge. Take care, as the print head may become very hot during use.

> *Access the Checklist tile on your CHOICE Course screen for reference information and job aids on How to Maintain Impact Printers.*

THERMAL PRINTERS

A **thermal printer** is a general term for any printer that uses a heating element to create the image on the paper with dye, ink from ribbons, or directly with pins while the feed assembly moves the media through the printer. There are several types of thermal printers that use significantly different technologies and are intended for different uses. The **dye sublimation** print process can be used for photo quality output and **thermal wax transfer** printers can be used as an alternative to color laser printing, but the most common type of thermal printer you are likely to have to support is the **direct thermal** printer.

A direct thermal receipt printer. (Image © 123RF.com).

Portable or small form factor direct thermal transfer printers are used for high volume barcode and label printing and also to print receipts. Such devices typically support 200-300 dpi, with some models able to print one or two colors. Print speeds are measured in inches per second.

COMPONENTS OF THERMAL PRINTERS

Most direct thermal print devices require special **thermal paper** that contains chemicals designed to react and change color as it is heated by the **heating element** within the printer to create images.

In the **feed assembly** on a direct thermal printer, paper is friction-fed through the print mechanism by a stepper motor turning a rubber-coated roller. Paper and labels may be fanfold or roll format.

DIRECT THERMAL PRINTER IMAGING PROCESS

Direct thermal printers have a heating element with heated pins that create an image directly onto special thermal paper.

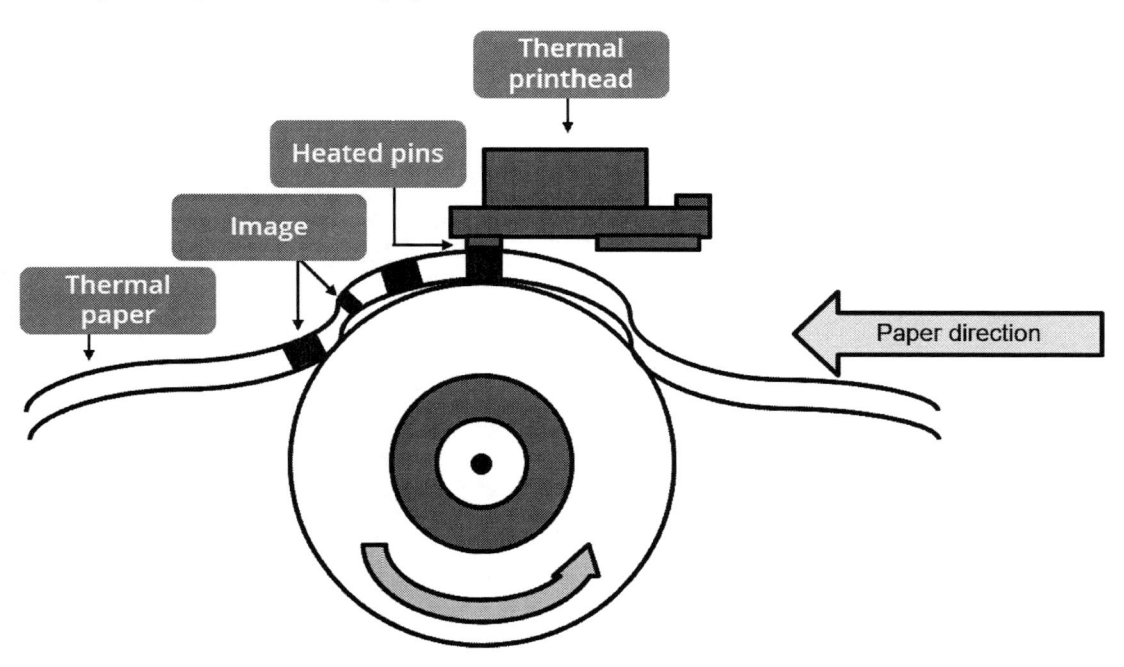

Direct thermal print process.

THERMAL TRANSFER PRINTER MAINTENANCE TIPS

Thermal printers are often used in cash registers and for printing labels. Both of these uses require the printer to be available at all times, and to keep up availability, you should perform regular maintenance.

When you are replacing the paper roll, you need to obtain the specific size and type for the brand and model of thermal printer you are using. The process is usually quite simple—just open the printer case, insert the roll, keeping the shiny print side facing outwards, then ensure that the end of the paper in held in place by the print head when closing the case again.

In receipt registers, the cashier rips the paper across the serrated teeth to give the receipt to the customer. This can lead to a build-up of paper dust in the printer from tearing off receipts. It can also lead to bits of paper debris becoming lodged in the mechanism if a clean slice is not made and bits of leftover paper fall into the printer.

Label printers can end up with sticky residue inside the printer. If labels are not loaded correctly, they can separate from the backing while being fed through the printer. You will need to ensure users know how to properly load the labels and how to clean up if labels get stuck inside the printer.

Use a vacuum or soft brush to remove any paper debris. Use a swab and appropriate cleaning fluid, such as Isopropyl Alcohol (IPA), to clean the print head (heating element) or any sticky residue inhibiting the feed mechanism. Alternatively, you can often purchase cleaning cards to feed through the printer to clean the print head safely. Only use cleaning cards when required, though, as they can be abrasive and wear down components.

Access the Checklist tile on your CHOICE Course screen for reference information and job aids on How to Maintain Thermal Printers.

3D PRINTERS

A **3D print process** builds a solid object from successive layers of material. The material is typically some sort of plastic but there are printer types that can work with rubber, carbon fiber, or metal alloys too. The range of materials that can be used is expanding quickly.

3D printing has very different use cases to printing to paper. It is most widely used in manufacturing, especially to create "proof of concept" working models from designs. The range of other applications is growing, however. For example, 3D printing can be used in healthcare (dentistry and prosthetics), clothing, and to make product samples and other marketing material.

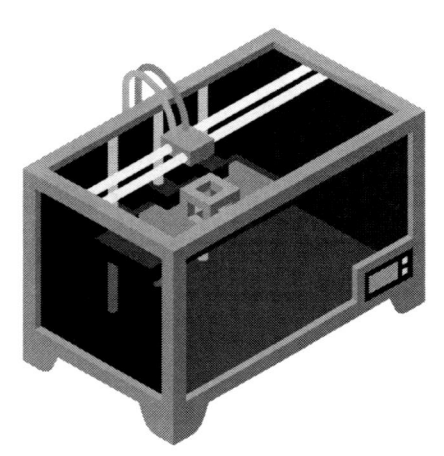

A 3D printer. (Image © 123RF.com.)

3D PRINTER IMAGING PROCESS

The **3D printer** imaging process begins with either a scan created by a **3D scanner** or by creating an object using **3D modeling software**. From either of these methods, you end up with a 3D model created in software and saved to a 3D model format.

This model is then **sliced** with **slicing software** into horizontal layers. The slicing software might be contained in the 3D modeling software or within the 3D printer. The result is a print job specifying how each layer in the finished object is to be deposited.

The sliced model is then fed to the 3D printer over a USB or Wi-Fi connection, or by inserting an SD card containing the file into the printer. The printer then melts the filament and extrudes it onto the build surface, creating layer upon layer based on the slices. The extruder (and sometimes the build bed) is moved as needed on X/Y/Z axes to create the build.

COMPONENTS OF 3D PRINTERS

There are several types of 3D printers. **Fused filament fabrication (FFF)**, also known as **fused deposition modeling (FDM)**, lays down layers of filament at high temperature. As layers are extruded, adjacent layers are allowed to cool and bond together before additional layers are added to the object. The main components in an FDM 3D printer are:

- **Print bed/build plate**—a flat glass plate onto which the material is extruded. The bed is usually heated to prevent the material from warping. The bed must be leveled for each print job—this is usually automated, but cheaper printer models require manual calibration. It is very important that the printer frame be strong and rigid enough to keep the bed as stable as possible. Any vibration will result in poor quality printing.
- **Bed/build surface**—a sheet placed onto the base plate to hold the object in position while printing, but also allow its removal on completion. The bed surface material may need to be matched to the filament material for best results.
- **Extruder**—the equivalent of a print head in an inkjet. A motor in the extruder draws filament from the "cold end" through to the nozzle (or "hot end"), where it is melted and squirted onto the object. Different size nozzles can be fitted to the extruder.
- **Gears/motors/motion control**—enable precise positioning of the extruder.
- **Fan**—cools the melted plastic where necessary to shape the object correctly.

The printer must be installed to a suitable environment. A stable, vibration-free floor and dust-free, humidity-controlled surroundings will ensure best results.

> *Note: 3D printing involves several possible safety risks. Components work at high temperatures, and use of sharp tools such as scrapers and finishing knives is required. Ideally, the 3D print facility should be accessible only to trained users.*

FILAMENT

The "ink" for a 3D printer is supplied as a spool of **filament**. Filament is provided either as 1.75 mm or 3 mm diameter. As noted earlier, there are various different filament materials. The two most popular plastics are Polylactic Acid (PLA) and Acrylonitrile Butadiene Styrene (ABS). Most printers can use a range of filament materials but it is best to check compatibility if a specific "exotic" is required for a project. Each material operates at different extruder and print bed temperatures.

To change a filament, the extruder must be heated to the appropriate temperature. Pull as much of the old filament out as possible—taking care not to burn yourself—then push the new filament through. Do not start printing until all of the old filament has been pushed out.

Filament spools require careful storage once opened. They should be kept free from heat and humidity.

3D PRINTER MAINTENANCE TIPS

3D printers require maintenance specific to the type of printing done. These printers do not print on paper, so have very different maintenance needs and consumables than traditional printers. Among the maintenance tasks you need to perform are:

- Remove any leftover filament from nozzles.
- Clean any residual plastic from the platform, nozzles, and other areas. There could also be glue left on the glass if your print process uses glue.

- If the documentation says to, apply grease to the moving parts that move the extruder on the X/Y/Z axes.
- Check tubes in the feeder mechanism to see if they need to be cleaned or replaced.
- Examine couplers to see if they have been damaged by the heat produced during the print process.
- Make sure only approved materials are used when printing.
- Check whether there are new versions of firmware available for the printer and whether you should apply them to the printer.

OTHER 3D PRINTER TYPES

There are two other common types of rapid prototype 3D printing.

Prototype	Description
SLA	**Stereolithography (SLA)** uses liquid plastic resin or **photopolymer** to create objects which are cured using an ultraviolet laser. Excess photopolymer is stored in a tank under the print bed. The print bed lowers into the tank as the object is created. A liquid solvent removes uncured polymer after the model is finished.
SLS	**Selective laser sintering (SLS)** fuses layers together using a pulse laser. The object is created from a powder and lowered into a tank as each layer is added. The powder can be plastic or metal.

Access the Checklist tile on your CHOICE Course screen for reference information and job aids on How to Maintain 3D Printers.

Activity 10-3
Discussing Impact, Thermal, and 3D Printer Maintenance

SCENARIO
Answer the following questions to check your understanding of the topic.

1. What type of printer technology is a dot matrix printer?

2. What types of paper/stationery can dot matrix printers use that laser and inkjet printers cannot?

3. Where are you must likely to encounter thermal printers?

4. You have been asked to perform basic maintenance on a printer in the Research and Development area. The dot matrix printer used to create shipping documents seems to be printing lighter than normal, and one of the pins seems to not be connecting near the center of the print head as there are blank areas in some letters and images.

   What maintenance should you perform?

5. A thermal printer used to create labels for parts bins, kits, and boxes is jammed due to a label coming loose during printing.

   How should you resolve this problem?

6. What do you need to create objects with an FDM-type 3D printer?

7. **What considerations for locating a 3D printer do you have to make?**

Topic D
Install and Configure Printers

EXAM OBJECTIVES COVERED
1001-3.10 Given a scenario, configure SOHO multifunction devices/printers and settings.
1001-3.11 Given a scenario, install and maintain various print technologies.

Because printers are such a fundamental component of almost every computing environment, it is almost guaranteed that you will be asked to set up and configure printing on devices, no matter what professional environment you are working in. Although the different technologies used in various printer types affect maintenance and troubleshooting, the type of printer does not substantially affect the way it is installed and configured in an operating system such as Windows or shared on a network. The skills you will learn in this topic should prepare you to install and configure a wide range of printer types efficiently and correctly.

WINDOWS PRINTERS

Windows applications that support printing are typically **WYSIWYG** (What You See Is What You Get), which means that the screen and print output are supposed to be the same. To achieve this, several components are required:

- The **print driver** provides an interface between the print device and Windows.
- Support for one or more **print languages** determines how accurate the output can be.
- The **technology** used by the printer determines the quality, speed, and cost of the output.

Note: There is a distinction between the software components that represent the printer and the physical printer itself. The software representation of the printer may be described as the "printer object," "logical printer," or simply "printer." Terms relating to the printer hardware include "print device" or "physical printer." Be aware that "printer" could mean either the physical print device or the software representation of that device. Pay attention to the context in which these terms are used.

WINDOWS PRINT PROCESS

Display and print functions for compatible applications are handled by the **Windows Presentation Foundation (WPF)**. A WPF print job is formatted and spooled as an **XML Print Specification (XPS)** file in the printer's spool folder (%SystemRoot%\System32\Spool\Printers\).

This spool file is then processed by the printer's device driver. It may either be output directly to an XPS-compatible print device or rendered using a different **Page Description Language (PDL)**, such as HP Printer Control Language or Adobe® PostScript®, and converted to a **raster**, or dot-by-bot description of where the printer should place ink.

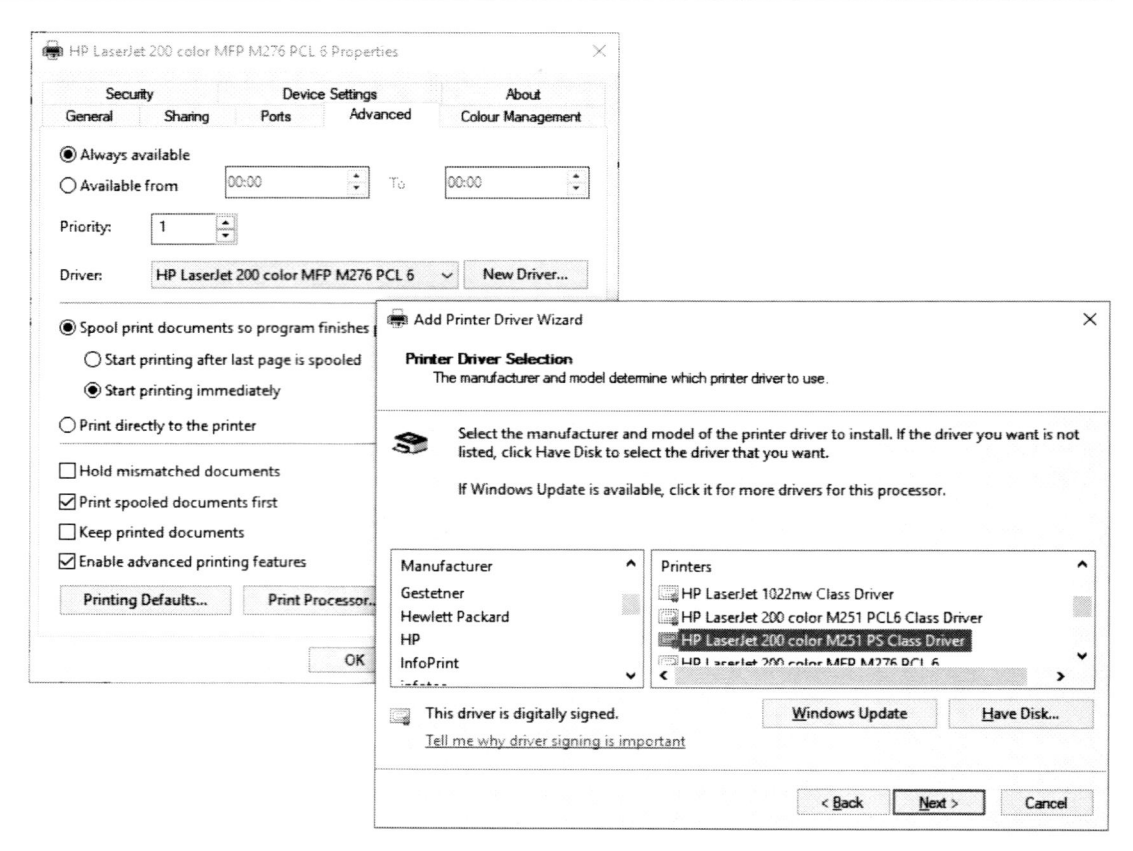

A print device might support more than one PDL—this HP printer supports both Printer Control Language (PCL) and PostScript (PS). (Screenshot used with permission from Microsoft.)

The **print monitor** transmits the print job to the printer and provides status information. Most print devices have their own memory and processor, enabling the print job to be transmitted more quickly and reliably. If a problem is encountered during printing, the print device sends a status message back to the print monitor, informing the user.

Applications and print devices that do not support WPF use the older **Graphics Device Interface (GDI)** print process. Under GDI, the print file can be spooled in one of two formats:

- **EMF (Enhanced Metafile)**—a small, efficient, printer-independent file type. As the file is smaller, it is written to disk more quickly, therefore freeing up resources. The printer must support EMF for this to work.
- **RAW**—this file type differs depending on your printer. RAW files must be formatted for the printer at the spooling stage, therefore it will take longer to spool the file and the file will be larger. The RAW spool format is a useful troubleshooting tool.

Users can also print to network printers. In this case, a redirector service on the local computer passes the print job from the locally spooled file to the spooler on the print server (the computer to which the network printer is connected). Note that a driver for the network device must be installed locally.

FEATURES OF PAGE DESCRIPTION LANGUAGES

PDLs support the following features:

- **Scalable fonts**—originally, characters were printed as bitmaps. This meant that the character could only be printed at sizes defined in the font (a bitmap font consists of a number of dot-by-dot images of each character at a particular font size). Scalable fonts are described by vectors. A **vector font** consists of a description of how each character should be drawn. This description can be scaled up or down to

different font sizes. All Windows printers support scalable TrueType or OpenType fonts. OpenType is an extension of TrueType, developed jointly by Microsoft and Adobe. OpenType offers portability between Windows and Mac OS®, better character (Unicode) support, and more advanced typographic options. PostScript compatible printers will also support PostScript outline fonts.
- Color printing—the color model used by display systems is different to that used by printers (**additive** versus **subtractive**). An additive model combines differently colored transmitted light (Red, Green, and Blue, for instance) to form different shades. A subtractive model works using the reflective properties of inks: Cyan, Magenta, and Yellow plus Black ink for "true" blacks. A color model provides an accurate translation between on-screen color and print output and ensures that different devices produce identical output.
- **Vector graphics**—as with fonts, scalable images are built from vectors, which describe how a line should be drawn, rather than providing a pixel-by-pixel description, as is the case with bitmap graphics.

VIRTUAL PRINTERS

There may be circumstances where you do not want to send a print job to a physical print device. Using a virtual printer means that the output is either a file containing instructions in some **page description language** or **bitmap image data**. Some of the reasons users might need to print to a virtual printer include:

- Sending a document from their computer to a fax server.
- Creating a document that cannot be purposely or inadvertently changed.
- Making the document content available outside of the application which originally created the document.
- Combining multiple documents into a single document.
- Testing how the document will appear when printed on paper from a physical printer.

When you are using a virtual print option, there may be a choice of file formats for the output:

- **Print to file**—this creates a file that can subsequently be sent to the print device. It basically means saving a copy of the file that would normally be spooled by the printer. This may be used in conjunction with the PostScript print language. Note that the output files are typically very large.
- **Print to PDF**—the Portable Document Format (PDF) was created by Adobe and later published as an open standard as a device-independent format for viewing and printing documents. Print (or export) to PDF functionality is available in many software applications.
- **Print to XPS**—as noted earlier, the XML Print Specification is the print language supported by Windows. An XPS format file should be printable on modern Windows-compatible printers.
- **Print to image**—some applications support directing the output to a bitmap image file format, such as PNG or JPEG. Vector text and art will be converted to a fixed resolution format.

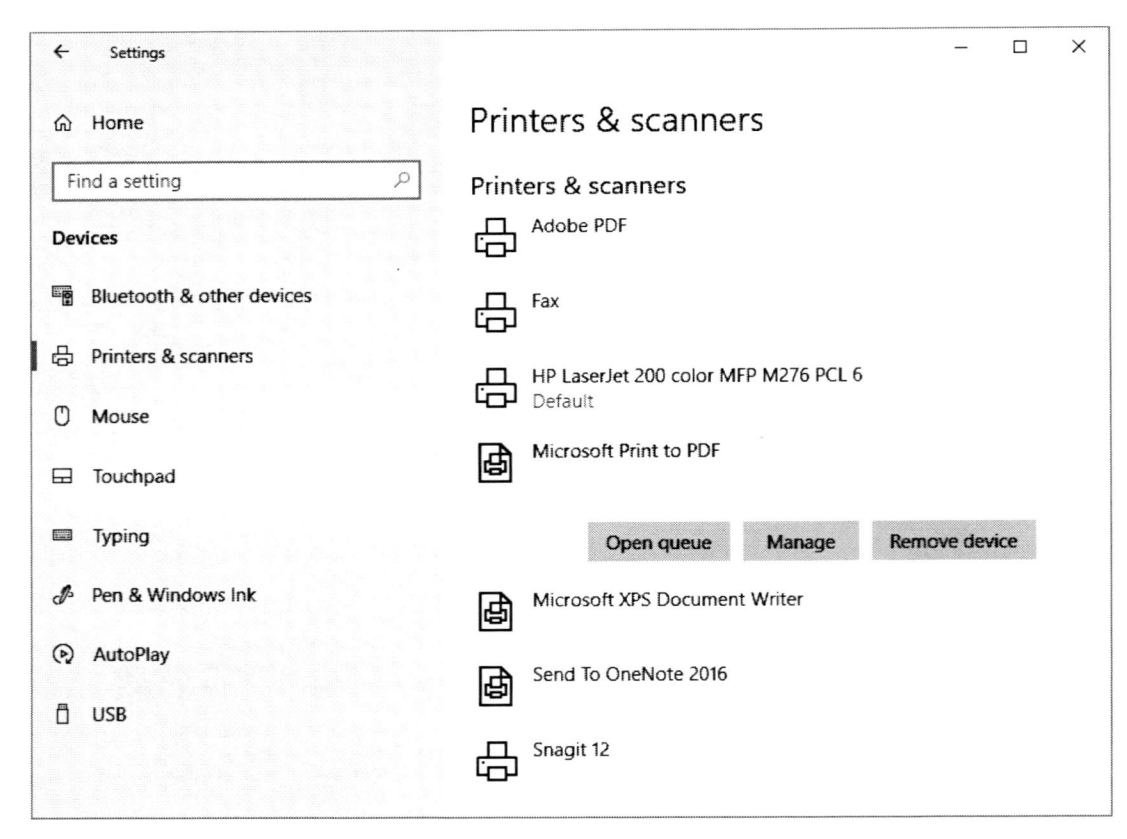

Windows 10 includes Print to PDF and XPS Document Writer virtual printers by default. (Screenshot used with permission from Microsoft.)

Note: *The PC in the previous figure also has Adobe PDF, Send to OneNote, and SnagIt virtual printers installed.*

LOCAL PRINTER CONNECTIONS

As with other PC peripherals, USB is now the dominant printer interface.

USB PORTS

To install a USB printer, connect the device plug (usually a Type B connector) to the printer's USB port and the Type A host plug to a free port on the computer. In most cases, Windows will detect the printer using Plug-and-Play and install the driver automatically. You can confirm that the printer is successfully installed and print a test page using the Devices and Printers or Settings applet.

Even though USB connections are powered, you will still need to connect the printer to mains power as it will draw down more power than USB can supply. Portable printers may have a battery supply.

In the following figure, notice that there is an option to print a test page. In the properties dialog box for the printer, you can see that the printer is connected via USB.

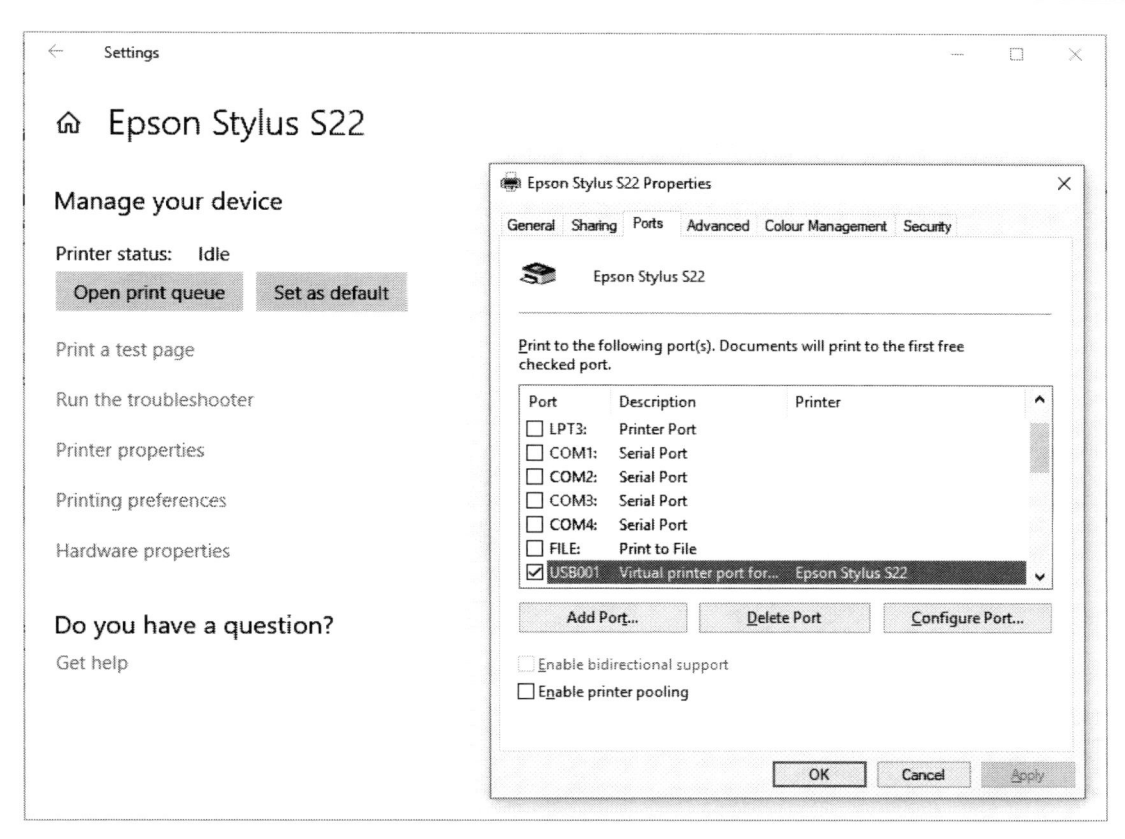

Using Windows Settings to verify printer installation. (Screenshot used with permission from Microsoft.)

ETHERNET

Some printers come equipped with a network adapter and RJ-45 port and can be connected directly to an Ethernet switch. Client devices can then either connect directly to the print device via its Internet Protocol (IP) address or the device can be managed and shared via a network print server.

SERIAL PORT

The serial (RS-232 or COM) port is a legacy port and does not support the bandwidth required by modern desktop printers. Certain Point-of-Sale (PoS) barcode printers and older impact printers are interfaced by serial ports, however.

Connect such a printer using an appropriate "null modem" serial cable; either 9-pin to 9-pin or 25-pin to 9-pin, depending on the printer model. Serial port drivers are unlikely to support Plug-and-Play, so you will need to complete the installation using the Device Setup wizard, selecting the appropriate COM port and driver. You may also need to configure custom COM port settings (via the **Ports** tab in the printer's property dialog box). Check the printer's setup guide for specific cable and connector requirements and installation procedures.

WIRELESS PRINT DEVICE INTERFACES

A cable-free connection to a printer offers a more flexible solution. Most wireless interfaces are built into the printer. Wi-Fi may be available as an installable upgrade. Another option is to connect a wireless print server via the printer's USB port. The two principal wireless printer interfaces are Bluetooth and Wi-Fi.

Bluetooth uses radio communications and supports speeds of up to 3 Mbps. It does not require line-of-sight and supports a maximum range of 10 m (30 feet), though signal strength will be very weak at this distance. To connect via Bluetooth, ensure that the printer is configured as discoverable, then use the **Bluetooth** applet in Control Panel or the **Devices** page in Windows Settings to add the device.

Wi-Fi (802.11) supports higher transfer rates. The printer should be configured with the appropriate WLAN settings (SSID and IP configuration) via its control panel. The main configuration choices are as follows:

- 802.11 standard—the printer's wireless adapter will support a particular 802.11 standard (a, b, g, n, or ac). Other devices connecting to it must support the same standard and be configured with the same security settings.
- Infrastructure versus ad-hoc—in infrastructure mode, the printer would be configured to connect to an access point and client connections would also be mediated by the access point. In ad-hoc mode, client devices would connect directly to the printer.

Using the printer control panel to join a Wi-Fi network (infrastructure mode).

Ad-hoc is a specific mode of peer-to-peer connection associated with legacy standards (802.11a/b/g). You are more likely to encounter devices supporting **Wi-Fi Direct**/Wireless Direct. With Wi-Fi Direct, the server device supports a software-implemented access point to facilitate connections to client devices.

Once the Wi-Fi link is established, you should then be able to connect to the printer from Windows like any other network printer.

PRINTER DRIVERS

Operating system printer drivers must be installed for a printer to function correctly. If the device is not detected automatically, the printer port can be selected, and drivers can be installed using the **Devices and Printers** applet or the **Windows Settings** app.

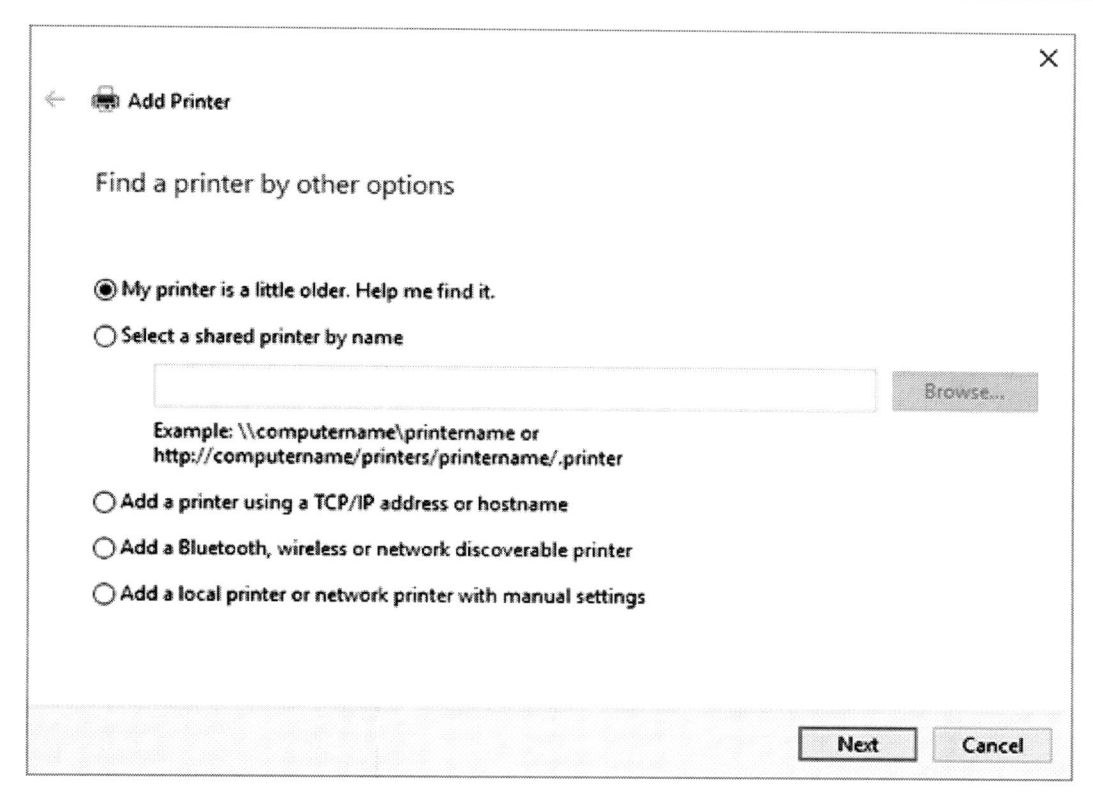

Add Printer Wizard—select a manual configuration if Windows does not detect the printer automatically. (Screenshot used with permission from Microsoft.)

Once the driver has been installed all applications will use it to send output to the printer. To test that the printer has installed correctly, open the **Printer Properties** dialog box (right-click the printer icon in the **Devices and Printers** applet) and select the **Print Test Page** button on the **General** tab.

> *Note:* Installing a new driver requires elevation (UAC). On a domain network, administrators can install approved drivers to designated servers then use group policy to allow standard users to install local printers using those drivers.

> *Note:* Make sure you obtain a 32-bit or 64-bit driver as appropriate. Many older print devices have become unusable as the vendor has not developed a 64-bit driver for them. If no up-to-date driver is available from Microsoft, download the driver from the printer vendor's website, extract it to a folder on your PC, then use the Have Disk option to install it.

CONFIGURATION SETTINGS

Print devices are configured and managed via the **Devices and Printers** folder (Windows 7 and 8) or the **Settings** app (Windows 10). The layout of these apps is slightly different, but they present similar options—view the print queue, open properties and preferences, set a default printer, start a troubleshooter, and so on.

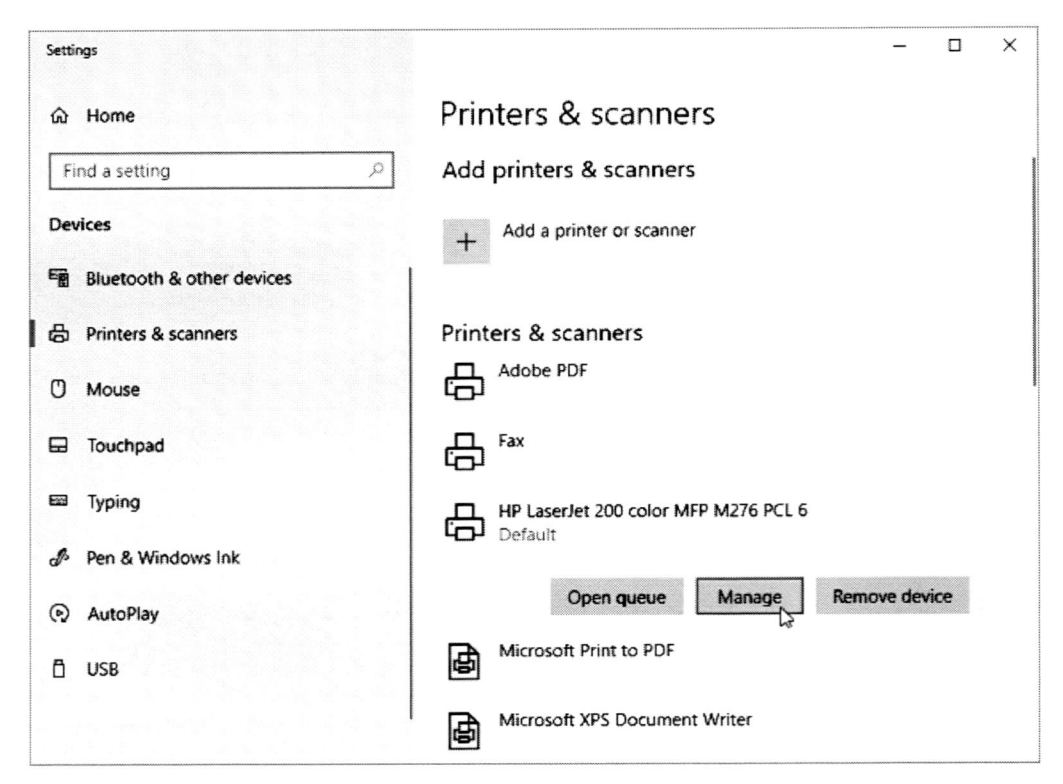

Viewing the print queue and configuring preferences through the Printers and Scanners Settings app page. (Screenshot used with permission from Microsoft.)

There are two main configuration dialog boxes for a local printer: **Printer Properties** and **Printing Preferences**.

> **Note:** *To adjust some device properties and options, you may have to select **Run as administrator** then **Printer Properties** or **Printing Preferences** as appropriate.*

PRINTER PROPERTIES

A printer's **Properties** dialog box allows you to manage configuration settings for the printer object and the underlying hardware, such as updating the driver, printing to a different port, sharing and permissions, setting basic device options (such as whether a duplex unit is installed), and configuring default paper types for different feed trays.

The **About** tab contains information about the driver and the printer vendor and may include links to support and troubleshooting tips and utilities.

> **Note:** *The options available for printing preferences and the layout of these dialog boxes is partly vendor-specific.*

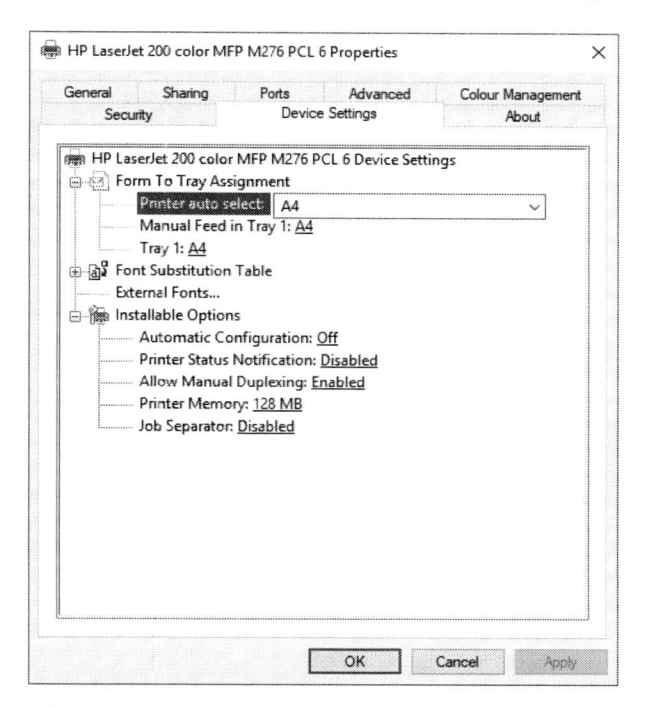

This HP printer allows defaults and installable options to be configured here. (Screenshot used with permission from Microsoft.)

PRINTING PREFERENCES

The **Preferences** dialog box sets the default **print job** options, such as the type and orientation of paper or whether to print in color or black and white.

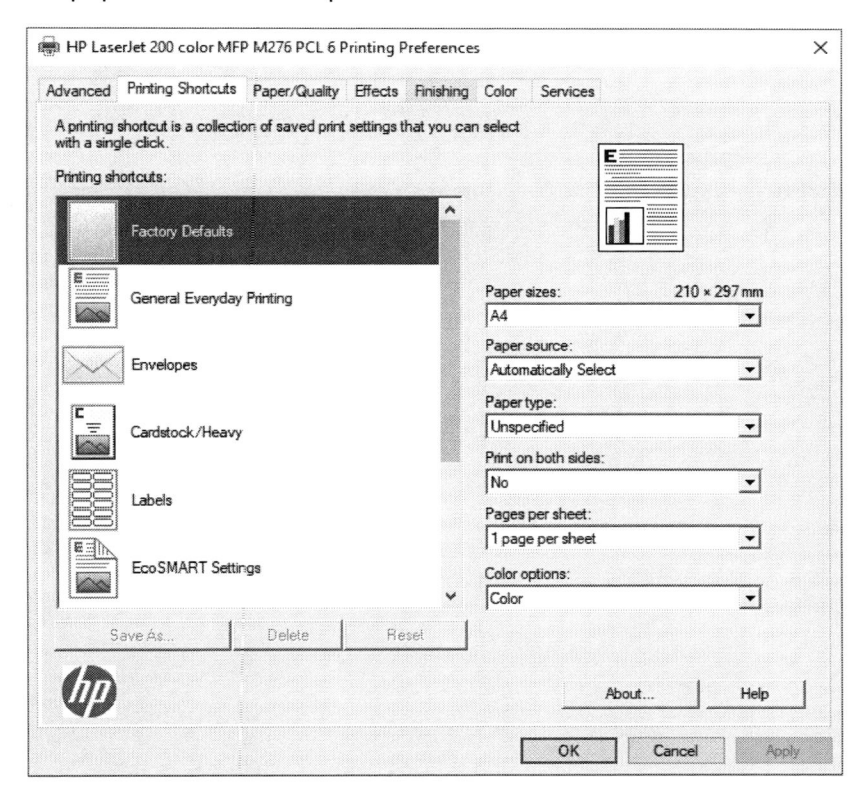

The shortcuts tab lets you select from preset option templates. (Screenshot used with permission from Microsoft.)

These settings can also be changed on a per-job basis by selecting the **Properties** button in the application's **Print** dialog box. Alternatively, the printer may come with management software that you can use to change settings.

PAPER/QUALITY

The **Paper/Quality** tab allows you to choose the type of paper stock (size and type) to use and whether to use an economy or draft mode to preserve ink/toner. You can also use the **Color** tab to select between color and grayscale printing.

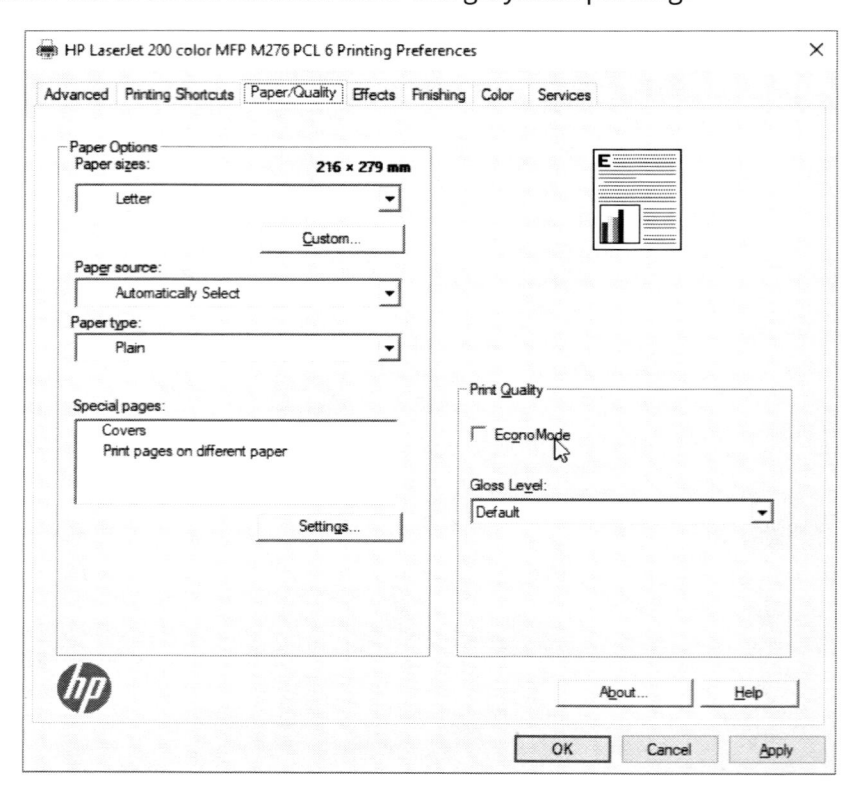

Use the Paper/Quality tab to configure the paper type and whether to use a reduced ink/toner economy mode. (Screenshot used with permission from Microsoft.)

FINISHING

The **Finishing** tab lets you select output options such as whether to print on both sides of the paper (duplex), print multiple images per sheet, and/or print in portrait or landscape orientation.

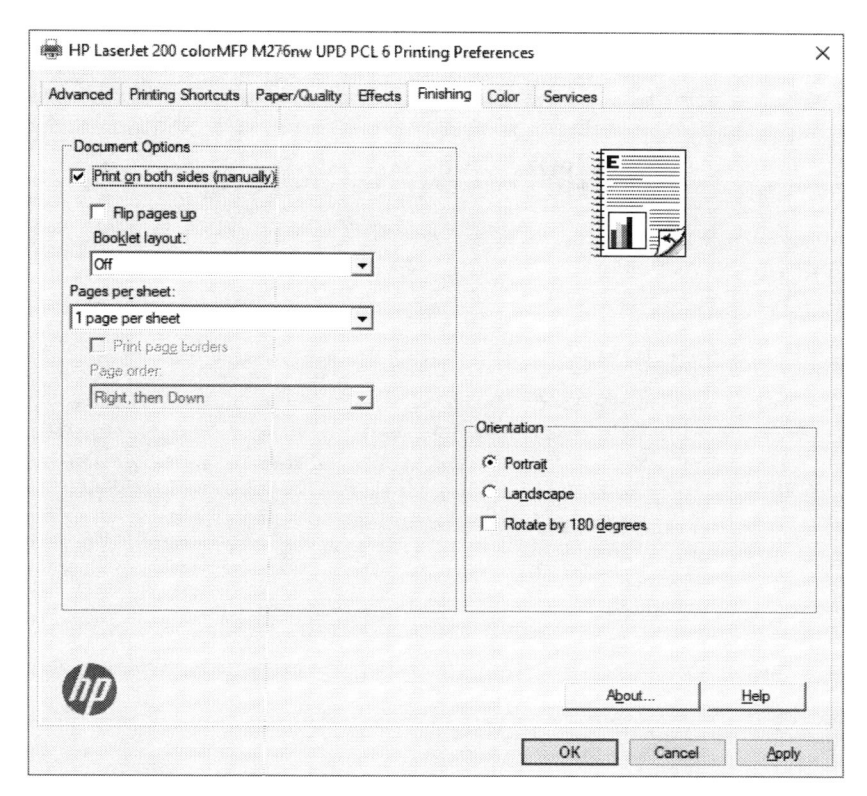

The Finishing tab allows you to select duplex output (this printer allows only manual duplex, where the stack must be flipped by the user and reinserted into the paper tray manually). (Screenshot used with permission from Microsoft.)

COPY COUNT AND COLLATED PRINTS

You can change the copy count and collation options using the **Advanced** tab.

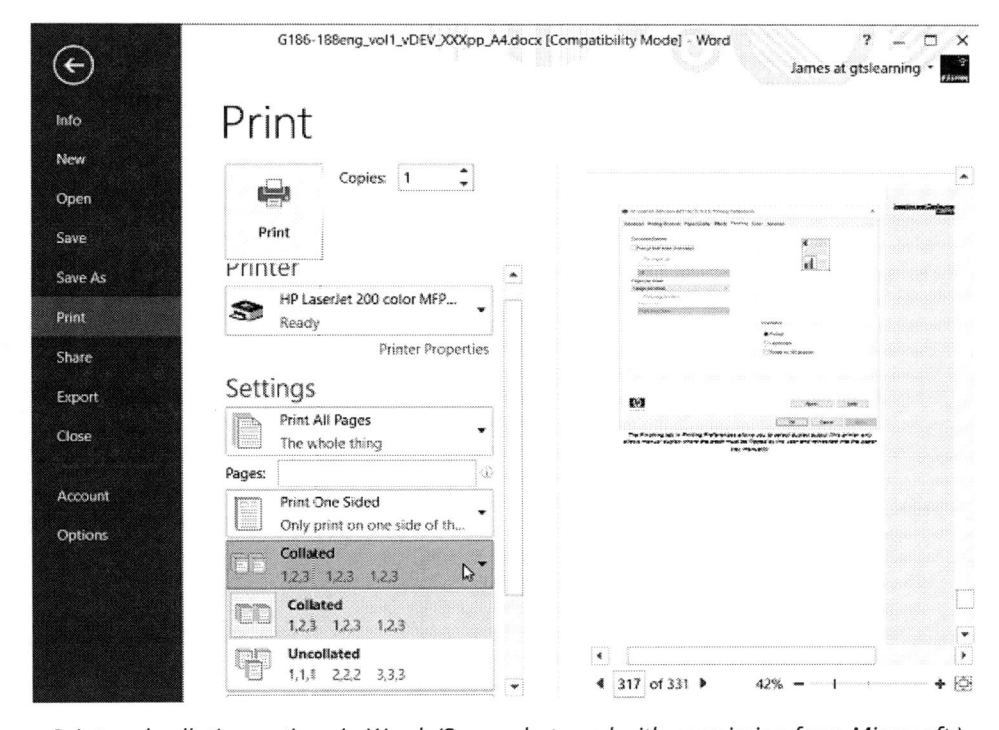

Print and collation options in Word. (Screenshot used with permission from Microsoft.)

A **collated** print job is one where all pages of the first copy are printed, followed by all pages of the second copy, and so on. If the **uncollated** option is selected, then all copies of page 1 are printed first, followed by all copies of page 2, and so on.

PRINTER SHARING AND NETWORKING

There are two main options for sharing a printer on the network:
- Windows printer sharing
- Hardware print server sharing

WINDOWS PRINT SERVER CONFIGURATION

An administrator can share any locally installed printer via its **Sharing** tab in the **Properties** dialog box. **Locally installed** means that Windows communicates with the print device directly over the relevant port. It does not matter whether the port is wired (USB, serial, or Ethernet) or wireless (Bluetooth or Wi-Fi). Drivers for different operating systems can also be installed locally so that clients can obtain the appropriate driver when they connect to the print share.

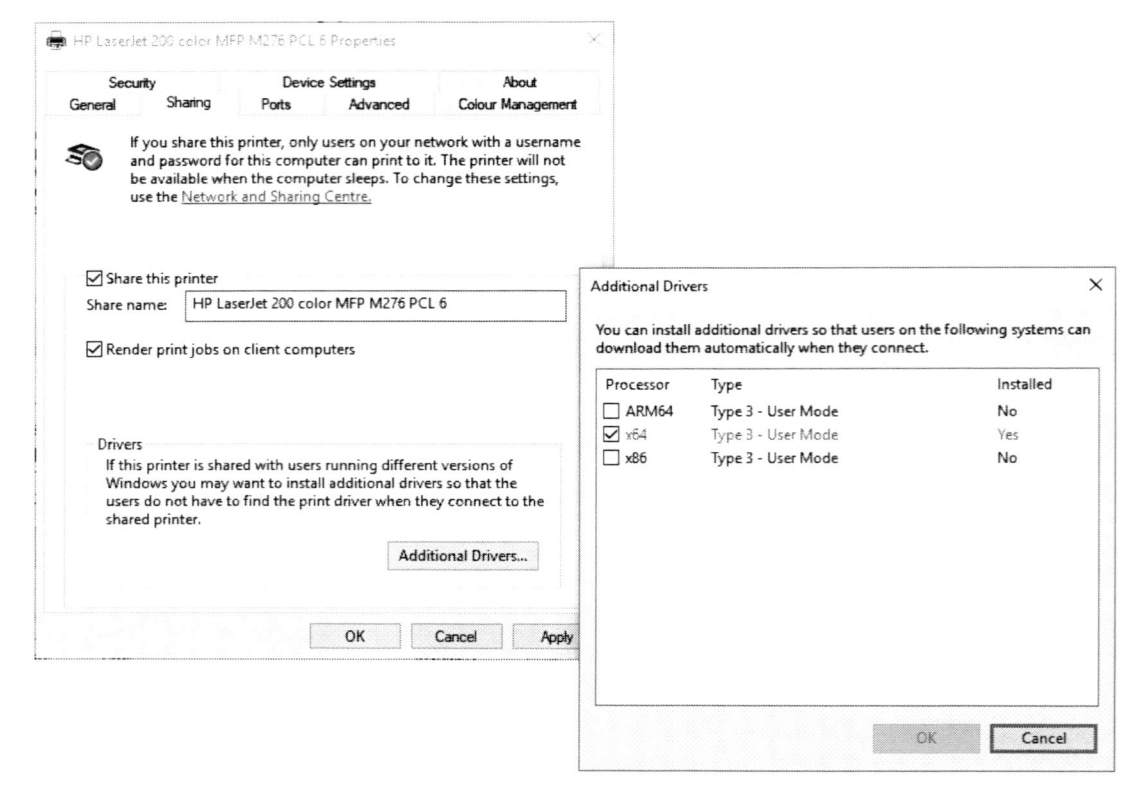

Sharing a printer via the Printer Properties dialog box. Use the Additional Drivers button from the Sharing page to install drivers for operating systems other than the host print server. (Screenshot used with permission from Microsoft.)

> **Note:** When you configure sharing, only one PC should be designated as the server for any one print device. If multiple PCs try to act as the server for the same print device, the result will be confusion.

If the network has clients running a mix of different operating systems, you need to consider how to make a printer driver available for each supported client. If the printer supports a "Type 3" driver, you need only add x86 (32-bit Windows) and/or x64 (64-bit Windows) support. For earlier "Type 2" drivers, each specific Windows version requires its own driver.

Note: *Windows 8 and 10 add support for Type 4 drivers. These are designed to move towards a print class driver framework, where a single driver will work with multiple devices. Where a specific print device driver is required, the client obtains it from Windows Update rather than the print server.*

SHARED PRINTER CONNECTIONS

An ordinary user can connect to a network printer (assuming that the printer administrator has given them permissions to use it). One way of doing this is to browse through the network resources using the **Network** object in **File Explorer**. Open the server computer hosting the printer, then right-click the required printer and select **Connect**.

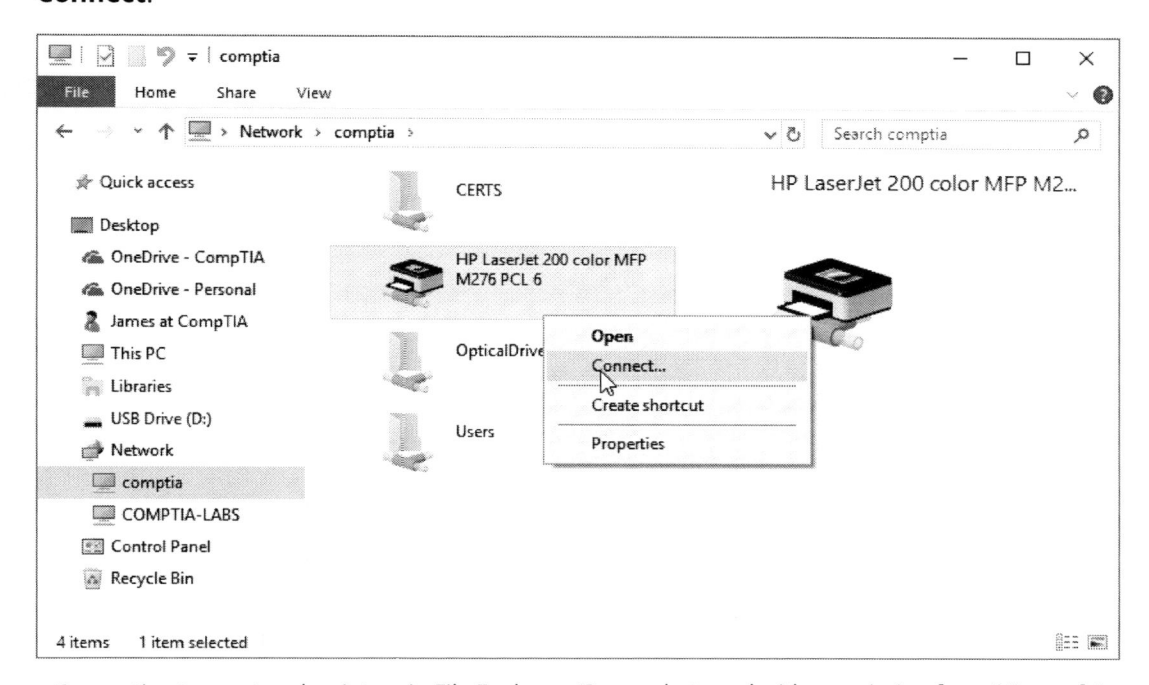

Connecting to a network printer via File Explorer. (Screenshot used with permission from Microsoft.)

INTEGRATED HARDWARE PRINT SERVERS/NAS

Some printers come with integrated or embedded print server hardware and firmware, allowing client computers to connect to them over the network without having to go via a server computer. You can also purchase print servers or use a solution such as a Network Attached Storage (NAS) appliance that supports print sharing. Many wireless Internet routers can be configured to work as a NAS/print server solution.

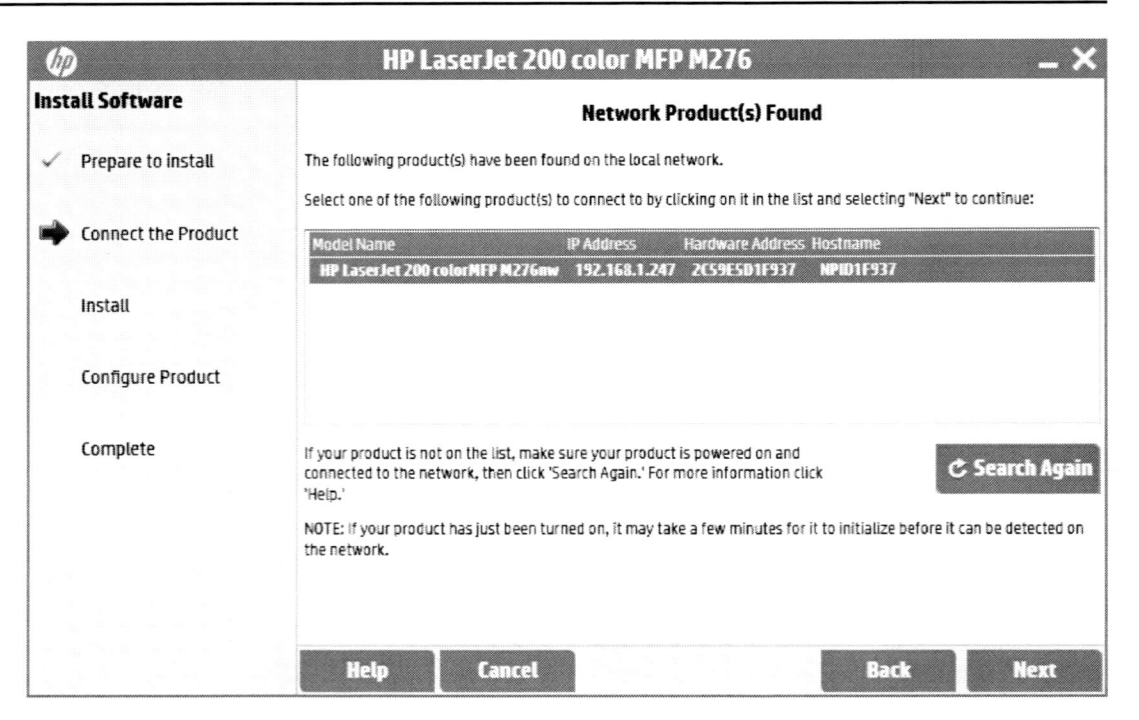

Installing a network printer using a vendor tool. The printer has been connected to the network via an Ethernet cable and been assigned an IP address by a DHCP server.

> **Note:** You can also purchase external print servers, such as HP's Jetdirect, that connect to a USB port on the printer and to the network via a standard port.

In place of a standard network card, a printer could be fitted with a Wi-Fi wireless adapter to make it available in a wireless network.

A network printer needs to be configured so that it has a valid address. On an IP network, you might set the printer to obtain an address automatically via a Dynamic Host Configuration Protocol (DHCP) server or configure it with a static IP address and subnet mask. The printer will need to communicate with computers over one or more Transmission Control Protocol (TCP) or User Datagram Protocol (UDP) network ports. If a network connection cannot be established, verify that these ports are not being blocked by a firewall or other security software.

Most printers provide a mechanism for locally configuring the printer. Usually, this is by means of a menu system which you navigate by using an LCD display and adjacent buttons or a touchscreen on the front of the printer.

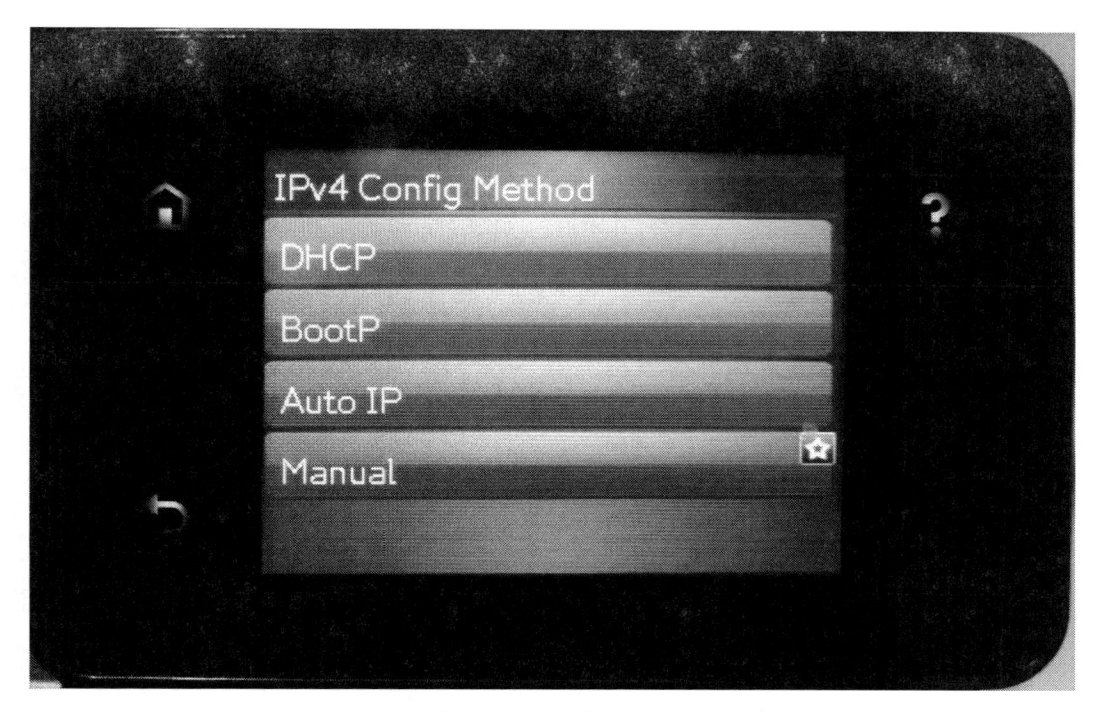

Setting the IP address configuration method via the printer's control panel.

This method is suitable for small office environments where you have few printers to manage. It is also useful in troubleshooting situations when the printer is inaccessible from the network. However, the printer vendor will usually supply a web-based utility to discover and manage their printers, whereas more advanced management suites are available for enterprise networks.

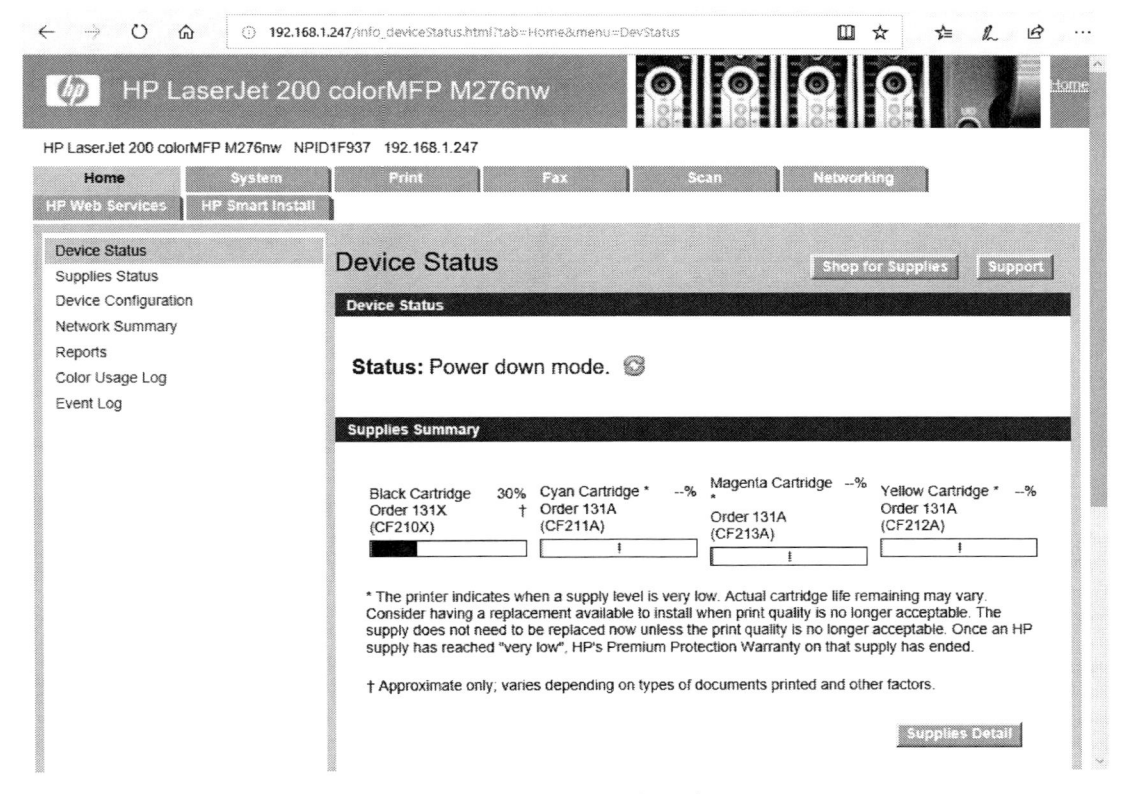

Managing an HP printer using a browser.

CLOUD AND REMOTE PRINTING

A networked printer can also be made available over the web using the HyperText Transfer Protocol (HTTP) and Internet Printing Protocol (IPP). For example, on an HP printer, you can use the management console to enable web services. This allows users to print to the device via HP's ePrint Center using a specially configured print path for the printer (identified by an email address). Alternatively, you could use third-party software, such as Google's Cloud Print™, which can connect to cloud-ready printers or support cloud printing for legacy devices.

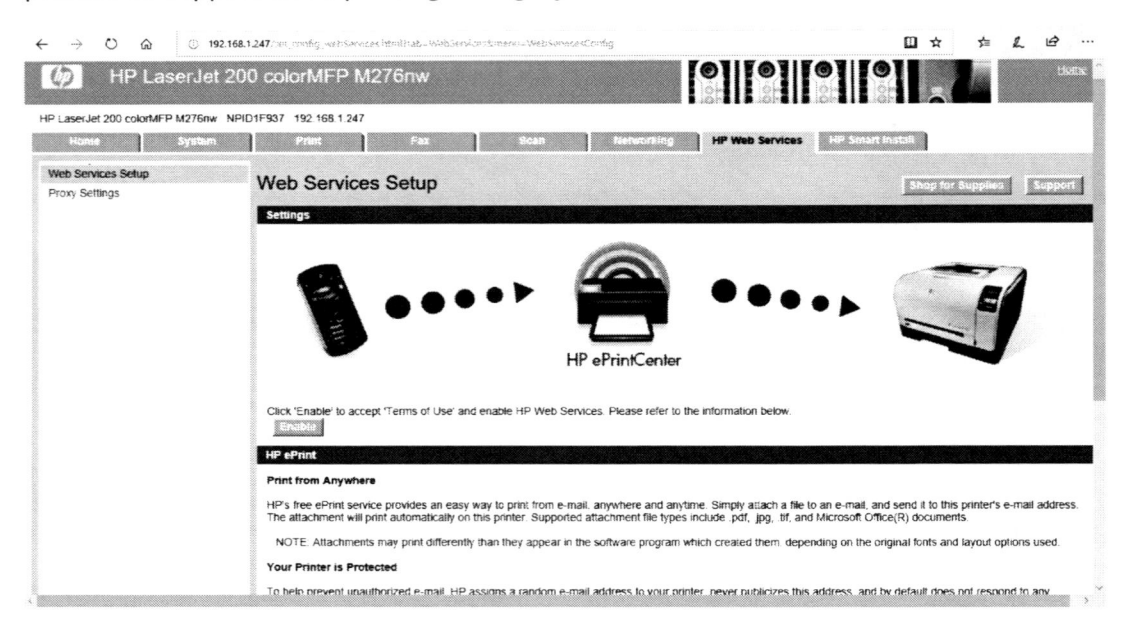

Configuring ePrint web services on an HP printer.

Users can send documents to the printer by logging into the cloud service. There are apps to support mobile devices as well as PCs and laptops.

Bonjour/AirPrint

You may also want to configure a network printer to support clients other than Windows. One option is to enable the **Bonjour** service to allow macOS PCs and iOS mobile devices to connect by using Apple **AirPrint**.

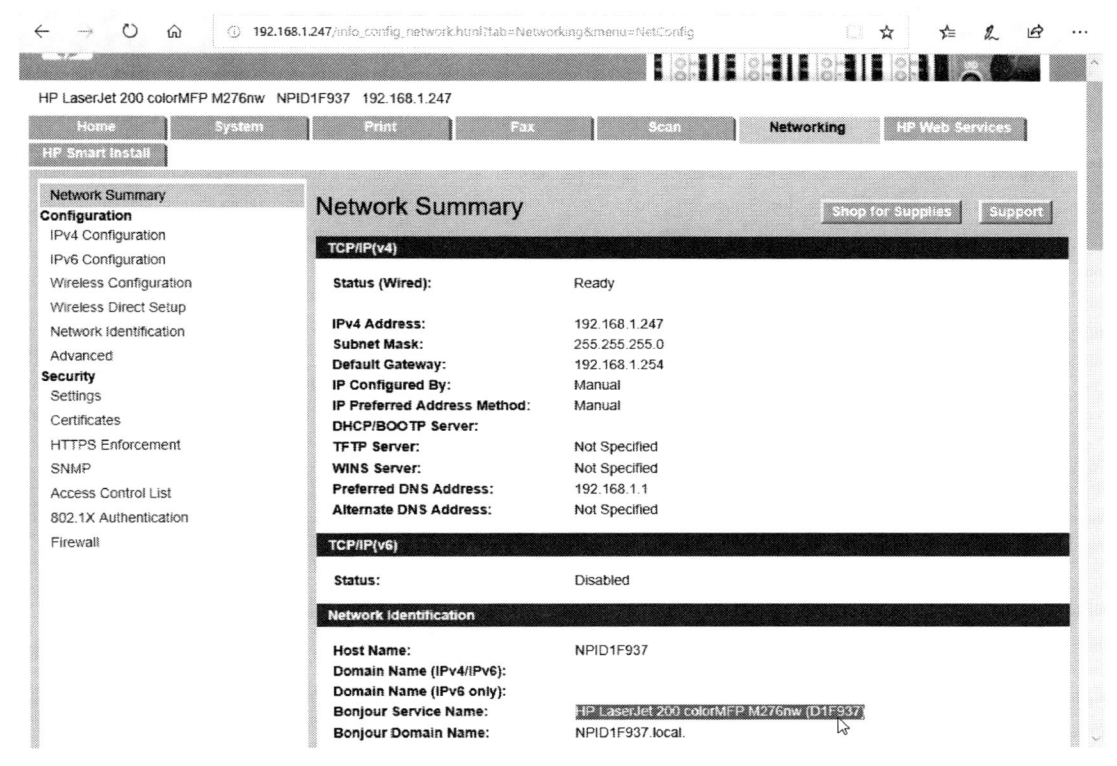

Bonjour services have been configured on this printer allowing macOS and iOS devices to connect to it wirelessly (using Apple AirPrint).

Bonjour is the server part of the solution, while AirPrint provides the client connectivity. Through Bonjour, users can locate printers and file servers. It uses DNS service records to locate the devices offering print and file sharing services. AirPrint is part of the macOS and iOS operating systems and supported by most third-party applications and apps.

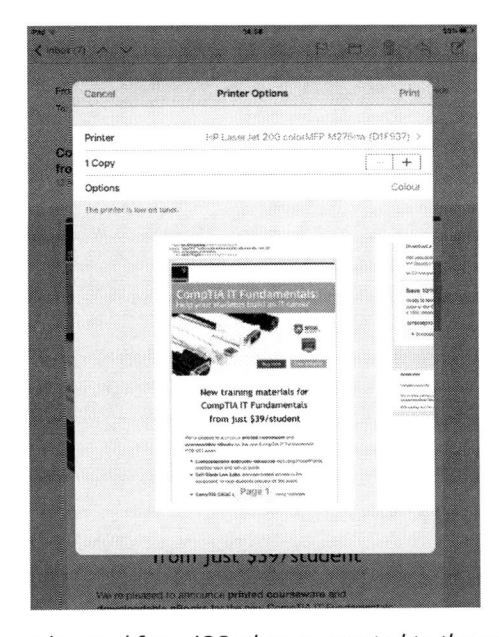

The printer can be used from iOS when connected to the same network.

DATA PRIVACY AND SECURITY ISSUES

You should be aware of some of the data privacy and security issues exposed by shared printers:

- **Hard drive caching**—most printers have a local storage device to use to cache print files. Someone with access to the device could be able to recover confidential information from the hard drive cache.
- **User authentication**—it may be necessary to prevent unauthorized use of a network or cloud-based printer. In a Windows network, the permissions system can be used to control access to the printer. Cloud-based services can also be configured to require user authentication.
- **Data privacy**—jobs sent over a network (such as via a cloud or remote print service) could potentially be intercepted and read, copied, or modified.

*Note: To learn more, check the **Video** tile on the CHOICE Course screen for any videos that supplement the content for this lesson.*

Access the Checklist tile on your CHOICE Course screen for reference information and job aids on How to Install and Configure Printers.

Activity 10-4
Discussing Printer Installation and Configuration

SCENARIO
Answer the following questions to check your understanding of the topic.

1. **When you are purchasing a new printer, what would you need to decide between as you evaluate connections?**

2. You use three Windows applications that need to print to a Canon BJC-4300 printer.

   How many printer drivers must you install?

3. You are setting up a print server and want to enable access for the widest range of Windows 7 machines possible.

   Should you install separate drivers for the Home and Enterprise editions?

4. **What tool can you use to confirm that basic print functionality is available?**

5. You have installed an automatic duplex unit in an office laser printer.

   What configuration setting would you change to make the unit available for print jobs?

6. **True or false? When you print 10 copies of an uncollated job, 10 copies of page one are printed, followed by 10 copies of page two, then 10 copies of page three, and so on.**

7. True or false? To enable printer sharing via Windows, the print device must be connected to the Windows PC via an Ethernet or Wi-Fi link.

8. What configuration information does a user need to use a print device connected to the same local network?

9. What service should a network print device run to enable an Apple iPad to use the device over Wi-Fi?

Activity 10-5
Installing and Configuring Printers

BEFORE YOU BEGIN

Complete this activity on your WORKBENCH PC. Check with your instructor for extra instructions.

SCENARIO

In the first part of this activity, you will compare and contrast various printers and print processes. There are several printers that are currently not deployed in your organization that are being stored in the IT department inventory cages. In order to determine which ones you will need when the time comes to replace currently deployed printers, you want to examine these printers to identify the features of each. You will then fill out a chart to identify which printers have which features.

In the second part of this activity, you will install and configure a printer. If a physical printer is not available, you can install a PostScript driver, which can be used to create print files that can be sent to any PostScript print device.

1. Examine the printers available to you, then fill out the following table. (Use the space on the bottom half of the page if necessary.)

Printer Type	Creates Images Using	Connection Method	Paper Handling Mechanism

2. Install a physical print device. If necessary, install the printer's driver software before connecting the print device.

    Your instructor will provide you with a print device and the necessary cabling.

a) If the printer comes with setup software that guides you through the installation process, follow the guided setup process.
b) Connect the power cable to an electrical outlet and switch on the print device.
c) Connect the printer cable to the appropriate port on the PC.

   You should hear a notification chime. Windows should locate the driver files and install the printer.
d) Click in the **Instant Search** box and type *printers*. Select the **Printers & scanners** link.
e) If your printer is not listed, select **Add a printer or scanner**.
f) If the printer is still not located, select the **The printer or scanner I want isn't listed** link.
g) Try the **My printer is a little older option** first. If this does not work, try **Add a local printer or network printer with manual settings**.

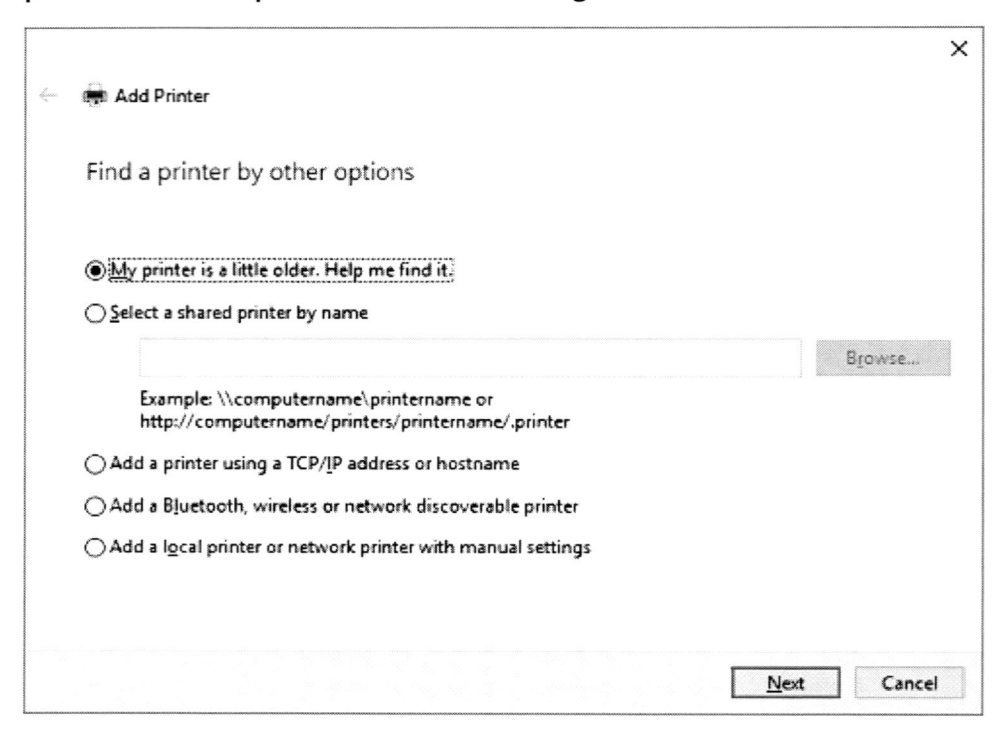

The Add Printer wizard—the wizard will usually detect any local or network printers available. (Screenshot used with permission from Microsoft.)

3. Install a driver to support Print to File.

   If a physical print device is not available, you can install a printer driver configured to output to a file.

   a) Click in the **Instant Search** box and type *printers*. Select the **Printers & scanners** link.
   b) Select **Add a printer or scanner**. When it appears, select the **The printer or scanner I want isn't listed** link.

      The **Add Printer** wizard starts.
   c) Select **Add a local printer or network printer with manual settings** and select **Next**.

d) From the **Use an existing port** box, select **FILE** and select **Next**.

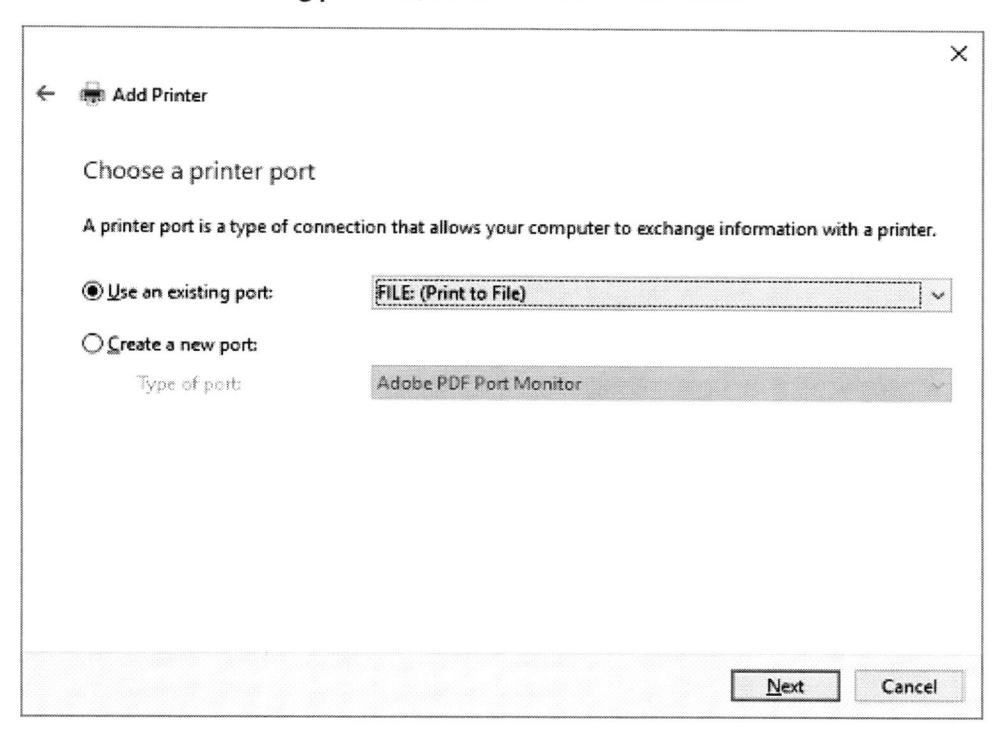

Configuring a printer to direct output to a file, rather than a device port. (Screenshot used with permission from Microsoft.)

e) From the **Manufacturer** box, select **Microsoft**, and then from the **Printers** box, select **Microsoft PS Class Driver**.

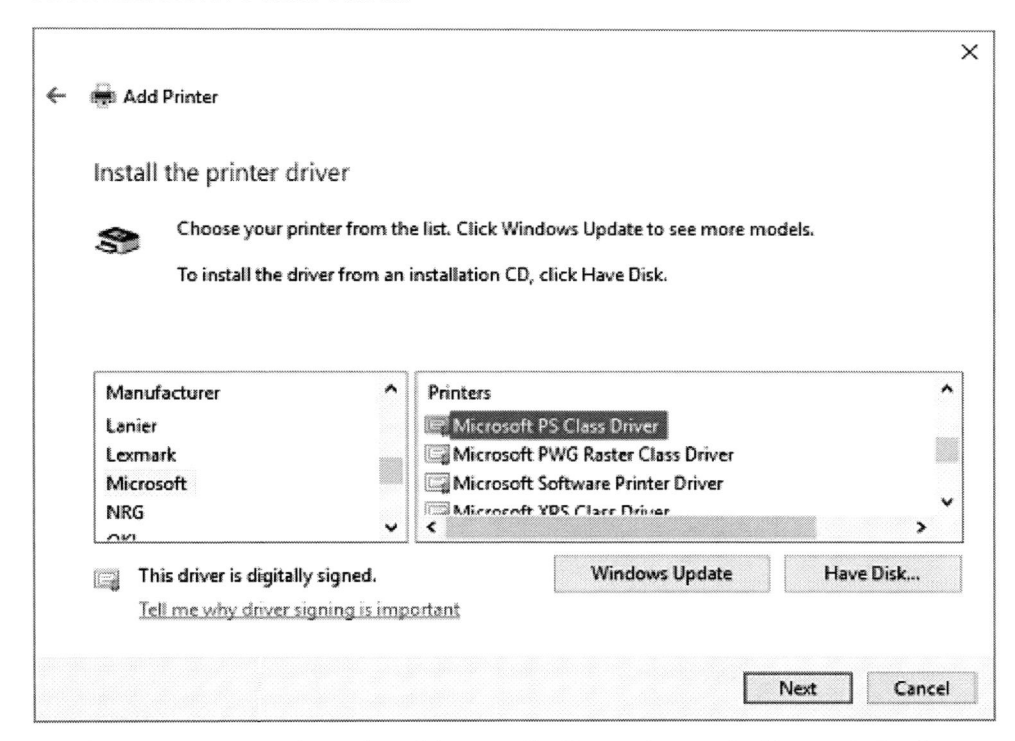

Selecting a printer make and model manually. (Screenshot used with permission from Microsoft.)

f) Select **Next**.
g) Select **Next**.

h) Accept the default **Printer name** and select **Next**.
   The printer driver files will be installed.
i) Select **Do not share this printer**, then select **Next**.
j) Select **Finish**.

4. Pause the print queue.
   a) If necessary, open **Printers & scanners** again.
   b) Observe the message on the printer indicating that it is the default.
   c) Select the printer and then select the **Manage** button.
      This shows status information and presents configuration options.

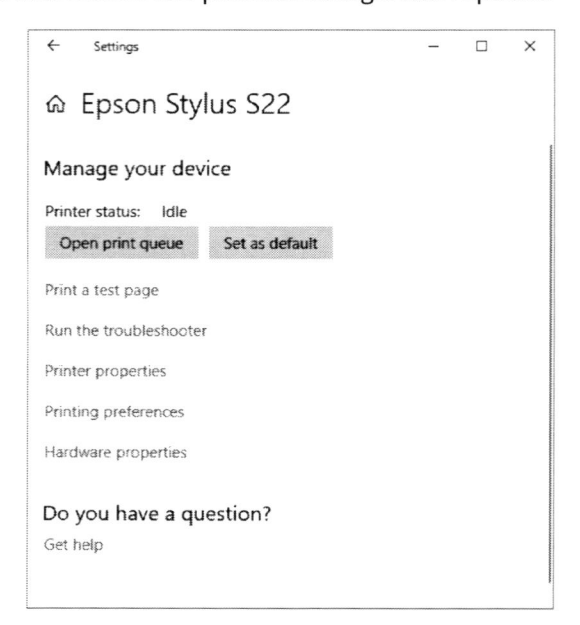

Device settings for an Epsom inkjet printer. (Screenshot used with permission from Microsoft.)

   d) Select **Open print queue** to open the print queue.
   e) Select **Printer→Pause Printing**.

      Note: *You will not be able to pause a virtual printer (when printing to a file).*

   f) Leave the print queue open.

5. View the print device's preferences, and configure it to use draft mode output.
   a) Switch back to the **Printers & scanners** app, and select **Printing preferences**.
   b) Configure the following options (most options will not be available if you configured the Print to File option):
      - Paper size: select **Letter**.
      - Paper type: select **plain paper** in the auto-feeder tray.
      - Print quality: set to **Draft/300 dpi**.
   c) Select **OK**.

6. Print a test page.
   a) Right-click the printer and select **Printer properties**.

      Note: *Select **Printer properties** not **Hardware properties**, as the latter option opens a different dialog box (Device Manager properties).*

b) Look through the options on the various tabs, then select the **General** tab and select **Print Test Page**. If you are printing to a file, save the file as ***test.oxps*** in the **Documents** folder.
c) Select **Close** to dismiss the message. Select **OK** to close the dialog box.

7. View the print queue and the printer's spool folder.
   a) Switch to the print queue and observe the job waiting for the print device to come online.

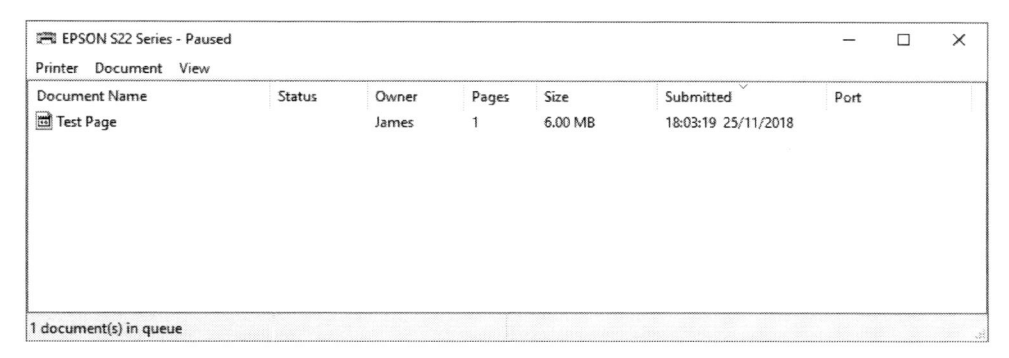

   Observing the print queue. (Screenshot used with permission from Microsoft.)

   b) In Explorer, open **C:\Windows\System32\Spool\PRINTERS**. If necessary, select **Continue** at the UAC prompt to get access to the folder. Observe the spooled job.
   c) Open another Explorer window and browse the **C:\COMPTIA-LABS\LABFILES** folder. Right-click the **comptia-logo.jpg** picture and select **Print** then confirm with **Print** again. If you are printing to a file, save it as ***sample.oxps*** in the **Documents** folder.
   d) Verify that the spooled files are listed in the **PRINTERS** folder.
   e) Verify that the printer is correctly loaded with paper.
   f) In the print queue, right-click the **Full page photo** job and select **Pause**. Select **Printer→Pause Printing**.
   g) When the job has printed, collect it from the printer.
   h) Look at the spooled files again—verify that they are now either 0 KB or deleted.
   i) Switch back to the print queue, right-click the **Full page photo** job, and select **Cancel**. Confirm by selecting **Yes**.
   j) Check the **PRINTERS** folder again—the spooled files should no longer be displayed.
   k) If you are printing to a file, browse the XPS format documents created in the **Documents** folder.

8. Uninstall the printer.
   a) Disconnect the printer from the port and switch it off.
   b) Look at **Printers & settings**.
      The printer should be listed as offline.
   c) Select the printer and select **Remove device**. Select **Yes** to confirm.
   d) Verify that another printer (if present) is automatically selected as the new default.
   e) If you installed the printer software, open **Settings→Apps→Apps & features**. Select the printer software and select **Uninstall**. Work through the remaining prompts to remove the software.

Topic E
Troubleshoot Print Device Issues

EXAM OBJECTIVES COVERED
1001-5.6 Given a scenario, troubleshoot printers.

As a support professional, you will be well aware that one of the most unpleasant problems for users is being unable to print. If users need hard copies of documents and the systems do not work, it can be very frustrating. Users will look to you to identify and resolve their problems quickly, so you will need to recognize common issues and to correct them efficiently when they occur.

PRINTER CONNECTIVITY TROUBLESHOOTING

Printers are usually simple devices to troubleshoot, as in most cases there will be an error message or code displayed on the printer's control panel telling you exactly where the error lies. You may need to look the error code up in the printer documentation to confirm what it means. Use the error code to guide your troubleshooting efforts.

USING PRINTER LOGS

You could also check for multiple failed jobs in the print server's log. For example, in Windows, use Event Viewer to open the **Applications and Services→Microsoft→Windows→Print Service→Operational** log.

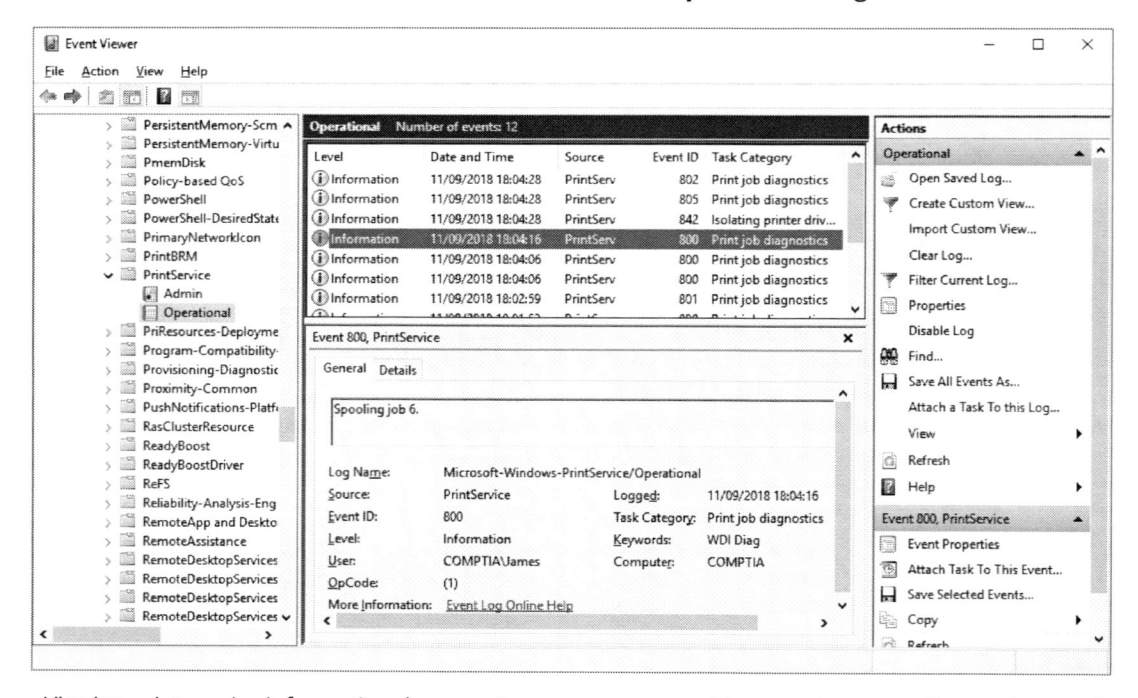

Viewing print service informational messaging—any errors would appear here, too. (Screenshot used with permission from Microsoft.)

Note: You need to right-click to enable the **Print Service—Operational** log before it starts recording events. Consider creating an administrative alert for error events so that you can be warned of and investigate problems quickly.

You may also be able to collect error logs from the device itself. Management software will be able to retrieve these logs and report them to a centralized console. Alternatively, you can view them manually using a vendor-supplied tool, such as the management URL for this HP printer.

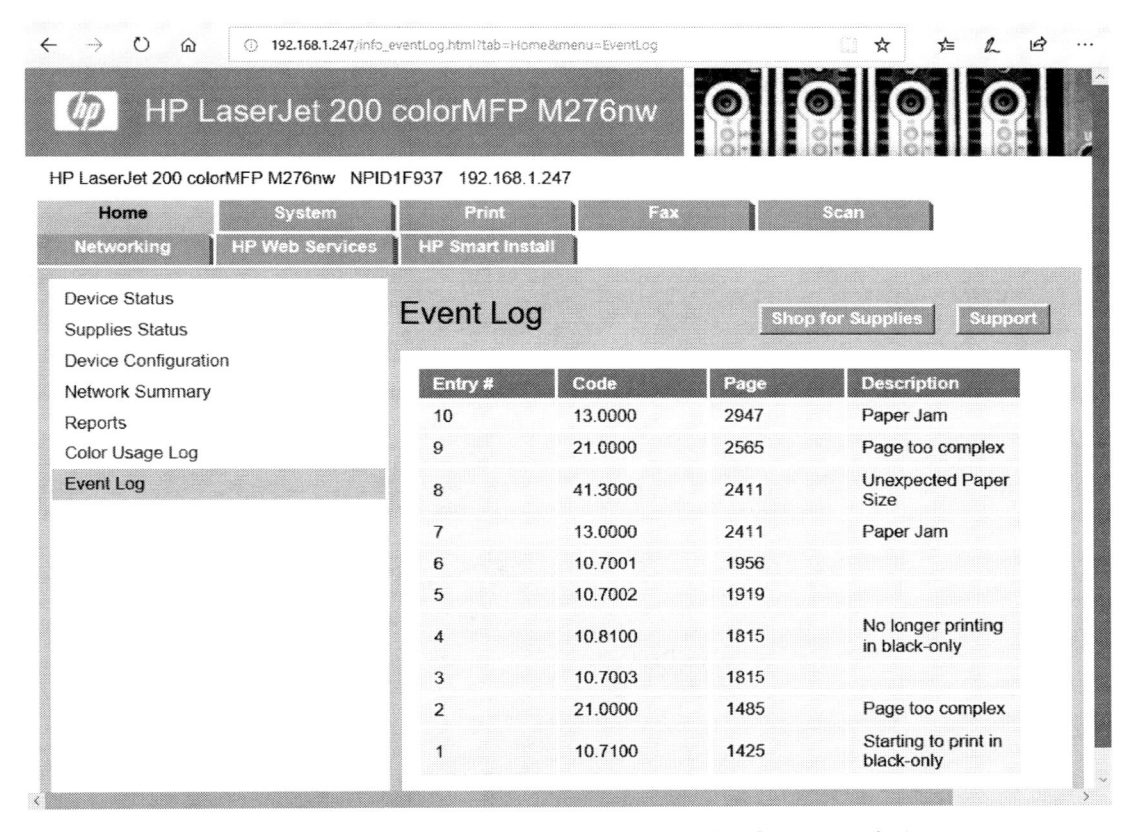

Using a web management tool to view the event log for a print device.

GENERAL TROUBLESHOOTING APPROACH

In the absence of any error code or descriptive error log, remember to test obvious things first:

- Is the printer switched on and loaded with paper?
- Is there sufficient ink or toner?
- Is the connection between the printer and PC good?
- Can you print a test page by using the printer's control panel and from within Windows?

Also check environmental conditions—a printer may malfunction if it overheats. Check that there is plenty of space around the printer for air to circulate (especially around the vents on the printer case) and that the environment is not excessively hot.

Remember to ask: "What has changed?" It is important to establish whether something has never worked or has just stopped working. If something never worked, then there has been an installation error; if something has stopped working, look for a configuration change or maintenance issue.

Note: *Also remember that Windows has several built-in troubleshooting tools, one of which covers printer problems.*

GUIDELINES FOR TROUBLESHOOTING PRINT DEVICE ISSUES

Note: *All of the Guidelines for this lesson are available as checklists from the **Checklist** tile on the CHOICE Course screen.*

Consider these guidelines as you troubleshoot printing problems in Windows.

NO IMAGE ON THE PRINTER DISPLAY

If there is no image on the printer display but the printer's power LED is lit:

- Verify that the printer has not gone into a power-saving sleep cycle. Pressing the power button or pressing the touchscreen will generally wake the printer.
- Try powering down the printer. Remove the power cord and any peripheral cables, and leave the printer switched off and unplugged for at least a minute. Then reconnect and restart the printer.
- If these steps do not resolve the issue, there is likely to be a hardware fault.

NO CONNECTIVITY

If documents do not print or if you see "Not available" messages relating to the printer you want to use:

- Verify that the printer is switched on and "online." A printer can be taken offline quite easily by pressing the button on the control panel. Often this happens by accident. A printer may also go offline because it is waiting for user intervention or because it has received corrupt print job data.
- Also check the connection between the host PC and printer. Make sure connectors are secure, that the network configuration is correct, or that there are no sources of interference blocking a wireless link, for instance.

Note: *Remember, cycling the power is a time-honored response to most troubleshooting scenarios involving end-user devices.*

PRINT QUEUE AND SPOOLER TROUBLESHOOTING

A **backed-up print queue** means that there are lots of jobs pending but not printing. This might occur because the printer is offline or out of paper or ink/toner. It could also occur because of an error processing a particular print job. If a particular job will not print:

- Open the **Devices and Printers** applet or Windows **Settings** to access the printer and open its print queue. Try restarting the job (right-click the document name and select **Restart**). You need permission to **Manage Documents** on the printer object to restart or cancel jobs.
- If that does not work, delete the print job and try printing it again.
- Many problems, including "Low memory" or "Out of memory" errors, can also be solved by cycling the power on the printer and clearing a backed up print queue.

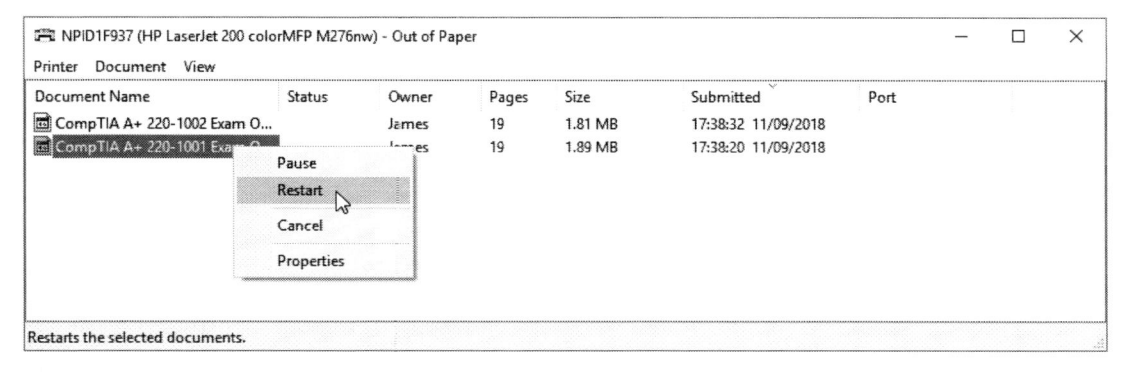

Use the print queue to manage jobs—in this instance, you should be loading the printer with some paper, rather than trying to restart the print job. (Screenshot used with permission from Microsoft.)

If you cannot delete a job (if the print queue is backed up or stalled), you will need to stop the **Print Spooler** service.

1. Open the **Computer Management** console, then expand **Services and Applications** and select **Services**.

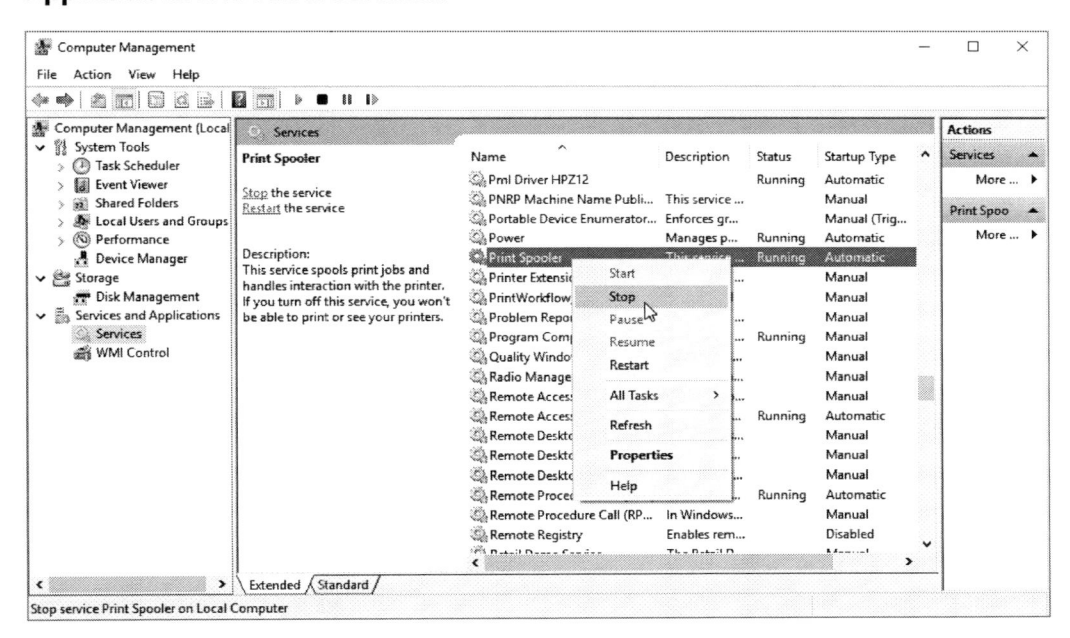

Managing the spooler service using the Computer Management console. (Screenshot used with permission from Microsoft.)

2. Right-click the **Print Spooler** service and select **Stop**.
3. Use Explorer to delete the spooled file from **%SystemRoot%\System32\Spool\Printers**. There will be a *.SPL file (the print job) and possibly a *.SHD file (status information), too.
4. Start the **Print Spooler** service again.

Alternatively, you can use `net` commands to manage the spooler service. Enter the commands `net stop spooler` and `net start spooler` in the **Run** dialog box or at a command prompt.

Another option is to try using different spool settings. Spool settings can be configured on the **Advanced** tab of the **Properties** dialog box. You might want to change these settings if there are problems spooling jobs. This page also lets you set the spooled file type between EMF and RAW (select **Print Processor**). In the **Printer Properties** dialog box, change the spool settings as follows, testing after each change:

- Change the spool data format to **RAW**.

- Turn off spooling (select **Print directly to printer**).

Also verify that there is plenty of free disk space on the volume hosting the spooler.

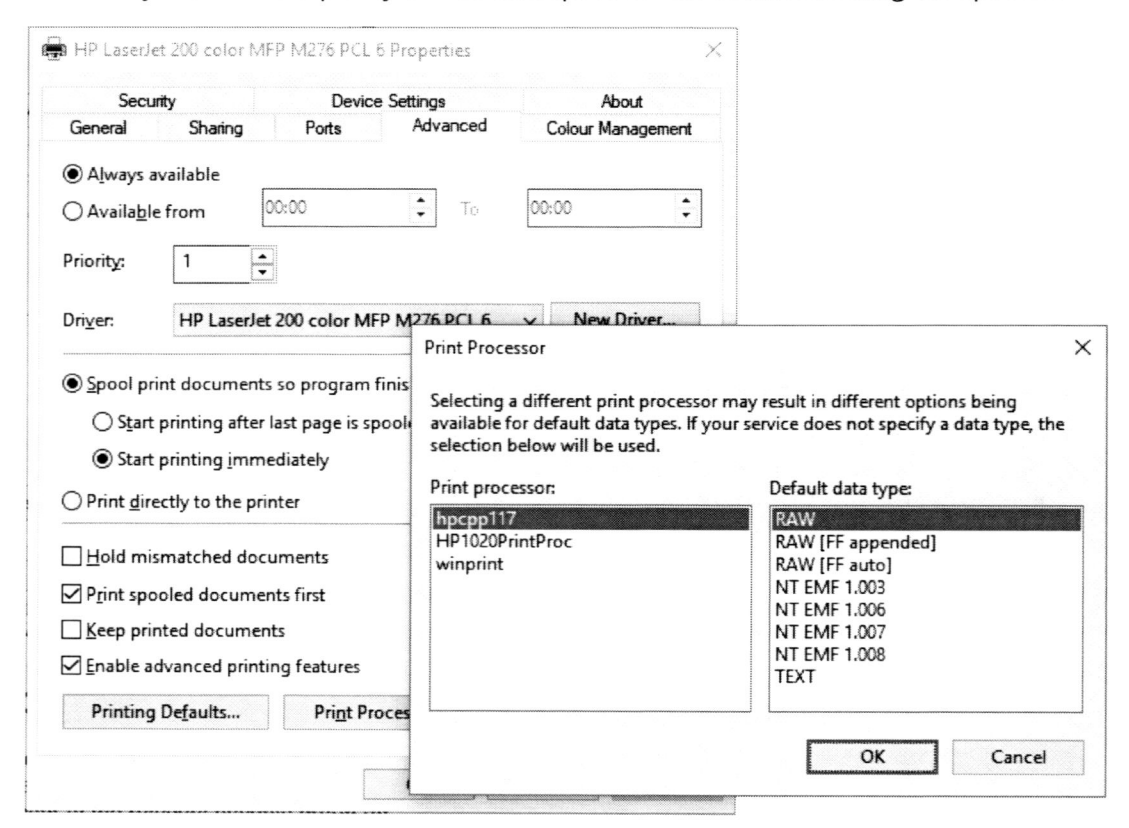

Spool and Print Processor settings in Printer Properties.

PERMISSION ISSUES TROUBLESHOOTING

There are several scenarios where permission issues can affect a user's ability to print documents.

ACCESS DENIED

If a user is accessing a printer that has been shared over a network, an **Access Denied** message means that the user account has not been configured with permission to print documents. Add the user to the relevant security group (or add the relevant security group or user object to the printer).

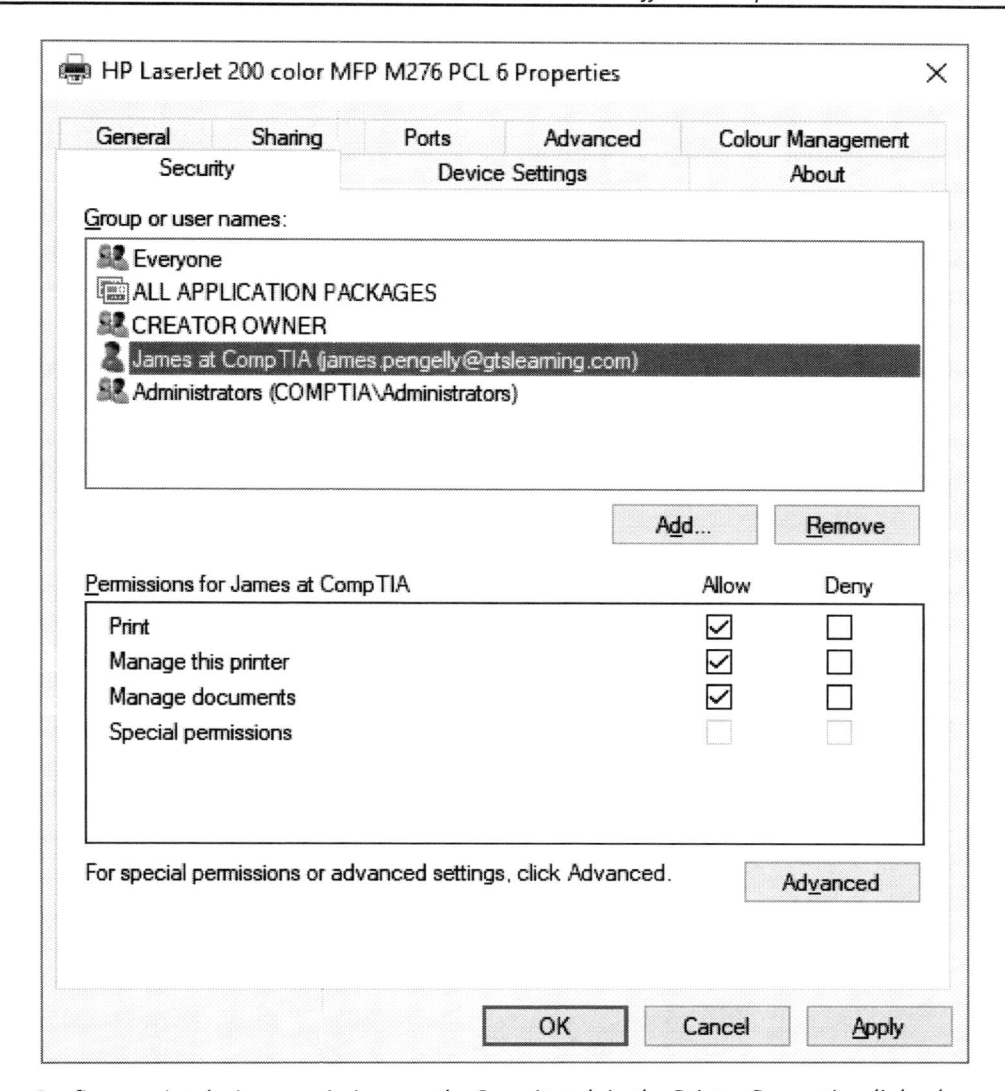

Configure print device permissions on the Security tab in the Printer Properties dialog box.

If the permissions are correct, verify that security software is not causing a problem by trying to scan the spool folder, and verify the permissions on the spool folder itself. You might also investigate the disk hosting the printer spool to ensure there is no problem there.

UNABLE TO INSTALL PRINTER

If a user cannot install a printer, it is likely to be because their account does not have sufficient permissions to install the printer driver. This sort of operation will normally have to be performed by an administrator, though it is possible to configure network security policies that allow users to install printers with signed drivers.

If the problem is not related to permissions, verify that you are attempting to install a driver for the correct version and type of Windows. In particular, remember that 32-bit printer drivers will not work with a 64-bit edition of Windows.

Also verify that the print spooler service is started.

> *Note: There's also the possibility that existing printer drivers are interfering with the one you're trying to install. Uninstall these other drivers, then try installing the new one. If you need these older drivers for other printers, try removing them from the default printer status, then install the new printer driver as the default.*

DRIVER AND GARBLED OUTPUT ISSUES

If a print job contains high-resolution graphics or multiple pages and printing is very slow, bear in mind that the printer may not have sufficient resources to handle the job and may display an error such as **Low memory** or **Out of memory**.

- Try clearing the print queue and sending the job again or cycling power on the printer.
- If there are persistent problems with printing from a specific application, check the vendor's troubleshooting website to determine if a driver update will fix the problem.

Use the printer's property sheet to print a test page. If the test page prints successfully, then the problem is related to the print function of a particular application. Try printing a different file from the same application; if this works, then you know that the problem is specific to a particular file. If the test page does not print, try using the printer's control panel to print it. If this works, there is some sort of communication problem between the print device and Windows.

One of the first options when trying to remedy most types of software print problem is to update the driver to the latest version or use a different driver (PostScript instead of PCL, for instance). Also check that the correct job options have been set (media type, input tray, duplex printing, monochrome or color, economy mode, and so on). Remember that print properties set through the application (by selecting **File→Print→Properties→Print Setup**) override those set as the default (either through the Printer object in Windows or through the device's control panel).

If a print job is garbage (if it emits many pages with a few characters on each or many blank pages):

1. Cancel the print job.
2. Clear the print queue.
3. Cycle the power on the printer (leaving it off for 30 seconds to clear the memory).
4. Try to print again.

If the problem persists, update the printer driver and check that the printer is set to use the correct control language (PCL or PostScript). You can also try changing the spool type from EMF to RAW or disabling spooling.

If printing is slow, use the **Advanced** property page to choose the **Start printing immediately** option. You can try changing the spool format from RAW to EMF.

If the characters in a document are different from those expected or if strange characters appear in an otherwise normal print, check that **fonts** specified in the document are available on the PC and/or printer. The software application should indicate whether the specified font is available or whether it is substituting it for the nearest match.

To view fonts installed on the computer, open the **Fonts** applet in Control Panel/Windows **Settings**. Each font family (such as Arial) often comes with a number of variants (such as Bold or Italic). If you open a font icon, a preview of the font at different sizes is shown. If a font is not shown here, use the **File** menu to locate and install it. Fonts are usually located in **C:\Windows\Fonts**, but some font manager applications may store fonts in another location.

> *Note: Most fonts require a license—you should not copy them between computers without making the proper licensing arrangements.*

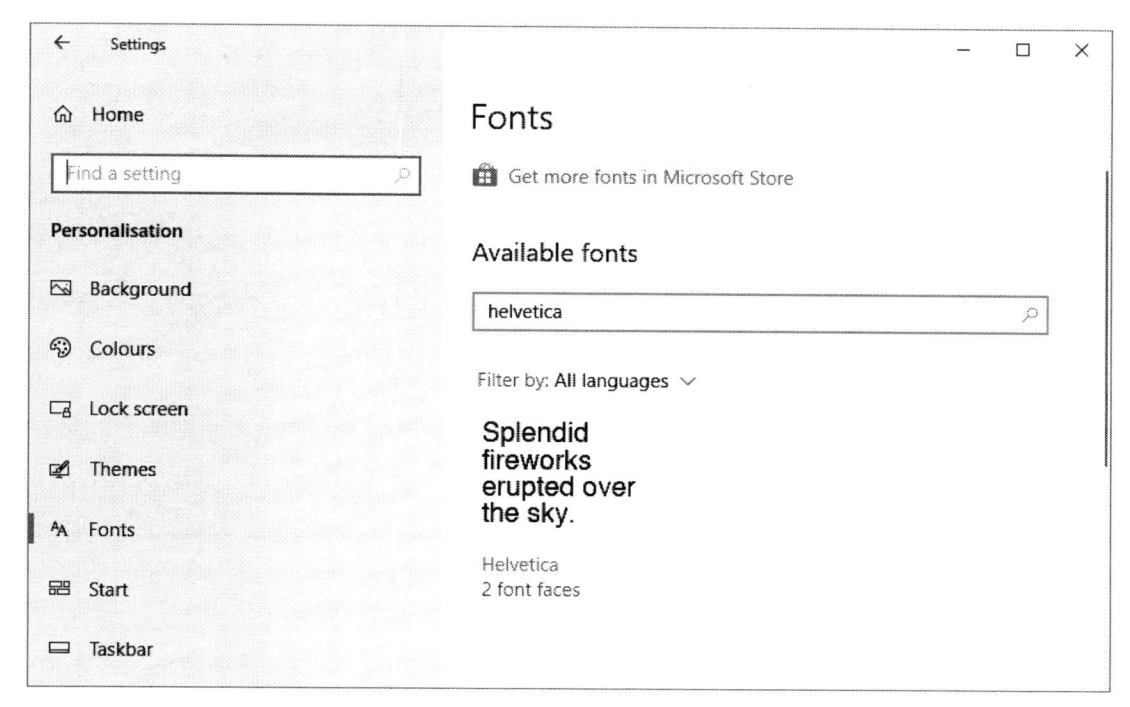

If characters do not appear correctly, check that the proper fonts are installed. (Screenshot used with permission from Microsoft.)

A PostScript printer may use internal fonts in preference to those installed on the PC. Check **Printing Preferences** to confirm that the printer is not using font substitution.

GENERAL PRINT DEFECT RESOLUTION

If a job prints from Windows but the output is smudged, faded, or arrives with unusual marks (print defects), the problem is likely to be a printer hardware or media fault. This section describes some of the common faults likely to be encountered. Always consult the manufacturer's documentation and troubleshooting notes.

> **Note:** *Working inside any electrical equipment, especially a laser printer, can be dangerous. If the cause of a problem is not easily found, you must seek advice from a qualified source. You should never defeat a safety interlock in order to operate a printer with protective covers removed.*

A **paper jam** is one of the most frequently occurring printer problems.

Fixing a paper jam is usually quite straightforward. The key point is to gain proper access to the stuck page. Do not use force to try to remove a sheet as you may cause further damage. Most sheets will pull free from most parts of the printer, but if a page is stuck in the fuser unit of a laser printer, you must use the release levers to get it out. Pulling the paper forcibly through the fuser can damage the rollers and, if the paper rips, leave paper debris on them.

If paper jams are frequent, you need to diagnose the problem, rather than simply fix the symptom each time. Most paper jams arise because the media (paper or labels) are not suitable for the printer or because a sheet is creased, folded, or not loaded properly in the tray. There could be a problem with a roller, too. Identify whether or not the jam occurs in the same place each time, and take appropriate preventive maintenance (clean or replace the part).

The printer control panel should identify the location of the paper jam.

If paper is not feeding into the printer or if the printer is feeding multiple sheets at the same time, verify that it is loaded in the tray properly and that it is of an appropriate weight (not too thick or thin). If you can discount a media problem, try changing the pickup rollers. In a laser printer, these are part of the maintenance kit.

> **Note:** *Fan the edge of a paper stack with your thumb to separate the sheets before loading the tray. Do not overdo this however—you can generate a static charge that will hold the sheets together.*

LASER PRINTER PRINT DEFECTS

The causes of print defects tend to be specific to the technology used by the imaging process. The following defects are common in laser printers:

- **Faded or faint prints**—if a simple cause such as the user choosing an option for low density (draft output) can be discounted, this is most likely to indicate that the toner cartridge needs replacing.
- **Blank pages**—as noted earlier, this is usually an application or driver problem, but it could indicate that a toner cartridge has been installed without removing its packing seals. Alternatively, if these simple causes can be discounted, this could also be a sign that the transfer roller (or secondary corona wire) is damaged (the image transfer stage fails).
- **Skewed output**—verify that the paper is inserted correctly and that media guides are well-positioned (not too tight and not too loose).
- **White stripes**—this indicates either that the toner is poorly distributed (give the cartridge a gentle shake) or that the transfer roller is dirty or damaged.
- **Black stripes or whole page black**—indicates that the primary transfer roller is dirty or damaged or that the High Voltage Power Supply to the developer unit is malfunctioning.
- **Toner specks**—if the output is "speckled," loose toner may be getting onto the paper. Clean the inside of the printer using an approved toner vacuum.
- **Persistent marks**—streaks, vertical or horizontal lines, and other marks that appear in the same place (referred to as repetitive defects) are often due to dirty

feed rollers (note that there are rollers in the toner cartridge and fuser unit, too) or a damaged or dirty photosensitive drum.
- **Toner not fused to paper**—if the output smudges easily, this indicates that the fuser needs replacing.
- **Wavy or wrinkled output**—make sure the paper is inserted correctly (try turning the stack over).
- **Ghost images**—this is a sign that the photosensitive drum has not been cleaned properly. The drum is smaller than the size of a sheet of paper, so if the image is not completely cleared it will repeat as a light "ghost" or dark "shadow" image farther down the page. Images may also appear from previous prints. Try printing a series of different images and see if the problem resolves itself. If not, replace the drum/toner cartridge.
- **Wrong color/color cast**—if prints come out in the wrong color (for example, if the whole print has a magenta tint), ensure that the toner cartridges have been installed in the correct location (for instance, that a Magenta cartridge hasn't been installed in the Cyan slot). Also ensure that there is sufficient toner in each cartridge. If there is a cast or shadow-like effect, one or all of the cartridges, rollers, or transfer belt are probably misaligned. Try reseating them and then run the printer calibration utility, and print a test page to verify the problem is solved.
- **Color missing**—if a color is completely missing, try replacing the cartridge. If this does not solve the issue, clean the contacts between the printer and cartridge.
- **Paper jams**—if the media and pickup rollers are good and if the jam occurs within the drum assembly but before the image is fused, the cause could be a faulty Static Eliminator Strip. Normally, this removes the high static charge from the paper as it leaves the transfer unit. If the strip fails, the paper may stick to the drum or curl as it enters the fuser unit.

*Note: To learn more, check the **Video** tile on the CHOICE Course screen for any videos that supplement the content for this lesson.*

INKJET AND DOT MATRIX PRINT DEFECTS

Defects in inkjet and dot matrix output tend to be concentrated around print head and media issues.

INKJET PRINTERS

Lines running through printouts indicate a dirty print head or blocked ink nozzle, which can usually be fixed by running a cleaning cycle. Most other print quality problems (output that smears easily, wavy or wrinkled output, or blurry output) is likely to be a media problem. As with laser printers, persistent marks on output probably indicate a dirty feed roller. If the print head jams, the printer will probably display a status message or show a flashing LED. Try turning the printer off and unplugging it then turning it back on. Inconsistent color output indicates that one of the ink reservoirs is running low (or that a print head for one of the color cartridges is completely blocked). If a document does not print in color, check that color printing has actually been selected.

DOT MATRIX PRINTERS

Lines in the output indicate a stuck pin in the print head. Output can also be affected by the platen position. The platen adjusts the gap between the paper and the print head to accommodate different paper types. Incorrect adjustment of the platen gap can cause faint printing (gap too wide) or smudging (too narrow). On more sophisticated printers, the platen gap is adjusted automatically. Use an Isopropyl Alcohol solution to clean the print head if necessary.

Activity 10-6
Troubleshooting Printer Issues

SCENARIO
Answer the following questions to check your understanding of the topic.

1. A user reports that the printed output is not up to the usual standards for her printer. You will need to resolve this issue so she can print her report.

   What is the overall process for troubleshooting this issue?

2. **If print jobs do not appear at the printer and the queue is clear, what could you try first to solve the problem?**

3. **Where on disk is the print file spooled in Windows?**

4. You need to restart the Print Spooler service on a Windows 7 machine. You have logged on as Administrator.

   What are your next steps?

5. **How would you track down the source of a paper jam?**

6. **What should you do if you cannot delete a job stuck in the print queue?**

7. Paper is jamming in an inkjet printer.

   What could be causing this?

8. What effect does a worn photosensitive drum have on printing?

9. A laser printer is producing white stripes on the paper.
   What could be causing this?

10. What effect does a dirty primary corona wire have on laser printing?

Activity 10-7
Maintaining and Troubleshooting Printers

SCENARIO
Depending on the equipment available, in this activity, you will complete some routine maintenance and troubleshooting of printers.

1. Read the printer service documentation provided by your instructor carefully.

2. Complete a maintenance cycle on a print device. For example, on a laser printer, complete the following tasks:
   a) Remove the toner cartridge and maintenance kit components from the laser printer.
   b) Clean the laser printer using the approved products available.
   c) Replace the maintenance kit components and toner cartridge.

3. Print a test page using the printer's configuration panel. If available, print the configuration page, too.

4. Depending on the facilities available in your training center, your instructor will create one or more printer issues to troubleshoot. For each scenario, record what you think the problem is and what action you should take. After confirming with the instructor, complete your plan to resolve the problem.
   a) Issue #1
      Problem: _____
      Action: _____
   b) Issue #2
      Problem: _____
      Action: _____
   c) Issue #3
      Problem: _____
      Action: _____
   d) Issue #4
      Problem: _____
      Action: _____

Topic F
Install and Configure Imaging Devices

EXAM OBJECTIVES COVERED
1001-3.6 Explain the purposes and uses of various peripheral types.

Printers are used to create output from a variety of sources. Some of those sources take the form of copying physical documents and photos. Another source might be from a barcode. Some printers include features that allow you to copy or scan an item to bring it into the computer as a file, or to take it directly from the source to output from the printer. In this topic, you will look at a variety of scanning devices.

IMAGING DEVICES

In a previous lesson, you learned about some imaging devices such as digital cameras and webcams. Another type of imaging device is scanners.

SCANNERS

A **scanner** is a digital imaging device, designed to create computer file data from a real-life object. Typically, scanners handle flat objects, like documents, receipts, or photographs. **Optical Character Recognition (OCR)** software can be used to convert scanned text into digital documents, ready for editing. Historically, scanners could be connected using the parallel port or via a SCSI bus. Nowadays, scanners are connected via USB or via an Ethernet network port (RJ-45) or wireless (Wi-Fi/802.11) network.

FLATBED SCANNERS

A **flatbed scanner** works by shining a bright light, usually from a **Cold Cathode Fluorescent Lamp (CCFL)**, at the object, which is placed on a protective glass surface. A system of mirrors reflects the illuminated image of the object onto a lens. The lens either uses a prism to split the image into its component colors (Red, Green, and Blue) or focuses it onto imaging sensors coated with different color filters.

There are two main types of imaging sensor: **Charge Coupled Device (CCD)** and **Complementary Metal Oxide Semiconductor (CMOS)**. Most flatbed scanners use CCD-type sensors.

A flatbed scanner. (Image © 123RF.com.)

SHEET-FED AND ADF SCANNERS

Contact Image Sensor (CIS)-based scanners use an array of LEDs (Light Emitting Diodes) that strobe between red, green, and blue light to illuminate the image. This is reflected via a rod-shaped lens onto an image sensor. CIS scanners are typically used in **sheet-fed scanners**. In a sheet-fed scanner or the scan component of an **Automatic Document Feeder (ADF)**, rather than passing the scan head under the paper, the paper is passed over a fixed scan head.

This design is much more compact and often used in "all-in-one" type MultiFunction Devices (MFDs).

MULTI-FUNCTION DEVICES

A **multi-function device (MFD)** is a piece of office equipment that performs the functions of a number of other specialized devices. MFDs typically include the functions of a printer, scanner, fax machine, and copier. However, there are MFDs that do not include fax functions. Although the multi-function device might not equal the performance or feature sets of the dedicated devices it replaces, multi-function devices are very powerful and can perform most tasks adequately and are an economical and popular choice for most home or small-office needs.

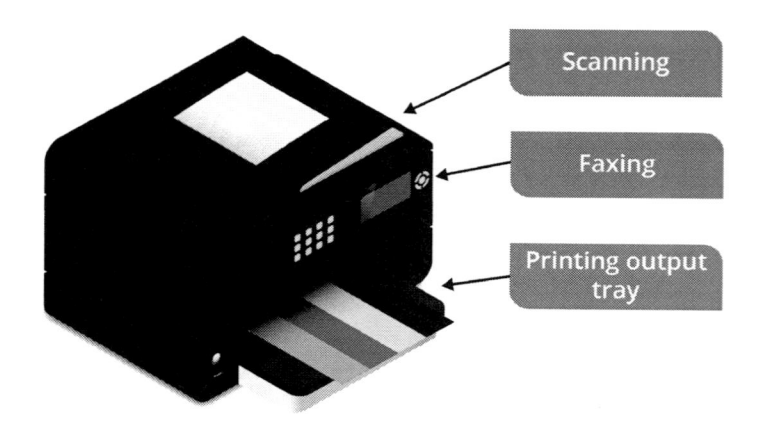

An MFD. (Image © 123RF.com.)

SCAN OPTIONS

When the scanner has been connected to the PC and configured by Plug-and-Play, it should become available to applications that can use the scan interface. Older scanners use **TWAIN**-based software; modern scanners are more likely to use **Windows Image Acquisition (WIA)**. The software will present options for the image output format (PDF or JPEG, for instance) and tools for selecting and correcting the image. Another option may be to use Optical Character Recognition (OCR) software to convert a text image into a computer-editable text document.

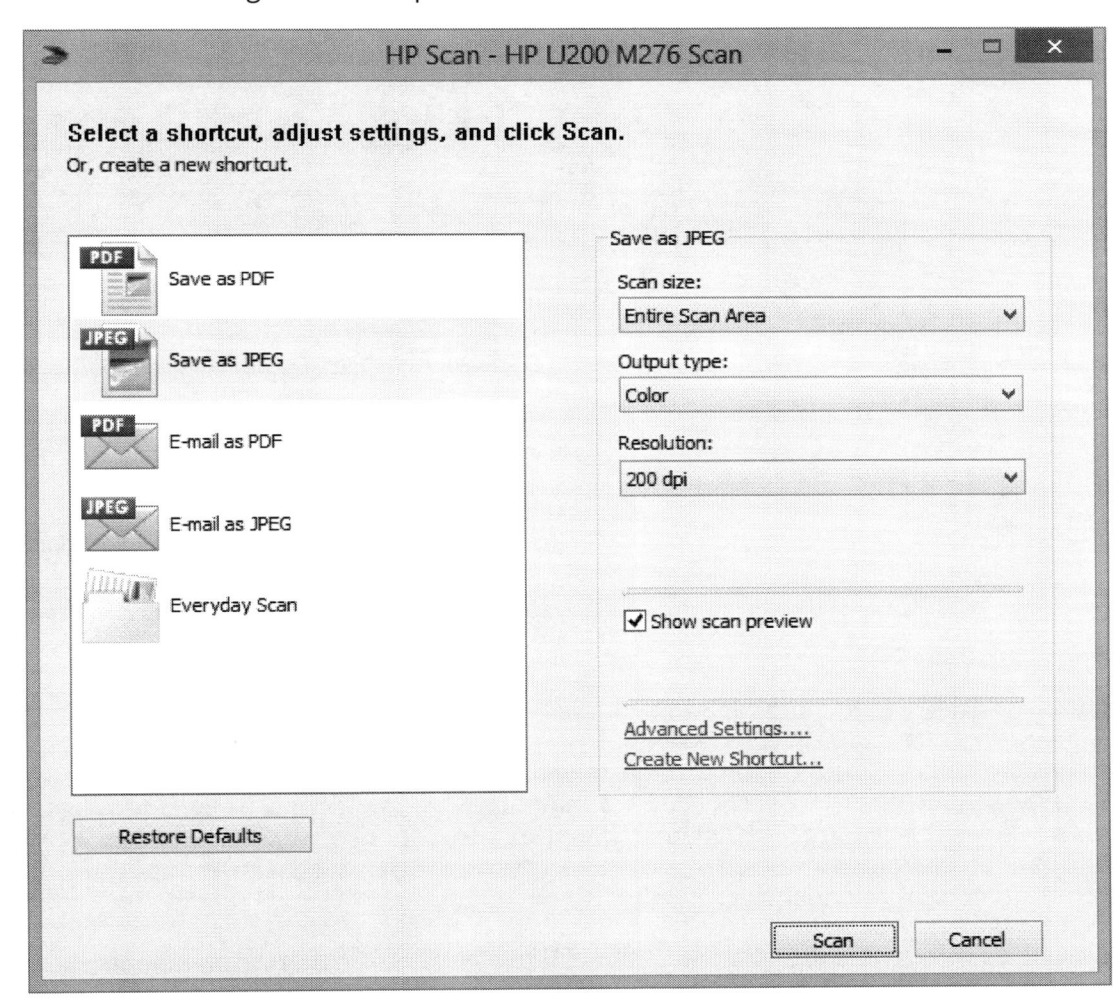

HP Scan image acquisition software.

Some scanners have the options available directly on the printer to specify what format to scan the item as, the resolution, and other options.

BARCODE SCANNERS

A **barcode scanner** is a handheld or pen-shaped device designed to scan barcodes. A barcode is a pattern of different sized parallel bars, typically representing a product number, such as an ISBN, IAN/EAN, or UPC. The reader uses a sensor mechanism (one of a photo diode, laser, or CCD) to read the intensity of light reflected back by the barcode. The reader then reports the number back to application software, which links it to a product database. Barcode scanners are connected to a computer using a USB port.

An example of a barcode scanner. (Image © 123RF.com.)

QR SCANNERS

Quick Response (QR) codes are a particular type of **2D barcode** that have been widely adopted for consumer-oriented uses. A QR code can be scanned using a smart phone camera, a normal digital camera, or webcam. There is no need to install special barcode scanning hardware. QR code scanning software can identify a QR code image directly from the camera and initiate the appropriate response in software to the information contained in the QR code. This might be to open a website or import a contact record or calendar event.

Note: Actually, a camera can be used to scan any type of barcode if the software to identify and interpret the barcode is available.

An example of a QR code you can scan with a QR scanner installed on your smart phone.

Note: *To learn more, check the **Video** tile on the CHOICE Course screen for any videos that supplement the content for this lesson.*

Access the Checklist tile on your CHOICE Course screen for reference information and job aids on How to Install and Configure Imaging Devices.

Activity 10-8
Discussing Imaging Device Installation and Configuration

SCENARIO
Answer the following questions to check your understanding of the topic.

1. What type of connection interface is a scanner most likely to use?

2. What type of sensor is used to capture an image for conversion to a digital file?

3. What is the function of OCR?

4. What type of imaging input device would be most useful for a Point-of-Sale (POS) system?

5. True or false? Any type of smartphone camera can be used to read a QR code.

Summary

In this lesson, you supported printers. Because printers enable users to transfer digital information to paper, they are among the most commonly used devices in almost every type of computing environment. As an A+ certified professional, you can use the skills and knowledge from this lesson when you are called upon to install, configure, or troubleshoot printers

When would you recommend to users that they use laser printers? Inkjet printers? Impact printers? Thermal printers?

Which printer maintenance tasks have you performed, on which types of printers? Which maintenance tasks are most important in your organization? Why are they so important?

Practice Question: Additional practice questions are available on the CompTIA CHOICE platform within the **Assessments** tile.

Course Follow-Up

Congratulations! You have completed *The Official CompTIA® A+® Core 1 (Exam 220-1001)* course. You have acquired the essential skills and information you will need to install, configure, optimize, troubleshoot, repair, upgrade, and perform preventive maintenance on PCs and digital devices.

What's Next?

Become a CompTIA A+ Certified Professional!

CompTIA A+ certified professionals are proven problem solvers. They support today's core technologies from security to cloud to data management and more. CompTIA A+ is the industry standard for launching IT careers into today's digital world. It is the only industry recognized credential with performance-based items to prove pros can think on their feet to perform critical IT support tasks in the moment. It is trusted by employers around the world to identify the go-to person in end point management and technical support roles. CompTIA A+ is regularly re-invented by IT experts to ensure that it validates core skills and abilities demanded in the workplace.

In order to become a CompTIA A+ Certified Professional, you must successfully pass both the A+ Core 1 exam (Exam Code 220-1001) and A+ Core 2 exam (Exam Code 220-1002). Therefore, your first next step might be completing *The Official CompTIA® A+® Core 2 (Exam 220-1002)* course.

In order to help you prepare for the exams, you may also want to invest in CompTIA's exam prep product, CertMaster Practice for A+.

CertMaster Practice is an online knowledge assessment and certification training companion tool specifically designed for those who have completed The Official CompTIA A+ Core 1 and Core 2 course. It helps reinforce and test what you know and close knowledge gaps prior to taking the exam.

CertMaster Practice features:

- Adaptive knowledge assessments with feedback, covering all domains of the A+ Core 1 or Core 2 exams.
- Practice tests with performance-based questions.
- Question-first design and smart refreshers to get feedback on the questions you get wrong.
- Learning analytics that track real-time knowledge gain and topic difficulty to help you learn intelligently.

Taking the Exams

When you think you have learned and practiced the material sufficiently, you can book a time to take the test.

Preparing for the Exams

We've tried to balance this course to reflect the percentages in the exam so that you have learned the appropriate level of detail about each topic to comfortably answer the exam questions. Read the following notes to find out what you need to do to register for the exam and get some tips on what to expect during the exam and how to prepare for it.

Questions in the exam are weighted by domain area as follows:

CompTIA A+ Core 1 (Exam 220-1001) Certification Domain Areas	Weighting
1.0 Mobile Devices	14%
2.0 Networking	20%

CompTIA A+ Core 1 (Exam 220-1001) Certification Domain Areas	Weighting
3.0 Hardware	27%
4.0 Virtualization and Cloud Computing	12%
5.0 Hardware and Network Troubleshooting	27%

For more information about how to register for and take your exam, please visit the CompTIA website: **https://certification.comptia.org/testing**.

Mapping Course Content to CompTIA® A+® Core 1 (Exam 220-1001)

Achieving CompTIA A+ certification requires candidates to pass exams 220-1001 and 220-1002. This table describes where the exam objectives for Core 1 (Exam 220-1001) are covered in this course.

Domain and Objective	Covered in
Domain 1.0 Mobile Devices	
1.1 Given a scenario, install and configure laptop hardware and components.	
• Hardware/device replacement	Topic 8B
• Keyboard	Topic 8B
• Hard drive	Topic 8B
• SSD vs. hybrid vs. magnetic disk	Topic 8B
• 1.8in vs. 2.5in	Topic 8B
• Memory	Topic 8B
• Smart card reader	Topic 8B
• Optical drive	Topic 8B
• Wireless card/Bluetooth module	Topic 8B
• Cellular card	Topic 8B
• Video card	Topic 8B
• Mini PCIe	Topic 8B
• Screen	Topic 8B
• DC jack	Topic 8B
• Battery	Topic 8B
• Touchpad	Topic 8B
• Plastics/frames	Topic 8B
• Speaker	Topic 8B
• System board	Topic 8B
• CPU	Topic 8B
1.2 Given a scenario, install components within the display of a laptop.	
• Types	Topic 8B
• LCD	Topic 8B
• OLED	Topic 8B
• Wi-Fi antenna connector/placement	Topic 8B
• Webcam	Topic 8B
• Microphone	Topic 8B
• Inverter	Topic 8B
• Digitizer/touchscreen	Topic 8B
1.3 Given a scenario, use appropriate laptop features.	
• Special function keys	Topic 8A
• Dual displays	Topic 8A
• Wireless (on/off)	Topic 8A
• Cellular (on/off)	Topic 8A
• Volume settings	Topic 8A

Domain and Objective	Covered in
• Screen brightness	Topic 8A
• Bluetooth (on/off)	Topic 8A
• Keyboard backlight	Topic 8A
• Touchpad (on/off)	Topic 8A
• Screen orientation	Topic 8A
• Media options (fast forward/rewind)	Topic 8A
• GPS (on/off)	Topic 8A
• Airplane mode	Topic 8A
• Docking station	Topic 8A
• Port replicator	Topic 8A
• Physical laptop lock and cable lock	Topic 8A
• Rotating/removable screens	Topic 8A
1.4 Compare and contrast characteristics of various types of other mobile devices.	
• Tablets	Topic 9A
• Smartphones	Topic 9A
• Wearable technology devices	Topic 9A
• Smart watches	Topic 9A
• Fitness monitors	Topic 9A
• VR/AR headsets	Topic 9A
• E-readers	Topic 9A
• GPS	Topic 9A
1.5 Given a scenario, connect and configure accessories and ports of other mobile devices.	
• Connection types	Topic 9B
• Wired	Topic 9B
• Micro-USB/Mini-USB/USB-C	Topic 9B
• Lightning	Topic 9B
• Tethering	Topic 9B
• Proprietary vendor-specific ports (communication/power)	Topic 9B
• Wireless	Topic 9B
• NFC	Topic 9B
• Bluetooth	Topic 9B
• IR	Topic 9B
• Hotspot	Topic 9B
• Accessories	Topic 9B
• Headsets	Topic 9B
• Speakers	Topic 9B
• Game pads	Topic 9B
• Extra battery packs/battery chargers	Topic 9B
• Protective covers/waterproofing	Topic 9B
• Credit card readers	Topic 9B
• Memory/MicroSD	Topic 9B

Domain and Objective	Covered in
1.6 Given a scenario, configure basic mobile device network connectivity and application support.	
• Wireless/cellular data network (enable/disable)	Topic 9C
• Hotspot	Topic 9C
• Tethering	Topic 9C
• Airplane mode	Topic 9C
• Bluetooth	Topic 9C
• Enable Bluetooth	Topic 9C
• Enable pairing	Topic 9C
• Find a device for pairing	Topic 9C
• Enter the appropriate pin code	Topic 9C
• Test connectivity	Topic 9C
• Corporate and ISP email configuration	Topic 9C
• POP3	Topic 9C
• IMAP	Topic 9C
• Port and SSL settings	Topic 9C
• S/MIME	Topic 9C
• Integrated commercial provider email configuration	Topic 9C
• iCloud	Topic 9C
• Google/Inbox	Topic 9C
• Exchange Online	Topic 9C
• Yahoo	Topic 9C
• PRI updates/PRL updates/ baseband updates	Topic 9C
• Radio firmware	Topic 9C
• IMEI vs. IMSI	Topic 9C
• VPN	Topic 9C
1.7 Given a scenario, use methods to perform mobile device synchronization.	
• Synchronization methods	Topic 9D
• Synchronize to the cloud	Topic 9D
• Synchronize to the desktop	Topic 9D
• Synchronize to the automobile	Topic 9D
• Types of data to synchronize	Topic 9D
• Contacts	Topic 9D
• Applications	Topic 9D
• Email	Topic 9D
• Pictures	Topic 9D
• Music	Topic 9D
• Videos	Topic 9D
• Calendar	Topic 9D
• Bookmarks	Topic 9D
• Documents	Topic 9D
• Location data	Topic 9D
• Social media data	Topic 9D

Domain and Objective	Covered in
• E-books	Topic 9D
• Passwords	Topic 9D
• Mutual authentication for multiple services (SSO)	Topic 9D
• Software requirements to install the application on the PC	Topic 9D
• Connection types to enable synchronization	Topic 9D

Domain 2.0 Networking

2.1 Compare and contrast TCP and UDP ports, protocols, and their purposes.

• Ports and protocols	Topic 5F
• 21 – FTP	Topic 5F
• 22 – SSH	Topics 5F, 6D
• 23 – Telnet	Topics 5F, 6D
• 25 – SMTP	Topic 5F
• 53 – DNS	Topic 5F
• 80 – HTTP	Topic 5F
• 110 – POP3	Topic 5F
• 143 – IMAP	Topic 5F
• 443 – HTTPS	Topic 5F
• 3389 – RDP	Topics 5F, 6D
• 137-139 – NetBIOS/NetBT	Topic 5F
• 445 – SMB/CIFS	Topic 5F
• 427 – SLP	Topic 5F
• 548 – AFP	Topic 5F
• 67/68 – DHCP	Topic 5F
• 389 – LDAP	Topic 5F
• 161/162 – SNMP	Topic 5F
• TCP vs. UDP	Topic 5F

2.2 Compare and contrast common networking hardware devices.

• Routers	Topic 5E
• Switches	Topic 5B
• Managed	Topic 5B
• Unmanaged	Topic 5B
• Access points	Topic 5C
• Cloud-based network controller	Topic 7B
• Firewall	Topic 6C
• Network interface card	Topic 5B
• Repeater	Topic 5B
• Hub	Topic 5B
• Cable/DSL modem	Topic 5D
• Bridge	Topic 5B
• Patch panel	Topic 5A
• Power over Ethernet (PoE)	Topic 5B
• Injectors	Topic 5B

Domain and Objective	Covered in
• Switch	Topic 5B
• Ethernet over Power	Topic 5B
2.3 Given a scenario, install and configure a basic wired/ wireless SOHO network.	
• Router/switch functionality	Topic 6B
• Access point settings	Topic 6B
• IP addressing	Topic 6A
• NIC configuration	Topic 6A
• Wired	Topic 6A
• Wireless	Topic 6A
• End-user device configuration	Topic 6A
• IoT device configuration	Topic 6F
• Thermostat	Topic 6F
• Light switches	Topic 6F
• Security cameras	Topic 6F
• Door locks	Topic 6F
• Voice-enabled, smart speaker/digital assistant	Topic 6F
• Cable/DSL modem configuration	Topic 6B
• Firewall settings	Topic 6C
• DMZ	Topic 6C
• Port forwarding	Topic 6C
• NAT	Topic 6C
• UPnP	Topic 6C
• Whitelist/blacklist	Topic 6C
• MAC filtering	Topic 6C
• QoS	Topic 6A
• Wireless settings	Topic 6B
• Encryption	Topic 6B
• Channels	Topic 6B
• QoS	Topic 6B
2.4 Compare and contrast wireless networking protocols.	
• 802.11a	Topic 5C
• 802.11b	Topic 5C
• 802.11g	Topic 5C
• 802.11n	Topic 5C
• 802.11ac	Topic 5C
• Frequencies	Topic 5C
• 2.4Ghz	Topic 5C
• 5Ghz	Topic 5C
• Channels	Topic 5C
• 1–11	Topic 5C
• Bluetooth	Topic 6F
• NFC	Topic 6F
• RFID	Topic 6F

Domain and Objective	Covered in
• Zigbee	Topic 6F
• Z-Wave	Topic 6F
• 3G	Topic 5D
• 4G	Topic 5D
• 5G	Topic 5D
• LTE	Topic 5D
2.5 Summarize the properties and purposes of services provided by networked hosts.	
• Server roles	Topic 5F
• Web server	Topic 5F
• File server	Topic 5F
• Print server	Topic 5F
• DHCP server	Topic 5F
• DNS server	Topic 5F
• Proxy server	Topic 5F
• Mail server	Topic 5F
• Authentication server	Topic 5F
• syslog	Topic 5F
• Internet appliance	Topic 5F
• UTM	Topic 5F
• IDS	Topic 5F
• IPS	Topic 5F
• End-point management server	Topic 5F
• Legacy/embedded systems	Topic 5F
2.6 Explain common network configuration concepts.	
• IP addressing	Topic 5E
• Static	Topic 5E
• Dynamic	Topic 5E
• APIPA	Topic 5E
• Link local	Topic 5E
• DNS	Topic 5E
• DHCP	Topic 5E
• Reservations	Topic 5E
• IPv4 vs. IPv6	Topic 5E
• Subnet mask	Topic 5E
• Gateway	Topic 5E
• VPN	Topic 5E
• VLAN	Topic 5E
• NAT	Topic 5E
2.7 Compare and contrast Internet connection types, network types, and their features.	Topic 5E
• Internet connection types	Topic 5D
• Cable	Topic 5D
• DSL	Topic 5D

Domain and Objective	Covered in
• Dial-up	Topic 5D
• Fiber	Topic 5D
• Satellite	Topic 5D
• ISDN	Topic 5D
• Cellular	Topic 9C
• Tethering	Topic 9B
• Mobile hotspot	Topic 9B
• Line-of-sight wireless Internet service	Topic 5D
• Network types	Topic 5A
• LAN	Topic 5A
• WAN	Topic 5A
• PAN	Topic 5C
• MAN	Topic 5A
• WMN	Topic 5C
2.8 Given a scenario, use appropriate networking tools.	
• Crimper	Topic 5A
• Cable stripper	Topic 5A
• Multimeter	Topic 5A
• Tone generator and probe	Topic 5A
• Cable tester	Topic 5A
• Loopback plug	Topic 5A
• Punchdown tool	Topic 5A
• WiFi analyzer	Topic 6E
Domain 3.0 Hardware	
3.1 Explain basic cable types, features, and their purposes.	
• Network cables	Topic 5A
• Ethernet	Topic 5A
• Cat 5	Topic 5A
• Cat 5e	Topic 5A
• Cat 6	Topic 5A
• Plenum	Topic 5A
• Shielded twisted pair	Topic 5A
• Unshielded twisted pair	Topic 5A
• 568A/B	Topic 5A
• Fiber	Topic 5A
• Coaxial	Topic 5A
• Speed and transmission limitations	Topic 5A
• Video cables	Topic 2A
• VGA	Topic 2A
• HDMI	Topic 2A
• Mini-HDMI	Topic 2A
• DisplayPort	Topic 2A
• DVI (DVI-D/DVI-I)	Topic 2A
• Multipurpose cables	Topic 1C

Domain and Objective	Covered in
• Lightning	Topic 1C
• Thunderbolt	Topic 1C
• USB	Topic 1C
• USB-C	Topic 1C
• USB 2.0	Topic 1C
• USB 3.0	Topic 1C
• Peripheral cables	Topic 1C
• Serial	Topic 1C
• Hard drive cables	Topic 3B
• SATA	Topic 3B
• IDE	Topic 3B
• SCSI	Topic 3B
• Adapters	Topic 2A
• DVI to HDMI	Topic 2A
• USB to Ethernet	Topic 8A
• DVI to VGA	Topic 2A
3.2 Identify common connector types.	
• RJ-11	Topic 1C
• RJ-45	Topic 1C
• RS-232	Topic 1C
• BNC	Topic 5A
• RG-59	Topic 5A
• RG-6	Topic 5A
• USB	Topic 1C
• Micro-USB	Topic 1C
• Mini-USB	Topic 1C
• USB-C	Topic 1C
• DB-9	Topic 1C
• Lightning	Topic 1C
• SCSI	Topic 1C
• eSATA	Topic 1C
• Molex	Topic 1C
3.3 Given a scenario, install RAM types.	Topic 3A
• RAM types	Topic 3A
• SODIMM	Topic 3A
• DDR2	Topic 3A
• DDR3	Topic 3A
• DDR4	Topic 3A
• Single channel	Topic 3A
• Dual channel	Topic 3A
• Triple channel	Topic 3A
• Error correcting	Topic 3A
• Parity vs. non-parity	Topic 3A

Domain and Objective	Covered in
3.4 Given a scenario, select, install and configure storage devices.	
• Optical drives	Topic 3C
• CD-ROM/CD-RW	Topic 3C
• DVD-ROM/DVD-RW/DVD-RW DL	Topic 3C
• Blu-ray	Topic 3C
• BD-R	Topic 3C
• BD-RE	Topic 3C
• Solid-state drives	Topic 3B
• M.2 drives	Topic 3B
• NVME	Topic 3B
• SATA 2.5	Topic 3B
• Magnetic hard drives	Topic 3B
• 5,400rpm	Topic 3B
• 7,200rpm	Topic 3B
• 10,000rpm	Topic 3B
• 15,000rpm	Topic 3B
• Sizes	Topic 3B
• 2.5	Topic 3B
• 3.5	Topic 3B
• Hybrid drives	Topic 3B
• Flash	Topic 3C
• SD card	Topic 3C
• CompactFlash	Topic 3C
• Micro-SD card	Topic 3C
• Mini-SD card	Topic 3C
• xD	Topic 3C
• Configurations	Topic 3D
• RAID 0, 1, 5, 10	Topic 3D
• Hot swappable	Topic 3D
3.5 Given a scenario, install and configure motherboards, CPUs, and add-on cards.	
• Motherboard form factor	Topic 1B
• ATX	Topic 1B
• mATX	Topic 1B
• ITX	Topic 1B
• mITX	Topic 1B
• Motherboard connector types	Topic 1B
• PCI	Topic 1B
• PCIe	Topic 1B
• Riser card	Topic 1B
• Socket types	Topic 1B
• SATA	Topic 1B
• IDE	Topic 1B

Domain and Objective	Covered in
• Front panel connector	Topic 1B
• Internal USB connector	Topic 1B
• BIOS/UEFI settings	Topic 4B
• Boot options	Topic 4B
• Firmware updates	Topic 4B
• Security settings	Topic 4B
• Interface configurations	Topic 4B
• Security	Topic 4B
• Passwords	Topic 4B
• Drive encryption	Topic 4B
• TPM	Topic 4B
• LoJack	Topic 4B
• Secure boot	Topic 4B
• CMOS battery	Topic 1B
• CPU features	Topic 4A
• Single-core	Topic 4A
• Multicore	Topic 4A
• Virtualization	Topic 4A
• Hyperthreading	Topic 4A
• Speeds	Topic 4A
• Overclocking	Topic 4A
• Integrated GPU	Topic 4A
• Compatibility	Topic 4A
• AMD	Topic 4A
• Intel	Topic 4A
• Cooling mechanism	Topic 4A
• Fans	Topic 4A
• Heat sink	Topic 4A
• Liquid	Topic 4A
• Thermal paste	Topic 4A
• Expansion cards	Topic 2A
• Video cards	Topic 2A
• Onboard	Topic 2A
• Add-on card	Topic 2A
• Sound cards	Topic 2C
• Network interface card	Topic 1C
• USB expansion card	Topic 1C
• eSATA card	Topic 1C
3.6 Explain the purposes and uses of various peripheral types.	
• Printer	Topic 10A
• ADF/flatbed scanner	Topic 10F
• Barcode scanner/QR scanner	Topic 10F
• Monitors	Topic 2A

Domain and Objective	Covered in
• VR headset	Topic 2A
• Optical drive types	Topic 3C
• Mouse	Topic 1D
• Keyboard	Topic 1D
• Touchpad	Topic 1D
• Signature pad	Topic 1D
• Game controllers	Topic1D
• Camera/webcam	Topic 2C
• Microphone	Topic 2C
• Speakers	Topic 2C
• Headset	Topic 2C
• Projector	Topic 2A
• Lumens/brightness	Topic 2A
• External storage drives	Topic 3C
• KVM	Topic 1D
• Magnetic reader/chip reader	Topic 1D
• NFC/tap pay device	Topic 1D
• Smart card reader	Topic 1D
3.7 Summarize power supply types and features.	
• Input 115V vs. 220V	Topic 4C
• Output 5V vs. 12V	Topic 4C
• 24-pin motherboard adapter	Topic 4C
• Wattage rating	Topic 4C
• Number of devices/types of devices to be powered	Topic 4C
3.8 Given a scenario, select and configure appropriate components for a custom PC configuration to meet customer specifications or needs.	
• Graphic/CAD/CAM design workstation	Topic 4E
• SSD	Topic 4E
• High-end video	Topic 4E
• Maximum RAM	Topic 4E
• Audio/video editing workstation	Topic 4E
• Specialized audio and video card	Topic 4E
• Large, fast hard drive	Topic 4E
• Dual monitors	Topic 4E
• Virtualization workstation	Topic 4E
• Maximum RAM and CPU cores	Topic 4E
• Gaming PC	Topic 4E
• SSD	Topic 4E
• High-end video/specialized GPU	Topic 4E
• High-definition sound card	Topic 4E
• High-end cooling	Topic 4E
• Network attached storage device	Topic 4E
• Media streaming	Topic 4E

Domain and Objective	Covered in
• File sharing	Topic 4E
• Gigabit NIC	Topic 4E
• RAID array	Topic 4E
• Hard drive	Topic 4E
• Standard thick client	Topic 4E
• Desktop applications	Topic 4E
• Meets recommended requirements for selected OS	Topic 4E
• Thin client	Topic 4E
• Basic applications	Topic 4E
• Meets minimum requirements for selected OS	Topic 4E
• Network connectivity	Topic 4E
3.9 Given a scenario, install and configure common devices.	
• Desktop	Topic 4E
• Thin client	Topic 4E
• Thick client	Topic 4E
• Account setup/settings	Topic 4E
• Laptop/common mobile devices	Topic 8A
• Touchpad configuration	Topic 8A
• Touchscreen configuration	Topic 8A
• Application installations/configurations	Topic 9D
• Synchronization settings	Topic 9D
• Account setup/settings	Topic 9D
• Wireless settings	Topic 9C
3.10 Given a scenario, configure SOHO multifunction devices/printers and settings.	
• Use appropriate drivers for a given operating system	Topic 10D
• Configuration settings	Topic 10D
• Duplex	Topic 10D
• Collate	Topic 10D
• Orientation	Topic 10D
• Quality	Topic 10D
• Device sharing	Topic 10D
• Wired	Topic 10D
• USB	Topic 10D
• Serial	Topic 10D
• Ethernet	Topic 10D
• Wireless	Topic 10D
• Bluetooth	Topic 10D
• 802.11(a , b, g, n, ac)	Topic 10D
• Infrastructure vs. ad hoc	Topic 10D
• Integrated print server (hardware)	Topic 10D
• Cloud printing/remote printing	Topic 10D
• Public/shared devices	Topic 10D

Domain and Objective	Covered in
• Sharing local/networked device via operating system settings	Topic 10D
• TCP/Bonjour/AirPrint	Topic 10D
• Data privacy	Topic 10D
• User authentication on the device	Topic 10D
• Hard drive caching	Topic 10D
3.11 Given a scenario, install and maintain various print technologies.	
• Laser	Topic 10A
• Imaging drum, fuser assembly, transfer belt, transfer roller, pickup rollers, separate pads, duplexing assembly	Topic 10A
• Imaging process: processing, charging, exposing, developing, transferring, fusing, and cleaning	Topic 10A
• Maintenance: Replace toner, apply maintenance kit, calibrate, clean	Topic 10A
• Inkjet	Topic 10B
• Ink cartridge, print head, roller, feeder, duplexing assembly, carriage, and belt	Topic 10B
• Calibrate	Topic 10B
• Maintenance: Clean heads, replace cartridges, calibrate, clear jams	Topic 10B
• Thermal	Topic 10C
• Feed assembly, heating element	Topic 10C
• Special thermal paper	Topic 10C
• Maintenance: Replace paper, clean heating element, remove debris	Topic 10C
• Impact	Topic 10C
• Print head, ribbon, tractor feed	Topic 10C
• Impact paper	Topic 10C
• Maintenance: Replace ribbon, replace print head, replace paper	Topic 10C
• Virtual	Topic 10D
• Print to file	Topic 10D
• Print to PDF	Topic 10D
• Print to XPS	Topic 10D
• Print to image	Topic 10D
• 3D printers	Topic 10C
• Plastic filament	Topic 10C
Domain 4.0 Virtualization and Cloud Computing	
4.1 Compare and contrast cloud computing concepts.	
• Common cloud models	Topic 7B
• IaaS	Topic 7B
• SaaS	Topic 7B
• PaaS	Topic 7B
• Public vs. private vs. hybrid vs. community	Topic 7B
• Shared resources	Topic 7B

Domain and Objective	Covered in
• Internal vs. external	Topic 7B
• Rapid elasticity	Topic 7B
• On-demand	Topic 7B
• Resource pooling	Topic 7B
• Measured service	Topic 7B
• Metered	Topic 7B
• Off-site email applications	Topic 7B
• Cloud file storage services	Topic 7B
• Synchronization apps	Topic 7B
• Virtual application streaming/cloud-based applications	Topic 7B
• Applications for cell phones/tablets	Topic 7B
• Applications for laptops/desktops	Topic 7B
• Virtual desktop	Topic 7B
• Virtual NIC	Topic 7B
4.2 Given a scenario, set up and configure client-side virtualization.	
• Purpose of virtual machines	Topic 7A
• Resource requirements	Topic 7A
• Emulator requirements	Topic 7A
• Security requirements	Topic 7A
• Network requirements	Topic 7A
• Hypervisor	Topic 7A
Domain 5.0 Hardware and Network Troubleshooting	
5.1 Given a scenario, use the best practice methodology to resolve problems.	
• Always consider corporate policies, procedures, and impacts before implementing changes	Topic 1E
• 1. Identify the problem	Topic 1E
• Question the user and identify user changes to computer and perform backups before making changes	Topic 1E
• Inquire regarding environmental or infrastructure changes	Topic 1E
• Review system and application logs	Topic 1E
• 2. Establish a theory of probable cause (question the obvious)	Topic 1E
• If necessary, conduct external or internal research based on symptoms	Topic 1E
• 3. Test the theory to determine cause	Topic 1E
• Once the theory is confirmed, determine the next steps to resolve problem	Topic 1E
• If theory is not confirmed re-establish new theory or escalate	Topic 1E
• 4. Establish a plan of action to resolve the problem and implement the solution	Topic 1E
• 5. Verify full system functionality and, if applicable, implement preventive measures	Topic 1E

Domain and Objective	Covered in
• 6. Document findings, actions, and outcomes	Topic 1E
5.2 Given a scenario, troubleshoot problems related to motherboards, RAM, CPUs, and power.	
• Common symptoms	Topic 4D
• Unexpected shutdowns	Topic 4D
• System lockups	Topic 4D
• POST code beeps	Topic 4D
• Blank screen on bootup	Topic 4D
• BIOS time and setting resets	Topic 4D
• Attempts to boot to incorrect device	Topic 4D
• Continuous reboots	Topic 4D
• No power	Topic 4D
• Overheating	Topic 4D
• Loud noise	Topic 4D
• Intermittent device failure	Topic 4D
• Fans spin – no power to other devices	Topic 4D
• Indicator lights	Topic 4D
• Smoke	Topic 4D
• Burning smell	Topic 4D
• Proprietary crash screens (BSOD/pin wheel)	Topic 4D
• Distended capacitors	Topic 4D
• Log entries and error messages	Topic 4D
5.3 Given a scenario, troubleshoot hard drives and RAID arrays.	
• Common symptoms	Topic 3E
• Read/write failure	Topic 3E
• Slow performance	Topic 3E
• Loud clicking noise	Topic 3E
• Failure to boot	Topic 3E
• Drive not recognized	Topic 3E
• OS not found	Topic 3E
• RAID not found	Topic 3E
• RAID stops working	Topic 3E
• Proprietary crash screens (BSOD/pin wheel)	Topic 3E
• S.M.A.R.T. errors	Topic 3E
5.4 Given a scenario, troubleshoot video, projector, and display issues.	Topic 2B
• Common symptoms	Topic 2B
• VGA mode	Topic 2B
• No image on screen	Topic 2B
• Overheat shutdown	Topic 2B
• Dead pixels	Topic 2B
• Artifacts	Topic 2B
• Incorrect color patterns	Topic 2B
• Dim image	Topic 2B

Domain and Objective	Covered in
• Flickering image	Topic 2B
• Distorted image	Topic 2B
• Distorted geometry	Topic 2B
• Burn-in	Topic 2B
• Oversized images and icons	Topic 2B
5.5 Given a scenario, troubleshoot common mobile device issues while adhering to the appropriate procedures.	
• Common symptoms	Topic 8C
• No display	Topic 8C
• Dim display	Topic 8C
• Flickering display	Topic 8C
• Sticking keys	Topic 8C
• Intermittent wireless	Topic 8C
• Battery not charging	Topic 8C
• Ghost cursor/pointer drift	Topic 8C
• No power	Topic 8C
• Num lock indicator lights	Topic 8C
• No wireless connectivity	Topic 8C
• No Bluetooth connectivity	Topic 8C
• Cannot display to external monitor	Topic 8C
• Touchscreen non-responsive	Topic 8C
• Apps not loading	Topic 8C
• Slow performance	Topic 8C
• Unable to decrypt email	Topic 8C
• Extremely short battery life	Topic 8C
• Overheating	Topic 8C
• Frozen system	Topic 8C
• No sound from speakers	Topic 8C
• GPS not functioning	Topic 8C
• Swollen battery	Topic 8C
• Disassembling processes for proper reassembly	Topic 8B
• Document and label cable and screw locations	Topic 8B
• Organize parts	Topic 8B
• Refer to manufacturer resources	Topic 8B
• Use appropriate hand tools	Topic 8B
5.6 Given a scenario, troubleshoot printers.	
• Common symptoms	Topic 10E
• Streaks	Topic 10E
• Faded prints	Topic 10E
• Ghost images	Topic 10E
• Toner not fused to the paper	Topic 10E
• Creased paper	Topic 10E
• Paper not feeding	Topic 10E
• Paper jam	Topic 10E

Domain and Objective	Covered in
• No connectivity	Topic 10E
• Garbled characters on paper	Topic 10E
• Vertical lines on page	Topic 10E
• Backed-up print queue	Topic 10E
• Low memory errors	Topic 10E
• Access denied	Topic 10E
• Printer will not print	Topic 10E
• Color prints in wrong print color	Topic 10E
• Unable to install printer	Topic 10E
• Error codes	Topic 10E
• Printing blank pages	Topic 10E
• No image on printer display	Topic 10E
• Multiple failed jobs in logs	Topic 10E

5.7 Given a scenario, troubleshoot common wired and wireless network problems.

• Common symptoms	Topic 6E
• Limited connectivity	Topic 6E
• Unavailable resources	Topic 6E
• Internet	Topic 6E
• Local resources	Topic 6E
• Shares	Topic 6E
• Printers	Topic 6E
• Email	Topic 6E
• No connectivity	Topic 6E
• APIPA/link local address	Topic 6E
• Intermittent connectivity	Topic 6E
• IP conflict	Topic 6E
• Slow transfer speeds	Topic 6E
• Low RF signal	Topic 6E
• SSID not found	Topic 6E

Solutions

Activity 1-1: Implementing an Anti-ESD Service Kit

1. **Describe the equipment you should use to prevent static electricity on your body from damaging the equipment on which you are working.**

   An anti-ESD service kit comprising an anti-ESD wrist strap, grounding cord and plug, and a conductive mat. The grounding plug should be connected to an earthed point.

3. **True or False? If you are using an anti-static floor mat, you do not need any other anti-ESD service equipment.**

   False. A mat should be used with a wrist strap. You may also need ESD-safe packaging for storing components.

4. **In which atmospheric conditions is the risk of ESD highest?**

   During cool, dry conditions when humidity is low. When humidity is high, the static electricity can dissipate through the moisture present in the air.

5. **Electrical injuries include electrocution, shock, and collateral injury. Would you be injured if you are not part of the electrical ground current?**

   Yes, you could receive a thermal burn from the head of an electric arc or electric equipment. Your clothes can catch on fire, or your skin can be burned.

6. **Which computer component presents the most danger from electrical shock?**

   ○ System boards
   ○ Hard drives
   ● Power supplies
   ○ System unit

7. **What component helps to protect users of electrical equipment against a short circuit?**

   ○ Resistor
   ● Fuse
   ○ Power supply
   ○ ESD wrist strap

8. **What care should you take when lifting a heavy object?**

   The main concern is damaging your back. Lift slowly using your legs for power not your back muscles.

9. What should you do before transporting a bulky object?

Check that there is a clear path to the destination point. If you cannot carry the object safely, get help or use a cart.

Activity 1-2: Discussing PC Components

1. Describe how you would open a PC case to access the motherboard.

Power down the PC and remove the power cable. With the power cable removed, hold the power button down for a few seconds to ensure PC is completely de-engergized. Then, remove any screws holding the case cover in place, and slide the cover out from the retaining clips. This should expose the motherboard. You would usually need to remove other panels only to access storage devices.

2. At the rear of a system case are slots for adapter card ports. Why should these be covered with blanking plates if not in use?

The fan system is designed to draw cool air across the motherboard and blow out warm air. Large holes in the chassis disrupt this air flow. Also dust will be able to settle on the system components more easily.

3. What is the most likely explanation?

The cable connecting the power button to the motherboard could have been disconnected and either not reconnected or not properly reconnected.

4. What is the main function of the chipset?

Provides controllers for the CPU to interface with other components (memory and expansion bus for instance) and adapters to provide functions such as video and audio, and Ethernet and wireless networking on the motherboard.

5. True or false? The Real Time Clock controls the timing of signals between the CPU and other components.

False. The system clock controls timing; the Real Time Clock keeps track of the calendar date and time.

6. What type of socket is used to install system memory?

Dual Inline Memory Module (DIMM).

7. You have a x8 PCIe storage adapter card—can you fit this in a x16 slot?

Yes—this is referred to as up-plugging. On some motherboards it may only function as a x1 device though.

8. What is the bandwidth of a PCIe v2.0 x16 graphics adapter?

8 GBps in each direction (full duplex). PCIe v2 supports 500 MBps per lane.

9. **What type of motherboard is displayed here, and what characteristics did you use to help you identify the board type?**

6.7 inches

6.7 inches

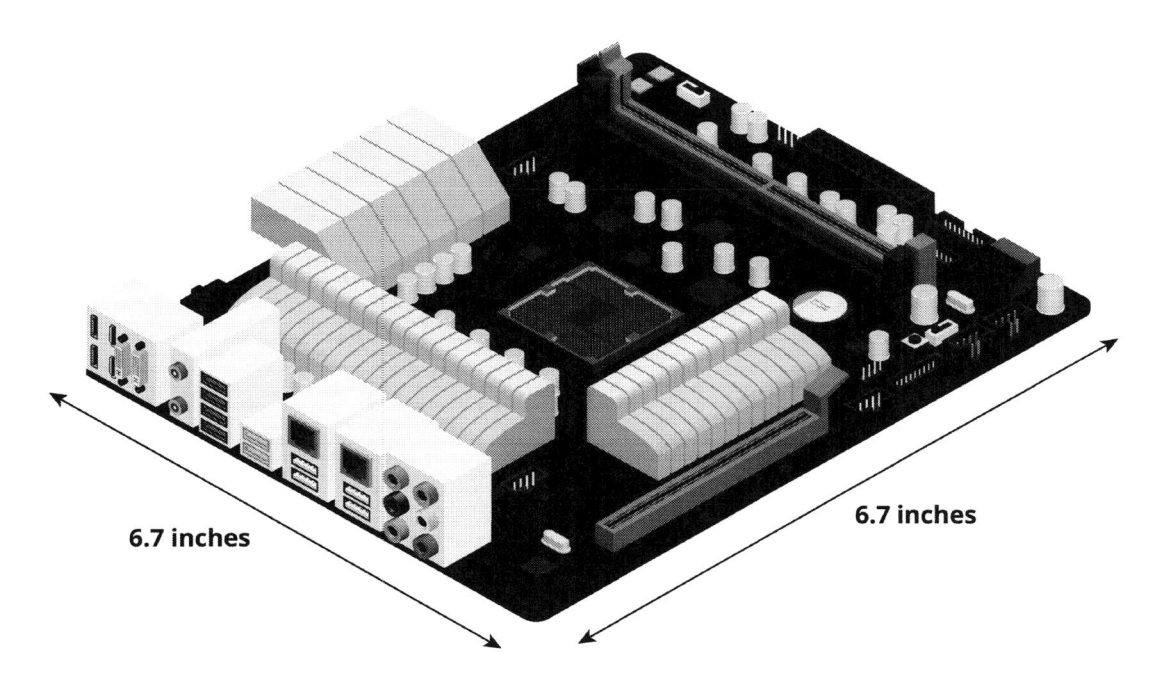

Based on its small size dimensions and compact component design, this motherboard is a mini-ITX.

10. **What type of motherboard is displayed here, and what characteristics did you use to help you identify the board type?**

12 inches

~10 inches

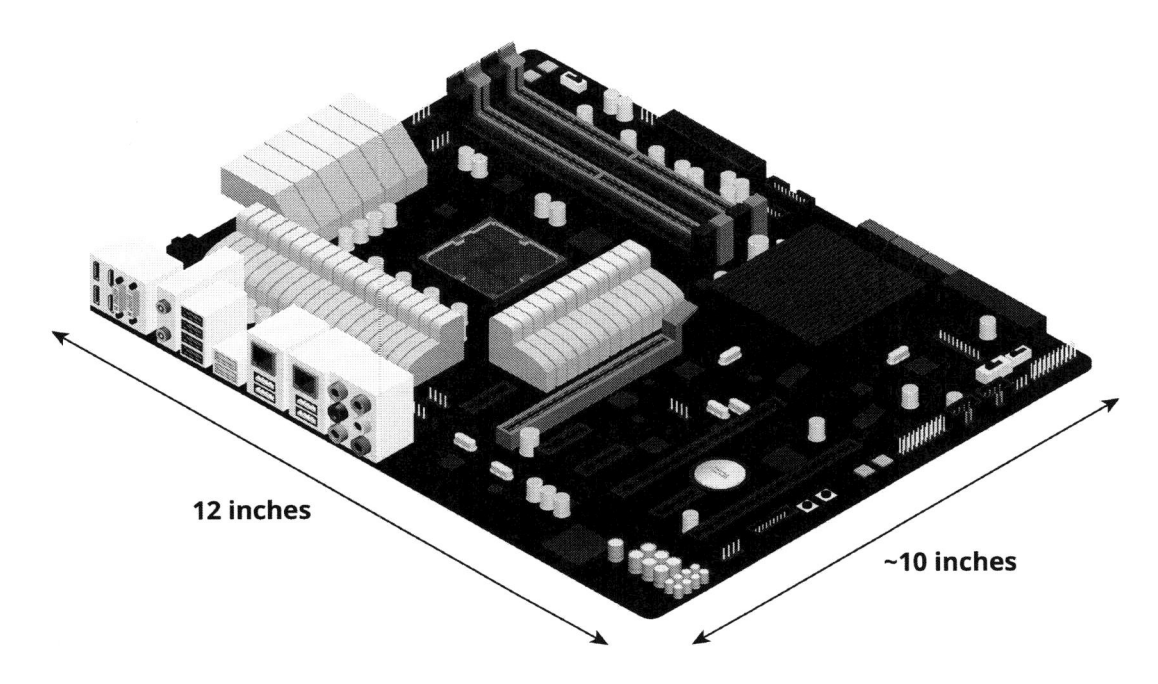

You can tell by the large size and large number of available components and slots that this motherboard is an ATX.

Activity 1-3: Identifying Connection Interfaces

1. **In this graphic, identify the (A) audio ports, (B) video ports, and (C) USB ports.**

   Moving from left to right, the components should be labeled: C, B, C, A.

2. **You are speaking with a junior technician. He is not sure what is meant by a "keyed" connector. Can you tell him?**

   A keyed connector has a catch or slot to ensure that it cannot be inserted the wrong way round or used with an incompatible port.

3. **What is the nominal data rate of a USB port supporting SuperSpeed+?**

   Normally 10 Gbps, but devices supporting USB 3.2 can use up to 20 Gbps over USB-C cabling.

4. **True or false? USB-C ports and cables are compatible with Apple Lightning ports and cables.**

   False.

5. **What type of device would you connect a Molex cable to?**

   A Molex cable is a power cable. Normally, devices such as disk drives and optical drives require more power than can be delivered over the data bus. Note that most drives actually use SATA power connectors these days.

6. **Why would you install an I/O adapter card?**

   To make more or different kinds of ports available (SCSI, USB, or SATA typically).

Activity 1-4: Demonstrating PC Disassembly and Reassembly

2. **Draw a diagram showing the layout of the components you identified above.**

   In the reference image, there are four DIMMs (DDR4 but the label is not legible), two of which are used. From top to bottom, the PCIe slots are x1, x16 (occupied by graphics adapter card), x4 (hard to see), and x16. There are two SATA ports on the right edge, connecting two HDDs. The card below them is an SSD connected to an M.2 port. There are actually two more SATA ports in the middle of the board, but these are obscured by the CPU heat sink—you can follow the cable back to the optical drive bay though. The RTC battery is just visible below the CPU, and learners should be able to make out the fan connections. The P1 connector is beneath the jumble of cables. Some of the front panel connectors on the bottom edge are easy to pick out from the cables. It isn't easy to identify their type, though (from left to right: audio in, USB, speaker). The connectors for another set of USB ports plus LED and power are beneath the cable ties.

3. **Write down any problems you might suspect with the way the system is built (for example, cables not connected to devices, scorch marks, excessive dust or dirt, and so on).**

   Responses will vary depending on the systems being examined.

6. **What ports can you identify?**

   USB 3 ports and plugs have blue tabs and usually an "SS" label for SuperSpeed. USB 2 ports and plugs are supposed to have white tabs but this is not so commonly observed. In the reference image, starting on the left there are two PS/2 ports (mouse and keyboard). Note that it is quite common for vendors to continue to include these on servers and workstations for use with KVM. Next to them is an RJ-45 port above two USB 2.0 ports. In the next block, there are two DP++ (DisplayPort) video ports and one DVI port. You haven't covered video ports yet, so don't worry if you can't identify the exact type. Next in the image are four USB 3 ports and finally the audio ports. The dedicated graphics adapter has a DVI and DP++ port.

Activity 1-5: Discussing Peripheral Device Installation

1. **What is the likely cause of this issue?**

   The appropriate keyboard layout has not been selected in **Settings**.

2. **What is your answer?**

   Yes, you can use a Keyboard Video Mouse (KVM) switch for this purpose.

3. **Which peripheral device types or functions should she consider?**

   A POS system reads the information stored on the customer's payment card or digital wallet. Historically, this information was stored in the card's magnetic strip. Most POS devices retain a magnetic reader as a backup mechanism. The majority of bank cards now also store the account information in an embedded chip, which can be read by inserting the card into the reader. This chip may also support contactless use or Near Field Communications (NFC). A customer can also store the card details in a smartphone and use the smartphone's NFC chip to make payments. Not all POS readers support contactless and it would carry a slight price premium, so your client should decide whether it is important to offer this payment method to her customers.

4. **What should you do before unplugging the stick?**

   Use the **Safely Remove Hardware** icon to stop the device.

Activity 1-6: Discussing Troubleshooting Methodology

1. **What should be your next troubleshooting step?**

   Test the theory to determine the cause.

2. **If you have to open the system case to troubleshoot a computer, what should you check before proceeding?**

   That data on the PC has been backed up. You should always verify that you have a backup before beginning any troubleshooting activities.

3. **What should be your first troubleshooting step?**

   Question the user to establish all the circumstances surrounding the problem.

4. **Why does it help to categorize a problem when troubleshooting?**

   A step-by-step analysis of the problem helps by making sure you approach it methodically and troubleshooting within a more limited area is simpler.

5. **If another technician says to you, "We'll have to strip this back to base?", what do they mean, and at which specific step of troubleshooting are you likely to be?**

   Bringing a system "back to base" means re-building a troublesome system from its core components. You can then add extra devices one by one until the source of the fault is revealed. This can be time-consuming so is likely to be something you would try if you are testing a theory of probable cause unsuccessfully, and you need to establish a new theory.

6. **What should you do if you cannot determine the cause of a problem?**

   You could consult a colleague, refer to product documentation, or search the web. It might also be appropriate to escalate the problem to more senior support staff.

7. **What should be your next troubleshooting step?**

   Identify any negative consequences in applying the software patch, then devise an implementation plan to install the file. You need to schedule the work so as to minimize disruption. You should also make a plan to rollback the installation, should that prove necessary.

8. **After applying a troubleshooting repair, replacement, or upgrade, what should you do next?**

   Test that the fix works and that the system as a whole is functional. You might also implement preventative measures to reduce the risk of the problem occurring again.

9. **What is the last step in the best practice methodology for troubleshooting and how might it be implemented?**

   Document findings, actions, and outcomes. You can use spreadsheet or database tools, but using ticket-based management system software to create incident logs is best.

Activity 2-1: Discussing Display Device Installation and Configuration

1. **What two types of display cabling can be connected to this laptop?**

   The image shows a VGA port and an HDMI port (with an RJ-45 network port between them). The USB ports could be used for a portable monitor.

2. **Which ports are present on the graphics card shown below?**

   The port on the left is DVI-I and the one on the right is DisplayPort.

3. **Which interfaces does the adapter cable shown below support?**

   DVI-I (left) and HDMI.

4. **A customer is shopping for a computer game for her daughter and wants to know if you can explain the reference to "DirectX" on the packaging?**

   DirectX is Microsoft's API (Application Programming Interface) for 3D and multimedia applications. Software such as a computer game will specify a minimum DirectX version. The graphics card must support this version to run the game. Vendors often provide support through driver updates, even for older card models.

5. **What should you configure in the Display dialog box?**

   Ensure the layout of the displays in the dialog box matches their physical location.

Activity 2-3: Discussing Display Device Troubleshooting

1. **Which component(s) would you prioritize for fault-finding?**

   The first thing to test is the display cable. If the original cable is properly inserted at the computer and monitor ends, try replacing it with a known good version. If this does not fix the problem, inspect the ports for signs of damage.

2. **What is the most likely cause of a flickering display?**

   On a CRT, flickering can occur if the refresh rate is set too low. On a TFT it could indicate a problem with the backlight. You should also verify that the connectors are secure and rule out other potential cabling problems.

3. **What would you do if the image from a projector appeared narrower at the top than at the bottom?**

   Ensure the projector lens is lined up with the whiteboard. You might be able to adjust the lens position using a knob or have to move the projector. If the projector or lens cannot be repositioned, there may be a digital keystone correction control.

4. **Which display connector types would be suitable?**

   DVI, HDMI, DisplayPort, and Thunderbolt.

Activity 2-5: Discussing Multimedia Device Installation and Configuration

1. **What size and color connector would you look for to plug a basic microphone into a PC?**

   3.5mm jack, which is often color coded pink.

2. **You have installed a new sound card in a computer designed for home entertainment. What type of connector would you use to connect a digital surround sound speaker system to the new card?**

   S/PDIF—optical or coax. Coax for audio uses RCA connectors. An optical S/PDIF connector is also sometimes referred to as TOSLINK. Note that a lot of home entertainment setups might just output audio over HDMI with the signal from the graphics adapter.

3. **What type of speaker unit is the ".1" in a 5.1 or 7.1 surround sound system and where do you suggest this speaker be placed?**

   Subwoofer for bass (low frequency) response. Start with placing it in the front of the room, but consider trying other locations to see where you get the best base response for the space in which the surround sound system is set up.

4. **What type of interface would allow a software program running on the PC to operate a synthesizer connected as a peripheral device?**

   MIDI (Musical Instrument Digital Interface).

5. **What sampling rate from a sound card would you require if you want to be able to record CD-quality sound?**

   16-bit @ 44.1 KHz.

Activity 3-1: Discussing System Memory Installation

1. **What are the principal characteristics of DRAM technology?**

   Each cell in Dynamic RAM must be refreshed periodically to preserve its charge. It is high density and low cost.

2. **Why is Synchronous DRAM so-called?**

   Because it works at the same speed as the motherboard.

3. **What is the clock speed of PC2100 DDR SDRAM?**

   133 MHz.

4. **How many pins are there on a DIMM stick of DDR2 SDRAM?**

   240

5. **How can you distinguish memory slots on the motherboard?**

   They have plastic clips at either end.

6. **How is laptop system memory typically packaged?**

   SODIMM.

7. **How would you determine which slots to use?**

   Check the system guide—most Intel boards would require the use of slots 1 and 3 to use both channels, but it's best not to proceed without consulting the vendor's documentation.

8. **Your PC's system bus is 800 MHz. You have one 1 GB stick of PC3-12800 installed already. You have a 1 GB stick of PC3-8500 available. Should you add it to the system?**

   You should realize that the whole memory bus will operate at the slower speed, but otherwise there is no definitive answer—it does depend on how the PC is used. The performance benefits of more RAM probably outweigh the speed penalty in most circumstances, though.

9. **What steps would you take to resolve this job ticket?**

   First, verify that the correct memory type was installed on the system and in the correct configuration (consider whether dual-channel memory was installed in the correct slots). Check that the new memory module is seated properly in its slot. Try swapping memory around in the memory slots.

Activity 3-3: Discussing Mass Storage Device Installation and Configuration

1. **True or false? The read/write heads on an HDD require regular cleaning to obtain optimum performance from the disk.**

   False.

2. **What basic factor might you look at in selecting a high-performance drive?**

   RPM—the speed at which it spins. Other factors to consider include the access and seek times, rotational latency, internal and external rater rates, and reliability.

3. **What is a S.M.A.R.T. hard disk?**

   One with Self Monitoring Analysis and Reporting Technology. This means that it can provide status reports to diagnostic software.

4. **True or false? SATA is an interface for hard drives only.**

   False.

5. **How many storage devices can be attached to a single SATA port?**

   One.

6. **In what two ways could a PC be configured to use an SSD cache?**

   Using a hybrid drive unit with both SSD and magnetic HDD devices or using a dual-drive configuration (with separate SSD / eMMC and HDD units).

7. **You are upgrading a drive. You have removed the main panel from the PC, disconnected the data and power cables, and removed the screws holding the drive to the cage, but it will not slide out. What is your next step?**

   Remove the second panel and check whether there are screws on the other side.

Activity 3-5: Discussing Removable Storage Device Installation and Configuration

1. **What is the primary benefit of using removable solid state storage?**

   Answers will vary, but should include the portability of thumb drives and flash memory cards plus easier and faster rewriting compared to optical media.

2. **Which two media types allow you to write to an optical disc only once?**

   - [ ] CD-ROM
   - [x] CD-R
   - [ ] CD+RW
   - [x] DVD+R
   - [ ] DVD-RW

3. **If a CD writer is 12x8x32x, what is the maximum transfer rate when creating a CD-R?**

   1.8 MBps (1800 KBps).

4. **True or false? DVD-RW media allows double-layer recording.**

   False. Only DVD, DVD-R, or DVD+R media can be double layer.

5. **What is the transfer rate of a 10x DVD drive?**

   13.21 MBps

6. **What is the capacity of a single Blu-ray dual-layer recordable disc?**

   50 GB (25 GB per layer).

7. **True or false? A memory card reader is needed to attach a USB flash memory drive to a PC.**

   False—the "drive" will plug into any USB port.

8. **Name the two main specifications for currently available memory card formats.**

   Secure Digital (SD) and Compact Flash (CF).

Activity 3-6: Discussing RAID Configuration

1. **If you have a computer with three hard disks, what type of RAID fault-tolerant configuration will make best use of them?**

   RAID 5 (striping with parity); RAID 0 is not fault-tolerant and RAID 1 and RAID 10 require an even number of disks.

2. **How much space will be available?**

   360 GB.

3. **What is the minimum number of disks required to implement RAID 10 and how much of the disks' total capacity will be available for the volume?**

   RAID 10 requires at least four disks (two mirrored pairs) and comes with a 50% capacity overhead so the volume will only be half the total disk capacity.

Activity 3-7: Discussing Storage Device Troubleshooting

1. **What would you suggest?**

   Do not use other applications at the same time as DVD writing, make sure that the source files are on the local hard disk (not a removable or network drive), or try using a slower write speed.

2. **What should you do?**

   Check the boot order in system setup is set correctly; check that the disc is not dirty or scratched.

3. **If you experience an error such as "BCD missing" when booting the computer, what action could you take?**

   Use the Startup Repair tool or run `bootrec /rebuildbcd`.

4. **A user reports hearing noises from the hard disk—does this indicate it is failing and should be replaced?**

   Not necessarily—hard disks do make noises but they are not all indicators of a problem. Question the user to find out what sort of noises are occurring or inspect the system yourself.

5. **What is the likely cause and how might you attempt to fix it?**

   The file system is corrupt. You can try using the Startup Repair tool or run bootrec /fixboot to recover it without losing data.

6. **What should be your first troubleshooting step?**

   Determine whether a data backup has been made. If not, try to make one.

7. **What command could you use to try to repair the error?**

   bootrec /fixmbr

8. **What should you do?**

   A degraded volume is still working but has lost one of its disks. In most RAID configurations, another disk failure would cause the volume to fail so you should add a new disk as soon as possible (though do note that rebuilding the array will reduce performance).

Activity 3-8: Troubleshooting Storage Devices

2. What is the possible cause and solution to this type of issue?

- ● The hard drive is physically damaged, so the drive must be replaced.
- ○ A virus has attacked the hard drive, so you can use antivirus software to mitigate the issues.
- ○ Data is corrupt on the drive, and the PC has not been shut down correctly.

3. What is the most likely cause of the problem?

The most likely cause of this problem is a bad hard drive—some of the sectors on the hard drive are probably damaged. You will probably need to replace the hard drive. If you do continue to use the drive, monitor it closely and ensure that the user backs up file data often.

4. What steps might you take to attempt to resolve this problem?

You could try running the Windows error-checking option in the **Tools** pane of the **Local Disk Properties** dialog box. Definitely back up the data if you can get to any of it. You can try using other software utilities to recover the data or take the drive to a data recovery facility.

5. What is the most likely cause of the problem?

If it is not caused by a virus, the most likely cause of this problem is a bad hard drive, and you will probably need to replace it. If you do continue to use the drive, monitor it closely and ensure that the user backs up file data often.

6. What steps might you take to attempt to resolve this problem?

You should isolate the system or drive and check for viruses, because the result of some infections looks like this problem. If you do not identify a security issue, use error checking tools, such as Windows `chkdsk`, to scan the file system. Back up the data if you can get to any of it. You can try using other software utilities to recover the data or take the drive to a data recovery facility.

Activity 4-1: Discussing CPU Upgrades

1. What limits upgrade potential for the system processor?

The type of CPU socket and chipset provided on the motherboard.

2. How can CPU performance be improved?

Overclocking—setting the processor to run at a higher clock speed than it was designed for.

3. Why can cache improve performance?

A CPU tends to repeat the same routines and access the same data over-and-over again. If these routines are stored in fast cache RAM, they can be accessed more quickly than instructions and data stored in system memory.

4. **What does SMP mean?**

   Symmetric Multiprocessing—installing more than one CPU. This requires a motherboard with multiple CPU sockets.

5. **How is the heat sink and fan assembly attached, and what problems can occur releasing it?**

   The heat sink is attached to the motherboard via a clip or push pins. There will also be a power connector for the fan. Clip mechanisms can be difficult to release; push pins are now more common and just require a half turn on each pin with a screwdriver to release. Another issue can arise where too much thermal paste has been applied, causing the heat sink to stick to the processor.

6. **What must you check when inserting a PGA CPU chip?**

   That pin 1 is aligned properly and that the pins on the package are aligned with the holes in the socket. Otherwise, you risk damaging the pins when the ZIF lever is lowered.

7. **What is the difference between a heat sink and a heat pipe?**

   A heat sink uses solid metal fins to dissipate heat through convection (often assisted by using fans to move air across the fins). A heat pipe contains fluid that evaporates in the area over the CPU, cools and condenses in a another part of the pipe, and then flows back to the area over the CPU to continue the cycle.

Activity 4-3: Discussing BIOS/UEFI Configuration and Updates

1. **What advantages does UEFI have over BIOS?**

   UEFI supports 64-bit CPU operation and better hardware support at boot. UEFI also allows for full GUI system utilities and mouse support plus better system startup security options (such as pre-OS boot authentication).

2. **Name three keys commonly used to run a PC's BIOS/UEFI system setup program.**

   Esc, Del, F1, F2, F10.

3. **What widely supported boot method is missing from the following list? HDD, FDD, Optical, USB.**

   Network/PXE (Pre-eXecution Environment)—obtaining boot information from a specially configured server over the network.

4. **Where should you launch a typical firmware upgrade utility—from system setup or from Windows?**

   If the option is available, it is safer to run a firmware upgrade from the system setup program as it reduces the risk of some other process interfering with the update.

5. **If you want to enforce TPM system security, what other BIOS feature should you enable?**

   A supervisor password to prevent the TPM keys from being accessed or cleared.

6. **True or false? Processor extensions such as VT are set by the vendor depending on the CPU model and cannot be enabled or disabled by the user.**

   Mostly false. A feature such as VT is sometimes disabled on some low-end models, but if it is available as a feature of that model, the user can choose whether it is enabled or disabled.

7. **A user's computer was recently installed with a new optical drive. The user now reports a "chassis" error message after the POST sequence. What might be the cause?**

   Intrusion detection is enabled in the BIOS.

8. **When you are configuring BIOS security, what is the difference between a supervisor password and a user password?**

   The user password allows the boot sequence to continue, while a supervisor password controls access to the firmware setup program.

9. **What security system allows system boot to be disabled if the computer is reported stolen?**

   LoJack for Laptops (other tracking software suites are available).

Activity 4-4: Discussing Power Supply Installation

1. **How would you calculate the power used by a component?**

   Multiply its voltage by the current it draws (W=V*I).

2. **What causes a fuse to blow—excessive voltage or excessive current?**

   Excess current.

3. **What is the significance of a PSU's power output when you are designing a custom build PC?**

   It determines the number of drives, expansion cards, and peripherals that the PC can support (assuming the peripherals do not have their own power supplies).

4. **Are you able to use a standard ATX12V PSU with a Mini-ITX motherboard?**

   Yes (assuming it fits in the case you have chosen).

5. **You have a power supply with an 8-pin connector on it. What is this for?**

   It supplies power to a PCI Express graphics card.

6. **You are connecting a new PSU. The PSU has a square 4-pin P4 cable but there is no square 4-pin receptacle on the motherboard. Should you leave the cable disconnected?**

   No; it will plug into an 8-pin EPS12V receptacle near the CPU. You should check the motherboard documentation for advice about which pins to plug the cable into.

7. **What setting should you check before installing a PSU?**

   That the voltage selector is set to the correct voltage (or if there is no selector, that the PSU is suitable for the voltage used by the building power).

8. **What do you think might be the cause?**

   You would need to open the case to investigate the problem. Perhaps when the upgrade was performed, one of the fan power connectors was not attached properly. If the PSU cabling was not secured with cable ties, it could disrupt air flow within the case, reducing the effectiveness of fans. There could be a fault with the fan on the new PSU.

Activity 4-6: Discussing System Component Troubleshooting

1. **What cause might you suspect if a PC experiences intermittent lockups?**

   Assuming the cause is not recent installation of faulty software or hardware, then thermal or power problems are most likely. Loose connections or faulty memory or CPU are also possibilities.

2. **How might you diagnose a thermal problem?**

   Feel if the system is hot to touch, check temperature gauges, watch for cyclic lockup/reboot problems.

3. **What measurement would you expect from a multimeter if a fuse is good?**

   Zero ohms.

4. **What might stop a POST from executing?**

   Faulty cabling and connections, poorly-seated chips, faulty interfaces and devices, logic errors, faulty CPU, motherboard, or PSU.

Activity 4-7: Diagnosing Power Problems

1. **What would you do to resolve this problem?**

   Unplug the power cord. Remove the system cover. Using compressed air, remove the dust from around the fan spindle. Verify that there is no obvious reason the fan is not spinning. Replace the power cord and restart the computer. Verify that the computer starts properly. If these actions did not fix the problem, you would need to replace the power supply. Leaving the problem alone would allow heat to build up to dangerous levels, causing serious damage to the system.

2. **What would you do to resolve this problem?**

   An odor coming from the power supply could be a sign that there is something wrong. Because you have just replaced the unit, verify that all the connections are secure and that the fan is functioning. Restart the machine and verify that the power supply is running as it should. Once the functionality of the unit is verified, then odor is probably a result of installing a new power supply unit. If the odor does not go away in a few days, then contact the power supply manufacturer.

4. **What would you do to resolve this problem?**

   Verify that the power cord is securely connected to the power supply and to the electrical outlet on the surge protector. Verify that the surge protector is turned on and plugged in. Verify that the surge protector is working by plugging in a known good electrical device and turning it on. If the device did not turn on, check to see whether any reset buttons need to be reset on the surge protector, or check the electric outlet's circuit breaker. Restart the computer. If these actions did not solve the problem, you would need to replace the power supply.

5. **Why is it so high?**

   A wrist strap must allow high voltage charges to leak from your body and clothing through the ground, but prevent large currents from flowing into your body and causing an electric shock. This is accomplished by a megaohm resistor.

6. **What does it mean if the reading is zero or over range?**

   The fuse has blown and must be replaced.

Activity 4-8: Diagnosing System Errors

1. **What initial steps should you take to identify and resolve a potential CPU problem?**

    ☐ Replace the CPU with a known-good processor.

    ☑ Verify that the CPU fan and other cooling systems are installed and functional.

    ☐ Replace the motherboard.

    ☑ If the CPU is overclocked, throttle it down to the manufacturer-rated clock speed.

2. **All other diagnostic and corrective steps have failed. You need to verify that it is the CPU itself that is defective. What should you do?**

    ● Replace the CPU with a known-good chip.

    ○ Remove all the adapter cards.

    ○ Reinstall the operating system.

    ○ Replace the motherboard.

Activity 4-9: Discussing Custom PC Configuration

1. **Which component is likely to be a performance bottleneck on a workstation used to edit digital movies?**

    The disk subsystem is most likely to cause the performance bottleneck. The files will be too large to be stored completely in system memory and so must be streamed from the disk, which will need to be both large and fast.

2. **For what type of workstation is a CPU with 4 or more cores particularly well suited?**

    Multiple cores benefit software that can take advantage of multi-threading. Examples include virtualization software and Rapid Application Development (RAD) tools.

3. **You are specifying a PC to act as a home theater. What multimedia outputs should it support?**

    Surround sound audio outputs to the speaker system and HDMI to the TV screen.

4. **Which factors are most likely to make a PC used for gaming require high-end cooling?**

    These PCs use at least two heavyweight processors: the CPU and GPU. Also, gamers are more likely than most other users to overclock components to improve performance. Overclocking requires very effective thermal management solutions.

5. **On a thin client, which component is more important: NIC or HDD?**

   Thin clients do not need much permanent storage at all—some can make do without any mass storage. They do not generate that much network traffic either but that said, the NIC is the more important component here.

6. **Why might high-spec components (CPU, memory, RAID) not be a good idea in a home theater PC?**

   These devices need to operate as quietly as possible and using high-spec components means heat, heat requires cooling, cooling usually means fans, and fans mean noise.

Activity 4-10: Selecting Components for Custom Workstations

1. **A user needs to be able to access the central employee data repository to run reports, but does not need access to any local applications used to create, edit, and manage the employee data. The employee data is managed on a server that can be accessed with a log in. What type of client is best in this case?**

   ● Thin client

   ○ Virtualization workstation

   ○ Thick client

2. **June has recently been put in charge of making updates to the Human Resource employee benefits website. She will be publishing a monthly newsletter and posting company-wide announcements, among other small updates and changes, on a regular basis. All changes to the website must be tested on a number of platforms and web browsers to verify that the changes are correct regardless of the operating system and browser. What type of client setup would you suggest for her?**

   Answers will vary, but will most likely include a virtualization workstation so that she can switch from different operating systems and test any website changes quickly.

3. **In order to properly support the HR employee benefits website, a new server running client VMs has been installed so that the environment that the application requires can be strictly administered by IT staff. Current PCs will be used to access the Client VM environment that is configured on the VM Server. What needs to be present at all PCs that will be accessing this new server and application?**

   ☑ Appropriately configured VM Client.

   ☑ Fast network connection to server hosting the VM environment.

   ☐ Upgrade to video cards.

4. **True or False? The HR manager's client computer must meet the recommended requirements to run Windows 10 so that she can access and use all of the HR-related applications used by the organization. In this case, the best client option is a thick client.**

   True

Activity 4-11: Selecting Components for Custom Personal Computers

1. **What type of computer setup would you suggest for this customer? What specific questions might you ask this customer about additional component needs?**

    Answers may vary, but will most likely include setting up a home server PC for easy file sharing among the household computing devices and to provide more speed to play movies from the PC. You may ask if they are in need of additional storage space and if they are looking for redundancy through a RAID array in the PC.

2. **What hardware and software requirements would you suggest for the graphic designer's workstation?**

    Answers may vary, but will most likely include a PC with a high-end, multicore processor, a high end video card, and the maximum RAM that the motherboard can handle. In addition, the motherboard should contain multiple high-speed ports for peripherals such as external hard drives or additional video cards. The applications will most likely include Adobe's Creative Cloud or similar graphic-design software.

3. **What would you check for first?**

    She needs to have a TV tuner card installed in the computer. The tuner card provides the port to connect the cable from the provider to the computer. You would also want to verify that the tuner card is correctly configured, and that all device drivers are installed and up-to-date.

Activity 5-1: Discussing Wired Networks

1. **Identify each type of network described here.**

    The global network is a WAN. The network at each site is a LAN. The sites within a city comprise a MAN.

2. **Is this the best choice?**

    Cat5e will meet the requirement and will cost the least. Cat6 might offer better performance without adding too much cost. Cat6A would be the best choice for supporting future requirements, but it is likely to cost more than the customer is budgeting for. You should also notify the customer if plenum-rated cabling will be required.

3. **What is the significance of network cabling marked "CMP/MMP"?**

    The cable is plenum cable, rated for use in plenum spaces (building voids used with HVAC systems).

4. **Which networking tool might help you?**

    A punch down tool. Remember that punch down tools are used to terminate solid core cabling to Insulation Displacement Connector (IDC) blocks in patch panels and wall plates, while crimpers are used to attach RJ-45 jacks to stranded patch cord cabling

5. **What type of tool provides comprehensive information about the properties of a network cable installation?**

    A cable certifier.

6. **What features of fiber optic cable make it more suitable for WANs than copper cabling?**

   It suffers less attenuation (and therefore longer range) and is immune to EMI and eavesdropping.

7. **What types of connector are often used with coaxial cable?**

   BNC connectors and F-connectors.

Activity 5-2: Discussing Network Hardware Devices

1. **What is a MAC address?**

   A unique 48-bit identifier coded into every network interface. This is also referred to as the physical or hardware address. A MAC address is expressed as 12 hex digits, usually with colon or hyphen delimiters between each byte value. For example: aa:bb:cc:00:11:22. Each hex digit expresses a 4-bit value using the characters 0 to 9 plus A, B, C, D, E, and F.

2. **What feature(s) should you check when ordering an Ethernet network card?**

   That it supports the correct speed (for example, Gigabit or 10GbE) and media type/connector (for example, RJ-45 for copper cabling or LC for fiber optic).

3. **Can this device be usefully deployed on a modern network?**

   No. Hubs support only half duplex mode and limited speed. There could be very specific circumstances in which you need to deploy a hub (to support some sort of legacy server equipment, for instance) but in general terms, using a hub along with modern switches and network adapters is likely to cause configuration errors and performance problems.

4. **What are the arguments for and against proceeding?**

   As it requires no configuration, an unmanaged switch should be simpler (and cheaper) to deploy. An unmanaged switch will not support configuration features such as Virtual LANs (VLANs), but these would not be required on such a small network. A managed switch would support a remote configuration and monitoring interface and security features that might be useful, however. You might also mention traffic prioritization as a good reason to deploy a managed switch (though the scenario does not specify supporting VoIP handsets).

5. **Can you explain the difference and identify which technology the customer needs?**

   The customer needs a switch supporting Power over Ethernet (PoE). This means that the switch sends power over the data cabling and RJ-45 port to the device. Ethernet over Power (or Powerline) is a means of networking devices by using building power outlets and circuits, rather than data cabling.

Activity 5-3: Discussing Wireless Networks

1. **What is the maximum transfer rate of an 802.11g Wi-Fi adapter?**

   54 Mbps.

2. **Why are 2.4 GHz networks more susceptible to interference than 5 GHz networks?**

   Each channel in a 2.4 GHz network is only 5 MHz wide while Wi-Fi requires about 20 MHz. Consequently, there is not much "space" for separate networks and the chances of overlap are high. There are also numerous other product types that work in the 2.4 GHz band.

3. **How does 802.11n achieve greater speeds than previous Wi-Fi standards?**

   Largely through using multiple reception and transmission antennas (MIMO) and channel bonding.

4. **Can 802.11ac achieve higher throughput by multiplexing the signals from both 2.4 and 5 GHz frequency bands? Why or why not?**

   No, because 802.11ac works only at 5 GHz.

5. **Why might a wireless mesh network topology be used?**

   Each station in a wireless mesh can be made capable of discovering other nodes on the network and forwarding traffic. This can be used to create a network that covers a wide area without deploying numerous access points or extenders.

Activity 5-4: Discussing Internet Connection Types

1. **If you have remote employees who need to connect to the corporate network but they are located in a remote area with no access to high-speed Internet service, what do you think is the best Internet connection method to use?**

   Satellite is the most likely option. A dial-up link is unlikely to provide sufficient bandwidth for a remote access VPN. In some cases, tethering to a cell phone or connecting to a wireless network device is an option, but this will depend on how remote the employees' location is and if they can get a strong cellular signal.

2. **True or false? Analog modems are required for dial-up and ISDN Internet access services.**

   False. Dial-up uses an analog modem but Integrated Services Digital Network (ISDN) uses digital not analog transmissions. The link is created via an adapter called an NT1. This may loosely be referred to as an "ISDN modem," but it is not an analog modem.

3. **What type of SOHO Internet access method offers the best bandwidth?**

   Fiber to the Premises is the best, but it is not always available. Fiber to the Curb and Hybrid Fiber Coax (cable) are the best options for the majority of residential subscribers.

4. **Which protocol enables a dial-up user to exchange frames of data with an ISP's access server?**

   Point-to-Point Protocol (PPP).

5. **What type of cabling is used with the WAN port of a cable modem?**

   Coax.

6. **What Internet access method would be suitable for a business requiring a high bandwidth connection where no cabled options exist?**

   Line-of-sight microwave radio from a Wireless Internet Service Provider (WISP).

Activity 5-5: Discussing Network Configuration Concepts

1. **What is the difference between a router and a modem?**

   A router is a device that can forward traffic between different logical networks. These networks might use different media and different ways of transporting frames across links. In an Ethernet network, a host interfaces with the local network (LAN) using a network adapter. When a link is point-to-point, using media such as a telephone line, a modem is used to convert the signals that can be carried over the media from the LAN format to the WAN format. Where a router is connected to such links, it may be installed with a modem, but the functions of the devices are separate. The modem makes a physical network link with the ISP network, functioning at the same level as a switch. The router can make decisions about forwarding between logical networks.

2. **What are those four layers called?**

   Link/Network Interface, Internet, Transport, and Application.

3. **What is meant by dotted decimal notation?**

   An IPv4 address is a 32-bit number expressed as four octets (bytes). A byte can be expressed as the decimal values 0 to 255, and these are used to represent the IP address, with dots between each decimal number. This scheme is easier for people to read than a binary number and reduces configuration errors.

4. **When is a default gateway required?**

   When a host needs to communicate with hosts located outside its own IP network.

5. **What is the host's subnet mask?**

   255.255.255.0.

6. **What is the purpose of a DHCP server?**

   A Dynamic Host Configuration Protocol (DHCP) server automatically allocates a TCP/IP configuration (IP address, subnet mask, default gateway, and DNS servers) to hosts when they join the network.

7. **What is special about an IP address that starts 169.254?**

   It is an APIPA address—that is, one automatically selected if the interface is configured to use DHCP but cannot contact a DHCP server.

8. **What is significant about this address?**

   It is a private address and cannot be reached directly over the Internet. The host must use a router with address translation or a proxy service to communicate on the Internet.

9. **What is the function of NAT?**

   Network Address Translation (NAT) enables a router to map private network IP addresses onto a public IP address. Private addressing keeps the local network more secure and reduces the demand for unique IP addresses.

10. **Apart from its length, what is the main difference between the structure of an IPv4 address and an IPv6 address?**

    Both types of IP address identify a host within a specific logical network. In an IPv4 address, the network ID portion is determined by applying a mask to the whole address. In an IPv6 address, the host portion is always the last 64 bits of the address. The first 64 bits are used with network prefixes to identify networks and subnetworks.

Activity 5-6: Discussing Network Services

1. **If a network application cannot tolerate a missing packet, what type of transport protocol should it use?**

   Transmission Control Protocol (TCP).

2. **True or false? Protocols that stream video and audio over the Internet are likely to be based on UDP.**

   True. UDP carries less overhead compared to Transmission Control Protocol (TCP), so is better suited to playing media files where small glitches due to lost packets are less of a problem than the whole video freezing.

3. **What is DNS?**

   Domain Name System—servers that map host and domain names to IP addresses.

4. **What configuration parameter must be entered to enable a client to use DNS?**

   The IP address of a DNS server on the local network or network reachable by the client.

5. **True or false? An HTTP application secured using the SSL/TLS protocol should use a different port to unencrypted HTTP.**

   True. By default HTTPS uses port 443. It is possible in theory to apply SSL/TLS to port 80 but most browsers would not support this configuration.

6. **What protocol would a mail client use to access the message store on a remote mail server?**

   Typically Post Office Protocol (POP3) or Internet Message Access Protocol (IMAP). A proprietary protocol such as MAPI (Microsoft Exchange) might also be used.

7. **If you want to configure a firewall on the mail server to allow clients to download email messages, which port(s) might you have to open?**

   Either TCP port 993 (IMAPS) or 995 (POP3S), depending on the mail access protocol in use (IMAP or POP). These are the default ports for secure connections. Unsecure default ports are TCP port 143 and TCP port 110. Port 25 (SMTP) is used to send mail between servers, not to access messages stored on a server. Port 587 is often used by a client to submit messages for delivery by an SMTP server.

8. **What file sharing protocol(s) could you use to allow access to Windows, Linux, and Apple macOS clients?**

   Most clients should support Server Message Block (SMB)/Common Internet File System (CIFS). You might want to configure Apple Filing Protocol to support older macOS clients. Another option is to configure File Transfer Protocol (FTP).

9. **What is the difference between SNMP and syslog?**

   The Simple Network Management Protocol (SNMP) provides a means for devices to report statistics to a management server. Syslog provides a means for devices to send log entries to a remote server.

10. What are the principal types and configuration options?

A network Intrusion Detection System (IDS) scans packet contents for signs of traffic that could violate security policies. An Intrusion Protection System (IPS) can effect some sort of action to block such traffic. An IPS is usually provisioned as a Unified Threat Management (UTM) appliance to include firewall, anti-malware, and other security functionality. Appliances with blocking functionality are typically deployed inline with the network, so that all traffic passes through the appliance. Alternatively, a tap or sensor can be attached to the network so that traffic is copied for the appliance to read.

Activity 6-1: Discussing Network Connection Configuration Settings

1. What steps do you need to follow?

Open **Device Manager** and the adapter's **Property** sheet. Select the **Advanced** tab and select the **Duplex** property (or **Speed and Duplex**). Change the value as required, and select **OK**.

2. True or false? If you want a computer to be available through Wake-on-LAN, you can disconnect it from the power supply but must leave it connected to the network data port.

False. The network adapter must be connected to standby power, and the computer could not start anyway if it were disconnected from the power supply.

3. Why is this?

It has been configured with an Alternate Configuration static IP address.

4. Why are IP addresses entered under DNS, and why should there be two of them?

These are the IP addresses of DNS servers that will process client requests to resolve host and domain names to IP addresses. DNS is a critical service on Windows networks and on the Internet, so a second server should always be specified for redundancy

5. What parameters do you need to specify to connect to a VPN?

Assuming you have a remote host topology, you need to establish a connection to a server over a public network such as the Internet. The VPN server then facilitates a connection to a local network. You need to specify the location of the VPN server as an IP address or Fully Qualified Domain Name (FQDN). If the VPN type is not detected automatically, you might need to configure extra settings or use third-party VPN client software. To connect to the VPN, the user must submit credentials, such as a user name and password.

Activity 6-2: Discussing SOHO Network Installation and Configuration

1. What type of cable and connectors are used to connect a modem to a phone port?

Twisted pair with RJ-11 connectors. In the UK, the phone port might use a BT-style connector though.

2. What is the function of a microfilter?

It screens noise from data signals on jacks for voice or fax devices if DSL equipment is connected.

3. **To configure a router/modem, what type of IP interface configuration should you apply to the computer you are using to access the device administration web app?**

   Set the adapter to obtain an IP address automatically. The router/modem will be running a Dynamic Host Configuration Protocol (DHCP) server that will allocate an appropriate IP address and DNS server.

4. **What is the effect of reducing transmit power when you are configuring an access point?**

   It reduces the supported range of the access point. You might do this to prevent interference between two access points in close proximity. You might also reduce power to prevent the network being accessible outside a particular area (such as making the network accessible to indoor users only).

5. **Which standard represents the best available wireless network security?**

   Wi-Fi Protected Access version 2 (WPA2). It is also worth noting that this can be configured in personal mode (using a passphrase shared between all users) or enterprise mode. Enterprise mode is more secure. Each user connects with his or her network credential, which is validated by an authentication server (typically RADIUS).

6. **How can QoS improve performance for SOHO Internet access?**

   A Quality of Service (QoS) mechanism allows you to elevate certain types of traffic to a higher priority to be processed by the router/modem. For example, you could create a rule reserving 80% of bandwidth for a Voice over IP (VoIP) protocol. This means that whenever the VoIP application is active, other protocols can use only 20% of the router's link bandwidth, making it less likely that ordinary file downloads or web browsing will interfere with a call.

Activity 6-4: Discussing SOHO Network Security

1. **True or false? A firewall can be configured to block hosts with selected IP address ranges from connecting to a particular TCP port on a server that is available to hosts in other IP address ranges.**

   True. A firewall's access control entry ruleset can combine any supported criteria.

2. **What sort of configuration options are available to apply parental controls, as opposed to packet filtering via a firewall?**

   You can set restrictions to block access at times of the day or night. You can blacklist web addresses (URLs), optionally on the basis of site rating schemes. You may also be able to block access on the basis of keyword filtering.

3. **What security method could you use to allow only specific hosts to connect to a SOHO router/modem?**

   You could configure a whitelist of permitted Media Access Control (MAC) addresses.

4. **How would you enable access?**

   Configure port forwarding on the router to send incoming connections on port 21 to the LAN computer.

5. **What feature on the router will simplify configuration of online multiplayer gaming?**

   Universal Plug and Play (UPnP).

6. **True or false? To allow a PC game to accept incoming connections over a custom port you need to configure the Advanced Security Firewall.**

   False. You can allow a process to connect via the basic firewall interface.

7. **What option on the General tab of the Internet Options dialog box is most relevant to user privacy?**

   Delete browsing history.

8. **How would you configure a Windows 7 computer to use a proxy server for web browsing?**

   Open the **Internet Options** dialog box, and select the **Connections** tab. Select **LAN Settings** and enter the address of the proxy.

Activity 6-5: Discussing Remote Access Configuration

1. **Which edition(s) of Windows support connecting to the local machine over Remote Desktop?**

   The Remote Desktop server functionality is available in Professional, Enterprise, and Ultimate editions.

2. **What is the goal of RDP Restricted Admin (RDPRA) Mode and Remote Credential Guard?**

   If the local machine is compromised, malware may be able to obtain the credentials of a user account connecting to the machine over Remote Desktop. RDPRA Mode and Remote Credential Guard are designed to mitigate this risk.

3. **True or false? SSH is not available for use with Windows.**

   False. Support for an SSH client and server is being included in feature updates to Windows 10, and there are numerous commercial and open source products.

4. **How can you confirm that you are connecting to a legitimate SSH server?**

   The server displays its host key on connection. You need to keep a record of valid host keys and compare the key presented by the server to the record you have.

Activity 6-6: Discussing Network Connection Troubleshooting

1. **What would you suspect the problem to be?**

   The computer's wireless adapter is not supported by the AP, the computer is not in range, or there is some sort of interference.

2. **What readings would you expect to gather with a Wi-Fi analyzer?**

   The signal strength of different Wi-Fi networks and their channels within range of the analyzer.

3. **What command would you use to refresh the IP configuration on Windows 7 client workstations?**

   `ipconfig /renew`

4. **What command can you use on a Linux computer to report the IP configuration?**

   Historically, this could be reported using the `ifconfig` tool. The `ip` command is now preferred.

5. **Where would you start troubleshooting?**

   You could test the PC's IP configuration, specifically the default gateway or name resolution, or you could check that the cable is good.

6. **What does this tell you?**

   If a DHCP server cannot be contacted, the machine should default to using an APIPA address (169.254.x.y). As it has not done this, something is wrong with the networking software installed on the machine (probably the DHCP client service, TCP/IP stack, or registry configuration, to be specific).

7. **If a host has a firewall configured to block outgoing ICMP traffic, what result would you expect from pinging the host (assuming that the path to the host is otherwise OK)?**

   Destination unreachable.

8. **What Windows tool is used to test the end-to-end path between two IP hosts on different IP networks?**

   `tracert`

9. **Which command produces the output shown in this graphic?**

   This is output from `netstat`. Specifically, it is `netstat -ano`. The switches show all connections, with ports in numeric format, and the PID of the process that opened the port.
   Command output exhibit. (Screenshot used with permission from Microsoft.)

Activity 6-7: Discussing IoT Devices

1. **What type of network topology is used by protocols such as Zigbee and Z-Wave?**

   A wireless mesh network topology.

2. **What types of home automation device might require specialist installer training?**

   A device such as a thermostat has to be wired safely and correctly to the heating controls, door locks must be fitted securely by a joiner or carpenter, and even a security camera would be better fitted by someone with the skills to evaluate the best placement. While a homeowner might attempt these as DIY jobs, a service or support company should not allow untrained staff to attempt this type of installation.

3. **What are the two main options for operating smart devices?**

   Using a smartphone/tablet app, or using a voice-enabled smart speaker. Some devices might also support configuration via a web app.

4. **True or false? Voice processing by a smart speaker is performed internally so these devices can be used without an Internet connection.**

   False. The speaker passes the voice data to a backend server for processing.

Activity 7-1: Discussing Client-Side Virtualization Configuration

1. **What is a Type 2 hypervisor?**

   Hypervisor software that must be installed to a host OS. A Type 1 (or bare metal) hypervisor is installed directly on the host PC.

2. **What is a guest OS?**

   An OS installed on a virtual machine running within the virtual environment.

3. **What system resources are most important on a system designed to host multiple virtual machines?**

   The CPU must support virtualization extensions (and ideally be multi-processor or multicore), and there must be plenty of system memory and disk space.

4. **What might you need to install to a guest OS to make full use of a hypervisor's features?**

   The drivers for the emulated hardware (often referred to as an extensions, additions, or integration components).

5. **True or false? VMs can be networked together by using a virtual switch, which is implemented in software by the hypervisor.**

   True.

6. **If users have access to virtualization tools, what network security controls might be required?**

   A VM needs to be subject to network access control and authorization, like any physical computer device. The VMs need to be checked to ensure they are not running malware, for instance.

7. **If you are using a normal antivirus product to protect a VM from malware, should you install the A-V product on the host to scan the VM disk image or on the VM itself?**

   On the VM. The A-V software will not be able to scan the disk image for malware and may lock the file and cause performance problems while trying to perform the scan.

Activity 7-2: Discussing Cloud Computing Concepts

1. **How do the five components of cloud computing defined by the NIST work together to provide users with cloud computing services?**

   Resource allocation is provided through rapid elasticity and resource pooling. Resource allocation is requested through on-demand self-service. Broad network access makes the resources available to the user. Measured service enables the provider to meter customer usage and bill the customer accordingly.

2. **Which type of cloud would your organization be likely to use?**

   Answers will vary. Depending on how much control you need over the storage or services provided through the cloud, you might select a private cloud solution as the most secure, and a community cloud solution as the least secure.

3. **What type of service should the provider run to enable these features?**

   A measured service with the resources to cope with changing demands.

4. **How would such a cloud solution be classed?**

   Offsite hosted private.

5. **What type of infrastructure is being deployed?**

   Virtual Desktop Infrastructure (VDI).

Activity 8-1: Discussing Laptop Features

1. **What feature would you expect to find on a modern touchpad, compared to older models?**

   Support for multi-touch.

2. **True or false? Touchpad settings would be configured via the Touch applet in Windows Control Panel.**

   False—the touchpad is configured via tabs in the **Mouse** applet.

3. **What two display settings would you expect to be able to control via a laptop's Fn keys?**

   Screen brightness, and toggling the output between the built-in screen and external display.

4. **What device would you use to extend the functionality of a laptop while sitting at a desk?**

   A docking station is used to extend functionality (allowing use of additional drives or adapters) but you could also mention a port replicator, which extends the number of connectivity options.

5. **What connectivity issue is resolved by providing a USB-to-RJ-45 dongle?**

   Ethernet/wired network connectivity.

6. **What is the brand name of the standard cable lock security system for laptops?**

   Kensington.

Activity 8-2: Discussing Laptop Hardware Installation and Configuration

1. **What is the process for installing memory in a laptop?**

   Verify that the DDR version of the upgrade module is supported by the motherboard. Take anti-static precautions. Locate the memory slot, which is usually accessed via a panel on the back cover. Move the connector up to 45° and insert the memory card, taking care to align it correctly. Push the card flat again.

2. **What type of standard adapter card might be used to connect internal FRU devices to the motherboard of a laptop?**

   Mini-PCIe, mSATA, or M.2.

3. **What distinguishes a magnetic hard drive designed for a laptop from one designed for a PC?**

   Laptop drives are 2.5" (or sometimes 1.8"), rather than 3.5". They also tend to be slower (5,400 rpm, rather than 7,200 or 10,000 rpm) and lower capacity. The largest at the time of writing is 5 TB, so this may not be a limiting factor in practice.

4. **Is this something you can easily repair?**

   Typically, the processor, the DC jack, and USB ports are attached directly on the board and cannot be replaced without replacing the whole laptop motherboard. If the other USB ports are functional, a USB hub could provide additional ports.

5. **Which items are most easily replaced in a laptop?**

   The fixed drive, system memory (RAM), and plug-in wireless card will be the easiest upgradable components to install. If items need repairing, fans, the screen, the battery, touchpad, and the keyboard should be straightforward to replace, if you can obtain compatible parts.

Activity 8-4: Troubleshooting Common Laptop Issues

1. **If the laptop can display an image on an external monitor but not the built-in one, which component do you know is working, and can you definitively say which is faulty?**

   The graphics adapter is working. The problem must exist either in the cabling to the built-in screen or with a screen component, such as an inverter, backlight, or the display panel itself. Further tests will be required to identify which (though it may be quicker to replace the whole screen assembly).

2. **What actions should you take in response to this issue?**

   Overheating can be a sign that dust and dirt is restricting the necessary airflow within the device, so start by cleaning the ventilation duct with compressed air, and then make sure that the device is getting proper air circulation around the outside of the case.

3. **What would you suggest is the problem?**

   The batteries in the keyboard have run down—replace them.

4. **What could be the cause?**

   The laptop could be using reduced performance settings to conserve battery life.

5. What do you suggest?

Batteries lose maximum charge over time. It may be possible to recondition the battery or to use power saving features, but the only real way to restore maximum battery life is to buy a new battery.

6. What might be the cause of this?

The user could be touching the touchpad while typing, or vibrations could be affecting the touchpad. Update the driver, or reduce the sensitivity/disable touch and tap events.

Activity 9-1: Discussing Mobile Device Types

1. What are the principal characteristics of the phablet form factor?

A phablet is essentially a smartphone with a screen size of more than approximately 5.5" but less than about 7". Phablets can make voice calls and use cellular data, while many tablets are limited to Wi-Fi connectivity.

2. What is the relevance of ARM to smartphones?

Advanced RISC Machines (ARM) produce the CPU designs most widely used in smartphones.

3. True or false? Smartphones use a type of memory technology that works both as system memory and as persistent storage.

False—like PCs, smartphones use a variant of DDR for system memory. This is volatile storage so a flash memory device is used for persistent storage.

4. What is meant by wearable technology?

Wearable technology is devices that the user doesn't need to hold (as they are affixed to the wearer via a band or clip) to provide uninterrupted interaction between computer and network systems and the user. Examples include Virtual Reality (VR) headsets, smartwatches (such as Apple's iWatch), and fitness monitors like FitBit.

5. What technology gives an e-Reader better battery life than a tablet?

The e-Ink display works without backlighting, producing little to no heat through resistance and better energy efficiency.

Activity 9-2: Discussing Mobile Device Accessory Connection and Configuration

1. What type of peripheral port would you expect to find on a current generation smartphone?

For Apple devices, the Lightning port. For Android and Windows, it will be USB—either Micro Type B or Type-C.

2. How would you upgrade storage capacity on a typical smartphone?

If the smartphone supports removable flash cards such as Micro-SD, you can add a larger card. Otherwise, the components in these devices are not field replaceable, so there are no upgrade options.

3. **What technology do smartphones use to facilitate payment at points of sale?**

   Near Field Communications (NFC) allows the user to touch a receiver for the phone to pass card data to a point of sale terminal.

4. **True or false? An IP67-rated smartwatch could be considered risk-free for wear while swimming in an indoor pool.**

   False—IP67 rates immersion up to 1 m (for up to 30 minutes), so wearing a device while swimming would be a significant risk.

Activity 9-3: Discussing Mobile Device Network Connectivity Configuration

1. **Why would a user be likely to disable cellular data access but leave Wi-Fi enabled?**

   To avoid data charges (especially when using the device abroad).

2. **What is tethering?**

   Tethering is the use of a smartphone as an Internet connectivity hub. It can share its Internet connection with a computer via either a cable, Bluetooth, or Wi-Fi.

3. **What serial number uniquely identifies a particular handset?**

   International Mobile Station Equipment Identity (IMEI) for handsets from GSM providers or Mobile Equipment ID (MEID) from CDMA providers.

4. **What is the function of a smartphone's baseband processor?**

   The baseband system is usually dedicated to providing radio modem functions, acting as an interface with the cell tower, access point, or other radio source to transmit signals.

5. **How do you configure an autodiscover-enabled email provider on a smartphone?**

   Just select the provider then enter the email address. If the account is detected, you will be prompted for the password.

6. **True or false? S/MIME is used to configure a secure connection to a mailbox server, so that your password cannot be intercepted when connecting over an open access point.**

   False—S/MIME is for encrypting messages. SSL/TLS is used to secure connections.

Activity 9-5: Discussing Mobile App Support

1. **Why must a vendor account usually be configured on a smartphone?**

   A vendor account, such as an Apple, Google, or Samsung account, is required to use the app store.

2. **What is sideloading?**

   Installing a mobile app without going through the app store. Android supports sideloading through the APK package format. Sideloading is not officially supported on iOS devices.

3. Which types of data might require mapping between fields when syncing between applications?

Contacts and calendar items.

4. What software is used to synchronize data files between an iOS device and a PC and what connection methods can it use?

iTunes. It can work over USB (with a USB-to-Apple cable) or Wi-Fi.

5. How might an app register users without implementing its own authentication process?

Through federated identity management, or as the user sees it, a "Sign in with..." feature. If the user's sign-in with the identity service (Google or Facebook, for example) is cached on the device, this will enable Single Sign On (SSO) with supported apps. This could also be referred to as mutual authentication, of a kind (the app and the sign-in provider must authorize one another).

Activity 10-1: Discussing Laser Printer Maintenance

1. Why is a laser printer better suited to most office printing tasks than an inkjet?

Laser printers are much faster, quieter, and better quality (the pages do not smear) than inkjets at this type of output. They also have lower running costs.

2. What makes the power supply in a printer different to that used in a PC?

A PC's Power Supply Unit (PSU) only needs to generate voltages up to 12 V DC. The charging and transfer corona wires/rollers in a laser printer require much higher voltages. To apply a 600 V charge to the drum, for instance, the corona wire must be charged to 1000 V.

3. How is the imaging drum in a laser printer charged?

Applying a uniform high charge to the photosensitive drum using the primary corona wire or roller.

4. What is the removal of the charge from the photosensitive drum by a laser called?

Laser imaging or writing.

5. What is the process of image transfer?

Passing paper between the photosensitive drum and the secondary or transfer corona wire or roller. This attracts the toner from the drum to the paper.

6. What must you do before installing a new toner cartridge into a printer?

Remove the packing strips. The printer should also be turned off, and the old cartridge should be removed and placed into a sealed bag for recycling.

7. Which components are provided as part of a laser printer maintenance kit?

The main component is a new fuser assembly. The kit will also usually contain a transfer/secondary charge roller plus paper transport rollers for each tray (pickup rollers and a new separation pad).

Activity 10-2: Discussing Inkjet Printer Maintenance

1. **Which inks are typically used in the color printing process?**

   Cyan, Magenta, Yellow, and Black (CMYK). Do be aware that some printers can use more inks. For example, a 6-color printer might add Light Cyan and Light Magenta inks, or Orange and Green inks (hexachrome).

2. **What two types of print heads are used by inkjet printers?**

   Thermal and piezoelectric. The thermal type is also known by Canon's Bubble Jet trademark because of the way the print head creates an ink bubble by heating. Most other printer vendors use thermal technology but Epson printers use their piezoelectric pump-like process.

3. **What would you do?**

   Try using the printer's built-in cleaning cycle, and then replacing the ink cartridge. If these do not work, try using an after market cleaning product. Try using the printer properties sheet to check for print head alignment, color settings, and other settings.

4. **Can inkjet printers use plain copy paper?**

   Yes, but this type of paper will not produce the best results. It is better to use paper designed for inkjets. There are different grades of inkjet paper. Higher-grade paper allows for glossy photo printing.

5. **What is an ASF?**

   An AutoSheet Feeder (ASF) allows the printer to load a sheet of paper from a tray, using pickup rollers to move the sheet and a separation pad to make sure only a single sheet is fed at one time.

Activity 10-3: Discussing Impact, Thermal, and 3D Printer Maintenance

1. **What type of printer technology is a dot matrix printer?**

   It is commonly described as an impact printer.

2. **What types of paper/stationery can dot matrix printers use that laser and inkjet printers cannot?**

   Multi-part or continuous tractor-fed stationery and carbon copy paper.

3. **Where are you must likely to encounter thermal printers?**

   Direct thermal printers are typically used as handheld receipt printers. There are other thermal printer types. For example, dye sublimation printers are often used for photo printing.

4. **What maintenance should you perform?**

   Using the steps in the printer documentation, replace the ribbon in the printer and clean the print head. If this does not fix the problem, replace the print head.

5. **How should you resolve this problem?**

   Open the printer and locate the label that came off the backing. Remove the label and if there is any sticky residue, clean it with isopropyl alcohol (IPA) applied to a swab. Ensure the roll of labels is properly loaded and that there are no loose labels that might come loose again.

6. **What do you need to create objects with an FDM-type 3D printer?**

   You will need spools of filament, usually made of some type of plastic, to create 3D objects on a print bed or build surface.

7. **What considerations for locating a 3D printer do you have to make?**

   The 3D print process is sensitive to movement and vibration, so the printer must be located on a firm and stable surface. The process can also be affected by dust and the ambient temperature and humidity (especially variations and drafts). Finally, some printer types are fully exposed so there is some risk of burns from the high-heat elements. Ideally, the printer should not be accessible to untrained staff.

Activity 10-4: Discussing Printer Installation and Configuration

1. **When you are purchasing a new printer, what would you need to decide between as you evaluate connections?**

   Almost all new printers use USB, so the main consideration would be whether you needed support for a wireless or Ethernet connection.

2. **How many printer drivers must you install?**

   One. Applications rely on the operating system to mediate access to devices. They do not need their own drivers.

3. **Should you install separate drivers for the Home and Enterprise editions?**

   No—there is no difference between editions in this regard. You do need to install drivers for x86 (32-bit) and x64 (64-bit) versions, though.

4. **What tool can you use to confirm that basic print functionality is available?**

   Print a test page by using the option in the setup wizard or on the **General** tab of the **Printer Properties** dialog box.

5. **What configuration setting would you change to make the unit available for print jobs?**

   From **Devices and Printers** or **Settings**, select **Printer Properties** and then select the **Device Settings** tab. Select the **Duplex Unit** setting and select **Installed**.

6. **True or false? When you print 10 copies of an uncollated job, 10 copies of page one are printed, followed by 10 copies of page two, then 10 copies of page three, and so on.**

   True.

7. **True or false? To enable printer sharing via Windows, the print device must be connected to the Windows PC via an Ethernet or Wi-Fi link.**

   False—any print device can be shared via printer properties. The print device can be connected to the Windows print server over USB, Bluetooth, Ethernet, or Wi-Fi. Other clients connect to the printer via the share, however, so the Windows PC must be kept on to facilitate printing.

8. **What configuration information does a user need to use a print device connected to the same local network?**

   The print device's IP address or host name. You might note that vendor utilities can search for a connected device on the local network, so "None" could also be a correct answer.

9. **What service should a network print device run to enable an Apple iPad to use the device over Wi-Fi?**

   The Bonjour service.

Activity 10-6: Troubleshooting Printer Issues

1. **What is the overall process for troubleshooting this issue?**

   Print out a test page to see if you can reproduce the problem the user reported. If you see the same problem as reported by the user, identify the print defect, based on the type of printer, to resolve the problem. Document the steps you took to resolve the problem.

2. **If print jobs do not appear at the printer and the queue is clear, what could you try first to solve the problem?**

   Cycle the power on the printer.

3. **Where on disk is the print file spooled in Windows?**

   %SystemRoot%\System32\Spool\Printers.

4. **What are your next steps?**

   Right-click **Computer** and select **Manage**. Select **Services and Applications→Services**. Right-click **Print Spooler** and select **Restart**.

5. **How would you track down the source of a paper jam?**

   Check the error message reported by the printer (this may be shown on the printer's console). It may indicate the location of the stuck pages. Otherwise, visually inspect the various feed and output mechanisms.

6. **What should you do if you cannot delete a job stuck in the print queue?**

   Stop the print spooler service, delete the spooled file, then restart the spooler.

7. **What could be causing this?**

   The paper might not be loaded squarely, there might be too much paper loaded into the tray, or the paper is creased or dirty.

8. **What effect does a worn photosensitive drum have on printing?**

   Faint printing.

9. **What could be causing this?**

   Poorly distributed toner or a damaged/worn transfer corona wire. If the secondary corona does not apply a charge evenly across the paper, less toner is attracted from the drum to the part of the sheet where charging failed. Note that if there are repetitive white or black marks (rather than stripes) that do not smudge, the issue is more likely to be dirt or grease on the drum.

10. **What effect does a dirty primary corona wire have on laser printing?**

    It leaves black stripes on the paper. If the charging corona does not apply the correct charge evenly to the drum, toner is attracted to the place where the charging failed, creating a black stripe all the way down the page.

Solutions

Activity 10-8: Discussing Imaging Device Installation and Configuration

1. **What type of connection interface is a scanner most likely to use?**

   All modern scanners will support USB. Some might have an Ethernet network port (RJ-45) or even wireless (Wi-Fi and/or Bluetooth), though this is more typical of Multifunction Devices (MFD) than standalone scanners.

2. **What type of sensor is used to capture an image for conversion to a digital file?**

   Charge Coupled Device (CCD) or Complementary Metal Oxide Semiconductor (CMOS).

3. **What is the function of OCR?**

   Optical Character Recognition (OCR) software can convert a scanned image of text into a digital text file that can be edited in a text editor or word processor.

4. **What type of imaging input device would be most useful for a Point-of-Sale (POS) system?**

   Barcode scanner.

5. **True or false? Any type of smartphone camera can be used to read a QR code.**

   True. The smartphone just needs to capture the image of the Quick Response (QR) code and be installed with software to decode it.

Glossary

*aaS
(Something as a Service) An ownership model for cloud services where the "something" can refer to infrastructure, network, platform, or software.

2D barcodes
See **QR codes**.

3D modeling software
Software that creates a model of a physical object using polygons, spline curves, and bezel curves.

3D print process
A printing process that builds a solid object from successive layers of material.

3D printer
Hardware device capable of small scale manufacturing. 3D printers use a variety of filament media (typically plastic) with different properties.

3D scanner
A scanner that can gather data about the shape and appearance of a physical object and save that information to a computer.

3D slicing software
Software in a 3D printer or in 3D modeling software that takes a 3D model and creates multiple horizontal layers of the model.

802.3af
PoE powered devices can draw up to about 13 W over the link. Power is supplied as 350mA@48V and limited to 15.4 W, but the voltage drop over the maximum 100 feet of cable results in usable power of around 13 W.

802.3at (PoE+)
PoE powered devices can draw up to about 25 W. PoE+ allows for a broader range of devices to be powered such as cameras with pan/tilt/zoom capabilities, door controllers, and thin client computers.

AC
(alternating current) When electricity is produced by a generator at the power station, the rotational movement of the magnetic coils causes the current produced to oscillate like a sine wave (it is said to alternate). Computers require direct current (at a constant voltage). A transformer is used to convert AC from the power outlet into the 3.3, 5, and 12 V DC supply required by the computer.

AC adapter
An external power supply used to power laptops and other portable devices.

accelerometer
Mobile technology that can determine the orientation of a device with a sensor that measures the acceleration of the device direction.

accelerometer/gyroscope
Components used in mobile devices to detect motion (accelerometer) and rotation (gyroscope). As well as switching screen orientation, this can be used as a control mechanism (for example, a driving game could allow the tablet itself to function as a steering wheel).

access time
The speed at which memory or a disk drive can be addressed and utilized (opened, read from, or written to).

ACL
(Access Control List) The permissions attached to or configured on a network resource, such as folder, file, or firewall. The ACL specifies which subjects (user accounts, host IP addresses, and so on)

are allowed or denied access and the privileges given over the object (read only, read/write, and so on).

ad-hoc mode
A temporary network mode in which devices connect to each other directly without an intermediary networking device.

ad-hoc network
A peer-to-peer network created for the current print session.

adapter card
Circuit board providing additional functionality to the computer system (video, sound, networking, modem, and so on). An adapter card fits a slot on the PC's expansion bus and often provides ports through slots cut into the back of the PC case. Different cards are designed for different slots (PCI or PCIe).

add-on card
An adapter card installed in a PCIe slot.

additive color printing
A color printing method that combines differently colored transmitted light to form different shades.

ADF
(Automatic Document Feeder) Device that feeds media automatically into a scanner or printer.

ADSL
(Asymmetrical DSL) A consumer version of DSL that provides a fast downlink but a slow uplink. The upstream rate is between 64 Kbps and 1 Mbps and the downstream rate it 500 Kbps to 8 Mbps.

AES
(Advanced Encryption Standard) Modern encryption suite providing symmetric encryption (the same key is used to encrypt and decrypt). AES is a very strong cipher with many applications, including being part of the WPA2 Wi-Fi encryption scheme.

AFP
(Apple Filing Protocol) Protocol supporting file sharing on macOS networks. AFP works over TCP port 548.

agent
A process running on an SNMP compatible network device that sends information to an SNMP manager.

AHCI
(Advanced Host Controller Interface) A logical interface used by SATA drives to communicate with the bus.

airplane mode
A toggle found on mobile devices enabling the user to disable and enable wireless functionality quickly.

all-in-one unit
A desktop computer in which all the computer components, except the keyboard and mouse, are contained within the monitor case.

ALU
(Arithmetic Logic Unit) A circuit in the CPU that performs integer-based calculations and performs bit-wise logical calculations.

AMD-V
Extensions in AMD-based systems that allow hardware virtualization.

AMD64
AMD's 64-bit instruction set that was also adopted by Intel for its 64-bit desktop and mobile line. Intel refers to it as EM64T or Intel 64.

analog display
A computer monitor that accepts continuously varying signals. CRT monitors use analog signals and are capable of supporting several output resolutions without losing quality.

Android application package
(APK) Third-party or custom programs that are installed directly through an APK file, giving users and business the flexibility to install apps directly on Android devices.

Android Auto
An Android phone feature that allows users to interact with their phone using voice commands and a vehicle's built-in display.

anti-glare cover
A display cover to deal with ambient lighting issues on the display.

antistatic bag
A packaging material containing anti-ESD shielding or dissipative materials to protect components from ESD damage.

AP
(Access Point) A device that provides connectivity between wireless devices and a cabled network. APs with Internet connectivity located in public buildings (cafes, libraries, and airports, for instance) are often referred to as hotspots.

APIPA
(Automatic Private IP Addressing) A means for Windows clients configured to obtain an address automatically that could not contact a DHCP server to communicate on the local subnet. The host randomly selects an address from the range 169.254.x.y. This is also called a link-local address.

App Store
The online site where Apple users can purchase or get free apps have been submitted to and approved by Apple before they are released to users.

Apple CarPlay
An iPhone feature that allows users to interact with their phone using voice commands and a vehicle's built-in display.

Application protocols layer
In the TCP/IP suite, numerous protocols used for network configuration, management, and services reside at this level. Application protocols use a TCP or UDP port to connect the client and server.

application virtualization
Rather than run the whole client desktop as a virtual platform, the client either accesses a particular application hosted on a server or streams the application from the server to the client for local processing.

apps
Installable programs that extend the functionality of the mobile device, that must be written and compiled for a particular mobile operating system (Apple iOS, Android, or Windows).

AR
(augmented reality) Using software and smartphone cameras or headsets to interact with real-world objects and images or change the way they appear in some way.

ARP
(Address Resolution Protocol) When two systems communicate using IP, an IP address is used to identify the destination machine. The IP address must be mapped to a device (the network adapter's MAC address). ARP performs the task of resolving an IP address to a hardware address. Each host caches known mappings in an ARP table for a few minutes. It is also a utility used to manage the ARP cache.

array
See **RAID**.

ASF
(AutoSheet Feeder) In an inkjet printer, the paper pickup mechanism to feed paper into the printer.

aspect ratio
A characteristic of display devices that indicates the ratio of width to height.

ATX
A standard PC case, motherboard, and power supply specification. Mini-, Micro-, and Flex-ATX specify smaller board designs.

audio subsystem
Made up of a sound card and one or more audio input and output devices.

authentication
A means for a user to prove their identity to a computer system. Authentication is implemented as either something you know (a username and password), something you have (a smart card or key fob), or something you are (biometric information). Often, more than one method is employed (2-factor authentication).

autodiscover
The ability of a mobile device to determine connection settings based on the user entering their email credentials.

back haul
A link or transit arrangement with another ISP to connect each Point of Presence to their core network infrastructure and one or more IXPs.

backed up print queue
A problem situation where there are lots of jobs pending but not printing.

backlight
Fluorescent lamp illuminating the image on a flat panel (LCD) screen. If the backlight or inverter fails, the screen image will go very, very dark.

barcode scanner
A barcode reader is a handheld or pen-shaped device designed to scan barcodes. A barcode is a pattern of different sized parallel bars, typically representing a product number, such as an ISBN, EAN, or UPC. The reader uses a sensor mechanism (typically either a photo diode, laser, or CCD) to read the intensity of light reflected back by the barcode. The reader then reports the number back to application software, which links it to a product database.

baseband update
Modification of the firmware of a cellular modem.

BD
(Blu-ray Disc) The latest generation of optical disc technology that uses a 405 mm blue laser for high density storage, with disc capacity of 25 GB per layer. Transfer rates are measured in multiples of 36 MBps.

biometric devices
Peripherals used to gather biometric data for comparison to data stored in a database.

biometrics
Identifying features stored as digital data can be used to authenticate a user. Typical features used include facial pattern, iris, retina, or fingerprint pattern, and signature recognition. This requires the relevant scanning device, such as a fingerprint reader, and a database of biometric information (template).

BIOS
(Basic Input/Output System) Firmware that contains programs and information relating to the basic operation of PC components such as drives, keyboard, video display, and ports. It also contains specific routines to allow set-up configuration to be viewed and edited and it contains the self-diagnostic Power-On Self-Test (POST) program used to detect fundamental faults in PC components. BIOS can also be used to secure components not protected by the OS by specifying a supervisor password (to prevent tampering with BIOS settings) and a user password (to boot the PC).

BIOS setup
(Basic Input/Output System setup) Another name for the setup program used to configure system firmware settings. Also known as CMOS setup or UEFI setup.

bitmap image data
A pixel-by-pixel image sent to a printer to print a file.

blacklisting
An address added to the black list is prohibited from connecting to any port.

blanking plate
Metal strips that cover unused adapter slots in the case so that proper air flow is maintained within the system case.

blaster
See **IR**.

BLE
(Bluetooth Low Energy) A radio-based technology designed for small battery-powered devices that transmit small amounts of data infrequently. BLE is not backwards-compatible with "classic" Bluetooth, though a device can support both standards simultaneously.

Blu-ray drive
An optical drive for reading, and if so equipped, writing to Blu-ray disc media.

Most drives can also read CD and DVD discs.

Bluetooth
Short-range radio-based technology, working at up to 10 m (30 feet) at up to 1 Mbps used to connect peripherals (such as mice, keyboards, and printers) and for communication between two devices (such as a laptop and smartphone).

bookmark
A record of a website or web page that you visited.

boot device priority
See **boot sequence**.

boot sequence
The order in which the system firmware searches devices for a boot manager.

BRI
(Basic Rate Interface) A class of ISDN service that provides two 64 Kbps (B channels) for data and one 16 Kbps (D channel) for link management control signals

bridge
A bridge can be used to divide an overloaded network into separate segments. Intrasegment traffic (traffic between devices on the same segment) remains within this segment and cannot affect the other segments. A bridge works most efficiently if the amount of intersegment traffic (traffic between devices on different segments) is kept low. Segments on either side of a bridge are in separate collision domains but the same broadcast domain. The function of bridges is now typically performed by switches.

broadband
The technical meaning of broadband is a transmission that divides the available media bandwidth into a number of transmission paths or channels. WAN signaling generally uses this form of transmission and consequently the term is used generally to refer to 2 MBps+ Internet links such as DSL or cable.

broadcast address
A packet sent to all hosts on the local network (or subnet). Routers do not ordinarily forward broadcast traffic. The broadcast address of IP is one where the host bits are all set to 1; at the MAC layer, it is the address ff:ff:ff:ff:ff:ff.

BSSID
(Basic Service Set Identifier) The MAC address of the access point.

Bubblejet
The term used by the Canon company to refer to their **thermal inkjet print method.**

burning
In optical discs, the process of using a special laser used to transform the dye to mimic the pits and lands of a premastered CD.

bus
Buses are the connections between components on the motherboard and peripheral devices attached to the computer. Buses are available in industry standard formats, each with its own advantages and disadvantages. The standard functions of a bus are to provide data sharing, memory addressing, power supply, and timing. Common bus types include PCI, PCI Express, and USB.

bus mastering
Feature of a bus allowing devices to communicate with one another without going through the CPU. Bus mastering is supported by most bus types, including PCI, SCSI, and ATA (in "Ultra DMA" modes).

cache
A small block of high-speed memory that enhances performance by pre-loading (caching) code and data from relatively slow system memory and passing it to the CPU on demand.

CAD
(Computer-Aided Design) Software that makes technical drawings and schematics easier to produce and revise.

calibration (printer)
The process by which the printer determines the appropriate print density or color balance, or how much toner to use.

CAM
(Computer Aided Manufacturing) Software that can control machine tools found in manufacturing environments.

CAN
(Campus area network) A network that spans multiple nearby buildings.

capacitor
An electrical component that stores electrical energy and is often used to regulate voltages. It can hold a charge after the power is removed.

CATV
(Cable Access TV) Access to television stations over a coaxial cable connected to a TV, set-top box, or computer.

CCD
(Charge Coupled Device) A type of microchip widely used as a digital image sensor. Each element in a CCD converts light captured by a photodiode into a proportional electric charge, which is then amplified, sampled, and stored as a digital value. The number of elements determines the resolution.

CCFL
(Cold Cathode Fluorescent Lamp) A type of lamp providing a bright, clear light source. CCFLs are used for LCD backlights and scanners.

CD drive
An optical drive consisting of a spindle motor to spin the disc, a laser and lens to read the disc, and a tracking system to move the laser and lens assembly.

CD-R
Compact disks containing a layer with photosensitive dye in which a laser transforms the dye to mimic the pits and lands of a premastered CD.

CD-ROM
(Compact Disc - Read Only Memory) An optical storage technology. The discs can normally hold 700 MB of data or 80 minutes of audio data. Recordable and re-writable CDs (and DVDs) are a popular backup solution for home users. They are also useful for archiving material. Unlike magnetic media, the data on the disc cannot be changed (assuming that the disc is closed to prevent further rewriting in the case of RW media). This makes them useful for preserving tamper-proof records.

CD-RW
Compact disks containing a heat sensitive compound whose properties can be changed between crystalline and amorphous by a special laser.

CDMA
(Code Division Multiple Access) Method of multiplexing a communications channel using a code to key the modulation of a particular signal. CDMA is associated with Sprint and Verizon cellular phone networks.

cellular data
Connecting to the Internet via the device's cell phone radio and the handset's cellular network provider.

cellular radio
A component in a mobile device that is capable of switching frequencies automatically when moving between network cells without losing the connection.

channels
Paths between PATA drives and motherboard, called IDE1 and IDE2, or primary (PRI IDE) and secondary (SEC IDE).

chassis
See **system case**.

chip creep
Cards can work free from a slot over time, though this is not common.

chipset
The chipset provides communications between different components by implementing various controllers (for memory, graphics, I/O, and so on). Historically, "fast" controllers (memory and video) were part of a "northbridge" chipset, placed close to the CPU and system memory. Slower buses were part of a "southbridge" chipset. In modern PC architecture, video and memory controllers are part of the CPU (on-die), the northbridge would mostly handle PCI

Express adapters, and the southbridge would host SATA, USB, audio and LAN functions, plus PCI/PATA legacy bus support.

CIFS
(Common Internet File System) Another term for **SMB**.

CIS
(Contact Image Sensor) A type of digital imaging sensor. An array of LEDs strobing between red, blue, and green light are used to illuminate an object. The reflected light is captured through a lens onto an image sensor.

cleaning blade
See **cleaning unit**.

cleaning unit
Parts such as a blade, roller, or brush that rest on the surface of a laser printer's photosensitive drum that are used to clean excess toner and remove residual charge from the photoconductor.

client-side virtualization
Any solution designed to run on desktops or workstations in which the user interacts with the virtualization host directly.

clock battery
See **RTC battery**.

closed network
A network where the elements of the network are all known to the system vendor and there is no connectivity to wider computer data networks.

cloud computing
Any environment where software (Software as a Service and Platform as a Service) or computer/network resources (Infrastructure as a Service and Network as a Service) are provided to an end user who has no knowledge of or responsibility for how the service is provided. Cloud services provide elasticity of resources and pay-per-use charging models. Cloud access arrangements can be public, hosted private, or private (this type of cloud could be onsite or offsite relative to the other business units).

cloud-based network controller
A cloud-based management system that enables registering and monitoring all of the organization's networks, clients, and servers.

CMOS
(complementary metal oxide semiconductor) A type of integrated circuit with a wide range of applications, including static RAM (for firmware and flash memory) and imaging sensors.

CMOS battery
(complementary metal oxide semiconductor battery) A battery designed to last 5 to 10 years to maintain CMOS settings.

CMOS setup
(complementary metal oxide semiconductor setup) Another name for the setup program used to configure system firmware settings. Also known as BIOS setup or UEFI setup.

CMP
(chip-level multiprocessing) Multiple processors combined on the same die.

CMTS
(Cable Modem Termination System) Equipment used by cable companies to allow computers to send and receive IP packets by inserting the packets into MPEG frames over an RF signal and reverses the process for data coming from a cable modem.

CMYK Color Model
(Cyan Magenta Yellow Key [Black] color model) Subtractive color model used by print devices. CMYK printing involves use of halftone screens. Four screens (or layers) of dots printed in each of the colors are overlaid. The size and density of the dots on each layer produces different shades of color and is viewed as a continuous tone image.

coaxial cable
Cable type using two separate conductors that share a common axis (hence the term co-axial). Coax cables are categorized using the Radio Grade (RG) "standard". Coax is considered obsolete in terms of LAN applications but is still widely used for

CCTV networks and as drop cables for cable TV (CATV).

collated
A print job where all pages of the first copy are printed, followed by all pages of the next copy.

collision domain
The network segment in which contention collisions occur.

color calibration
The process of adjusting display and scanner settings so that color input and output are balanced.

color depth
Each pixel in a digital image can be one of a number of colors. The range of colors available for each pixel is referred to as the color depth. Providing a greater range of colors requires more memory. If 1-bit is allowed for color depth, two colors (white and black) are allowed. A VGA video system supports 4-bit color (16 possible colors). SVGA supports 8-bit (256 colors), 16-bit (65,536 colors), 24-bit (16,777,216 colors), and 32-bit (deep color).

COM port
(communications port) Windows' representation of a computer's serial port(s), numbered sequentially (COM1, COM2...).

conductor
A material that is good at conducting electricity, such as gold, copper, or tin. These are used for wires and contacts.

connections
The physical access points that enable a computer to communicate with internal or external devices.

contact
A record with fields for name, address, email address(es), phone numbers, notes, and other information related to the entity defined in the record.

container virtualization
A virtualization method that doesn't use a hypervisor and instead enforces resources separate at the operating system level with isolated containers for each user instance to run in with its own allocated CPU and memory resources, but all processes are run through the native OS kernel.

contention
A media access method in which nodes compete or cooperate among themselves for media access time. Also called competitive media access.

contrast ratio
A measure of the ratio of luminance (brightness) of whites to blacks, indicating the color performance of a display or scanner. A device supporting a higher contrast ratio is able to display a wider range of colors and deliver "true" black.

Control Center
An iOS feature that is accessed by swiping up from the bottom of the display to access iOS feature settings.

core clock speed
The speed at which the CPU runs internal processes and accesses L1 and L2 cache.

corona
An assembly within a laser printer that contains a wire (the corona wire), which is responsible for charging the paper.

corporate mail gateway
A connection between mail servers that use different communications protocols or between two networks that use the same or different protocols.

cover
The removable portion of the system case that allows access to the motherboard and internal components.

CPU
(Central Processing Unit) The principal microprocessor in a computer or smartphone responsible for running operating system and applications software.

CPU form factor
(central processing unit form factor) The size, shape, and connection method of the CPU.

critical update
A widely released, non-security update to fix a critical issue.

CRM
(Customer Relationship Management) Software designed to manage an organization's customer (and potential customer) relationships and interactions.

crossover cable
A twisted pair cable wired as T568A on one end and as T568B on the other end.

CSV
(Comma Separated Values) A file format in which data is stored using commas or another character to separate fields in the data. Typically, data has been exported from a spreadsheet or a database.

current
The actual flow of electrons, measured in Amps (I).

cylinder
The aggregate of all tracks that reside in the same location on every disk surface.

DAC
(Digital-to-Analog Converter) A sound card component that converts the digital signals generated by the CPU to an analog electrical signal that can drive the speakers.

daughter board
A circuit board that connects to the motherboard to provide extra expansion slots or connectors. Typically, these are used in slimline case designs so that adapter cards can be installed parallel to the motherboard, reducing the height of the case.

DB-9
Although the original serial port used a 25-pin male D connector, most PCs today use a male DB-9 (9-pin) port. (See also **serial port**.)

DC
(direct current) PCs and most computer components function by using power supplied in the form of direct current. This is normally at low voltage and is produced by stepping down the voltage from the building supply. Direct current, unlike alternating current, does not oscillate between positive and negative states.

DDR SDRAM
(Double Data Rate Synchronous Dynamic Random Access Memory) A standard for SDRAM where data is transferred twice per clock cycle (making the maximum data rate 64x the bus speed in bps). DDR2/DDR3/DDR4 SDRAM uses lower voltage chips and higher bus speeds.

default gateway
The default gateway is an IP configuration parameter that identifies the location of a router on the local subnet that the host can use to contact other networks.

default mask
In the early days of IP addressing, the network ID was determined automatically from the first octet of the address. When subnet masks were introduced, the "default" masks (255.0.0.0, 255.255.0.0, and 255.255.255.0) that corresponded to treating the first octet as classful were commonly described as "class A", "class B", and "class C" masks. The Internet no longer uses classful addressing but many LANs use the private IP address ranges and the default masks.

defense in depth
Configuring security controls on hosts (endpoints) as well as providing network (perimeter) security, physical security, and administrative controls.

defragmentation
See **disk defragmentation**.

desktop computer
A computing device designed to be placed on or near a user's desk.

detac corona
A strip that removes the charge to prevent paper curl in a laser printer.

developer roller
A magnetized roller to which toner adheres during the printing process. See also **developer unit**.

developer unit
Assembly that applies toner to areas of the photoconductor where charge has been removed by the laser. The main components are a toner hopper, transfer roller, waste toner hopper, a screw or blade to stir the toner, and a doctor blade to ensure the correct level of toner on the developer roller.

DHCP Server
(Dynamic Host Configuration Protocol server) A networking service that allows a client to request an appropriate IP configuration from a server. The server is configured with a range of addresses to lease. Hosts can be allocated an IP address dynamically or be assigned a reserved IP address, based on the host's MAC address. The server can also provide other configuration information, such as the location of DNS servers. DHCP utilizes UDP ports 67 and 68. It is important to monitor the network to ensure that only valid DHCP servers are running on the network.

dial-up
A remote network access method that utilizes the local telephone line (Plain Old Telephone System [POTS]) to establish a connection between two computers fitted with modems. Dial-up is a legacy method of Internet access. It may still be deployed for special administrative purposes or as an emergency backup connection method. Configuration is generally a case of setting the telephone number, username, and password.

die
The area on a silicon chip containing millions of transistors and signal pathways created by the hoping process.

digital assistant
A voice interface designed to respond to natural language commands and queries.

digital camera
A version of a 35mm film camera where the film is replaced by light-sensitive diodes (an array of CCDs [Charge Coupled Devices]) and electronic storage media (typically a flash memory card). The sensitivity of the array determines the maximum resolution of the image, measured in megapixels.

digital display
A computer monitor that accepts a digital signal. Flat-panel monitors use digital signals and only support lower resolutions by interpolating the image, which can make it appear fuzzy.

digitizer
As part of a touchscreen assembly, the digitizer is a touch-sensitive glass panel covering the LCD. The panel converts touch events to digital signals that can be interpreted as different types of input.

dim display
When a mobile device has the **backlight**set to its lowest setting and the automatic light adjustment is disabled, or the phone is set to conserve power by auto-dimming the light.

DIMM
(Dual In-line Memory Module) The standard packaging for system memory. There are different pin configurations for different RAM types (DDR SDRAM [184], DDR2/3 SDRAM [240], and DDR4 SDRAM [288]).

diode
A valve, allowing current to flow in one direction only. These are used in a computer's power supply and as protection for components.

direct thermal printer
A thermal printer that uses heated pins to form images directly onto specially coated thermal paper.

disk defragmentation
Fragmentation occurs when a data file is not saved to contiguous sectors on a disk. This decreases performance by making the disk read/write heads move between fragments. Defragmentation is a software routine that compacts files back into contiguous areas of the disk. The process can be run from a command-line using the defrag utility, but it is more often run from Windows.

disk mirroring
See **mirroring**.

disk striping
A disk array access pattern where data is written in stripes to two or more disks sequentially, improving performance. Note that a RAID 0 striped volume provides no redundancy, and if any of the physical disks in the set fails, the whole volume will be lost.

disk thrashing
A state in which the main memory is filled up, pages are swapped in and out of virtual memory—which needs to be written to the hard disk—in rapid succession, leading to possible early drive failure.

DisplayPort
Digital A/V interface developed by VESA. DisplayPort supports some cross-compatibility with DVI and HDMI devices.

distended capacitors
Capacitors that are swollen or bulging or emitting residue indicates that they have been damaged or could have failed due to a manufacturing defect.

distinguished name
A unique identifier for any given resource within the LDAP directory.

DLP (video)
(Digital Light Processing) Mirror-based projector technology developed by Texas Instruments.

DMZ
(Demilitarized Zone) A private network connected to the Internet must be protected against intrusion from the Internet. However, certain services may need to be made publicly accessible from the Internet (web and email, for instance). One solution is to put such servers in a DMZ. The idea of a DMZ is that traffic cannot pass through it. If communication is required between hosts on either side of a DMZ, a host within the DMZ acts as a proxy. It takes the request and checks it. If the request is valid, it re-transmits it to the destination. External hosts have no idea about what (if anything) is behind the DMZ. A DMZ is implemented using either two firewalls (screened subnet) or a single three-legged firewall (one with three network ports).

DNS
(Domain Name System) A network service that provides names to IP address mapping services on the Internet and large intranets. DNS name servers host the database for domains for which they are authoritative. Root servers hold details of the top-level domains. DNS resolvers perform queries or lookups to service client requests. The DNS protocol utilizes TCP/UDP port 53.

docking station
A sophisticated type of port replicator designed to provide additional ports (such as network or USB) and functionality (such as expansion slots and drives) to a portable computer when used at a desk.

DOCSIS
(Data Over Cable Service Interface Specification) A global telecommunications standard that enables data to be sent over cable modems in a CATV system.

domain name
The unique and officially registered name that identifies a company, organization, or individual.

DoS
(Denial of Service) A network attack that aims to disrupt a service, usually by overloading it.

dot matrix printer
A type of impact printer that uses a set of pins to strike the ribbon to create printed characters and images using combinations of dots.

dotted decimal notation
32 bit addresses displayed in human readable format using base-10 numbering.

DRAM
(Dynamic Random Access Memory) A type of volatile memory that stores each bit of data as a charge within a single transistor. Each transistor must be refreshed periodically. Standard DRAM is the lowest common denominator of the DRAM types. Modern PCs use a DRAM derivative to store data (Double Data Rate **SDRAM**).

drive controller
The controller is the circuitry in the disk unit that allows it to put data on the bus, which the HBA shuttles to the CPU or RAM.

drive enclosure
An external case that holds one or more disks and typically connects to the computer through USB or Thunderbolt ports.

drive encryption
The entire contents of the drive (or volume), including system files and folders, are encrypted.

driver
Software that creates an interface between a device and the operating system. It may also include tools for configuring and optimizing the device.

drop cable
Solid cables used for permanent links such as cable running through walls.

DSL
(Digital Subscriber Line) A technology for transferring data over voice-grade telephone lines. DSL uses the higher frequencies available in a copper telephone line as a communications channel. The use of a filter prevents this from contaminating voice traffic with noise. There are various "flavors" of DSL, notably S(ymmetric)DSL, A(symmetric)DSL, and V(ery HIgh Bit Rate)DSL.

DSLAM
(DSL Access Multiplier) A network device at the telecommunications central office that connects subscribers with the Internet.

DSLR
(Digital Single Lens Reflex) A digital camera that replicates the features of compact 35mm film cameras, preserving the traditional viewfinder method of picture composition and supporting replaceable lenses and manual adjustments.

DSP chip
(Digital Signal Processor chip) The basis of a sound card containing one or more DACs. It also provides functions for playing digital sound (synthesis) and driving MIDI compatible devices.

DTLS
(Datagram Transport Layer Security) TLS used with UDP applications, such as some VPN solutions.

DTP
(Desktop Publishing) An application similar to word processing but with more emphasis on the formatting and layout of documents than on editing the text.

dual heat pipe
Two **heat pipe** tubes to provide better cooling.

dual rail
A power supply with two +12 V rails.

dual-channel memory
Memory controller with two pathways through the bus to the CPU so that 128 bits of data can be transferred per transaction.

duplexing assembly
A device that enables a printer or scanner to use both sides of a page automatically.

DVD
(Digital Video/Versatile Disk) An optical storage technology. DVDs offer higher capacities (4.7 GB per layer) than the preceding CD-ROM format. As with CDs, recordable and re-writable forms of DVD exist, though there are numerous competing formats (notably ±R and ±RW and DVD-RAM).

DVD drive
An optical drive similar to a CD drive, but with a different encoding method and a shorter wavelength laser. Typically can read and burn CD and DVD media.

DVI
(Digital Video Interface) A video adapter designed to replace the VGA port used by CRT monitors. The DVI interface supports digital only or digital and analog signaling.

dye sublimation printer
See **thermal dye transfer printer**.

e-ink
(electrophoretic ink) Micro-encapsulated black and white particles, electronically

manipulated to create images and text on an **e-reader**.

e-magazine
A digital magazine that can be read on an electronic device such as an **e-reader**, smartphone, tablet, or computer.

e-newspaper
A digital newspaper that can be read on an electronic device such as an **e-reader**, smartphone, tablet, or computer.

e-reader
A tablet-sized device designed for reading rather than general-purpose computing.

EAP
(Extensible Authentication Protocol) Framework for negotiating authentication methods, supporting a range of authentication devices. EAP-TLS uses PKI certificates, Protected EAP (PEAP) creates a TLS-protected tunnel between the supplicant and authenticator to secure the user authentication method, and Lightweight EAP (LEAP) is a password-based mechanism used by Cisco.

early-life failure rate
A method of calculating how quickly a device will fail through accelerated testing.

EAS
(Exchange ActiveSync) Microsoft's synchronization protocol that enables mobile devices to connect to an Exchange Server to access mail, calendar, and contacts.

ebook
A digital book that can be read on an electronic device such as an **e-reader**, smartphone, tablet, or computer.

ECC
(Error Checking and Correcting [or Error Correcting Code]) System memory (RAM) with built-in error correction security. It is more expensive than normal memory and requires motherboard support. It is typically only used in servers.

EDR
(Enhanced Data Rate) An option in the Bluetooth specification that allows faster data rates and potentially better battery life.

EIR database
(Equipment Identity Register database) A database where **IMEI** numbers are stored. A lost or stolen device IMEI is marked as invalid.

Electrostatic discharge
See **ESD**.

electrostatic latent image
Representation of the image to be printed created as a series of raster lines with charge/no-charge areas.

embedded system
A computer system that is designed to perform a specific, dedicated function, such as a microcontroller in a medical drip or components in a control system managing a water treatment plant.

EMF
(Enhanced MetaFile) When using EMF, the software application and GDI quickly produce a partial print job. Control is then released back to the user while spooling continues in the background (GDI and the print driver are called to complete the processing of the job).

encryption
Scrambling the characters used in a message so that the message can be seen but not understood or modified unless it can be deciphered. Encryption provides for a secure means of transmitting data and authenticating users. It is also used to store data securely. Encryption uses different types of cipher and one or more keys. The size of the key is one factor in determining the strength of the encryption product.

encryption key
A specific piece of information that is used with an algorithm to perform encryption and decryption in cryptography.

Endpoint Management Server
Facilitates the defense in depth process by identifying computing devices running on the network and ensuring that they are securely configured. This can include applying OS and antivirus updates

automatically, cataloging software applications installed on each device, applying security policies, retrieving and analyzing log files, and monitoring performance and other status alerts.

energy
The amount of power consumed by a device over time, measured in Watt-hours (or more typically Kilowatt-hours [kWh]).

EP drum
(Electrostatic Photographic drum) The component in a laser printer that carries the electrical charge to attract toner and then to transfer the toner to the paper.

EPD
(Electronic Paper Display) A low-power display using **e-ink** to create a display that mimics the look of text on paper without using a backlight or glossy surface.

EPS specification
(Entry-level Power Supply specification) 8-pin +12 V connectors developed initially for server-class hardware.

EPT
(Extended Page Table) The term used for SLAT extensions by Intel.

erase lamp
See **cleaning unit**.

eSATA
(external Serial Advanced Technology Attachment) An external interface for SATA connections, enabling you to connect external SATA drives to PCs.

eSATAp
A non-standard powered port used by some vendors that is compatible with both USB and SATA (with an eSATAp cable).

ESD
(electrostatic discharge) The release of a charge from a metal or plastic surface that occurs when a potential difference is formed between the charged object and an oppositely charged conductive object. This electrical discharge can damage silicon chips and computer components if they are exposed to it.

Ethernet
A family of networking technologies that provide connectivity by using Ethernet network adapters, contention-based media access, and twisted pair, coax, or fiber media.

evil twin
In an evil twin attack, the attacker creates a malicious wireless access point masquerading as a genuine one, enabling the attacker to harvest confidential information as users connect via the AP.

Exchange
Microsoft Exchange is a client-based email system that allows mobile devices to sync with the server.

expansion bus
The external bus that allows additional components to be connected to the computer.

expansion cards
A printed circuit board that is installed in a slot on a system board to provide special functions for customizing or extending a computer's capabilities. Also referred to as adapter card, I/O card, add-in, add-on, or board.

expansion slots
Connection slots on the motherboard in which adapter cards can be installed to extend the range of functions the computer can perform.

Extended Service Set
Basic service sets can be grouped into an extended service set.

external transfer rate
A measure of how fast data can be transferred to the CPU across the bus.

extranet
A network of semi-trusted hosts, typically representing business partners, suppliers, or customers. Hosts must authenticate to join the extranet.

fast charge
A general technology for quickly charging mobile devices using varying voltages to speed up charging times.

FDE
(full disk encryption) Encryption of all data on a disk (including system files, temporary files, and the pagefile) can be accomplished via a supported OS, third-party software, or at the controller level by the disk device itself. Used with a strong authentication method, this mitigates against data theft in the event that the device is lost or stolen. The key used to encrypt the disk can either be stored on a USB stick or smart card or in a Trusted Platform Module.

FDM
(fused deposition modeling) See **FFF**.

federated identity management
An agreement between enterprises to allow users to authenticate using the same information to all networks within the agreed upon group.

feed assembly
In a thermal printer, a stepper motor turns a rubber-coated roller to feed the paper through the print mechanism using friction feed.

feed roller
Roller that works with a separation roller or pad to feed just one sheet of paper (or other media) into the printer mechanism.

female port
A port that has hole connectors.

FFF
(fused filament fabrication) A 3D printing method which lays down each layer of filament at high temperature, and as layers are extruded, adjacent layers are allowed to cool and bond together before additional layers are added to the object.

filament
In 3D printing, the spool of plastic or other material used to create the three-dimensional object.

firewall
Hardware or software that filters traffic passing into or out of a network. A basic packet-filtering firewall works at Layer 3 (Network). Packets can be filtered depending on several criteria (inbound or outbound, IP address, and port number). More advanced firewalls (proxy and stateful inspection) can examine higher layer information, to provide enhanced security.

firmware
This refers to software instructions stored semi-permanently (embedded) on a hardware device. Modern types of firmware are stored in flash memory and can be updated more easily than legacy programmable Read Only Memory (ROM) types.

flash memory
Flash RAM is similar to a ROM chip in that it retains information even when power is removed, but it adds flexibility in that it can be reprogrammed with new contents quickly. Flash memory is used in USB thumb drives and memory cards for removable storage and in Solid State Drives (SSDs), designed to replicate the function of hard drives.

flatbed scanner
A type of scanner where the object is placed on a glass faceplate and the scan head moved underneath it.

fonts
The display and word processing programs can make use of any typeface designs (fonts) installed on the local system. Most Windows fonts are OpenType (replacing the earlier TrueType) but some design programs and printers also use Adobe Type 1 fonts.

force stop
An Android option to close an unresponsive app.

formatter board
In a laser printer, the unit that exposes and processes all of the data received from the computer and coordinates the steps needed to produce the finished page.

FPU
(Floating Point Unit) A math co-processor built into the CPU that performs calculations on floating point numbers.

FQDN
(Fully Qualified Domain Name) The full name of any host which reflects the hierarchy from most specific (the host) to the least specific (the top level domain followed by the root).

frame rate
The number of times the image in a video stream changes per second. This can be expressed in Hertz or Frames per Second (fps).

frequency response
The volume that can be produced at different frequencies.

friction feed
An impact printer mechanism that uses two rolls placed one on top of the other to force individual cut sheets of paper or envelopes through the paper path.

front panel
The portion of the system case that provides access to removable media drives, power switch, and LEDs to indicate driver operation.

FRU
(field replaceable unit) An adapter or other component that can be replaced by a technician on-site. Most PC and laptop components are FRUs, while the components of smartphones are not.

FTP
(File Transfer Protocol) A protocol used to transfer files across the Internet. Variants include S(ecure)FTP, FTP with SSL (FTPS and FTPES), and T(rivial)FTP. FTP utilizes ports 20 and 21.

FTTC
(Fiber to the Curb/Cabinet) A fiber optic solution which places the connection on a pole or cabinet at the curb, then coax or twisted pair cables carry the signal from this point to the home or business.

FTTH
(Fiber to the Home) A fiber optic solution which places the connection inside the home or residence.

FTTN
(Fiber to the Node) A fiber optic solution which places the connection within one mile of customers with the final connections made using existing phone or cable lines.

FTTP
(Fiber to the Premises) A fiber optic solution which places the connection inside the premises.

fuse
A circuit breaker designed to protect the device and users of the device from faulty wiring or supply of power (overcurrent protection).

fuser assembly
The part of a laser printer that fixes toner to media. This is typically a combination of a heat and pressure roller, though non-contact flash fusing using xenon lamps is found on some high-end printers.

game pad
A controller containing multiple buttons and toggles, each of which controls a different action in a video game or program, typically held and manipulated with two hands.

gaming rig
A computer used for standalone or online gaming, often connected to surround sound speakers or headphones, sometimes integrated with virtual reality goggles. May use specialized gaming equipment such as gaming controllers, joysticks, gaming mouse, and keyboard.

GDI
(Graphics Device Interface) The Windows XP component responsible for drawing graphics objects. Cheaper printers use GDI as the print processor. Windows Vista and later have a redesigned display/print architecture called Windows Presentation Foundation, but retain compatibility with GDI applications.

geolocation
The process of identifying the real-world geographic location of an object, often by associating a location such as a street address with an IP address, hardware address, Wi-Fi positioning system, GPS

coordinates, or some other form of information.

global address
In an IPv6 address, an address that is unique on the Internet (equivalent to public addresses in IPv4).

gloss coating
A display coating that helps the display appear richer, but reflects more light, which can cause problems with screen glare and reflections of background objects. Compare with **matte coating**.

Google account
An account from Google used to access an Android device and related online services.

Gov Cloud
A Google cloud service that can be used by branches of the U.S. government, but is not available to other consumers or businesses.

GP registers
(General Purpose registers) Registers that store data from the CPU's basic instruction set. 32-bit processors have 32-bit GP registers for the x86/IA-32 instruction set; 64-bit processors are so-called because they have 64-bit GP registers. CPUs also support larger registers to optimize graphics processing.

GPS
(Global Positioning System) Means of determining a receiver's position on the Earth based on information received from GPS satellites. The receiver must have line-of-sight to the GPS satellites.

GPT
(GUID Partition Table) A modern disk partitioning system allowing large numbers of partitions and very large partition sizes.

GPU
(Graphics Processing Unit) a Type of microprocessor used on dedicated video adapter cards or within a CPU with integrated graphics capability.

graphics adapter
See **video card**.

grounded
An equipment ground provides a safe path for electrical current to flow away in the event that a device or cable is faulty. Self-grounding removes any static potential difference between a technician's clothes and body and a device they are handling, reducing the risk of damaging the component through Electrostatic Discharge (ESD).

GSM
(Global System for Mobile Communication) Standard for cellular radio communications and data transfer. GSM phones use a SIM card to identify the subscriber and network provider. 4G and later data standards are developed for GSM.

gyroscope
Mobile device technology that can determine the rotation of a device with a sensor that measures the rotation of the device. (See also **accelerometer/gyroscope**).

haptic feedback
Tactile response on a touchscreen device, typically a slight vibration of the surface, although the entire device can vibrate in certain responses.

hard copy
Printer output of electronic documents onto paper.

hardware RAID solution
A method of creating volumes from an array of physical disks by using a plug-in controller card or the motherboard, independently of the installed OS.

HAV
(Hardware Assisted Virtualization) Instruction set extensions (Intel VT-x and AMD-V) that facilitate the operation of virtual machines.

HBA
(host bus adapter) A component allowing storage devices to exchange data with a computer system using a particular interface (PATA, SATA, SCSI, and so on). Motherboards will come with built-in host adapters and more can be added as expansion cards if necessary.

HDD
(Hard Disk Drive) A device providing persistent mass storage for a PC (saving data when the computer is turned off). Data is stored using platters with a magnetic coating that are spun under disk heads that can read and write to locations on each platter (sectors). A HDD installed within a PC is referred to as the fixed disk. HDDs are often used with enclosures as portable storage or as Network Attached Storage (NAS).

HDMI
(High Definition Multimedia Interface) High-specification digital connector for audio-video equipment.

head unit
In a car, the unified hardware interface for the audio system and related components.

headset
A device that combines headphones and microphone in a single device.

heat pipe
A sealed tube containing water or ethanol coolant. The liquid close to the heat source evaporates then condenses at a cooler point in the pipe and flows back towards the heat source.

heat sink
A passive heat exchanger that dissipates heat from a source such as a CPU and transfers it, normally via an enlarged surface area, to another medium such as air or water.

heat spreader
Similar to a **heat pipe** except it is a flat container rather than a pipe.

heating element
In a thermal printer, the component within the printer that is heated to react to chemicals in **thermal paper** to change color, creating images on the thermal paper.

heuristic
Monitoring technique that allows dynamic pattern matching based on past experience rather than relying on pre-loaded signatures.

HFC Cable
(Hybrid Fiber Coax cable) A cable Internet connection is usually available along with a cable telephone/television service (Cable Access TV [CATV]). These networks are often described as Hybrid Fiber Coax (HFC) as they combine a fiber optic core network with coax links to consumer premises equipment, but are more simply just described as "cable." Consumers interface with the service via a cable "modem" (actually functioning more like a bridge).

HIDs
(Human Interface Devices) Peripherals that enable the user to enter data and select commands.

home server PC
Either a **home theater PC (HTPC)** with a slightly expanded role or a repurposed desktop or low-end PC server used primarily for file storage, media streaming, and printer sharing.

host controller
A hardware component of the USB subsystem responsible for recognizing when a USB device is attached or removed from the system, monitors the device status, provides power to the USB devices, and controls the flow of data between the USB host and USB devices.

host firewall
See **personal firewall**.

host ID
In an IP address, the portion of the address that uniquely identifies a host on a particular IP network

host name
The description name assigned to a computer.

host-hinted mode
A SATA standard (version 3.2) that defines a set of commands to allow the host computer to specify how the cache should be used.

hot swappable
A device that can be added or removed without having to restart the operating system.

hotspot
A location served by some sort of device offering Internet access via Wi-Fi.

HT
(HyperThreading) Intel CPU architecture implemented on many Pentium 4 models. HT exposes two or more logical processors to the OS, delivering performance benefits similar to SMP.

HTPC
(Home Theater PC) A PC used in place of consumer appliances such as Personal Video Recorders (PVRs) to watch and record TV broadcasts and play movies and music.

HTT
(HyperThreading technology) Intel's term for HyperThreading.

HTTP
(HyperText Transfer Protocol) The protocol used to provide web content to browsers. HTTP uses port 80. HTTPS(ecure) provides for encrypted transfers, using SSL/TLS and port 443.

HTTPS
(HTTP Secure) A protocol that provides for encrypted transfers, using SSL/TLS and port 443.

hub
An OSI layer 1 (Physical) network device used to implement a star network topology on legacy Ethernet networks. Hubs may also be known as "multiport repeaters" or concentrators. They are the central points of connection for segments and act like repeaters so that every segment receives signals sent from any other segment.

HVAC
(Heating, Ventilation, and Air Conditioning) The building environmental heating and cooling services and the control of those systems.

hybrid drive
A drive in which a portion is SSD, which functions as a large cache, containing frequently accessed data and a magnetic disk portion which is only spun up when non-cached data is accessed.

I/O addresses
(Input/Output addresses) Input/output peripherals have a special area of memory in the range 0000-FFFF set aside to allow data reading and writing functions. This is normally configured by Plug-and-Play but can be set manually using Device Manager.

I/O port
A device connection through which data can be sent and received.

IA-32
See **x86-32**.

IA-64
The 64-bit instruction set developed by Intel for its Itanium server CPU platform that never gained acceptance in the PC market.

IaaS
(Infrastructure as a Service) A cloud computing service that enables a consumer to outsource computing equipment purchases and running their own data center.

IC
(integrated circuit) A **silicon chip** embedded on a ceramic plate.

ICMP
(Internet Control Message Protocol) IP-level protocol for reporting errors and status information supporting the function of troubleshooting utilities such as ping.

IDE
(Integrated Development Environment) A programming environment that typically includes a code editor containing an autocomplete feature to help you write code, a debugger to help you find coding errors, and an **interpreter** that translates the **script file** code into machine readable code the computer can **execute**.

IDS
(Intrusion Detection System) Software or security appliance designed to monitor network traffic (NIDS) or configuration files and logs on a host (HIDS) to record and detect unusual activity. Many systems can automatically take preventive action (Intrusion Prevention System [IPS]).

Detection is either signature-based or anomaly-based (or both). IDS software typically requires a lengthy period of configuration and "training" to recognize baseline "normal" activity.

IEEE 802.11
A series of Wi-Fi standards used to implement Wireless Local Area Networks.

illuminance
The light projecting power. Compare with **luminance**.

imaging drum
See **EP drum**.

IMAP
(Internet Message Access Protocol) A TCP/IP application protocol providing a means for a client to access email messages stored in a mailbox on a remote server. Unlike POP3, messages persist on the server after the client has downloaded them. IMAP also supports mailbox management functions, such as creating subfolders and access to the same mailbox by more than one client at the same time. IMAP4 utilizes TCP port number 143.

IMEI number
(International Mobile Equipment Identity number) A number that uniquely identifies a mobile device on a GSM network.

impact printer
Typically, a dot matrix printer, this uses pressure to transfer ink from a ribbon onto paper in a particular pattern, similar to the mechanism of a typewriter.

IMSI number
(International Mobile Subscriber Identity number) A number that uniquely identifies a mobile subscriber.

incident
Something that is not normal and disrupts regular operations in the computing environment.

infrastructure mode
Wi-Fi network configuration in which each client device or station is configured to connect to the network via an access point.

ink cartridge
In an inkjet printer, a cartridge containing an ink reservoir and sensors to detect the amount of remaining ink, typically with separate cartridges for cyan, magenta, yellow, and black ink. Most ink cartridges also contain the print head for the printer.

ink dispersion printer
Better known as inkjets, this is a type of printer where colored ink is sprayed onto the paper using microscopic nozzles in the print head. There are two main types of ink dispersion system: thermal shock (heating the ink to form a bubble that bursts through the nozzles) and piezoelectric (using a tiny element that changes shape to act as a pump).

ink jet printer
See **ink dispersion printer**.

input voltage
A PSU setting to set North American power supplies to 115 V and UK power supplies to 240 V.

instruction set
The machine language code and commands the CPU can process.

insulator
A material that does not conduct electricity, such as rubber or plastic.

integrated GPU
(integrated graphics processing unit) A graphics adapter built into the motherboard or the CPU.

interface
The point at which two devices connect and communicate with each other.

internal transfer rate
A measure of how fast read/write operations are performed on the disk platters. Also known as data or disk transfer rate.

Internet backbone
The major infrastructure of the Internet.

intranet
A network designed for information processing within a company or organization. An intranet uses the same

technologies as the Internet but is owned and managed by a company or organization.

inventory management
An inventory is a list of things, usually stored in a database. Inventories are usually compiled for assets.

IoT
(Internet of Things) The global network of personal devices (such as phones, tablets, and fitness trackers), home appliances, home control systems, vehicles, and other items that have been equipped with sensors, software, and network connectivity.

IP
(Internet Protocol) The network (Internet) layer protocol in the TCP/IP suite providing packet addressing and routing for all higher level protocols in the suite.

IP scale
(ingress protection scale) An international standard to determine how well electrical enclosures are sealed against dust, water, moisture, and other intrusive materials from entering the enclosure. The ratings scale is defined in the British EN60529:1992 and European IEC 60509:1989 standards.

IPS
(in-plane switching) An LCD panel technology designed to resolve the quality issues inherent in TN panel technology, including strong viewing angle dependence and low-quality color reproduction.

IPS
(Intrusion Protection System) Systems that can automatically take preventive action using signature-based or anomaly-based detection. Also known as network IDS (NIDS).

IPS
(Indoor Positioning Systems) A system that works out a device's location by triangulating its proximity to other radio sources, such as Wi-Fi access points or Bluetooth beacons.

IPSec
(Internet Protocol Security) Layer 3 protocol suite providing security for TCP/IP. It can be used in two modes (transport, where only the data payload is encrypted, and tunnel, where the entire IP packet is encrypted and a new IP header added). IPsec can provide confidentiality and/or integrity. Encryption can be applied using a number of hash (MD5 or SHA) and symmetric (DES or AES) algorithms. Key exchange and security associations are handled by the Internet Key Exchange Protocol. Hosts can be authenticated by a shared secret, PKI, or Kerberos.

IR
(Infrared) Infrared Data Association (IrDA) was a wireless networking standard supporting speeds up to about 4 Mbps. Infrared (IR) sensors are used in mobile devices and with IR blasters to control appliances.

IRQ
(Interrupt Request) A communications channel between a hardware device and the system processor. Originally, when hardware was added to the computer it had to be manually configured with a unique interrupt number (between 0 and 15). Plug-and-Play compatible systems configure resources automatically. The PCI bus introduced IRQ steering, which allowed IRQs to be shared. Modern computers use programmable interrupt controllers, allowing for hundreds of interrupts.

ISDN
(Integrated Services Digital Network) A digital phone/fax/data service used to provide Internet connectivity. There are two classes of ISDN: Basic Rate Interface (BRI) provides two 64 Kbps (B channels) for data and one 16 Kbps (D channel) for link management control signals; Primary Rate Interface (PRI) provides either T1 or E1 capacity levels (23B or 30B) channels, depending on location in the world, and one 64 Kbps D channel.

ISP
(Internet Service Provider) An organization that provides a connection to the Internet and other web- and email-related services. A connection to the ISP's Internet routing

equipment can be made using a variety of methods.

IXPs
(Internet eXchange Points) High bandwidth trunks that connect to the Internet backbone.

jailbreaking
Removing manufacturer restrictions on a device to allow other software, operating systems, or networks to work with a device. Typically refers to iPhone devices.

jitter
A variation in the time it takes for a signal to reach the recipient. Jitter manifests itself as an inconsistent rate of packet delivery. If packet loss or delay is excessive, then noticeable audio or video problems (artifacts) are experienced by users.

joystick
A pivoting stick or lever attached to a base that is used to control movement on a device.

jumper
A small plastic clip containing a metal conductor that fits over two contacts to complete a circuit that configures the motherboard or adapter card one way or another.

keyboard
The oldest PC input device and still fundamental to operating a computer. There are many different designs and layouts for different countries. Some keyboards feature special keys.

keyed port
A port with physical attributes that prevent a connector from being inserted into the port the wrong way around.

KVM switch
(Keyboard Video Mouse switch) A switch supporting a single set of input and output devices controlling a number of PCs. KVM are more typically used with servers but 2-port versions allow a single keyboard, mouse, and display to be used with two PCs.

LAN
(Local Area Network) A network in which all the nodes or hosts participating in the network are directly connected with cables or short-range wireless media.

lands
In optical storage media, raised areas on the disk.

lanes
In PCIe, two wire pairs (four wires in total) using low voltage differential signaling, with one pair used to transmit and the other pair to receive (bi-directional).

laptop
A portable computer offering similar functionality to a desktop computer. Laptops come with built-in LCD screens and input devices (keyboard and touchpad), and can be powered from building power (via an AC adapter) or by a battery.

laser printer
A type of printer that develops an image on a drum using electrical charges to attract special toner then applying it to paper. The toner is then fixed to the paper using a high-heat and pressure roller (fuser). The process can be used with black toner only or four color toner cartridges (Cyan, Magenta, Yellow, and Black) to create full-color prints. Monochrome laser printers are the "workhorses" of office printing solutions.

latency
The time it takes for a signal to reach the recipient. A video application can support a latency of about 80 ms, while typical latency on the Internet can reach 1000 ms at peak times. Latency is a particular problem for 2-way applications, such as VoIP (telephone) and online conferencing.

LC
(Lucent Connector) Small Form Factor version of the SC push-pull fiber optic connector; available in simplex and duplex versions.

LCD panel
(Liquid Crystal Display panel) A display technology where the image is made up of liquid crystal cells controlled using

electrical charges. LCD panels are used on laptops and have replaced CRT monitors as the main type of computer display screen.

LDAP
(Lightweight Directory Access Protocol) Standard for accessing and updating information in an X.500-style network resource directory. LDAP uses port 389. Unless secure communications are used, LDAP is vulnerable to packet sniffing and Man-in-the-Middle attacks. It is also usually necessary to configure user permissions on the directory. LDAP version 3 supports simple authentication or Simple Authentication and Security Layer, which integrates it with Kerberos or TLS.

LED
(Light Emitting Diode) Small, low-power lamps used both as diagnostic indicators, LCD backlights, and (as Organic LEDs) in high-quality flat panels.

LED printer
(light emitting diode printer) A type of printer that uses LEDs to print.

legacy system
A computer system that is no longer supported by its vendor and so no longer provided with security updates and patches.

LGA
(Land Grid Array) A CPU form factor used by Intel where the pins that connect the CPU and socket are located on the socket.

life expectancy
The length of time for which a device can be expected to remain reliable.

light sensors
Sensors in a mobile device used to dim and brighten the display based on ambient conditions.

Lightning ports
Proprietary connector and interface for Apple devices.

link
Point-to-point connections in PCIe.

link-local address
Addresses used by IPv6 for network housekeeping traffic. Link-local addresses span a single subnet (they are not forwarded by routers).

load roller
In an inkjet printer, a roller that turns against the paper stack to move the top sheet, while a separation roller prevents more than one sheet from entering the printer.

local bus
The internal bus that links components directly to the processor, resulting in the highest possible data speed as required by components such as the video display.

locally installed printer
A printer that Windows communicates with directly over the relevant port.

locked out
When a user is unable to access a device because the device has been disabled either by means of the user forgetting the passcode too many times or remotely using an app that locks the device if it is reported lost or stolen.

LoJack tracking software
"Rootkit"-style software that enables a stolen laptop to be traced or remotely locked down or wiped in the event of theft.

loopback plug
A special connector used for diagnosing network transmission problems that redirects electrical signals back to the transmitting system.

LoS
(Line of Sight) A wireless connection method using ground-based microwave antennas aligned with one another.

low level format
A "proper" low level format creates cylinders and sectors on the disk. This can generally only be done at the factory. The disk utilities just clean data from each sector; they don't re-create the sector layout.

LTE
(Long Term Evolution) A packet data communications specification providing an upgrade path for both GSM and CDMA2000 cellular networks. LTE Advanced is designed to provide 4G standard network access.

LTE-A
(LTE Advanced) LTE Advanced is designed to provide 4G standard network access

luminance
The perceived brightness of a display screen, measured in candelas per square meter (cd/m²).

MAC address
A unique physical hardware address for each Ethernet network adapter that is composed of 12 hexadecimal digits.

MAC filtering
(media access control filtering) Applying an access control list to a switch or access point so that only clients with approved MAC addresses can connect to it.

Machine to Machine (M2M)
Internet of Things feature that allows objects to communicate and pass data between themselves and other traditional systems like computer servers.

main board
See **motherboard**.

main connector
The adapter from the power supply that supplies power to the motherboard.

maintenance kit
A set of replacement feed rollers, new transfer roller, and a new fuser unit for a laser printer.

male port
A port that has pin connectors.

managed_switch
Works as an **unmanaged switch** out-of-the-box but an administrator can connect to it over a management port, configure security settings, and then choose options for the switch's more advanced functionality.

MAPI
(Message Application Programming Interface) A Windows messaging interface used primarily by the email client software Outlook to communicate with an Exchange mail server.

mass storage device
Non-volatile storage devices that are able to hold data when the system is powered off.

matte coating
A display coating that is best suited to office work. Compare with **gloss coating**.

MBR
(Master Boot Record) A sector on a hard disk storing information about partitions configured on the disk.

MDM
(Mobile Device Management) Software suites designed to manage use of smartphones and tablets within an enterprise.

measured service
A provider's ability to control and bill a customer's use of resources such as CPU, memory, disk, and network bandwidth through metering.

media center
A computer used for media streaming, often connected to surround sound speakers, and capable of recording TV shows.

media guides
In a paper tray, the movable components that can be adjusted to hold the paper in the proper position for feeding through the printer.

megapixels
A unit of measure for the number of pixels a digital camera is capable of producing.

MEID
(Mobile Equipment ID) A number that uniquely identifies a mobile device on a CDMA network.

memory card
Flash drives typically used for digital cameras and smartphones; typically small and flat.

memory card reader
A device containing one or more slots to accommodate reading (and writing) memory cards.

memory module
A printed circuit board that holds a group of memory chips that act as a single unit.

MFD
(multifunction device) Any device that performs more than one function. This typically refers to either SOHO Internet routers/access points or print devices that can also scan and fax.

MIB
(Management Information Base) A database used by SNMP in which agents maintain configuration and usage data and identifies what information the managed system offers.

microATX
Introduced in late 1997, and is often referred to as μATX, and has a maximum size of 9.6 inches by 9.6 inches.

microprocessor
A programmable **integrated circuit (IC)**.

microsegmentation
Each switch port is a separate collision domain. In effect, the switch establishes a point-to-point link called a virtual circuit between any two network nodes.

MIDI
(Musical Instrument Digital Interface) Allows a computer with a sound card to drive MIDI compatible musical instruments, such as synthesizers, samplers, and drum machines (or [vice versa] for a synthesizer to drive a computer audio application [such as a sampler]).

MIME
(Multi-purpose Internet Mail Extensions) A protocol specifying Internet mail message formats and attachments.

MIMO/MU-MIMO
(Multiple Input Multiple Output/Multiple User MIMO) Wireless technology used in 802.11n/ac and 4G standards. MIMO is the use of multiple reception and transmission antennas to boost bandwidth. A Multi-user MIMO (MU-MIMO)-capable access point can use separate streams to connect multiple MU-MIMO-capable stations simultaneously, providing the stations are not on the same directional path.

mini-ITX
A small compact board that fits the same form factor as the ATX and the micro-ATX boards. They have a maximum size of 6.7 inches by 6.6 inches.

mirroring
Mirroring is a type of RAID (RAID 1) using two hard disks, providing the simplest way of protecting a single disk against failure. Data is written to both disks and can be read from either disk.

MMF
(Multimode Fiber) A category of fiber optic cable. Compared to SMF, MMF is cheaper (using LED optics rather than lasers), but supports shorter distances (up to about 500 m).

mobile device synchronization
Copying data back and forth between a mobile device and another device such as another mobile device, tablet, laptop, PC, or cloud service to keep the information up-to-date on all of the devices.

mobile hotspot
See **tethering**.

mobile VPN
A **VPN** that can maintain the VPN link across multiple carrier networks, where the IP address assigned to the mobile device may change often.

mobile VR headset
(mobile Virtual Reality headset) A VR device designed to be used with specific smartphones.

mobo
See **motherboard**.

modem
(modulator/demodulator) A network device that is used to interface a computer with the telephone network for data and fax communications, modulating digital data for transmission as an analog signal and demodulating incoming analog transmissions. Broadband modems are used to transmit signals over telephone (DSL) or cable TV networks.

Molex connector
A power connector that is used to supply power to Parallel Advanced Technology Attachment (PATA) drives, optical drives, and SCSI drives.

motherboard
The computer motherboard, also called the system board, provides the basic foundation for all of the computer's hardware, including the processor, RAM, firmware, and expansion cards. Several motherboard standards are available, each with a different layout and associated advantages.

mouse
The essential device to implement a WIMP GUI, a mouse simply controls the movement of a cursor that can be used to select objects from the screen. All Windows mice feature two click buttons, which are configured to perform different actions. Many mice also feature a scroll wheel.

MTBF
(Mean Time Between Failures) The rating on a device or component that predicts the expected time between failures.

multimedia
Multimedia refers to PC components that can playback and record sound and video (or to sound and video files). There are numerous sound and video file formats, including legacy Windows-specific formats such as WAV (for audio) or AVI (for video and audio). The preferred file format for Windows Media Player is ASF (Advanced Systems Format), which is usually compressed (WMA or WMV). Other file formats include those used for Apple's QuickTime player (MOV and QT), Apple's iTunes format (AIFF), and RealNetworks player (RA or RAM). The most popular standards-based format is MPEG.

multimeter
An electrical meter capable of measuring voltage, resistance, and current. Voltage readings can be used to determine whether, for example, a power supply unit is functioning correctly. Resistance readings can be used to determine whether a fuse or network cable is functioning correctly.

multiport repeater
See **hub**.

multitasking
The ability of an operating system to run multiple programs, or tasks, at one time. DOS was a single tasking operating system. Windows 3.x was a cooperative multitasking operating system, while Windows 9x and higher provide pre-emptive multitasking. Cooperative multitasking relies on the applications to share CPU cycles with one another and to voluntarily relinquish the processor to other tasks, which has reliability implications.

multithreaded
Software that runs multiple parallel threads within a process.

multitouch
A touchscreen or touchpad capable of interpreting gestures, such as pinching or swiping.

mutual authentication for multiple services
(SSO [Single Sign On]) One service accepts the credentials from another service. Also known as **federated identity management**.

NAPT
(Network Address Port Translation) Similar to NAT, it (or PAT or NAT overloading) maps private host IP addresses onto a single public IP address. Each host is tracked by assigning it a random high TCP port for communications.

NAS
(Network Attached Storage) A storage device with an embedded OS that

supports typical network file access protocols (TCP/IP and SMB, for instance). These may be subject to exploit attacks (though using an embedded OS is often thought of as more secure as it exposes a smaller attack "footprint"). The unauthorized connection of such devices to the network is also a concern.

NAT
(Network Address Translation) A network service provided by router or proxy server to map private local addresses to one or more publicly accessible IP addresses. NAT can use static mappings but is most commonly implemented as Network Address Port Translation (NAPT) or NAT overloading, where a few public IP addresses are mapped to multiple LAN hosts using port allocations.

native resolution
The fixed resolution for LCD or other flat panel display devices.

Negative Acknowledgement
(NACK) On a TCP/IP network, when using TCP and the data is delivered in a damaged state, a NACK packet is sent back to the sender to force retransmission of the data.

NetBEUI
A proprietary Microsoft network transport protocol typically found in non-routed networks. Fast and efficient, but not widely supported by third parties. Largely forgotten in these days of TCP/IP.

NetBIOS
NetBIOS is a session management protocol used to provide name registration and resolution services on legacy Microsoft networks. WINS provides NetBIOS name resolution. See also **NetBEUI**.

NetBT
(NetBIOS over TCP/IP) NetBIOS that was re-engineered to work over the TCP and UDP protocols.

network
Two or more computer systems linked together by some form of transmission medium that enables them to share information.

network firewall
A firewall placed inline in the network that inspects all traffic that passes through it.

network ID
In an IP address, the portion of the address that is common to all hosts on the same IP network.

Network Interface layer
In the TCP/IP suite, the layer responsible for putting frames onto the physical network.

NFC
(Near Field Communications) A Standard for peer-to-peer (2-way) radio communications over very short (around 4") distances, facilitating contactless payment and similar technologies. NFC is based on RFID.

NIC
(Network interface Card) An expansion card that enables a PC to connect to a LAN. Also referred to as a network adapter.

NIST
(National Institute of Standards and Technology) Develops computer security standards used by US federal agencies and publishes cybersecurity best practice guides and research.

NLA
(Network Level Authentication) An RDP technology requiring users to authenticate before a server session is created.

non-parity
System memory that does not perform error checking (except for the startup memory count).

notification shade
An Android feature that is accessed by swiping down from the top of the display to access Android OS feature settings.

NVMe
(Non-volatile Memory Express) An interface for connecting flash memory devices, such as SSDs, directly to a PCI Express bus. NVMe allows much higher transfer rates than SATA/AHCI.

NVMHCI
(Non-Volatile Memory Host Controller Interface specification) A logical interface used by PCIe-based SSD drives to communicate with the bus.

OCP
(Overcurrent Protection) A power supply rail safety feature that cuts the circuit if the power exceeds a safe limit.

OCR
(Optical Character Recognition) Software that can identify the shapes of characters and digits to convert them from printed images to electronic data files that can be modified in a word processing program. Intelligent Character Recognition (ICR) is an advanced type of OCR, focusing on handwritten text.

octet
32 bit addresses subdivided into four groups of 8 bits (1 byte).

OLED display
(organic light emitting diode display) A type of LED flat panel display device that uses organic compounds that emit light when subjected to an electric current.

onboard adapter
A low-end adapter included with the motherboard or as part of the CPU itself.

online social lives
An online way to interact with other people using sites such as Facebook, Twitter, and Instagram.

OSD
(on-screen display) Display configuration menus that show up on the monitor and that you interact with by using buttons on the monitor case.

OTP
(one time password) A password that is generated for use in one specific session and becomes invalid after the session ends.

overclocking
Manually setting the CPU and chipset to run at a faster speed than advised by the manufacturer. Some CPUs are better suited to overclocking than others and the system will generally need a better cooling system to cope with the increased thermal output.

PaaS
(Platform as a Service) A cloud computing service that enables consumers to rent fully configured systems that are set up for specific purposes.

packet filtering
A type of firewall that inspects the headers of IP packets and can perform filtering on IP address, protocol type, and port numbers.

page description language
(PDL) A high-level computer language used to describe the contents and the layout of the information to be printed on a page through PDL commands.

PAN
(Personal Area Network) Close range networking (usually based on Bluetooth or NFC) allowing communications between personal devices, such as smartphones, laptops, and printers/peripheral devices.

paper jam
Occurs when paper does not feed through the printer properly, resulting in pages that are stuck within the paper feed mechanism, often crumpled or torn.

parity checking
An error checking method where each byte of data in memory is accompanied by a ninth bit used to check for corrupted data.

passive cooling device
A CPU generates a large amount of heat that must be dissipated to prevent damage to the chip. Generally, a CPU will be fitted with a heatsink (a metal block with fins) and fan. Thermal compound is used at the contact point between the chip and the heatsink to ensure good heat transfer. The PSU also incorporates a fan to expel warm air from the system. Modern motherboards have temperature sensors that provide warning of overheating before damage can occur. Very high performance or overclocked systems or systems designed for quiet operation may require more sophisticated

cooling systems, such as liquid cooling. Cooling systems that work without electricity are described as passive; those requiring a power source are classed as active.

PAT
(portable appliance testing) In the UK, Australia, and New Zealand, the process for inspecting and testing electrical equipment to ensure its safety.

PAT
(port address translation) Another term for NAT overloading or NAPT.

PATA
(Parallel Advanced Technology Attachment) Used to be the main disk interface for PCs. The interface was very commonly called IDE (Integrated Drive Electronics) or Enhanced IDE (EIDE). Each PATA adapter supports two devices, commonly called master and slave. A drive is connected to the bus by a 40-pin ribbon cable. The PATA interface has been replaced by SATA.

PCI bus
(Peripheral Component Interconnect bus) Introduced in 1995 with the Pentium processor, it connects the CPU, memory, and peripherals to a 32-bit working at 33 MHz. PCI supports bus mastering, IRQ steering, and Plug-and-Play. Later versions defined 64-bit operation and 66 MHz clock but were not widely adopted on desktop PCs.

PCIe
(PCI Express) An expansion bus standard using serial communications. Each device on the bus can create a point-to-point link with the I/O controller or another device. The link comprises one or more lanes (x1, x2, x4, x8, x12, x16, or x32). Each lane supports a full-duplex transfer rate of 250 MBps (v1.0), 500 MBps (v2.0), or 1 GBps (v3.0). The standard is software compatible with PCI, allowing for motherboards with both types of connectors.

permissions
To access files and folders on a volume, the administrator of the computer will need to grant file permissions to the user (or a group to which the user belongs). File permissions are supported by NTFS-based Windows systems.

personal firewall
A firewall implemented as applications software running on the host. Personal software firewalls can provide sophisticated filtering of network traffic and also block processes at the application level. However, as a user-mode application they are more vulnerable to attack and evasion than kernel mode firewalls or network firewall appliances.

PGA
(Pin Grid Array) A CPU socket form factor where pins are located on the bottom of the processor to fit in the matching holes in the motherboard socket. PGA-type sockets are still used by AMD but Intel has switched to Land Grid Array (LGA), where the pins are located on the socket rather than the chip.

PGP
(Pretty Good Privacy) Email encryption product providing message confidentiality and integrity using web of trust PGP certificates.

photopolymer
A polymer material that is sensitive to light, and changes its properties when exposed to a light source.

pickup roller
Roller that turns above a stack of paper to feed a sheet into the feed roller.

piezoelectric printing
Ink delivery system in an **inkjet** printer that uses a tiny element that changes shape to act as a pump used in Epson printers.

pits
In optical storage media, recessed areas on the disk.

pixel
The smallest discrete element on a display. A single pixel is composed of a red, a blue, and a green dot.

plenum
An air handling space, including ducts and other parts of the HVAC system in a building.

plenum cable
A grade of cable that does not give off noxious or poisonous gases when burned. Unlike PVC cable, plenum cable can be run through the plenum and firebreak walls.

Plug and Play
See **UPnP**.

PoE
(Power over Ethernet) Specification allowing power to be supplied via switch ports and ordinary data cabling to devices such as VoIP handsets and wireless access points. Devices can draw up to about 13 W (or 25 W for PoE+).

pointing device
A peripheral used to move a cursor to select and manipulate objects on the screen.

PoP
(Point of Presence) The equipment that allows a location, facility, home, or other point-of-access to connect to the Internet.

POP 3
(Post Office Protocol) A TCP/IP application protocol providing a means for a client to access email messages stored in a mailbox on a remote server. The server usually deletes messages once the client has downloaded them. POP3 utilizes TCP port 110.

port (logical)
In TCP and UDP applications, a port is a unique number assigned to a particular application protocol (such as HTTP or SMTP). The port number (with the IP address) forms a socket between client and server. A socket is a bi-directional pipe for the exchange of data. For security, it is important to allow only the ports required to be open (ports can be blocked using a firewall).

port (physical)
A hardware connection interface on a personal computer that enables devices to be connected to the computer.

port forwarding
Port forwarding means that a router takes requests from the Internet for a particular application (say, HTTP/port 80) and sends them to a designated host on the LAN.

port number
The number between 0 and 65535 assigned to each type of network application so that the transport layer can identify it.

port replicator
A simple device to extend the range of ports (for example, USB, DVI, HDMI, Thunderbolt, network, and so on) available for a laptop computer when it is used at a desk.

port triggering
Port triggering is used to configure access through a firewall for applications that require more than one port. Basically, when the firewall detects activity on outbound port A destined for a given external IP address, it opens inbound access for the external IP address on port B for a set period.

POST
(Power-On Self-Test) A hardware checking routine built into the PC firmware. This test sequentially monitors the state of the memory chips, the processor, system clock, display, and firmware itself. Errors that occur within vital components such as these are signified by beep codes emitted by the internal speaker of the computer. Further tests are then performed and any errors displayed as on-screen error codes and messages.

POTS
(Plain Old Telephone System) Parts of a telephone network "local loop" using voice-grade cabling. Analog data transfer over POTS using dial-up modems is slow (33.3 Kbps). DSL technologies make better use of the bandwidth available, but are not accessible over all of the network.

power
The rate at which electricity is drawn from the supply by the device using it, measured in Watts.

power injector
Used when an existing switch does not support PoE. When a device is connected to a port on a PoE switch, the switch goes through a detection phase to determine whether the device is PoE-enabled. If not, it does not supply power over the port and therefore does not damage non-PoE devices. If so, it determines the device's power consumption and sets the supply voltage level appropriately.

power management
Computers and hardware supporting a power management specification such as ACPI (Advanced Configuration Power Interface) can enter power-saving or standby modes that can be reactivated from the host.

power rating
The maximum power output available from a PC power supply, measured in watts, calculated as voltage multiplied by current.

power supply tester
A type of meter designed to test PC Power Supply Units.

PPP
(Point-to-Point Protocol) Dial-up protocol working at layer 2 (Data Link) used to connect devices remotely to networks. Often used to connect to an ISP's routers and out to the Internet. PPPoE (PPP over Ethernet) or PPPoA (PPP over ATM) are used to provide broadband connections (over DSL or cable Internet, for instance).

PPPoA
(PPP over ATM) The PPP protocol is used with the ATM transport protocol by DSL providers.

PPPoE
(PPP over Ethernet) PPP packets are encapsulated within Ethernet frames for transport by DSL providers.

PRI
(Preferred Roaming Index) An index that works with the PRL to provide the best data/voice quality to a phone while roaming.

PRI
(Primary Rate Interface) A class of ISDN service that provides either T1 or E1 capacity levels (23B or 30B) channels, depending on location in the world, and one 64 Kbps D channel.

primary charge roller
See **cleaning unit**.

print driver
Software that provides an interface between the print device and Windows.

print head
In a dot matrix printer, pins that are fired by solenoids are secured to a moving carriage that sweeps across the paper and the pins make contact with the **ribbon** to press it against the paper to create images. In an inkjet printer, the print head is typically contained in the **ink cartridge** although Epson inkjet printers include the printhead as part of the printer instead.

print job
The output produced by an application and passed to the printer, and then to the print device via a print monitor and port.

print languages
The language used by printers to interpret output from the computer as printable text and images. Some printers can use multiple print languages.

print monitor
In Windows, the print monitor is a process that checks the print queue (%SystemRoot%\System32\Spool\Printers\) for print jobs. When they arrive, they are processed, if necessary, then passed via a print port to the print device.

printer
An output device that produces text and images from electronic content onto physical media such as paper or transparency film.

printer technology
The mechanism used in a printer to create images on paper. It determines the quality, speed, and cost of the output.

printer type
The mechanism used to make images on the paper. Also referred to as printer technology.

privacy filter
A filter to fit over a display screen so that it can only be viewed straight-on.

private address
IP addresses in ranges defined by RFC1928 which are not allowed to route traffic over the Internet, with those addressed being confined to private LANs.

PRL
(Preferred Roaming List) A database built by CDMA service carriers to indicate which radio bands should be used when connecting to a cell tower.

problem management
A method of identifying, prioritizing, and establishing ownership of **incidents**.

processor
See **CPU**.

prosumer
A combination of the words professional and consumer, typically referring to an amateur user who uses professional level devices.

protocol
Rules and formats enabling systems to exchange data. A single network will involve the use of many different protocols. In general terms, a protocol defines header fields to describe each packet, a maximum length for the payload, and methods of processing information from the headers.

protocol suite
A collection of several protocols used for networking are designed to work together.

proxy server
A server that mediates the communications between a client and another server. The proxy server can filter and often modify communications as well as provide caching services to improve performance.

PSE
(Power Sourcing Equipment) Network switches that provide power through the Ethernet cable to connected devices.

PSK
(Pre-shared Key) Symmetric encryption technologies, such as those used for WEP, require both parties to use the same private key. This key must be kept a secret known only to those authorized to use the network. A pre-shared key is normally generated from a passphrase.

PSTN
(Public Switched Telephone Network) National telecommunications systems have evolved and combined over the years to create a global (and indeed extra-terrestrial) communications network This is referred to as the Public Switched Telephone Network (PSTN) but it is capable of carrying more than simply voice-call services. The basis of PSTN is a circuit-switched network, but the infrastructure can also carry packet-switched data services.

PSU
(Power Supply Unit) Transformer that converts AC mains power into 3.3 V, 5 V, and 12 V DC to power components on the motherboard. The type of PSU must match the case and motherboard form factor.

PVR
(personal video recorder) Software installed on a **home theater PC (HTPC)** to record and watch TV broadcasts.

QC
(Quick Charge) A Qualcomm **fast charging** technology that also has a second chip for power management that allows higher wattage than is allowed by the USB standard without overheating.

QoS
(Quality of Service) Systems that differentiate data passing over the network that can reserve bandwidth for particular applications. A system that cannot guarantee a level of available bandwidth is often described as Class of Service (CoS).

QR codes
(Quick Response codes) A 2D barcode created of black and white squares used to store information that can be read using a barcode scanner or the camera on a smartphone that has a barcode scanning app installed.

Quick Response codes
See **QR codes**.

radio firmware
An operating system that is separate from the end-user operating system in a mobile device.

RADIUS
(Remote Authentication Dial-in User Service) Used to manage remote and wireless authentication infrastructure. Users supply authentication information to RADIUS client devices, such as wireless access points. The client device then passes the authentication data to an AAA (Authentication, Authorization, and Accounting) server, which processes the request.

RAID
(Redundant Array of Independent/Inexpensive Disks) A set of vendor-independent specifications for fault-tolerant configurations on multiple-disk systems.

RAM
(Random Access Memory) The principal storage space for computer data and program instructions. RAM is described as being volatile in the sense that once power has been removed or the computer has been rebooted, data is lost.

range extender
See **wireless range extender**.

rapid elasticity
The ability to scale cloud computing resources quickly to meet peak demand and just as quickly remove resources if they are not currently needed.

raster
A bitmap image of a page for printing. See also **Raster Image Processing**.

RAW
When applied to a print job, RAW means the job is fully rendered and ready to be passed to the print device without further processing.

RDPRA Mode
(RDP Restricted Admin Mode) A method of mitigating the risk of using Remote Desktop.

real time
The date and time that are maintained by the Real Time Clock.

rear panel
The portion of the system case with cut-out slots aligned with the position of adapter card slots.

refresh rate
The picture displayed on a CRT monitor is updated (by vertical refreshing) many times per second. The more times the image is refreshed, the more stable and flicker-free the picture. On flat panels, there is no flicker as each pixel is not redrawn but only updated. Flat panels can suffer from motion blur and ghosting, however, and better refresh rates can reduce these issues.

register
Registers are temporary storage areas in the CPU that can hold data prior to processing by the Arithmetic Logic Unit (ALU) and other components of the processor. A CPU can incorporate a number of different registers, but the most important are the **General Purpose (GP) registers**.

registration roller
Roller equipped with a sensor that feeds paper into the print engine.

relative distinguished name
In an LDAP directory, the most specific attribute in the distinguished name that uniquely identifies the object within the context of successive (parent) attribute values.

Remote Assistance
A Windows remote support feature allowing a user to invite a technical support professional to help them over a

network using chat. The user can also grant the support professional control over their desktop. Remote Assistance uses the same RDP protocol as Remote Desktop.

Remote Credential Guard
A method of mitigating the risk of using Remote Desktop.

Remote Desktop
The Windows feature that allows a remote user to initiate a connection at any time and sign on to the local machine using an authorized account.

removable storage
A storage device that can be removed from the computer, or the removable media that can be inserted in a drive, to store portable data.

repeater
A repeater is a layer 1 device that takes a signal and repeats it to the devices that are connected to it. Repeaters can be used to maintain signal integrity and amplitude across a connection or a network.

reserve
In DHCP servers, particular IP addresses are set aside for and assigned to specific devices so that those devices receive the same IP address each time.

resistance
Resistance (R) describes the property of a material to prevent electrical flow through itself. Metals have little electrical resistance whereas plastics and rubber have very high resistance and in most cases will not allow electrical current to pass through them. The resistance of a body to electrical current is measured in Ohms (Ω or R) and is related to potential difference (V) and current (I) by the equation V=IR.

resistor
A component that opposes the flow of current without blocking it completely and is used to manage electronic circuits.

resolution
A measure of the number of picture elements (pixels) that an imaging device can use to sample or display the image, measured in pixels per inch (ppi). On a digital printer, the resolution is the number of toner or ink dots that the print engine can put on paper (measured in dots per inch [dpi]). Note that sometimes dpi is used interchangeably with ppi to describe scanner or monitor resolution, but image pixels and printer dots are not equivalent, as multiple print dots are required to represent a single image pixel accurately.

resolution (digital camera)
The number of megapixels a digital camera is capable of producing.

resource pooling
A cloud provider's data center hardware is not dedicated or reserved for a particular customer account, allowing the provider to provision more resources through management software rather than physically altering hardware to allocate or deallocate resources for a customer.

response rate
The time taken for a pixel to change color, measured in milliseconds (ms).

RF
(Radio Frequency) Radio waves propagate at different frequencies and wavelengths. Wi-Fi network products work at 2.4 GHz or 5 GHz.

RFID
(Radio Frequency Identification) A chip allowing data to be read wirelessly. RFID tags are used in barcodes and smart cards.

RFID tag
A tag containing an RFID chip programmed with asset data.

ribbon
In an impact printer, the inked medium against which pins press to create the image.

RIP
(Raster Image Processing) The component responsible for converting instructions in the Page Description Language (PDL) to instructions that control the print engine (an inkjet's ink dispersion nozzles or a laser printer's developer laser, for instance). A PDL might contain instructions

for printing vector graphics and fonts; the RIP translates these instructions into a pattern of dots (raster) at the required resolution.

riser card
A space-saving feature of some motherboards, a riser card puts the PC's expansion slots on a separate board installed at right-angles to the main board. This allows the system components to fit within a slimline case.

RJ connector
(Registered Jack connector) A connector used for twisted pair cabling. 4-pair network cabling uses the larger RJ-45 connector. Modem/telephone 2-pair cabling uses the RJ-11 connector.

RJ-11 connector
A six-position connector that uses just one pair of wires. It is used in telephone system connections.

RJ-45 connector
An eight-position connector that uses all four pairs of wires. It is usually used for network connectivity.

rogue access point
An unauthorized wireless access point on a corporate or private network, which allows unauthorized individuals to connect to the network.

rogue VM
(rogue virtual machine) A virtual machine that has been installed without authorization.

rooting
Gaining privileged level or root level access to an Android device to enable modifying code or installing software not intended for the device.

rotational latency
The time it takes for the read/write head to find a sector location.

router
A network device that links dissimilar networks and can support multiple alternate paths between locations based upon the parameters of speed, traffic loads, and cost. A router works at layer 3 (Network) of the OSI model. Routers form the basic connections of the Internet. They allow data to take multiple paths to reach a destination (reducing the likelihood of transmission failure). Routers can access source and destination addresses within packets and can keep track of multiple active paths within a given source and destination network. TCP/IP routers on a LAN can also be used to divide the network into logical subnets.

RS-232
A serial port that uses a 25-pin male D connector. (See also **serial port**).

RSSI
(Received Signal Strength Indicator) For a wireless signal, an index level calculated from the signal strength level.

RTC
(real time clock) Part of the system chipset that keeps track of the date and time. The RTC is powered by a battery so the PC keeps track of the time even when it is powered down. If the computer starts losing time, it is a sign that the battery is failing.

RTC battery
(real time clock battery) The battery that powers the chipset that keeps track of date and time for the system.

RTOS
(real-time operating system) An OS that is optimized for use in embedded or real-time apps.

RVI
(Rapid Virtualization Indexing) The term used for SLAT extensions by AMD.

S.M.A.R.T.
(Self Monitoring Analysis and Reporting Technology) Technology designed to alert the user to possible hard disk failures before the disk becomes unusable.

S/MIME
(Secure Multipurpose Internet Mail Extensions) Email encryption standard (Cryptographic Message Standard) using PKI (X.509) certificates for confidentiality (digital envelopes) and integrity (digital

signatures). S/MIME provides extensions for standard MIME headers.

S/PDIF
(Sony/Phillips Digital Interface) A high-quality audio port that uses coax cabling with RCA connectors or fiber optic cabling and connectors. S/PDIF supports surround sound speakers.

SaaS
(Software as a Service) A cloud computing service that enables a service provider to make applications available over the Internet.

sample
A sound pattern stored in a wave table.

Samsung account
An account created for Samsung Android devices used to access the Samsung devices and related online services.

SAS
(Serial Attached SCSI) Developed from parallel SCSI, SAS represents the highest performing hard disk interface available.

SATA
(Serial ATA) The most widely used interface for hard disks on desktop and laptop computers. It uses a 7-pin data connector with one device per port. There are three SATA standards specifying bandwidths of 1.5 Gbps, 3 Gbps, and 6 Gbps, respectively. SATA drives also use a new 15-pin power connector, though adapters for the old style 4-pin Molex connectors are available. External drives are also supported via the eSATA interface.

SC
(Subscriber Connector) Push/pull connector used with fiber optic cabling.

scalable fonts
Fonts that are **vector based**.

scanner
A type of photocopier that can convert the image of a physical object into an electronic data file. The two main components of a scanner are the lamp, which illuminates the object, and the recording device, an array of CCDs (Charge Coupled Devices). There are flatbed and sheet-fed versions, with sheet-fed versions typically being incorporated with a printer and fax machine into a multifunction device. Scanners can output images directly to a printer or to a suitable file format (such as JPEG, PNG, or TIFF). Scanners can also interface with applications software using one of several interfaces (TWAIN, WIA, SANE, or ISIS).

script file
A text file containing commands or instructions that are performed by a program on the computer rather than by the computer itself.

SCSI
(Small Computer Systems Interface) A legacy expansion bus standard allowing for the connection of internal and external devices. SCSI 1 defines the original 8-bit bus with a transfer rate of 5 MBps. SCSI 2 features a 16-bit data bus implementation (Wide SCSI) and a faster transfer rate (Fast SCSI) while maintaining backward compatibility with most of the original devices. SCSI 3 introduces further data rate enhancements (Ultra SCSI) and a serial SCSI standard (Firewire). Each device on a SCSI bus must be allocated a unique ID. The bus must also be terminated at both ends.

SDK
(Software Development Kit) A set of resources provided by a platform vendor for programmers to use when creating software to work with the vendor's platform.

SDN
(Software Defined Networking) Application Programming Interfaces (API) and compatible hardware allowing for programmable network appliances and systems.

SDRAM
(Synchronous Dynamic Random Access Memory) A variant on the DRAM chip designed to run at the speed of the system clock, thus accelerating the periodic refresh cycle times. SDRAM can run at much higher clock speeds than previous types of DRAM. Basic SDRAM is now obsolete and has been replaced by DDR/DDR2/3 SDRAM.

sector
The regularly sized subdivision of a drive track. During low-level formatting, the size and position of the sectors is written to the disk so that the data can be placed into uniform spots that the drive head can easily access.

secure boot
A security system offered by UEFI that is designed to prevent a computer from being hijacked by malware.

seek time
The time it takes for the read/write head to locate a particular track position.

self-grounding
Manual dissipation of static buildup by touching a grounded object prior to touching any electronic equipment.

semiconductor
A material that can act as both a conductor and an insulator, which provides switch-like functionality, where a circuit can be opened and closed, used to represent binary (on/off) digits.

separation pad
A stationary pad in a paper tray that pushes the stack of paper back, allowing only a single sheet of paper to be fed into the printer.

separation roller
A roller in a paper tray that pushes the stack of paper back, allowing only a single sheet of paper to be fed into the printer.

serial port
Asynchronous serial transmission (RS-232) is one of the oldest PC bus standards. A serial port is a legacy port that can be used to connect devices such as modems, mice, and Uninterruptible Power Supplies (UPS). Serial ports transmit data bit-by-bit using a single data line at a speed of up to about 115 Kbps. Although the original serial port used a 25-pin male D connector, most PCs today use a male DB9 (9-pin) port. The serial port is now little used but does provide an "out-of-band" means of configuring network appliances such as switches and routers.

server consolidation
Using virtual servers, make more efficient use of system resources and hardware since most servers' capacity is not fully utilized.

server-side virtualization
A solution in which one or more virtual servers are created on a physical server in which each virtual server acts like it was a separate computer.

SFF
(Small Form Factor) Motherboards and connectors that are designed to take up less space.

sheet-fed scanner
A scanner in which the paper is passed over a fixed scan head.

sideload
See **Android application package**.

silicon chip
A wafer of purified silicon doped with a metal oxide (typically copper or aluminum).

SIM
(Subscriber Identity Module) A small chip card that identifies the user and phone number of a mobile device via an International Mobile Subscriber Identity (ISMI). A SIM card also provides a limited amount of local storage for contacts.

single-channel memory
Memory with one 64-bit bus between the CPU and RAM.

SLA
(stereolithography) A 3D printing method which uses a resin or **photopolymer** to create objects which are cured using an ultraviolet laser.

SLAT
(Second Level Address Translation) A feature of virtualization software designed to improve the management of virtual (paged) memory.

slicing
Creating horizontal layers to use in 3D modeling and 3D printers.

SLS
(selective laser sintering) A 3D printing method which fuses layers together using a pulse laser, creating the object from a plastic or metal powder with the model being lowered into a tank as each layer is added.

smart card
A card with a chip containing data on it. Smart cards are typically used for authentication, with the chip storing authentication data such as a digital certificate.

smart card reader
A device, either built-in or attached as a peripheral, that uses a slot or NFC to interact with a smart card.

SMB
(Server Message Block) A protocol used for requesting files from Windows servers and delivering them to clients. SMB allows machines to share files and printers, thus making them available for other machines to use. SMB client software is available for UNIX-based systems. Samba software allows UNIX and Linux servers or NAS appliances to run SMB services for Windows clients.

SMF
(Single Mode Fiber) A category of fiber optic cable. SMF is more expensive than MMF (using high quality cable and optics) and supports much longer distances (up to about 70 km).

SMP
(symmetric multiprocessing) A condition where two or more physical CPUs that share a common OS and memory execute instructions simultaneously.

SMT
(Simultaneous Multithreading) Processing of multiple threads simultaneously.

SMTP
(Simple Mail Transfer Protocol) The protocol used to send mail between hosts on the Internet. Messages are sent over TCP port 25.

SNMP
(Simple Network Management Protocol) A protocol for monitoring and managing network devices. A management system collates data sent by agents running on each device. The agents maintain a Management Information Base of configuration and usage data. An agent can also generate a trap, alerting the management system of some notable event (such as a printer being out of paper). SNMP works over UDP ports 161 and 162 by default.

Snort
An intrusion detection program.

SNR
(Signal-to-Noise Ratio) A sound measurement that is expressed in decibels that compares the signal power with the noise power.

SODIMM
(Small Outline Dual In-line Memory Module) Memory that is half the size of DIMMs, are available in 32- or 64-bit data paths, and are commonly found in laptops and iMac systems.

soft reset
Power cycling a mobile device in an attempt to resolve issues the user is experiencing.

SOHO network
(small office/home office network) A small network that provides connectivity and resource sharing for a small office or home office.

solid state storage
Any type of persistent digital storage technology that does not use mechanical parts.

sound card
An add-on card or built-in adapter to process audio signals and provide interfaces for connecting audio devices.

SSD
(solid state drive) A personal computer storage device that stores data in non-volatile special memory instead of on disks or tape.

SSH
(Secure Shell) A remote administration and file copy program that is flexible enough to support VPNs too (using port forwarding). SSH runs on TCP port 22.

SSID
(Service Set ID) Identifies a particular Wireless LAN (WLAN). This "network name" can be used to connect to the correct network. When multiple APs are configured with the same SSID, this is referred to as an E(xtended)SSID.

SSL
(Secure Sockets Layer) A security protocol developed by Netscape to provide privacy and authentication over the Internet. It is application independent (working at layer 5 [Session]) and can be used with a variety of protocols, such as HTTP or FTP. Client and server set up a secure connection through PKI (X.509) certificates (optionally, both client and server can authenticate to one another). The protocol is now being developed as Transport Layer Security (TLS).

SSO
(Single Sign-on) Any authentication technology that allows a user to authenticate once and receive authorizations for multiple services. Kerberos is a typical example of an authentication technology providing SSO.

SSTP
(Secure Socket Tunneling Protocol) Uses the HTTP over SSL protocol and encapsulates an IP packet with an SSTP header.

ST Connector
(Straight Tip connector) Bayonet-style twist-and-lock connector for fiber optic cabling.

standard client
A business computer that performs most or all computing functions on its own. Also referred to as a thick client or a fat client.

standoffs
Used to firmly attach the motherboard to the case, ensuring no other part of the motherboard touches the case.

static eliminator
See **detac corona**.

storage bus
A special type of expansion bus dedicated to communicating with storage devices.

STP
(Shielded Twisted Pair cabling) A type of network cabling used where protection from interference is required. Insulation is installed around all four pairs of twisted cables.

structured cabling system
The use of patch cords, permanent links, and patch panels.

subnet mask
An IP address consists of a Network ID and a Host ID. The subnet mask is used in IPv4 to distinguish these two components within a single IP address. The typical format for a mask is 255.255.0.0. Classless network addresses can also be expressed in the format 169.254.0.0/16, where /16 is the number of bits in the mask. IPv6 uses the same /nn notation to indicate the length of the network prefix.

subtractive color printing
A color printing method that uses the reflective properties of inks.

superpipelining
Superscalar architectures feature longer pipelines with multiple stages but shorter actions (micro-ops) at each stage.

superscalar architecture
CPUs process multiple instructions at the same time (for example, while one instruction is fetched, another is being decoded, another is being executed, and another is being written back to memory).

Suricata
An intrusion detection program.

surround sound
Placement of multiple speakers positioned around the listener to provide a cinematic audio experience.

Glossary

SVGA
(Super VGA) A variant of the VGA standard that supported 800x600 pixel resolution with 4-bit or 8-bit color.

Swift
Apple's programming language for developing mobile apps.

switch
Ethernet switches are at the heart of most local networks. A switch receives incoming data into a buffer, then the destination MAC address is compared with an address table. The data is then only sent out to the port with the corresponding MAC address. In a switched network, each port is in a separate collision domain (microsegmentation). Advanced switches perform routing at layers 3 (IP), 4 (TCP), or 7 (Application). Switches routing at layer 4/7 are referred to as load balancers and content switches.

syslog
Used in UNIX and Linux, log files that allow for centralized collection of events from multiple sources.

system board
See **motherboard**.

system case
A plastic and metal box that houses components such as the motherboard, Central Processing Unit (CPU), memory, adapter cards, disk drives, and power supply unit. System units are also often referred to as boxes, main units, or base units.

system clock
The computer's timing mechanism that synchronizes the operation of all parts of the computer and provides the basic timing signal for the CPU; measured in MHz or GHz.

system firmware
Low-level code to allow the computer components to be initialized and load the main operating system software.

system memory
The main storage area for programs and data when the computer is running.

system resources
Settings that enable a device to communicate with the CPU and memory without the device conflicting with other devices.

T568A
A legacy twisted pair standard that was used in commercial buildings and cabling systems that support data networks, voice, and video. It further defines cable performance and technical requirements.

T568B
A twisted pair standard that defines the standards for preferred cable types that provide the minimum acceptable performance levels for home-based networks.

TA
(Terminal Adapter) An external appliance or a plug-in card for a PC or compatible router that facilitates an ISDN connection.

TB
(Thunderbolt) It can be used as a display interface (like DisplayPort) and as a general peripheral interface (like USB 3). The latest version uses USB-C connectors.

TCO
(total cost of ownership) The cost of a device over its lifetime, including the cost of replacement components and consumables.

TCP
(Transmission Control Protocol) A protocol in the TCP/IP suite operating at the transport layer to provide connection-oriented, guaranteed delivery of packets. Hosts establish a session to exchange data and confirm delivery of packets using acknowledgements. This overhead means the system is relatively slow.

TCP/IP Suite
(Transmission Control Protocol/Internet Protocol suite) The network protocol suite used by most operating systems and the Internet. It is widely adopted, industry standard, vendor independent, and open. It uses a 4-layer network model that corresponds roughly to the OSI model as follows: Network Interface (Physical/Data Link), Internet (Network), Transport

(Transport), Application (Session, Presentation, Application).

telnet
TCP/IP application protocol supporting remote command-line administration of a host (terminal emulation). Telnet is unauthenticated and has therefore been superseded by SSH or graphical remote configuration utilities. Telnet runs over TCP port 23.

tethered VR headset
(tethered Virtual Reality headset) A self-contained VR device.

tethering
Using the cellular data plan of a mobile device to provide Internet access to a laptop or PC. The PC can be tethered to the mobile by USB, Bluetooth, or Wi-Fi (a mobile hotspot).

TFT Active Matrix Display
(Thin Film Transistor active matrix display) The TFT display provides the best resolution of all of the currently available flat-panel Liquid Crystal Display (LCD) designs, although they are also the most expensive. TFT displays offer very high image clarity, contrast ratios of between 150:1 to 200:1, fast refresh rates, and wide viewing angles.

THD
(Total Harmonic Distortion) A sound measurement that is expressed as a percentage that compares input and output audio signals, which indicates the amount of distortion in the output signal.

thermal dye transfer printer
A sophisticated type of color printer that uses heat to diffuse dye from color ribbons onto special paper or transparency blanks to produce continuous-tone output similar in quality to a photographic print. Also called dye sublimation printer.

thermal inkjet print method
Ink delivery system in an inkjet printer that uses **thermal shock**.

thermal paper
Paper that contains a chemical designed to react with the heating element of a thermal printer to create images on paper.

thermal paste
A paste that is used to connect a heat sink to a CPU to provide a liquid thermally conductive compound gel that fills any gaps between the CPU and the heat sink to permit a more efficient transference of heat from the processor to the heat sink.

thermal printer
A type of printer that uses a thermal (high heat) print head to fuse or transfer wax-based ink onto paper or selectively heats specially treated paper to form the image. Most thermal printers are handheld devices used for printing labels or receipts.

thermal shock
An ink delivery system where the ink is heated to form a bubble that bursts through the nozzles.

thermal wax transfer printer
A printer that uses a thermal printhead to melt wax-based ink from a transfer ribbon onto the paper.

thick client
A business computer that performs most or all computing functions on its own. Also referred to as a standard client or a fat client.

thin client
A business computer that relies heavily on another system, typically a server, to run most of its programs, processes, and services.

thrashed
See **disk thrashing**.

thread
A stream of instructions generated by a software application. Most applications run a single process in a single thread.

throttling
Technology that allows the CPU to slow down if thermal output reaches a critical level or to improve power performance. Intel's throttling technology is called SpeedStep; AMD's is called PowerNow!.

TKIP
(Temporal Key Integrity Protocol) Mechanism used in the first version of WPA to improve the security of wireless encryption mechanisms, compared to the flawed WEP standard.

TLS
(Transport Layer Security) A security protocol that protects sensitive communication from eavesdropping and tampering by using a secure, encrypted, and authenticated channel over a TCP/IP connection.

TN
(Twisted Nematic) An LCD panel technology where the panel is black when no electric current is running through the liquid crystal cells because the cells align themselves in a twisted state. When an electric current is applied, the liquid crystal cells untwist, allowing light to pass through, resulting in a white display screen.

tone generator and probe
The tone generator is an electronic device that sends an electrical signal through one set of UTP cables. The tone probe (or tone locator) is an electronic device that emits an audible tone when it detects a signal sent by the tone generator in a set of wires.

toner
Specially formulated compound to impart dye to paper through an electrographic process (used by laser printers and photocopiers). The key properties of toner are the colorant (dye), ability to fuse (wax or plastic), and ability to hold a charge. There are three main types of toner, distinguished by the mechanism of applying the toner to the developer roller: dual component (where the toner is mixed with a separate magnetic developer), mono-component (where the toner itself is magnetic), and non-magnetic mono-component (where the toner is transferred using static properties).

Top Level Domains
(TLD) In the DNS hierarchy, the level immediately below the root.

touchpad
Input device used on most laptops to replace the mouse. The touchpad allows the user to control the cursor by moving a finger over the pad's surface. There are usually buttons too but the pad may also recognize "tap" events and have scroll areas.

touchscreen
A display screen combined with a digitizer that is responsive to touch input.

tower case
A desktop computer designed to sit vertically on a surface so that it is taller than it is wide. Tower cases come in four basic sizes: full, mid, mini, and slim line.

TPM
(Trusted Platform Module) A specification for hardware-based storage of digital certificates, keys, hashed passwords, and other user and platform identification information. Essentially, it functions as a smart card embedded on a motherboard.

traces
Wires etched on to the motherboard to provide electrical pathways.

track
When data is written onto a drive, it is stored as magnetic changes in the structure of the disk. These alterations are written as concentric rings as the disk spins. Each of these rings is termed a track.

tractor feed
An impact printer mechanism that uses pairs of wheels with pins evenly spaced around the circumference at a set spacing to feed continuous roll paper with matching holes that fit over the pins.

transfer belt
In a color printer, combining colors to print in one pass.

transfer roller
See **transfer unit**.

transfer unit
Roller, corona wire, or belt assembly that applies a charge to the media (paper) so that it attracts toner from the

photoconductor. A detac strip then removes the charge to prevent paper curl. On a color laser printer, the transfer unit is usually a belt.

transistor
In computers, semiconductor switches used to create logic devices.

trickle charge
Charging a device that has been fully charged at the rate at which the charge discharges, keeping the device fully charged without overcharging the battery.

trip hazard
Any object placed in pathways where people walk.

tunneling
A tunneling (or encapsulation) protocol wraps up data from one protocol for transfer over a different type of network. For example, PPP can carry TCP/IP data over a dial-up line, enabling a remote computer to communicate with the LAN.

TWAIN
Standard "driver" model for interfacing scanner hardware with applications software.

Type 1 hypervisor
A bare metal hypervisor in which you install directly on the server's hardware.

Type 2 hypervisor
A host-based hypervisor in which you install the host operating system first, then install the hypervisor.

UDP
(User Datagram Protocol) A protocol in the TCP/IP suite operating at the transport layer to provide connectionless, non-guaranteed communication with no sequencing or flow control. Faster than TCP, but does not provide reliability.

UEFI
(Unified Extensible Firmware Interface) A type of system firmware providing support for 64-bit CPU operation at boot, full GUI and mouse operation at boot, and better boot security.

UEFI setup
(Unified Extensible Firmware Interface setup) Another name for the setup program used to configure system firmware settings. Also known as BIOS setup.

unauthorized account access
When someone other than an authorized user gains access to an online account.

uncollated
A print job where all copies of page 1 are printed first, followed by all copies of page 2, and so on.

unicast addressing
A packet addressed to a single host. If the host is not on the local subnet, the packet must be sent via one or more routers.

unmanaged_switch
Performs microsegmentation without requiring any sort of configuration.

UPnP
(Universal Plug-and-Play) A protocol framework allowing network devices to autoconfigure services, such as allowing a games console to request appropriate settings from a firewall.

URL
(Uniform Resource Locator/Identifier) An application-level addressing scheme for TCP/IP, allowing for human-readable resource addressing. For example: protocol://server/file, where "protocol" is the type of resource (HTTP, FTP), "server" is the name of the computer (www.microsoft.com), and "file" is the name of the resource you wish to access.

USB
(Universal Serial Bus) The main type of connection interface used on PCs. A larger Type A connector attaches to a port on the host; Type B and Mini- or Micro-Type B connectors are used for devices. USB 1.1 supports 12 Mbps while USB 2.0 supports 480 Mbps and is backward compatible with 1.1 devices (which run at the slower speed). USB devices are hot swappable. A device can draw up to 2.5 W of power. USB 3.0 and 3.1 define 5 Gbps (SuperSpeed) and 10 Gbps (SuperSpeed+) rates and can deliver 4.5 W of power.

USB 2.0 (HighSpeed) standard
A USB standard that operates at up to 480 Mbps.

USB hub
A device that connects to a USB port to allow additional USB devices to be connected to the PC, essentially increasing the number of USB ports available.

USB On the Go (OTG)
A USB standard that allows a port to function as either a host or as a device.

USB SuperSpeed
The USB 3.0 standard that operates at up to 5 Gbps and makes the link full duplex.

USB SuperSpeed+
The USB 3.1 standard that operates at up to 10 Gbps.

UTM
(Unified Threat Management) All-in-one security appliances and technologies that combine the functions of a firewall, malware scanner, intrusion detection, vulnerability scanner, Data Loss Prevention, content filtering, and so on.

UTP
(Unshielded Twisted Pair cabling) The type of cabling typically used for computer networking, composed of eight insulated copper wires grouped into four pairs with each pair twisted to reduce interference between wires.

vCard
The digital equivalent of a business card.

VDE
(Virtual Desktop Environment) A virtual environment in which users can customize and update the environment as if it was a physical environment.

VDI
(Virtual Desktop Infrastructure) Hosting user desktops as virtual machines on a centralized server or cloud infrastructure. The desktop OS plus applications software is delivered to the client device (often a thin client) over the network as an image.

VDSL
(Very High Bitrate DSL) A high speed version of DSL with an upstream rate between 1.5 Mbps and 2.5 Mbps and a downstream rate between 50 Mbps and 55 Mbps.

vector font
A font that consists of a description of how each character should be drawn that can be scaled up or down to different font sizes.

vector graphics
Scalable images that are created from vectors which describe how a line should be drawn.

VGA
(Video Graphics Array). A standard for the resolution and color depth of computer displays. VGA specifies a resolution of 640x480 with 16 colors (4-bit color) at 60 Hz.

VGA Connector
(Video Graphics Array connector) A 15-pin HD connector has been used to connect the graphics adapter to a monitor since 1987. The use of digital flat-panel displays rather than CRTs means that as an analog connector, it is fast becoming obsolete.

video card
Provides the interface between the graphics components of the computer and the display device. A number of connectors may be provided for the display, including VGA, DVI, and HDMI. Most adapters come with their own processor (Graphics Processing Unit [GPU]) and onboard memory.

video projector
A large format display in which the image is projected onto a screen or wall using a lens system.

virtual application streaming
Just enough of an application is installed on the end user device for the system to recognize that the application is available to the user, and when the user accesses the application, additional portions of the code are downloaded to the device.

virtual assistant
Another term for a **digital assistant**.

virtual memory
An area on the hard disk allocated to contain pages of memory. When the operating system doesn't have sufficient physical memory (RAM) to perform a task, pages of memory are swapped to the paging file. This frees physical RAM to enable the task to be completed. When the paged RAM is needed again, it is re-read into memory.

virtual switch
A software application that enables communication between VMs.

virtualization
Software allowing a single computer (the host) to run multiple "guest" operating systems (or Virtual Machines [VMs]). The VMs are configured via a hypervisor or VM Monitor (VMM). VMs can be connected using virtual networks (vSwitch) or leverage the host's network interface(s). It is also possible for the VMs to share data with the host (via shared folders or the clipboard, for instance). VT is now used as major infrastructure in data centers as well as for testing and training.

VLAN
(Virtual LAN) A logically separate network, created using switching technology. Even though hosts on two VLANs may be physically connected to the same cabling, local traffic is isolated to each VLAN so they must use a router to communicate.

VM
(Virtual Machine) A guest operating system installed on a host computer using virtualization software (a hypervisor), such as Microsoft Hyper-V or VMware.

VM escaping
(virtual machine escaping) Malware running on a guest OS jumping to another guest or to the host.

VM sprawl
(virtual machine sprawl) The uncontrolled development of more and more virtual machines.

VNC
(Virtual Network Computing) Remote access tool and protocol. VNC is the basis of macOS screen sharing.

volatile
A type of memory where data cannot be stored without power being supplied.

voltage
The potential difference between two points (often likened to pressure in a water pipe) measured in Volts (V). In the US, grid power is 114-126 VAC. In Europe, grid power is referred to as mains electricity and is supplied at 220-240 VAC.

voltage regulators
Voltage Regulator Modules ensure that the motherboard delivers the voltage required by the CPU. When CPUs changed from 5 V to 3.3 V operation, VRMs were provided as plug-in modules. Most modern CPUs use around 1.5 - 2 V and the voltage regulators are built into the motherboard.

VPN
(Virtual Private Network) A secure tunnel created between two endpoints connected via an unsecure network (typically the Internet). VPNs are typically created using SSL/TLS or IPsec. Encryption software is used to ensure privacy of data as messages transit through the public network.

VR
(Virtual Reality) A computer-generated, simulated environment experienced via a headset connected to a PC or powered by a smartphone.

VR headset
(Virtual Reality headset) A headset worn like goggles to interact with images displayed in the headset.

VSAT
(Very Small Aperture Terminal) A microwave antenna aligned to an orbital satellite that can either relay signals between sites directly or via another satellite.

VT-x
Extensions in Intel-based systems that allow hardware virtualization.

walled garden
A closed software system in which the user's access to content and services is controlled by the user's mobile carrier or by a service provider.

WAN
(Wide Area Network) A network that spans multiple geographic locations.

wear leveling
Routines used by flash drives to prevent any single storage location from being overused and to optimize the life of the device.

web server
HTTP servers host websites. A basic website consists of static HTML pages but many sites are developed as front-end applications for databases. Web servers are popular targets for attack, particularly DoS, spoofing, and software exploits. Many companies use hosted web servers but if not, the server should be located in a DMZ. Web servers are also commonly used for intranet services, especially on Microsoft networks.

webcam
A webcam can be used to stream and record video. There are many types, from devices built into laptops to standalone units. While early devices were only capable of low resolutions, most webcams are now HD-capable.

WEP
(Wired Equivalent Privacy) A mechanism for encrypting data sent over a wireless connection. WEP is considered flawed (that is, a determined and well-resourced attack could probably break the encryption). Apart from problems with the cipher, the use and distribution of a pre-shared key (effectively a password) depends on good user practice. WEP has been replaced by WPA.

whitelisting
An address added to the white list is permitted to connect to any port.

Wi-Fi
IEEE standard for wireless networking based on spread spectrum radio transmission in the 2.4 GHz and 5 GHz bands. The standard has five main iterations (a, b, g, n, and ac), describing different modulation techniques, supported distances, and data rates.

Wi-Fi analyzer
A Wi-Fi spectrum analyzer used to detect devices and points of interference, as well as analyze and troubleshoot network issues on a WLAN or other wireless networks.

Wi-Fi Direct
Technology that enables two mobile devices to connect to each other without a wireless access point.

WIA
(Windows Image Acquisition) Driver model and API (Application Programming Interface) for interfacing scanner hardware with applications software on Windows PCs.

Wireless Range Extender
Designed to repeat the signal from an access point to extend the range of a WLAN.

WISP
(Wireless Internet Service Provider) An ISP offering Internet access over ground-based Line of Sight (LoS) microwave transmitters.

WMN
(Wireless Mesh Network) Wireless network topology where all nodes—including client stations—are capable of providing forwarding and path discovery. This improves coverage and throughput compared to using just fixed access points and extenders.

WoL
(Wake on LAN) Where a host has a compatible network card, a network server can be configured to transmit a "magic packet" that causes the host to power up.

workstation
Client devices connecting to the network represent one of the most vulnerable points as they are usually harder to monitor than centrally located equipment, such as servers and switches. As well as secure configuration of the OS and

applications, workstations should be protected with anti-malware software. Users should be trained in security best practices and educated about common threats.

WoWLAN
(Wake-on-Wireless LAN) A wireless version of WoL that is not widely implemented.

WPA
(Wi-Fi Protected Access) An improved encryption scheme for protecting Wi-Fi communications, designed to replace WEP. The original version of WPA was subsequently updated (to WPA2) following the completion of the 802.11i security standard. WPA features an improved method of key distribution and authentication for enterprise networks, though the pre-shared key method is still available for home and small office networks. WPA2 uses the improved AES cipher, replacing TKIP and RC4.

WPF
(Windows Presentation Foundation) In Windows, handles the display and print functions for compatible applications.

WPS
(Wi-Fi Protected Setup) Mechanism for auto-configuring a WLAN securely for home users. On compatible equipment, users just have to push a button on the access point and connecting adapters to associate them securely.

WWAN
(Wireless Wide Area Network) A large wireless network, such as a cellular data network or line-of-sight microwave transmission.

WYSIWYG
(What You See Is What You Get) The screen and print output are supposed to be the same.

x64
See **x86-64**.

x86-32
The instruction set used by IBM PC compatible CPUs.

x86-64
Another term for the **AMD64** instruction set.

Xcode
Apple's **SDK** for macOS and iOS software development.

XML
(eXtensible Markup Language) A system for structuring documents so that they are human- and machine-readable. Information within the document is placed within tags, which describe how information within the document is structured.

XPS
(XML Print Specification) A file format based on **XML** that describes one or more pages and how the information should appear on the page.

Z-Wave
Low-power wireless communications protocol used primarily for home automation. Z-Wave uses radio frequencies in the high 800 to low 900 MHz range and a mesh topology.

ZIF socket
(Zero Insertion Force socket) A processor socket type allowing the chip to be placed in the socket with as little risk of damaging the pins on the processor chip as possible.

Zigbee
Low-power wireless communications open source protocol used primarily for home automation. Zigbee uses radio frequencies in the 2.4 GHz band and a mesh topology.

Index

2D barcode *562*
3D modeling software *516*
3D printers *516*
3D scanner *516*
802.3af *260*
802.3at *260*
    See also PoE+

A

AC *197*
accelerometers *457*
Access Control Lists, *See* ACLs
Access Point, *See* AP
access time *129*
ACLs *347*
adapter cards
    slots *15*
additive *523*
add-on cards *44*, *88*
addressing *171*
Address Resolution Protocol, *See* ARP
ADF *560*
Advanced Encryption Standard, *See* AES
Advanced Host Controller Interface, *See* AHCI
Advanced Technology Extended, *See* ATX
AES *335*
AFP *300*
agent *303*
AHCI *131*
airplane mode *477*
all-in-one units *14*
Alternating Current, *See* AC
ALU *171*
AMD64 *171*
analog displays *79*
Android Auto *490*
anti-glare covers *80*
antistatic bags *10*
AP *267*
APIPA *285*

Apple CarPlay *490*
Apple Filing Protocol, *See* AFP
Apple ID *483*
Application protocols *281*
application virtualization *412*
AR *460*
Arithmetic Logic Unit, *See* ALU
ARP *281*
ASF *509*
aspect ratio *79*
ATX *17*
audio subsystems *104*
Augmented Reality, *See* AR
autodiscover *477*
Automatic Document Feeder, *See* ADF
Automatic Private IP Addressing, *See* APIPA
AutoSheet Feeder, *See* ASF

B

backed-up print queue *548*
backhaul *270*
barcode scanners *561*
baseband updates *473*
Basic Input/Output System, *See* BIOS
Basic Rate Interface, *See* BRI
Basic Service Set Identifier, *See* BSSID
BDs *141*
biometric devices *57*
biometrics *57*
BIOS *185*
BIOS setup *185*
bitmap image data *523*
blanking plates *15*
blaster *465*
BLE *387*
Bluetooth *387*, *474*
Bluetooth Low Energy, *See* BLE
Blu-ray Discs, *See* BDs
Blu-ray drives *144*
bookmarks *487*
boot device priority *189*

boot sequence *189*
BRI *274*
bridges *256*
broadband *271*
broadcast address *284*
BSSID *267*
bus
    expansion *22*
    internal *22*
    local *22*
bus mastering *24*

C

Cable Access TV, *See* CATV
Cable Modem Termination System, *See* CMTS
CAD *225*
CAM *225*
Campus Area Networks, *See* CANs
CANs *236*
capacitor *198*
CATV *272*
CCD *559*
CCFL *559*
CCFL bulb *77*
CD drives *144*
CDMA *275*, *471*
CD-R *140*
CD-RW *141*
CDs
    burning *140*
cellular data
    networks *470*
cellular radios *471*
Central Processing Unit, *See* CPU
channels *133*
Charge Coupled Device, *See* CCD
chassis *13*
chip creep *215*
Chip Level Multiprocessing, *See* CMP
chipsets *20*
CIFS *300*
CIS *560*
cleaning blade *500*
client-side virtualization *404*
clock battery *21*
closed network *304*
cloud *407*
cloud-based network controller *414*
CMOS
    battery *21*

CMOS setup *185*
CMP *173*
CMTS *272*
CMYK *523*
coatings
    gloss *80*
    matte *80*
coax cable *249*
coaxial cable, *See* coax cable
Code Division Multiple Access, *See* CDMA
Cold Cathode Fluorescent bulb, *See* CCFL bulb
Cold Cathode Fluorescent Lamp, *See* CCFL
collision domains *256*
color depth *79*
Comma Separated Values
    CSVs *486*
Common Internet File System, *See* CIFS
compact discs, *See* CDs
Complementary Metal Oxide Semiconductor, *See* CMOS
CompTIA A+ Troubleshooting Model *64*
Computer Aided Design, *See* CAD
Computer Aided Manufacturing, *See* CAM
conductor *197*
connections
    keyed *35*
    USB *36*
Contact Image Sensor, *See* CIS
contacts *486*
container virtualization *413*
contention *256*
contrast ratio *79*
Control Center *477*
core clock speed *173*
corporate mail gateway *478*
CPU
    architectures *171*
    form factor *175*
    installation considerations *180*
CPU sockets *18*
critical updates *193*
CRM *410*
crossover cables *243*
CSVs *486*
current *197*

Customer Relationship Management, *See* CRM
Cyan, Magenta, Yellow, and Black, *See* CMYK

D

DACs *104*
Data Over Cable Service Interface Specification, *See* DOCSIS
daughter boards *23*
DC *197*
DDR SDRAM *115*
default gateway *284*
default masks *282*
defense in depth *303*
Demilitarized Zone, *See* DMZ
Denial of Service, *See* DoS
desktop computers *13*
Desktop Publishing, *See* DTP
detac corona *500*
developer roller *499*
DHCP *284*
dial-up connection *322*
die *170*
digital assistants *390*
digital cameras *109*
digital displays *79*
Digital Light Processing, *See* DLP
Digital Signal Processor chips, *See* DSP chips
Digital Single Lens Reflex, *See* DSLR
Digital Subscriber Line, *See* DSL
Digital-to-Analog Converters, *See* DACs
digital versatile discs, *See* DVDs
Digital Visual Interface, *See* DVI
digitizer *430*
DIMM *117*
diode *198*
Direct Current, *See* DC
direct thermal printers *514*
disk defragmentation *160*
disk mirroring *150*
disk striping *149*
disk thrashing *156*
DisplayPort *84*
distended capacitors *216*
Distinguished Name *302*
DLP *78*
DMZ *351*
DNS *284*, *295*
docking stations *423*

DOCSIS *272*
domain names *296*
Domain Name System, *See* DNS
DoS *405*
dot matrix printers *512*
dotted decimal notation *281*
Double Data Rate SDRAM, *See* DDR SDRAM
DRAM *115*
drive controllers *129*
drive enclosures *146*
drive encryption *192*
drivers *60*
drives
    hot swappable *154*
drop cables *243*
DSL *271*
DSL Access Multiplier, *See* DSLAM
DSLAM *271*
DSLR *110*
DSP chips *104*
DTP *225*
dual-channel memory *118*
dual heat pipes *179*
Dual Inline Memory Module, *See* DIMM
dual rails *200*
duplexing assembly *500*, *509*
DVD drives *144*
DVDs *140*
DVI *82*
dye sublimation *514*
Dynamic Host Configuration Protocol, *See* DHCP
Dynamic RAM, *See* DRAM

E

Early-life Failure Rate *129*
e-books *487*
ECC memory *119*
EDR *463*
EIR database *472*
Electronic Paper Displays, *See* EPDs
electrostatic discharge, *See* ESD
electrostatic latent images *499*
electrostatic photographic drum, *See* EP drum
embedded system *304*
encryption keys *479*
Endpoint Management Server *304*
energy *197*
Enhanced Data Rate, *See* EDR

Entry-level Power Supply, See EPS
EP drum 498
EPDs 458
EPS 202
EPT 174, 401
Equipment Identity Register database, See EIR database
erase lamp 500
e-readers 458
Error Checking and Correcting memory, See ECC memory
eSATA standard 41
ESD 8
ESS 267
Ethernet 238
Exchange
    ActiveSync 478
expansion bus 22
expansion cards 44
    See also add-on cards
expansion slots 22
Extended Page Table, See EPT
Extended Service Set, See ESS
external transfer rate 129
extranets 297

F

fast-charged 468
FDE 192
FDM 517
federated identity management 491
feed 499
FFF 517
Fiber to the Curb/Cabinet, See FTTC
Fiber to the Home, See FTTH
Fiber to the Node, See FTTN
Fiber to the Premises, See FTTP
field replaceable units, See FRUs
File Transfer Protocol, See FTP
firewalls
    host 347
    network 347
firmware
    system 185
flash memory 144
flatbed scanners 559
Floating Point Unit, See FPU
FPU 171
FQDN 296
frame rate 79
frames 254

frequency response 104
friction feed 513
FRUs 10, 16, 427
FTP 300
FTTC 272
FTTH 272
FTTN 272
FTTP 272
Full Disk Encryption, See FDE
Fully Qualified Domain Name, See FQDN
fuse 198
fused deposition modeling, See FDM
fused filament fabrication, See FFF
fuser assembly 500
fuses 3

G

game pads 56
gaming rigs 225
General Purpose registers, See GP registers
geolocation 487
global address 289
Global Positioning System, See GPS
Global System for Mobile Communication, See GSM
Gov Cloud 409
GP registers 171
GPS 461
GPU 88
graphics adapters 87
Graphics Processing Unit, See GPU
grounding
    equipment 4
GSM 275, 471
gyroscopes 457

H

haptic feedback 457
hard disk drive, See HDD
hardware-assisted virtualization 174
hardware RAID solution 153
HBAs 129
HDD
    performance factors 128
HDMI 82
headsets 107
head unit 490

Heating, Ventilation, and Air Conditioning, See HVAC
heat pipes 179
heat sinks 177
heat spreader 179
HFC 272
HIDs 52
High Definition Multimedia Interface, See HDMI
home server PC 226
home theater PC, See HTPC
Host Bus Adapters, See HBAs
host controller 36
host firewalls 347
host-hinted mode 132
host ID 282
host names 296
hotspots 474
hot swappable 129
hot swappable drives 154
HT 172
HTML 297
HTPC 226
HTT 172
HTTP 297
HTTP Over SSL, See HTTPS
HTTPS 298
HTTP Secure, See HTTPS
hubs 36, 256
Human Interface Devices, See HIDs
HVAC 242
hybrid drives 132
Hybrid Fiber Coax, See HFC
HyperText Markup Language, See HTML
HyperText Transfer Protocol, See HTTP
HyperThreading 401
  See also HT
HyperThreading Technology, See HTT
hypervisors 399

I

I/O address 60
IA-32 171
IA-64 171
IaaS 410
ICMP 281, 379
IDS 305
IEEE 802.11 238
illuminance 80
IMAP 299, 478
IMEI 472
impact printers
  paper feeding 513
IMSI number 472
incidents 63
infrared, See IR
Infrastructure as a Service, See IaaS
infrastructure mode 267
Ingress Protection scales, See IP scales
ink dispersion printers 496, 506
inkjet printers 496, 506
In-Plane Switching, See IPS
input devices 52
input voltage 199
instruction sets
  x86-32 171
insulator 198
Integrated Development Environments, See IDEs
Integrated Services Digital Network, See ISDN
interfaces 34
internal transfer rate 129
International Mobile Station Equipment Identity, See IMEI
International Mobile Subscriber Identity number, See IMSI number
Internet backbone 270
Internet Control Message Protocol, See ICMP
Internet eXchange Points, See IXPs
Internet Mail Access Protocol, See IMAP
Internet Message Access Protocol, See IMAP
Internet of Things, See IoT
Internet Protocol, See IP
Internet Service Providers, See ISPs
Interrupt Request, See IRQ
intranets 297
Intrusion Detection System, See IDS
Intrusion Protection System, See IPS
inventory management 303
IoT 387
IP 280
IPS 76, 305
IP scales 467
IPSec 474
IR 465
IRQ 60
ISDN 273
ISPs 270, 478

IXPs 270

J

jailbreaking 473
jitter 338
joysticks 56
jumpers 29

K

Keyboard, Video, Mouse switches, See KVM switches
keyboards 52, 420
KVM switches 56

L

Land Grid Array, See LGA
lands 140
lanes 26, 131
LANs 236
laptops 418
laser printers
    process 498
latency 338
LC 249
LDAP 302
LED printers 500
LEDs 208
legacy system 304
LGA 175
life expectancy 129
Light Emitting Diodes, See LEDs
Lightning 39
Lightweight Directory Access Protocol, See LDAP
Line of Sight, See LoS
link-local addresses 290
links 26
Liquid Crystal Displays, See LCDs
Local Area Networks, See LANs
Local Connector, See LC
LoJack tracking software 193
Long Term Evolution, See LTE
loopback plugs 248
LoS 274
LTE 276
LTE-A 276
LTE Advanced, See LTE-A
luminance 79

M

MAC 255
main board 17
main connector 200
maintenance kits 503
managed switches 259
Management Information Base, See MIB
MANs 237
MAPI 298, 478
mass storage devices 127
MDM 479
Mean Time Between Failure, See MTBF
measured service 408
Media Access Control, See MAC
media centers 225
media guides 499
megapixels, See MPs
MEID 472
memory cards
    readers 145
memory modules 117
Message Application Programming Interface, See MAPI
Messaging Application Programming Interface, See MAPI
Metropolitan Area Networks, See MANs
MFDs 497, 560
MIB 303
Micro-ATX 17
microprocessors 170
microsegmentation 257
MIDI 107
MIME 298
MIMO 266
Mini-ITX 18
mirroring 150
MMF 249
Mobile Device Management, See MDM
mobile device synchronization 486
Mobile Equipment ID, See MEID
mobile hotspots 465
mobile VPNs 474
mobo 17
Molex connectors 42, 201
monitors
    LCD 76
motherboards
See also main board
    connector types 18

form factors *17*
    See also main board
mouse *54*
MPs *110*
MTBF *129*, *405*
Multi-Function Devices, See MFDs
multimeters *210*, *246*
Multi-Mode Fiber, See MMF
Multiple-Input-Multiple-Output, See MIMO
multiport repeater *256*
Multipurpose Internet Mail Extension, See MIME
multitasking *172*
multitouch *457*
Musical Instrument Digital Interface, See MIDI
mutual authentication for multiple services (SSO) *491*

N

NACK *294*
NAPT *286*
NAS *146*, *226*
NAT *286*, *349*
National Institute of Standards and Technology, See NIST
native resolution *79*
Near Field Communications, See NFC
Near Field Communications protocol, See NFC protocol
Negative Acknowledgement, See NACK
NetBIOS *302*
NetBIOS over TCP/IP, See NetBT
NetBT *302*
Network Address Port Translation, See NAPT
Network Address Translation, See NAT
Network Attached Storage, See NAS
Network Basic Input/Output System, See NetBIOS
network firewalls *347*
network ID *282*
Network Interface Cards, See NICs
Network Interface layer *280*
Network Level Authentication, See NLA
networks *236*
NFC *388*, *464*
NFC protocol *58*
NICs *254*
NIST *407*

NLA *367*
non-parity *119*
Non-Volatile Memory Host Controller Interface Specification, See NVMHCI
notification shade *477*
NVMe *131*
NVM Express, See NVMe
NVMHCI *131*

O

OCP *200*
OCR *559*
OLED
    display *457*
onboard adapters *88*
On-Screen Display, See OSD
Optical Character Recognition, See OCR
Organic LED, See OLED
OSD *90*
OTG *37*
overclocking *173*
Overcurrent Protection, See OCP

P

PaaS *410*
packet filtering *347*
Page Description Language, See PDL
PANs *268*, *463*
paper jams *553*
Parallel Advanced Technology Attachment, See PATA
parity checking *119*
passive cooling device *177*
PAT *3*, *349*
PATA *133*
PCI bus *23*
PCIe bus *25*
PCI Express bus, See PCIe bus
PDL *521*
Peripheral Component Interconnect bus, See PCI bus
Personal Area Networks, See PANs
PGA *176*
PGP *479*
photopolymer *518*
pickup roller *499*
picture elements, See pixels
piezoelectric *507*
Pin Grid Array, See PGA
pits *140*

pixels *79*
Plain Old Telephone Service, *See* POTS
Platform as a Service, *See* PaaS
plenum *242*
Plug-and-Play *59*
PoE *260*
PoE+ *260*
pointing devices *54*
Point of Presence, *See* PoP
Point-to-Point Protocol, *See* PPP
PoP *270*
POP3 *299, 478*
portable appliance testing, *See* PAT
Port Address Translation, *See* PAT
port forwarding *350*
port number *293*
port replicators *423*
ports
    female *35*
    I/O *35*
    keyed *35*
    male *35*
port triggering *351*
POST *212*
Post Office Protocol, *See* POP3
POTS *270*
power *197*
power management *188*
Power On Self Test, *See* POST
Power over Ethernet, *See* PoE
Power Sourcing Equipment, *See* PSE
Power Supply Tester *211*
Power Supply Unit, *See* PSU
PPP *271*
PPPoA *271*
PPPoE *271*
PPP over ATM, *See* PPPoA
PPP over Ethernet, *See* PPPoE
Preferred Roaming List, *See* PRL
Pre-shared Key, *See* PSK
Pretty Good Privacy, *See* PGP
PRI *274*
primary charge roller *500*
Primary Rate Interface, *See* PRI
printer drivers *526*
printers
    3D *516*
    direct thermal *514*
    dot matrix *512*
    impact *512*
    ink dispersion *496, 506*
    inkjet *496, 506*
    laser *496, 497*
    LED *500*
    thermal *514*
    virtual *523*
    Windows *521*
printer types *496*
print jobs *529*
privacy filters *80*
private addresses *286*
PRL *472*
probable causes
    determining *67*
problem management *63*
problems
    escalating *68*
    identifying *65*
protocols *279*
protocol suite *279*
proxy server *306*
PSE *260*
PSK *336*
PSTN *270*
PSU
    adapter types *200*
    form factors *198*
    output voltages *200*
    power ratings *199*
Public Switched Telephone Network, *See* PSTN

Q

QC *467*
QoS *313, 338*
QR codes *562*
QR scanners *562*
Quality of Service, *See* QoS
Quick Charge, *See* QC
Quick Response codes, *See* QR codes

R

radio firmware *473*
Radio Frequency, *See* RF
Radio Frequency ID, *See* RFID
RADIUS *336*
RAID
    configuration options *153*
    levels *149*
RAM *19, 114*
Random Access Memory, *See* RAM

range extender *267*
rapid elasticity *408*
Rapid Virtualization Indexing, *See* RVI
RDPRA *367*
RDP Restricted Admin, *See* RDPRA
real time *189*
Real Time Clock, *See* RTC
Realtime Operating System, *See* RTOS
Received Signal Strength Indicator, *See* RSSI
recordable CD, *See* CD-R
Redundant Array of Independent Disks, *See* RAID
refresh rate *79*
Registered Jack connectors, *See* RJ connectors
registers *171*
registration roller *500*
Relative Distinguished Name *302*
Remote Assistance *366*
Remote Authentication Dial-in User Service, *See* RADIUS
Remote Credential Guard *367*
Remote Desktop *366*
removable storage *140*
repeaters *256*
resistance *197*
resistor *198*
resolution *79*, *110*
resource pooling *408*
response rate *79*
rewritable CD, *See* CD-RW
RF *375*
RFID *58*, *388*
riser cards *22*
RJ-11 connectors *44*
RJ-45 *242*
RJ-45 connectors *43*
RJ connectors *43*
rogue VMs *404*
rooting *473*
rotational latency *128*
routers *278*
RSSI *376*
RTC *21*
RTC battery *21*
RTOS *473*
RVI *174*, *401*

S

S/MIME *479*
S/PDIF jacks *105*
S.M.A.R.T. *129*
SaaS *410*
sample *107*
sampling *107*
SAS *130*
SATA *41*, *129*
SC *249*
scalable fonts *522*
scanners
    barcode *561*
    flatbed *559*
    QR *562*
    sheet-fed *560*
SCSI *42*, *134*
SDK *484*
SDN *414*
SDRAM *115*
Second Level Address Translation, *See* SLAT
sectors *128*
secure boot *193*
Secure Multipart Internet Mail Extensions, *See* S/MIME
Secure Shell, *See* SSH
Secure Sockets Layer, *See* SSL
Secure Sockets Tunneling Protocol, *See* SSTP
seek time *129*
selective laser sintering, *See* SLS
self-grounding *8*
Self-Monitoring Analysis and Reporting Technology, *See* S.M.A.R.T.
semiconductor *198*
separation pad *499*
separation roller *499*, *509*
Serial Advanced Technology Attachment, *See* SATA
Serial Attached SCSI, *See* SAS
server consolidation *404*
Server Message Block, *See* SMB
server-side virtualization *404*
Service Set ID, *See* SSID
SFF case *14*
sheet-fed scanners *560*
Shielded Twisted Pair, *See* STP
Signal-to-Noise Ratio, *See* SNR
silicon chips *170*
SIM cards *472*
Simple Mail Transfer Protocol, *See* SMTP

Simple Network Management Protocol, *See* SNMP
Simultaneous Multithreading, *See* SMT
single-channel memory *118*
Single-Mode Fiber, *See* SMF
Single Sign On, *See* SSO
SLA *518*
SLAT *174, 401*
slicing software *516*
SLS *518*
Small Computer Systems Interface, *See* SCSI
Small Form Factor case, *See* SFF case
Small Office Home Office, *See* SOHO
Small Outline DIMM, *See* SODIMM
smart card readers *57*
smart cards *57*
SMB *300*
SMF *249*
SMP *173, 401*
SMT *172*
SMTP *298, 478*
SNMP *303*
SNR *107*
SODIMM *118, 428*
Software as a Service, *See* SaaS
Software Defined Networking, *See* SDN
Software Development Kit, *See* SDK
SOHO *239, 327*
Solid State Drives, *See* SSDs
solid state storage *144*
Sony/Phillips Digital Interface jacks, *See* S/PDIF jacks
sound cards *104*
SSDs *131*
SSH *371*
SSID *336*
SSL *298, 478*
SSO *491*
SSTP *474*
ST *249*
standard clients *223*
    See also thick clients
standoffs *17*
static eliminator *500*
stereolithography, *See* SLA
storage bus *27*
STP *242*
Straight Tip, *See* ST
striping *149*
structured cabling system *244*

subnet mask *282*
Subscriber Connector, *See* SC
Subscriber Identity Module cards, *See* SIM cards
subtractive *523*
superpipelining *172*
superscalar architecture *172*
SuperSpeed+ mode *37*
SuperSpeed mode *37*
Super VGA, *See* SVGA
surround sound *106*
SVGA *80*
switches
    managed *259*
    unmanaged *259*
Symmetric Multiprocessing, *See* SMP
Synchronous DRAM, *See* SDRAM
syslog *304*
system board *17*
system case
See also chassis
    cover *15*
    front panel *15*
    rear cover *15*
    See also chassis
system clock *23*
system memory
    volatile *114*
system resources *60*

T

TA *274*
TB *39*
TCO *497*
TCP *280, 294*
TCP/IP *279*
Telnet *370*
Terminal Adapter, *See* TA
tethering *465*
TFT *76*
THD *107*
thermal paper *515*
thermal paste *177*
thermal printers *514*
thermal wax transfer *514*
thick clients *223*
thin clients *223*
Thin Film Transistor, *See* TFT
thrashed *227*
threads *172*
throttling *174*

Thunderbolt, *See* TB
TLDs *295*
TLS *298*
TN *76*
tone generator and probe *247*
Top Level Domains, *See* TLDs
Total Cost of Ownership, *See* TCO
Total Harmonic Distortion, *See* THD
touchpads *55*, *419*
touchscreens *421*, *457*
tower case *13*
TPM *192*
traces *21*
tracks *128*
transfer belt *500*
transfer roller *500*
transistor *198*
Transmission Control Protocol, *See* TCP
Transmission Control Protocol/Internet Protocol, *See* TCP/IP
Transport Control Protocol, *See* TCP
Transport Layer Security, *See* TLS
trickle charge *468*
trip hazards *6*
troubleshooting
    basics *63*
Trusted Platform Module, *See* TPM
TWAIN *561*
Twisted Nematic, *See* TN
Type 1 hypervisors *400*
Type 2 hypervisors *400*

U

UDP *280*, *294*
UEFI *185*
UEFI setup *185*
unicast addressing *284*
Unified Extensible Firmware Interface, *See* UEFI
Unified Threat Management, *See* UTM
Uniform Resource Locator, *See* URL
Universal Plug-and-Play, *See* UPnP
Universal Serial Bus, *See* USB
unmanaged switches *259*
Unshielded Twisted Pair, *See* UTP
UPnP *352*
URL *297*
USB *36*
USB 2.0 (HighSpeed) standard *36*
USB On the Go, *See* OTG
user accounts *223*

User Datagram Protocol, *See* UDP
UTM *305*
UTP *240*

V

vCards *486*
VDE *411*
VDI *223*, *411*
vector fonts *522*
vector graphics *523*
Very Small Aperture Terminal, *See* VSAT
VGA
    port *81*
video cards *87*
    See also graphics adapters
Video Graphics Array, *See* VGA
video projectors *77*
virtual application streaming *412*
virtual assistants *390*
Virtual Desktop Environment, *See* VDE
Virtual Desktop Infrastructure, *See* VDI
virtualization
    client-side *404*
    server-side *404*
Virtualization Technology, *See* VT-x
Virtual LANs, *See* VLANs
Virtual Machines, *See* VMs
virtual memory *115*
Virtual Network Computing, *See* VNC
virtual printers *523*
Virtual Private Network, *See* VPN
virtual reality, *See* VR
Virtual Reality headsets, *See* VR headsets
virtual switches, *See* vSwitches
VLANs *259*, *279*
VM escaping *405*
VMs *174*, *224*
VM sprawl *404*
VNC *372*
voltage *197*
voltage regulators *200*
VPN *287*, *474*
VR *78*
VR headsets
    mobile *78*
    tethered *78*
VSAT *274*
vSwitches *402*
VT-x *401*

W

Wake on LAN, *See* WoL
Wake-on-Wireless LAN, *See* WoWLAN
walled garden model *484*
WANs *237*
wearable technology *458*
wear leveling *132*
webcams *109*
web servers *297*
WEP *335*
What You See Is What You Get, *See* WYSIWYG
WIA *561*
Wide Area Networks, *See* WANs
Wi-Fi *264*
Wi-Fi Analyzer *377*
Wi-Fi Direct *526*
Wi-Fi Protected Access, *See* WPA
Wi-Fi Protected Setup, *See* WPS
Windows Firewall *353*
Windows Image Acquisition, *See* WIA
Windows Presentation Foundation, *See* WPF
Windows printers *521*
Wired Equivalent Privacy, *See* WEP
Wireless Internet Service Provider, *See* WISP
Wireless LANs, *See* WLANs
Wireless Mesh Network, *See* WMN
Wireless Wide Area Network, *See* WWAN
WISP *275*
WLANs *264*
WMN *267*
WoL *315*
workstations *224*
WoWLAN *315*
WPA *335*
WPF *521*
WPS *332*
WWAN *323*
WYSIWYG *521*

X

x64 *171*
x86-32 *171*
    See also IA-32
x86-64 *171*
    See also x64
XML Print Specification, *See* XPS
XPS *521*

Z

Zero Insertion Force socket, *See* ZIF socket
ZIF socket *176*
Zigbee *388*
Z-Wave *388*

ISBN-13 978-1-6427-4131-5
ISBN-10 1-6427-4131-0